A TREASURY OF
CHRISTIAN
WISDOM

Also by Tony Castle

Traditional Christian Names
A Treasury of Prayer

A TREASURY OF
CHRISTIAN
WISDOM

TWO THOUSAND YEARS OF
CHRISTIAN LIVES AND QUOTATIONS

TONY CASTLE

Hodder & Stoughton

Originally published as two separate titles: *The Hodder Book of
Christian Quotations* (first published in 1982) and *The Hodder &
Stoughton Book of Famous Christians* (first published in 1988).

Copyright © 2001, 1988, 1982 Tony Castle

This edition first published in Great Britain in 2001

The right of Tony Castle to be identified as the Author of
the Work has been asserted by him in accordance with
the Copyright, Designs and Patents Act 1988.

10 9 8 7 6 5 4 3 2 1

British Library Cataloguing in Publication Data
A record for this book is available from the British Library

ISBN 0 340 78550 0

Typeset by Avon Dataset Ltd, Bidford-on-Avon, Warks

Printed and bound in Great Britain by
Clays Ltd, St Ives plc

Hodder & Stoughton
A Division of Hodder Headline Ltd
338 Euston Road
London NW1 3BH

Dedicated

to

each and every one of the
students of my Year 11
Religious Studies class
(2000–2001),
particularly
Dionne, Julia, Maria and Natasha.

May they grow in Christian wisdom.

Contents

Introduction   3

Christian Quotations   5
Index to Quotations   259

Christian Lives   277

Introduction

In this Internet age the world is awash with information and knowledge. The vast volume of facts, figures, projections and predictions that are available at the touch of a keyboard is truly amazing. Knowledge appears to be the key to everything. But is it? Is knowledge the same as wisdom? That is not the view found throughout the Bible. Knowledge and right judgment, or wisdom, are viewed as separate entities; as any concordance will reveal. Wisdom, as distinct from knowledge, is seen as so fundamentally important that there is even a deutero-canonical book of the Bible dedicated to it. Wisdom is the ability to use knowledge prudently, drawing on common sense and experience.

The 'wisdom' gathered together here, in the form of persons and useful quotations, is a distinctly different collection from anything available on the Internet or elsewhere. This compilation began many years ago when, as a student, I was learning the art of public speaking. I started a small collection of useful sayings and inspiring quotations, arranged thematically in a simple school exercise book. They totalled no more than a hundred and included not just quotations from famous Christians, but also quotations that I could use, in public speaking, to draw out or illustrate a point. That modest interest and pastoral aid was the origin and basis of the present compilation. The approach has remained practical and pastoral. Given the source and historico-cultural context of a few of the quotations, they cannot all be considered *Christian*; but they are sayings that a Christian speaker or writer may find wise use for.

As radio telescopes and satellites probe deep space for other intelligent life forms, young people are conditioned through their education, their computers and their leisure pursuits to look to the scientific advances of this new century for enlightenment and excitement. Our age is impatient with the accumulated wisdom of previous generations that, lacking the micro-chip, is often ignored and even scorned. But the Christian faith has long and firm roots in history and cherishes the word of God, and the light shed upon it by persons of accepted standing in the Christian community. The quotations in this collection have won a place because they are seen to cast some light upon revealed truth and the mysteries and exigencies of life.

In the selection of the famous Christians who have reflected the wisdom of God in their lives and in these quotations, I have attempted to maintain a balance between each of the Christian traditions, and also between ancient and modern times. Quotations can be found from every century and, where possible, the author's dates are given in the index to locate the quotation in its own social and historical context. Much effort has been made to ascribe the quotations correctly and no anonymous material has been accepted.

Tony Castle

Christian Quotations

Abandonment

(*See also* Providence, Trust and Will of God)

The Lord doesn't want the first place in my life, he wants all of my life.
HOWARD AMERDING

The greatness of a man's power is the measure of his surrender.
WILLIAM BOOTH

There is but one thing to do: to purify our hearts, to detach ourselves from creatures, and abandon ourselves entirely to God.
JEAN PIERRE DE CAUSSADE

While he strips of everything the souls who give themselves absolutely to him, God gives them something which takes the place of all; of light, wisdom, life and force: this gift is his love.
JEAN PIERRE DE CAUSSADE

God is the master of the scenes; we must not choose what part we shall act; it concerns us only to be careful that we do it well, always saying, 'If this please God, let it be as it is.'
JEREMY TAYLOR

Ability

(*See also* Talents)

If people knew how hard I have to work to gain my mastery, it would not seem wonderful at all.
MICHELANGELO BUONARROTI

The winds and waves are always on the side of the ablest navigators.
EDWARD GIBBON

Alas for those who never sing, but die with all their music in them.
OLIVER WENDELL HOLMES

It is a fine thing to have ability, but the ability to discover ability in others is the true test.
ELBERT KIPLING

Behind an able man there are always other able men.
CHINESE PROVERB

Do what you can, with what you have, where you are.
THEODORE ROOSEVELT

A man must not deny his manifest abilities, for that is to evade his obligations.
ROBERT LOUIS STEVENSON

Acceptance

As in a game of cards, so in the game of life we must play with what is dealt out to us; and the glory consists not so much in winning as in playing a poor hand well.
JOSH BILLINGS

To live by the law of Christ and accept him in our hearts is to turn a giant floodlight of hope into our valleys of trouble.
CHARLES R. HEMBREE

A man can accept what Christ has done without knowing how it works; indeed, he certainly won't know how it works *until* he's accepted it.
C. S. LEWIS

Acceptance says, True, this is my situation at the moment. I'll look unblinkingly at the reality of it. But I'll also open my hands to accept willingly whatever a loving Father sends.
CATHERINE MARSHALL

I have accepted all and I am free. The inner chains are broken as well as those outside.
CHARLES F. RAMUZ

The task ahead of us is to know ourselves as not acceptable. And to accept that knowledge.
SIMON TUGWELL

If we stand in the openings of the present moment, with all the length and breadth of our faculties unselfishly adjusted to what it reveals, we are in the best condition to receive what God is always ready to communicate.
T. C. UPHAM

You are not accepted by God because you deserve to be, or because you have worked hard for Him; but because Jesus died for you.
COLIN URQUHART

Achievement

(*See also* Success)

Having once decided to achieve a certain task, achieve it at all costs of tedium and distaste. The gain in self-confidence of having accomplished a tiresome labour is immense.
ARNOLD BENNETT

Nothing great was ever achieved without enthusiasm.
RALPH WALDO EMERSON

No great thing is created suddenly, any more than a bunch of grapes or a fig. If you tell me that you desire a fig, I answer you that there must be time. Let it first blossom, then bear fruit, then ripen.
EPICTETUS

I am only one, but still I am one. I cannot do everything, but still I can do something; and because I cannot do everything, I will not refuse to do something that I can do.
EDWARD EVERETT HALE

We judge ourselves by what we feel capable of doing; others judge us by what we have done.
HENRY W. LONGFELLOW

Praise the ripe field not the green corn.
IRISH PROVERB

Four steps to achievement. Plan purposefully. Prepare prayerfully. Proceed positively. Pursue persistently.
WILLIAM A. WARD

Active Life

Happy persons seldom think of happiness. They are too busy losing their lives in the meaningful sacrifices of service.
DAVID AUGSBURGER

We do the works, but God works in us the doing of the works.
ST. AUGUSTINE OF HIPPO

Christian action should be defined as an action of God mediated through a person.
ANTHONY BLOOM

I do not believe in a fate that falls on men however they act; but I do believe in a fate that falls on men unless they act.
G. K. CHESTERTON

Action may not always bring happiness; but there is no happiness without action.
BENJAMIN DISRAELI

Love's secret is always to be doing things for God, and not to mind because they are such very little ones.
FREDERICK W. FABER

It is possible to be so active in the service of Christ as to forget to love him.
P. T. FORSYTH

Our problem is not that we take refuge from action in spiritual things, but that we take refuge from spiritual things in action.
MONICA FURLONG

We ascend to the heights of contemplation by the steps of the active life.
POPE ST. GREGORY I

A Christian should always remember that the value of his good works is not based on their number and excellence, but on the love of God which prompts him to do these things.
ST. JOHN OF THE CROSS

Act well at the moment, and you have performed a good action to all eternity.
JOHANN K. LAVATER

The Christian who tugs on the oars hasn't time to rock the boat.
AUSTIN ALEXANDER LEWIS

Our own actions are our security, not others' judgments.
ENGLISH PROVERB

To live is not merely to breathe; it is to act.
JEAN JACQUES ROUSSEAU

The princes among us are those who forget themselves and serve mankind.
WOODROW WILSON

Adam

(*See also* Fall of Man and Original Sin)

Oh, he didn't believe in Adam or Eve,
He put no faith therein;
His doubts began with the fall of man,
And he laughed at original sin.
HILAIRE BELLOC

The man without a navel still lives in me.
SIR THOMAS BROWNE

Adam, whiles he spake not, had paradise at will.
WILLIAM LANGLAND

When Adam delved and Eve span, who was then a gentleman?
ENGLISH PROVERB

Adam ate the apple and our teeth still ache.
HUNGARIAN PROVERB

Adam and Eve had many advantages, but the principal one was that they escaped teething.
MARK TWAIN

Adam was but human – this explains it all. He did not want the apple for the apple's sake; he wanted it only because it was forbidden. The mistake was in not forbidding the serpent – then he would have eaten the serpent.
MARK TWAIN

I sometimes think that if Adam and Eve had been merely engaged, she would not have talked with the serpent; and the world had been saved an infinity of misery.
H. G. WELLS

Adoption

(*See also* Baptism)

Our adoptive sonship is in its super-natural reality a reflection of the sonship of the Word. God has not communi-cated to us the whole of his nature but a participation of it.
R. GARRIGOU-LAGRANGE

Christians are made, not born.
ST. JEROME

The Spirit is the Spirit of adoption, since He is the Spirit received in baptism, whereby Christians are adopted into the household of God as joint-heirs with Christ.
ALAN RICHARDSON

For children to be baptised implies that they be brought into a whole new set of relationships with the triune God: sons and daughters of the *Father*, reborn in the likeness of Christ, the *Son of God*, to be his faithful witnesses, united to him and adopted by the *Father* through the power of the *Spirit*.
MARK SEARLE

Adoration

(*See also* Praise and Worship)

At my devotion I love to use the civility of my knee, my hat and hand.
SIR THOMAS BROWNE

If we would understand Divine things, we must cultivate an attitude of humble adoration. Who does not begin by kneeling down, runs every possible risk.
ERNEST HELLO

It is magnificent to be clothed like the lilies of the field . . . but the supreme glory is to be nothingness in adoration.
SØREN KIERKEGAARD

Man is most truly himself, as the Eastern Church well knows, not when he toils but when he adores. And we are learning more and more that all innocent joy in life may be a form of adoration.
VIDA P. SCUDDER

To pray is less than to adore.
CLARENCE WALWORTH

Adversity

(*See also* Affliction and Suffering)

Take the cross *he* sends, as it is, and not as *you* imagine it to be.
CORNELIA CONNELLY

God instructs the heart not by ideas, but by pains and contradictions.
JEAN PIERRE DE CAUSSADE

There is no education like adversity.
BENJAMIN DISRAELI

Adversity is the trial of principle. Without it a man hardly knows whether he is honest or not.
HENRY FIELDING

No man is fit to comprehend heavenly things who hath not resigned himself to suffer adversities for Christ.
THOMAS À KEMPIS

Adversity not only draws people together but brings forth that beautiful inward friendship, just as the cold winter forms ice-figures on the window-panes which the warmth of the sun effaces.
SØREN KIERKEGAARD

Adversity is the diamond dust Heaven polishes its jewels with.
ROBERT LEIGHTON

The hardness of God is kinder than the softness of men, and his compulsion is our liberation.
C. S. LEWIS

It has done me good to be somewhat parched by the heat and drenched by the rain of life.
HENRY WORDSWORTH
LONGFELLOW

Adversity is not necessarily an evil. Beethoven composed his deepest music after becoming totally deaf. Pascal set down his most searching observations about God and man, life and death, in brief intervals of release from a prostrating illness.
ROBERT MCCRACKEN

Adversity makes a man wise, not rich.
ENGLISH PROVERB

Many can bear adversity, but few contempt.
ENGLISH PROVERB

The stars are constantly shining, but often we do not see them until the dark hours.
EARL RINEY

As sure as ever God puts his children in the furnace he will be in the furnace with them.
CHARLES H. SPURGEON

Too much sunshine in life makes a desert.
GUSTAV J. WHITE

Advice

Whenever my advice is followed I confess that I always feel oppressed with a greater burden of responsibility, and I can never be confident, and always await the outcome with anxiety.
ST. BERNARD OF CLAIRVAUX

Advice is seldom welcome; and those who want it the most always like it the least.
LORD CHESTERFIELD

Advice is like snow; the softer it falls, the longer it dwells upon, and the deeper it sinks into the mind.
SAMUEL TAYLOR COLERIDGE

To ask advice is in nine cases out of ten to tout for flattery.
JOHN CHURTON COLLINS

To profit from good advice requires more wisdom than to give it.
JOHN CHURTON COLLINS

An honest man may take a fool's advice.
JOHN DRYDEN

No gift is more precious than good advice.
DESIDERIUS ERASMUS

11

He that won't be counselled can't be helped.
BENJAMIN FRANKLIN

I have often heard that it is more safe to hear and to take counsel than to give it.
THOMAS À KEMPIS

He who builds according to every man's advice will have a crooked house.
DANISH PROVERB

No one wants advice – only corroboration.
JOHN STEINBECK

Affliction

(*See also* Adversity and Suffering)

One and the same violence of affliction proves, purifies and melts the good, and condemns, wastes and casts out the bad.
ST. AUGUSTINE OF HIPPO

God measures out affliction to our need.
ST. JOHN CHRYSOSTOM

The truly loving heart loves God's good pleasure not in consolations only, but, and especially, in afflictions also.
ST. FRANCIS DE SALES

Affliction can be a treasure. Absolutely functional, it triggers life's greatest insights and accomplishments.
FRED GREVE

Strength is born in the deep silence of long-suffering hearts, not amid joy.
FELICIA HEMANS

Afflictions are but the shadow of God's wings.
GEORGE MACDONALD

Whenever I find myself in the cellar of affliction, I always look about for the wine.
SAMUEL RUTHERFORD

The Lord gets his best soldiers out of the highlands of affliction.
CHARLES H. SPURGEON

Afterlife

(*See also* Eternity and Immortality)

I cannot conceive that (God) could make such a species as the human merely to live and die on this earth. If I did not believe in a future state, I should believe in no God.
JOHN ADAMS

Those who hope for no other life are dead even for this.
JOHANN WOLFGANG VON GOETHE

I know as much about the afterlife as you do – nothing. I must wait and see.
WILLIAM RALPH INGE

Before I started working with dying patients, I did not believe in a life after death. I now believe in a life after death, beyond a shadow of a doubt.
ELIZABETH KUEBLER-ROSS

The seed dies into a new life, and so does man.
GEORGE MACDONALD

The only ultimate disaster that can befall us is to feel ourselves at home on this earth.
MALCOLM MUGGERIDGE

Those who live in the Lord never see each other for the last time.
GERMAN PROVERB

We maintain that after life has passed away, thou still remainest in existence, and look forward to a day of judgment, and according to thy deserts, art assigned to misery or bliss.
QUINTUS TERTULLIAN

I have never seen what to me seemed an atom of proof that there is a future life. And yet – I am strongly inclined to expect one.
MARK TWAIN

Age and Ages of Man

(*See also* Old Age and Youth)

To know how to grow old is the master work of wisdom, and one of the most difficult chapters in the great art of living.
HENRI FRÉDÉRIC AMIEL

They shall grow not old, as we that are left grow old. Age shall not weary them, nor the years condemn. At the going down of the sun and in the morning we will remember them.
LAURENCE BINYON

To grow old is to pass from passion to compassion.
ALBERT CAMUS

The old may be out-run but not out-reasoned.
GEOFFREY CHAUCER

You know you're getting old when the candles cost more than the cake.
BOB HOPE

Forty is the old age of youth; fifty the youth of old age.
VICTOR HUGO

The evening of a well-spent life brings its lamps with it.
JOSEPH JOUBERT

The older the fiddle the sweeter the tune.
ENGLISH PROVERB

The old forget, the young don't know.
GERMAN PROVERB

The old age of an eagle is better than the youth of a sparrow.
GREEK PROVERB

For the ignorant, old age is as winter; for the learned, it is a harvest.
JEWISH PROVERB

The young man who has not wept is a savage; the old man who will not laugh is a fool.
GEORGE SANTAYANA

A man of fifty is responsible for his face.
FRANK L. STANTON

No wise man ever wished to be younger.
JONATHAN SWIFT

None are so old as those who have outlived enthusiasm.
HENRY DAVID THOREAU

Agnosticism

(*See also* Doubt and Unbelief)

The mystery of the beginning of all things is insoluble by us; and I for one must be content to remain an agnostic.
CHARLES DARWIN

Agnosticism simply means that a man shall not say he knows or believes that for which he has no grounds for professing to believe.
THOMAS HENRY HUXLEY

Agnosticism solves not, but merely shelves the mysteries of life. When agnosticism has done its withering work in the mind of man, the mysteries remain as before; all that has been added to them is a settled despair.
VINCENT MCNABB

Agnosticism leads inevitably to moral indifference. It denies us all power to esteem or to understand moral values, because it severs our spiritual contact with God who alone is the source of all morality.
THOMAS MERTON

I do not see much difference between avowing that there is no God, and implying that nothing definite can for certain be known about him.
JOHN HENRY NEWMAN

The agnostic's prayer: 'O God, if there is a god, save my soul, if I have a soul.'
JOSEPH ERNEST RENAN

Alms

(*See also* Gifts and Giving)

It is possible to give without loving, but it is impossible to love without giving.
RICHARD BRAUNSTEIN

The more he cast away the more he had.
JOHN BUNYAN

We make a living by what we get, but we make a life by what we give.
SIR WINSTON CHURCHILL

Our prayers and fastings are of less avail, unless they are aided by almsgiving.
ST. CYPRIAN

Alms are but the vehicles of prayer.
JOHN DRYDEN

Alms never make poor.
ENGLISH PROVERB

The little alms are the best alms.
FRENCH PROVERB

Offer your prayers and alms and do all things according to the Gospel of our Lord.
TEACHING OF THE TWELVE APOSTLES

Ambition

Ambition is like hunger; it obeys no law but its appetite.
JOSH BILLINGS

Well is it known that ambition can creep as well as soar.
EDMUND BURKE

All ambitions are lawful except those which climb upward on the miseries or credulities of mankind.
JOSEPH CONRAD

Ambition is the mind's immodesty.
SIR WILLIAM DAVENANT

Most of the trouble in the world is caused by people wanting to be important.
T. S. ELIOT

Nothing is humbler than ambition when it is about to climb.
BENJAMIN FRANKLIN

Hew not too high lest the chip fall in thine eye.
JOHN HEYWOOD

Ambition is pitiless; any merit that it cannot use it finds despicable.
JOSEPH JOUBERT

Most people would suceed in small things if they were not troubled by great ambitions.
HENRY WORDSWORTH LONGFELLOW

Every eel hopes to become a whale.
GERMAN PROVERB

Ambition destroys its possessor.
HEBREW PROVERB

You may get to the very top of the ladder, and then find it has not been leaning against the right wall.
A. RAINE

You cannot be anything if you want to be everything.
SOLOMON SCHECHTER

Angels

The servants of Christ are protected by invisible, rather than visible, beings. But if these guard you, they do so because they have been summoned by your prayers.
ST. AMBROSE

Angels mean messengers and ministers. Their function is to execute the plan of divine providence, even in earthly things.
ST. THOMAS AQUINAS

Angels can fly because they take themselves lightly.
G. K. CHESTERTON

There are nine orders of angels, to wit, angels, archangels, virtues, powers, principalities, dominations, thrones, cherubim and seraphim.
POPE ST. GREGORY I

They take different forms at the bidding of their master, God, and thus reveal themselves to men and unveil the divine mysteries to them.
ST. JOHN OF DAMASCUS

An angel is a spiritual creature created by God without a body, for the services of Christendom and of the Church.
MARTIN LUTHER

Millions of spiritual creatures walk the earth unseen, both when we sleep and when we awake.
JOHN MILTON

The question of how many angels could dance on the point of a pin no longer is absurd in molecular physics, with its discovery of how broad that point actually is, and what a part invisible electronic 'messengers' play in the dance of life.
LEWIS MUMFORD

Man is neither angel nor beast; and the misfortune is that he who would act the angel acts the beast.
BLAISE PASCAL

In these days you must go to Heaven to find an angel.
POLISH PROVERB

Anger

Anger is quieted by a gentle word just as fire is quenched by water.
JEAN PIERRE CAMUS

There is no sin nor wrong that gives a man such a foretaste of Hell in this life as anger and impatience.
ST. CATHERINE OF SIENA

There is a holy anger, excited by zeal, which moves us to reprove with warmth those whom our mildness failed to correct.
JEAN BAPTISTE DE LA SALLE

Anger is never without a reason, but seldom with a good one.
BENJAMIN FRANKLIN

Anger is one of the sinews of the soul. He who lacks it hath a maimed mind.
THOMAS FULLER

To be angry is to revenge the fault of others upon ourselves.
ALEXANDER POPE

Anger is often more hurtful than the injury that caused it.
AMERICAN PROVERB

Anger and haste hinder good counsel.
ENGLISH PROVERB

People who fly into a rage always make a bad landing.
WILL ROGERS

He that would be angry and sin not must not be angry with anything but sin.
THOMAS SECKER

Animals

A robin redbreast in a cage puts all heaven in a rage. A skylark wounded in the wing doth make a cherub cease to sing. He who shall hurt the little wren shall never be beloved by men.
WILLIAM BLAKE

Monkeys are superior to men in this: when a monkey looks into a mirror, he sees a monkey.
MALCOLM DE CHAZAL

Swans have an air of being proud, stupid, and mischievous – three qualities that go well together.
DENIS DIDEROT

Animals are such agreeable friends – they ask no questions, they pass no criticisms.
GEORGE ELIOT

A cat can be trusted to purr when she is pleased, which is more than can be said about human beings.
WILLIAM RALPH INGE

I tend to be suspicious of people whose love of animals is exaggerated; they are often frustrated in their relationships with humans.
CAMILLA KOFFLER

When an animal has nothing to do, it goes to sleep. When a man has nothing to do, he may ask questions.
BERNARD J. F. LONERGAN

No animal admires another animal.
BLAISE PASCAL

In training animals and children, the same principles apply; be fair, be firm, be fun.
BARBARA WOODHOUSE

Anxiety

(*See also* Worry)

Drones make more noise than bees, but all they make is the wax, not the honey. Those who torment themselves with eagerness and anxiety do little, and that badly.
ST. FRANCIS DE SALES

Anxiety is the natural result when our hopes are centred in anything short of God and his will for us.
BILLY GRAHAM

Anxiety is not only a pain which we must ask God to assuage but also a weakness we must ask him to pardon – for he's told us to take no care for the morrow.
C. S. LEWIS

Anxiety does not empty tomorrow of its sorrows, but only empties today of its strength.
CHARLES H. SPURGEON

Beware of anxiety. Next to sin, there is nothing that so troubles the mind, strains the heart, distresses the soul and confuses the judgment.
WILLIAM ULLATHORNE

Apathy

(*See also* Indifference)

The hottest places in Hell are reserved for those who in time of great moral crisis maintain their neutrality.
DANTE ALIGHIERI

The only thing necessary for the triumph of evil is for good men to do nothing.
EDMUND BURKE

Science may have found a cure for most evils; but it has found no remedy for the worst of them all – the apathy of human beings.
HELEN KELLER

Bad officials are elected by good citizens who do not vote.
GEORGE JEAN NATHAN

Appreciation

(*See also* Gratitude and Thanksgiving)

The deepest principle in human nature is the craving to be appreciated.
WILLIAM JAMES

Brains are like hearts – they go where they are appreciated.
ROBERT MCNAMARA

I have yet to find the man, however exalted his station, who did not do better work and put forth greater effort under a spirit of approval than under a spirit of criticism.
CHARLES M. SCHWAB

The best things in life are appreciated most after they have been lost.
ROY L. SMITH

Next to excellence is the appreciation of it.
WILLIAM MAKEPEACE THACKERAY

Architecture

It has been said that Gothic architecture represents the soul aspiring to God, and the Renaissance or Romanseque architecture represents God tabernacling with men.
ROBERT H. BENSON

Architecture is frozen music.
JOHANN WOLFGANG VON GOETHE

One of the big problems for an architect in our time is that for a hundred and fifty years men have been building churches as if a church could not belong to our time. A church has to look as if it were left over from some other age. I think that such an assumption is based on an implicit confession of atheism – as if God did not belong to all ages and as if religion were really only a pleasant, necessary social formality, preserved from past time in order to give our society an air of respectability.
THOMAS MERTON

However my reason may go with Gothic, my heart has ever gone with Grecian.
JOHN HENRY NEWMAN

Varieties of uniformities make complete beauty.
CHRISTOPHER WREN

Art

The aim of art is to represent not the outward appearance of things, but their inward significance.
ARISTOTLE

Art is the signature of man.
G. K. CHESTERTON

There has never been a boy painter, nor can there be. The art requires a long apprenticeship, being mechanical as well as intellectual.
JOHN CONSTABLE

Where the spirit does not work with the hand there is no art.
LEONARDO DA VINCI

One always has to spoil a picture a little bit, in order to finish it.
DELACROIX

Art is a collaboration between God and the artist, and the less the artist does the better.
ANDRÉ GIDE

All art is propaganda, for it is in fact impossible to do anything, to make anything, which is not expressive of 'value'.
ERIC GILL

What is the work of art? A word made flesh. That is the truth, in the clearest sense of the text. A word, that which emanates from the mind. Made flesh; a thing, a thing seen, a thing known, the immeasurable translated into terms of the measurable. From the highest to the lowest that is the substance of works of art.
ERIC GILL

Art is nothing more than the shadow of humanity.
HENRY JAMES

Art is the gift of God, and must be used unto his glory.
HENRY WORDSWORTH LONGFELLOW

Art is beauty made a sacrament. Art is finite human expression made infinite by love.
VINCENT MCNABB

Art is the telling of truth, and is the only available method for telling of certain truths.
IRIS MURDOCH

The novel is practically a Protestant form of art; it is a product of the free mind, of the autonomous individual.
GEORGE ORWELL

A good spectator also creates.
SWISS PROVERB

All great art is the expression of man's delight in God's work, not his own.
JOHN RUSKIN

We should comport ourselves with the masterpieces of art as with exalted personages – stand quietly before them and wait till they speak to us.
ARTHUR SCHOPENHAUER

Asceticism

(*See also* Self-Denial)

The sacrifice most acceptable to God is complete renunciation of the body and its passions. This is the only real piety.
ST. CLEMENT OF ALEXANDRIA

We can only reach the delicate truth of mysticism through the commonplace sincerities of asceticism.
FREDERICK W. FABER

The true ascetic counts nothing his own save his harp.
JOACHIM OF FLORA

The only asceticism known to Christian history is one that multiplies desire till the ascetic with something like divine avarice covets a kingdom beyond even the stars.
VINCENT MCNABB

Atheism

(*See also* Unbelief)

A little philosophy inclineth a man's mind to atheism, but depth in philosophy bringeth men's minds about to religion.
FRANCIS BACON

Atheism is rather in the lip than in the heart of man.
FRANCIS BACON

Where there is no God, there is no man.
NIKOLAI BERDYAEV

A man cannot become an atheist merely by wishing it.
NAPOLEON BONAPARTE

Nobody talks so constantly about God as those who insist there is no God.
HEYWOOD BROUN

An atheist is a man without any invisible means of support.
JOHN BUCHAN

There are no atheists in fox-holes.
WILLIAM T. CUMMINGS

Some are atheists only in fair weather.
THOMAS FULLER

Every effort to prove there is no God is in itself an effort to reach for God.
CHARLES EDWARD LOCKE

If Christianity cannot be based on atheism one must nevertheless acknowledge that the challenge of atheism is a constant safeguard against idolatry.
JOHN MACQUARRIE

Atheism thrives where religion is most debated.
WELSH PROVERB

To believe means to recognise that we must wait until the veil shall be removed. Unbelief prematurely unveils itself.
EUGEN ROSENSTOCK-HUESSY

The worst moment for the atheist is when he is really thankful and has nobody to thank.
DANTE GABRIEL ROSSETTI

Christianity founds hospitals, and atheists are cured in them, never knowing that they owe their cure to Christ.
WILLIAM TEMPLE

An atheist is a man who believes himself an accident.
FRANCIS THOMPSON

The religion of the atheist has a God-shaped blank at its heart.
H. G. WELLS

Atonement

(*See also* Reconciliation)

Christ's Passion is the true and proper cause of the forgiveness of sins.
ST. THOMAS AQUINAS

For the sake of each of us he laid down his life – worth no less than the universe. He demands of us in return our lives for the sake of each other.
ST. CLEMENT OF
ALEXANDRIA

In the cross, God descends to bear in his own heart the sins of the world. In Jesus, he atones at unimaginable cost to himself.
WOODROW A. GEIER

A great many people are trying to make peace, but that has already been done. God has not left it for us to do; all we have to do is to enter into it.
DWIGHT L. MOODY

When God pardons, he consigns the offence to everlasting forgetfulness.
MERV. ROSELL

A heavy guilt rests upon us for what the whites of all nations have done to the coloured peoples. When we do good to them, it is not benevolence – it is atonement.
ALBERT SCHWEITZER

Attributes of God

God is that, the greater than which cannot be conceived.
ST. ANSELM OF CANTERBURY

God alone knows the depths and the riches of his Godhead, and divine wisdom alone can declare his secrets.
ST. THOMAS AQUINAS

We can know what God is not, but we cannot know what he is.
ST. AUGUSTINE OF HIPPO

God is within all things, but not included; outside all things, but not excluded; above all things, but not beyond their reach.
POPE ST. GREGORY I

Change and decay in all around I see;
O thou, who changest not, abide with
me.
HENRY FRANCIS LYTE

The attributes of God, though intelligible to us on their surface yet, for the very reason that they are infinite, transcend our comprehension, when they are dwelt upon, when they are followed out, and can only be received by faith.
JOHN HENRY NEWMAN

The word 'God' is a theology in itself, indivisibly one, inexhaustibly various, from the vastness and the simplicity of its meaning.
JOHN HENRY NEWMAN

To him no high, no low, no great, no small; he fills, he bounds, connects and equals all!
ALEXANDER POPE

A comprehended God is not God at all.
GERHARD TERSTEEGEN

One might lay it down as a postulate: all conceptions of God which are incompatible with a movement of pure charity are false. All other conceptions of him, in varying degrees, are true.
SIMONE WEIL

Authority

No authority has power to impose error, and if it resists the truth, the truth must be upheld until it is admitted.
JOHN ACTON

The man who cannot control himself becomes absurd when he wants to rule over others.
ISAAC ARAMA

It is right to submit to higher authority whenever a command of God would not be violated.
ST. BASIL

Cast away authority, and authority shall forsake you!
ROBERT H. BENSON

I am convinced that people are open to the Christian message if it is seasoned with authority and proclaimed as God's own Word.
BILLY GRAHAM

Authority is not a short way to the truth; it is the only way to many truths; and for men on earth, it is the only way to divine truths.
VINCENT MCNABB

Men desire authority for its own sake that they may bear a rule, command and control other men, and live uncommanded and uncontrolled themselves.
SIR THOMAS MORE

If you accept the authority of Jesus in your life, then you accept the authority of His words.
COLIN URQUHART

Baptism

No athlete is admitted to the contest of virtue, unless he has first been washed of all stains of sins and consecrated with the gift of heavenly grace.
ST. AMBROSE

According to the New Testament, all men have in principle received baptism long ago, namely on Golgotha, at Good Friday and Easter.
OSCAR CULLMAN

If any man receive not baptism, he hath no salvation; except only martyrs, who even without water receive the kingdom.
ST. CYRIL OF JERUSALEM

When the Church baptises a child, that action concerns me, for that child is thereby connected to that which is my head too, and ingrafted into that body whereof I am a member.
JOHN DONNE

You have been baptised, but think not that you are straightway a Christian . . . The flesh is touched with salt: what then if the mind remains unsalted? The body is anointed, yet the mind remains un-anointed. But if you are buried with Christ within, and already practise walking with Him in newness of life, I acknowledge you as a Christian.
DESIDERIUS ERASMUS

Baptism signifies that the old Adam in us is to be drowned by daily sorrow and repentance, and perish with all sins and evil lusts; and that the new man should daily come forth again and rise, who shall live before God in righteousness and purity forever.
MARTIN LUTHER

Baptism points back to the work of God, and forward to the life of faith.
J. A. MOTYER

In baptism, the direction is indicated rather than the arrival.
FREDERICH REST

Baptism seemed such an integral part of New Testament Christianity and I couldn't imagine a droplet of water dribbled on my head when I was a baby could be a proper substitute for that adult symbol of submission and obedience.
CLIFF RICHARD

After their baptism in the Holy Spirit Christians walk in newness of life, the life of the new creation, the life of the Age to Come.
ALAN RICHARDSON

Baptise as follows: After first explaining all these points, baptise in the name of the Father and of the Son and of the Holy Spirit, in running water. But if you have no running water, baptise in other water; and if you cannot in cold, then in warm. But if you have neither, pour water on the head three times in the name of the Father and of the Son and of the Holy Spirit.
TEACHING OF THE TWELVE APOSTLES

Happy is our sacrament of water, in that by washing away the sins of our early blindness, we are set free and admitted into eternal life . . . But we, little fishes, after the example of our ICHTHYS (Jesous Christos Theou Uios Soter: Jesus Christ Son of God Saviour) are born in water, nor have we safety in any other way than by permanently abiding in water.
QUINTUS TERTULLIAN

The Passover provides the day of most solemnity for baptism, for then was accomplished our Lord's Passion, and into it we are baptised.
QUINTUS TERTULLIAN

Beatitudes

If the Sermon on the Mount is the précis of all Christian doctrine, the eight beatitudes are the précis of the whole of the Sermon on the Mount.
JACQUES B. BOSSUET

Blessed is he who does good to others and desires not that others should do good to him.
BROTHER GILES

Jesus clothes the beatitudes with his own life.
CARL F. HENRY

The more we live and try to practise the Sermon on the Mount, the more shall we experience blessing.
MARTYN LLOYD-JONES

It is not written, blessed is he that feedeth the poor, but he that considereth the poor. A little thought and a little kindness are often worth more than a great deal of money.
JOHN RUSKIN

The beatitudes are a call to us to see ourselves, to live with ourselves, in a way that probably does not come easily to most of us.
SIMON TUGWELL

Beauty

Beauty and the beautiful – these are one and the same in God.
ST. THOMAS AQUINAS

Beauty is indeed a good gift of God; but that the good may not think it a great good, God dispenses it even to the wicked.
ST. AUGUSTINE OF HIPPO

Wherever ugliness is kept at bay, there the Spirit of God, who is the God of Beauty, is doing His creative and re-creative labour.
DONALD COGGAN

When beauty fires the blood, how love exalts the mind.
JOHN DRYDEN

Beauty is the mark God sets upon virtue.
RALPH WALDO EMERSON

Though we travel the world over to find the beautiful, we must carry it with us or we find it not.
RALPH WALDO EMERSON

Spring is God thinking in gold, laughing in blue, and speaking in green.
FRANK JOHNSON

A thing of beauty is a joy for ever.
JOHN KEATS

God's fingers can touch nothing but to mould it into loveliness.
GEORGE MACDONALD

Beauty is the radiance of truth; the fragrance of goodness.
VINCENT MCNABB

If you want a golden rule that will fit everybody, this is it: Have nothing in your houses that you do not know to be useful, or believe to be beautiful.
WILLIAM MORRIS

Beauty may have fair leaves, yet bitter fruit.
ENGLISH PROVERB

The crow thinketh her own birds fairest in the wood.
ENGLISH PROVERB

Beauty without virtue is a flower without perfume.
FRENCH PROVERB

The saying that beauty is but skin deep is but a skin-deep saying.
HERBERT SPENCER

Behaviour

(*See also* Courtesy and Manners)

The sum of behaviour is to retain a man's own dignity, without intruding upon the liberty of others.
FRANCIS BACON

We are turning out machines that act like men, and men that act like machines.
ERICH FROMM

The quality of moral behaviour varies in inverse ratio to the number of human beings involved.
ALDOUS HUXLEY

Would to God we had behaved ourselves well in this world, even for one day.
THOMAS À KEMPIS

Strive to be like a well-regulated watch, of pure gold, with open face, busy hands and full of good works.
DAVID NEWQUIST

Belief

(*See also* Conviction and Faith)

A belief is not true because it is useful.
HENRI FRÉDÉRIC AMIEL

If you believe in the Gospel what you like, and reject what you don't like, it is not the Gospel you believe, but yourself.
ST. AUGUSTINE OF HIPPO

Understanding is the reward of faith. Therefore seek not to understand that you may believe, but believe that you may understand.
ST. AUGUSTINE OF HIPPO

Man is what he believes.
ANTON CHEKHOV

The point of having an open mind, like having an open mouth, is to close it on something solid.
G. K. CHESTERTON

He that will believe only what he can fully comprehend must have a very long head or a very short creed.
CHARLES CALEB COLTON

Belief consists in accepting the affirmations of the soul; unbelief in denying them.
RALPH WALDO EMERSON

You never know how much you really believe anything until its truth or falsehood becomes a matter of life and death to you.
C. S. LEWIS

Believing in God means getting down on your knees.
MARTIN LUTHER

It is as absurd to argue men, as to torture them, into believing.
JOHN HENRY NEWMAN

There are three roads to belief: reason, habit, revelation.
BLAISE PASCAL

Believe not all that you see nor half what you hear.
ENGLISH PROVERB

To believe means to recognise that we must wait until the veil shall be removed. Unbelief prematurely unveils itself.
EUGEN ROSENSTOCK-HUESSY

Bereavement

(*See also* Death and Grief)

The true way to mourn the dead is to take care of the living who belong to them.
EDMUND BURKE

The house of mourning teaches charity and wisdom.
ST. JOHN CHRYSOSTOM

A deep plunge into the waters of sorrow is the hopefullest way of getting through them on one's daily road of life again. No one can help another very much in these crises of life; but love and sympathy count for something.
THOMAS HENRY HUXLEY

A man's dying is more the survivors' affair than his own.
THOMAS MANN

You cannot prevent the birds of sorrow from flying over your head, but you can prevent them from building nests in your hair.
CHINESE PROVERB

Those who live in the Lord never see each other for the last time.
GERMAN PROVERB

Ah, why should we wear black for the guests of God.
JOHN RUSKIN

But, oh, for the touch of a vanished hand, And the sound of a voice that is still!
ALFRED, LORD TENNYSON

Bible

(*See also* Scripture)

In the Old Testament the New lies hidden, in the New Testament the Old is laid open.
ST. AUGUSTINE OF HIPPO

In the twentieth century our highest praise is to call the Bible 'the World's Best-Seller'. And it has come to be more and more difficult to say whether we think it is a best-seller because it is great, or vice versa.
D. BOORSTIN

The Bible is a window in this prison-world, through which we may look into eternity.
T. DWIGHT

The word of God is in the Bible as the soul is in the body.
P. T. FORSYTH

What you bring away from the Bible depends to some extent on what you carry to it.
OLIVER WENDELL HOLMES

Lay hold on the Bible until the Bible lays hold on you.
WILLIAM H. HOUGHTON

Men do not reject the Bible because it contradicts itself but because it contradicts them.
E. PAUL HOVEY

England has two books, the Bible and Shakespeare. England made Shakespeare but the Bible made England.
VICTOR HUGO

If a man's Bible is coming apart, it is an indication that he himself is fairly well put together.
JAMES JENNINGS

The Bible is an inexhaustible fountain of all truths. The existence of the Bible is the greatest blessing which humanity ever experienced.
IMMANUEL KANT

If thou knewest the whole Bible by heart, and the sayings of all the philosophers, what would it profit thee without the love of God and without grace?
THOMAS À KEMPIS

The Bible is alive, it speaks to me; it has feet, it runs after me; it has hands, it lays hold on me.
MARTIN LUTHER

The Bible was written for a man with a head upon his shoulders.
MARTIN LUTHER

One of the many divine qualities of the Bible is this, that it does not yield its secrets to the irreverent and censorious.
J. I. PACKER

We must not only pause to reflect upon passages from the Bible, but upon 'slices of life', too, relating them together, and to the will of the Risen Christ for us.
MICHEL QUOIST

If a man is not familiar with the Bible, he has suffered a loss which he had better make all possible haste to correct.
THEODORE ROOSEVELT

We need never tremble *for* the word of God, though we may tremble *at* it and the demands which it makes upon our faith and courage.
WILLIAM ROBERTSON SMITH

When you have read the Bible, you will know it is the word of God, because you will have found it the key to your own heart, your own happiness and your own duty.
WOODROW WILSON

Bigotry

(*See also* Blindness, Spiritual)

Wisdom never has made a bigot, but learning has.
JOSH BILLINGS

Bigotry may be roughly defined as the anger of men who have no opinions.
G. K. CHESTERTON

The mind of a bigot is like the pupil of the eye; the more light you pour upon it, the more it will contract.
OLIVER WENDELL HOLMES

The experience of many ages proves that men may be ready to fight to the death, and to persecute without pity, for a religion whose creed they do not understand, and whose precepts they habitually disobey.
THOMAS B. MACAULAY

Bigotry is the infliction of our own unproved first principles on others, and treating others with scorn or hatred for not accepting them.
JOHN HENRY NEWMAN

Men never do evil so completely and cheerfully as when they do it from religious conviction.
BLAISE PASCAL

No physician can cure the blind in mind.
JEWISH PROVERB

If we believe absurdities we shall commit atrocities.
FRANÇOIS MARIE VOLTAIRE

Birth

Those who are born drive out those who preceded them. But there, in the hereafter, we shall all live on together. There will be no successors there, for neither will there be departures.
ST. AUGUSTINE OF HIPPO

If you grieve for the dead, mourn also for those who are born into the world; for as the one thing is of nature, so is the other too of nature.
ST. JOHN CHRYSOSTOM

Birth is the beginning of death.
THOMAS FULLER

Our birth made us mortal, our death will make us immortal.
ENGLISH PROVERB

He who is born, yells; he who dies is silent.
RUSSIAN PROVERB

Bishop

(*See also* Clergy)

'For you, I am Bishop,' said St. Augustine to his people, 'but with you, I am a Christian. The first is an office accepted, the second a grace received; one a danger, the other safety. If then I am gladder by far to be redeemed with you than I am to be placed over you, I shall, as the Lord commanded, be more completely your servant.'
ST. AUGUSTINE OF HIPPO

Whoever is sent by the Master to run his house, we ought to receive him as we would receive the Master himself. It is obvious, therefore, that we ought to regard the bishop as we would the Lord himself.
ST. IGNATIUS OF ANTIOCH

The bishop is the chief of the priests . . . For he ordains priests and deacons. He has power over all ranks of the clergy; he points out what each one should do.
ST. ISIDORE OF SEVILLE

To be a bishop (sacerdos) is much, to deserve to be one is more.
ST. JEROME

A bishop should die preaching.
JOHN JEWEL

The very conception of Israel or the Church as a flock involves the institution of pastoral rule and oversight; the flock must have shepherds who rule it and feed it under the ultimate supervision of the Chief Shepherd himself.
ALAN RICHARDSON

Now hear an allusion: a mitre, you know, is divided above, but united below. If this you consider, our emblem is right; the bishops divide, but the clergy unite.
JONATHAN SWIFT

Blasphemy

Blasphemy itself could not survive religion; if anyone doubts that, let him try to blaspheme Odin.
G. K. CHESTERTON

There is nothing worse than blasphemy.
ST. JOHN CHRYSOSTOM

All great truths begin as blasphemies.
GEORGE BERNARD SHAW

Blessing

Our real blessings often appear to us in the shape of pains, losses and disappointments; but let us have patience, and we soon shall see them in their proper figures.
JOSEPH ADDISON

Blessedness consists in the accomplishment of our desires, and in our having only regular desires.
ST. AUGUSTINE OF HIPPO

Prosperity is the blessing of the Old Testament; adversity is the blessing of the New.
FRANCIS BACON

Reflect upon your present blessings, of which every man has many; not on your past misfortunes, of which all men have some.
CHARLES DICKENS

Never undertake anything for which you wouldn't have the courage to ask the blessings of heaven.
GEORGE C. LICHTENBERG

It is not God's way that great blessings should descend without the sacrifice first of great sufferings.
JOHN HENRY NEWMAN

Blessings ever wait on virtuous deeds.
ENGLISH PROVERB

Blessings we enjoy daily, and for the most of them, because they be so common, men forget to pay their praises. But let not us, because it is a sacrifice so pleasing to him who still protects us, and gives us flowers, and showers, and meat and content.
IZAAK WALTON

The more we count the blessings we have, the less we crave the luxuries we haven't.
WILLIAM A. WARD

Blindness, Spiritual

(*See also* Bigotry, Darkness and Light)

Blind men should judge no colours.
JOHN HEYWOOD

The devil is ready to put out men's eyes that are content willing to wax blind.
SIR THOMAS MORE

None so blind as those who won't see.
ENGLISH PROVERB

When the blind man carries the banner, woe to those who follow.
FRENCH PROVERB

Blood

Let us fix our gaze on the blood of Christ and realise how precious it is to the Father, seeing that it was poured out for our salvation.
POPE ST. CLEMENT I

Human blood is all of one colour.
THOMAS FULLER

Blood is thicker than water.
ENGLISH PROVERB

It is His 'blood', the symbol of the laying down of His life, which can cleanse us from our sins today.
JOHN R. W. STOTT

We multiply whenever we are mown down by you; the blood of Christians is seed.
QUINTUS TERTULLIAN

Body and Soul

(*See also* Wholeness)

Despise the flesh, for it passes away; be solicitous for your soul which will never die.
ST. BASIL

The body is a vital source of gratification which we ignore or dismiss only at the risk of violating our integrity.
JACK DOMINIAN

We take excellent care of our bodies, which we have for only a lifetime; yet we let our souls shrivel, which we will have for eternity.
BILLY GRAHAM

The soul, like the body, lives by what it feeds on.
JOSIAH GILBERT HOLLAND

Even a cursory reading of the New Testament leaves a convincing impression that Jesus was typically Hebrew in his view of man: he did not divide man into body and soul, but he saw him as a whole person.
FRANCIS MacNUTT

The body is sooner dressed than the soul.
ENGLISH PROVERB

What soap is for the body, tears are for the soul.
JEWISH PROVERB

Conscience is the voice of the soul, as the passions are the voice of the body. No wonder they often contradict each other.
JEAN JACQUES ROUSSEAU

Body and soul are twins: God only knows which is which.
CHARLES A. SWINBURNE

Body and soul are not two substances but one. They are man becoming aware of himself in two different ways.
C. F. VON WEIZSACKER

Boredom

We are seldom tiresome to ourselves.
SAMUEL JOHNSON

One cure for boredom is to forget yourself through activities which bring you in touch with people and ideas outside yourself.
BLANCHE McKEOUN

The average male gets his living by such depressing devices that boredom becomes a sort of natural state to him.
HENRY L. MENCKEN

Is not life a hundred times too short for us to bore ourselves.
FRIEDRICH NIETZSCHE

There is nothing so insupportable to man as complete repose, without passion, occupation, amusement, care. Then it is that he feels his nothingness, his isolation, his insufficiency, his dependence, his impotence, his emptiness.
BLAISE PASCAL

We often forgive those who bore us, but we cannot forgive those whom we bore.
FRANÇOIS DE LA ROCHEFOUCAULD

The most bored people in life are not the underprivileged but the overprivileged.
FULTON J. SHEEN

Bread

(*See also* Communion, Holy and Eucharist)

Therefore you hear that as often as sacrifice is offered, the Lord's death, the Lord's resurrection, the Lord's ascension and the remission of sins is signified, and will you not take the Bread of Life daily? He who has a wound needs medicine. The wound is that we are under sin; the medicine is the heavenly and venerable Sacrament.
ST. AMBROSE

The question of bread for myself is a material question; but the question of bread for my neighbour, for everybody, is a spiritual and a religious question.
NIKOLAI BERDYAEV

The history of man from the beginning has been the history of the struggle for daily bread.
JESUS DE CASTRO

Here is bread, which strengthens man's heart, and therefore called the staff of life.
MATTHEW HENRY

When God gives us bread, men will supply the butter.
YIDDISH PROVERB

Bread is worth all, it is the staff of life.
ENGLISH PROVERB

He who turns up his nose at his work quarrels with his bread and butter.
CHARLES H. SPURGEON

Brokenness

God can never make us wine if we object to the fingers he uses to crush us with. If God would only use his own fingers, and make us broken bread and poured out wine in a special way! But when he uses someone whom we dislike, or some set of circumstances to which we said we would never submit, and makes those the crushers, we object.
OSWALD CHAMBERS

God creates out of nothing. Therefore until a man is nothing, God can make nothing out of him.
MARTIN LUTHER

Broken bones well set become stronger.
ENGLISH PROVERB

We must be broken into life.
CHARLES E. RAVEN

Brokenness is not revival; it is a vital and indispensable step toward it.
ARTHUR WALLIS

How else but through a broken heart may the Lord Christ enter in.
OSCAR WILDE

Brotherhood

(*See also* Community)

Men became what they are, sons of God, by becoming what they are, brothers of their brothers.
MARTIN BUBER

The mystic bond of brotherhood makes all men one.
THOMAS CARLYLE

Until you have become really, in actual fact, the brother of everyone, brotherhood will not come to pass.
FEODOR DOSTOEVSKI

There is no brotherhood of man without the fatherhood of God.
HENRY MARTYN FIELD

If you really believe in the brotherhood of man, and you want to come into its fold, you've got to let everyone else in too.
OSCAR HAMMERSTEIN

It is through fraternity that liberty is saved.
VICTOR HUGO

The world has narrowed into a neighbourhood before it has broadened into a brotherhood.
LYNDON B. JOHNSON

Human brotherhood is not just a goal. It is a condition on which our way of life depends.
JOHN F. KENNEDY

The race of mankind would perish from the earth did they cease to aid each other.
SIR WALTER SCOTT

In all my travels the thing that has impressed me most is the universal brotherhood of man – what there is of it.
MARK TWAIN

Business

The society of money and exploitation has never been charged, so far as I know, with assuring the triumph of freedom and justice.
ALBERT CAMUS

Do other men for they would do you. That's the true business precept.
CHARLES DICKENS

Make yourself a seller when you are buying, and a buyer when you are selling, and then you will sell and buy justly.
ST. FRANCIS DE SALES

Business is the salt of life.
ENGLISH PROVERB

The buyer needs a hundred eyes, the seller but one.
ITALIAN PROVERB

To my mind the best investment a young man starting out in business could possibly make is to give all his time, all his energies to work, just plain, hard work.
CHARLES M. SCHWAB

I think that there is nothing, not even crime, more opposed to poetry, to philosophy, ay, to life itself than this incessant business.
HENRY DAVID THOREAU

Business underlies everything in our national life, including our spiritual life. Witness the fact that in the Lord's Prayer the first petition is for daily bread. No one can worship God or love his neighbour on an empty stomach.
WOODROW WILSON

Capitalism

(*See also* Business)

All the denominations have fallen prey to the capitalist machine. With what remnant of moral authority can we demand structural change if our own institutes are linked to the old structures?
HELDER CAMARA

What horror has the world come to when it uses profit as the prime incentive in human progress, and competition as the supreme law of economics?
HELDER CAMARA

The inherent vice of capitalism is the unequal sharing of blessings, the inherent vice of socialism is the equal sharing of miseries.
SIR WINSTON CHURCHILL

The fear of capitalism has compelled socialism to widen freedom, and the fear of socialism has compelled capitalism to increase equality.
WILL DURANT

Capital as such is not evil; it is its wrong use that is evil.
MOHANDAS GANDHI

It is just that any man who does service to society and increases the general wealth should himself have a due share of the increased public riches, provided always that he respects the laws of God and the rights of his neighbour.
POPE PIUS XI

Under capitalism man exploits man; under socialism the reverse is true.
POLISH PROVERB

Catholic

The Church has four marks, being one, holy, catholic or universal, and strong or lasting.
ST. THOMAS AQUINAS

For the whole Church which is throughout the whole world possesses one and the same faith.
ST. IRENAEUS

The fact of the missions reveals the Church's faith in herself as the catholic unity of mankind.
J. C. MURRAY

It seems to me that catholicity is not only one of the notes of the Church, but, according to the divine purposes, one of its securities.
JOHN HENRY NEWMAN

True catholicity is commensurate with the wants of the human mind; but persons are often to be found who are surprised that they cannot persuade all men to follow them, and cannot destroy dissent, by preaching a portion of the divine system, instead of the whole of it.
JOHN HENRY NEWMAN

Locality, nationality, particularity are essential marks of the universal Church; the local congregation is the embodiment at a given place and time of the Church of all the world.
ALAN RICHARDSON

Change

(*See also* Reform)

All great changes are irksome to the human mind, especially those which are attended with great dangers and uncertain effects.
JOHN ADAMS

We can change, slowly and steadily, if we set our will to it.
ROBERT H. BENSON

We must all obey the great law of change. It is the most powerful law of nature.
EDMUND BURKE

He who shall introduce into public affairs the principles of primitive Christianity will change the face of the world.
BENJAMIN FRANKLIN

There is danger in reckless change; but greater danger in blind conservation.
HENRY GEORGE

There is nothing permanent except change.
HERACLITUS

In a higher world it is otherwise; but here below to live is to change, and to be perfect is to have changed often.
JOHN HENRY NEWMAN

The more change, the more of the same old thing.
FRENCH PROVERB

Those who cannot change their minds cannot change anything.
GEORGE BERNARD SHAW

Character

(*See also* Personality)

Character is better than ancestry, and personal conduct is of more importance than the highest parentage.
DR. BARNARDO

At death, if at any time, we see ourselves as we are, and display our true characters.
ROBERT H. BENSON

Just as good literature and good art raise and ennoble character, so bad literature and bad art degrade it.
DONALD COGGAN

A man is what he thinks about all day long.
RALPH WALDO EMERSON

A character, no more than a fence, can be strengthened by whitewash.
PAUL FROST

The discipline of desire is the background of character.
JOHN LOCKE

Character is what you are in the dark.
DWIGHT L. MOODY

Reputation is what men and women think of us. Character is what God and the angels know of us.
THOMAS PAINE

You cannot carve rotten wood.
CHINESE PROVERB

A man never shows his own character so plainly as by the way he describes another's.
JEAN PAUL RICHTER

Men best show their character in trifles, where they are not on their guard.
ARTHUR SCHOPENHAUER

Character is not in the mind. It is in the will.
FULTON J. SHEEN

Character is a by-product, it is produced in the great manufacture of daily duty.
WOODROW WILSON

Charity

(*See also* Love of Neighbour)

Charity is the form, mover, mother and root of all the virtues.
ST. THOMAS AQUINAS

Charity is that with which no man is lost, and without which no man is saved.
ST. ROBERT BELLARMINE

No sound ought to be heard in the Church but the healing voice of Christian charity.
EDMUND BURKE

Charity is the pure gold which makes us rich in eternal wealth.
JEAN PIERRE CAMUS

Charity begins at home, and justice begins next door.
CHARLES DICKENS

This is charity, to do all, all that we can.
JOHN DONNE

To love our neighbour in charity is to love God in man.
ST. FRANCIS DE SALES

Perhaps with charity one shouldn't think. Charity like love should be blind.
GRAHAM GREENE

All other gifts of God and works of man are common to good and bad, to the elect and the reprobate, but the gift of charity belongs only to the good and the elect.
WALTER HILTON

True charity means returning good for evil – always.
MARY MAZZARELLO

He who has charity is far from all sin.
POLYCARP

Charity and pride do both feed the poor.
ENGLISH PROVERB

It is certain that God cannot, will not, never did, reject a charitable man in his greatest needs and in his most passionate prayers; for God himself is love, and every degree of charity that dwells in us is the participation of the Divine Nature.
JEREMY TAYLOR

Chastity

(*See also* Modesty and Purity)

Do not say that you have chaste minds if you have unchaste eyes, because an unchaste eye is the messenger of an unchaste heart.
ST. AUGUSTINE OF HIPPO

The essence of chastity is not the suppression of lust, but the total orientation of one's life towards a goal. Without such a goal, chastity is bound to become ridiculous. Chastity is the sine qua non of lucidity and concentration.
DIETRICH BONHOEFFER

To be chaste is to have the body in the keeping of the heart. Their divorce is the one thing which in the end makes unchastity.
FRANCIS H. BRADLEY

Chastity is the longed for house of Christ and the earthly heaven of the heart.
ST. JOHN CLIMACUS

Vigilance and prayer are the safeguards of chastity.
JEAN BAPTISTE DE LA SALLE

If anyone is able to persevere in chastity to the honour of the flesh of the Lord, let him do so in all humility.
ST. IGNATIUS OF ANTIOCH

The virtue of chastity does not mean that we are insensible to the urge of concupiscence, but that we subordinate it to reason and the law of grace, by striving wholeheartedly after what is noblest in human and Christian life.
POPE PIUS XII

We Christians regard a stain upon our chastity as more dreadful than any punishment, or even than death itself.
QUINTUS TERTULLIAN

Cheerfulness

(*See also* Contentment, Happiness and Joy)

Cheerfulness and content are great beautifiers, and are famous preservers of good looks.
CHARLES DICKENS

Cheerfulness is among the most laudable virtues. It gains you the good will and friendship of others. It blesses those who practise it and those upon whom it is bestowed.
B. C. FORBES

A cheerful look makes a dish a feast.
GEORGE HERBERT

Christian cheerfulness is that modest, hopeful and peaceful joy which springs from charity and is protected by patience.
WILLIAM ULLATHORNE

Cheerfulness in most cheerful people is the rich and satisfying result of strenuous discipline.
EDWIN PERCY WHIPPLE

Children

(*See also* Family)

I cannot bear the crying of children, but when my child cries, I don't hear.
ANTON CHEKHOV

Children are our most valuable natural resource.
HERBERT HOOVER

One laugh of a child will make the holiest day more sacred still.
ROBERT G. INGERSOLL

You can learn many things from children. How much patience you have, for instance.
FRANKLIN P. JONES

Children have more need of models than of critics.
JOSEPH JOUBERT

The one thing children wear out faster than shoes is parents.
JOHN PLOMP

Children should be seen and not heard.
ENGLISH PROVERB

Children suck the mother when they are young, and the father when they are old.
ENGLISH PROVERB

The best brought-up children are those who have seen their parents as they are. Hypocrisy is not the parents' first duty.
GEORGE BERNARD SHAW

Children are very adept at comprehending modern statistics. When they say, 'Everyone else is allowed to', it is usually based on a survey of one.
PAUL SWEENEY

As the twig is bent the tree inclines.
PUBLIUS VIRGIL

Give me a child for the first seven years, and you may do what you like with him afterwards.
FRANCIS XAVIER

Children can forgive their parents for being wrong, but weakness sends them elsewhere for strength.
LEONTINE YOUNG

Choice

(*See also* Free Will)

The strongest principle of growth lies in human choice.
GEORGE ELIOT

In darkness there is no choice. It is light that enables us to see the differences between things; and it is Christ who gives us light.
AUGUSTUS W. HARE

When you have to make a choice and don't make it, that is in itself a choice.
WILLIAM JAMES

The power of choosing good or evil is within the reach of all.
ORIGEN OF ALEXANDRIA

Christian

(*See also* Discipleship)

All diseases of Christians are to be ascribed to demons.
ST. AUGUSTINE OF HIPPO

A Christian is someone who shares the sufferings of God in the world.
DIETRICH BONHOEFFER

If you were arrested for being a Christian, would there be enough evidence to convict you?
DAVID OTIS FULLER

Being a Christian is more than just an instantaneous conversion – it is a daily process whereby you grow to be more and more like Christ.
BILLY GRAHAM

Christian life is the life of Christ in man and man in Christ.
ROMANO GUARDINI

A Christian is not his own master, since all his time belongs to God.
ST. IGNATIUS OF ANTIOCH

To be a Christian is the great thing, not merely to seem one. And somehow or other those please the world most who please Christ least.
ST. JEROME

A true Christian may be almost defined as one who has a ruling sense of God's presence within him.
JOHN HENRY NEWMAN

To be like Christ is to be a Christian.
WILLIAM PENN

The Christian should resemble a fruit tree, not a Christmas tree! For the gaudy decorations of a Christmas tree are only tied on, whereas fruit grows on a fruit tree.
JOHN R. W. STOTT

No one is wise, no one is faithful, no one excels in dignity, but the Christian; and no one is a Christian but he who perseveres even to the end.
QUINTUS TERTULLIAN

Christianity

Two things about the Christian religion must surely be clear to anybody with eyes in his head. One is that men cannot do without it; the other, that they cannot do with it as it is.
MATTHEW ARNOLD

The essential fact of Christianity is that God thought all men worth the sacrifice of his Son.
WILLIAM BARCLAY

Christianity has died many times and risen again; for it had a God who knew the way out of the grave.
G. K. CHESTERTON

He who begins by loving Christianity better than truth will proceed by loving his own sect or church better than Christianity and end in loving himself better than all.
SAMUEL TAYLOR COLERIDGE

The essence of Christianity is simply and solely belief in the unification of the world in God through the Incarnation.
P. TEILHARD DE CHARDIN

Christianity is completed Judaism, or it is nothing.
BENJAMIN DISRAELI

The great part of Christianity is wholeheartedly to want to become a Christian.
DESIDERIUS ERASMUS

It is unnatural for Christianity to be popular.
BILLY GRAHAM

There is no more profound or more dangerous enemy to Christianity than anything which shrinks it and makes it narrow.
ABBÉ HUVELIN

Christianity is the highest perfection of humanity.
SAMUEL JOHNSON

Organised Christianity has probably done more to retard the ideals that were its founder's than any other agency in the world.
RICHARD LE GALLIENNE

Christianity, if false, is of no importance, and if true, of infinite importance. The one thing it cannot be is moderately important.
C. S. LEWIS

True Christianity is love in action.
DAVID O. MCKAY

Christianity is more than a doctrine. It is Christ Himself, living in those whom He has united to Himself in One Mystical Body.
THOMAS MERTON

For a religion to be true it must have knowledge of our nature. It must know its greatness and its meaning, and the cause of both. What religion but Christianity knows that?
BLAISE PASCAL

Christianity is like electricity. It cannot enter a person unless it can pass through.
RICHARD C. RAINES

Christ cannot live his life today in this world without our mouth, without our eyes, without our going and coming, without our heart. When we love, it is Christ loving through us. This is Christianity.
LEON JOSEPH SUENENS

The primary declaration of Christianity is not 'This do!' but 'This happened!'
EVELYN UNDERHILL

Christianity can be condensed into four words: admit, submit, commit and transmit.
SAMUEL WILBERFORCE

Christmas

(*See also* Incarnation)

The fact of Jesus' coming is the final and unanswerable proof that God cares.
WILLIAM BARCLAY

The character of the Creator cannot be less than the highest He has created, and the highest is that babe born to Mary on that first Christmas morning.
A. IAN BURNETT

It is good to be children sometimes, and never better than at Christmas, when its mighty Founder was a child Himself.
CHARLES DICKENS

Christmas is the season for kindling the fire of hospitality in the hall, the genial flame of charity in the heart.
WASHINGTON IRVING

To us Christians, the first Christmas Day is the solstice or bottleneck of history. Things got worse till then, ever since we had lost paradise; things are to get better since then, till we reach paradise once more. History is shaped like an X.
RONALD A. KNOX

You can never truly enjoy Christmas until you can look up into the Father's face and tell him you have received his Christmas gift.
JOHN R. RICE

The simple shepherds heard the voice of an angel and found their Lamb; the wise men saw the light of a star and found their Wisdom.
FULTON J. SHEEN

Christmas is the day that holds all time together.
ALEXANDER SMITH

A good many people with houses half empty on Christmas Eve have blamed the little innkeeper of Bethlehem because his place was full.
ROY L. SMITH

The coming of Christ by way of a Bethlehem manger seems strange and stunning. But when we take him out of the manger and invite him into our hearts, then the meaning unfolds and the strangeness vanishes.
NEIL C. STRAIT

After all, Christmas is but a big love affair to remove the wrinkles of the year with kindly remembrances.
JOHN WANAMAKER

Church

(*See also* Communion of Saints)

He cannot have God for his father who refuses to have the Church for his mother.
ST. AUGUSTINE OF HIPPO

The Church of Christ is not an institution; it is a new life with Christ and in Christ, guided by the Holy Spirit.
SERGIUS BULGAKOV

Every man may err, but not the whole gathered together; for the whole hath a promise.
ROBERT H. BENSON

What matters in the Church is not religion but the form of Christ, and its taking form amidst a band of men.
DIETRICH BONHOEFFER

Wherever we see the Word of God purely preached and heard, there a Church of God exists, even if it swarms with many faults.
JOHN CALVIN

The purpose of the Church in the world is to be the worshipping and witnessing spearhead of all that is in accordance with the will of God as it has been revealed in Jesus Christ.
DONALD COGGAN

The Church is the family of God. It is seen in miniature in each family.
JOHN FERGUSON

The Church of Christ is the world's only social hope and the sole promise of world peace.
SIR DOUGLAS HAIG

The Church is in Christ as Eve was in Adam.
RICHARD HOOKER

God pity the nation whose factory chimneys rise higher than her church spires.
JOHN KELMAN

The Church is the only institution in the world that has lower entrance requirements than those for getting on a bus.
WILLIAM LAROE

God never intended his Church to be a refrigerator in which to preserve perishable piety. He intended it to be an incubator in which to hatch converts.
F. LINCICOME

The Church is failing in her mission if her dual conception of sin and joy is defective and inadequate.
MARTYN LLOYD-JONES

It may take a crucified Church to bring a crucified Christ before the eyes of the world.
WILLIAM E. ORCHARD

The Church is an anvil that has worn out many hammers.
ENGLISH PROVERB

He who is near the church is often far from God.
FRENCH PROVERB

The Church is not a finished, solidly built and furnished house, in which all that changes is the successive generations who live in it. The Church is a living reality which has had a history of its own and still has one.
KARL RAHNER

The Christian Church is the one organisation in the world that exists purely for the benefit of non-members.
WILLIAM TEMPLE

Where three are gathered together, there is a Church, even though they be laymen.
QUINTUS TERTULLIAN

Citizen

(*See also* Civic Duty)

The health of a democratic society may be measured by the quality of functions performed by private citizens.
ALEXIS DE TOCQUEVILLE

Morality is the very soul of good citizenship.
JOHN IRELAND

Citizens pay their taxes, and then they abdicate. They have lost their skills as citizens; they have contracted them out to public employees.
E. S. SAVAS

Whatever makes men good Christians makes them good citizens.
DANIEL WEBSTER

Civic Duty

(*See also* Citizen)

No personal consideration should stand in the way of performing a public duty.
ULYSSES S. GRANT

When a man assumes a public trust, he should consider himself as public property.
THOMAS JEFFERSON

No better citizen is there, whether in time of peace or war, than the Christian who is mindful of his duty; but such a one should be ready to suffer all things, even death itself, rather than abandon the cause of God or of the Church.
POPE LEO XIII

The worth of a state, in the long run, is the worth of the individuals composing it.
JOHN STUART MILL

Civilisation

(*See also* Culture)

The test of every civilisation is the point below which the weakest and most unfortunate are not allowed to fall.
HERBERT HENRY ASQUITH

Religion is the main determining element in the formation of a culture or civilisation.
HILAIRE BELLOC

Civilisation in the best sense merely means the full authority of the human spirit over all externals.
G. K. CHESTERTON

Intelligent discontent is the mainspring of civilisation.
EUGENE V. DEBS

No true civilisation can be expected permanently to continue which is not based on the great principles of Christianity.
TYRON EDWARDS

The true test of civilisation is, not the census, nor the size of cities, nor the crops, but the kind of man that the country turns out.
RALPH WALDO EMERSON

What has destroyed every previous civilisation has been the tendency to the unequal distribution of wealth and power.
HENRY GEORGE

The true civilisation is where every man gives to every other every right that he claims for himself.
ROBERT G. INGERSOLL

We must each of us be humbled by this fresh wind of the Spirit that has come to lift us up from the nadir our civilisation has reached.
GEORGE MACLEOD

What is called Western civilisation is in an advanced stage of decomposition.
MALCOLM MUGGERIDGE

A visitor from Mars could easily pick out the civilised nations. They have the best implements of war.
HERBERT V. PROCHNOW

Civilisation is always in danger when those who have never learned to obey are given the right to command.
FULTON J. SHEEN

Civilisation is a movement and not a condition, a voyage and not a harbour.
ARNOLD TOYNBEE

All that is best in the civilisation of today is the fruit of Christ's appearance among men.
DANIEL WEBSTER

Clergy

(*See also* Bishop and Priesthood)

Too many clergymen have become keepers of an aquarium instead of fishers of men – and often they are just swiping each other's fish.
M. S. AUGSBURGER

There is not in the universe a more ridiculous, nor a more contemptible animal, than a proud clergyman.
HENRY FIELDING

People expect the clergy to have the grace of a swan, the friendliness of a sparrow, the strength of an eagle, and the night hours of an owl – and some people expect such a bird to live on the food of a canary.
EDWARD JEFFREY

That clergyman soon becomes an object of contempt who being often asked out to dinner never refuses to go.
ST. JEROME

I have always considered a clergyman as the father of a larger family than he is able to maintain.
SAMUEL JOHNSON

The greatest clerks be not the wisest men.
ENGLISH PROVERB

The duty of the clergyman is to remind people in an eloquent manner of the existence of God.
JOHN RUSKIN

Popular religion may be summed up as respect for ecclesiastics.
BARUCH DE SPINOZA

Comfort

(*See also* Hope)

God does not comfort us to make us comfortable, but to make us comforters.
JOHN HENRY JOWETT

All human comfort is vain and short.
THOMAS À KEMPIS

Comfort in tribulation can be secured only on the sure ground of faith holding as true the words of Scripture and the teaching of the Church.
SIR THOMAS MORE

The comforter's head never aches.
ENGLISH PROVERB

Comfort is better than pride.
FRENCH PROVERB

Commandments

(*See also* Law)

What else are the laws of God written in our hearts but the very presence of the Holy Ghost?
ST. AUGUSTINE OF HIPPO

No man can break any of the Ten Commandments. He can only break himself against them.
G. K. CHESTERTON

The Ten Commandments, completed by the evangelical precepts of justice and charity, constitute the framework of individual and collective survival.
POPE JOHN XXIII

I am not sure whether ethical absolutes exist. But I am sure that we have to act as if they existed or civilisation perishes.
ARTHUR KOESTLER

The Ten Commandments, when written on tablets of stone and given to man did not then first begin to belong to him; they had their existence in man and lay as a seed hidden in the form and make of his soul.
WILLIAM LAW

Communication

(*See also* Conversation, Media and Talk)

The best argument is that which seems merely an explanation.
DALE CARNEGIE

The freedom to communicate also requires in a Christian community not only a response of integrity but one of love.
JACK DOMINIAN

The way from God to a human heart is through a human heart.
SAMUEL GORDON

Good words quench more than a bucket of water.
GEORGE HERBERT

The most immutable barrier in nature is between one man's thoughts and another's.
WILLIAM JAMES

Communication is something so simple and difficult that we can never put it in simple words.
T. S. MATTHEWS

Communion, Holy

(*See also* Bread and Eucharist)

A soul can do nothing that is more pleasing to God than to communicate in a state of grace.
ST. ALPHONSUS LIGUORI

We eat the Body of Christ that we may be able to be partakers of eternal life.
ST. AMBROSE

Christ is so united to us in the sacrament of Communion that he acts as if he were ourselves.
MARTIN LUTHER

Holy Communion is the shortest and safest way to heaven.
POPE ST. PIUS X

The heart preparing for Communion should be as a crystal vial filled with clear water in which the least mote of uncleanness will be seen.
ELIZABETH SETON

The bread and wine of Communion are visible, tangible emblems of Christ's body given and blood shed on the cross for our sins.
JOHN R. W. STOTT

The reality of our communion with Christ and in him with one another is the increase of love in our hearts.
WILLIAM TEMPLE

Communion of Saints

(*See also* Church)

The union of men with God is the union of men with one another.
ST. THOMAS AQUINAS

In God and in his Church there is no difference between living and dead, and all are one in the love of the Father. Even the generations yet to be born are part of this one divine humanity.
SERGIUS BULGAKOV

In that Mystical Body, thanks to the communion of saints, no good can be done, no virtue practised by individual members, without its contributing something also to the salvation of all.
POPE PIUS XII

The primary and full Bride of Christ never is, nor can be, the individual man at prayer, but only this complete organism of all faithful people throughout time and space.
FRIEDRICH VON HUGEL

Communism

Beware of invoking the fear of Communism as an excuse for avoiding a change in the structures which confine millions of the sons of God in a subhuman condition.
HELDER CAMARA

Communism is the Franciscan movement without the moderating balance of the Church.
G. K. CHESTERTON

Radio talks, pamphlets, pious aspirations are not going to defeat Communism – the only answer to it is a just social order.
JOSEPH FITZSIMMONS

One does not have to keep bad governments in to keep Communists out.
JOHN K. GALBRAITH

Society cannot leap into Communism from Capitalism without going through a socialist stage of development. Socialism is the first stage to Communism.
NIKITA S. KHRUSHCHEV

Communism is not love. Communism is a hammer which we use to crush the enemy. We are always revolutionists and never reformers.
MAO TSE-TUNG

One of the analogies between Communism and Roman Catholicism is that only the 'educated' are completely orthodox.
GEORGE ORWELL

Socialism is workable only in heaven where it isn't needed, and in hell where they've got it.
CECIL PALMER

Communism is by its nature anti-religious. It considers religion as 'the opiate of the people' because the principles of religion which speak of a life beyond the grave dissuade the proletariat from the dream of a soviet paradise which is of this world.
POPE PIUS XI

The Communist Party cannot be neutral towards religion. It stands for science, and all religion is opposed to science.
JOSEPH STALIN

So we, who are united in mind and soul, have no hesitation about sharing property. All is commun among us – except our wives.
QUINTUS TERTULLIAN

Communism is an ideal that can be achieved only when people cease to be selfish and greedy and when everyone receives according to his needs from communal production. But that is a long way off.
MARSHAL TITO

Communism is a religion and only as we see it as a religion, though a secular religion, will we understand its power.
ELTON TRUEBLOOD

Community

(*See also* Family)

Community is viable if it is the outgrowth of a deep involvement in a purpose which is other than, or above, that of being a community.
BRUNO BETTELHEIM

The individual man himself does not have the essence of man in himself as a moral or a thinking being. The essence of man is found only in the community, in the unity of man with man.
LUDWIG FEUERBACH

The community stagnates without the impulse of the individual. The impulse dies away without the sympathy of the community.
WILLIAM JAMES

Man, the social being, naturally, and in the sense helplessly, depends on his communities. Sundered from them, he has neither worth nor wit, but wanders in waste places, and, when he returns, finds the lonely house of his individual life empty, swept, and garnished.
JOSIAH ROYCE

Community life brings a painful revelation of our limitations, weaknesses and darkness, the unexpected discovery of the monsters within us is hard to accept.
JEAN VANIER

Compassion

(*See also* Pity)

Compassion will cure more sins than condemnation.
HENRY WARD BEECHER

We must learn to regard people less in the light of what they do or omit to do, and more in the light of what they suffer.
DIETRICH BONHOEFFER

Man may dismiss compassion from his heart, but God will never.
WILLIAM COWPER

God tempers the wind to the shorn lamb.
HENRI ESTIENNE

Man is never nearer the Divine than in his compassionate moments.
JOSEPH H. HERTZ

The existence of compassion in man proves the existence of compassion in God.
CHRISTOPHER HOLLIS

Though our saviour's Passion is over, his compassion is not.
WILLIAM PENN

One heart is mirror to another.
JEWISH PROVERB

The compassion that you see in the kind-hearted is God's compassion: he has given it to them to protect the helpless.
SRI RAMAKRISHNA

Compassion is the basis of all morality.
ARTHUR SCHOPENHAUER

When a man has compassion for others, God has compassion for him.
THE TALMUD

Compromise

All government – indeed, every human benefit and enjoyment, every virtue and every prudent act – is founded on compromise and barter.
EDMUND BURKE

An appeaser is one who feeds a crocodile – hoping it will eat him last.
SIR WINSTON CHURCHILL

Everything yields. The very glaciers are viscous, or regulate into conformity, and the stiffest patriots falter and compromise.
RALPH WALDO EMERSON

Life cannot subsist in society but by reciprocal concessions.
SAMUEL JOHNSON

Better bend than break.
SCOTTISH PROVERB

Conceit

(*See also* Pride and Vanity)

Conceit is God's gift to little men.
BRUCE BARTON

Conceit is the most incurable disease that is known to the human soul.
HENRY WARD BEECHER

The world tolerates conceit from those who are successful, but not from anybody else.
JOHN BLAKE

Talk to a man about himself and he will listen for hours.
BENJAMIN DISRAELI

I've never any pity for conceited people, because I think they carry their comfort about with them.
GEORGE ELIOT

Failures are usually the most conceited of men.
D. H. LAWRENCE

Conceit may puff a man up, but never prop him up.
JOHN RUSKIN

Confession

(*See also* Reconciliation)

The confession of evil works is the first beginning of good works.
ST. AUGUSTINE OF HIPPO

Daily in one's prayer, with tears and sighs, to confess one's past sins to God; to amend those sins for the future.
ST. BENEDICT

Our brother has been given to us to help us. He hears the confession of our sins in Christ's stead and he forgives our sins in Christ's name.
DIETRICH BONHOEFFER

It is better for a man to confess his sins than to harden his heart.
POPE ST. CLEMENT I

Confession is the first step to repentance.
EDMUND GAYTON

For him who confesses, shams are over and realities have begun.
WILLIAM JAMES

A fault confessed is a new virtue added to a man.
JAMES S. KNOWLES

That which you confess today, you will perceive tomorrow.
COVENTRY PATMORE

Open confession is good for the soul.
SCOTTISH PROVERB

Confidence

(*See also* Trust)

The greater and more persistent your confidence in God, the more abundantly you will receive all that you ask.
ST. ALBERT THE GREAT

Confidence as an outgoing act is directness and courage in meeting the facts of life, trusting them to bring instruction and support to a developing self.
JOHN DEWEY

In sorrow and suffering, go straight to God with confidence, and you will be strengthened, enlightened and instructed.
ST. JOHN OF THE CROSS

Confidence in others' honesty is no light testimony to one's own integrity.
MICHEL DE MONTAIGNE

Confidence is a plant of slow growth.
ENGLISH PROVERB

Confidence begets confidence.
LATIN PROVERB

Our confidence in Christ does not make us lazy, negligent, or careless, but on the contrary it awakens us, urges us on, and makes us active in living righteous lives and doing good. There is no self-confidence to compare with this.
ULRICH ZWINGLI

Confirmation

The Holy Spirit gave at the font all that is needed for innocence: at confirmation he gives an increase for grace, for in this world those who survive through the different stages of life, must walk among dangers and invisible enemies.
FAUSTUS

The bishop . . . after pouring oil and laying his hand on his head shall say: I anoint thee with holy oil in God the Father Almighty and Christ Jesus and the Holy Ghost.
ST. HIPPOLYTUS

As to the anointing of neophytes, it is clear that this cannot be done by any save the bishop.
POPE ST. INNOCENT I

Confirmation is the sacrament of the common priesthood of the laity.
GERALD VANN

Conflict

All men have in them an instinct for conflict: at least, all healthy men.
HILAIRE BELLOC

You are but a poor soldier of Christ if you think you can overcome without fighting, and suppose you can have the crown without the conflict.
ST. JOHN CHRYSOSTOM

When one ceases from conflict, whether because he has won, because he has lost, or because he cares no more for the game, the virtue passes out of him.
CHARLES H. COOLEY

I am sure that most of us, looking back, would admit that whatever we have achieved in character we have achieved through conflict.
J. WALLACE HAMILTON

No doubt there are other important things in life besides conflict, but there are not many other things so inevitably interesting. The very saints interest us most when we think of them as engaged in a conflict with the Devil.
ROBERT LYND

Conformity

(*See also* Orthodoxy)

We should not conform with human traditions to the extent of setting aside the command of God.
ST. BASIL

For one man who thanks God that he is not as other men there are a thousand to offer thanks that they are as other men, sufficiently as others to escape attention.
JOHN DEWEY

We cannot help conforming ourselves to what we love.
ST. FRANCIS DE SALES

We would know mankind better if we were not so anxious to resemble one another.
JOHANN WOLFGANG VON GOETHE

To deny self is to become a noncon-formist. The Bible tells us not to be conformed to this world either physic-ally or intellectually or spiritually.
BILLY GRAHAM

The essence of true holiness consists in conformity to the nature and will of God.
SAMUEL LUCAS

We are half ruined by conformity; but we should be wholly ruined without it.
CHARLES D. WARNER

Conscience

(*See also* Free Will)

Conscience and reputation are two things. Conscience is due to yourself, reputation to your neighbour.
ST. AUGUSTINE OF HIPPO

Conscience illuminated by the presence of Jesus Christ in the heart must be the guide of every man.
ROBERT H. BENSON

A good conscience is a mine of wealth. And in truth, what greater riches can there be, what thing more sweet than a good conscience?
ST. BERNARD OF CLAIRVAUX

A sleeping pill will never take the place of a clear conscience.
EDDIE CANTOR

Conscience is the royalty and prerogative of every private man.
JOHN DRYDEN

Most of us follow our conscience as we follow a wheelbarrow. We push it in front of us in the direction we want to go.
BILLY GRAHAM

What we call conscience is the voice of Divine love in the deep of our being, desiring union with our will.
J. P. GREAVES

The testimony of a good conscience is the glory of a good man; have a good conscience and thou shalt ever have gladness.
THOMAS À KEMPIS

My conscience is captive to the Word of God.
MARTIN LUTHER

Conscience is nearer to me than any other means of knowledge.
JOHN HENRY NEWMAN

All too often a clear conscience is merely the result of a bad memory.
ANCIENT PROVERB

There is no pillow so soft as a clear conscience.
FRENCH PROVERB

A bad conscience is a snake in one's heart.
YIDDISH PROVERB

Conscience is the voice of the soul, as the passions are the voice of the body. No wonder they often contradict each other.
JEAN JACQUES ROUSSEAU

Conscience warns us as a friend before it punishes us as a judge.
KING STANISLAS I

Labour to keep alive in your breast that little spark of celestial fire called conscience.
GEORGE WASHINGTON

Conservation

(*See also* Ecology and Nature)

Such prosperity as we have known it up to the present is the consequence of rapidly spending the planet's irreplaceable capital.
ALDOUS HUXLEY

Government cannot close its eyes to the pollution of waters, to the erosion of soil, to the slashing of forests any more than it can close its eyes to the need for slum clearance and schools.
FRANKLIN D. ROOSEVELT

Man is a complex being; he makes deserts bloom – and lakes die.
GIL STERN

Contemplation

(*See also* Meditation and Mysticism)

The contemplation of God is promised to us as the goal of all our acts and the eternal consummation of all our joys.
ST. AUGUSTINE OF HIPPO

Too late I loved you, O beauty so ancient yet ever new! Too late I loved you! And, behold, you were within me, and I out of myself and there I searched for you.
ST. AUGUSTINE OF HIPPO

If we hope to move beyond the superficialities of our culture – including our religious culture – we must be willing to go down into the recreating silences, into the inner world of contemplation.
RICHARD FOSTER

To live according to the spirit is to think, speak and act according to the virtues that are in the spirit, and not according to the sense and sentiments which are in the flesh.
ST. FRANCIS DE SALES

He that contemplates hath a day without night.
GEORGE HERBERT

Contemplation is nothing else but a secret, peaceful, and loving infusion of God, which, if admitted, will set the soul on fire with the Spirit of love.
ST. JOHN OF THE CROSS

Seek in reading and thou shalt find in meditation; knock in prayer and it shall be opened to thee in contemplation.
ST. JOHN OF THE CROSS

We become contemplatives when God discovers Himself in us.
THOMAS MERTON

The love which we bear to others remains the mark of the authenticity of our contemplation.
ROGER SCHUTZ

The acts of contemplation are four: to seek after God, to find Him, to feel His sacred touch in the soul, and to be united with Him and to enjoy Him.
WILLIAM ULLATHORNE

Contentment

(*See also* Cheerfulness, Happiness and Joy)

The utmost we can hope for in this world is contentment.
JOSEPH ADDISON

Contentment is a pearl of great price, and whoever procures it at the expense of ten thousand desires makes a wise and a happy purchase.
JOHN BALGUY

True contentment is a real, even an active, virtue – not only affirmative but creative. It is the power of getting out of any situation all there is in it.
G. K. CHESTERTON

I am always content with what happens, for I know that what God chooses is better than what I choose.
EPICTETUS

Those who face that which is actually before them, unburdened by the past, undistracted by the future, these are they who live, who make the best use of their lives; these are those who have found the secret of contentment.
ALBAN GOODIER

It is right to be contented with what we have, but never with what we are.
JAMES MACKINTOSH

Better a handful of dry dates and content therewith than to own the Gate of Peacocks and be kicked in the eye by a broody camel.
ARAB PROVERB

A contented mind is a continual feast.
ENGLISH PROVERB

When we cannot find contentment in ourselves it is useless to seek it elsewhere.
FRANÇOIS DE LA ROCHEFOUCAULD

Contentment with the divine will is the best remedy we can apply to misfortune.
WILLIAM TEMPLE

Controversy

Controversy, for the most part, disfigures the question it seeks to elucidate.
FREDERICK W. FABER

Controversy equalises fools and wise men in the same way – and the fools know it.
OLIVER WENDELL HOLMES

Nothing dies harder than a theological difference.
RONALD A. KNOX

Half the controversies in the world are verbal ones; and could they be brought to a plain issue, they would be brought to a prompt termination.
JOHN HENRY NEWMAN

When men understand each other's meaning, they see, for the most part, that controversy is either superfluous or hopeless.
JOHN HENRY NEWMAN

Conversation

(*See also* Talk)

The mark of good conversation is that every member of the company takes part in it, and that all discuss the same theme.
JOHN ERSKINE

Be at peace regarding what is said or done in conversations: for if good, you have something to praise God for, and if bad, something in which to serve God by turning your heart away from it.
ST. FRANCIS DE SALES

The marvellous thing about good conversation is that it brings to birth so many half-realised thoughts of our own – besides sowing the seeds of innumerable other thought-plants.
DAVID GRAYSON

Be humble and gentle in your conversation; and of few words, I charge you; but always pertinent when you speak.
WILLIAM PENN

Though conversing face to face, their hearts have a thousand miles between them.
CHINESE PROVERB

What a strange scene if the surge of conversation could suddenly ebb like the tide, and show us the real state of people's minds.
SIR WALTER SCOTT

Ultimately the bond of all companionship, whether in marriage or in friendship, is conversation.
OSCAR WILDE

Conversion

Conversion has to materialise in small actions as well as in great.
ROBERT H. BENSON

The Church is a house with a hundred gates: and no two men enter at exactly the same angle.
G. K. CHESTERTON

Conversion may occur in an instant, but the process of coming from sinfulness into a new life can be a long and arduous journey.
CHARLES COLSON

Conversion is but the first step in the divine life. As long as we live we should more and more be turning from all that is evil, and to all that is good.
TYRON EDWARDS

No inferior form of energy can be simply converted into a superior form unless at the same time a source of higher value lends its support.
CARL GUSTAV JUNG

Every story of conversion is the story of a blessed defeat.
C. S. LEWIS

Knox once remarked that the Church gets on by hook or crook, by the hook of the fisherman and the crook of the shepherd.
ARNOLD LUNN

I went to Africa that I might be able to sin to my heart's content. I was a wild beast on the coast of Africa till the Lord caught and tamed me.
JOHN NEWTON

Nothing is more expensive than a start.
FRIEDRICH NIETZSCHE

Men often mistake their imagination for the promptings of their heart, and believe they are converted the moment they think of conversion.
BLAISE PASCAL

A good beginning makes a good ending.
ENGLISH PROVERB

It is better to begin in the evening than not at all.
ENGLISH PROVERB

For a web begun, God sends thread.
ITALIAN PROVERB

Conviction

(*See also* Belief)

Conviction, were it never so excellent, is worthless till it convert itself into conduct.
THOMAS CARLYLE

Never, for sake of peace and quiet, deny your own experience or convictions.
DAG HAMMARSKJOLD

Convictions are the mainsprings of action, the driving powers of life. What a man lives are his convictions.
FRANCIS C. KILLEY

Every man, wherever he goes, is encompassed by a cloud of comforting convictions, which move with him like flies on a summer day.
BERTRAND RUSSELL

As life goes on we discover that certain thoughts sustain us in defeat, or give us victory, whether over ourselves or others, and it is these thoughts, tested by passion, that we call convictions.
W. B. YEATS

Courage

Mere physical courage – the absence of fear – simply is not worth calling bravery. It's the bravery of the tiger, not the moral bravery of the man.
ROBERT H. BENSON

Have plenty of courage. God is stronger than the Devil. We are on the winning side.
JOHN CHAPMAN

Courage is almost a contradiction in terms. It means a strong desire to live taking the form of a readiness to die.
G. K. CHESTERTON

To see what is right, and not to do it, is want of courage.
CONFUCIUS

Most acts of assent require far more courage than most acts of protest, since courage is clearly a readiness to risk self-humiliation.
NIGEL DENNIS

Courage is a virtue only insofar as it is directed by prudence.
FRANÇOIS FENELON

Fear can keep a man out of danger, but courage can support him in it.
THOMAS FULLER

Courage is grace under pressure.
ERNEST HEMINGWAY

Have courage for the great sorrows of life, and patience for the small ones. And when you have laboriously accomplished your daily task, go to sleep in peace. God is awake.
VICTOR HUGO

Courage consists not in hazarding without fear, but being resolutely minded in a just cause.
PLUTARCH

To a brave heart nothing is impossible.
FRENCH PROVERB

It is better to live one day as a lion than a hundred years as a sheep.
ITALIAN PROVERB

Courage consists not in blindly overlooking danger, but in seeing it and conquering it.
JEAN PAUL RICHTER

Courtesy

(*See also* Behaviour and Manners)

The grace of God is in courtesy.
HILAIRE BELLOC

Nothing is more becoming in a great man than courtesy and forbearance.
MARCUS TULLIUS CICERO

Know, most dearly beloved brother, that courtesy is one of the properties of God, who gives His sun and rain to the just and the unjust by courtesy; and courtesy is the sister of charity, by which hatred is vanquished and love is cherished.
ST. FRANCIS OF ASSISI

There is a politeness of the heart, and it is allied to love. It produces the most agreeable politeness of outward behaviour.
JOHANN WOLFGANG VON GOETHE

Genuine courtesy is a splinter from the true cross.
JOHN ANDREW HOLMES

The habit of courtesy, when once acquired, is almost impossible to get rid of.
ROBERT LYND

Courtesy on one side only lasts not long.
ENGLISH PROVERB

The courteous learns his courtesy from the discourteous.
TURKISH PROVERB

Politeness is to human nature what warmth is to wax.
ARTHUR SCHOPENHAUER

Hail the small sweet courtesies of life, for smooth do they make the road of it.
LAURENCE STERNE

Covetousness

(*See also* Envy)

Nothing lies on our hands with such uneasiness as time. Wretched and thoughtless creatures! In the only place where covetousness were a virtue we turn prodigals.
JOSEPH ADDISON

Covetousness often starves other vices.
ENGLISH PROVERB

Abundance consists not so much in material possessions, but in an uncovetous spirit.
JOHN SELDEN

Covetousness is both the beginning and end of the devil's alphabet – the first vice in corrupt nature that moves, and the last which dies.
ROBERT SOUTH

Covetousness is the root of all evil, the ground of all vice.
LEONARD WRIGHT

Creation

(*See also* Universe)

To create is to bring a thing into existence without any previous material at all to work on.
ST. THOMAS AQUINAS

Thus does the world forget You, its Creator, and falls in love with what You have created instead of with You.
ST. AUGUSTINE OF HIPPO

The probability of life originating from accident is comparable to the probability of the unabridged dictionary resulting from an explosion in a printing shop.
EDWIN CONKLIN

We can in fact get at the Creator only through the world.
THOMAS CORBISHLEY

It is for this we are created: that we may give a new and individual expression of the absolute in our own peculiar character.
ISAAC T. HECKER

We are not our own, any more than what we possess is our own. We did not make ourselves; we cannot be supreme over ourselves. We cannot be our own masters. We are God's property by creation, by redemption, by regeneration.
JOHN HENRY NEWMAN

Posterity will some day laugh at the foolishness of modern materialistic philosophy. The more I study nature, the more I am amazed at the Creator.
LOUIS PASTEUR

We depend upon God every moment for our existence: creatures only remain in being through the constant exercise of His upholding power.
J. I. POWER

It has been said that the highest praise of God consists in the denial of Him by the atheist, who finds creation so perfect that he can dispense with a creator.
MARCEL PROUST

God made us and we wonder at it.
SPANISH PROVERB

God as Creator is concerned about the whole quality of men's lives, not only with the personal conversion, important though that is.
DAVID SHEPPARD

The spiritual interest in the doctrine of Creation lies solely in the assertion of the dependence of all existence upon the will of God.
WILLIAM TEMPLE

Creativity

(*See also* Genius and Talent)

The greatest mystery of life is that satisfaction is felt not by those who take and make demands but by those who give and make sacrifices. In them alone the energy of life does not fail, and this is precisely what is meant by creativity.
NIKOLAI BERDYAEV

To raise new questions, new possibilities, to regard old problems from a new angle requires creative imagination and marks real advances in science.
ALBERT EINSTEIN

If you would create something, you must be something.
JOHANN WOLFGANG VON GOETHE

Creative life is characterised by spontaneous mutability: it brings forth the unknown, impossible to preconceive.
D. H. LAWRENCE

Creativity is so delicate a flower that praise tends to make it bloom, while discouragement often nips it in the bud. Any of us will put out more and better ideas if our efforts are truly appreciated.
ALEXANDER F. OSBORN

Creeds

(*See also* Dogma)

If you have a Bible creed, it is well; but is it filled out and inspired by Christian love?
J. F. BRODIE

The Athanasian Creed is the most splendid ecclesiastical lyric ever poured forth by the genius of man.
BENJAMIN DISRAELI

A man's liberty to travel is not cramped by signposts: on the contrary, they save his time by showing what roads he must avoid if he wishes to reach his destination. The creeds perform the same function.
C. B. MOSS

The proper question to be asked about any creed is not, 'Is it pleasant?' but, 'Is it true?'
DOROTHY L. SAYERS

There lives more faith in honest doubt, Believe me, than in half the creeds.
ALFRED, LORD TENNYSON

Truth has never been, can never be, contained in any one creed.
MARY AUGUSTA WARD

Crime and Punishment

Heaven takes care that no man secures happiness by crime.
VITTORIO ALFIERI

Poverty is the mother of crime.
MARCUS AURELIUS

The real significance of crime is in its being a breach of faith with the community of mankind.
JOSEPH CONRAD

Capital punishment is as fundamentally wrong as a cure for crime as charity is wrong as a cure for poverty.
HENRY FORD

Whoever meditates a crime has all the guiltiness of the deed.
DECIMUS JUVENAL

Distrust all men in whom the impulse to punish is powerful.
FRIEDRICH NIETZSCHE

No crime is rooted out once for all.
QUINTUS TERTULLIAN

Criticism

(*See also* Advice)

It is ridiculous for any man to criticise the works of another if he has not distinguished himself by his own performance.
JOSEPH ADDISON

A thick skin is a gift from God.
KONRAD ADENAUER

Never forget what a man says to you when he is angry.
HENRY WARD BEECHER

I love criticism just so long as it's unqualified praise.
NOEL COWARD

It is much easier to be critical than to be correct.
BENJAMIN DISRAELI

We resent all criticism which denies us anything that lies in our line of advance.
RALPH WALDO EMERSON

To escape criticism – do nothing, say nothing, be nothing.
ELBERT HUBBARD

You will never be an inwardly religious and devout man unless you pass over in silence the shortcomings of your fellow men, and diligently examine your own weaknesses.
THOMAS À KEMPIS

Criticism is asserted superiority.
HENRY E. MANNING

It is salutary to train oneself to be no more affected by censure than by praise.
W. SOMERSET MAUGHAM

It is easier to bear some abuse if I reflect, 'I do not deserve this reproach but I do deserve others that have not been made.'
FRANÇOIS MAURIAC

If you want to help other people you have got to make up your mind to write things that some men will condemn.
THOMAS MERTON

Nothing would be done at all, if a man waited till he could do it so well that no one could find fault with it.
JOHN HENRY NEWMAN

Cross

Our Lord who saved the world through the cross, will only work for the good of souls through the cross.
MADELEINE SOPHIE BARAT

It has been said that the cross is the symbol of absolutely endless expansion; it is never content. It points for ever and ever to four indefinitely receding points.
ROBERT H. BENSON

In the cross of Christ excess in men is met by excess in God, excess of evil is mastered by excess of love.
LOUIS BOURDALOUE

The crosses that we shape for ourselves are always lighter than the ones laid upon us.
JEAN PIERRE CAMUS

The cross cannot be defeated for it is defeat.
G. K. CHESTERTON

We have not to carry the cross of others, but our own.
ST. FRANCIS DE SALES

We do not attach any intrinsic virtue to the cross; this would be sinful and idolatrous. Our veneration is referred to Him who died upon it.
JAMES GIBBONS

Everyone who accepts God in Christ accepts him through the cross.
POPE JOHN PAUL II

In the cross is the height of virtue; in the cross is the perfection of sanctity. There is no health of the soul nor hope of eternal life but in the cross.
THOMAS À KEMPIS

The cross is a way of life; the way of love meeting all hate with love, all evil with good, all negatives with positives.
RUFUS MOSELEY

Bear the cross and do not make the cross bear you.
PHILIP NERI

Crosses are ladders that lead to Heaven.
ENGLISH PROVERB

No cross, no crown.
ENGLISH PROVERB

There are no crown-wearers in Heaven who were not cross-bearers here below.
CHARLES H. SPURGEON

In all our actions, when we come in or go out, when we dress, when we wash, at our meals, before retiring to sleep, we make on our foreheads the sign of the cross. These practices are not committed by a formal law of Scripture, but tradition teaches them, custom confirms them, faith observes them.
QUINTUS TERTULLIAN

What other society has as its symbol a horrifying instrument of torture and death – especially when the marks of that society are meant to be love and peace.
DAVID WATSON

Culture

Culture is to know the best that has been said and thought in the world.
MATTHEW ARNOLD

The great law of culture: let each become all that he was created capable of being.
THOMAS CARLYLE

There are moments when one is more ashamed of what is called culture than anyone can ever be of ignorance.
EDWARD V. LUCAS

Those who find beautiful meanings in beautiful things are the cultivated. For these there is hope.
OSCAR WILDE

Custom

(*See also* Tradition)

The customs of God's people and the institutions of our ancestors are to be considered as laws. And those who throw contempt on the customs of the

Church ought to be punished as those who disobey the law of God.
ST. AUGUSTINE OF HIPPO

Custom is a kind of law, having its origin in usage, which takes the place of law when law fails.
ST. ISIDORE OF SEVILLE

The perpetual obstacle to human advancement is custom.
JOHN STUART MILL

Custom without reason is but ancient error.
ENGLISH PROVERB

Some of the roads most used lead nowhere.
JEWISH PROVERB

Custom will often blind one to the good as well as to the evil effects of any long-established system.
RICHARD WHATELY

Cynicism

We can destroy ourselves by cynicism and disillusion, just as effectively as by bombs.
KENNETH CLARK

The habit of thinking ill of everything and everyone is tiresome to ourselves and to all around us.
POPE JOHN XXIII

Cynicism is disappointed idealism.
HARRY KEMELMAN

I hate cynicism a great deal worse than I do the devil, unless, perhaps, the two were the same thing.
ROBERT LOUIS STEVENSON

Cynicism is humour in ill-health.
H. G. WELLS

A cynic is a man who knows the price of everything and the value of nothing.
OSCAR WILDE

Daily Living

(*See also* Day and Life)

Consider every day that you are then for the first time – as it were – beginning; and always act with the same fervour as on the first day you began.
ST. ANTHONY OF PADUA

If a man cannot be a Christian where he is, he cannot be a Christian anywhere.
HENRY WARD BEECHER

I find a heaven in the midst of saucepans and brooms.
STANISLAUS KOSTKA

Relying on God has to begin all over again every day as if nothing had yet been done.
C. S. LEWIS

We die daily. Happy those who daily come to life as well.
GEORGE MACDONALD

Every day is a messenger of God.
RUSSIAN PROVERB

You will become a saint by complying exactly with your daily duties.
MARY JOSEPH ROSSELLO

Our task as moral beings is to lead a 'dying life'; to rest on our oars would mean a 'living death', a very different thing.
A. E. TAYLOR

Darkness

(*See also* Blindness and Light)

It is one thing to be blind, and another to be in darkness.
COVENTRY PATMORE

To see one's darkness proves the presence of a great light.
RAOUL PIUS

Don't curse the darkness – light a candle.
CHINESE PROVERB

The darkest hour is that before the dawn.
ENGLISH PROVERB

Whate'er my darkness be, 'Tis not, O Lord, of Thee: The light is Thine alone; The shadows, all my own.
J. B. TABB

In darkness there is no choice. It is light that enables us to see the differences between things; and it is Christ who gives us light.
C. T. WHITMELL

Day

(*See also* Daily Living and Time)

Write it on your heart that every day is the best day in the year. No man has learned anything rightly until he knows that every day is Doomsday.
RALPH WALDO EMERSON

To sensible men, every day is a day of reckoning.
JOHN W. GARDNER

They deem me mad because I will not sell my days for gold; and I deem them mad because they think my days have a price.
KAHLIL GIBRAN

Better the day, better the deed.
THOMAS MIDDLETON

Be the day never so long, at length cometh evensong.
ENGLISH PROVERB

Every day should be passed as if it were to be our last.
PUBLILIUS SYRUS

Death

The foolish fear death as the greatest of evils, the wise desire it as a rest after labours and the end of ills.
ST. AMBROSE

For man is by nature afraid of death and of the dissolution of the body; but there is this most startling fact, that he who has put on the faith of the cross despises even what is naturally fearful, and for Christ's sake is not afraid of death.
ST. ATHANASIUS

Death is but a sharp corner near the beginning of life's procession down eternity.
JOHN AYSCOUGH

Men fear death as children fear to go in the dark; and as that natural fear in children is increased with tales, so is the other.
FRANCIS BACON

Death is the great adventure, beside which moon landings and space trips pale into insignificance.
JOSEPH BAYLY

At death, if at any time, we see ourselves as we are, and display our true characters.
ROBERT H. BENSON

What is death at most? It is a journey for a season: a sleep longer than usual. If thou fearest death, thou shouldest also fear sleep.
ST. JOHN CHRYSOSTOM

The final heartbeat for the Christian is not the mysterious conclusion to a meaningless existence. It is, rather, the grand beginning to a life that will never end.
JAMES DOBSON

Death has nothing terrible which life has not made so. A faithful Christian life in this world is the best preparation for the next.
TYRON EDWARDS

Blessed be God for our sister, the death of the body.
ST. FRANCIS OF ASSISI

Death takes no bribes.
BENJAMIN FRANKLIN

We are not entirely present to ourselves until the day of our death.
LOUIS LAVELLE

If after I depart this vale, you ever remember me and have thought to please my ghost, forgive some sinner and wink your eye at some homely girl.
HENRY L. MENCKEN

Death devours lambs as well as sheep.
ENGLISH PROVERB

To die well is the chief part of virtue.
GREEK PROVERB

A good death does honour to a whole life.
ITALIAN PROVERB

Death does not take the old but the ripe.
RUSSIAN PROVERB

The angel of Death has many eyes.
YIDDISH PROVERB

Death is the side of life which is turned away from us.
RAINER MARIA RILKE

When a man dies he clutches in his hands only that which he has given away in his lifetime.
JEAN JACQUES ROUSSEAU

We understand death for the first time when he puts his hand upon one whom we love.
ANNE L. DE STAEL

It is a poor thing for anyone to fear that which is inevitable.
QUINTUS TERTULLIAN

Why is it that we rejoice at a birth and grieve at a funeral? It is because we are not the person involved.
MARK TWAIN

Deception

(*See also* Lying)

I have met with many that would deceive; who would be deceived, no one.
ST. AUGUSTINE OF HIPPO

Do you hate to be deceived? Then never deceive another.
ST. JOHN CHRYSOSTOM

Human beings seem to have an almost unlimited capacity to deceive themselves, and to deceive themselves into taking their own lies for truth.
R. D. LAING

Indeed, it is not in human nature to deceive others for any long time, without in a measure deceiving ourselves too.
JOHN HENRY NEWMAN

To deceive a deceiver is no deceit.
ENGLISH PROVERB

The wolf will hire himself out very cheaply as a shepherd.
RUSSIAN PROVERB

Decision

(*See also* Free Will)

The man who insists upon seeing with perfect clearness before he decides never decides.
HENRI FRÉDÉRIC AMIEL

We make our decisions, and then our decisions turn around and make us.
F. W. BOREHAM

Not to decide is to decide.
HARVEY COX

Some persons are very decisive when it comes to avoiding decisions.
BRENDAN FRANCIS

There is a time when we must firmly choose the course we will follow, or the relentless drift of events will make the decision.
HERBERT V. PROCHNOW

No one learns to make right decisions without being free to make wrong ones.
KENNETH SOLLITT

Deed

(*See also* Active Life)

Our deeds act upon us as much as we act upon them.
GEORGE ELIOT

Deeds done, when viewed in themselves, and not simply as means to ends, are also to be regarded as things made.
ERIC GILL

Everyone knows that it is much harder to turn word into deed than deed into word.
MAXIM GORKY

Deeds are fruits, words are but leaves.
ENGLISH PROVERB

They will be hushed by a good deed who laugh at a wise speech.
FRENCH PROVERB

Defeat

(*See also* Failure)

God is never defeated. Though He may be opposed, attacked, resisted, still the ultimate outcome can never be in doubt.
BROTHER ANDREW

There's no defeat in truth, save from within.
HENRY AUSTIN

Defeat is never more assured for an individual than at the moment when he resigns himself to it.
O. A. BATTISTA

It is remarkable that in so many great wars it is the defeated who have won. The people who were left worst at the end of the war were generally the people who were left best at the end of the whole business.
G. K. CHESTERTON

Democracy

(*See also* Government and Politics)

We are justified, from the point of view of exegesis, in regarding the democratic conception of the state as an expansion of the thought of the New Testament.
KARL BARTH

Democracy doesn't give the average man any real power at all. It swamps him among his fellows – that is to say, it kills his individuality; and his individuality is the one thing he has which is worth anything.
ROBERT H. BENSON

That Christianity is identical with democracy, is the hardest of gospels; there is nothing that so strikes men with fear as the saying that they are all the sons of God.
G. K. CHESTERTON

Democracy is the worst system ever invented – except for all the rest.
SIR WINSTON CHURCHILL

Democracy assumes that there are extraordinary possibilities in ordinary people.
HARRY EMERSON FOSDICK

Democracy always makes for materialism, because the only kind of equality that you can guarantee to a whole people is, broadly speaking, physical.
KATHERINE FULLERTON GEROULD

Democracy is the very child of Jesus' teachings of the infinite worth of every personality.
FRANCIS J. MCCONNELL

Man's capacity for justice makes democracy possible. His inclination to injustice makes democracy necessary.
REINHOLD NIEBUHR

Desire

For desire never ceases to pray even though the tongue be silent. If ever desiring, then ever praying.
ST. AUGUSTINE OF HIPPO

It is by that which he longs for, that every man knows and apprehends the quality with which he has to serve God.
MARTIN BUBER

To desire to love God is to love to desire Him, and hence to love Him, for love is the root of all desire.
JEAN PIERRE CAMUS

Humble hearts have humble desires.
GEORGE HERBERT

Remove every evil desire and clothe yourself with good and holy desire. For if you are clothed with good desire, you will hate evil desire and bridle it as you please.
SHEPHERD OF HERMAS

Desires are nourished by delays.
ENGLISH PROVERB

He who likes cherries soon learns to climb.
GERMAN PROVERB

They that desire but a few things can be crossed but in a few.
GERMAN PROVERB

None of us ever desired anything more ardently than God desires to bring men to a knowledge of himself.
JOHNN TAULER

If we go down into ourselves we find that we possess exactly what we desire.
SIMONE WEIL

Any unmortified desire which a man allows in will effectually drive and keep Christ out of the heart.
CHARLES WESLEY

Despair

Despair ruins some, presumption many.
BENJAMIN FRANKLIN

I have plumbed the depths of despair and have found them not bottomless.
THOMAS HARDY

I once counselled a man in despair to do what I myself did in similar circumstances: to live for short terms. Come, I said to myself at that time, at any rate you can bear it for a quarter of an hour!
THEODOR HOECKER

Despair is the absolute extreme of self-love. It is reached when a man deliberately turns his back on all help from anyone else in order to taste the rotten luxury of knowing himself to be lost.
THOMAS MERTON

Despair is vinegar from the wine of hope.
AUSTIN O'MALLEY

Despair gives courage to a coward.
ENGLISH PROVERB

It is impossible for that man to despair who remembers that his helper is omnipotent.
JEREMY TAYLOR

Destiny

(*See also* Predestination)

I felt as if I were walking with destiny, and that all my past life had been but a preparation for this hour and this trial.
SIR WINSTON CHURCHILL

Destiny waits in the hand of God, not in the hands of statesmen.
T. S. ELIOT

We are not permitted to choose the frame of our destiny. But what we put into it is ours.
DAG HAMMARSKJOLD

Every man has his own destiny: the only imperative is to follow it, to accept it, no matter where it leads him.
HENRY MILLER

One meets his destiny often in the road he takes to avoid it.
FRENCH PROVERB

Devil

(*See also* Satan)

The Devil's snare does not catch you, unless you are first caught by the Devil's bait.
ST. AMBROSE

When the Devil is called the god of this world, it is not because he made it, but because we serve him with our worldliness.
ST. THOMAS AQUINAS

The Devil may also make use of morality.
KARL BARTH

I do not know a description of a devil in literature which does not leave one with some sense of sympathy. Milton's devils are admirable; Dante's devils stir our pity; Goethe's devil makes us feel what a good thing has been wasted. Human nature seems incapable of imagining that which is wholly bad, just because it is not wholly bad itself.
ALBAN GOODIER

The Devil has got to be resisted, not merely deprecated.
MICHAEL GREEN

The Devil cannot lord it over those who are servants of God with their whole heart and who place their hope in Him. The Devil can wrestle with, but not overcome them.
SHEPHERD OF HERMAS

The Devil appeared to St. Bridget and she asked him: 'What is your name?' 'Coldness itself.'
ABBÉ HUVELIN

When you close your eyes to the Devil, be sure that it is not a wink.
JOHN C. KULP

The Devil is a gentleman who never goes where he is not welcome.
JOHN L. LINCOLN

For where God built a church, there the Devil would also build a chapel.
MARTIN LUTHER

Francis Thompson said that the Devil doesn't know how to sing, only how to howl.
VINCENT MCNABB

The Devil dances in an empty pocket.
ENGLISH PROVERB

The Devil paints himself black, but we see him rose-coloured.
FINNISH PROVERB

The Devil's boots don't creak.
SCOTTISH PROVERB

The Devil has three children: pride, falsehood and envy.
WELSH PROVERB

The Devil tries to shake truth by pretending to defend it.
QUINTUS TERTULLIAN

The Devil only tempts those souls that wish to abandon sin and those that are in a state of grace. The others belong to him: he has no need to tempt them.
JOHN VIANNEY

Dignity

It is only people of small moral stature who have to stand on their dignity.
ARNOLD BENNETT

To behave with dignity is nothing less than to allow others freely to be themselves.
SOL CHANELES

I know of no case where a man added to his dignity by standing on it.
SIR WINSTON CHURCHILL

What is dignity without honesty?
MARCUS TULLIUS CICERO

Let not a man guard his dignity, but let his dignity guard him.
RALPH WALDO EMERSON

Man is more interesting than men. God made him and not them in his image. Each one is more precious than all.
ANDRÉ GIDE

Scrubbing floors and emptying bedpans has as much dignity as the Presidency.
RICHARD M. NIXON

The easiest way to dignity is humility.
ENGLISH PROVERB

Perhaps the only true dignity of man is his capacity to despise himself.
GEORGE SANTAYANA

Discipleship

(*See also* Christian)

Happy are they who know that discipleship simply means the life which springs from grace, and that grace simply means discipleship.
DIETRICH BONHOEFFER

I have inevitably and increasingly been driven to the conclusion, almost against my own will, that for a West European whose life and background and traditions are in terms of Western European Christian civilisation, the only answer lies in the person and life and teaching of Christ.
MALCOLM MUGGERIDGE

On account of him there have come to be many Christs in the world, even all who, like him, loved righteousness and hated inquity.
ORIGEN OF ALEXANDRIA

The attempts of Christians to be Christians now are almost as ridiculous as the attempts of the first men to be human.
G. A. STUDDERT-KENNEDY

The world around us will recognise us as disciples of Jesus when they see our prayers being answered.
COLIN URQUHART

If we were willing to learn the meaning of real discipleship and actually to become disciples, the Church in the West would be transformed, and the resultant impact on society would be staggering.
DAVID WATSON

Divinity of Christ

(See also God and Jesus Christ)

The Son is the Image of the invisible God. All things that belong to the Father He expresses as the Image; all things that are the Father's He illumines as the splendour of His glory and manifests to us.
ST. AMBROSE

Just as every human being is one person, that is, a rational soul and body, so, too, is Christ one Person, the Word and Man.
ST. AUGUSTINE OF HIPPO

If Socrates would enter the room, we should rise and do him honour. But if Jesus Christ came into the room, we should fall down on our knees and worship him.
NAPOLEON BONAPARTE

If Jesus Christ is not true God, how could he help us? If he is not true man, how could he help us?
DIETRICH BONHOEFFER

I consider the Gospels to be thoroughly genuine; for in them there is the effective reflection of a sublimity which emanated from the Person of Christ; and this is as Divine as ever the divine appeared on earth.
JOHANN WOLFGANG VON GOETHE

There is one Doctor active in both body and soul, begotten and yet unbegotten, God in man, true Life in death, Son of Mary, and Son of God, first able to suffer and then unable to suffer, Jesus Christ our Lord.
ST. IGNATIUS OF ANTIOCH

If the life and death of Socrates were those of a man, the life and death of Jesus were those of God.
JEAN JACQUES ROUSSEAU

He that cried in the manger, that sucked the paps of a woman, that hath exposed himself to poverty, and a world of inconveniences, is the Son of the Living God, of the same substance with his Father, begotten before all ages, before the morning stars; he is God eternal.
JEREMY TAYLOR

Jesus acts with the manifest authority of God; he is the creative Word of God. In him we are to see what is the purpose of God in making the world and in making us.
WILLIAM TEMPLE

They should have known that (Christ) was God. His patience should have proved that to them.
QUINTUS TERTULLIAN

Dogma

(*See also* Creeds)

No dogmas nail your faith.
ROBERT BROWNING

Dogma is the anatomy of thought. As scientists tell you, even a bad doctrine is better than none at all. You can test it, differ from it, your mind has something to bite on. You need the rock to plan the lighthouse.
JOYCE CARY

Dogma means the serious satisfaction of the mind. Dogma does not mean the absence of thought, but the end of thought.
G. K. CHESTERTON

Truths turn into dogmas the moment they are disputed.
G. K. CHESTERTON

Religion cannot but be dogmatic; it ever has been. All religions have had doctrines; all have professed to carry with them benefits which could be enjoyed only on condition of believing the word of a supernatural informant, that is, of embracing some doctrines or other.
JOHN HENRY NEWMAN

Doubt

Doubt charms me no less than knowledge.
DANTE ALIGHIERI

If only God would give me some clear sign! Like making a large deposit in my name at a Swiss bank.
WOODY ALLEN

Every step toward Christ kills a doubt.
THEODORE CUYLER

Should we feel at times disheartened and discouraged, a confiding thought, a simple movement of heart towards God will renew our powers. Whatever he may demand of us, he will give us at the moment the strength and the courage that we need.
FRANÇOIS FENELON

Doubt is a pain too lonely to know that faith is his twin brother.
KAHLIL GIBRAN

Give me the benefit of your convictions if you have any, but keep your doubts to yourself, for I have enough of my own.
JOHANN WOLFGANG VON GOETHE

Time trieth truth in every doubt.
JOHN HEYWOOD

Doubt comes in at the window when enquiry is denied at the door.
BENJAMIN JOWETT

There are two ways to slide easily through life: to believe everything or to doubt everything; both ways save us from thinking.
ALFRED KORZYBSKI

He is a dull man who is always sure, and a sure man who is always dull.
HENRY L. MENCKEN

Underlying all life is the ground of doubt and self-questioning which sooner or later must bring us face to face with the ultimate meaning of our life.
THOMAS MERTON

Ten thousand difficulties do not make one doubt, as I understand the subject; difficulty and doubt are incommensurate.
JOHN HENRY NEWMAN

When in doubt do nowt.
ENGLISH PROVERB

Who knows nothing doubts nothing.
FRENCH PROVERB

The wise are prone to doubt.
GREEK PROVERB

To believe with certainty we must begin with doubting.
POLISH PROVERB

Our doubts are traitors
And make us lose the good we oft might win
By fearing to attempt.
WILLIAM SHAKESPEARE

There lives more faith in honest doubt, believe me, than in half the creeds.
ALFRED, LORD TENNYSON

Faith keeps many doubts in her pay. If I could not doubt, I should not believe.
HENRY DAVID THOREAU

Duty

We need to restore the full meaning of the old word, duty. It is the other side of rights.
PEARL BUCK

Exactness in little duties is a wonderful source of cheerfulness.
FREDERICK W. FABER

Do what you can to do what you ought, and leave hoping and fearing alone.
THOMAS HENRY HUXLEY

Let us have faith that right makes might, and in that faith let us to the end dare to do our duty as we understand it.
ABRAHAM LINCOLN

The right, practical divinity is this: believe in Christ, and do your duty in that state of life to which God has called you.
MARTIN LUTHER

You would not think any duty small if you yourself were great.
GEORGE MACDONALD

Duty does not have to be dull. Love can make it beautiful and fill it with life.
THOMAS MERTON

Never think yourself safe because you do your duty in ninety-nine points; it is the hundredth which is to be the ground of your self-denial.
JOHN HENRY NEWMAN

The path of duty lies in what is near at hand, but men seek for it in what is remote.
JAPANESE PROVERB

You will become a saint by complying exactly with your daily duties.
MARY JOSEPH ROSSELLO

Every duty which we omit, obscures some truth which we should have known.
JOHN RUSKIN

God never imposes a duty without giving time to do it.
JOHN RUSKIN

Easter

(*See also* Resurrection)

The stone at the tomb of Jesus was a pebble to the Rock of Ages inside.
FREDERICK BECK

The great Easter truth is not that we are to live newly after death, but that we are to be new here and now by the power of the resurrection.
PHILLIPS BROOKS

Many meetings and conferences with bishops were held on this point, and all unanimously formulated in their letters the doctrine of the Church for those in every country, that the mystery of the Lord's resurrection from the dead could be celebrated on no day save Sunday, and that on that day alone we should celebrate the end of the paschal feast.
EUSEBIUS OF CAESAREA

Easter says you can put truth in a grave, but it won't stay there.
CLARENCE W. HULL

The night of Easter is spent in keeping the vigil (pervigilia) because of the coming of our King and Lord, that the time of His resurrection may not find us sleeping, but awake. The reason for this night is twofold: either because He then received back His life when He suffered, or because He is later to come for judgment at the same hour at which He arose.
ST. ISIDORE

Easter, like all deep things, begins in mystery and it ends like all high things, in great courage.
BLISS PERRY

At Easter let your clothes be new, or else be sure you will it rue.
ENGLISH PROVERB

Ecology

(*See also* Conservation and Nature)

Every flower of the field, every fibre of a plant, every particle of an insect, carries with it the impress of its Maker, and can – if duly considered – read us lectures of ethics of divinity.
THOMAS POPE BLOUNT

An ecologist wants to clean up the world; an environmentalist wants you to clean up your garden.
BILL COPELAND

Due to man's destruction of the forests and woodlands and his pollution of the rivers and air, one species of the animal kingdom per day is lost; goes into extinction. By the 1990s it will be one species an hour!
GERALD DURRELL

The sun, the moon and the stars would have disappeared long ago, had they happened to be within reach of predatory human hands.
HAVELOCK ELLIS

There is a sufficiency in the world for man's need but not for man's greed.
MOHANDAS GANDHI

We won't have a society if we destroy the environment.
MARGARET MEAD

The ground is holy, being even as it came from the Creator. Keep it, guard it, care for it, for it keeps men, guards men, cares for men. Destroy it and man is destroyed.
ALAN PATON

If you want to clear the stream, get the hog out of the spring.
AMERICAN PROVERB

Man has mastered nature, but, in doing that, he has enslaved himself to the new man-made environment that he has conjured up all around him. Man has condemned himself now to live in cities and to make his living by working in factories and offices.
ARNOLD TOYNBEE

Ecstasy

(*See also* Joy)

The height of love's esctasy is to have our will not in its own contentment but in God's.
ST. FRANCIS DE SALES

Ecstasy is naught but the going forth of a soul from itself and its being caught up in God, and this is what happens to the soul that is obedient, namely, that it goes forth from itself and from its own desires, and thus lightened, becomes immersed in God.
ST. JOHN OF THE CROSS

For God's sake, mistrust and beware of these states of exaltation and ecstasy. They send you, anyone, swaying so far beyond the centre of gravity in one direction, there is the inevitable swing back with greater velocity in the other direction, and in the end you exceed the limits of your own soul's elasticity, and go smash, like a tower that has swung too far.
D. H. LAWRENCE

The ecstasy of religion, the ecstasy of art, and the ecstasy of love are the only things worth thinking about or experiencing.
DON MARQUIS

I wish I could explain with the help of God, wherein union differs from rapture, or from transport, or from flight of the spirit, as they say, or from a trance, which are all one. I mean that all these are only different names for one and the same thing, which is also called ecstasy.
ST. TERESA OF AVILA

Ecumenism

The real ecumenical crisis today is not between Catholic and Protestants but between traditional and experimental forms of Church life.
HARVEY COX

I do not want the walls of separation between different orders of Christians to be destroyed, but only lowered, that we may shake hands a little easier over them.
ROWLAND HILL

Church unity is like peace, we are all for it, but we are not willing to pay the price.
DR. VISSER'T HOOFT

Form all together one choir, so that, with the symphony of your feelings and having all taken the tone of God, you may sing with one voice to the Father through Jesus Christ, that He may listen to you and know you from your chant as the canticle of His only Son.
ST. IGNATIUS OF ANTIOCH

Our divisions prevent our neighbours from hearing the Gospel as they should.
JOHN PAUL II

Putting all the ecclesiastical corpses into one graveyard will not bring about a resurrection.
MARTYN LLOYD-JONES

Some of us worked long enough in a shipbuilding district to know that welding is impossible except the materials to be joined are at white heat. When you try to weld them, they only fall apart.
GEORGE F. MACLEOD

None understand better the nature of real distinction than those who have entered into unity.
JOHN TAULER

Education

(*See also* Learning)

A teacher affects eternity; he can never tell where his influence stops.
HENRY ADAMS

To train a citizen is to train a critic. The whole point of education is that it should give a man abstract and eternal standards, by which he can judge material and fugitive conditions.
G. K. CHESTERTON

What greater work is there than training the mind and forming the habits of the young.
ST. JOHN CHRYSOSTOM

Education is the systematic, purposeful reconstruction of experience.
JOHN DEWEY

The secret of education lies in respecting the pupil.
RALPH WALDO EMERSON

Education is helping the child realise his potentialities.
ERICH FROMM

We must learn to get on in the world – not in the commercial and materialistic sense – but as a means to getting Heavenwards. Any education which neglects this fact, and to the extent to which it neglects it, is false education, because it is false to man.
ERIC GILL

The supreme end of education is expert discernment in all things – the power to tell the good from the bad, the genuine from the counterfeit, and to prefer the good and the genuine to the bad and the counterfeit.
SAMUEL JOHNSON

Education without religion, as useful as it is, seems rather to make man a more clever devil.
C. S. LEWIS

I respect faith, but doubt is what gets you an education.
WILSON MIZNER

Every method of education founded wholly, or in part, on the denial or forgetfulness of original sin and grace, and relying solely on the powers of human nature, is unsound.
POPE PIUS XI

An education which is not religious is atheistic; there is no middle way. If you give to children an account of the world from which God is left out, you are teaching them to understand the world without reference to God.
WILLIAM TEMPLE

Effort

(*See also* Active Life)

God only asks you to do your best.
ROBERT H. BENSON

The trite objects of human efforts – possessions, outward success, luxury – have always seemed to me contemptible.
ALBERT EINSTEIN

We strain hardest for things which are almost but not quite within our reach.
FREDERICK W. FABER

No one knows what is in him till he tries, and many would never try if they were not forced to.
BASIL W. MATURIN

Pray to God, but keep rowing to the shore.
RUSSIAN PROVERB

All effort is in the last analysis sustained by faith that it is worth making.
ORDWAY TEAD

Egoism

(*See also* Conceit and Self-Love)

The burden of the absolute ego is the chief agony of life.
WALDO FRANK

There's only one really nice thing about egotists, they don't talk about other people.
PAUL FROST

We talk little if we do not talk about ourselves.
WILLIAM HAZLITT

There's only one thing that can keep growing without nourishment: the human ego.
MARSHALL LUMSDEN

The egoist does not tolerate egoism.
JOSEPH ROUX

When a man is wrapped up in himself, he makes a pretty small package.
JOHN RUSKIN

Emotion

(*See also* Sentiment)

Emotions should be servants, not masters – or at least not tyrants.
ROBERT H. BENSON

'What do you think of God?' the teacher asked. After a pause the young pupil replied 'He's not a think, He's a feel'.
PAUL FROST

Emotion may vary in religious experience. Some people are stoical and others are demonstrative, but the feeling will be there. There is going to be a tug at the heart.
BILLY GRAHAM

Trust not to thy feelings, for whatever it be now, it will quickly be changed into another thing.
THOMAS À KEMPIS

The only thing men have not learned to do is to stick up for their own instinctive feelings, against the things they are taught.
D. H. LAWRENCE

Emotion is not the Cinderella of our inner life, to be kept in her place among the cinders in the kitchen. Our emotional life is *us* in a way our intellectual life cannot be.
JOHN MACMURRAY

Each of us makes his own weather, determines the colour of the skies in the emotional universe which he inhabits.
FULTON J. SHEEN

It is so many years before one can believe enough in what one feels even to know what the feeling is.
W. B. YEATS

Encouragement

Encouragement is oxygen to the soul.
GEORGE M. ADAMS

One of the highest of human duties is the duty of encouragement. There is a regulation of the Royal Navy which says: 'No officer shall speak discouragingly to another officer in the discharge of his duties.'
WILLIAM BARCLAY

Correction does much, but encouragement does more. Encouragement after censure is as the sun after a shower.
JOHANN WOLFGANG VON GOETHE

There is a point with me in matters of any size when I must absolutely have encouragement as much as crops rain: afterwards I am independent.
GERARO MANLEY HOPKINS

The deepest principle in human nature is the craving to be appreciated.
WILLIAM JAMES

Endurance

(*See also* Perseverance)

Patient endurance is the perfection of charity.
ST. AMBROSE

There remain times when one can only endure. One lives on, one doesn't die, and the only thing that one can do, is to fill one's mind and time as far as possible with the concerns of other people. It doesn't bring immediate peace, but it brings the dawn nearer.
ARTHUR C. BENSON

Nothing great was ever done without much enduring.
ST. CATHERINE OF SIENA

He that endures is not overcome.
ENGLISH PROVERB

What can's be cured must be endured.
ENGLISH PROVERB

One can go a long way after one is tired.
FRENCH PROVERB

He that can't endure the bad, will not live to see the good.
YIDDISH PROVERB

Enemy

(*See also* Charity and Love of Neighbour)

Everyone is his own enemy.
ST. BERNARD OF CLAIRVAUX

The Bible tells us to love our neighbours, and also to love our enemies; probably because they are generally the same people.
G. K. CHESTERTON

Love your enemies, for they tell you your faults.
BENJAMIN FRANKLIN

If we are bound to forgive an enemy, we are not bound to trust him.
THOMAS FULLER

Love will conquer hate.
MOHANDAS GANDHI

I owe much to my friends, but all things considered, it strikes me that I owe even more to my enemies. The real person springs to life under a sting, even better than under a caress.
ANDRÉ GIDE

If you have no enemies, you are apt to be in the same predicament in regard to friends.
ELBERT HUBBARD

Where there is no love, pour love in, and you will draw out love.
ST. JOHN OF THE CROSS

Never cease loving a person, and never give up hope for him, for even the Prodigal Son who had fallen most low, could still be saved. The bitterest enemy and also he who was your friend could again be your friend; love that has grown cold can kindle again.
SØREN KIERKEGAARD

Could we read the secret history of our enemies, we should find in each man's life, sorrow and suffering enough to disarm all hostility.
HENRY WORDSWORTH LONGFELLOW

Often we attack and make ourselves enemies, to conceal that we are vulnerable.
FRIEDRICH NIETZSCHE

An enemy may chance to give good counsel.
ENGLISH PROVERB

If you would make an enemy, lend a man money, and ask it of him again.
ENGLISH PROVERB

Love makes all hard hearts gentle.
ENGLISH PROVERB

The first duty of love is to listen.
PAUL TILLICH

Enjoyment

(*See also* Happiness and Pleasure)

Everybody knows how to weep, but it takes a fine texture of mind to know thoroughly how to enjoy the bright and happy things of life.
OLIVER BELL BUNCE

Nobody who looks as though he enjoyed life is ever called distinguished, though he is a man in a million.
ROBERTSON DAVIES

Enjoy what you can and endure what you must.
JOHANN WOLFGANG VON GOETHE

Enthusiasm

(*See also* Zeal)

Nothing great was ever achieved without enthusiasm.
RALPH WALDO EMERSON

Enthusiasm is the key not only to the achievement of great things but to the accomplishment of anything that is worthwhile.
SAMUEL GOLDWYN

The enthusiastic, to those who are not, are always something of a trial.
ALBAN GOODIER

Be not afraid of enthusiasm; you need it; you can do nothing effectively without it.
FRANCOIS GUIZAT

Enthusiasm finds the opportunities, and energy makes the most of them.
HENRY S. HUSKINS

Apathy can only be overcome by enthusiasm, and enthusiasm can only be aroused by two things; first, an ideal which takes the imagination by storm, and second, a definite intelligible plan for carrying that ideal into practice.
ARNOLD TOYNBEE

Enthusiasm is that temper of the mind in which the imagination has got the better of the judgment.
WILLIAM WARBURTON

Envy

(*See also* Jealousy)

Show me what a man envies the least in others and I will show you what he has got the most of himself.
JOSH BILLINGS

Envy and fear are the only passions to which no pleasure is attached.
JOHN CHURTON COLLINS

Envy takes the joy, happiness, and contentment out of living.
BILLY GRAHAM

Better be envied than pitied.
JOHN HEYWOOD

Too many Christians envy the sinners their pleasure and the saints their joy, because they don't have either one.
MARTIN LUTHER

Men always hate most what they envy most.
HENRY L. MENCKEN

If envy were a fever, all the world would be ill.
DANISH PROVERB

Envy never enriched any man.
ENGLISH PROVERB

Envy eats nothing but its own heart.
GERMAN PROVERB

Beggars do not envy millionaires, though of course they will envy other beggars who are more successful.
BERTRAND RUSSELL

Envy comes from people's ignorance of, or lack of belief in, their own gifts.
JEAN VANIER

Equality

Equality consists in the same treatment of similar persons.
ARISTOTLE

The only stable state is the one in which all men are equal before the law.
ARISTOTLE

The defect of equality is that we only desire it with our superiors.
HENRY BECQUE

All men are equal on the turf and under it.
GEORGE BENTINCK

In sport, in courage, and the sight of Heaven, all men meet on equal terms.
SIR WINSTON CHURCHILL

Equality is a mortuary word.
CHRISTOPHER FRY

It is not true that some human beings are by nature superior and others inferior. All men are equal in their natural dignity.
POPE JOHN XXIII

All men are born equal but the tough job is to outgrow it.
DON LEARY

Equality is a quantitative term and, therefore, love knows nothing of it. Authority exercised with humility, and obedience accepted with delight are the very lines along which our spirits live.
C. S. LEWIS

All animals are equal, but some animals are more equal than others.
GEORGE ORWELL

Equality begins in the grave.
FRENCH PROVERB

Before God and the bus driver we are all equal.
GERMAN PROVERB

In the public baths, all men are equal.
YIDDISH PROVERB

The Lord so constituted everybody that no matter what colour you are, you require the same amount of nourishment.
WILL ROGERS

Equality of opportunity is an equal opportunity to prove unequal talents.
HERBERT SAMUEL

There is no merit in equality, unless it be equality with the best.
JOHN LANCASTER SPALDING

Error

(*See also* Heresy and Mistakes)

An error is the more dangerous in proportion to the degree of truth which it contains.
HENRI FRÉDÉRIC AMIEL

It is human to err; it is devilish to remain wilfully in error.
ST. AUGUSTINE OF HIPPO

Who errs and mends, to God himself commends.
MIGUEL DE CERVANTES

One must never confuse error and the person who errs.
POPE JOHN XXIII

Error is just as important a condition of life as truth.
CARL GUSTAV JUNG

It is one thing to show a man that he is in error, and another to put him in possession of truth.
JOHN LOCKE

A wavering or shallow mind does perhaps as much harm to others as a mind that is consistent in error.
JOHN HENRY NEWMAN

To err is human, to forgive divine.
ALEXANDER POPE

Error is always in a hurry.
ENGLISH PROVERB

An old error is always more popular than a new truth.
GERMAN PROVERB

The error which we hold enquiringly, striving to find what element of fact there be in it, is worth more to us than the truth which we accept mechanically and retain with indifference.
JOHN LANCASTER SPALDING

Eternity

(*See also* Afterlife)

As eternity is the proper measure of permanent being, so time is the proper measure of movement.
ST. THOMAS AQUINAS

The sole purpose of life in time is to gain merit for life in eternity.
ST. AUGUSTINE OF HIPPO

He who has no vision of eternity will never get a true hold of time.
THOMAS CARLYLE

For a small living, men run a great way; for eternal life, many will scarce move a single foot from the ground.
THOMAS À KEMPIS

There really are two ideas, life which goes on and life which has some quality or value in it which lifts it above time. We might use 'everlasting' for the first idea and 'eternal' for the second.
W. R. MATTHEWS

We have all eternity to celebrate our victories, but only one short hour before sunset in which to win them.
ROBERT MOFFAT

In the presence of eternity, the mountains are as transient as the clouds.
ENGLISH PROVERB

The life of faith does not earn eternal life; it is eternal life. And Christ is its vehicle.
WILLIAM TEMPLE

He who provides for this life, but takes no care for eternity, is wise for a moment, but a fool forever.
JOHN TILLOTSON

Ethics

(*See also* Morality)

There are no pastel shades in the Christian ethic.
ARNOLD LOWE

The essence of the ethics of Jesus is not law, but a relationship of persons to God.
MICHAEL RAMSEY

The idea of vocation is the central concept of Christian ethics.
N. H. G. ROBINSON

Ethical behaviour is concerned above all with human values, not with legalisms.
A. M. SULLIVAN

An ethical man is a Christian holding four aces.
MARK TWAIN

Eucharist

(*See also* Bread and Communion, Holy)

When it comes to the consecration of this venerable sacrament, the priest no longer uses his own language, but he uses the language of Christ. Therefore, the word of Christ consecrates this sacrament.
ST. AMBROSE

The noblest sacrament, consequently, is that wherein His Body is really present. The Eucharist crowns all the other sacraments.
ST. THOMAS AQUINAS

The appropriateness of the name 'Eucharist' rests upon the giving of thanks by Jesus at the Last Supper and upon the character of the rite itself which is the supreme act of Christian thanksgiving.
J. G. DAVIES

The sheer stupendous quantity of the love of God which this ever repeated action has drawn from obscure Christian multitudes through the centuries is in itself an overwhelming thought.
GREGORY DIX

Let that Eucharist be held valid which is offered by the bishop or by one to whom the bishop has committed this charge.
ST. IGNATIUS OF ANTIOCH

Be zealous, then, in the observance of one Eucharist. For there is one Flesh of our Lord, Jesus Christ, and one Chalice that brings union in His Blood. There is one altar, as there is one bishop with the priests and deacons, who are my fellow workers. And so, whatever you do, let it be done in the name of the Lord.
ST. IGNATIUS OF ANTIOCH

Every Eucharist proclaims the beginning of the time of God's salvation.
J. JEREMIAS

The Eucharist is the Church at her best.
GABRIEL MORAN

The Eucharist is the means whereby those who once received the Spirit in baptism are constantly renewed in the Spirit until their life's end.
ALAN RICHARDSON

Evangelism

(*See also* Mission)

The way from God to a human heart is through a human heart.
SAMUEL GORDON

God will hold us responsible as to how well we fulfil our responsibilities to this age and take advantage of our opportunities.
BILLY GRAHAM

These early Christians (in the Book of Acts) were led by the Spirit to the main task of bringing people to God through Christ, and were not permitted to enjoy fascinating sidetracks.
J. B. PHILLIPS

The Church has many tasks but only one mission.
ARTHUR PRESTON

There is no expeditious road
To pack and label men for God,
And save them by the barrel-load.
FRANCIS THOMPSON

The Church has nothing to do but to save souls; therefore spend and be spent in this work. It is not your business to speak so many times, but to save souls as you can; to bring as many sinners as you possibly can to repentance.
JOHN WESLEY

When social action is mistaken for evangelism the Church has ceased to manufacture its own blood cells and is dying of leukemia.
SHERWOOD WIRT

Evil

(*See also* Good and Evil)

Just as a little fresh water is blown away by a storm of wind and dust, in like manner the good deeds, that we think we do in this life, are overwhelmed by the multitude of evils.
ST. BASIL

For evil to triumph, it is only necessary for good men to do nothing.
EDMUND BURKE

It is tempting to deny the existence of evil since denying it obviates the need to fight it.
ALEXIS CARREL

Although it be with truth thou speakest evil, this is also a crime.
ST. JOHN CHRYSOSTOM

If evil is due to ignorance, then all professors should be saints.
RICHARD S. EMRICH

Indifference to evil is more insidious than evil itself; it is more universal, more contagious, more dangerous.
ABRAHAM JESCHEL

Never tell evil of a man, if you do not know it for certainty, and if you know it for a certainty, then ask yourself, 'Why should I tell it?'
JOHANN K. LAVATER

We who live beneath a sky still streaked with the smoke of crematoria, have paid a high price to find out that evil is really evil.
FRANÇOIS MAURIAC

Evil communications corrupt good manners.
MENANDER

Of evil grain, no good seed can come.
ENGLISH PROVERB

One does evil enough when one does nothing good.
GERMAN PROVERB

An evil-speaker differs from an evil-doer only in the lack of opportunity.
MARCUS FABIUS QUINTILIAN

There is some soul of goodness in things evil, would men observingly distil it out.
WILLIAM SHAKESPEARE

The word is grown so bad, that wrens make prey where eagles dare not perch.
WILLIAM SHAKESPEARE

Nature throws a veil either of fear or shame over all evil.
QUINTUS TERTULLIAN

Evolution

(*See also* Science)

The evolutionists seem to know everything about the missing link except the fact that it is missing.
G. K. CHESTERTON

Man with all his noble qualities . . . still bears in his bodily frame the indelible stamp of his lowly origin.
CHARLES DARWIN

A creation of evolutionary type (God making things make themselves) has for long seemed to some great minds the most beautiful form imaginable in which God could act in the universe.
PIERRE TEILHARD DE CHARDIN

If evolution works, how come mothers still have only two hands?
ED. DUSSAULT

In Jesus we see the point in the evolution of the universe when the divine consciousness took possession of a human soul and body and the plan of God in creation from the beginning was revealed.
BEDE GRIFFITHS

Evolution is far more a philosophical concept than a strictly scientific one.
ELTON TRUEBLOOD

Example

Example is the school of mankind, and they will learn at no other.
EDMUND BURKE

No man is so insignificant as to be sure his example can do no hurt.
EDWARD CLARENDON

No force the free-born spirit can constrain, but charity and great example gain.
JOHN DRYDEN

People seldom improve when they have no other model but themselves to copy after.
OLIVER GOLDSMITH

It would scarcely be necessary to expound doctrine if our lives were radiant enough. If we behaved like true Christians, there would be no pagans.
POPE JOHN XXIII

Example is always more efficacious than precept.
SAMUEL JOHNSON

There is just one way to bring up a child in the way he should go and that is to travel that way yourself.
ABRAHAM LINCOLN

A holy life will produce the deepest impression. Lighthouses blow no horns; they only shine.
DWIGHT L. MOODY

A child's life is like a piece of paper on which every passer-by leaves a mark.
CHINESE PROVERB

Example is the greatest of all seducers.
FRENCH PROVERB

Precept begins, example accomplishes.
FRENCH PROVERB

Example is not the main thing in influencing others – it is the only thing.
ALBERT SCHWEITZER

I am a part of all that I have met.
ALFRED, LORD TENNYSON

If you try to improve one person by being a good example, you're improving two. If you try to improve someone without being a good example, you won't improve anybody.
JAMES THOM

If you would convince a man that he does wrong, do right. Men will believe what they see. Let them see.
HENRY DAVID THOREAU

Few things are harder to put up with than the annoyance of a good example.
MARK TWAIN

There are two ways of spreading light; to be a candle, or the mirror that reflects it.
EDITH WHARTON

Existence

(*See also* Life)

To know any man is not merely to be sure of his existence, but to have some conception of what his existence signifies, and what it is for.
PHILLIPS BROOKS

The great majority of men exist but do not live.
BENJAMIN DISRAELI

Man can only find meaning for his existence in something outside himself.
VIKTOR E. FRANKL

The more unintelligent a man is, the less mysterious existence seems to him.
ARTHUR SCHOPENHAUER

Every existing thing is equally upheld in its existence by God's creative love. The friends of God should love him to the point of merging their love into his with regard to all things here below.
SIMONE WEIL

Experience

All experience is an arch, to build upon.
HENRY ADAMS

You cannot acquire experience by making experiments. You cannot create experience. You must undergo it.
ALBERT CAMUS

Experience is the best of schoolmasters, only the school fees are heavy.
THOMAS CARLYLE

Nothing which has entered into our experience is ever lost.
WILLIAM ELLERY CHANNING

The years teach much which the days never knew.
RALPH WALDO EMERSON

We cannot afford to forget any experience, even the most painful.
DAG HAMMARSKJOLD

Experience is not what happens to a man. It is what a man does with what happens to him.
ALDOUS HUXLEY

One thorn of experience is worth a whole wilderness of warning.
JAMES RUSSELL LOWELL

Experience is the comb that Nature gives us when we are bald.
BELGIAN PROVERB

Blacksmith's children are not afraid of sparks.
DANISH PROVERB

A new broom sweeps clean, but the old brush knows the corners.
IRISH PROVERB

Experience is always experience of oneself: it cannot, therefore, make others wise.
JOHN LANCASTER SPALDING

To reach something good it is very useful to have gone astray, and thus acquire experience.
ST. TERESA OF AVILA

The long experience of the Church is more likely to lead to correct answers than is the experience of the lone individual.
ELTON TRUEBLOOD

Failure

(*See also* Mistakes)

Failure sometimes enlarges the spirit. You have to fall back upon humanity and God.
CHARLES H. COOLEY

Show me a thoroughly satisfied man – and I will show you a failure.
THOMAS A. EDISON

One of the reasons mature people stop learning is that they become less and less willing to risk failure.
JOHN W. GARDNER

A failure is a man who has blundered but is not able to cash in the experience.
ELBERT HUBBARD

It is not a disgrace to fail. Failing is one of the greatest arts in the world.
CHARLES KETTERING

When we can begin to take our failures non-seriously, it means we are ceasing to be afraid of them. It is of immense importance to learn to laugh at ourselves.
KATHERINE MANSFIELD

Failure teaches success.
ENGLISH PROVERB

The greatest failure is the failure to try.
WILLIAM A. WARD

Faith

(*See also* Faith and Good Works)

Do not rejoice in earthly reality, rejoice in Christ, rejoice in his word, rejoice in his law... There will be peace and tranquility in the Christian heart; but only as long as our faith is watchful; if, however, our faith sleeps, we are in danger.
ST. AUGUSTINE OF HIPPO

For what is faith unless it is to believe what you do not see.
ST. AUGUSTINE OF HIPPO

People only think a thing's worth believing in if it's hard to believe.
ARMIGER BARCLAY

Faith is never identical with piety.
KARL BARTH

Faith is a gift which can be given or withdrawn; it is something infused into us, not produced by us.
ROBERT H. BENSON

Those who have the faith of children have also the troubles of children.
ROBERT H. BENSON

A faith that cannot survive collision with the truth is not worth many regrets.
ARTHUR C. CLARKE

Faith has need of the whole truth.
P. TEILHARD DE CHARDIN

Believe that you have it, and you have it.
DESIDERIUS ERASMUS

It is cynicism and fear that freeze life; it is faith that thaws it out, releases it, sets it free.
HARRY EMERSON FOSDICK

If we really believe in something, we have no choice but to go further.
GRAHAM GREENE

For faith is the beginning and the end is love, and God is the two of them brought into unity. After these comes whatever else makes up a Christian gentleman.
ST. IGNATIUS OF ANTIOCH

Human reason is weak, and may be deceived, but true faith cannot be deceived.
THOMAS À KEMPIS

I do not want merely to possess a faith; I want a faith that possesses me.
CHARLES KINGSLEY

Faith always shows itself in the whole personality.
MARTYN LLOYD-JONES

Faith, like light, should always be simple, and unbending; while love, like warmth, should beam forth on every side, and bend to every necessity of our brethren.
MARTIN LUTHER

Faith is the sight of the inward eye.
ALEXANDER MACLAREN

The deep secret of the mystery of faith lies in the fact that it is a 'baptism' in the death and sacrifice of Christ. We can only give ourselves to God when Christ, by His grace, dies and rises again spiritually within us.
THOMAS MERTON

Ultimately, faith is the only key to the universe. The final meaning of human existence, and the answers to the questions on which all our happiness depends cannot be found in any other way.
THOMAS MERTON

Faith is illuminative, not operative; it does not force obedience, though it increases responsibility; it heightens guilt, it does not prevent sin; the will is the source of action.
JOHN HENRY NEWMAN

Belief is a truth held in the mind. Faith is a fire in the heart.
JOSEPH NEWTON

Faith declares what the senses do not see, but not the contrary of what they see. It is above them, not contrary to them.
BLAISE PASCAL

Faith essentially means taking someone at their word.
DAVID WATSON

Faith and Good Works

To be active in works and unfaithful in heart is like raising a beautiful and lofty building on an unsound foundation. The higher the building, the greater the fall. Without the support of faith, good works cannot stand.
ST. AMBROSE

If a man believes and knows God, he can no longer ask, 'What is the meaning of my life?' But by believing he actually lives the meaning of his life.
KARL BARTH

He who would obey the gospel must first be purged of all defilement of the flesh and the spirit that so he may be acceptable to God in the good works of holiness.
ST. BASIL

For faith without works cannot please, nor can good works without faith.
THE VENERABLE BEDE

You do right when you offer faith to God: you do right when you offer works. But if you separate the two, then you do wrong. For faith without works is dead; and lack of charity in action murders faith, just as Cain murdered Abel, so that God cannot respect your offering.
ST. BERNARD OF CLAIRVAUX

You can do very little with faith, but you can do nothing without it.
NICHOLAS M. BUTLER

You must live with people to know their problems, and live with God in order to solve them.
PETER T. FORSYTH

We must learn that to expect God to do everything while we do nothing is not faith, but superstition.
MARTIN LUTHER KING, JR.

Faith sees by the ears.
ENGLISH PROVERB

All work that is worth anything is done in faith.
ALBERT SCHWEITZER

As the flower is before the fruit, so is faith before good works.
RICHARD WHATELY

Faith is the root of works. A root that produces nothing is dead.
THOMAS WILSON

Fall of Man

(*See also* Adam and Original Sin)

The desire of power in excess caused the angels to fall; the desire of knowledge in excess caused man to fall.
FRANCIS BACON

The fall of man stands as a lie before Beethoven, a truth before Hitler.
GREGORY CORSO

The fruit of the tree of knowledge always drives man from some paradise or other.
WILLIAM R. INGE

Adam whiles he spake not, had paradise at will.
WILLIAM LANGLAND

Fame

The more inward a man's greatness, in proportion to the external show of it, the more substantial, and therefore lasting, his fame.
JOHN AYSCOUGH

Fame always brings loneliness. Success is as ice cold and lonely as the north pole.
VICKI BAUM

All men desire fame. I have never known a single exception to that rule, and I doubt if anyone else has.
HILAIRE BELLOC

A man comes to be famous because he has the matter of fame within him. To seek for, to hunt after fame, is a vain endeavour.
JOHANN WOLFGANG VON GOETHE

If fame is to come only after death, I am in no hurry for it.
MARCUS VALERIUS MARTIAL

All the fame I look for in life is to have lived it quietly.
MICHEL DE MONTAIGNE

For what is fame in itself but the blast of another man's mouth as soon passed as spoken?
SIR THOMAS MORE

All fame is dangerous: good brings envy; bad, shame.
ENGLISH PROVERB

The desire of glory clings even to the best men longer than any other passion.
CAIUS CORNELIUS TACITUS

Family

Wife and children are a kind of discipline of humanity.
FRANCIS BACON

The union of the family lies in love; and love is the only reconciliation of authority and liberty.
ROBERT H. BENSON

Where does the family start? It starts with a young man falling in love with a girl – no superior alternative has yet been found.
SIR WINSTON CHURCHILL

What a father says to his children is not heard by the world, but it will be heard by posterity.
JEAN PAUL EIXHTER

Few are born to do the great work of the world, but the work that all can do is to make a small home circle brighter and better.
GEORGE ELIOT

Every effort to make society sensitive to the importance of the family is a great service to humanity.
POPE JOHN PAUL II

No matter how many communes anybody invents, the family always creeps back.
MARGARET MEAD

That man will never be unwelcome to others who makes himself agreeable to his own family.
FITUS PLAUTUS

Nobody's family can hang out the sign 'Nothing the matter here.'
CHINESE PROVERB

There are no praises and no blessings for those who are ashamed of their families.
JEWISH PROVERB

None but a mule denies his family.
MOROCCAN PROVERB

All happy families resemble one another; every unhappy family is unhappy in its own way.
COUNT LEO TOLSTOY

Loving relationships are a family's best protection against the challenges of the world.
BERNIE WIEBE

Fanaticism

It is part of the nature of fanaticism that it loses sight of the totality of evil and rushes like a bull at the red cloth instead of at the man who holds it.
DIETRICH BONHOEFFER

Earth's fanatics make too frequently heaven's saints.
ELIZABETH BARRETT BROWNING

A fanatic is one who can't change his mind and won't change the subject.
SIR WINSTON CHURCHILL

Fanaticism is the false fire of an overheated mind.
WILLIAM COWPER

There is no strong performance without a little fanaticism in the performer.
RALPH WALDO EMERSON

Fanatics seldom laugh. They never laugh at themselves.
JAMES M. GILLIS

History teaches us that no one feels so disgustingly certain of victory, or is so unteachably sure, and immune to reason, as the fanatic, and that no one is so absolutely certain of ultimate defeat.
THEODOR HAECKER

Father, God The

If we address him as children, it is because he tells us he is our Father. If we unbosom ourselves to him as a friend, it is because he calls us friends.
WILLIAM COWPER

The Moslem Faith has ninety-nine names for God, but 'Our Father' is not among them.
PAUL FROST

The Father is our Fount and Origin, in whom our life and being is begun.
JOHN OF RUYSBROECK

Whatever may happen to you, God is your Father, and He is interested in you, and that is His attitude towards you.
MARTYN LLOYD-JONES

Our Heavenly Father never takes anything from His children unless He means to give them something better.
GEORGE MÜLLER

More than a projection of the qualities of earthly fathers, it is a name that demands its own definition, by the Father Himself, through His Son.
LLOYD JOHN OGILVIE

Be content to be a child, and let the Father proportion out daily to thee what light, what power, what exercises, what straits, what fears, what troubles He sees fit for there.
I. PENINGTON

God is a kind Father. He sets us all in the places where He wishes us to be employed; and that employment is truly 'Our Father's business'.
JOHN RUSKIN

Fatherhood

(*See also* Family)

There is something ultimate in a father's love, something that cannot fail, something to be believed against the whole world. We almost attribute practical omnipotence to our father in the days of our childhood.
FREDERICK W. FABER

I could not point to any need in childhood as strong as that for a father's protection.
SIGMUND FREUD

It is easier for a father to have children than for children to have a real father.
POPE JOHN XXIII

The father in praising his son extols himself.
CHINESE PROVERB

You have to dig deep to bury your Daddy.
GYPSY PROVERB

The best gift a father can give to his son is the gift of himself – his time. For material things mean little, if there is not someone to share them with.
NEIL C. STRAIT

Faults

(*See also* Sin)

The greatest of faults, I should say, is to be conscious of none.
THOMAS CARLYLE

There is only one way of getting rid of one's faults and that is to acquire the habits contradictory to them.
ERNEST DIMNET

We like to find fault ourselves; but we are never attracted to another man who finds fault. It is the last refuge of our good humour that we like to have a monopoly of censure.
FREDERICK W. FABER

The business of finding fault is very easy, and that of doing better very difficult.
ST. FRANCIS DE SALES

Think of your own faults the first part of the night when you are awake, and of the faults of others the latter part of the night when you are asleep.
CHINESE PROVERB

Faults are thick where love is thin.
DANISH PROVERB

Make peace with men and quarrel with your faults.
RUSSIAN PROVERB

Do not think of the faults of others but of what is good in them and faulty in yourself.
ST. TERESA OF AVILA

A fault which humbles a man is of more use to him than a good action which puffs him up.
THOMAS WILSON

Fear

If thou hast a fearful thought, share it not with a weakling, whisper it to thy saddle-bow, and ride forth singing.
ALFRED THE GREAT

Fear is never a good counsellor and victory over fear is the first spiritual duty of man.
NIKOLAI BERDYAEV

We must fear God through love, not love Him through fear.
JEAN PIERRE CAMUS

Servile fear is no honour to God; for what father feels honoured by his son's dread of the rod?
WALTER ELLIOTT

The wise man in the storm prays God, not for safety from danger, but for deliverance from fear. It is the storm within which endangers him, not the storm without.
RALPH WALDO EMERSON

We must not fear fear.
ST. FRANCIS DE SALES

Fear nothing but sin.
GEORGE HERBERT

Fear the Lord, then, and you will do everything well.
SHEPHERD OF HERMAS

All fear is bondage.
ENGLISH PROVERB

Things never go so well that one should have no fear, and never so ill that one should have no hope.
TURKISH PROVERB

The only thing we have to fear is fear itself.
FRANKLIN D. ROOSEVELT

Keep your fears to yourself; share your courage with others.
ROBERT LOUIS STEVENSON

Fellowship

(*See also* Community and Friendship)

Individuals cannot cohere closely unless they sacrifice something of their individuality.
ROBERT H. BENSON

We are all strings in the concert of his joy.
JACOB BOEHME

The only basis for real fellowship with God and man is to live out in the open with both.
ROY HESSION

To live in prayer together is to walk in love together.
MARGARET MOORE JACOBS

God calls us not to solitary sainthood but to fellowship in a company of committed men.
DAVID SCHULLER

Flattery

(*See also* Conceit and Vanity)

Flattery is praise insincerely given for an interested purpose.
HENRY WARD BEECHER

Flattery corrupts both the receiver and giver.
EDMUND BURKE

He who cannot love must learn to flatter.
JOHANN WOLFGANG VON GOETHE

Words really flattering are not those which we prepare but those which escape us unthinkingly.
NINON DE LENELOS

I hate careless flattery, the kind that exhausts you in your effort to believe it.
WILSON MIZNER

In vain does flattery swell a little virtue to a mountain; self-love can swallow it like a mustard seed.
J. PETIT-SENN

What really flatters a man is that you think him worth flattering.
GEORGE BERNARD SHAW

Baloney is the unvarnished lie laid on so thick you hate it. Blarney is flattery laid on so thin you love it.
FULTON J. SHEEN

Food

(*See also* Bread)

God never sendeth mouth but He sendeth meat.
JOHN HEYWOOD

Strange to see how a good dinner and feasting reconciles everybody.
SAMUEL PEPYS

He who cannot cut the bread evenly cannot get on well with people.
CZECH PROVERB

The way one eats is the way one works.
CZECH PROVERB

When God gives hard bread He gives sharp teeth.
GERMAN PROVERB

Foolishness

We were deceived by the wisdom of the serpent, but we are freed by the foolishness of God.
ST. AUGUSTINE OF HIPPO

The greatest lesson in life is to know that even fools are right sometimes.
SIR WINSTON CHURCHILL

If fifty million people say a foolish thing, it is still a foolish thing.
ANATOLE FRANCE

Fools and wise folk are alike harmless. It is the half-wise and the half-foolish, who are most dangerous.
JOHANN WOLFGANG VON GOETHE

Suffer fools gladly. They may be right.
HOLBROOK JACKSON

The fellow who is always declaring he's no fool usually has his suspicions.
WILSON MIZNER

Fools rush in where angels fear to tread.
ALEXANDER POPE

Nothing looks so like a man of sense as a fool who holds his tongue.
GERMAN PROVERB

There is no fool who has not his own kind of sense.
IRISH PROVERB

Forgiveness

(*See also* Confession and Reconciliation)

'I can forgive, but I cannot forget,' is only another way of saying 'I cannot forgive.'
HENRY WARD BEECHER

There is not one moral virtue that Jesus inculcated but Plato and Cicero did inculcate before him. What then did Christ inculcate? Forgiveness of sins. This alone is the Gospel, and this is the life and immortality brought to life by Jesus.
WILLIAM BLAKE

Forgiveness is man's deepest need and highest achievement.
HORACE BUSHNELL

Nothing in this lost world bears the impress of the Son of God so surely as forgiveness.
ALICE CAREY

The more a man knows, the more he forgives.
CATHERINE THE GREAT

He that cannot forgive others breaks the bridge over which he must pass himself; for every man has need to be forgiven.
THOMAS FULLER

There's no point in burying a hatchet if you're going to put up a marker on the site.
SYDNEY HARRIS

The only true forgiveness is that which is offered and extended even before the offender has apologised and sought it.
SØREN KIERKEGAARD

Everyone says forgiveness is a lovely idea, until they have something to forgive.
C. S. LEWIS

The man who is truly forgiven and knows it, is a man who forgives.
MARTYN LLOYD-JONES

He who forgives ends the quarrel.
AFRICAN PROVERB

The noblest vengeance is to forgive.
ENGLISH PROVERB

They who forgive most shall be most forgiven.
ENGLISH PROVERB

To forgive is beautiful.
GREEK PROVERB

Forgiving the unrepentant is like drawing pictures on water.
JAPANESE PROVERB

Humanity is never so beautiful as when praying for forgiveness or else forgiving another.
JEAN PAUL RICHTER

Only one petition in the Lord's Prayer has any condition attached to it; it is the petition for forgiveness.
WILLIAM TEMPLE

It is very easy to forgive others their mistakes; it takes more grit and gumption to forgive them for having witnessed your own.
JESSAMYN WEST

Freedom

(*See also* Free Will and Liberty)

One hallmark of freedom is the sound of laughter.
HARRY ASHMORE

The free man is he who does not fear to go to the end of his thought.
LEON BLUM

Freedom! No word was ever spoken that has held greater hope, demanded greater sacrifice, needed more to be nurtured, blessed more the giver . . . or come closer to being God's will on earth.
OMAR N. BRADLEY

No man in this world attains to freedom from any slavery except by entrance into some higher servitude. There is no such thing as an entirely free man conceivable.
PHILLIPS BROOKS

The real problem for the world today is how to preserve freedom, because for most people social justice is more important. People are prepared to abandon freedom for social justice. But then all that happens is that you get a new form of social injustice.
ALBERT CAMUS

God forces no one, for love cannot compel, and God's service, therefore, is a thing of perfect freedom.
HANS DENK

Freedom is not worth having if it does not include the freedom to make mistakes.
MOHANDAS GANDHI

Freedom is to be in possession of oneself.
GEORGE W. F. HEGEL

When people are free to do as they please, they usually imitate each other.
ERIC HOFFER

It is better for a man to go wrong in freedom than to go right in chains.
THOMAS HENRY HUXLEY

One should never put on one's best trousers to go out to battle for freedom and truth.
HENRIK IBSEN

Freedom is that faculty which enlarges the usefulness of all other faculties.
IMMANUEL KANT

There are two freedoms – the false, where a man is free to do what he likes; the true, where a man is free to do what he ought.
CHARLES KINGSLEY

Men are free when they belong to a living, organic, believing community, active in fulfilling some unfulfilled, perhaps some unrealised purpose.
D. H. LAWRENCE

Free Will

(*See also* Freedom and Liberty)

We are not constrained by servile necessity, but act with free will, whether we are disposed to virtue or incline to vice.
ST. AMBROSE

There are no galley slaves in the royal vessel of divine love – every man works his oar voluntarily.
JEAN PIERRE CAMUS

God, having placed good and evil in our power, has given us full freedom of choice; he does not keep back the unwilling, but embraces the willing.
ST. JOHN CHRYSOSTOM

We have freedom to do good or evil; yet to make choice of evil, is not to use, but to abuse our freedom.
ST. FRANCIS DE SALES

He who has a firm will moulds the world to himself.
JOHANN WOLFGANG VON GOETHE

People do not lack strength; they lack will.
VICTOR HUGO

He who deliberates fully before taking a step will spend his entire life on one leg.
CHINESE PROVERB

Man is essentially a freedom-event. As established by God, and in his very nature, he is unfinished. He freely determines his own everlasting nature and bears ultimate responsibility for it.
KARL RAHNER

Without our faith in free will the earth would be the scene not only of the most horrible nonsense but also of the most intolerable boredom.
ARTHUR SCHNITZLER

God is omnipotent – but powerless still
To stop my heart from wishing what it will.
ANGELUS SILESIUS

There is no such thing as free will. The mind is induced to wish this or that by some cause, and that cause is determined by another cause, and so on back to infinity.
BENEDICT DE SPINOZA

You must recognise as brothers and sisters all who live; and free to will, free to act, free to enjoy, you shall know the worth of existence.
RICHARD WAGNER

I think that our power of conscious origination is where free will comes in . . . We are continually choosing between the good and the less good, whether aware of it or not.
ALFRED NORTH WHITEHEAD

Friendship

A friendship that makes the least noise is very often the most useful; for which reason I prefer a prudent friend to a zealous one.
JOSEPH ADDISON

Every man should keep a fair-sized cemetery, in which to bury the faults of his friends.
HENRY WARD BEECHER

The essence of a perfect friendship is that each friend reveals himself utterly to the other, flings aside his reserves, and shows himself for what he truly is.
ROBERT H. BENSON

Friendship is in loving rather than in being loved.
ROBERT BRIDGES

Friendship is like money, easier made than kept.
SAMUEL BUTLER

You make more friends by becoming interested in other people than by trying to interest other people in yourself.
DALE CARNEGIE

True friendship is like sound health, the value of it is seldom known until it be lost.
CHARLES CALEB COLTON

God evidently does not intend us all to be rich or powerful or great, but He does intend us all to be friends.
RALPH WALDO EMERSON

Friendships begun in this world will be taken up again, never to be broken off.
ST. FRANCIS DE SALES

To know someone here or there with whom you feel there is understanding in spite of distances or thoughts unexpressed – that can make of this earth a garden.
JOHANN WOLFGANG VON GOETHE

Friendship is a disinterested commerce between equals.
OLIVER GOLDSMITH

True friendship ought never to conceal what it thinks.
ST. JEROME

It is mutual respect which makes friendship lasting.
JOHN HENRY NEWMAN

Do not use a hatchet to remove a fly from your friend's forehead.
CHINESE PROVERB

A friend in need is a friend indeed.
ENGLISH PROVERB

Friendship is the marriage of the soul.
FRENCH PROVERB

Hold a true friend with both your hands.
NIGERIAN PROVERB

Blessed is he who hungers for friends –
for though he may not realise it, his soul
is crying out for God.
HABIB SAHABIB

The impulse of love that leads us to the
doorway of a friend is the voice of God
within and we need not be afraid to
follow it.
AGNES SANFORD

A friend should bear his friend's infirm-
ities.
WILLIAM SHAKESPEARE

No one can develop freely in this world
and find a full life without feeling understood by at least one person.
PAUL TOURNIER

True friendship is a plant of slow growth,
and must undergo and withstand the
shocks of adversity before it is entitled
to the appellation.
GEORGE WASHINGTON

Future

(*See also* Time)

Most men prefer and strive for the
present, we for the future.
ST. AMBROSE

I never think of the future. It comes soon
enough.
ALBERT EINSTEIN

The only light upon the future is faith.
THEODOR HOECKER

We should all be concerned about the
future because we will have to spend the
rest of our lives there.
CHARLES KETTERING

The best thing about the future is that it
comes only one day at a time.
ABRAHAM LINCOLN

The most effective way to ensure the
value of the future is to confront the
present courageously and constructively.
ROLLO MAY

Gambling

The Devil invented gambling.
ST. AUGUSTINE OF HIPPO

Gaming, women, and wine, while they
laugh they make men pine.
GEORGE HERBERT

Gambling is a disease of barbarians
superficially civilised.
WILLIAM R. INGE

Italians come to ruin most generally in
one of three ways – women, gambling,
and farming. My family chose the
slowest one.
POPE JOHN XXIII

Generosity

Too many people have decided to do
without generosity in order to practise
charity.
ALBERT CAMUS

Generosity is not in giving me that
which I need more than you do, but it is
in giving me that which you need more
than I do.
KAHLIL GIBRAN

If you are not generous with a meagre income, you will never be generous with abundance.
HAROLD NYE

The quickest generosity is the best.
ARAB PROVERB

A willing helper does not wait to be called.
DANISH PROVERB

The hand that gives, gathers.
ENGLISH PROVERB

No one is so generous as he who has nothing to give.
FRENCH PROVERB

The man who gives little with a smile gives more than the man who gives much with a frown.
JEWISH PROVERB

You do not have to be rich to be generous. If he has the spirit of true generosity, a pauper can give like a prince.
CORRINE V. WELLS

Genius

(*See also* Creativity and Talents)

Genius is the ability to think in a very large number of categories.
HILAIRE BELLOC

The world is always ready to receive talent with open arms. Very often it does not know what to do with genius.
OLIVER WENDELL HOLMES

The principal mark of genius is not perfection but originality, the opening of new frontiers.
ARTHUR KOESTLER

Great things are done by devotion to one idea; there is one class of geniuses, who would never be what they are, could they grasp a second.
JOHN HENRY NEWMAN

Genius makes its way with so much difficulty, because this lower world is in the hands of two omnipotences – that of the wicked and that of the fools.
JOSEPH ROUX

Gentleness

(*See also* Meekness)

Good manners and soft words have brought many a difficult thing to pass.
AESOP

It takes more oil than vinegar to make a good salad.
JEAN PIERRE CAMUS

Nothing appeases an enraged elephant so much as the sight of a little lamb.
ST. FRANCIS DE SALES

Nothing is so strong as gentleness, nothing so gentle as real strength.
ST. FRANCIS DE SALES

If you would reap praise, sow the seeds;
Gentle words and useful deeds.
BENJAMIN FRANKLIN

A real gentleman is a combination of gentle strength and strong gentleness.
GEORGE MONAGHAN

This is the final test of a gentleman: his respect for those who can be of no possible service to him.
WILLIAM L. PHELPS

Kind words don't wear out the tongue.
DANISH PROVERB

Gentle is that gentle does.
ENGLISH PROVERB

A gentle hand may lead the elephant
with a hair.
PERSIAN PROVERB

Well bred thinking means kindly and
sensitive thoughts.
FRANÇOIS DE LA
ROCHEFOUCAULD

Gifts and Giving

What brings joy to the heart is not so
much the friend's gift as the friend's love.
ST. AILRED OF RIEVAULX

It is easy to want things from the Lord
and yet not want the Lord Himself; as
though the gift could ever be preferable
to the Giver.
ST. AUGUSTINE OF HIPPO

The more he cast away the more he had.
JOHN BUNYAN

We make a living by what we get, but
we make a life by what we give.
SIR WINSTON CHURCHILL

Complete possession is proved only
by giving. All you are unable to give
possesses you.
ANDRÉ GIDE

God has given us two hands – one for
receiving and the other for giving.
BILLY GRAHAM

We must not only give what we *have*;
we must also give what we *are*.
DÉSIRÉ JOSEPH MERCIER

He who gives to me teaches me to give.
DANISH PROVERB

Give and spend, and God will send.
ENGLISH PROVERB

He gives twice who gives quickly.
ENGLISH PROVERB

Many look with one eye at what they
give and with seven at what they receive.
GERMAN PROVERB

Glory

Verily, here must the spirit rise to grace,
or else neither the body nor it shall there
rise to glory.
LANCELOT ANDREWES

Grace is but glory begun, and glory is
but grace perfected.
JONATHAN EDWARDS

Provided that God be glorified, we must
not care by whom.
ST. FRANCIS DE SALES

The paths of glory lead but to the grave.
THOMAS GRAY

Short is the glory that is given and taken
by men; and sorrow followeth ever the
glory of this world . . .
   . . . But true glory and holy joy is to
glory in Thee and not in one's self; to
rejoice in Thy name, and not to be
delighted in one's own virtue, nor in any
creature, save only for Thy sake.
THOMAS À KEMPIS

By faith we know his existence; in glory
we shall know his nature.
BLAISE PASCAL

If the glory of God is to break out in your service, you must be ready to go out into the night.
M. BASILEA SCHLINK

Gluttony

Gluttony is an emotional escape, a sign something is eating us.
PETER DE VRIES

In general, mankind, since the improvement of cookery, eats twice as much as nature requires.
BENJAMIN FRANKLIN

Gluttony kills more than the sword.
ENGLISH PROVERB

Gluttons dig their graves with their teeth.
JEWISH PROVERB

God

(*See also* One God and Trinity)

People who tell me there is no God are like a six-year-old boy saying there is no such thing as passionate love – they just haven't experienced it.
WILLIAM ALFRED

God? The imagination reels.
CHARLES AZNAVOUR

The atheist staring from his attic window is often nearer to God than the believer caught up in his own false image of God.
MARTIN BUBER

What we make in our minds we call God, but in reality He dwells in our hearts.
SIR WINSTON CHURCHILL

Things are all the same in God: they are God himself.
MEISTER ECKHART

The presence of a superior reasoning power revealed in the incomprehensible universe, forms my idea of God.
ALBERT EINSTEIN

God is not an idea, or a definition that we have committed to memory, he is a presence which we experience in our hearts.
LOUIS EVELY

There are innumerable definitions of God because his manifestations are innumerable. They overwhelm me . . . stun me.
MOHANDAS GANDHI

The world is so empty if one thinks only of mountains, rivers and cities, but to know someone here and there who thinks and feels with us and who, though distant, is close to us in spirit, this makes the earth for us an inhabited garden.
JOHANN WOLFGANG VON GOETHE

We die on the day when our lives cease to be illumined by the steady radiance renewed daily, of a wonder, the source of which is beyond reason.
DAG HAMMERSKJOLD

There is a native, elemental homing instinct in our souls which turns us to God as naturally as the flower turns to the sun.
RUFUS M. JONES

We know God easily, if we do not constrain ourselves to define him.
JOSEPH JOUBERT

We expect too much of God, but He always seems ready.
JOHN F. KENNEDY

The hardness of God is kinder than the softness of men, and His compulsion is our liberation.
C. S. LEWIS

Change and decay in all around I see;
O thou, who changest not, abide with me.
HENRY FRANCIS LYTE

Two men please God – who serves Him with all his heart because he knows Him; who seeks Him with all his heart because he knows Him not.
PANIN

If a man is not made for God, why is he happy only in God? If man is made for God, why is he opposed to God?
BLAISE PASCAL

God often visits us, but most of the time we are not at home.
FRENCH PROVERB

God is an utterable sigh, planted in the depths of the soul.
JEAN PAUL RICHTER

Anything that makes religion a second object makes it no object. He who offers to God a second place offers him no place.
JOHN RUSKIN

I used to ask God to help me. Then I asked if I might help him. I ended up by asking him to do his work through me.
HUDSON TAYLOR

God is he without whom one cannot live.
COUNT LEO TOLSTOY

If God did not exist, it would be necessary to invent him.
FRANÇOIS M. VOLTAIRE

Religion is the first thing and the last thing, and until a man has found God, and been found by God, he begins at no beginning and works to no end.
H. G. WELLS

Good/Goodness

(*See also* Good and Evil)

Most men are not as good as they pretend to be, or as bad as their enemies paint them.
MORRIS ABRAM

For that which every man seeketh most after, is by him esteemed his greatest good. Which is all one with happiness.
AMICIUS M. S. BOETHIUS

The word *good* has many meanings. For example, if a man were to shoot his grandmother at a range of five hundred yards, I should call him a good shot, but not *necessarily* a good man.
G. K. CHESTERTON

The first condition of human goodness is something to love; the second, something to reverence.
GEORGE ELIOT

It is very hard to be simple enough to be good.
RALPH WALDO EMERSON

We are sometimes so occupied with being good angels that we neglect to be good men and women.
ST. FRANCIS DE SALES

Goodness is something so simple: Always live for others, never to seek one's own advantage.
DAG HAMMARSKJOLD

There is no creature so little and con-. temptible as not to manifest the goodness of God.
THOMAS À KEMPIS

We must first be made good before we can do good; we must first be made just before our works can please God.
HUGH LATIMER

An act of goodness, the least act of true goodness, is indeed the best proof of the existence of God.
JACQUES MARITAIN

Good, the more communicated, more abundant grows.
JOHN MILTON

Good and quickly seldom meet.
ENGLISH PROVERB

The cross has revealed to good men that their goodness has not been good enough.
JOHANN H. SCHROEDER

Anyone who proposes to do good must not expect people to roll stones out of his way, but must accept his lot calmly if they even roll a few more upon it.
ALBERT SCHWEITZER

Good and Evil

(*See also* Evil and Good)

Non-cooperation with evil is as much a duty as is cooperation with good.
MOHANDAS GANDHI

Good is that which makes for unity; evil is that which makes for separateness.
ALDOUS HUXLEY

Man knows not how to rejoice aright or how to grieve aught, for he understands not the distance that there is between good and evil.
ST. JOHN OF THE CROSS

A good word costs no more than a bad one.
ENGLISH PROVERB

Evil communications corrupt good manners.
ENGLISH PROVERB

One does evil enough when one does nothing good.
GERMAN PROVERB

The first prison I ever saw had inscribed on it, 'Cease to do evil: learn to do well,' but as the inscription was on the outside, the prisoners could not read it. It should have been addressed to the self-righteous free spectator in the street, and should have run 'All have sinned, and fallen short of the glory of God.'
GEORGE BERNARD SHAW

Gospel

(*See also* Bible and Scripture)

Thanks be to be the gospel, by means of which we also, who did not see Christ when He came into this world, seem to be with Him when we read His deeds.
ST. AMBROSE

Because it was the message of God to humanity, the gospel could only reveal itself in the simplest of garments.
ADOLF DEISSMANN

Cry the gospel with your whole life.
CHARLES DE FOUCAULD

Talk about the questions of the day; there is but one question, and that is the gospel. It can and will correct everything needing correction.
WILLIAM E. GLADSTONE

The gospel was not good advice but good news.
WILLIAM RALPH INGE

The glory of the gospel is that when the Church is absolutely different from the world, she invariably attracts it.
MARTYN LLOYD-JONES

God writes the gospel not in the Bible alone, but on trees, and flowers, and clouds, and stars.
MARTIN LUTHER

The gospel is neither a discussion or a debate. It is an announcement.
PAUL S. REES

How petty are the books of the philosophers with all their pomp, compared with the Gospels!
JEAN JACQUES ROUSSEAU

Humble and self-forgetting we must be always but diffident and apologetic about the gospel never.
JAMES S. STEWART

Our reading of the gospel story can be and should be an act of personal communion with the living Lord.
WILLIAM TEMPLE

Gossip

(*See also* Scandal and Talk)

Truly unexpected tidings make both ears tingle.
ST. BASIL

A real Christian is a person who can give his pet parrot to the town gossip.
BILLY GRAHAM

I am grateful that my worst offences have not been found out. We all complain about gossip, but gossip is merciful to all of us in that it does not know all.
EDGAR W. HOWE

Gossip is vice enjoyed vicariously.
ELBERT HUBBARD

Never listen to accounts of the frailties of others; and if anyone should complain to you of another, humbly ask him not to speak of him at all.
ST. JOHN OF THE CROSS

I always prefer to believe the best of everybody; it saves so much trouble.
RUDYARD KIPLING

If all men knew what each said of the other, there would not be four friends in the world.
BLAISE PASCAL

Whoever gossips to you will gossip of you.
SPANISH PROVERB

Government

(*See also* Democracy and Politics)

Christianity introduced no new forms of government, but a new spirit, which totally transformed the old ones.
JOHN ACTON

As the happiness of the people is the sole end of government, so the consent of the people is the only foundation of it.
JOHN ADAMS

If therefore, it is natural for man to live in society of many, it is necessary that there exist among men some means by which the group may be governed. For where there are many men together, and each one is looking after his own interest, the group would be broken up and scattered unless there were also someone to take care of what appertains to the common weal.
ST. THOMAS AQUINAS

Government is a contrivance of human wisdom to provide for human wants.
EDMUND BURKE

When one is in office one has no idea how damnable things can feel to the ordinary rank and file of the public.
SIR WINSTON CHURCHILL

All free governments are managed by the combined wisdom and folly of the people.
JAMES A. GARFIELD

No matter how noble the objectives of a government, if it blurs decency and kindness, cheapens human life, and breeds ill will and suspicion − it is an evil government.
ERIC HOFFER

That government is best which governs the least, because its people discipline themselves.
THOMAS JEFFERSON

When a man assumes a public trust, he should consider himself as public property.
THOMAS JEFFERSON

The most successful government is that which leads its subjects to the highest aim by means of the greatest freedom.
VINCENT MCNABB

Even a fool can govern if nothing happens.
GERMAN PROVERB

The people's government is made for the people, made by the people, and is answerable to the people.
DANIEL WEBSTER

Grace

No athlete is admitted to the contest of virtue, unless he has first been washed of all stains of sins and consecrated with the gift of heavenly grace.
ST. AMBROSE

Grace does not destroy nature, it perfects it.
ST. THOMAS AQUINAS

This grace of Christ without which neither infants nor adults can be saved, is not rendered for any merits, but is given gratis, on account of which it is also called grace.
ST. AUGUSTINE OF HIPPO

Let grace be the beginning, grace the consummation, grace the crown.
THE VENERABLE BEDE

There is no such way to attain to a greater measure of grace as for a man to live up to the little grace he has.
PHILLIPS BROOKS

Glory is perfected grace.
MEISTER ECKHART

A state of mind that sees God in everything is evidence of growth in grace and a thankful heart.
CHARLES G. FINNEY

Grace is not sought nor bought nor wrought. It is a free gift of Almighty God to needy mankind.
BILLY GRAHAM

They travel lightly whom God's grace carries.
THOMAS À KEMPIS

All men who live with any degree of serenity live by some assurance of grace.
REINHOLD NIEBUHR

God does not refuse grace to one who does what he can.
LATIN PROVERB

Grace grows best in the winter.
SAMUEL RUTHERFORD

Grace is love that cares and stoops and rescues.
JOHN R. W. STOTT

The burden of life is from ourselves, its lightness from the grace of Christ and the love of God.
WILLIAM ULLATHORNE

Grace is God himself, his loving energy at work within his Church and within our souls.
EVELYN UNDERHILL

Gratitude

(*See also* Thanksgiving)

A true Christian is a man who never for a moment forgets what God has done for him in Christ, and whose whole comportment and whole activity have their root in the sentiment of gratitude.
JOHN BAILLIE

Ingratitude is the soul's enemy; it empties it of merit, scatters its virtues, and deprives it of graces.
ST. BERNARD OF CLAIRVAUX

Gratitude is heaven itself.
WILLIAM BLAKE

In ordinary life we hardly realise that we receive a great deal more than we give, and that it is only with gratitude that life becomes rich. It is very easy to overestimate the importance of our own achievements in comparison with what we owe others.
DIETRICH BONHOEFFER

Gratitude is not only the greatest of virtues, but the parent of all the others.
MARCUS TULLIUS CICERO

The obligation of gratitude may easily become a trap, and the young are often caught and maimed in it.
ERIC GILL

Thou hast given so much to me . . . Give one thing more – a grateful heart.
GEORGE HERBERT

How happy a person is depends upon the depth of his gratitude.
JOHN MILLER

Gratitude is the heart's memory.
FRENCH PROVERB

One finds little ingratitude so long as one is in a position to grant favours.
FRENCH PROVERB

Gratitude to God makes even a temporal blessing a taste of heaven.
WILLIAM ROMAINE

He who receives a benefit with gratitude repays the first instalment on his debt.
SENECA

Gratitude is not only the memory but the homage of the heart – rendered to God for his goodness.
NATHANIEL PARKER WILLIS

Greatness

Greatness after all, in spite of its name, appears to be not so much a certain size as a certain quality in human lives. It may be present in lives whose range is very small.
PHILLIPS BROOKS

There is a great man who makes every man feel small. But the really great man is the man who makes every man feel great.
G. K. CHESTERTON

The price of greatness is responsibility.
SIR WINSTON CHURCHILL

We all go to our graves unknown, worlds of unsuspected greatness.
FREDERICK W. FABER

He who stays not in his littleness, loses his greatness.
ST. FRANCIS DE SALES

It is a grand mistake to think of being great without goodness; and I pronounce it as certain that there was never yet a truly great man that was not at the same time truly virtuous.
BENJAMIN FRANKLIN

Great hopes make great men.
THOMAS FULLER

He who comes up to his own idea of greatness must always have had a very low standard of it in his mind.
WILLIAM HAZLITT

Nothing can make a man truly great but being truly good and partaking of God's holiness.
MATTHEW HENRY

The world is charged with the grandeur of God.
GERARD MANLEY HOPKINS

There is a greatness that can come to all of us, but it is a greatness that comes to us through prayer.
HAROLD LINDSELL

One of the marks of true greatness is the ability to develop greatness in others.
J. C. MACAULAY

It is no sign of intellectual greatness to hold other men cheaply. A great intellect takes for granted that other men are more or less like itself.
HENRY E. MANNING

Persons and things look great at a distance, which are not so when seen close.
JOHN HENRY NEWMAN

Goodness is not tied to greatness, but greatness to goodness.
GREEK PROVERB

Great without small makes a bad wall.
GREEK PROVERB

For us the great men are not those who solved the problems, but those who discovered them.
ALBERT SCHWEITZER

Be not afraid of greatness: some are born great, some achieve greatness and some have greatness thrust upon 'em.
WILLIAM SHAKESPEARE

Greed

(*See also* Gluttony)

It is an excellent rule to banish greed beyond the reach of scandal, and not only to be innocent of it.
ST. BERNARD OF CLAIRVAUX

If you would abolish avarice, you must abolish its mother, luxury.
MARCUS TULLIUS CICERO

Greed has three facets: love of things, love of fame, and love of pleasure; and these can be attacked directly with frugality, anonymity, and moderation.
PAUL MARTIN

Greedy folks have long arms.
ENGLISH PROVERB

One of the weaknesses of our age is our apparent inability to distinguish our needs from our greeds.
DON ROBINSON

Grief

(*See also* Sadness and Sorrow)

There is no greater grief than, in misery, to recall happier times.
DANTE ALIGHIERI

Genuine grief is like penitence, not clamorous, but subdued.
JOSH BILLINGS

The true way to mourn the dead is to take care of the living who belong to them.
EDMUND BURKE

Grief and death were born of sin, and devour sin.
ST. JOHN CHRYSOSTOM

There is no grief which time does not lessen and soften.
MARCUS TULLIUS CICERO

Grief knits two hearts in closer bonds than happiness ever can, and common suffering is a far stronger link than common joy.
ALPHONSE DE LAMARTINE

Grief is the agony of an instant; the indulgence of grief, the blunder of a life.
BENJAMIN DISRAELI

Sorrow makes us all children again, destroys all differences in intellect. The wisest knows nothing.
RALPH WALDO EMERSON

Happiness is beneficial for the body but it is grief that develops the powers of the mind.
MARCEL PROUST

You cannot prevent the birds of sorrow from flying over your head, but you can prevent them from building nests in your hair.
CHINESE PROVERB

He who would have no trouble in this world must not be born in it.
ITALIAN PROVERB

He that conceals his grief finds no remedy for it.
TURKISH PROVERB

To weep is to make less the depth of grief.
WILLIAM SHAKESPEARE

Growth

(*See also* Maturity)

In this world, things that are naturally to endure for a long time, are the slowest in reaching maturity.
VINCENT DE PAUL

The great majority of men are bundles of beginnings.
RALPH WALDO EMERSON

Growth is the only evidence of life.
JOHN HENRY NEWMAN

Be not afraid of growing slowly, be afraid only of standing still.
CHINESE PROVERB

What grows makes no noise.
GERMAN PROVERB

I am learning to see I do not know why it is, but everything penetrates more deeply within me, and no longer stops at the place, where until now, it always used to finish.
RAINER MARIA RILKE

He is only advancing in life, whose heart is getting softer, his blood warmer, his brain quicker, and his spirit entering into living peace.
JOHN RUSKIN

Growth begins when we start to accept our own weakness.
JEAN VANIER

Guilt

The act of sin may pass, and yet the guilt remain.
ST. THOMAS AQUINAS

It is better that ten guilty persons escape than one innocent suffer.
WILLIAM BLACKSTONE

Too many of our securities are guilt-edged.
MARIANNE CRISWELL

Guilt has very quick ears to an accusation.
HENRY FIELDING

A guilty conscience needs no accuser.
ENGLISH PROVERB

Man today attempts to escape his guilt through the electrifying effects of consumer society, through seeking different ways of being amused, through the merchandising of peace by commercial means.
ROGER SCHUTZ

Every man is guilty of all the good he didn't do.
FRANÇOIS MARIE VOLTAIRE

Habit

(*See also* Custom)

Habits, like fish-hooks, are lots easier to get caught than uncaught.
FRANK A. CLARK

Two quite opposite qualities equally bias our minds – habit and novelty.
JEAN DE LA BRUYÈRE

Habit and routine have an unbelievable power to waste and destroy.
HENRI DE LUBAC

We first make our habits, then our habits make us.
JOHN DRYDEN

But oftentimes if we brace ourselves with strong energy against the incitements of evil habits, we turn even those very evil habits to the account of virtue.
POPE ST. GREGORY I

Habit is overcome by habit.
THOMAS À KEMPIS

I never knew a man to overcome a bad habit gradually.
JOHN R. MOTT

The strength of a man's virtue should not be measured by his special exertions, but by his habitual acts.
BLAISE PASCAL

Habit is a shirt made of iron.
CZECH PROVERB

The best way to break a bad habit is to drop it.
D. S. YODER

Happiness

(*See also* Contentment and Joy)

Happiness is living by inner purpose, not by outer pressures. Happiness is a happening-with-God.
DAVID AUGSBURGER

Happiness consists in the attainment of our desires, and in our having only right desires.
ST. AUGUSTINE OF HIPPO

Those who bring sunshine to the lives of others cannot keep it from themselves.
JAMES M. BARRIE

If you ever find happiness by hunting for it, you will find it, as the old woman did her best spectacles, safe on her own nose all the time.
JOSH BILLINGS

Men are made for happiness, and anyone who is completely happy has a right to say to himself 'I am doing God's will on earth.'
ANTON CHEKHOV

Happiness is the practice of the virtues.
ST. CLEMENT OF ALEXANDRIA

The happiest man is he who learns from nature the lesson of worship.
RALPH WALDO EMERSON

It is the chiefest point of happiness that a man is willing to be what he is.
DESIDERIUS ERASMUS

The supreme happiness of life is the conviction of being loved for yourself, or, more correctly, of being loved in spite of yourself.
VICTOR HUGO

God cannot give us happiness and peace apart from himself, because it is not there. There is no such thing.
C. S. LEWIS

Most of us believe in trying to make other people happy only if they can be happy in ways which we approve.
ROBERT S. LYND

A happiness that is sought for ourselves alone can never be found: for a happiness that is diminished by being shared is not big enough to make us happy.
THOMAS MERTON

Happiness is the harvest of a quiet eye.
AUSTIN O'MALLEY

Happiness is neither within us only, or without us; it is the union of ourselves with God.
BLAISE PASCAL

Two happy days are seldom brothers.
BULGARIAN PROVERB

When a man is happy he does not hear the clock strike.
GERMAN PROVERB

Happiness is not a horse; you cannot harness it.
RUSSIAN PROVERB

Happiness is not a state to arrive at, but a manner of travelling.
MARGARET LEE RUNBECK

Happiness is a great love and much serving.
OLIVE SCHREINER

Happiness? That's nothing more than health and a poor memory.
ALBERT SCHWEITZER

Much happiness is overlooked because it doesn't cost anything.
OSCAR WILDE

Hate

Hatred is self-punishment.
HOSEA BALLOU

We hate what we fear and so where hate is, fear is lurking.
CYRIL CONNOLLY

Hatred is like fire; it makes even light rubbish deadly.
GEORGE ELIOT

Love blinds us to faults, but hatred blinds us to virtues.
MOSES IBN EZRA

Hating people is like burning down your own house to get rid of a rat.
HARRY EMERSON FOSDICK

The important thing is not to oneself be poisoned. Now, hatred poisons.
ANDRÉ GIDE

When you visualised a man or a woman carefully, you could always begin to feel pity . . . That was a quality God's image carried with it . . . When you saw the lines at the corners of the eyes, the shape of the mouth, how the hair grew, it was impossible to hate. Hate was just a failure of imagination.
GRAHAM GREENE

These two sins, hatred and pride, deck and trim themselves out as the devil clothed himself in the Godhead. Hatred will be Godlike; pride will be truth. These two are deadly sins: hatred is killing, pride is lying.
MARTIN LUTHER

Hate cannot wise thee worse
Than guilt and shame have made thee.
THOMAS MOORE

Short is the road that leads from fear to hate.
ITALIAN PROVERB

You shall not hate any man; but some you shall admonish, and pray for others, and still others you shall love more than your own life.
TEACHING OF THE TWELVE APOSTLES

Healing

(*See also* Health)

The good Instructor, the Wisdom, the Word of the Father, who made man, cares for the whole nature of his creature. The all-sufficient Physician of humanity, the Saviour, heals both our body and soul, which are the proper man.
ST. CLEMENT OF ALEXANDRIA

The prayer that reforms the sinner and heals the sick is an absolute faith that all things are possible to God – a spiritual understanding of Him, an unselfed love.
MARY BAKER EDDY

The temperature of the spiritual life of the Church is the index of her power to heal.
EVELYN FROST

Christian thinkers cannot consider experiences of healing today because of the tacit acceptance of a world view which allows no place for a breakthrough of 'divine power' into the space-time world.
MORTON T. KELSEY

In healing one can concentrate on either of two attributes: the power of God or the love of God. In every healing there is a manifestation of both.
FRANCIS MacNUTT

The healing acts of Jesus were themselves the message that he had come to set men free.
FRANCIS MacNUTT

Stronger than all the evils in the soul is the Word, and the healing power that dwells in him.
ORIGEN OF ALEXANDRIA

Only the Holy Spirit can safely direct our healing power. And if we will listen to the voice of God within, we will be shown for whom to pray.
AGNES SANFORD

Hear further, O man, of the work of resurrection going on in yourself, even though you were unaware of it. For perhaps you have sometimes fallen sick, and lost flesh, and strength, and beauty; but when you received again from God mercy and healing, you picked up again in flesh and appearance and recovered also your strength.
THEOPHILUS OF ANTIOCH

Health

(*See also* Body and Soul and Healing)

Health and cheerfulness mutually beget each other.
JOSEPH ADDISON

Half the spiritual difficulties that men and women suffer arise from a morbid state of health.
HENRY WARD BEECHER

Be careful to preserve your health. It is a trick of the devil, which he employs to deceive good souls, to incite them to do more than they are able, in order that they may no longer be able to do anything.
ST. VINCENT DE PAUL

Take care of your health, that it may serve you to serve God.
ST. FRANCIS DE SALES

The secret of the physical well-being of the Christian is the vitality of the divine life welling up within by virtue of his incorporation into Christ.
EVELYN FROST

Do the best you can, without straining yourself too much and too continuously, and leave the rest to God. If you strain yourself too much you'll have to ask God to patch you up. And for all you know, patching you up may take time that it was planned to use some other way.
DON MARQUIS

He who has health has hope; and he who has hope has everything.
ARAB PROVERB

Health is better than wealth.
ENGLISH PROVERB

Health is not valued till sickness comes.
ENGLISH PROVERB

He who has health is rich and does not know it.
ITALIAN PROVERB

All sorts of bodily diseases are produced by half-used minds.
GEORGE BERNARD SHAW

Look at your health: and if you have it, praise God, and value it next to a good conscience.
IZAAK WALTON

Heart

A man's first care should be to avoid the reproaches of his own heart.
JOSEPH ADDISON

To my God, a heart of flame; to my fellow men, a heart of love; to myself, a heart of steel.
ST. AUGUSTINE OF HIPPO

The heart is as divine a gift as the mind; and to neglect it in the search for God is to seek ruin.
ROBERT H. BENSON

Let us learn to cast our hearts into God.
ST. BERNARD OF CLAIRVAUX

A man's heart gets cold if he does not keep it warm by living in it; and a censorious man is one who ordinarily lives out of his own heart.
FREDERICK W. FABER

What a number of the dead we carry in our hearts. Each of us bears his cemetery within.
GUSTAVE FLAUBERT

Plato located the soul of man in the head; Christ located it in the heart.
ST. JEROME

The heart of a good man is the sanctuary of God in this world.
MADAME NECKER

When the heart is crowded, it has most room; when empty, it can find place for no new guest.
AUSTIN O'MALLEY

The heart has its reasons which reason does not understand.
BLAISE PASCAL

When the heart is afire, some sparks will fly out of the mouth.
ENGLISH PROVERB

Nowhere are there more hiding places than in the heart.
GERMAN PROVERB

The capital of Heaven is the heart in which Jesus Christ is enthroned as king.
SADHU SUNDAR SINGH

Heaven

If you insist on having your own way, you will get it. Hell is the enjoyment of your own way forever. If you really want God's way with you, you will get it in Heaven.
DANTE ALIGHIERI

Heaven is not to be looked upon only as the reward, but as the natural effect of a religious life.
JOSEPH ADDISON

People sometimes say to youth, 'The world is at your feet!' But this is not true unless Heaven is in your heart.
P. AINSWORTH

Heaven will be the endless portion of every man who has Heaven in his soul.
HENRY WARD BEECHER

To believe in Heaven is not to run away from life; it is to run towards it.
JOSEPH D. BLINCO

God may not give us an easy journey to the Promised Land, but He will give us a safe one.
ANDREW BONAR

A man's reach should exceed his grasp, or what's a Heaven for?
ROBERT BROWNING

All the way to Heaven is Heaven.
ST. CATHERINE OF SIENA

Heaven means to be one with God.
CONFUCIUS

The main object of religion is not to get a man into Heaven; but to get Heaven into him.
THOMAS HARDY

I would not give one moment of Heaven for all the joys and riches of the world, even if it lasted for thousands and thousands of years.
MARTIN LUTHER

Earth hath no sorrow that Heaven cannot heal.
THOMAS MOORE

Love of Heaven is the only way to Heaven.
JOHN HENRY NEWMAN

Men go laughing to Heaven.
DUTCH PROVERB

If God were not willing to forgive sin Heaven would be empty.
GERMAN PROVERB

Heaven is mine if God says amen.
SPANISH PROVERB

One day, in my despair, I threw myself into a chair in the consulting room and groaned out, 'What a blockhead I was to come out here to doctor savages like these!' Whereupon Joseph quietly remarked, 'Yes, doctor, here on earth you are a great blockhead, but not in Heaven.'
ALBERT SCHWEITZER

Heaven is God and God is in my soul.
ELISABETH DE LA TRINITÉ

Hell

I found the original of my Hell in the world which we inhabit.
DANTE ALIGHIERI

Hell is not to love anymore.
GEORGE BERNANOS

What is Hell? . . . The suffering that comes from the consciousness that one is no longer able to love.
FEODOR DOSTOEVSKI

Hell is truth seen too late – duty neglected in its season.
TYRON EDWARDS

Hell was not prepared for man. God never meant that man would ever go to Hell. Hell was prepared for the devil and his angels, but man rebelled against God and followed the devil.
BILLY GRAHAM

There is nobody will go to Hell for company.
GEORGE HERBERT

Men are not in Hell because God is angry with them: they are in wrath and darkness because they have done to the light, which infinitely flows forth from God, as that man does to the light of the sun who puts out his own eyes.
WILLIAM LAW

The safest road to Hell is the gradual one – the gentle slope, soft underfoot, without sudden turnings, without milestones, without signposts.
C. S. LEWIS

The one principle of Hell is 'I am my own.'
GEORGE MACDONALD

When the world dissolves, all places will be Hell that are not Heaven.
CHRISTOPHER MARLOWE

Heaven would be Hell to an irreligious man.
JOHN HENRY NEWMAN

Heaven for climate; Hell for society.
GERMAN PROVERB

Hell is paved with good intentions and roofed with lost opportunities.
PORTUGUESE PROVERB

Fierce and poisonous animals were created for terrifying man, in order that he might be made aware of the final judgment in Hell.
JOHN WESLEY

Help

He who sees a need and waits to be asked for help is as unkind as if he had refused it.
DANTE ALIGHIERI

God's help is nearer than the door.
WILLIAM G. BENHAM

A willing helper does not wait to be called.
DANISH PROVERB

Help your brother's boat across, and your own will reach the shore.
HINDU PROVERB

To help all created things, that is the measure of our responsibility; to be helped by all, that is the measure of our hope.
GERALD VANN

Heresy

(*See also* Error)

For you are not to suppose, brethren, that heresies could be produced through any little souls. None save great men have been the authors of heresies.
ST. AUGUSTINE OF HIPPO

We should detest and prohibit in heretics not those common beliefs in which they are with us and not against us, but those divisions of peace contrary to truth by which they are against us and do not follow.
THE VENERABLE BEDE

The heretic is not a man who loves truth too much; no man can love truth too much. The heretic is a man who loves his truth more than truth itself. He prefers the half-truth that he has found to the whole truth which humanity has found.
G. K. CHESTERTON

Ignorance is the mark of the heathen, knowledge of the true Church, and conceit of the heretics.
ST. CLEMENT OF ALEXANDRIA

A heretic was one who was pertinacious, or sinfully obstinate, in his rejection of revealed doctrine. To speak of a heretic in good faith would have seemed as odd to the medieval thinkers as to speak of a murderer in good faith seems to us.
CHARLES DAVIS

When doctrines meet with general approbation, it is not heresy, but reformation.
DAVID GARRICK

Heresy is the school of pride.
GEORGE HERBERT

They that approve a private opinion, call it opinion, but they that mislike it, heresy, and yet heresy signifies no more than private opinion.
THOMAS HOBBES

It is a shorter thing, and sooner done, to write heresies, than to answer them.
SIR THOMAS MORE

In reading ecclesiastical history, when I was an Anglican, it used to be forcibly brought home to me how the initial error of what afterwards became heresy was the urging forward some truth against the prohibition of authority at an unseasonable time.
JOHN HENRY NEWMAN

History

God cannot alter the past, but historians can.
SAMUEL BUTLER

Perhaps history is a thing that would stop happening if God held His breath, or could be imagined as turning away to think of something else.
HERBERT BUTTERFIELD

One of the deepest impulses in man is the impulse to record – to scratch a drawing on a tusk or keep a diary, to collect sagas and heap cairns. This instinct as to the enduring value of the past is, one might say, the very basis of civilisation.
JOHN JAY CHAPMAN

History unfolds itself by strange and unpredictable paths. We have little control over the future; and none at all over the past.
SIR WINSTON CHURCHILL

What are all histories but God manifesting himself.
OLIVER CROMWELL

There is no history; only biography.
RALPH WALDO EMERSON

Man writes histories; goodness is silent. History is, indeed, little more than the register of the crimes, follies, and misfortunes of mankind.
EDWARD GIBBON

The lesson of history tells us that no state or government devised by man can flourish forever.
BILLY GRAHAM

The historian cannot choose his villains like the poet, nor invent them. At a particular time they are 'given'. Given, as it were, perfectly clearly, by a higher power.
THEODOR HAECKER

The first law of history is not to dare to utter falsehood; the second, not to fear to speak the truth.
POPE LEO XIII

In truth, every event of this world is a type of those that follow, history proceeding forward as a circle ever enlarging.
JOHN HENRY NEWMAN

Hegel was right when he said that we learn from history that men never learn anything from history.
GEORGE BERNARD SHAW

Holiness

(*See also* Perfection, Spiritual Life and Wholeness)

There is no single definition of holiness: there are dozens, hundreds. But there is one I am particularly fond of; being holy means getting up immediately every time you fall, with humility and joy. It doesn't mean never falling into sin. It means being able to say, 'Yes, Lord, I have fallen a thousand times. But thanks to you I have got up again a thousand and one times.' That's all. I like thinking about that.
HELDER CAMARA

The beauty of holiness has done more, and will do more, to regenerate the world and bring in everlasting righteousness than all the other agencies put together.
THOMAS CHALMERS

All of us can attain to Christian virtue and holiness, no matter in what condition of life we live and no matter what our life-work may be.
ST. FRANCIS DE SALES

Sanctify yourself and you will sanctify society.
ST. FRANCIS OF ASSISI

There is no true holiness without humility.
THOMAS FULLER

In our era the road to holiness necessarily passes through the world of action.
DAG HAMMERSKJOLD

We have become too spiritual in a 'holy' 'holy' sense, whereas we should be Biblically holy – that means facing up to the totality of life, in the power of the Cross.
GEORGE MACLEOD

To know what holiness is you have to be holy.
DONALD NICHOLL

Holiness is not an optional extra to the process of creation but rather the whole point of it.
DONALD NICHOLL

You must be holy in the way God asks you to be holy. God does not ask you to be a Trappist monk or a hermit. He wills that you sanctify the world and your everyday life.
VINCENT PALLOTTI

The serene beauty of a holy life is the most powerful influence in the world next to the power of God.
BLAISE PASCAL

Humour is one of the three H's that link Holiness to Humility.
T. D. ROBERTS

Holy Spirit

(*See also* Holy Trinity and Indwelling Spirit)

Love can be used either as an essential name of the divine nature or as a personal name of a divine person – then it is the proper name of the Holy Ghost, as Word is the proper name of the Son.
ST. THOMAS AQUINAS

The Holy Spirit Himself, which also operates in the prophets, we assert to be an effluence of God, flowing from Him and returning back again like a beam of the sun.
ATHENAGORAS

As 'to be born' is, for the Son, to be from the Father, so, for the Holy Spirit, 'to be the gift of God' is to proceed from Father and Son.
ST. AUGUSTINE OF HIPPO

I should as soon attempt to raise flowers if there were no atmosphere, or produce fruits if there were neither light nor heat, as to regenerate men if I did not believe there was a Holy Ghost.
HENRY WARD BEECHER

The Holy Spirit is the living interiority of God.
ROMANO GUARDINI

The whole future of the human race depends on bringing the individual soul more completely and perfectly under the sway of the Holy Spirit.
ISAAC T. HECKER

Those who have the gale of the Holy Spirit go forward even in sleep.
BROTHER LAWRENCE

The Spirit of God first imparts love; he next inspires hope, and then gives liberty; and that is about the last thing we have in many of our churches.
DWIGHT L. MOODY

Every time we say 'I believe in the Holy Spirit,' we mean that we believe there is a living God able and willing to enter human personality and change it.
J. B. PHILLIPS

Home

(*See also* Family)

The strength of a nation is derived from the integrity of its homes.
CONFUCIUS

A home is no home unless it contains food and fire for the mind as well as for the body.
MARGARET FULLER

He is the happiest, be he king or peasant, who finds peace in his home.
JOHANN WOLFGANG VON GOETHE

Home is where the heart is.
PLINY THE ELDER

Better be kind at home than burn incense in a far place.
CHINESE PROVERB

It takes patience to appreciate domestic bliss; volatile spirits prefer unhappiness.
GEORGE SANTAYANA

Happiness is to be found only in the home where God is loved and honoured, where each one loves, and helps, and cares for the others.
THEOPHANE VÉNARD

The home must be in accord with the Church, that all harmful influences be withheld from the souls of children. Where there is true piety in the home, purity of morals reigns supreme.
JOHN VIANNEY

Honesty

(*See also* Integrity)

How desperately difficult it is to be honest with oneself. It is much easier to be honest with other people.
EDWARD BENSON

He who says there is no such thing as an honest man, you may be sure is himself a knave.
GEORGE BERKELEY

Honesty is the first chapter of the book of wisdom.
THOMAS JEFFERSON

An honest man's the noblest work of God.
ALEXANDER POPE

Honesty may be dear bought, but can never be an ill pennyworth.
ENGLISH PROVERB

No honest man ever repented of his honesty.
GERMAN PROVERB

I hope I shall possess firmness and virtue enough to maintain what I consider the most enviable of all titles, the character of an honest man.
GEORGE WASHINGTON

Honesty is the best policy; but he who is governed by that maxim is not an honest man.
RICHARD WHATELY

Honour

Dignity does not consist in possessing honours, but in deserving them.
ARISTOTLE

Honour is like a rocky island without a landing place; once we leave it we can't get back.
NICOLAS BOILEAU-DESPREAUX

The louder he talked of his honour, the faster we counted our spoons.
RALPH WALDO EMERSON

When one has to seek the honour that comes from God only, he will take the withholding of the honour that comes from men very quietly indeed.
GEORGE MACDONALD

Whoever would not die to preserve his honour would be infamous.
BLAISE PASCAL

He who has lost honour can lose nothing more.
PUBLILIUS SYRUS

It is better to deserve honours and not have them than to have them and not deserve them.
MARK TWAIN

Hope

(*See also* Encouragement)

No man is able of himself to grasp the supreme good of eternal life; he needs divine help. Hence there is here a two-fold object, the eternal life we hoped for, and the divine help we hope by.
ST. THOMAS AQUINAS

Other men see only a hopeless end, but the Christian rejoices in an endless hope.
GILBERT BRENKEN

What oxygen is to the lungs, such is hope for the meaning of life.
EMIL BRUNNER

As long as matters are really hopeful, hope is a mere flattery or platitude; it is only when everything is hopeless that hope begins to be a strength at all. Like all the Christian virtues, it is as unreasonable as it is indispensable.
G. K. CHESTERTON

Hope is one of the principal springs that keep mankind in motion.
ANDREW FULLER

The word which God has written on the brow of every man is Hope.
VICTOR HUGO

Hope is itself a species of happiness, and perhaps, the chief happiness which the world affords.
SAMUEL JOHNSON

Hope is the struggle of the soul, breaking loose from what is perishable, and attesting her eternity.
HERMAN MELVILLE

The coffin of every hope is the cradle of a good experience.
FLORENCE NIGHTINGALE

Hope springs eternal in the human breast.
ALEXANDER POPE

If it were not for hope the heart would break.
ENGLISH PROVERB

While there is life there is hope.
LATIN PROVERB

We promise according to our hopes, and perform according to our fears.
FRANÇOIS DE LA ROCHEFOUCAULD

I am a man of hope, not for human reasons nor from any natural optimism, but because I believe the Holy Spirit is at work in the Church and in the World, even when His name remains unheard.
LEON JOSEPH SUENENS

Hope is the only good that is common to all men; those who have nothing else possess hope still.
THALES

Hospitality

The Christian should offer his brethren simple and unpretentious hospitality.
ST. BASIL

It is a sin against hospitality to open your doors and shut up your countenance.
ENGLISH PROVERB

Hospitality is one form of worship.
JEWISH PROVERB

To give our Lord a perfect hospitality, Mary and Martha must combine.
ST. TERESA OF AVILA

Human Condition

(*See also* Original Sin)

The goodness of God knows how to use our disordered wishes and actions, often lovingly turning them to our advantage while always preserving the beauty of His order.
ST. BERNARD OF CLAIRVAUX

We are all as God made us, and oftentimes a great deal worse.
MIGUEL DE CERVANTES

Do you think anything on earth can be done without trouble?
MOHANDAS GANDHI

There is no crime of which one cannot imagine oneself to be the author.
JOHANN WOLFGANG VON GOETHE

The world owes all its onward impulse to men ill at ease. The happy man inevitably confines himself within ancient limits.
NATHANIEL HAWTHORNE

The children of Israel did not find in the manna all the sweetness and strength they might have found in it; not because the manna did not contain them, but because they longed for other meat.
ST. JOHN OF THE CROSS

He who makes a beast of himself gets rid of the pain of being a man.
SAMUEL JOHNSON

From such crooked wood as that which man is made of, nothing straight can be fashioned.
IMMANUEL KANT

Humanity does not pass through phases as a train passes through a station: being alive, it has the privilege of always moving yet never leaving anything behind. Whatever we have been, in some sort we are still.
C. S. LEWIS

If there be a God, *since* there is a God, the human race is implicated in some terrible aboriginal calamity. It is out of joint with the purposes of its Creator.
JOHN HENRY NEWMAN

To what shall I compare this life of ours? Even before I can say, 'It is like a lightning flash or a dewdrop,' it is no more.
SENGAI

We are not part of a nice neat creation, set in motion by a loving God; we are part of a mutinous world where rebellion against God is the order of the day.
SAMUEL M. SHOEMAKER

Humanity

(*See also* Man)

Our humanity were a poor thing were it not for the divinity that stirs within us.
FRANCIS BACON

I know of no rights of race superior to the rights of humanity.
FREDERICK DOUGLAS

It is easier to love humanity as a whole than to love one's neighbour.
ERIC HOFFER

Whenever there is lost the consciousness that every man is an object of concern for us just because he is a man, civilisation and morals are shaken, and the advance to fully developed inhumanity is only a question of time.
ALBERT SCHWEITZER

Only on paper has humanity yet achieved glory, beauty, truth, knowledge, virtue, and abiding love.
GEORGE BERNARD SHAW

Humanity of Christ

(*See also* Jesus Christ)

He became what we are that he might make us what he is.
ST. ATHANASIUS

Christ as God is the fatherland where we are going. Christ as man is the way by which we go.
ST. AUGUSTINE OF HIPPO

To know Jesus and Him crucified is my philosophy, and there is none higher.
ST. BERNARD OF CLAIRVAUX

God clothed himself in vile man's flesh so He might be weak enough to suffer woe.
JOHN DONNE

By a Carpenter mankind was created and made, and by a Carpenter meet it was that man should be repaired.
DESIDERIUS ERASMUS

Tell me the picture of Jesus you have reached and I will tell you some important traits about your nature.
OSCAR PFISTER

He is a man who acts like a man.
DANISH PROVERB

'Gentle Jesus, meek and mild,' is a snivelling modern invention, with no warrant in the Gospels.
GEORGE BERNARD SHAW

Poor creature though I be, I am the hand and foot of Christ. I move my hand and my hand is wholly Christ's hand, for deity is become inseparably one with me. I move my foot, and it is aglow with God.
ST. SYMEON THE NEW THEOLOGIAN

God's only Son doth hug humanity into his very person.
EDWARD TAYLOR

Christ did not die a martyr. He died – infinitely more humbly – a common criminal.
SIMONE WEIL

Human Nature

It will be very generally found that those who will sneer habitually at human nature, and affect to despise it, are among its worst and least pleasant samples.
CHARLES DICKENS

It is human nature to think wisely and act foolishly.
ANATOLE FRANCE

Human nature will find itself only when it fully realises that to be human it has to cease to be beastly or brutal.
MOHANDAS GANDHI

Human action can be modified to some extent, but human nature cannot be changed.
ABRAHAM LINCOLN

Human nature is like a drunk peasant. Lift him into the saddle on one side, over he topples on the other side.
MARTIN LUTHER

Left to itself, human nature tends to death, and utter apostasy from God, however plausible it may look externally.
JOHN HENRY NEWMAN

We were made to be human beings here, and when people try to be anything else, they generally get into some sort of scrapes.
HANNAH WHITHALL SMITH

Human Rights

(*See also* Right)

Rights that do not flow from duty well performed are not worth having.
MOHANDAS GANDHI

Wherever there is a human being, I see God-given rights inherent in that being, whatever may be the sex or complexion.
WILLIAM L. GARRISON

I am the inferior of any man whose rights I trample under foot.
ROBERT G. INGERSOLL

They have rights who dare maintain them.
JAMES RUSSELL LOWELL

No one can be perfectly free till all are free, no one can be perfectly moral till all are moral; no one can be perfectly happy till all are happy.
HERBERT SPENCER

A right is worth fighting for only when it can be put into operation.
WOODROW WILSON

Humility

(*See also* Modesty)

Pride is the cold mountain peak, sterile and bleak; humility is the quiet valley fertile and abounding in life, and peace lives there.
ANNE AUSTIN

You grow up the day you have your first real laugh at yourself.
ETHEL BARRYMORE

To feel extraordinarily small and unimportant is always a wholesome feeling.
ROBERT H. BENSON

Humility is the mother of salvation.
ST. BERNARD OF CLAIRVAUX

Humility is the truth about ourselves loved.
C. CAREY-ELWES

Humility in oneself is not attractive, though it is attractive in others.
JOHN CHAPMAN

It is always the secure who are humble.
G. K. CHESTERTON

The reason why God is so great a Lover of humility is because He is the great Lover of truth. Now humility is nothing but truth, while pride is nothing but lying.
ST. VINCENT DE PAUL

True humility makes no pretence of being humble, and scarcely ever utters words of humility.
ST. FRANCIS DE SALES

The humble knowledge of yourself is a surer way to God than the deepest search after science.
THOMAS À KEMPIS

In the sight of God no man can look at himself except when he is down on his knees.
FRANÇOIS MAURIAC

If there were no humility in the world, everybody would long ago have committed suicide.
THOMAS MERTON

The humble man receives praise the way a clean window takes the light of the sun. The truer and more intense the light is, the less you see of the glass.
THOMAS MERTON

I used to think that God's gifts were on shelves one above the other and that the taller we grew in Christian character the more easily we could reach them. I now find that God's gifts are on shelves one beneath the other and that it is not a question of growing taller but of stooping lower.
F. B. MEYER

Golden deeds kept out of sight are most laudable.
BLAISE PASCAL

An able yet humble man is a jewel worth a kingdom.
WILLIAM PENN

Too much humility is pride.
GERMAN PROVERB

Don't make yourself so big. You are not so small.
JEWISH PROVERB

Reflect that true humility consists to a great extent in being ready for what the Lord desires to do with you, and happy that He should do it, and in always considering yourselves unworthy to be called His servants.
ST. TERESA OF AVILA

Humility like darkness reveals the heavenly lights.
HENRY DAVID THOREAU

Humour

(*See also* Joy and Laughter)

A clown may be the first in the Kingdom of Heaven, if he has helped lessen the sadness of human life.
RABBI BAROKA

True humour springs not more from the head than from the heart; it is not contempt, its essence is love.
THOMAS CARLYLE

It is the test of a good religion whether you can make a joke of it.
G. K. CHESTERTON

Whom the gods would make bigots, they first deprive of humour.
JAMES M. GILLIS

There is of course something wrong with a man who is only partly humorous, or is only humorous at times, for humour ought to be a yeast, working through the whole of a man and his bearing.
THEODOR HAECKER

I have never understood why it should be considered derogatory to the Creator to suppose that he has a sense of humour.
WILLIAM RALPH INGE

Humour is the harmony of the heart.
DOUGLAS JERROLD

Humour distorts nothing, and only false gods are laughed off their earthly pedestals.
AGNES PEPPLIER

Hunger

(*See also* Poverty)

There's no sauce in the world like hunger.
MIGUEL DE CERVANTES

There is no reason that the senseless Temples of God should abound in riches, and the living Temples of the Holy Spirit starve for hunger.
ETHELWOLD, BISHOP OF WINCHESTER

Hunger makes hard beans sweet.
ENGLISH PROVERB

Hungry bellies have no ears.
ENGLISH PROVERB

The road to Jericho today, the road of the Good Samaritan, runs through every under-developed country.
MICHEL QUOIST

Husband

(*See also* Family and Marriage)

Being a husband is a full-time job. That is why so many husbands fail. They cannot give their entire attention to it.
ARNOLD BENNETT

Husbands who have the courage to be tender, enjoy marriages that mellow through the years.
BRENDAN FRANCIS

The only compliment some husbands pay their wives is to marry them.
ARNOLD GLASGOW

To make a good husband, make a good wife.
JOHN HEYWOOD

And the woman must realise that the man is a boy always, and will take his pleasures always as a boy. He must have his own circle of fellow-men. That is his way of pleasure. That is how he escapes. Sports, games, recreation – he is a boy again; living a boy's memories even to old age.
BEDE JARRETT

Marriage is not harmed by seducers, but by cowardly husbands.
SØREN KIERKEGAARD

Husbands are in heaven whose wives scold not.
ENGLISH PROVERB

In the husband wisdom, in the wife gentleness.
ENGLISH PROVERB

Christian husband! Imitate St. Joseph by beginning your day's work with God, and ending it for Him. Cherish those belonging to you as the holy foster father did Jesus, and be their faithful protector.
JOHN VIANNEY

Hypocrisy

(*See also* Deception)

Don't stay away from church because there are so many hypocrities. There's always room for one more.
ARTHUR R. ADAMS

A bad man is worse when he pretends to be a saint.
FRANCIS BACON

Hypocrisy – prejudice with a halo.
AMBROSE BIERCE

No man, for any considerable period, can wear one face to himself and another to the multitude, without finally getting bewildered as to which may be the true.
NATHANIEL HAWTHORNE

It is no fault of Christianity if a hypocrite falls into sin.
ST. JEROME

Solemn prayers, rapturous devotions, are but repeated hypocrisies unless the heart and mind be conformable to them.
WILLIAM LAW

Better be a sinner than a hypocrite.
DANISH PROVERB

When the fox preaches, look to your geese.
GERMAN PROVERB

Hypocrisy is the homage which vice pays to virtue.
FRANÇOIS DE LA ROCHEFOUCAULD

One may smile, and smile, and be a villain.
WILLIAM SHAKESPEARE

The old-style hypocrite was a person who tried to appear better than he actually was: the new-style hypocrite tries to appear worse than he or she is.
CHARLES TEMPLETON

Idealism

There is only one really startling thing to be done with the ideal, and that is to do it.
G. K. CHESTERTON

If we put an absurdly high ideal before us, it ceases to be an ideal at all, because we have no idea of acting upon it.
FREDERICK W. FABER

Men find in Jesus a reflection of their own ideals.
GRANVILLE HICKS

The test of an ideal or rather of an idealist, is the power to hold to it and get one's inspiration from it under difficulties.
OLIVER WENDELL HOLMES

Some men can live up to their loftiest ideals without ever going higher than a basement.
THEODORE ROOSEVELT

Ideals are like the stars – we never reach them, but like the mariners of the sea we chart our course by them.
CARL SCHURZ

Idleness

Idleness is the enemy of the soul.
ST. BENEDICT

Sloth, like rust, consumes faster than labour wears.
BENJAMIN FRANKLIN

To have too much to do is for most men safer than to have too little.
HENRY E. MANNING

The devil tempts all but the idle man tempts the devil.
ENGLISH PROVERB

How beautiful it is to do nothing, and then rest afterward.
SPANISH PROVERB

He is not only idle who does nothing but he is idle who might be better employed.
SOCRATES

To be idle requires a strong sense of personal identity.
ROBERT LOUIS STEVENSON

Idolatry

The Church is society's permanent rampart against idolatry. This is the ultimate, in a sense it is the only, sin, the root of all disorder.
AELRED GRAHAM

We easily fall into idolatry, for we are inclined to it by nature; and coming to us by inheritance, it seems pleasant.
MARTIN LUTHER

Christians can be more prone to idolatry than they realise, and their idolatries take the form of fetishism, the devotional attachment to facts, words or concepts which are not themselves final and are not themselves God.
MICHAEL RAMSEY

When men have gone so far as to talk as though their idols have come to life, it is time that someone broke them.
RICHARD H. TAWNEY

Whatever a man seeks, honours, or exalts more than God, this is the god of idolatry.
WILLIAM ULLATHORNE

Ignorance

There are more fools than wise men and even in the wise man himself there is more folly than wisdom.
NICOLAS DE CHAMFORT

A young levite once remarked to his professor: 'God can dispense with my learning.' 'Yes,' was the reply, 'but He has still less need of your ignorance.'
JAMES GIBBONS

There is nothing more frightful than ignorance in action.
JOHANN WOLFGANG VON GOETHE

Ignorance is preferable to error; and he is less remote from truth who believes nothing, than he who believes what is wrong.
THOMAS JEFFERSON

Nothing is so firmly believed as that which is least known.
FRANCIS JEFFREY

We must make up our minds to be ignorant of much, if we would know anything.
JOHN HENRY NEWMAN

Herein is the evil of ignorance, that he who is neither good nor wise is nevertheless satisfied with himself: he has no desire for that of which he feels no want.
SOCRATES

I believe in the forgiveness of sins and the redemption of ignorance.
ADLAI STEVENSON

Not ignorance, but ignorance of ignorance, is the death of knowledge.
ALFRED NORTH WHITEHEAD

Imagination

The soul without imagination is what an observatory would be without a telescope.
HENRY WARD BEECHER

Imagination is not a talent of some men but is the health of every man.
RALPH WALDO EMERSON

He who has imagination without learning has wings and no feet.
JOSEPH JOUBERT

Always be on your guard against your imagination. How many lions it creates in our paths, and so easily! And we suffer so much if we do not turn a deaf ear to its tales and suggestions.
GEORGE PORTER

Imagination and fiction make up more than three-quarters of our real life. Rare indeed are the true contacts with good and evil.
SIMONE WEIL

Immortality

(*See also* Afterlife and Eternity)

If there is a sin against life, it lies perhaps less in despairing of it than in hoping for another and evading the implacable grandeur of the one we have.
ALBERT CAMUS

To be immortal is to share in Divinity.
ST. CLEMENT OF ALEXANDRIA

There is nothing innocent or good that dies and is forgotten: let us hold to that faith or none.
CHARLES DICKENS

Here in this world He bids us come, there in the next He shall bid us welcome.
JOHN DONNE

Our dissatisfaction with any other solution is the blazing evidence of immortality.
RALPH WALDO EMERSON

We cannot resist the conviction that this world is for us only the porch of another and more magnificent temple of the Creator's majesty.
FREDERICK W. FABER

The average man does not know what to do with this life, yet wants another one that will last forever.
ANATOLE FRANCE

Without love immortality would be frightful and horrible.
THEODOR HAECKER

Our Creator would never have made such lovely days, and have given us the deep hearts to enjoy them above and beyond all thought, unless we were meant to be immortal.
NATHANIEL HAWTHORNE

Surely God would not have created such a being as man . . . to exist only for a day! No, no, man was made for immortality.
ABRAHAM LINCOLN

The universe is a stairway leading no-where unless man is immortal.
EDGAR YOUNG MULLINS

Those who live in the Lord never see each other for the last time.
GERMAN PROVERB

Spring – an experience in immortality.
HENRY DAVID THOREAU

I have never seen what to me seemed an atom of proof that there is a future life. And yet – I am strongly inclined to expect one.
MARK TWAIN

There is only one way I can get ready for immortality, and that is to love this life, and live it bravely and cheerfully and as faithfully as I can.
HENRY VAN DYKE

Incarnation

(*See also* Christmas)

I think that the purpose and cause of the Incarnation was that God might illuminate the world by his wisdom and excite it to the love of himself.
PETER ABELARD

In order that the body of Christ might be shown to be a real body, he was born of a woman; but in order that his Godhead might be made clear he was born of a virgin.
ST. THOMAS AQUINAS

The greatness of God was not cast off, but the slightness of human nature was put on.
ST. THOMAS AQUINAS

Every thought, word, action, silence, and self-repression in the incarnate life of the Word of God is full of spiritual significance and effectiveness.
ROBERT H. BENSON

The Word of God became man that you also may learn from a man how a man becomes a God.
ST. CLEMENT OF ALEXANDRIA

The Incarnation would be equally a miracle however Jesus entered the world.
P. T. FORSYTH

If Jesus Christ is God incarnate, no fuller disclosure of God in terms of manhood than is given in his person is conceivable or possible.
CHARLES GORE

The Word of God, Jesus Christ, on account of His great love for mankind, became what we are in order to make us what He is himself.
ST. IRENAEUS

The Incarnation is not an event; but an institution. What Jesus once took up He never laid down.
VINCENT MCNABB

On account of Him there have come to be many Christs in the world, even all who, like Him, loved righteousness and hated iniquity.
ORIGEN OF ALEXANDRIA

We are far too apt to limit and mechandise the great doctrine of the Incarnation, which forms the centre of the Christian faith. Whatever it may mean, it means at least this – that in the conditions of human life we have access, as nowhere else, to the inmost nature of the divine.
A. S. PRINGLE-PATTISON

What happened at the Incarnation is that God, the power of nature and history, the logos or principle of the evolutionary process, began to be represented in a new way.
JOHN A. T. ROBINSON

Independence

Independence, like honour, is a rocky island without a beach.
NAPOLEON BONAPARTE

Let every tub stand upon its own bottom.
JOHN BUNYAN

There is a great deal of self-will in the world, but very little genuine independence of character.
FREDERICK W. FABER

Christianity promises to make men free; it never promises to make them independent.
WILLIAM RALPH INGE

It is tragic how few people ever 'possess their souls' before they die. 'Nothing is more rare in any man,' says Emerson, 'than an act of his own.' It is quite true. Most people are other people. Their thoughts are someone else's opinions, their lives a mimicry, their passions a quotation.
OSCAR WILDE

Indifference

(*See also* Apathy)

Holy indifference goes beyond resignation: for it loves nothing except for the love of God's will.
ST. FRANCIS DE SALES

The opposite of love is not hate; it is something much worse than that; hate with all its negation and emotion at least takes the other into account; the opposite of love is something much cooler, more pallid, and really much more cruel, the opposite of love is indifference.
WILLIAM HAGUE

Most of us have no real loves and no real hatreds. Blessed is love, less blessed is hatred, but thrice accursed is that indifference which is neither one nor the other.
MARK RUTHERFORD

The worst sin toward our fellow creatures is not to hate them, but to be indifferent to them.
GEORGE BERNARD SHAW

Individuality

The real man is a maze of a million notes: the label is all one note.
HILAIRE BELLOC

It is often all our own individuality that hinders us from becoming aware of the individualities of others to their full extent.
JOHANN WOLFGANG VON GOETHE

The way of salvation cannot lie in melting people down into a mass, but on the contrary in their separation and individuation.
THEODOR HAECKER

It is because of the devotion or sacrifice of individuals that causes become of value.
JULIAN HUXLEY

Every man must do two things alone: he must do his own believing, and his own dying.
MARTIN LUTHER

The only ultimate reason why man as man has individual significance is that Christ died for him.
GEORGE F. MACLEOD

At bottom every man knows well enough that he is a unique being, only once on this earth; and by no extraordinary chance will such a marvellously picturesque piece of diversity in unity as he is, ever be put together a second time.
FRIEDRICH NIETZSCHE

Indwelling Spirit

(*See also* Spiritual Life)

For it is not by themselves being so that men are gods, but they become gods by participation in that one God who is the true God.
ST. AUGUSTINE OF HIPPO

The indwelling of God is this – to hold God ever in memory, His shrine established within us.
ST. BASIL

The seed of God is in us. Given an intelligent and hard-working farmer, it will thrive and grow up to God, whose seed it is; and accordingly its fruits will be God-nature. Pear seeds grow into pear trees, nut seeds into nut trees, and God seeds into God.
MEISTER ECKHART

The very best and utmost of attainment in this life is to remain still and let God act and speak in thee.
MEISTER ECKHART

What lies behind us and what lies before us are tiny matters compared to what lies within us.
RALPH WALDO EMERSON

The gift of the Holy Ghost closes the last gap between the life of God and ours . . . When we allow the love of God to move in us, we can no longer distinguish ours and his; he becomes us, he lives us. It is the first fruits of the spirit, the beginning of our being made divine.
AUSTIN FARRER

For what is more consoling to a soul on earth than to be withdrawn by grace from the trouble of worldly affairs, from the defilement of desiring and the vanity of loving creatures, into the peace and sweetness of spiritual love, where it inwardly perceives God's presence and is satisfied with the light of His countenance?
WALTER HILTON

Your treasure house is within. It contains all you will ever need. Use it fully instead of seeking vainly outside yourself.
HUI HAI

The centre of the soul is God, and when the soul has attained to him according to the whole capacity of its being, and according to the force of its operation, it will have reached the last and deep centre of the soul, which will be when with all its powers it loves and understands and enjoys God.
ST. JOHN OF THE CROSS

Too few people have experienced the divine image as the innermost possession of their own souls. Christ only meets them from without, never from within the soul.
CARL GUSTAV JUNG

Every time we say, 'I believe in the Holy Spirit,' we mean that we believe that there is a living God able and willing to enter human personality and change it.
J. B. PHILLIPS

God is nigh unto thee. He is with thee. He is within thee. There is no good man but hath God within him.
SENECA

Father! replenish with Thy grace
This longing heart of mine;
Make it Thy quiet dwelling-place,
Thy sacred inmost shrine!
ANGELUS SILESIUS

Influence

Every life is a profession of faith, and exercises an inevitable and silent influence.
HENRI FRÉDÉRIC AMIEL

No man should think himself a zero, and think he can do nothing about the state of the world.
BERNARD M. BARUCH

We live at the mercy of a malevolent word. A sound, a mere disturbance of the air, sinks into our very soul sometimes.
JOSEPH CONRAD

Blessed is the influence of one true, loving soul on another.
GEORGE ELIOT

He who goes with wolves learns to howl.
SPANISH PROVERB

Innocence

Innocence always calls mutely for protection, when we would be so much wiser to guard ourselves against it; innocence is like a dumb leper who has lost his bell, wandering the world, meaning no harm.
GRAHAM GREENE

Hold fast to simplicity of heart and innocence. Yes, be as infants who do not know the wickedness that destroys the life of men.
SHEPHERD OF HERMAS

Innocence comes in contact with evil and doesn't know it; it baffles temptation; it is protected where no one else is.
BASIL W. MATURIN

Innocent actions carry their warrant with them.
ENGLISH PROVERB

What hope is there for innocence if it is not recognised?
SIMONE WEIL

Insight

A moment's insight is sometimes worth a life's experience.
OLIVER WENDELL HOLMES

Where man sees but withered leaves God sees sweet flowers growing.
ALBERT LAIGHTON

The longer the field of activity the personality has, the greater will be its insights into reality.
WILLIAM F. LYNCH

It is not easy to repent of anything that has given us truer insight.
JOHN LANCASTER SPALDING

One of the first things for which we have to pray is a true insight into our condition.
OLIVE WYON

Inspiration

Look well into yourself; there is a source which will always spring up if you will search there.
MARCUS ANTONIUS

No man was ever great without some portion of divine inspiration.
MARCUS TULLIUS CICERO

Inspirations never go in for long engagements; they demand immediate marriage to action.
BRENDAN FRANCIS

Inspiration is the name of that all-comprehensive operation of the Holy Spirit whereby he has bestowed on the Church a complete and infallible Scripture.
ABRAHAM KUYPER

The ultimate reason why God has inspired certain books is that through them he should be present in our midst.
HUBERT J. RICHARDS

You ask if inspiration can be lost; no, when creation has started (then it goes on like the child in the womb).
W. B. YEATS

Instinct

We know very little indeed about the inner working of our own selves. There's instinct, for instance. We know nothing about that, except that it is so.
ROBERT H. BENSON

Beasts obey the prescript of their natures, and live up to the height of that instinct that Providence hath given them.
RICHARD POWER

Instinct is a great matter, I was a coward on instinct.
WILLIAM SHAKESPEARE

Few of us have vitality enough to make any of our instincts imperious.
GEORGE BERNARD SHAW

Integrity

(*See also* Honesty)

Always vote for a principle, though you vote alone, and you may cherish the sweet reflection that your vote is never lost.
JOHN QUINCY ADAMS

Live so that the preacher can tell the truth at your funeral.
K. BECKSTROM

My worth to God in public is what I am in private.
OSWALD CHAMBERS

He that is good at making excuses is seldom good at anything else.
BENJAMIN FRANKLIN

Integrity without knowledge is weak and useless, and knowledge without integrity is dangerous and dreadful.
SAMUEL JOHNSON

Some people are likeable in spite of their unswerving integrity!
DON MARQUIS

Live among men as if God beheld you; speak with God as if men were listening.
SENECA

Intelligence

Intelligence is not something possessed once for all. It is in constant process of forming, and its retention requires constant alertness in observing consequences, an open-minded will to learn and courage in readjustment.
JOHN DEWEY

I do not feel obliged to believe that that same God who has endowed us with sense, reason, and intellect has intended us to forego their use.
GALILEO GALILEI

True intelligence very readily conceives of an intelligence superior to its own; and this is why truly intelligent men are modest.
ANDRÉ GIDE

The more intelligent a man is, the more originality he discovers in men. Ordinary people see no difference between men.
BLAISE PASCAL

Christianity has need of thought that it may come to the consciousness of its real self. For centuries it treasured the great commandment of love and mercy as traditional truth without recognising it as a reason for opposing slavery, witch-burning, torture, and all the other ancient and medieval forms of inhumanity.
ALBERT SCHWEITZER

Intention

(*See also* Motivation)

God looks at the intention of the heart rather than the gifts He is offered.
JEAN PIERRE CAMUS

The consciousness of good intentions is the greatest solace in misfortune.
MARCUS TULLIUS CICERO

One of the most excellent intentions that we can possibly have in all our actions, is to do them because our Lord did them.
ST. FRANCIS DE SALES

Man beholds the face, but God looks upon the heart. Man considers the actions, but God weighs the intentions.
THOMAS À KEMPIS

One often sees good intentions, if pushed beyond moderation, bring about very vicious results.
MICHEL DE MONTAIGNE

Involvement

Behold the turtle; he makes progress only when he sticks his neck out.
JAMES BRYANT CONANT

The Church as a whole must be concerned with both evangelism and social action. It is not a case of either-or; it is both-and. Anything less is only a partial Gospel, not the whole counsel of God.
ROBERT D. DE HAAN

Be to the world a sign that while we as Christians do not have all the answers, we do know and care about the questions.
BILLY GRAHAM

Jealousy

(*See also* Envy)

As to the green-eyed monster jealousy... set on him at once and poison him with extra doses of kindness to the person whom he wants to turn you against.
GEORGE PORTER

Frenzy, heresy, and jealousy, seldom cured.
ENGLISH PROVERB

In jealousy there is more self-love than love.
FRANÇOIS DE LA ROCHEFOUCAULD

Moral indignation is jealousy with a halo.
H. G. WELLS

Jesus Christ

(*See also* Divinity of Christ and Humanity of Christ)

Jesus Christ will be Lord of all or he will not be Lord at all.
ST. AUGUSTINE OF HIPPO

If Jesus Christ is not true God, how could he *help* us? If he is not true man, how could he help *us*?
DIETRICH BONHOEFFER

Christ did not love humanity. He never said that he loved humanity. He loved men.
G. K. CHESTERTON

As Gregory of Nyssa pictures it, He entered paradise bringing with Him His bride, Humanity, whom He had just wedded on the Cross.
JEAN DANIELOU

Who can deny that Jesus of Nazareth, the incarnate Son of the most High God, is the eternal glory of the Jewish Race?
BENJAMIN DISRAELI

I believe there is no one lovelier, deeper, more sympathetic and more perfect than Jesus. I say to myself that not only is there no one else like him, but there could never be any one like him.
FEODOR DOSTOEVSKI

A Christian has a union with Jesus Christ more noble, more intimate and more perfect than the members of a human body have with their head.
JOHN EUDES

Jesus Christ is God's everything for man's total need.
RICHARD HALVERSON

Had the doctrines of Jesus been preached always as pure as they came from his lips, the whole civilised world would now have been Christian.
THOMAS JEFFERSON

We get no deeper into Christ than we allow him to get into us.
JOHN HENRY JOWETT

In his life Christ is an example, showing us how to live; in his death he is a sacrifice, satisfying for our sins; in his resurrection, a conqueror; in his ascension, a king; in his intercession, a high priest.
MARTIN LUTHER

We can hardly think of Jesus Christ without thinking of the sparrows, the grass, fig trees, sheep.
VINCENT MCNABB

A radical revolution, embracing even nature itself, was the fundamental idea of Jesus.
JOSEPH ERNEST RENAN

I have a great need for Christ; I have a great Christ for my need.
CHARLES H. SPURGEON

Jews

The Hebrews have done more to civilise men than any other nation. If I were an atheist, and believed in blind eternal fate, I should still believe that fate had ordained the Jews to be the most essential instrument for civilising the nations.
JOHN QUINCY ADAMS

To be a Jew is a destiny.
VICKI BAUM

In Israel, in order to be a realist you must believe in miracles.
DAVID BEN-GURION

If my theory of relativity is proven successful, Germany will claim me as a German and France will declare that I am a citizen of the world. Should my theory prove untrue, France will say that I am a German and Germany will declare that I am a Jew.
ALBERT EINSTEIN

The pursuit of knowledge for its own sake, an almost fanatical love of justice, and a desire for personal independence – these are features of the Jewish tradition which make me thank my stars that I belong to it.
ALBERT EINSTEIN

The race of the Hebrews is not new but is honoured among all men for its antiquity and is itself well known to all.
EUSEBIUS OF CAESAREA

The Jew's home has rarely been his 'castle'; throughout the ages it has been something far higher – his sanctuary.
JOSEPH H. HERTZ

Spiritually we are all Semites.
POPE PIUS XI

No Jew is a fool, no hare is lazy.
SPANISH PROVERB

Even Moses couldn't get along with the Jews.
YIDDISH PROVERB

No misfortune avoids a Jew.
YIDDISH PROVERB

For others a knowledge of the history of their people is a civic duty, while for Jews it is a sacred duty.
MAURICE SAMUEL

The Jews generally give value. They make you pay; but they deliver the goods. In my experience the men who want something for nothing are invariably Christians.
GEORGE BERNARD SHAW

Joy

(*See also* Happiness, Humour and Laughter)

Those who bring sunshine to the lives of others cannot keep it from themselves.
JAMES M. BARRIE

To be able to find joy in another's joy, that is the secret of happiness.
GEORGE BERNANOS

Joy is the most infallible sign of the presence of God.
LEON BLOY

We are all strings in the concert of his joy.
JAKOB BOEHME

The joy that Jesus gives is the result of our disposition being at one with his own disposition.
OSWALD CHAMBERS

The life without festival is a long road without an inn
DEMOCRITUS OF ABDERA

It is good if man can bring about that God sings within him.
RABBI ELIMELEKH

When I think upon my God, my heart is so full of joy that the notes dance and leap from my pen; and since God has given me a cheerful heart, it will be pardoned me that I serve Him with a cheerful spirit.
FRANZ JOSEF HAYDN

There is no law which lays it down that you must smile! But you can make a gift of your smile; you can be the heaven of kindness in your family.
POPE JOHN PAUL II

If there is joy in the world, surely the man of pure heart possesses it.
THOMAS À KEMPIS

Joy is never in our power, and pleasure is. I doubt whether anyone who has tasted joy would ever, if both were in his power, exchange it for all the pleasure in the world.
C. S. LEWIS

Joy is the serious business of heaven.
C. S. LEWIS

Only joyous love redeems.
CATHERINE MARSHALL

One joy dispels a hundred cares.
ORIENTAL PROVERB

Joy is the heavenly 'okay' of the inner life of power.
AGNES SANFORD

The surest mark of a Christian is not faith, or even love, but joy.
SAMUEL M. SHOEMAKER

This is the secret of joy. We shall no longer strive for our own way; but commit ourselves, easily and simply, to God's way, acquiesce in his will and in so doing find our peace.
EVELYN UNDERHILL

Judging Others

(*See also* Judgment)

We must neither judge nor suspect evil of our neighbour, without good grounds.
ST. ALPHONSUS LIGUORI

It is well, when one is judging a friend, to remember that he is judging you with the same godlike and superior impartiality.
ARNOLD BENNETT

When it seems that God shows us the faults of others, keep on the safer side. It may be that thy judgment is false.
ST. CATHERINE OF SIENA

You will not become a saint through other people's sins.
ANTON CHEKHOV

How rarely we weigh our neighbour in the same balance in which we weigh ourselves.
THOMAS À KEMPIS

Our duty is to believe that for which we have sufficient evidence, and to suspend judgment when we have not.
SIR JOHN LUBBOCK

Never a sound judgment without charity. When man judges man, charity is less a bounty from our mercy than just allowance for the insensible leeway of human fallibility.
HERMAN MELVILLE

A man's judgment of another depends more on the judging and on his passions than on the one being judged and his conduct.
PAUL TOURNIER

Judgment

(*See also* Judging others)

For when the judgment is finished, this heaven and earth shall cease to be, and there will be a new heaven and a new earth. For this world shall pass away by transmutation, not by absolute destruction.
ST. AUGUSTINE OF HIPPO

It may be that the day of judgment will dawn tomorrow; in that case, we shall gladly stop working for a better future. But not before.
DIETRICH BONHOEFFER

If we judge ourselves, we will not be judged by God.
JEAN PIERRE CAMUS

God himself, sir, does not propose to judge man until the end of his days.
SAMUEL JOHNSON

God postpones the collapse and dissolution of the universe (through which the bad angels, the demons, and men would cease to exist), because of the Christian seed, which He knows to be the cause in nature of the World's preservation.
ST. JUSTIN MARTYR

Who judges others condemns himself.
ENGLISH PROVERB

The judgment of God is going on wherever the word of God is being proclaimed; men are judging themselves, according to their acceptance or rejection of the Gospel.
ALAN RICHARDSON

Justice

(*See also* Judgment)

Justice discards party, friendship, kindred, and is always, therefore, represented as blind.
JOSEPH ADDISON

The rule of justice is plain, namely, that a good man ought not to swerve from the truth, not to inflict any unjust loss on anyone, nor to act in any way deceitfully or fraudulently.
ST. AMBROSE

Let justice be done though the world perish.
ST. AUGUSTINE OF HIPPO

Children are innocent and love justice, while most adults are wicked and prefer mercy.
G. K. CHESTERTON

Justice is truth in action.
BENJAMIN DISRAELI

The perfection of justice implies charity, because we have a right to be loved.
AUSTIN O'MALLEY

The Christian demand for justice does not come from Karl Marx. It comes from Jesus Christ and the Hebrew prophets.
G. BROMLEY OXNAM

Justice and power must be brought together, so that whatever is just may be powerful, and whatever is powerful may be just.
BLAISE PASCAL

One hour of justice is worth a hundred of prayer.
ARAB PROVERB

In times when the government imprisons any unjustly, the true place for a just man is also the prison.
HENRY DAVID THOREAU

Kindness

(*See also* Love)

The greatest thing a man can do for his Heavenly Father is to be kind to some of His other children.
HENRY DRUMMOND

Kindness has converted more sinners than zeal, eloquence and learning.
FREDERICK W. FABER

There is a grace of kind listening, as well as a grace of kind speaking.
FREDERICK W. FABER

If you would reap praise, sow the seeds; gentle words and useful deeds.
BENJAMIN FRANKLIN

Kindness is the golden chain by which society is bound together.
JOHANN WOLFGANG VON
GOETHE

Wise sayings often fall on barren ground; but a kind word is never thrown away.
ARTHUR HELPS

Sign in a little shop: 'Kindness spoken here.'
MILDRED E. KORDENAT

Kindness which is betowed on the good is never lost.
PLATO

One kind word can warm three winter months.
JAPANESE PROVERB

One can pay back the loan of gold, but one dies forever in debt to those who are kind.
MALAYAN PROVERB

To give pleasure to a single heart by a single kind act is better than a thousand head-bowings in prayer.
SAADI

Be kind; everyone you meet is fighting a hard battle.
JOHN WATSON

That best portion of a good man's life –
His little, nameless unremembered acts of kindness and of love.
WILLIAM WORDSWORTH

Kingdom of God

The Kingdom of God will not come in a day; it will not be left with the morning milk.
S. PARKES CADMAN

Wherever the bounds of beauty, truth and goodness are advanced there the Kingdom comes.
DONALD COGGAN

Is the Kingdom of God a big family? Yes, in a sense it is. But in another sense it is a prodigious biological operation – that of the Redeeming Incarnation.
P. TEILHARD DE CHARDIN

To accept His Kingdom and to enter in brings blessedness, because the best conceivable thing is that we should be in obedience to the will of God.
C. H. DODD

The Kingdom of God is a kingdom of love; and love is never a stagnant pool.
HENRY W. DU BOSE

To want all that God wants, always to want it, for all occasions and without reservations, this is the Kingdom of God which is all within.
FRANÇOIS FENELON

Wherever God rules over the human heart as King, there is the Kingdom of God established.
PAUL W. HARRISON

The core of all that Jesus teaches about the Kingdom is the immediate apprehension and acceptance of God as King in his own life.
T. W. MASON

In the Gospel, Jesus is *autobasileia*, the Kingdom himself.
ORIGEN OF ALEXANDRIA

Eighty-six years I have served Him, and He has done me no wrong. How can I blaspheme my King who has saved me?
ST. POLYCARP TO HIS
EXECUTIONERS

If only we knew how to look at life as God sees it, we should realise that nothing is secular in the world, but that everything contributes to the building of the Kingdom of God.
MICHEL QUOIST

If you do not wish for His kingdom, don't pray for it. But if you do, you must do more than pray for it; you must work for it.
JOHN RUSKIN

Power in complete subordination to love – that is something like a definition of the Kingdom of God.
WILLIAM TEMPLE

There is no structural organisation of society which can bring about the coming of the Kingdom of God on earth, since all systems can be perverted by the selfishness of man.
WILLIAM TEMPLE

Jesus never speaks of the Kingdom of God as previously existing. To him the Kingdom is throughout something new, now first to be realised.
GEERHARDUS VOS

Knowledge

(*See also* Knowledge of God and Omniscience)

A scrap of knowledge about sublime things is worth more than any amount about trivialities.
ST. THOMAS AQUINAS

Let knowledge be applied to a kind of scaffolding, making it possible for the edifice of charity to rise, to endure for ever, even when knowledge is done away with.
ST. AUGUSTINE OF HIPPO

The knower and the known are one. Simple people imagine that they should see God, as if He stood there and they here. This is not so. God and I, we are one in knowledge.
MEISTER ECKHART

It is in the matter of knowledge that a man is most haunted with a sense of inevitable limitation.
JOSEPH FARRELL

If you have knowledge, let others light their candles at it.
MARGARET FULLER

Wonder rather than doubt is the root of knowledge.
ABRAHAM JOSHUA HESCHEL

Knowledge without integrity is dangerous and dreadful.
SAMUEL JOHNSON

All men naturally desire to know, but what doth knowledge avail without the fear of God?
THOMAS À KEMPIS

All knowledge is sterile which does not lead to action and end in charity.
DÉSIRÉ JOSEPH MERCIER

Quarry the granite rock with razors, or moor the vessel with a thread of silk; then may you hope with such keen and delicate instruments as human knowledge and human reason to contend against those giants, the passion and the pride of man.
JOHN HENRY NEWMAN

Where there is the tree of knowledge, there is always Paradise: so say the most ancient and the most modern serpents.
FRIEDERICH NIETZSCHE

Knowledge is folly, except grace guide it.
ENGLISH PROVERB

Knowledge without conscience is the ruination of the soul.
FRANCIS RABELAIS

Knowledge unused for the good of others is more vain than unused gold.
JOHN RUSKIN

Knowledge of God

(*See also* God and Omniscience)

If by knowledge only, and reason, we could come to God, then none should come but they that are learned and have good wits . . . But God hath made His way 'via Regiam' – the King's Highway.
LANCELOT ANDREWES

God alone knows the depths and the riches of His Godhead, and divine wisdom alone can declare his secrets.
ST. THOMAS AQUINAS

There is but one thing in the world really worth pursuing – the knowledge of God.
ROBERT H. BENSON

By faith we know his existence; in glory we shall know his nature.
BLAISE PASCAL

The way through to the vision of the Son of man and the knowledge of God, which is the heart of contemplative prayer, is by unconditional love of the neighbour, of 'the nearest *Thou* to hand'.
JOHN A. T. ROBINSON

He truly knows God perfectly that finds Him incomprehensible and unable to be known.
RICHARD ROLLE

All living knowledge of God rests upon this foundation: that we experience him in our lives as Will-to-Love.
ALBERT SCHWEITZER

The best way to know God is to love many things.
VINCENT VAN GOGH

We can no more find a method for knowing God than for making God, because the knowledge of God is God himself dwelling in the soul. The most we can do is to prepare for his entry, to get out of his way, to remove the barriers, for until God acts in us there is nothing positive that we can do in this direction.
ALAN W. WATTS

Laughter

(*See also* Humour and Joy)

Keep company with the more cheerful sort of the Godly; there is no mirth like the mirth of believers.
RICHARD BAXTER

Genuine laughter is the physical effect produced in the rational being by what suddenly strikes his immortal soul as being damned funny.
HILAIRE BELLOC

A laugh is like a love affair in that it carries a man completely off his feet; a laugh is like a creed or a church in that it asks that a man should trust himself to it.
G. K. CHESTERTON

Laughter with us is still suspect to this extent at least, that not yet do we without a shock think of God laughing.
ARTHUR G. CLUTTON-BROCK

God cannot be solemn, or he would not have blessed man with the incalculable gift of laughter.
SYDNEY HARRIS

Man is the only animal that laughs and weeps: for he is the only animal that is struck by the difference between what things are and what they might have been.
WILLIAM HAZLITT

Shared laughter creates a bond of friendship. When people laugh together, they cease to be young and old, master and pupils, worker and driver. They have become a single group of human beings, enjoying their existence.
W. GRANT LEE

If you're not allowed to laugh in Heaven, I don't want to go there.
MARTIN LUTHER

God is the creator of laughter that is good.
PHILO

He is not laughed at that laughs at himself first.
ENGLISH PROVERB

One who is always laughing is a fool, and one who never laughs a knave.
SPANISH PROVERB

Law

(*See also* Commandments)

All law is directed to the common well-being. From this it draws its force and meaning, and to the extent that it falls short of this it does not oblige in conscience.
ST. THOMAS AQUINAS

The law is reason free from passion.
ARISTOTLE

The law's final justification is in the good it does or fails to do to the society of a given place and time.
ALBERT CAMUS

Probably all laws are useless; for good men do not need laws at all, and bad men are made no better by them.
DEMONAX THE CYNIC

The law, in its majestic equality, forbids the rich as well as the poor to sleep under bridges, to beg in the streets, and to steal bread.
ANATOLE FRANCE

Moral law is more than a test, it is for man's own good. Every law that God has given has been for man's benefit. If man breaks it, he is not only rebelling against God, he is hurting himself.
BILLY GRAHAM

Wherever law ends, tyranny begins.
JOHN LOCKE

Men of most renowned virtue have sometimes by transgressing most truly kept the law.
JOHN MILTON

There is nothing more necessary for the national or international community than respect for the majesty of the law and the salutary thought that the law is also sacred and protected, so that whoever breaks it is punishable and will be punished.
POPE PIUS XII

The beginning and the end of the law is kindness.
JEWISH PROVERB

Nobody has a more sacred obligation to obey the law than those who make the law.
SOPHOCLES

Law is a common, just and stable precept, which has been sufficiently promulgated.
F. SUAREZ

Law never made men a whit more just.
HENRY DAVID THOREAU

Leadership

There is no worse mistake in public leadership than to hold out false hopes soon to be swept away.
SIR WINSTON CHURCHILL

If in order to succeed in an enterprise, I were obliged to choose between fifty deer commanded by a lion, and fifty lions commanded by a deer, I should consider myself more certain of success with the first group than with the second.
ST. VINCENT DE PAUL

In the simplest terms, a leader is one who knows where he wants to go, and gets up, and goes.
JOHN ERSKINE

A good leader takes a little more than his share of blame; a little less than his share of credit.
ARNOLD H. GLASGOW

The final test of a leader is that he leaves behind him in other men the conviction and the will to carry on.
WALTER LIPPMANN

To command is to serve, nothing more and nothing less.
ANDRÉ MALRAUX

In this world no one rules by mere love; if you are but amiable, you are no hero; to be powerful, you must be strong, and to have dominion you must have a genius for organising.
JOHN HENRY NEWMAN

Beware of the chief seat, because it shifts.
JEWISH PROVERB

Reason and calm judgment are the qualities of a leader.
CAIUS CORNELIUS TACITUS

To be a leader means to have determination. It means to be resolute inside and outside, with ourselves and with others.
LECH WALESA

Leadership is a serving relationship that has the effect of facilitating human development.
TED WARD

Learning

(*See also* Education)

Anyone who stops learning is old, whether at twenty or eighty. Anyone who keeps learning stays young. The greatest thing in life is to keep your mind young.
HENRY FORD

One of the reasons mature people stop learning is that they become less and less willing to risk failure.
JOHN W. GARDNER

I have learned silence from the talkative, toleration from the intolerant, and kindness from the unkind; yet strange, I am ungrateful to these teachers.
KAHLIL GIBRAN

Learning is not to be blamed, nor the mere knowledge of anything which is good in itself and ordained by God; but a good conscience and a virtuous life are always to be preferred before it.
THOMAS À KEMPIS

I've known countless people who were reservoirs of learning yet never had a thought.
WILSON MIZNER

He who is afraid of asking is ashamed of learning.
DANISH PROVERB

Learning is the eye of the mind.
ENGLISH PROVERB

Leisure

(*See also* Pleasure)

One ought, every day at least, to hear a little song, read a good poem, see a fine picture, and, if it were possible, to speak a few reasonable words.
JOHANN WOLFGANG VON GOETHE

Leisure, like its sister peace, is among those things which are internally felt rather than seen from the outside.
VERNON LEE

Leisure nourishes the body and the mind.
OVID

To be for one day entirely at leisure is to be for one day an immortal.
CHINESE PROVERB

Too much leisure with too much money has been the dread of societies across the ages. That is when nations cave in from within.
WILLIAM RUSSELL

Life lived amidst tension and business needs leisure. Leisure that re-creates and renews. Leisure should be a time to think new thoughts, not ponder old ills.
NEIL C. STRAIT

He enjoys true leisure who has time to improve his soul's estate.
HENRY DAVID THOREAU

To be able to fill leisure intelligently is the last product of civilisation.
ARNOLD TOYNBEE

Liberty

(*See also* Freedom and Free Will)

There is no true liberty except the liberty of the happy who cleave to the eternal law.
ST. AUGUSTINE OF HIPPO

The condition upon which God hath given liberty to man is eternal vigilance.
JOHN PHILPOT CURRAN

Freedom is not worth having if it does not connote freedom to err.
MOHANDAS GANDHI

The love of liberty is the love of others; the love of power is the love of ourselves.
WILLIAM HAZLITT

The world has never had a good definition of the word liberty.
ABRAHAM LINCOLN

God grants liberty only to those who love it.
DANIEL WEBSTER

Liberty is the only thing you can't have unless you give it to others.
WILLIAM ALLEN WHITE

Life

A blessed life may be defined as consisting simply and solely in the possession of goodness and truth.
ST. AMBROSE

The man who has no inner life is the slave to his surroundings.
HENRI FRÉDÉRIC AMIEL

All life is meeting.
MARTIN BUBER

If, after all, men cannot always make history have a meaning, they can always act so that their own lives have one.
ALBERT CAMUS

One life, a little gleam of time between two eternities.
THOMAS CARLYLE

One person who has mastered life is better than a thousand persons who have mastered only the contents of books, but no one can get anything out of life without God.
MEISTER ECKHART

Is life so wretched? Isn't it rather your hands which are too small, your vision which is muddied? You are the one who must grow up.
DAG HAMMARSKJOLD

Living a good, decent, Christian life is what's important, live that life and the rest will follow.
SPIKE MILLIGAN

Fear not that your life shall come to an end, but rather that it shall never have a beginning.
JOHN HENRY NEWMAN

Life is filled with meaning as soon as Jesus Christ enters into it.
STEPHEN NEILL

Life is a hard fight, a struggle, a wrestling with the principle of evil, hand to hand, foot to foot. Every inch of the way is disputed. The night is given us to take breath and to pray, to drink deep at the fountain of power. The day, to use the strength which has been given us, to go forth to work with it till the evening.
FLORENCE NIGHTINGALE

Life is an onion which one peels crying.
FRENCH PROVERB

The tragedy of life is what dies inside a man while he lives.
ALBERT SCHWEITZER

Life is a flame that is always burning itself out, but it catches fire again every time a child is born.
GEORGE BERNARD SHAW

The only significance of life consists in helping to establish the Kingdom of God; and this can be done only by means of the acknowledgment and profession of the truth by each one of us.
COUNT LEO TOLSTOY

Let us endeavour so to live that when we come to die even the undertaker will be sorry.
MARK TWAIN

After all it is those who have a deep and real inner life who are best able to deal with the 'irritating details of outer life'.
EVELYN UNDERHILL

God wants us to approach life, full of expectancy that God is going to be at work in every situation as we release our faith in Him.
COLIN URQUHART

How melancholy it is that we must often bolster up our will to live and strive by the thought that someone else is in an even worse plight than we are ourselves.
OSCAR WILDE

Light

Light, even though it passes through pollution, is not polluted.
ST. AUGUSTINE OF HIPPO

The first creature of God, in the works of the days, was the light of the sense, the last was the light of reason.
FRANCIS BACON

To the Church, Pentecost brought light, power, joy. There came to each illumination of mind, assurance of heart, intensity of love, fulness of power, exuberance of joy. No one needed to ask if they had received the Holy Ghost. Fire is self-evident. So is power!
SAMUEL CHADWICK

And I saw that there was an Ocean of Darkness and Death; but an infinite Ocean of Light and Love flowed over the Ocean of Darkness; and in that I saw the infinite love of God.
GEORGE FOX

There is more light than can be seen through the window.
RUSSIAN PROVERB

In darkness there is no choice. It is light that enables us to see the differences between things; and it is Christ who gives us light.
C. T. WHITMELL

Little Things

From a little spark may burst a mighty flame.
DANTE ALIGHIERI

By gnawing through a dike, even a rat may drown a nation.
EDMUND BURKE

We are too fond of our own will. We want to be doing what we fancy mighty things; but the great point is to do small things, when called to them, in a right spirit.
RICHARD CECIL

Faithfulness in little things is a big thing.
ST. JOHN CHRYSOSTOM

Exactness in little duties is a wonderful source of cheerfulness.
FREDERICK W. FABER

There is nothing small in the service of God.
ST. FRANCIS DE SALES

God does not want us to do extraordinary things; He wants us to do the ordinary things extraordinarily well.
CHARLES GORE

Little things come daily, hourly, within our reach, and they are not less calculated to set forward our growth in holiness than are the greater occasions which occur but rarely. Moreover, fidelity in trifles, and an earnest seeking to please God in little matters, is a test of real devotion and love. Let our aim be to please our dear Lord perfectly in little things, and to attain a spirit of childlike simplicity and dependence.
JEAN NICOLAS GROU

He does most in God's great world who does his best in his own little world.
THOMAS JEFFERSON

We can do little things for God: I turn the cake that is frying on the pan, for love of him; and that done, if there is nothing else to call me, I prostrate myself in worship before him who has given me grace to work; afterwards I rise happier than a king.
BROTHER LAWRENCE

He who is faithful over a few things is a lord of cities. It does not matter whether you preach in Westminster Abbey, or teach a ragged class, so you be faithful. The faithfulness is all.
GEORGE MACDONALD

There may be living and habitual conversation in heaven, under the aspect of the most simple, ordinary life. Let us always remember that holiness does not consist in doing uncommon things, but in doing everything with purity of heart.
HENRY E. MANNING

Do little things as if they were great, because of the majesty of the Lord Jesus Christ who dwells in thee.
BLAISE PASCAL

Nothing is too little to be ordered by our father; nothing too little in which to see His hand; nothing, which touches our souls, too little to accept from Him; nothing too little to be done to Him.
EDWARD B. PUSEY

Between the great things we cannot do and the little things we will not do, the danger is that we will do nothing.
H. G. WEAVER

Liturgy

(*See also* Worship)

If liturgy is to become a reality in the life of the Church it will have to be taken outside the Church precincts and become a formative element in the lives of Christians.
JAMES D. CRICHTON

The liturgy is the 'prayer' of the ecclesiastical community, a community which is forever moving towards the Lord and striving for a new fullness by continually searching to deepen its faith, strengthen its love, and solidify its hope in a world that is perpetually in a state of flux.
LUCIEN DEISS

Without the worship of the heart liturgical prayer becomes a matter of formal routine.
AELRED GRAHAM

The great danger is that liturgy creates a world of things over against the secular, instead of a vision of the sacredness of the secular.
ERIC JAMES

Great liturgies cannot be manufactured; they grow.
ARNOLD LUNN

It is superstition to found your hopes on ceremonies, but it is pride to refuse to submit to them.
BLAISE PASCAL

Liturgy can only really live, worship can only truly express joy, sorrow, hope, faith and love if it is firmly rooted in the actual lives and experience of the people who are worshipping.
IANTHE PRATT

Liturgy and evangelism are simply the inside and the outside of the one act of 'proclaiming the Lord's death'.
JOHN A. T. ROBINSON

The praise of Christ expressed by the liturgy is effective in so far as it continues to inform the humblest tasks.
ROGER SCHUTZ

Logic

Logic is like the sword – those who appeal to it shall perish by it.
SAMUEL BUTLER

Logic never attracts men to the point of carrying them away.
ALEXIS CARREL

One truth does not displace another. Even apparently contradictory truths do not displace one another. Logic is far too coarse to make the subtle distinctions life demands.
D. H. LAWRENCE

In formal logic, a contradiction is the signal of defeat: but in the evolution of real knowledge it marks the first step in progress towards a victory.
ALFRED NORTH WHITEHEAD

People who lean on logic and philosophy and rational exposition end by starving the best part of the mind.
J. B. YEATS

Loneliness

Men love because they are afraid of themselves, afraid of the loneliness that lives in them, and need someone in whom they can lose themselves as smoke loses itself in the sky.
V. F. CALVERTON

There is none more lonely than the man who loves only himself.
ABRAHAM IBN ESRA

At the innermost core of all loneliness is a deep and powerful yearning for union with one's lost self.
BRENDAN FRANCIS

The deepest need of man is the need to overcome his separateness, to leave the prison of his aloneness.
ERICH FROMM

It isn't the Devil in humanity that makes man a lonely creature, it's his God-likeness. It's the fullness of the Good that can't get out or can't find its proper 'other place' that makes for loneliness.
FYNN

We are born helpless. As soon as we are fully conscious we discover loneliness. We need others physically, emotionally, intellectually; we need them if we are to know anything, even ourselves.
C. S. LEWIS

People are lonely because they build walls instead of bridges.
JOSEPH F. NEWTON

Better be quarrelling than lonesome.
IRISH PROVERB

Language has created the word *loneliness* to express the pain of being alone, and the word *solitude* to express the glory of being alone.
PAUL TILLICH

We all carry our own deep wound, which is the wound of our loneliness.
JEAN VANIER

The soul hardly ever realises it, but whether he is a believer or not, his loneliness is really a homesickness for God.
HUBERT VAN ZELLER

Loneliness, far from being a rare and curious phenomenon peculiar to myself and to a few other solitary men, is the central and inevitable fact of human existence.
THOMAS WOLFE

Lord's Prayer

The prayer 'Thy Kingdom come', if we only knew it, is asking God to conduct a major operation.
GEORGE BUTTRICK

What deep mysteries, my dearest brothers, are contained in the Lord's Prayer! How many and great they are! They are expressed in a few words but they are rich in spiritual power so that nothing is left out; every petition and prayer we have to make is included. It is a compendium of heavenly doctrine.
ST. CYPRIAN

The 'Our Father' is a very personal prayer which nevertheless brings those praying closely together in the opening words. It is a very simple prayer of petition, but wholly concentrated on essentials, on God's cause which appears to be inextricably linked with man's cause.
HANS KUNG

The Lord's Prayer is the prayer above all prayers. It is a prayer which the most high Master taught us, wherein are comprehended all spiritual and temporal blessings, and the strongest comforts in all trials, temptations and troubles, even in the hour of death.
MARTIN LUTHER

The Lord's Prayer may be committed to memory quickly, but it is slowly learnt by heart.
FREDERICK D. MAURICE

The Lord's Prayer contains the sum total of religion and morals.
ARTHUR WELLESLEY
(DUKE OF WELLINGTON)

Love

Take away love and our earth is a tomb.
ROBERT BROWNING

It is love which gives things their value. It makes sense of the difficulty of spending hours and hours on one's knees praying while so many men need looking after in the world.
CARLO CARRETTO

Some day, after mastering the winds, the waves, the tides, and gravity, we shall harness for God the energies of love, and then, for the second time in the history of the world, man will have discovered fire.
P. TEILHARD DE CHARDIN

Only love can bring individual beings to their perfect completion as individuals because only love takes possession of them and unites them by what lies deepest within them.
P. TEILHARD DE CHARDIN

The love of a man and a woman gains immeasurably in power when placed under divine restraint.
ELISABETH ELLIOT

To love is to admire with the heart; to admire is to love with the mind.
THEOPHILE GAUTIER

To be loved for what one is, is the greatest exception. The great majority love in another only what they lend him, their own selves, their version of him.
JOHANN WOLFGANG VON GOETHE

We are shaped and fashioned by what we love.
JOHANN WOLFGANG VON GOETHE

In the evening of our lives we shall be examined in love.
ST. JOHN OF THE CROSS

Only love lasts forever. Alone, it constructs the shape of eternity in the earthly and short-lived dimensions of the history of man on the earth.
POPE JOHN PAUL II

I have decided to stick with love. Hate is too great a burden to bear.
MARTIN LUTHER KING, JR.

Love is infallible; it has no errors, for all errors are the want of love.
WILLIAM LAW

Love makes everything lovely; hate concentrates itself on the one thing hated.
GEORGE MACDONALD

Love cures people – both the ones who give it and the ones who receive it.
CARL MENNINGER

Love seeks one thing only: the good of the one loved. It leaves all the other secondary effects to take care of themselves. Love, therefore, is its own reward.
THOMAS MERTON

Joy is love exalted; peace is love in repose; long-suffering is love enduring; gentleness is love in society; goodness is love in action; faith is love on the battlefield; meekness is love in school; and temperance is love in training.
DWIGHT L. MOODY

Love does not consist in gazing at each other but in looking outward together in the same direction.
ANTOINE DE SAINT-EXUPÉRY

Love is the only spiritual power that can overcome the self-centredness that is inherent in being alive. Love is the thing that makes life possible or, indeed, tolerable.
ARNOLD TOYNBEE

Love is the greatest of all risks ... the giving of myself. But dare I take this risk, diving into the swirling waters of loving fidelity?
JEAN VANIER

Love of God

(*See also* God, Love and One God)

To love God is something greater than to know him.
ST. THOMAS AQUINAS

We should love God because he is God, and the measure of our love should be to love him without measure.
ST. BERNARD OF CLAIRVAUX

Give me such love for God and men, as will blot out all hatred and bitterness.
DIETRICH BONHOEFFER

He who loves his fellow man is loving God the best he can.
ALICE CARY

The reason why God's servants love creatures so much is that they see how much Christ loves them, and it is one of the properties of love to love what is loved by the person we love.
ST. CATHERINE OF SIENA

If God takes your lump of clay and remoulds it, it will be on the basis of love and not on the basis of power over you.
JAMES CONWAY

Love is the movement, effusion and advancement of the heart toward the good.
ST. FRANCIS DE SALES

When men are animated by the love of Christ they feel united, and the needs, sufferings and joys of others are felt as their own.
POPE JOHN XXIII

He is not to be gotten or holden by thought, but only by love.
JULIAN OF NORWICH

Human beings must be known to be loved, but divine things must be loved to be known.
BLAISE PASCAL

It is the heart which experiences God and not the reason.
BLAISE PASCAL

God does not love us because we are valuable. We are valuable because God loves us.
FULTON J. SHEEN

Our love for God is tested by the question of whether we seek Him or His gifts.
RALPH W. SOCKMAN

Love is the greatest thing that God can give us; for He Himself is love: and it is the greatest thing we can give to God.
JEREMY TAYLOR

Short arm needs man to reach to Heaven, so ready is Heaven to stoop to him.
FRANCIS THOMPSON

It is always springtime in the heart that loves God.
JOHN VIANNEY

Love of Neighbour

(*See also* Charity)

He alone loves the Creator perfectly who manifests a pure love for his neighbour.
THE VENERABLE BEDE

No man can be a friend of Jesus Christ who is not a friend to his neighbour.
ROBERT H. BENSON

We make our friends; we make our enemies; but God makes our next door neighbour.
G. K. CHESTERTON

We never love our neighbour so truly as when our love for him is prompted by the love of God.
FRANÇOIS FENELON

To love our neighbour in charity is to love God in man.
ST. FRANCIS DE SALES

We can live without our friends but not without our neighbours.
THOMAS FULLER

Man becomes great exactly in the degree in which he works for the welfare of his fellow-men.
MOHANDAS GANDHI

All is well with him who is beloved of his neighbours.
GEORGE HERBERT

Your neighbour is the man who needs you.
ELBERT HUBBARD

The good neighbour looks beyond the external accidents and discerns those inner qualities that make all men human and, therefore, brothers.
MARTIN LUTHER KING, JR.

Next to the Blessed Sacrament itself, your neighbour is the holiest object presented to your senses. If he is your Christian neighbour, he is holy in almost the same way, for in him also Christ vere latitat – the glorified, Glory Himself, is truly hidden.
C. S. LEWIS

The love of our neighbour is the only door out of the dungeon of self.
GEORGE MACDONALD

Happy is the man who is able to love all men alike.
MAXIMUS THE CONFESSOR

The camel never sees its own hump; but its neighbour's hump is ever before its eyes.
ARAB PROVERB

No one is rich enough to do without a neighbour.
DANISH PROVERB

He who prays for his neighbour will be loved for himself.
HEBREW PROVERB

Love thy neighbour, even when he plays the trombone.
JEWISH PROVERB

Love your neighbour, but don't pull down the hedge.
SWISS PROVERB

Have a deaf ear for unkind remarks about others, and a blind eye to the trivial faults of your brethren.
SIR WALTER SCOTT

Though we do not have our Lord with us in bodily presence, we have our neighbour, who, for the ends of love and loving service, is as good as our Lord himself.
ST. TERESA OF AVILA

Man becomes a holy thing, a neighbour, only if we realise that he is the property of God and that Jesus Christ died for him.
HELMUT THIELECKE

Loyalty

(*See also* Patriotism)

Loyalty means not that I *am* you, or that I *agree* with everything you say or that I believe you are always right. Loyalty means that I share a common ideal with you and that regardless of minor differences we fight for it, shoulder to shoulder, confident in one another's good faith, trust, constancy, and affection.
CARL MENNINGER

It is better to be faithful than famous.
THEODORE ROOSEVELT

Loyalty is the holiest good in the human heart.
SENECA

Cursed be that loyalty which reaches so far as to go against the law of God.
ST. TERESA OF AVILA

Luxury

Comfort comes as a guest, lingers to become a host and stays to enslave.
LEE BICKMORE

We act as though comfort and luxury were the chief requirements of life, when all that we need to make us really happy is something to be enthusiastic about.
CHARLES KINGSLEY

Avarice and luxury, those pests which have ever been the ruin of every great state.
LIVY

Luxury is the first, second, and third cause of ruin of reputation. It is the vampire which soothes us into a fatal slumber while it sucks the lifeblood of our veins.
HAMILTON MABIE

Luxury makes a man so soft, that it is hard to please him, and easy to trouble him; so that his pleasures at last become his burden. Luxury is a nice master, hard to be pleased.
COMPTON MACKENZIE

There has never yet been a man in our history who led a life of ease whose name is worth remembering.
THEODORE ROOSEVELT

Luxuries are what other people buy.
DAVID WHITE

Lying

(*See also* Deception)

To hide a fault with a lie is to replace a blot by a hole.
MARCUS AURELIUS

It is a sovereign remedy against lying to unsay the lie on the spot.
ST. FRANCIS DE SALES

We lie loudest when we lie to ourselves.
ERIC HOFFER

He who permits himself to tell a lie once finds it much easier to do it a second and a third time till at length it becomes habitual.
THOMAS JEFFERSON

No man has a good enough memory to make a successful liar.
ABRAHAM LINCOLN

With lies you may go ahead in the world – but you can never go back.
RUSSIAN PROVERB

The cruellest lies are often told in silence.
ROBERT LOUIS STEVENSON

A lie can travel halfway around the world while the truth is putting on its shoes.
MARK TWAIN

Man

(*See also* Age and Ages of Man, Human Condition and Humanity)

European man strode into history full of confidence in himself and his creature powers. Today he leaves it to pass into an unknown epoch, discouraged, his faith in shreds.
NIKOLAI BERDYAEV

Man will become better only when you will make him see what he is like.
ANTON CHEKHOV

The more we really look at man as an animal, the less he will look.
G. K. CHESTERTON

What a man is in the sight of God, so much he is and no more.
ST. FRANCIS OF ASSISI

Whenever two people meet there are really six people present. There is each man as he sees himself, each man as the other person sees him, and each man as he really is.
WILLIAM JAMES

Man lives a really human life thanks to culture.
POPE JOHN PAUL II

Now man cannot live without some vision of himself. But still less can he live without a vision that is true to his inner experience and inner feeling.
D. H. LAWRENCE

Man is but a reed, the most weak in nature, but he is a thinking reed.
BLAISE PASCAL

Man is harder than rock, and more fragile than an egg.
YUGOSLAV PROVERB

Made in God's image, man was made to be great, he was made to be beautiful and he was made to be creative in life and art. But his rebellion has led him into making himself into nothing but a machine.
FRANCIS A. SCHAEFFER

The salvation of mankind lies only in making everything the concern of all.
ALEXANDER I. SOLZHENITSYN

We must not reject man in favour of God, nor reject God in favour of man; for the glory of God is man alive, supremely in Christ.
LEON JOSEPH SUENENS

Man is the only animal that blushes. Or needs to.
MARK TWAIN

Man is a peculiar, puzzling paradox, groping for God and hoping to hide from Him at the selfsame time.
WILLIAM A. WARD

Man is like nothing so much as a lump of muddy earth plunged into a very clear, pure brook.
ULRICH ZWINGLI

Manners

(*See also* Behaviour and Courtesy)

Good manners are made up of petty sacrifices.
RALPH WALDO EMERSON

Manners are the happy ways of doing things . . . if they are superficial, so are the dewdrops, which give such a depth to the morning meadow.
RALPH WALDO EMERSON

It is superstitious to put one's faith in conventions; but it is arrogance not to submit to them.
BLAISE PASCAL

Manners make the man.
ENGLISH PROVERB

Marriage

Marriage is our last, best chance to grow up.
JOSEPH BARTH

Success in marriage is more than finding the right person: it is a matter of being the right person.
RABBI B. R. BRICKNER

The desire to be instantly understood and accurately responded to remains with us through life and is one of the clearest expressions of closeness and love between people.
JACK DOMINIAN

Marriage resembles a pair of shears, so joined that they cannot be separated, often moving in opposite directions yet always punishing anyone who comes between them.
P. FONTAINE

The state of marriage is one that requires more virtue and constancy than any other; it is a perpetual exercise of mortification.
ST. FRANCIS DE SALES

A successful marriage demands a divorce; a divorce from your own self-love.
PAUL FROST

The sum which two married people owe to one another defies calculation. It is an infinite debt, which can only be discharged through all eternity.
JOHANN WOLFGANG VON GOETHE

When men and women marry, the union should be made with the consent of the bishop, so that the marriage may be according to the Lord and not merely out of lust. Let all be done to the glory of God.
ST. IGNATIUS OF ANTIOCH

A successful marriage is an edifice that must be rebuilt every day.
ANDRÉ MAUROIS

There is no lonelier person than the one who lives with a spouse with whom he or she cannot communicate.
MARGARET MEAD

Successful marriage is always a triangle: a man, a woman, and God.
CECIL MYERS

Every man who is happily married is a successful man, even if he has failed in everything else.
WILLIAM LYON PHELPS

A good husband should be deaf and a good wife blind.
FRENCH PROVERB

Don't praise marriage on the third day, but after the third year.
RUSSIAN PROVERB

A happy marriage is the union of two good forgivers.
ROBERT QUILLEN

One of the great similarities between Christianity and marriage is that, for Christians, they both get better as we get older.
JEAN REES

A good marriage is that in which each appoints the other guardian of his solitude.
RAINER MARIA RILKE

Marriage is like twirling a baton, turning handsprings, or eating with chopsticks; it looks so easy till you try it.
HELEN ROWLAND

And when will there be an end of marrying? I suppose, when there is an end of living.
QUINTUS TERTULLIAN

Martyrdom

The martyrs were bound, imprisoned, scourged, racked, burnt, rent, butchered – and they multiplied.
ST. AUGUSTINE OF HIPPO

A tear is an intellectual thing,
And a sigh is the sword of an Angel King,
And the bitter groan of the martyr's woe
Is an arrow from the Almighty's bow.
WILLIAM BLAKE

Pain is superficial and therefore fear is. The torments of martyrdom are probably most keenly felt by the bystanders.
RALPH WALDO EMERSON

Let others wear the martyr's crown; I am not worthy of this honour.
DESIDERIUS ERASMUS

Fire and cross and battling with wild beasts, their clawing and tearing, the breaking of bones and mangling of members, the grinding of my whole body, the wicked torments of the devil – let them assail me, so long as I get to Jesus Christ.
ST. IGNATIUS OF ANTIOCH

The only method by which religious truth can be established is by martyrdom.
SAMUEL JOHNSON

No one is a martyr for a conclusion, no one is a martyr for an opinion; it is faith that makes martyrs.
JOHN HENRY NEWMAN

It is not suffering but the cause which makes a martyr.
ENGLISH PROVERB

Martyrdom has always been a proof of the intensity, never of the correctness of a belief.
ARTHUR SCHNITZLER

We multiply whenever we are mown down by you; the blood of Christians is seed.
QUINTUS TERTULLIAN

Love makes the whole difference between an execution and a martyrdom.
EVELYN UNDERHILL

Mary, Mother of Christ

In order that the body of Christ might be shown to be a real body, he was born of a woman: but in order that his Godhead might be made clear he was born of a virgin.
ST. THOMAS AQUINAS

If the Son is a King, the Mother who begot Him is rightly and truly considered a Queen and Sovereign.
ST. ATHANASIUS OF ALEXANDRIA

Let us not imagine that we obscure the glory of the Son by the praise we lavish on the Mother; for the more she is honoured, the greater is the glory of her Son.
ST. BERNARD OF CLAIRVAUX

'Behold thy mother' (Jn. 19:26). By these words, Mary, by reason of the love she bore them, became the Mother, not only of St. John, but of all men.
ST. BERNARDINE OF SIENA

To work a wonder, God would have her shown, at once, a Bud, and yet a Rose full-blown.
ROBERT HERRICK

Popular piety, normally, connected with devotion to Our Lady, certainly needs to be enlightened, guided, and purified. But as it is a devotion 'of the simple and poor', it generally expresses a certain 'thirst for God'. And then it is not necessarily a value sentiment, or an inferior form of religious expression. In fact it often contains a deep sense of God and his attributes, such as fatherhood, providence, loving presence, and mercy.
POPE JOHN PAUL II

The feast we call *Annunciatio Mariae*, when the angel came to Mary and brought her the message from God, may be fitly called the Feast of Christ's Humanity, for then began our deliverance.
MARTIN LUTHER

Since God has revealed very little to us about Mary, men who know nothing of who and what she was only reveal themselves when they try to add something to what God has told us about her.
THOMAS MERTON

Mary's humble acceptance of the divine will is the starting point of the story of the redemption of the human race from sin.
ALAN RICHARDSON

Our tainted nature's solitary boast.
WILLIAM WORDSWORTH

Materialism

(*See also* Possessions and Riches)

Materialism is our great enemy. It is the chief 'ism' we have to combat and conquer. It is the mother of all the 'isms'.
FRANK BUCHMAN

For every one hundred men who can stand adversity there is only one who can withstand prosperity.
THOMAS CARLYLE

Lives based on having are less free than lives based either on doing or on being.
WILLIAM JAMES

When money speaks, the truth is silent.
RUSSIAN PROVERB

Theology must pay greater attention to the creational character and hence the high value of matter, of the material and sensible world.
MARCEL REDING

Be sure, as long as worldly fancies you pursue, you are a hollow man – a pauper lives in you.
ANGELUS SILESIUS

If you want to destroy a nation, give it too much – make it greedy, miserable and sick.
JOHN STEINBECK

Unless our civilisation is redeemed spiritually, it cannot endure materially.
WOODROW WILSON

Maturity

(*See also* Character)

Most great men and women are not perfectly rounded in their personalities, but are instead people whose one driving enthusiasm is so great it makes their faults seem insignificant.
CHARLES A. CERAMI

God instructs the heart, not by ideas, but by pains and contradictions.
JEAN PIERRE DE CAUSSADE

The greater the difficulty, the more glory in surmounting it. Skillful pilots gain their reputation from storms and tempests.
EPICURUS

God will not look you over for medals, degrees, or diplomas, but for scars.
ELBERT HUBBARD

Spiritual maturity comes not by erudition, but by compliance with the known will of God.
D. W. LAMBERT

If God sends us on stony paths, he will provide us with strong shoes.
ALEXANDER MACLAREN

Maturity begins to grow when you can sense your concern for others outweighing your concern for yourself.
JOHN MACNAUGHTON

Blisters are a painful experience, but if you get enough blisters in the same place, they will eventually produce a callus. That is what we call maturity.
HERBERT MILLER

One of the marks of a mature person is the ability to dissent without creating dissension.
DON ROBINSON

It takes a long time to bring excellence to maturity.
PUBLILIUS SYRUS

Isn't it the greatest possible disaster, when you are wrestling with God, not to be beaten?
SIMONE WEIL

Media

Children who have been taught, or conditioned, to listen passively most of the day to the warm verbal communications coming from the TV screen, to the deep emotional appeal of the so-called TV personality, are often unable to respond to real persons because they arouse so much less feeling than the skilled actor.
BRUNO BETTELHEIM

If newspapers are useful in overthrowing tyrants, it is only to establish a tyranny of their own.
JAMES FENIMORE COOPER

Parents generally pay vigilant attention to the type of friends with whom their children associate, but do not exercise a similar vigilance regarding the ideas which the radio, the television, records, papers and comics carry into the 'protected' and 'safe' intimacy of their homes.
POPE JOHN PAUL II

Newspapers always excite curiosity. No one ever lays one down without a feeling of disappointment.
CHARLES LAMB

We are drowning our youngsters in violence, cynicism and sadism piped into the living room and even the nursery. The grandchildren of the kids who used to weep because the Little Match Girl froze to death, now feel cheated if she isn't slugged, raped and thrown into a Bessemer converter.
JENKIN LLOYD JONES

I find television very educating. Every time somebody turns on the set I go into the other room and read a book.
GROUCHO MARX

I don't think that television has corrupted me. But I do think that man has invented it to flee from reality.
MALCOLM MUGGERIDGE

Journalism is the ability to meet the challenge of filling space.
REBECCA WEST

Meditation

(*See also* Contemplation and Prayer)

To meditate on the life and sufferings of Jesus Christ I have called wisdom; in these I have placed the perfection of righteousness for me, the fulness of knowledge, the abundance of merits, the riches of salvation.
ST. BERNARD OF CLAIRVAUX

Meditate daily on the words of your Creator. Learn the heart of God in the words of God, that your soul may be kindled with greater longings for heavenly joys.
POPE ST. GREGORY I

Meditation is the attempt to provide the soul with a proper environment in which to grow and become.
MORTON T. KELSEY

The all-important aim in Christian meditation is to allow God's mysterious and silent presence within us to become more and more not only a reality, but the reality in our lives; to let it become that reality which gives meaning and shape and purpose to everything we do; to everything we are.
JOHN MAIN

Every man has a train of thought on which he rides when he is alone. The dignity and nobility of his life, as well as his happiness, depend upon the direction in which that train is going, the baggage it carries, and the scenery through which it travels.
JOSEPH FORT NEWTON

The world is to the meditative man what the mulberry plant is to the silkworm.
ALEXANDER SMITH

Proficiency in meditation lies not in thinking much, but in loving much. It is a way of seeking the divine companionship, the 'closer walk'. Thus it is that meditation has come to be called 'the mother of love'.
RICHARDSON WRIGHT

Meekness

(*See also* Gentleness)

Meekness is not weakness.
WILLIAM G. BENHAM

Meekness takes injuries like pills, not chewing, but swallowing them down.
SIR THOMAS BROWNE

Learn the blessedness of the unoffended in the face of the unexplainable.
AMY CARMICHAEL

Meekness is love at school, at the school of Christ. It is the disciple learning to know, and fear, and distrust himself, and learning of him who is meek and lowly of heart, and so finding rest to his soul.
JAMES HAMILTON

Meek endurance and meek obedience, the accepting of His dealings, of whatever complexion they are and however they may tear and desolate our hearts, without murmuring, without sulking, without rebellion or resistance, is the deepest conception of the meekness which Christ pronounced blessed.
ALEXANDER MACLAREN

Mercy

Mercy, also, is a good thing, for it makes men perfect, in that it imitates the perfect Father. Nothing graces the Christian soul so much as mercy.
ST. AMBROSE

The mercy of God may be found between the bridge and the stream.
ST. AUGUSTINE OF HIPPO

Among the attributes of God, although they are all equal, mercy shines with even more brilliancy than justice.
MIGUEL DE CERVANTES

For Mercy is a greater thing than right.
GEOFFREY CHAUCER

Mercy imitates God and disappoints Satan.
ST. JOHN CHRYSOSTOM

Reason to rule, but mercy to forgive: The first is law, the last prerogative.
JOHN DRYDEN

We hand folks over to God's mercy, and show none ourselves.
GEORGE ELIOT

Whoever falls from God's right hand is caught in his left.
EDWIN MARKHAM

Teach me to feel another's woe, to hide the fault I see; that mercy I to others show, that mercy show to me.
ALEXANDER POPE

Mercy is better than vengeance.
GREEK PROVERB

As freely as the firmament embraces the world, so mercy must encircle friend and foe.
JOHANN C. F. VON SCHILLER

If we refuse mercy here, we shall have justice in eternity.
JEREMY TAYLOR

Mind

(*See also* Intelligence)

No mind, however loving, could bear to see plainly into all the recesses of another mind.
ARNOLD BENNETT

I am incurably of the opinion that the object of opening the mind, as of opening the mouth, is to shut it again on something solid.
G. K. CHESTERTON

There is no salvation save in truth, and the royal road of truth is by the mind.
MARTIN C. D'ARCY

To the quiet mind all things are possible. What is the quiet mind? A quiet mind is one which nothing weighs on, nothing worries, which, free from ties and from all self-seeking, is wholly merged into the will of God and dead to its own.
MEISTER ECKHART

The human mind is so constructed that it resists vigour and yields to gentleness.
ST. FRANCIS DE SALES

An open scent bottle soon loses its scent. An open mind is often a vacant mind. There is something to be said for corks.
ARNOLD LUNN

Our minds are like crows. They pick up everything that glitters, no matter how uncomfortable our nests get with all that metal in them.
THOMAS MERTON

Almighty God influences us and works in us, through our minds, not without them or in spite of them.
JOHN HENRY NEWMAN

If you keep your mind sufficiently open, people will throw a lot of rubbish into it.
WILLIAM A. ORTON

No one would allow garbage at his table, but many allow it served into their minds.
FULTON J. SHEEN

Untilled ground, however rich, will bring forth thistles and thorns; so also the mind of man.
ST. TERESA OF AVILA

Ministry

(*See also* Clergy and Priesthood)

An upright minister asks, *what* recommends a man; a corrupt minister, *who*.
CHARLES CALEB COLTON

The Lord opened unto me that being bred at Oxford or Cambridge was not enough to fit and qualify men to be ministers of Christ.
GEORGE FOX

The life of a pious minister is visible rhetoric.
HERMAN HOOKER

In God's house we must try to accept any job: cook or kitchen boy waiter, stable boy, baker. If it pleases the king to call us into his private council, then we must go there, but without being too excited, for we know that our rewards depend not on the job itself but on the faithfulness with which we serve him.
POPE JOHN PAUL I

The Lord did not promise a ministry free of trials. He simply assured us that he had overcome the forces of evil at work in man.
POPE JOHN PAUL II

The Christian ministry is the worst of all trades, but the best of all professions.
JOSEPH FORT NEWTON

Miracles

(*See also* Wonder)

I should not be a Christian but for the miracles.
ST. AUGUSTINE OF HIPPO

It is only two years ago that the keeping of records was begun here in Hippo, and already, at this writing, we have nearly seventy attested miracles.
ST. AUGUSTINE OF HIPPO

A miracle in the sense of the New Testament is not so much a breach of the laws of nature, but rather a remarkable or exceptional occurrence which brought an undeniable sense of the presence and power of God.
C. H. DODD

All miracles are simply feeble lights like beacons on our way to the port where shines the light, the total light of the resurrection.
JACQUES ELLUL

I cannot understand people having historical difficulties about miracles. For, once you grant that miracles can happen, all the historical evidence at our disposal bids us believe that sometimes they do.
RONALD A. KNOX

The divine art of miracle is not an art of suspending the pattern to which events confirm, but of feeding new events into that pattern.
C. S. LEWIS

Miracles are important, and are only important because they provide evidence of the fact that the universe is not a closed system, and that effects in the natural world can be produced by the reactions of non-human will.
ARNOLD LUNN

The miracles of Jesus were the ordinary works of his Father, wrought small and swift that we might take them in.
GEORGE MACDONALD

Jesus was himself the one convincing and permanent miracle.
IAN MACLAREN

The Incarnation is the most stupendous event which ever can take place on earth; and after it and henceforth, I do not see how we can scruple at any miracle on the mere ground of it being unlikely to happen.
JOHN HENRY NEWMAN

It would have approached nearer to the idea of miracle if Jonah had swallowed the whale.
THOMAS PAINE

It is impossible on reasonable grounds to disbelieve miracles.
BLAISE PASCAL

Little saints also perform miracles.
DANISH PROVERB

A miracle in the Biblical sense is an event which happens in a manner contrary to the regularly observed processes of nature ... It may happen according to higher laws as yet but dimly discerned by scientists, and therefore must not be thought of as an irrational irruption of divine power into the orderly realm of nature.
ALAN RICHARDSON

Mission

(*See also* Missionary)

If people ask 'Why did he not appear by means of other parts of creation, and use some nobler instrument, as the sun or moon or stars or fire or air, instead of man merely?' let them know that the Lord came not to make a display, but to teach and heal those who were suffering.
ST. ATHANASIUS OF
ALEXANDRIA

Your love has a broken wing if it cannot fly across the sea.
MALTBIE D. BABCOCK

The Church exists by mission, as fire exists by burning.
EMIL BRUNNER

Our primary task is to create the space for the word of God once again to cut into our daily life experience, in order to redeem and liberate it.
THOMAS CULLINAN

To practical people like Americans there is no oral or written evidence of the true religion so valid as the spectacle of its power to change bad men into good ones. Such a people will not accept arguments from history and from Scripture, but those of a moral kind they demand, they must see the theories at work. A mission is a microcosm of the Church as a moral force.
WALTER ELLIOTT

The Spirit of Christ is the spirit of missions, and the nearer we get to him the more intensely missionary we must become.
HENRY MARTYN

The fact of the missions reveals the Church's faith in herself as the Catholic unity of mankind.
JOHN C. MURRAY

Mission will not happen unless the Church goes beyond its own life out into active care in the local neighbourhood.
DAVID SHEPPARD

Missionary

(*See also* Mission)

We are the children of the converts of foreign missionaries; and fairness means that I must do to others as men once did to me.
MALTBIE D. BABCOCK

If God calls you to be a missionary, don't stoop to be a king.
JORDON GROOMS

The Bible is a missionary book. Jesus Christ is the Father's missionary to a lost world.
HAROLD LINDSELL

God had an only Son, and he was a missionary and a physician.
DAVID LIVINGSTONE

The Spirit of Christ is the spirit of missions, and the nearer we get to Him the more intensely missionary we must become.
HENRY MARTYN

Mistakes

(*See also* Error)

A man who has committed a mistake and doesn't correct it is committing another mistake.
CONFUCIUS

The greatest mistake you can make in this life is to be continually fearing you will make one.
ELBERT HUBBARD

An error no wider than a hair will lead a hundred miles away from the goal.
GERMAN PROVERB

He is always right who suspects that he makes mistakes.
SPANISH PROVERB

The only man who never makes a mistake is the man who never does anything.
THEODORE ROOSEVELT

More people would learn from their mistakes if they weren't so busy denying them.
HAROLD J. SMITH

Modesty

(*See also* Chastity, Purity and Virginity)

Modesty is always the sign and safeguard of a mystery. It is explained by its contrary – profanation.
HENRI FRÉDÉRIC AMIEL

Guard your eyes, since they are the windows through which sin enters into the soul. Never look curiously on those things which are contrary to modesty, even slightly.
JOHN BOSCO

Modesty is to merit what shade is to figures in a picture; it gives it strength and makes it stand out.
JEAN DE LA BRUYÈRE

Modesty in human beings is praised because it is not a matter of nature, but of will.
LACTANTIUS

To Christian modesty it is not enough to be so, but to seem so too.
QUINTUS TERTULLIAN

Money

(*See also* Riches and Wealth)

Money is like muck, no good except it be spread.
FRANCIS BACON

If you would know what the Lord God thinks of money, you have only to look at those to whom he gives it.
MAURICE BARING

The golden age only comes to men when they have forgotten gold.
G. K. CHESTERTON

If you make money your god, it will plague you like the devil.
HENRY FIELDING

If a person gets his attitude toward money straight, it will help straighten out almost every other area in his life.
BILLY GRAHAM

Money can buy the husk of many things, but not the kernel. It brings you food, but not appetite; medicine, but not health; acquaintances, but not friends; servants, but not faithfulness; days of joy, but not peace and happiness.
HENRIK IBSEN

He who has money to spare has it always in his power to benefit others: and of such power a good man must always be desirous.
SAMUEL JOHNSON

The real measure of our wealth is how much we'd we worth if we lost all our money.
JOHN HENRY JOWETT

It cuts off from life, from vitality, from the alive sun and the alive earth, as *nothing* can. Nothing, not even the most fanatical dogmas of an iron-bound religion, can insulate us from the inrush of life and inspiration, as money can.
D. H. LAWRENCE

If a man's religion does not affect his use of money, that man's religion is vain.
HUGH MARTIN

Getting money is like digging with a needle; spending it is like water soaking into sand.
JAPANESE PROVERB

Money really adds no more to the wise than clothes can to the beautiful.
JEWISH PROVERB

We can hardly respect money enough for the blood and toil it represents. Money is frightening. It can serve or destroy man.
MICHEL QUOIST

Money has never yet made anyone rich.
SENECA

Nothing that is God's is obtainable by money.
QUINTUS TERTULLIAN

Make all you can, save all you can, give all you can.
JOHN WESLEY

Morality

(*See also* Ethics)

Love and *then* what you will, do.
ST. AUGUSTINE OF HIPPO

The moral good is not a goal but an inner force which lights up man's life from within.
NIKOLAI BERDYAEV

To deny the freedom of the will is to make morality impossible.
JAMES A. FROUDE

All moral obligation resolves itself into the obligation of conformity to the will of God.
CHARLES HODGE

Morality is not properly the doctrine of how we may make ourselves happy, but how we may make ourselves worthy of happiness.
IMMANUEL KANT

Strive we then to think aright: that is the first principle of moral life.
BLAISE PASCAL

Right is right, even if everyone is against it; and wrong is wrong, even if everyone is for it.
WILLIAM PENN

Motherhood

It was because my salvation was at stake that (my mother) loved Ambrose greatly and he loved her because of her fervent life of devotion, which took the form of good works and frequent churchgoing. Sometimes when he saw me he would break out in praise of her and congratulate me on having such a mother – not knowing what a son she had!
ST. AUGUSTINE OF HIPPO

The God to whom little boys say their prayers has a face very like their mother's.
JAMES M. BARRIE

I think it must somewhere be written, that the virtues of the mothers shall be visited on their children as well as the sins of the fathers.
CHARLES DICKENS

The child, in the decisive first years of his life, has the experience of his mother, as an all-enveloping, protective, nourishing power. Mother is food; she is love; she is warmth; she is earth. To be loved by her means to be alive, to be rooted, to be at home.
ERICH FROMM

The commonest fallacy among women is that simply having children makes one a mother – which is as absurd as believing that having a piano makes one a musician.
SYDNEY HARRIS

No man is poor who has had a godly mother.
ABRAHAM LINCOLN

God could not be everywhere, so He made mothers.
JEWISH PROVERB

In the eyes of its mother every beetle is a gazelle.
MOROCCAN PROVERB

An ounce of mother is worth a pound of clergy.
SPANISH PROVERB

Mother is the name of God in the lips and hearts of little children.
WILLIAM MAKEPEACE THACKERAY

The loveliest masterpiece of the heart of God is the heart of a mother.
ST. THÉRÈSE OF LISIEUX

Motivation

(*See also* Intention)

Lord, grant that I may always desire more than I can accomplish.
MICHELANGELO BUONARROTI

Pure motives will make a clear flame. Impure motives are the smoke that clogs the flame.
SIDNEY COOK

The biggest gap in the world is the gap between the justice of a cause and the motives of the people pushing it.
JOHN P. GRIER

If no action is to be deemed virtuous for which malice can imagine a sinister motive, then there never was a virtuous action.
THOMAS JEFFERSON

Man sees your actions, but God your motives.
THOMAS À KEMPIS

If a man does not keep pace with his companions, perhaps it is because he hears a different drummer.
HENRY DAVID THOREAU

Music

Music is a part of us, and either ennobles or degrades our behaviour.
AMICIUS M. S. BOETHIUS

Take then, you, that smile on strings,
those nobler sounds than mine,
The words that never lie, or brag,
or
flatter or malign.
G. K. CHESTERTON

So is music an asylum. It takes us out of the actual and whispers to us dim secrets that startle our wonder as to who we are, and for what, whence, and whereto, all the great interrogatories, like questioning angels, float in on its waves of sound.
RALPH WALDO EMERSON

Next to theology I give to music the highest place and honour. Music is the art of the prophets, the only art that can calm the agitations of the soul; it is one of the most magnificent and delightful presents God has given us.
MARTIN LUTHER

God save me from a bad neighbour and a beginner on the fiddle.
ITALIAN PROVERB

The thought of the eternal efflorescence of music is a comforting one, and comes like a messenger of peace in the midst of universal disturbance.
ROMAIN ROLLAND

The only time that our blessed Lord ever is recorded as having sung is the night that He went out to His death.
FULTON J. SHEEN

A painter paints his pictures on canvas. But musicians paint their pictures on silence. We provide the music and you provide the silence.
LEOPOLD STOKOWSKI

Bach opens a vista to the universe. After experiencing him, people feel there is meaning to life after all.
HELMUT WALCHA

Mystery

We are hemmed round with mystery, and the greatest mysteries are contained in what we see and do every day.
HENRI FRÉDÉRIC AMIEL

The most beautiful experience we can have is the mysterious. It is the fundamental emotion which stands at the cradle of true art and true science.
ALBERT EINSTEIN

The mysterious is always attractive. People will always follow a veil.
BEDE JARRETT

If the works of God were such as might be easily comprehended by human reason, they could not be called wonderful or unspeakable.
THOMAS À KEMPIS

A revelation is religious doctrine viewed on its illuminated side; a mystery is the selfsame doctrine viewed on the side unilluminated.
JOHN HENRY NEWMAN

The more unintelligent a man is, the less mysterious existence seems to him.
ARTHUR SCHOPENHAUER

Mysticism

(*See also* Contemplation)

Only on the wings of mysticism can the spirit soar to its full height.
ALEXIS CARREL

For the mystic especially it is important that theology should flourish and good theologians abound, for in the guidance which objective theology supplies lies the mystic's sole certainty of escaping self-delusion.
PHILIP HUGHES

One of the greatest paradoxes of the mystical life is this: that a man cannot enter into the deepest centre of himself and pass through that centre into God, unless he is able to pass entirely out of himself and empty himself and give himself to other people in the purity of a selfless love.
THOMAS MERTON

Any profound view of the world is mysticism, in that it brings men into a spiritual relation with the Infinite.
ALBERT SCHWEITZER

Name

Remember that man's name is to him the sweetest and most important sound in the English language.
DALE CARNEGIE

A nickname is the hardest stone that the devil can throw at a man.
WILLIAM HAZLITT

Thy name, O Lord, is for me oil poured out. For the grace of Thy visitation makes me fully understand the true meaning of Thy name, which is Jesus, Saviour.
WALTER HILTON

Do not concern yourself with anxiety for the show of a great name.
THOMAS À KEMPIS

Nature

(*See also* Ecology)

Nature knows nothing of rights. She knows only laws. Man, on the other hand, has ideals and aspirations.
JAMES TRUSLOW ADAMS

Nature, the vicar of th' Almightie Lord.
GEOFFREY CHAUCER

Nature is but a name for an effect whose cause is God.
WILLIAM COWPER

Let us permit nature to have her way; she understands her business better than we do.
MICHEL DE MONTAIGNE

Nature has some perfections, to show that she is the image of God; and some defects, to show that she is only his image.
BLAISE PASCAL

All are but parts of one stupendous whole,
Whose body Nature is, and God the soul.
ALEXANDER POPE

Nature does nothing in vain.
ENGLISH PROVERB

It is through the natural that we encounter the supernatural, although the supernatural eludes the ability of the natural to exhaust its meaning.
MICHAEL RAMSEY

The losing of Paradise is enacted over and over again by the children of Adam and Eve. We clothe our souls with messages and doctrines and lose the touch of the great life in the naked breast of Nature.
RABINDRANATH TAGORE

Obedience

The first degree of humility is obedience without delay.
ST. BENEDICT

Thirty years of Our Lord's life are hidden in these words of the gospel: 'He was subject unto them.'
JACQUES B. BOSSUET

How will you find good? It is not a thing of choices; it is a river that flows from the foot of the invisible throne, and flows by the path of obedience.
GEORGE ELIOT

It is vain thought to flee from the work that God appoints us, for the sake of finding a greater blessing, instead of seeking it where alone it is to be found – in loving obedience.
GEORGE ELIOT

We need only obey. There is guidance for each of us, and by lowly listening we shall hear the right word.
RALPH WALDO EMERSON

Obedience to God is the most infallible evidence of sincere and supreme love to him.
NATHANAEL EMMONS

Blessed are the obedient, for God will never suffer them to go astray.
ST. FRANCIS DE SALES

Don't listen to friends when the Friend inside you says, 'Do this!'
MOHANDAS GANDHI

No man securely commands but he who has learned to obey.
THOMAS À KEMPIS

Every duty, even the least duty, involves the whole principle of obedience. And little duties make the will dutiful, that is supple and prompt to obey. Little obediences lead into great.
HENRY E. MANNING

Obedience is all over the Gospels. The pliability of an obedient heart must be complete from the set of our will right on through to our actions.
CATHERINE MARSHALL

Justice is the insurance we have on our lives, and obedience is the premium we pay for it.
WILLIAM PENN

Obedience is the mother of success, the wife of safety.
GREEK PROVERB

No one can rule except one who can be ruled.
LATIN PROVERB

Obedience is the fruit of faith; patience the bloom on the fruit.
CHRISTINA ROSSETTI

We are born subjects, and to obey God is perfect liberty. He that does this shall be free, safe, and happy.
SENECA

Every revelation of God is a demand, and the way to knowledge of God is by obedience.
WILLIAM TEMPLE

Every great person has first learned how to obey, whom to obey, and when to obey.
WILLIAM A. WARD

Old Age

(*See also* Age and Maturity)

To know how to grow old is the master work of wisdom, and one of the most difficult chapters in the great art of living.
HENRI FRÉDÉRIC AMIEL

It is this very awareness that one is no longer an attractive object that makes life so unbearable for so many elderly people.
SIMONE DE BEAUVOIR

The care of the old is a vocation as delicate and difficult as the care of the young.
JAMES DOUGLAS

Life is a country that the old have seen, and lived in. Those who have to travel through it can only learn from them.
JOSEPH JOUBERT

The older I grow the more I distrust the familiar doctrine that age brings wisdom.
HENRY L. MENCKEN

To see a young couple loving each other is no wonder; but to see an old couple loving each other is the best sight of all.
WILLIAM MAKEPEACE THACKERAY

Omnipotence

(*See also* Power)

What is impossible to God? Not that which is difficult to His power, but that which is contrary to His nature.
ST. AMBROSE

God is called omnipotent because He can do all things that are possible absolutely.
ST. THOMAS AQUINAS

God is not in need of anything, but all things are in need of Him.
MARCIANUS ARISTIDES

There is nothing that God cannot accomplish.
MARCUS TULLIUS CICERO

God's omnipotence means power to do all that is intrinsically possible, not to do the intrinsically impossible. You may attribute miracles to him, but not nonsense.
C. S. LEWIS

Calvary is the key to an omnipotence which works only and always through sacrificial love.
MICHAEL RAMSEY

Omnipresence

(*See also* God and Omniscience)

God is in all things; not, indeed, as part of their essence, nor as an accident; but as an agent is present to that upon which it works.
ST. THOMAS AQUINAS

It must therefore be acknowledged that God is everywhere by the presence of His Divinity but not everywhere by the indwelling of His grace.
ST. AUGUSTINE OF HIPPO

A sense of Deity is inscribed on every heart.
JOHN CALVIN

Could we pierce the veil, and were we vigilant and attentive, God would reveal Himself continuously to us and we should rejoice in His actions in everything that happened to us.
JEAN PIERRE DE CAUSSADE

The remarkable thing about the way in which people talk about God, or about their relation to God, is that it seems to escape them completely that God hears what they are saying.
SØREN KIERKEGAARD

God is always with us, why should we not always be with God?
WILLIAM ULLATHORNE

Omniscience

(*See also* Knowledge of God)

God alone knows the depths and the riches of His Godhead, and divine wisdom alone can declare His secrets.
ST. THOMAS AQUINAS

What man is there who can comprehend that wisdom by which God knows all things, in such wise that neither what we call things past are past therein, nor what we call things future are therein looked for as coming, as though they were absent; but both past and future things together with those actually present are all present?
ST. AUGUSTINE OF HIPPO

We cannot too often think there is a never-sleeping eye which reads the heart and registers our thoughts.
FRANCIS BACON

If we consider the immensity and singleness of God's wisdom, it is one, simple, and indivisible; if the great number of things with which it has to do, it is manifold and diverse.
JOHN OF SALISBURY

There are three things that only God knows: the beginning of things, the cause of things, and the end of things.
WELSH PROVERB

One God

(*See also* God and Trinity)

God has many names though he is only one being.
ARISTOTLE

God is an infinite circle whose centre is everywhere and whose circumference is nowhere.
ST. AUGUSTINE OF HIPPO

God is the Thou which by its very nature cannot become it.
MARTIN BUBER

He who has gotten the whole world plus God has gotten no more than God by himself.
MEISTER ECKHART

It has been the universal opinion of mankind from ancient times, from the earliest tradition of the protoplast, that there is one God, the Maker of heaven and earth ... For nature reveals its Author, the work suggests the Artist, and the world manifests its Designer. But the whole Church throughout the world has received this tradition from the apostles.
ST. IRENAEUS

One sole God; One sole ruler – his Law; One sole interpreter of that Law – Humanity.
GIUSEPPE MAZZINI

God is one; what He does, sees none.
YIDDISH PROVERB

The name of this infinite and inexhaustible depth and ground of all being is God.
PAUL TILLICH

Opinion

Opinion is that exercise of the human will which helps us to make a decision without information.
JOHN ERSKINE

We are all of us, more or less, the slaves of opinion.
WILLIAM HAZLITT

Rulers who prefer popular opinion to truth have as much power as robbers in the desert.
ST. JUSTIN MARTYR

Opinion in good men is but knowledge in the making.
JOHN MILTON

Opportunity

A wise man will make more opportunities than he finds.
FRANCIS BACON

The secret of success in life is for a man to be ready for his opportunity when it comes.
BENJAMIN DISRAELI

He who refuses to embrace an unique opportunity loses the prize as surely as if he had failed.
WILLIAM JAMES

God often gives in one brief moment that which he has for a long time denied.
THOMAS À KEMPIS

Dawn does not come twice to awaken a man.
ARAB PROVERB

Opportunity makes the thief.
ENGLISH PROVERB

Order

Good order is the foundation of all good things.
EDMUND BURKE

Put things into their places, and they will put you in your place.
ARAB PROVERB

Order is heaven's first law.
ENGLISH PROVERB

The art of progress is to preserve order amid change, and to preserve change amid order. Life refuses to be embalmed alive.
ALFRED NORTH WHITEHEAD

Original Sin

(*See also* Fall of Man)

What history does is to uncover man's universal sin.
HERBERT BUTTERFIELD

God has not been taken by surprise or forced to change his plans. He permitted original sin only because He had decided to remedy it by the wonderful gift of salvation.
CHARLES DAVIS

Original sin is what results in us by reason of our birth into this condition of sin which precedes our own personal and conscious choices.
PETER DE ROSA

All men find themselves born into an historical order where sin is there before them, dragging them down.
JOHN A. T. ROBINSON

Orthodoxy

(*See also* Dogma)

Tradition by itself is not enough; it must be perpetually criticised and brought up to date under the supervision of what I call orthodoxy.
T. S. ELIOT

By identifying the new learning with heresy we make orthodoxy synonymous with ignorance.
DESIDERIUS ERASMUS

Orthodoxy is my doxy; heterodoxy is another man's doxy.
WILLIAM WARBURTON

You may be as orthodox as the devil, and as wicked.
JOHN WESLEY

Pain

(*See also* Suffering)

Pain is no evil, unless it conquer us.
CHARLES KINGSLEY

God whispers in our pleasures but shouts in our pain.
C. S. LEWIS

When pain is to be borne, a little courage helps more than much knowledge, a little human sympathy more than much courage, and the least tincture of the love of God more than all.
C. S. LEWIS

Pain and sorrow are the almost necessary medicines of the impetuosity of nature. Without these, men, though men, are like spoilt children; they act as if they considered everything must give way to their own wishes and conveniences.
JOHN HENRY NEWMAN

Pain is the price that God putteth upon all things.
ENGLISH PROVERB

Although today He prunes my twigs with pain, Yet doth His blood nourish and warm my root: Tomorrow I shall put forth buds again And clothe myself with fruit.
CHRISTINA ROSSETTI

The pain of the mind is worse than the pain of the body.
PUBLILIUS SYRUS

Nothing begins, and nothing ends,
That is not paid with moan;
For we are born in other's pain,
And perish in our own.
FRANCIS THOMPSON

Behind joy and laughter there may be a temperament, coarse, hard and callous. But behind sorrow there is always sorrow. Pain, unlike pleasure, wears no mask.
OSCAR WILDE

Paradise

(*See also* Heaven)

She is an all-pure soul who cannot love the paradise of God, but only the God of paradise.
ST. FRANCIS DE SALES

He that will enter into Paradise must come with the right key.
THOMAS FULLER

Can there be Paradise for any while there is Hell, conceived as unending torment, for some? Each supposedly damned soul was born into the world as a mother's child, and Paradise cannot be Paradise for her if her child is in such a Hell.
WILLIAM TEMPLE

There is no expeditious road
To pack and label men for God,
And save them by the barrel-load.
Some may perchance, with strange surprise,
Have blundered into Paradise.
FRANCIS THOMPSON

Pardon

(*See also* Forgiveness and Reconciliation)

The Lord is loving unto man, and swift to pardon, but slow to punish. Let no man therefore despair of his own salvation.
ST. CYRIL OF JERUSALEM

Know all and you will pardon all.
THOMAS À KEMPIS

One pardons in the degree that one loves.
FRANÇOIS DE LA ROCHEFOUCAULD

Pardon, not wrath, is God's best attribute.
JAMES BAYARD TAYLOR

How inconsistent it is to expect pardon of sins to be granted to a repentance which they have not fulfilled. This is to hold out your hand for merchandise, but not produce the price. For repentance is the price at which the Lord has determined to award pardon.
QUINTUS TERTULLIAN

Parents

(*See also* Family, Fatherhood and Motherhood)

The religion of a child depends on what its mother and father are, and not on what they say.
HENRI FRÉDÉRIC AMIEL

The joys of parents are secret; and so are their griefs and fears.
FRANCIS BACON

We never know the love of the parent until we become parents ourselves.
HENRY WARD BEECHER

Parents' influence is inevitable and continuous; they cannot be passive if they would. You cannot really *neglect* your children, you can *destroy* them.
FREDERICK W. FABER

Parents have little time for children and a great vacuum has developed and into that vacuum is going to move some kind of ideology.
BILLY GRAHAM

The most important thing a father can do for his children is to love their mother.
THEODORE M. HESBURGH

Every word and deed of a parent is a fibre woven into the character of a child, which ultimately determines how that child fits into the fabric of society.
DAVID WILKERSON

Passion

(*See also* Emotion)

A movement of the soul contrary to nature in the sense of disobedience to reason, that is what passions are.
ST. CLEMENT OF ALEXANDRIA

Passions are vices or virtues in their highest powers.
JOHANN WOLFGANG VON GOETHE

True quietness of heart is won by resisting our passions, not by obeying them.
THOMAS À KEMPIS

We should employ our passions in the service of life, not spend life in the service of our passions.
RICHARD STEELE

The happiness of a man in this life does not consist in the absence but in the mastery of his passions.
ALFRED, LORD TENNYSON

Patience

(*See also* Perseverance)

Patient endurance is the perfection of charity.
ST. AMBROSE

Patience is the companion of wisdom.
ST. AUGUSTINE OF HIPPO

Patience is not good, if when you may be free you allow yourself to become a slave.
ST. BERNARD OF CLAIRVAUX

Beware the fury of a patient man.
JOHN DRYDEN

Possess your soul with patience.
JOHN DRYDEN

We must wait for God, long, meekly, in the wind and wet, in the thunder and lightning, in the cold and the dark. Wait, and he will come. He never comes to those who do not wait.
FREDERICK W. FABER

Be patient with every one, but above all with yourself. I mean, do not be disturbed because of your imperfections, and always rise up bravely from a fall.
ST. FRANCIS DE SALES

The virtue of patience is the one which most assures us of perfection.
ST. FRANCIS DE SALES

'Take your needle, my child, and work at your pattern; it will come out a rose by and by.' Life is like that; one stitch at a time taken patiently, and the pattern will come out all right like embroidery.
OLIVER WENDELL HOLMES

All men commend patience, although few be willing to practise it.
THOMAS À KEMPIS

Patience and diligence, like faith, remove mountains.
WILLIAM PENN

One moment of patience may ward off great disaster, one moment of impatience may ruin a whole life.
CHINESE PROVERB

Patience is power; with time and patience the mulberry leaf becomes silk.
CHINESE PROVERB

Patience is a plaster for all sores.
ENGLISH PROVERB

Patience is bitter, but its fruit is sweet.
JEAN JACQUES ROUSSEAU

Patience is the ability to put up with people you'd like to put down.
ULRIKE RUFFERT

It takes patience to appreciate domestic bliss; volatile spirits prefer unhappiness.
GEORGE SANTAYANA

On every level of life from housework to heights of prayer, in all judgment and all efforts to get things done, hurry and impatience are sure marks of the amateur.
EVELYN UNDERHILL

Patience with ourselves is a duty for Christians and the only humility. For it means patience with a growing creature whom God has taken in hand and whose completion he will effect in his own time and way.
EVELYN UNDERHILL

Patriotism

(*See also* Loyalty)

Standing as I do in view of God and eternity, I realise that patriotism is not enough. I must have no hatred or bitterness for anyone.
EDITH CAVELL

True patriotism does not exclude an understanding of the patriotism of others.
QUEEN ELIZABETH II

Love for one's country which is not part of one's love for humanity is not love, but idolatrous worship.
ERICH FROMM

Men and women who would shrink from doing anything dishonourable in the sphere of personal relationships are ready to lie and swindle, to steal, and even murder when they are representing their country.
ALDOUS HUXLEY

Patriotism is the last refuge of a scoundrel.
SAMUEL JOHNSON

Ask not what your country can do for you; ask what you can do for your country.
JOHN F. KENNEDY

To me, it seems a dreadful indignity to have a soul controlled by geography.
GEORGE SANTAYANA

Patriotism is your conviction that this country is superior to all other countries because you were born in it.
GEORGE BERNARD SHAW

You'll never have a quiet world till you knock patriotism out of the human race.
GEORGE BERNARD SHAW

Peace

When Christ came into the world, peace was sung; and when He went out of the world, peace was bequeathed.
FRANCIS BACON

Peace is liberty in tranquillity.
MARCUS TULLIUS CICERO

If we will have peace without a worm in it, lay we the foundation of justice and good will.
OLIVER CROMWELL

If the basis of peace is God, the secret of peace is trust.
J. B. FIGGIS

My religion is based on truth and non-violence. Truth is my God and non-violence is the means to reach Him.
MOHANDAS GANDHI

God takes life's pieces and gives us unbroken peace.
W. D. GOUGH

Peace is such a precious jewel that I would give anything for it but truth.
MATTHEW HENRY

Where there is peace, God is.
GEORGE HERBERT

Peace is not made at the council tables, or by treaties, but in the hearts of men.
HERBERT HOOVER

Only a world that is truly human can be a world that is peaceful and strong.
POPE JOHN PAUL II

Thy peace shall be in much patience.
THOMAS À KEMPIS

We should have much peace if we would not busy ourselves with the sayings and doing of others.
THOMAS À KEMPIS

We have to make peace without limitations.
HAROLD LINDSELL

The springs of human conflict cannot be eradicated through institutions, but only through the reform of the individual human being.
DOUGLAS MACARTHUR

If we wish to have true peace, we must give it a soul. The soul of peace is love, which for us believers comes from the love of God and expresses itself in love for men.
POPE PAUL VI

Peace within makes beauty without.
ENGLISH PROVERB

Peace without truth is poison.
GERMAN PROVERB

Peace is not an absence of war, it is a virtue, a state of mind, a disposition for benevolence, confidence, justice.
BENEDICT DE SPINOZA

Thinking about interior peace destroys interior peace. The patient who constantly feels his pulse is not getting any better.
HUBERT VAN ZELLER

People

The People, though we think of a great entity when we use the word, means nothing more than so many millions of individual men.
JAMES BRYCE

The problems of the world reflect the people who live in it. Remake people and nations are remade.
FRANK BUCHMAN

Men of integrity, by their very existence, rekindle the belief that as a people we can live above the level of moral squalor.
JOHN W. GARDNER

God must love the common man; he made so many of them.
ABRAHAM LINCOLN

Whatever you may be sure of, be sure of this, that you are dreadfully like other people.
JAMES RUSSELL LOWELL

To try too hard to make people good is one way to make them worse; the only way to make them good is to be good.
GEORGE MACDONALD

The voice of the people, the voice of God.
LATIN PROVERB

We must begin with people where they are, and not where we like them to be. They are not where our fathers were.
LORD SOPER

Perfection

(*See also* Holiness)

Each and everything is said to be perfect in so far as it attains to its proper end; and this is its ultimate perfection.
ST. THOMAS AQUINAS

No one is suddenly made perfect.
THE VENERABLE BEDE

No man can advance three paces on the road to perfection unless Jesus Christ walks beside him.
ROBERT H. BENSON

Perfection does not consist in lacerating or killing the body, but in killing our perverse self-will.
ST. CATHERINE OF SIENA

Bachelors' wives and old maids' children are always perfect.
NICOLAS CHAMFORT

It is only imperfection that complains of what is imperfect. The more perfect we are, the more gentle and quiet we become towards the defects of others.
FRANÇOIS FENELON

Perfection does not lie in not seeing the world, but in not tasting or relishing it.
ST. FRANCIS DE SALES

Wherever we find ourselves we not only may, but should seek perfection.
ST. FRANCIS DE SALES

True perfection consists ... in having but one fear, the loss of God's friendship.
ST. GREGORY OF NYSSA

That soul is perfect which is guided habitually by the instinct of the Holy Spirit.
ISAAC HECKER

He who would fully and feelingly understand the words of Christ, must study to make his whole life conformable to that of Christ.
THOMAS À KEMPIS

It is right to be contented with what we have but never with what we are.
JAMES MACKINTOSH

There are many people living in the midst of unattractive circumstances, amid hardships, toil, and disease, whose daily life breathes out most gentle music that blesses others about them.
J. F. MILLAR

The diamond cannot be polished without friction, nor the man perfected without trials.
CHINESE PROVERB

Perfection is being, not doing; it is not to effect an act but to achieve a character.
FULTON J. SHEEN

If thou canst bear the whole yoke of the Lord, thou wilt be perfect, but if thou canst not, do what thou canst.
TEACHING OF THE TWELVE APOSTLES

What is Christian perfection? Loving God with all our heart, mind, soul and strength.
JOHN WESLEY

The divine nature is perfection; and to be nearest to the divine nature is to be nearest to perfection.
XENOPHON

Persecution

(*See also* Martyrdom)

To flee persecution implies no fault in him who flees but in him who persecutes.
ST. BERNARD OF CLAIRVAUX

Religious persecution may shield itself under the guise of a mistaken and over-zealous piety.
EDMUND BURKE

Opposition may become sweet to a man when he has christened it persecution.
GEORGE ELIOT

Whenever you see persecution, there is more than a probability that truth is on the persecuted side.
HUGH LATIMER

Perseverance

(*See also* Patience)

We cannot command our final perseverance, but must ask it from God.
ST. THOMAS AQUINAS

Genius, that power which dazzles mortal eyes,
Is oft but perseverance in disguise.
HENRY AUSTIN

Every noble work is at first impossible.
THOMAS CARLYLE

Never give in! Never give in! Never, Never, Never, Never – in anything great or small, large or petty – never give in except to convictions of honour and good sense.
SIR WINSTON CHURCHILL

Even the woodpecker owes his success to the fact that he uses his head and keeps pecking away until he finishes the job he starts.
COLEMAN COX

He greatly deceives himself who thinks that prayer perfects one without perseverance and obedience.
ST. FRANCIS DE SALES

Though perseverance does not come from our power, yet it comes within our power.
ST. FRANCIS DE SALES

A tree is shown by its fruits, and in the same way those who profess to belong to Christ will be seen by what they do. For what is needed is not mere present profession, but perseverance to the end in the power of faith.
ST. IGNATIUS OF ANTIOCH

Great works are performed not by strength but by perseverance.
SAMUEL JOHNSON

He said not, 'Thou shalt not be tempested, thou shalt not be travailed, thou shalt not be afflicted,' but he said, 'Thou shalt not be overcome.'
JULIAN OF NORWICH

The man who removed the mountain began by carrying away small stones.
CHINESE PROVERB

The will to persevere is often the difference between failure and success.
DAVID SARNOFF

By perseverance the snail reached the ark.
CHARLES H. SPURGEON

'Tis known as perseverance in a good cause, and obstinacy in a bad one.
LAURENCE STERNE

Personality

(*See also* Character)

Personality should reside in the will as in a castle, and issue orders to the passions and intellectual apprehensions, who, in their turn, should inform their master of external happenings and await his decision.
ROBERT H. BENSON

Human personality and individuality written and signed by God on each human countenance . . . is something altogether sacred, something for the resurrection, for eternal life.
LEON BLOY

Only when the Spirit of God takes possession of the 'old' man to transform him is the man made whole again. It is only when this threshold is crossed that personality takes on full meaning and significance.
ÉMILE CAILLIET

Man's main task in life is to give birth to himself, to become what he potentially is. The most important product of his effort is his own personality.
ERICH FROMM

It is a very significant fact that the idea of human personality, and also the practical recognition of the dignity of human personality, developed only during those centuries in which the dogmas of the Trinity and of the Incarnation were teaching Christendom the truths of divine personality.
JACQUES MARITAIN

Personality is that being which has power over itself.
PAUL TILLICH

Personality is born out of pain. It is the fire shut up in the flint.
J. B. YEATS

Philosophy

Philosophy is merely thought that has been thought out. It is often a great bore. But man has no alternative, except between being influenced by thought that has been thought out and being influenced by thought that has not been thought out. The latter is what we commonly call culture and enlightenment.
G. K. CHESTERTON

Is this not the task of philosophy to enquire about the divine?
ST. JUSTIN MARTYR

Two things fill the mind with ever new and increasing wonder and awe – the starry heavens above me, and the moral law within me.
IMMANUEL KANT

Philosophy does not seek to overthrow revelation; it seeks rather to defend it against assailants.
POPE LEO XIII

Philosophy is the science of the limitations of the human mind. When you know philosophy, you know what you cannot know.
JOSEPH RICKABY

Philosophy asks the simple question: What is it all about?
ALFRED NORTH WHITEHEAD

Piety

(*See also* Holiness and Perfection)

Genuine piety is the spring of peace of mind.
JEAN DE LA BRUYÈRE

Do not, therefore, please yourself with thinking how piously you would act and submit to God in a plague, a famine, or persecution, but be intent upon the perfection of the present day, and be assured that the best way of showing a true zeal is to make little things the occasion of great piety.
WILLIAM LAW

Piety requires us to renounce no ways of life where we can act reasonably and offer what we do to the glory of God.
WILLIAM LAW

The moods and phrases of evangelical piety can substitute a kind of self-contemplation for the self-forgetful contemplation of God and obedience to him.
MICHAEL RAMSEY

The consciousness that the human spirit is derived and responsible, that all its functions are heritages and trusts, involves a sentiment of gratitude and duty we may call piety.
GEORGE SANTAYANA

He who is pious does not contend but teaches in love.
ULRICH ZWINGLI

Pilgrimage

The pilgrim who spends all his time counting his steps will make little progress.
JEAN PIERRE CAMUS

When the sweet showers of April fall and shoot
Down through the drought of March to pierce the root,
Then people long to go on pilgrimages
And palmers long to seek the stranger strands
Of far-off saints, hallowed in sundry lands,
And specially, from every shire's end
In England, down to Canterbury they wend
To seek the holy blissful martyr, quick
In giving help to them when they were sick.
GEOFFREY CHAUCER

God knows well which are the best pilgrims.
ENGLISH PROVERB

God made the moon as well as the sun: and when he does not see fit to grant us the sunlight, he means us to guide our steps as well as we can by moonlight.
RICHARD WHATELY

Pity

(*See also* Sympathy)

Justice seeks out the merits of the case, but pity only regards the need.
ST. BERNARD OF CLAIRVAUX

Pity melts the mind to love.
JOHN DRYDEN

He that pities another remembers himself.
GEORGE HERBERT

To pity the unhappy is not contrary to selfish desire; on the other hand, we are glad of the occasion to thus testify friendship and attract to ourselves the reputation of tenderness, without giving anything.
BLAISE PASCAL

Pity is akin to love.
ENGLISH PROVERB

For pity, more than any other feeling, is a 'learned' emotion; a child will have it least of all.
THOMAS WOLFE

Pleasure

(*See also* Leisure)

It is nonsense to speak of 'higher' and 'lower' pleasures. To a hungry man it is, rightly, more important that he eats than that he philosophise.
W. H. AUDEN

In diving to the bottom of pleasure we bring up more gravel than pearls.
HONORÉ DE BALZAC

We must be able to find pleasure in ourselves when alone, and in our neighbour when in his company.
JEAN PIERRE CAMUS

There is something self-defeating in the too conscious pursuit of pleasure.
MAX EASTMAN

The inward pleasure of imparting pleasure, that is the choicest of all.
NATHANIEL HAWTHORNE

No display of virtue gives an act distinction if its origin is rooted in pleasure.
JOHN OF SALISBURY

Pleasure-seeking is a barren business; happiness is never found till we have the grace to stop looking for it, and to give our attention to persons and matters external to ourselves.
J. I. PACKER

Pleasure is frail like a dewdrop, while it laughs it dies.
RABINDRANATH TAGORE

Politics

(*See also* Democracy and Government)

Political life neither provides our final end nor contains the happiness we seek for ourselves or others . . . The purpose of temporal tranquility, which well-ordered policies establish and maintain, is to give opportunities for contemplating truth.
ST. THOMAS AQUINAS

The good of man must be the end of the science of politics.
ARISTOTLE

Nothing doth more hurt in a state than that cunning men pass for wise.
FRANCIS BACON

All the politics-as-usual of today seems so terribly antiquated; it lags so sadly behind the actual situation of man – and behind even our present knowledge of man.
WILLIAM BARRETT

Politics, and the fate of mankind, are shaped by men without ideals and without greatness. Men who have greatness within them don't go in for politics.
ALBERT CAMUS

Since a politician never believes what he says, he is always astonished when others do.
CHARLES DE GAULLE

He who shall introduce into public affairs the principles of primitive Christianity will revolutionise the world.
BENJAMIN FRANKLIN

We know that separation of State and Church is a source of strength, but the conscience of our nation does not call for separation between men of state and faith in the Supreme Being.
LYNDON B. JOHNSON

Christian political action does not mean waiting for the orders of the bishop or campaigning under the banner of the Church; rather, it means bringing to politics a sense of Christian responsibility.
FRANZISKUS KOENIG

Politics are a part of morals.
HENRY E. MANNING

Nothing is politically right which is morally wrong.
DANIEL O'CONNELL

The penalty that good men pay for not being interested in politics is to be governed by men worse than themselves.
PLATO

Bishops and Christians generally should beware of simply following politicians. A politician has an excuse for compromising, but it seems to me a Christian bishop has not.
T. D. ROBERTS

Poor in Spirit

(*See also* Beatitudes)

If any person, because of his state of life, cannot do without wealth and position, let him at least keep his heart empty of love of them.
ST. ANGELA

The man who is poor in spirit is the man who has realised that things mean nothing, and that God means everything.
WILLIAM BARCLAY

He is rich in spirit who has his riches in his spirit or his spirit in his riches; he is poor in spirit who has no riches in his spirit, nor his spirit in his riches.
ST. FRANCIS DE SALES

He is rich enough who is poor with Christ.
ST. JEROME

'Poor in spirit' refers, not precisely to humility, but to an attitude of dependence on God and detachment from earthly supports.
RONALD KNOX

He is not poor that hath little, but he that desireth much.
ENGLISH PROVERB

The poor man, rich in faith, who toils for the love of God and is generous of the little fruit of his labours, is much nearer to Heaven than the rich man who spends a fortune in good works from no higher motive than his natural inclination to benevolence.
WILLIAM ULLATHORNE

Possessions

(*See also* Materialism, Riches and Wealth)

It is easier to renounce worldly possessions than it is to renounce the love of them.
WALTER HILTON

Let temporal things serve thy use, but the eternal be the object of thy desire.
THOMAS À KEMPIS

To pretend to satisfy one's desires by possession is like using straw to put out a fire.
CHINESE PROVERB

All that we possess is qualified by what we are.
JOHN LANCASTER SPALDING

Poverty

(*See also* Hunger)

Poverty is an anomaly to rich people; it is difficult to make out why people who want dinner do not ring the bell.
WALTER BAGEHOT

A poor man with nothing in his belly needs hope and illusion, more than bread.
GEORGE BERNANOS

No man should praise poverty but he who is poor.
ST. BERNARD OF CLAIRVAUX

The conspicuously wealthy turn up urging the character-building value of privation for the poor.
JOHN K. GALBRAITH

Man is God's image; but a poor man is Christ's stamp to boot.
GEORGE HERBERT

If a free society cannot help the many who are poor, it cannot save the few who are rich.
JOHN F. KENNEDY

The rich will do everything for the poor but get off their backs.
KARL MARX

Satan now is wiser than of yore,
And tempts by making rich,
not making poor.
ALEXANDER POPE

Whoso stoppeth his ear at the poor shall cry himself and not be heard.
HEBREW PROVERB

Poverty is a blessing hated by all men.
ITALIAN PROVERB

It is no disgrace to be poor – which is the only good thing you can say about it.
JEWISH PROVERB

Not he who has little, but he who wishes for more, is poor.
LATIN PROVERB

Must the hunger become anger and the anger fury before anything will be done?
JOHN STEINBECK

Power

(*See also* Omnipotence)

Power is not revealed by striking hard or often, but by striking true.
HONORÉ DE BALZAC

We are the wire, God is the current. Our only power is to let the current pass through us.
CARLO CARRETTO

I have never been able to conceive how any rational being could propose happiness to himself from the exercise of power over others.
THOMAS JEFFERSON

There is one source of power that is stronger than every disappointment, bitterness or ingrained mistrust, and that power is Jesus Christ, who brought forgiveness and reconciliation to the world.
POPE JOHN PAUL II

Real power in prayer flows only when man's spirit touches God's spirit.
CATHERINE MARSHALL

No man can do the work of God until he has the Holy Spirit and is endued with power. It is impossible to preach the Gospel save in the power of the Spirit.
G. CAMPBELL MORGAN

The same power that brought Christ back from the dead is operative within those who are Christ's. The resurrection is an ongoing thing.
LEON MORRIS

Power undirected by high purpose spells calamity; and high purpose by itself is utterly useless if the power to put it into effect is lacking.
THEODORE ROOSEVELT

Next to power without honour, the most dangerous thing in the world is power without humour.
ERIC SEVAREID

In order to obtain and hold power a man must love it. Thus the effort to get it is not likely to be coupled with goodness, but with the opposite qualities of pride, craft, and cruelty.
COUNT LEO TOLSTOY

Praise

(*See also* Worship)

Modesty is the only sure bait when you angle for praise.
G. K. CHESTERTON

You don't have to be afraid of praising God too much; unlike humans He never gets a big head.
PAUL DIBBLE

Praise makes good men better and bad men worse.
THOMAS FULLER

Neither praise or dispraise thyself, thy actions serve the turn.
GEORGE HERBERT

Praise I call the product of the singing heart. It is the inner man responding – the moment you begin to delight in beauty, your heart and mind are raised.
BASIL HUME

The trouble with most of us is that we would rather be ruined by praise than saved by criticism.
NORMAN VINCENT PEALE

Let every man praise the bridge he goes over.
ENGLISH PROVERB

If one man praises you, a thousand will repeat the praise.
JAPANESE PROVERB

It is a sure sign of mediocrity to be niggardly with praise.
MARQUIS DE VAUVENARGUES

Prayer

(*See also* Contemplation and Meditation)

He prays best who does not know that he is praying.
ST. ANTHONY OF PADUA

Do not let us fail one another in interest, care and practical help; but supremely we must not fail one another in prayer.
MICHAEL BAUGHEN

If you are swept off your feet, it's time to get on your knees.
FREDERICK BECK

A prayer in its simplest definition is merely a wish turned Godward.
PHILLIPS BROOKS

In prayer it is better to have a heart without words, than words without a heart.
JOHN BUNYAN

Prayer is a shield to the soul, a sacrifice to God, and a scourge to Satan.
JOHN BUNYAN

Prayer is and remains always a native and deep impulse of the soul of man.
THOMAS CARLYLE

The degree of our faith is the degree of our prayer.
The strength of our hope is the strength of our prayer.
The warmth of our charity is the warmth of our prayer.
CARLO CARRETTO

Pray as you can and do not try to pray as you can't.
JOHN CHAPMAN

The biggest problem in prayer is how to 'let go and let God'.
GLENN CLARK

Prayer is conversation with God.
ST. CLEMENT OF ALEXANDRIA

Really to pray is to stand to attention in the presence of the King and to be prepared to take orders from Him.
DONALD COGGAN

Keep praying, but be thankful that God's answers are wiser than your prayers!
WILLIAM CULBERTSON

When we have learned to offer up every duty connected with our situation in life as a sacrifice to God, a settled employment becomes just a settled habit of prayer.
THOMAS ERSKINE

Talk to him in prayer of all your wants, your troubles, even of the weariness you feel in serving him. You cannot speak too freely, too trustfully, to him.
FRANÇOIS FENELON

A good prayer, though often used, is still fresh and fair in the eyes and ears of heaven.
THOMAS FULLER

He causes his prayers to be of more avail to himself, who offers them also for others.
POPE ST. GREGORY I

Prayer is the breath of the new-born soul, and there can be no Christian life without it.
ROWLAND HILL

Certain thoughts are prayers. There are moments when, whatever be the attitude of the body, the soul is on its knees.
VICTOR HUGO

Perfume all your actions with the life-giving breath of prayer.
POPE JOHN XXIII

God loves us to pray to him, and he very much dislikes our making prayer an excuse for neglecting the effort of doing good works.
POPE JOHN PAUL I

He who has learned to pray has learned the greatest secret of a holy and a happy life.
WILLIAM LAW

You need not cry very loud; he is nearer to us than we think.
BROTHER LAWRENCE

Prayer is the most important thing in my life. If I should neglect prayer for a single day, I should lose a great deal of the fire of faith.
MARTIN LUTHER

God insists that we ask, not because *He* needs to know our situation, but because *we* need the spiritual discipline of asking.
CATHERINE MARSHALL

The purpose of all prayer is to find God's will and to make that will our prayer.
CATHERINE MARSHALL

In a single day I have prayed as many as a hundred times, and in the night almost as often.
ST. PATRICK

Prayer is the pillow of religion.
ARAB PROVERB

Pray to God in the storm – but keep on rowing.
DANISH PROVERB

Pray as though no work would help, and work as though no prayer would help.
GERMAN PROVERB

If you pray for another, you will be helped yourself.
YIDDISH PROVERB

What's important is that God is so much part and parcel of life that spontaneous mental chat becomes second nature.
CLIFF RICHARD

The man of prayer finds his happiness in continually creating, searching, being with Christ.
ROGER SCHUTZ

Whether we like it or not, asking is the rule of the Kingdom.
CHARLES H. SPURGEON

Prayer if it is real is an acknowledgement of our finitude, our need, our openness to be changed, our readiness to be surprised, yes astonished by the 'beams of love'.
DOUGLAS STEERE

Prayer enlarges the heart until it is capable of containing God's gift of himself.
MOTHER TERESA

All that should be sought for in the exercise of prayer is conformity of our will and the divine will, in which consists the highest perfection.
ST. TERESA OF AVILA

We are always in the presence of God, yet it seems to me that those who pray are in his presence in a very different sense.
ST. TERESA OF AVILA

If your prayer is selfish, the answer will be something that will rebuke your selfishness. You may not recognise it as having come at all, but it is sure to be there.
WILLIAM TEMPLE

I have so much to do that I must spend several hours in prayer before I am able to do it.
JOHN WESLEY

Preaching

(*See also* Ministry)

Preaching is truth through personality.
PHILLIPS BROOKS

To love to preach is one thing – to love those to whom we preach, quite another.
RICHARD CECIL

No man has a right so to preach as to send his hearers away on flat tyres. A discouraged man is not an asset but a liability.
CLOVIS G. CHAPPELL

The authority of those who preach is often an obstacle to those who wish to learn.
MARCUS TULLIUS CICERO

The expertise of the pulpit can only be learned slowly and, it may well be, with a strange mixture of pain and joy.
DONALD COGGAN

Avoid showing, if you can help it, any sign of displeasure when you are preaching, or at least anger, as I did one day when they rang the bell before I had finished.
ST. FRANCIS DE SALES

It is no use walking anywhere to preach unless we preach as we walk.
ST. FRANCIS OF ASSISI

The test of a preacher is that his congregation goes away saying, not 'What a lovely sermon!' but 'I will do something.'
ST. FRANCIS DE SALES

Wherever the Gospel is preached, no matter how crudely, there are bound to be results.
BILLY GRAHAM

When I preach I regard neither doctors nor magistrates, of whom I have above forty in my congregation; I have all my eyes on the servant maids and on the children. And if the learned men are not well pleased with what they hear, well, the door is open.
MARTIN LUTHER

It is very important to live your faith by confessing it, and one of the best ways to confess it is to preach it.
THOMAS MERTON

My grand point in preaching is to break the hard heart and to heal the broken one.
JOHN NEWTON

The half-baked sermon causes spiritual indigestion.
AUSTIN O'MALLEY

A sermon is a proclamation of the generous love of God in Christ, or it is not a Christian sermon.
NORMAN PITTENGER

Those having torches will pass them on to others.
GREEK PROVERB

The teacher is like the candle, which lights others in consuming itself.
ITALIAN PROVERB

When you preach the Gospel, beware of preaching it as the religion which explains everything.
ALBERT SCHWEITZER

Give me one hundred preachers who fear nothing but sin and desire nothing but God, and I care not a straw whether they be clergymen or laymen, such alone will shake the gates of hell and set up the Kingdom of God upon earth.
JOHN WESLEY

Predestination

(*See also* Destiny)

The reason for the predestination of some, and reprobation of others, must be sought for in the goodness of God.
ST. THOMAS AQUINAS

God chose us in Christ before the foundation of the world, predestinating us to the adoption of children, not because we were going to be ourselves holy and immaculate, but He chose and predestinated us that we might be so.
ST. AUGUSTINE OF HIPPO

God has an exasperating habit of laying his hands on the wrong man.
JOSEPH D. BLINCO

It must be borne in mind that God foreknows but does not predetermine everything, since He foreknows all that is in us, but does not predetermine it all.
ST. JOHN OF DAMASCUS

God is preparing his heroes; and when the opportunity comes, he can fit them into their places in a moment, and the world will wonder where they came from.
A. B. SIMPSON

Prejudice

(*See also* Bigotry)

Prejudgments become prejudices only if they are not reversible when exposed to new knowledge.
GORDON W. ALLPORT

A prejudice is a vagrant opinion without visible means of support.
AMBROSE BIERCE

The man who never alters his opinion is like standing water, and breeds reptiles of the mind.
WILLIAM BLAKE

The chief cause of human errors is to be found in the prejudices picked up in childhood.
RENE DESCARTES

Ignorance is less remote from the truth than prejudice.
DENIS DIDEROT

She spoke of heaven and an angelic host;
She spoke of God and the Holy Ghost;
She spoke of Christ's teachings of man's brotherhood;
Yet when she had to sit beside a negro once – she stood.
ELIZABETH HART

Prejudice is never easy unless it can pass itself off for reason.
WILLIAM HAZLITT

Prejudice is the child of ignorance.
WILLIAM HAZLITT

Dogs bark at every one they do not know.
HERACLITUS

A great many people think they are thinking when they are merely rearranging their prejudices.
WILLIAM JAMES

Prejudice, not being founded on reason, cannot be removed by argument.
SAMUEL JOHNSON

Nothing is so firmly believed as that which is least known.
MICHEL DE MONTAIGNE

It is with narrow-minded people as with narrow-necked bottles; the less they have in them, the more noise they make in pouring it out.
ALEXANDER POPE

Drive out prejudices by the door, they will come back by the window.
FRENCH PROVERB

No physician can cure the blind in mind.
JEWISH PROVERB

Very few people take the trouble to use their brains as long as their prejudices are in working condition.
ROY L. SMITH

Never try to reason the prejudice out of a man. It was not reasoned into him and cannot be reasoned out.
SYDNEY SMITH

It is never too late to give up your prejudices.
HENRY DAVID THOREAU

Prejudices are what rule the vulgar crowd.
FRANÇOIS MARIE VOLTAIRE

Pride

(*See also* Vanity)

Pride strives for perverse excellence, a very special sin when God is despised, but also present whenever our neighbour is despised.
ST. THOMAS AQUINAS

Pride is the ground in which all the other sins grow, and the parent from which all the other sins come.
WILLIAM BARCLAY

The just estimate of ourselves at the moment of triumph is the most eminent renunciation of pride.
WILLIAM ELLERY CHANNING

Pride and grace dwell never in one place.
THOMAS FULLER

You can have no greater sign of a confirmed pride than when you think you are humble enough.
WILLIAM LAW

A proud man is always looking down on things and people; and, of course, as long as you're looking down, you can't see something that's above you.
C. S. LEWIS

God sends no one away empty except those who are full of themselves.
DWIGHT L. MOODY

Pride is at the bottom of all great mistakes.
JOHN RUSKIN

Pride is an established conviction of one's own paramount worth in some particular respect; while vanity is the desire of rousing such a conviction in others.
ARTHUR SCHOPENHAUER

Be not proud of race, face, place or grace.
CHARLES H. SPURGEON

Priesthood

(*See also* Ministry and Clergy)

I always like to associate with a lot of priests because it makes me understand anti-clerical things so well.
HILAIRE BELLOC

The priesthood requires a great soul; for the priest has many harassing troubles of his own, and has need of innumerable eyes on all sides.
ST. JOHN CHRYSOSTOM

He cannot have the ordination of the Church who does not hold the unity of the Church.
ST. CYPRIAN

But now I see well the old proverb is true:
That parish priest forgetteth that ever he was clerk!
JOHN HEYWOOD

The priesthood is the spiritual power conferred on the ministers of the Church by Christ for the purpose of dispensing the sacraments to the faithful.
JOHN OF PARIS

A constant danger with priests, even zealous priests, is that they become so immersed in the work of the Lord that they neglect the Lord of the work.
POPE JOHN PAUL II

A blot upon a layman's coat is little seen; a spot upon an alb cannot be hid.
HENRY E. MANNING

A priest ought to be no place where his Master would not go, nor employ in anything which his Master would not do.
HENRY E. MANNING

Principles

It is easier to fight for one's principles than to live up to them.
ALFRED ADLER

Nothing can bring you peace but the triumph of principle.
RALPH WALDO EMERSON

One cannot found a religion by putting together principles.
ERICH FROMM

Principles always become a matter of vehement discussion when practice is at ebb.
GEORGE GISSING

In matters of principle, stand like a rock; in matters of taste, swim with the current.
THOMAS JEFFERSON

Procrastination

The effect of my procrastination is that, always busy with the preliminaries and antecedents, I am never able to begin to produce.
HENRI FRÉDÉRIC AMIEL

I could give no reply except a lazy and drowsy, 'Yes, Lord, yes. I'll get to it right away; just don't bother me for a little while.' But 'right away' didn't happen right away; and 'a little while' turned out to be a very long while.
ST. AUGUSTINE OF HIPPO

Procrastination is the art of keeping up with yesterday.
DON MARQUIS

Tomorrow is often the busiest day of the week.
SPANISH PROVERB

Procrastination is the thief of time.
EDWARD YOUNG

Progress

What we call progress is the exchange of one nuisance for another nuisance.
GEORGE ELIOT

All that is human must retrograde if it does not advance.
EDWARD GIBBON

I consider that the way of life in urbanised, rich countries, as it exists today, and as it is likely to go on developing, is probably the most degraded and unillumined ever to come to pass on earth.
MALCOLM MUGGERIDGE

Progress may have been all right once, but it's gone on too long.
OGDEN NASH

The test of our progress is not whether we add more to the abundance of those who have much; it is whether we provide enough for those who have too little.
FRANKLIN D. ROOSEVELT

Those who speak most of progress measure it by quantity and not by quality.
GEORGE SANTAYANA

Promise

Promises may get friends, but it is performance that must nurse and keep them.
OWEN FELTHAM

God's promises are like the stars; the darker the night the brighter they shine.
DAVID NICHOLAS

From the promise to the deed is a day's journey.
BULGARIAN PROVERB

He that promises too much means nothing.
ENGLISH PROVERB

He who is slow in making a promise is most likely to be faithful in the performance of it.
JEAN JACQUES ROUSSEAU

God is the God of promise. He keeps His word, even when that seems impossible; even when the circumstances seem to point to the opposite.
COLIN URQUHART

Proof

The proof of the pudding is the eating.
MIGUEL DE CERVANTES

A Christianity which does not prove its worth in practice degenerates into dry scholasticism and idle talk.
ABRAHAM KUYPER

Confidence in the goodness of another is good proof of one's own goodness.
MICHEL DE MONTAIGNE

For when one's proofs are aptly chosen, Four are as valid as four dozen.
MATTHEW PRIOR

Prophecy

(*See also* Revelation)

Every honest man is a prophet; he utters his opinion both of private and public matters. Thus, if you go on so, the result is so. He never says, such a thing will happen let you do what you will. A prophet is a seer, not an arbitrary dictator.
WILLIAM BLAKE

The task of prophecy has been to 'discern the signs of the times,' to see what God is bringing to pass as the history of peoples and societies unfolds, to point to the judgment he brings upon all institutions.
JOHN B. COBURN

If we do not listen to the prophets we shall have to listen to Providence.
A. C. CRAIG

The prophet is to be no mere announcer, he is rather God's agent who by the 'word' accomplishes what he foretells, whether good or bad.
FLEMING JAMES

Prophets were twice stoned – first in anger, then, after their death, with a handsome slab in the graveyard.
CHRISTOPHER MORLEY

Not everyone who speaks in the spirit is a prophet, but only if he follows the conduct of the Lord.
TEACHING OF THE TWELVE APOSTLES

The prophet is primarily the man, not to whom God has communicated certain thoughts, but whose mind is illuminated by the divine spirit to interpret right the divine acts; and the act is primary.
WILLIAM TEMPLE

Providence

(*See also* Abandonment and Will of God)

Trust the past to the mercy of God, the present to his love, and the future to his Providence.
ST. AUGUSTINE OF HIPPO

Men must pursue things which are just in present, and leave the future to the divine Providence.
FRANCIS BACON

Behind the frowning Providence
He hides a smiling face.
WILLIAM COWPER

Accept the place the Divine Providence has found for you, the society of your contemporaries, the connection of events.
RALPH WALDO EMERSON

We sleep in peace in the arms of God, when we yield ourselves up to his Providence.
FRANÇOIS FENELON

Providence is the care God takes of all existing things.
JOHN OF DAMASCUS

God wishes each of us to work as hard as we can, holding nothing back but giving ourselves to the utmost, and when we can do no more, then is the moment when the hand of Divine Providence is stretched out to us and takes over.
DON ORIONE

What God sends is better than what men ask for.
CROATIAN PROVERB

Providence assists not the idle.
LATIN PROVERB

God builds the nest of the blind bird.
TURKISH PROVERB

He who gives us teeth will give us bread.
YIDDISH PROVERB

There's a divinity that shapes our ends,
Rough-hew them how we will.
WILLIAM SHAKESPEARE

God tempers the wind to the shorn lamb.
LAURENCE STERNE

In all created things discern the Providence and wisdom of God, and in all things give Him thanks.
ST. TERESA OF AVILA

Providence has at all times been my only dependence, for all other resources seem to have failed us.
GEORGE WASHINGTON

I firmly believe in Divine Providence. Without it, I think I should go crazy. Without God the world would be a maze without a clue.
WOODROW WILSON

Prudence

(*See also* Wisdom)

No man is prudent who is ignorant of God.
ST. AMBROSE

Few pay attention to prudence because few possess it.
ST. BERNARD OF CLAIRVAUX

The man who would truly love, and know to the full what it means, will beware of that timid limping thing which sometimes parades, and hides its littleness, under the name of prudence.
ALBAN GOODIER

Whose house is glass must not throw stones at another.
GEORGE HERBERT

We must not trust every word of others or feeling within ourselves, but cautiously and patiently try the matter, whether it be of God.
THOMAS À KEMPIS

Better is to bow than break.
ENGLISH PROVERB

Always wise men go back to leap the further.
FRENCH PROVERB

Purity

(*See also* Chastity and Modesty)

Purity means that we put on the likeness of God, as far as is humanly possible.
ST. JOHN CLIMACUS

Still to the lowly soul
He doth Himself impart,
And for His cradle and His throne
Chooseth the pure in heart.
JOHN KEBLE

A pure heart penetrates Heaven and Hell.
THOMAS À KEMPIS

The impure then cannot love God; and those who are without love of God cannot really be pure. Purity prepares the soul for love, and love confirms the soul in purity.
JOHN HENRY NEWMAN

The stream is always purer at its source.
BLAISE PASCAL

The pure soul is a beautiful rose, and the Three Divine Persons descend from Heaven to inhale its fragrance.
JOHN VIANNEY

Purity is the power to contemplate defilement.
SIMONE WEIL

Purpose

(*See also* Intention)

A good archer is not known by his arrows but his aim.
THOMAS FULLER

Purpose is what gives life a meaning.
C. H. PARKHURST

Continuity of purpose is one of the most essential ingredients of happiness in the long run, and for most men this comes chiefly through their work.
BERTRAND RUSSELL

Man, made in the image of God, has a purpose – to be in relationship to God, who is there. Man forgets his purpose and thus he forgets who he is and what life means.
FRANCIS A. SCHAEFFER

Every life should have a purpose to which it can give the energies of its mind and the enthusiasms of its heart. That life without a purpose will be prey to the perverted ways waiting for the uncommitted life.
NEIL C. STRAIT

Quietness

(*See also* Silence and Solitude)

If we have not quiet in our minds, outward comfort will do no more for us than a golden slipper on a gouty foot.
JOHN BUNYAN

O God, make us children of quietness, and heirs of peace.
ST. CLEMENT OF ALEXANDRIA

A little with quiet
Is the only diet.
GEORGE HERBERT

Happiness is the harvest of a quiet eye.
AUSTIN O'MALLEY

All the troubles of life come upon us because we refuse to sit quietly for a while each day in our rooms.
BLAISE PASCAL

It is difficult to be quiet if you have nothing to do.
ARTHUR SCHOPENHAUER

God is a tranquil Being, and abides in a tranquil eternity. So must thy spirit become a tranquil and clear little pool, wherein the serene light of God can be mirrored.
GERHARD TERSTEEGEN

Race

The easiest idea to sell anyone is that he is better than someone else. The appeal of the Ku Klux Klan and racist agitators rests on this type of salesmanship.
GORDON W. ALLPORT

Skin colour does not matter to God, for he is looking upon the heart ... When men are standing at the foot of the cross there are no racial barriers.
BILLY GRAHAM

Racism is man's gravest threat to man – the maximum of hatred for a minimum of reason.
ABRAHAM JOSHUA HESCHEL

We must recognise that the motives and forces behind racism are the Anti-Christ, denying that man is made in the divine image.
TREVOR HUDDLESTON

Even though human beings differ from one another by virtue of their ethnic peculiarities, they all possess certain common elements and are inclined by nature to meet each other in the world of spiritual values.
POPE JOHN XXIII

After all, there is but one race – humanity.
GEORGE MOORE

A heavy guilt rests upon us for what the whites of all nations have done to the coloured peoples. When we do good to them, it is not benevolence – it is atonement.
ALBERT SCHWEITZER

There is no more evil thing in this world than race prejudice ... It justifies and holds together more baseness, cruelty, and abomination than any other sort of error in the world.
H. G. WELLS

Reality

Make the application of Christianity to present-day life a reality, and none will support it with more zeal than the workers.
JAMES KEIR HARDIE

Facts call us to reflect, even as the tossings of a capsizing vessel cause the crew to rush on deck and to climb the masts.
ALBERT SCHWEITZER

Christ moves among the pots and pans.
ST. TERESA OF AVILA

A test of what is real is that it is hard and rough. Joys are found in it, not pleasure. What is pleasant belongs to dreams.
SIMONE WEIL

Reason

(*See also* Philosophy)

Reason in man is rather like God in the world.
ST. THOMAS AQUINAS

Reason is a light that God has kindled in the soul.
ARISTOTLE

Natural reason is a good tree which God has planted in us; the fruits which spring from it cannot but be good.
ST. FRANCIS DE SALES

Your own reason is the only oracle given you by heaven, and you are answerable for, not the rightness, but the uprightness of the decision.
THOMAS JEFFERSON

Reason, or the exercise of reason, is a living spontaneous energy within, not an art.
JOHN HENRY NEWMAN

Reconciliation

(*See also* Forgiveness and Repentance)

'Forgiving' as well as 'giving' is painful, penitential; perhaps if the Church can be seen as a forgiving and reconciling community, it will be possible to persuade people of the need for penitence.
JAMES D. CRICHTON

It takes two sides to make a lasting peace, but it only takes one to make the first step.
EDWARD M. KENNEDY

Reconciliation sounds a large theological term, but it simply means coming to ourselves and arising and going to our Father.
JOHN OMAN

A love of reconciliation is not weakness or cowardice. It demands courage, nobility, generosity, sometimes heroism, an overcoming of oneself rather than of one's adversary. At times it may even seem like dishonour, but it never offends against true justice or denies the rights of the poor. In reality, it is the patient, wise art of peace, of loving, of living with one's fellows, after the example of Christ, with a strength of heart and mind modelled on his.
POPE PAUL VI

Redemption

(*See also* Atonement and Salvation)

For no one is redeemed except through unmerited mercy, and no one is condemned except through merited judgment.
ST. AUGUSTINE OF HIPPO

And now without redemption all mankind
Must have been lost, adjudge'd to Death and Hell
By doom severe.
JOHN MILTON

Redemption does not only look back to Calvary. It looks forward to the freedom in which the redeemed stand. Precisely because they have been redeemed at such a cost, believers must be God's men.
LEON MORRIS

People will never take evil seriously nor even see much need to tap the resources of God until they join in with the costly redemptive purposes of love.
J. B. PHILLIPS

Reform

(*See also* Reformation and Revolution)

All zeal for a reform, that gives offence
To peace and charity, is mere pretence.
WILLIAM COWPER

Every reform movement has a lunatic fringe.
THEODORE ROOSEVELT

The best reformers the world has ever seen are those who commence on themselves.
GEORGE BERNARD SHAW

All reformers, however strict their social conscience, live in houses just as big as they can pay for.
LOGAN PEARSALL SMITH

Reformation

It cannot be denied that corruption of morals prevailed in the sixteenth century to such an extent as to call for a sweeping reformation, and that laxity of discipline invaded even the sanctuary.
JAMES GIBBONS

The question most disputed at the time of the Reformation, namely justification by faith alone, now leaves people in the Protestant Churches just as cold as those in the Catholic Church.
HANS KUNG

The authors and protagonists saw the Reformation as the recovery of the pure revelation of primitive Christianity, the 'word of God undefiled', while the Catholic Church of the time saw it mainly as a rejection of Christian truth.
JOSEPH LORTZ

To make a crooked stick straight, we bend it the contrary way.
MICHEL DE MONTAIGNE

Every reformation must have its victims. You can't expect the fatted calf to share the enthusiasm of the angels over the prodigal's return.
H. H. MUNRO

Every generation needs re-generation.
CHARLES H. SPURGEON

Every church should be engaged in continuous self-reformation, scrutinising its traditions in the light of Scripture and where necessary modifying them.
JOHN R. W. STOTT

Relationships

(*See also* Friendship, Love, and Love of Neighbour)

Nothing is a greater impediment to being on good terms with others than being ill at ease with yourself.
HONORÉ DE BALZAC

Have a heart that never hardens, and a temper that never tires, and a touch that never hurts.
CHARLES DICKENS

I think people ought to fulfil sacredly their desires. And this means fulfilling the deepest desire, which is a desire to live unhampered by things that are extraneous, a desire for pure relationships and living truth.
D. H. LAWRENCE

Once the realisation is accepted that even between the closest human beings infinite distances continue to exist, a wonderful living side by side can grow up, if they succeed in loving the distance between them which makes it possible for each to see the other whole against the sky.
RAINER MARIA RILKE

Christianity is not a religion, it is a relationship.
DR. THIEME

It is better to be alone than in bad company.
GEORGE WASHINGTON

Kissing is a means of getting two people so close together that they can't see anything wrong with each other.
GENE YASENAK

Religion

For true religion is that by which the soul is united to God so that it binds itself again by reconciliation to Him from Whom it had broken off, as it were, by sin.
ST. AUGUSTINE OF HIPPO

A religion that is small enough for our understanding is not great enough for our need.
ARTHUR JAMES BALFOUR

Religion is excellent stuff for keeping common people quiet.
NAPOLEON BONAPARTE

It is the root of all religion that a man knows that he is nothing in order to thank God that he is something.
G. K. CHESTERTON

Let your religion be less of a theory and more of a love affair.
G. K. CHESTERTON

Religion has its origins in the depths of the soul and it can be understood only by those who are prepared to take the plunge.
CHRISTOPHER DAWSON

Science without religion is lame, religion without science is blind.
ALBERT EINSTEIN

Religions are man's search for God; the Gospel is God's search for man. There are many religions, but one Gospel.
E. STANLEY JONES

The heart of religion lies in its personal pronouns.
MARTIN LUTHER

We have been dosing our people with religion when what they need is not that but the living God.
FREDERICK D. MAURICE

A man who is religious, is religious morning, noon, and night; his religion is a certain character, a mould in which his thoughts, words, and actions are cast, all forming parts of one and the same whole.
JOHN HENRY NEWMAN

What a travesty to think religion means saving my little soul through my little good deeds and the rest of the world go hang.
GERALD VANN

How poor and thin a things is all purely personal religion. Religion to be deep and rich must be historical.
FRIEDRICH VON HUGEL

Some people have just enough religion to make them uncomfortable.
JOHN WESLEY

Repentance

(*See also* Forgiveness)

To him who still remains in this world no repentance is too late. The approach to God's mercy is open, and the access is easy to those who seek and apprehend the truth.
ST. CYPRIAN

Sleep with clean hands, either kept clean all day by integrity or washed clean at night by repentance.
JOHN DONNE

When thou attackest the roots of sin, fix thy thought upon the God whom thou desirest rather than upon the sin which thou abhorrest.
WALTER HILTON

For right as by the courtesy of God He forgets our sins when we repent, right so will He that we forget our sin, and all our heaviness, and all our doubtful dreads.
JULIAN OF NORWICH

To do so no more is the truest repentance.
MARTIN LUTHER

It is never too late to repent.
ENGLISH PROVERB

Our repentance is not so much regret for the ill we have done as fear of the ill that may happen to us in consequence.
FRANÇOIS DE LA ROCHEFOUCAULD

The world, as we live in it, is like a shop window into which some mischievous person has got overnight, and shifted all the price-labels so that the cheap things have the high price-labels on them, and the really precious things are priced low. We let ourselves be taken in. Repentance means getting those price-labels back in the right place.
WILLIAM TEMPLE

Repentance must be something more than mere remorse for sins: it comprehends a change of nature befitting heavens.
LEW WALLACE

It can take less than a minute to commit a sin. It takes not as long to obtain God's forgiveness. Penitence and amendment should take a lifetime.
HUBERT VAN ZELLER

Reputation

(*See also* Character)

A good name is better than great riches.
MIGUEL DE CERVANTES

Excessive fear of losing a good name indicates a great distrust of its foundation, which is the truth of a good life.
ST. FRANCIS DE SALES

Reputation is but a signboard to show where virtue lodges.
ST. FRANCIS DE SALES

Glass, china, and reputation, are easily cracked and never well mended.
BENJAMIN FRANKLIN

What people say behind your back is your standing in the community.
EDGAR W. HOWE

Many a man's reputation would not know his character if they met on the street.
ELBERT HUBBARD

Good will, like a good name, is got by many actions, and lost by one.
FRANCIS JEFFREY

The reputation of a man is like his shadow; it sometimes follows and sometimes precedes him; it is sometimes longer and sometimes shorter than his natural size.
FRENCH PROVERB

Responsibility

(*See also* Duty)

Our main business is not to see what lies dimly at a distance, but to do what lies clearly at hand.
THOMAS CARLYLE

When you have saved a boy from the possibility of making any mistake, you have also prevented him from developing initiative.
JOHN ERSKINE

To let oneself be bound by a duty from the moment you see it approaching is part of the integrity that alone justifies responsibility.
DAG HAMMARSKJOLD

To be a man is, precisely, to be responsible.
ANTOINE DE SAINT-EXUPÉRY

Man must cease attributing his problems to his environment, and learn again to exercise his will – his personal responsibility in the realm of faith and morals.
ALBERT SCHWEITZER

Few things help an individual more than to place responsibility upon him, and to let him know that you trust him.
BOOKER T. WASHINGTON

The most important thought I ever had was that of my individual responsibility to God.
DANIEL WEBSTER

Resurrection

(*See also* Easter)

I know of no one fact in the history of mankind which is proved by better evidence of every sort, to the understanding of a fair enquirer, than the great sign which God has given us that Christ died and rose again from the dead.
THOMAS ARNOLD

Christ has turned all our sunsets into dawns.
ST. CLEMENT OF ALEXANDRIA

Let us consider, beloved, how the Lord is continually revealing to us the resurrection that is to be. Of this He has constituted the Lord Jesus Christ the first-fruits, by raising Him from the dead.
POPE ST. CLEMENT II

By virtue of the Resurrection, nothing any longer kills inevitably but everything is capable of becoming the blessed touch of the divine hands, the blessed influence of the will of God upon our lives.
P. TEILHARD DE CHARDIN

The entire New Testament is witness that the real presence of Christ was not withdrawn when the Resurrection 'appearances' ceased. The unique and evanescent meetings with the risen Lord triggered off a new kind of relation which proved permanent.
C. H. DODD

Our Lord has written the promise of the Resurrection, not in books alone, but in every leaf in springtime.
MARTIN LUTHER

The birth and rapid rise of the Christian Church therefore remain an unsolved enigma for any historian who refuses to take seriously the only explanation offered by the Church itself.
C. F. D. MOULE

To renounce all is to gain all; to descend is to rise; to die is to live.
KARL RAHNER

Christianity is a religion of miracle, and the miracle of Christ's Resurrection is the living centre and object of Christian faith.
ALAN RICHARDSON

Christian theology has never suggested that the 'fact' of Christ's Resurrection could be known apart from faith.
ALAN RICHARDSON

Every parting gives a foretaste of death; every coming together again a foretaste of the Resurrection.
ARTHUR SCHOPENHAUER

Christianity is in its very essence a resurrection religion. The concept of resurrection lies at its heart. If you remove it, Christianity is destroyed.
JOHN R. W. STOTT

If Christ be not risen, the dreadful consequence is not that death ends life, but that we are still in our sins.
G. A. STUDDERT-KENNEDY

Fellowship with Christ is participation in the divine life which finds its fullest expression in triumph over death. Life is a larger word than Resurrection; but Resurrection is, so to speak, the crucial quality of life.
WILLIAM TEMPLE

The Gospels do not explain the Resurrection; the Resurrection explains the Gospels. Belief in the Resurrection is not an appendage to the Christian faith, it *is* the Christian faith.
JOHN S. WHALE

The background of resurrection is always impossibility. And with impossibility staring us in the face, the prelude to resurrection is invariably doubt, confusion, strife, and the cynical smile which is our defence against them. Resurrection is always the defiance of the absurd.
H. A. WILLIAMS

Revelation

Human salvation demands the divine disclosure of truths surpassing reason.
ST. THOMAS AQUINAS

To see a World in a Grain of Sand,
And a Heaven in a Wild Flower,
Hold Infinity in the palm of your hand,
And Eternity in an hour.
WILLIAM BLAKE

The first and most important thing we know about God is that we know nothing about him except what he himself makes known.
EMIL BRUNNER

Man cannot cover what God would reveal.
THOMAS CAMPBELL

A Christian cannot live by philosophy. Only the light of Christian revelation gives the end as well as the means of life. It is the same for you as for me and the man in the street. If one has more learning, another has more grace, it is all one.
JOHN CHAPMAN

Every revelation of truth felt with interior savour and spiritual joy is a secret whispering of God in the ear of a pure soul.
WALTER HILTON

Revelation is the act of communicating divine knowledge by the Spirit to the mind. Inspiration is the act of the same Spirit, controlling those who make the truth known.
CHARLES HODGE

Knowing all things, therefore, and providing for what is profitable for each one, He revealed that which it was to our profit to know; but what we were unable to bear He kept secret.
ST. JOHN OF DAMASCUS

Revelation consists of the initiative of God, who personally came to meet man, in order to open with him a dialogue of salvation. It was God who began the talk, and it is God who carries it forward.
POPE JOHN PAUL II

The core of Christian revelation is that Jesus Christ is the sole legitimate Lord of all human lives.
H. KRAEMER

Every act formed by charity is a revelation of God. Every word of truth and love, every hand extended in kindness, echoes the inner life of the Trinity.
GABRIEL MORAN

We do not believe that God has added, or ever will add, anything to His revelation in His Son. But we can now see many things in that revelation which could not be seen by those who first received it. Each generation of Christians, and each people to which the Christian Gospel is preached, makes its own contribution to the understanding of the riches of Jesus Christ.
C. B. MOSS

As prayer is the voice of man to God, so revelation is the voice of God to man.
JOHN HENRY NEWMAN

In revelation, God is the agent as well as the object. It is not just that men speak about God, or for God; God speaks for Himself, and talks to us in person.
J. I. PACKER

Man is the revelation of the Infinite, and it does not become finite in him. It remains the Infinite.
MARK RUTHERFORD

Only because the Word, as love, has already been spoken and understood, can man give a loving answer, an answer which simply means making 'free passage' for the Word.
HANS URS VON BALTHASAR

Revenge

The noblest vengeance is to forgive.
HENRY G. BOHN

Revenge is the abject pleasure of an abject mind.
DECIMUS JUVENAL

Perhaps because our passions are less strong, perhaps even because the teaching of Christ has at least penetrated our thick heads, we look upon revenge as discreditable.
W. SOMERSET MAUGHAM

Revenge is a dish that should be eaten cold.
ENGLISH PROVERB

The smallest revenge will poison the soul.
JEWISH PROVERB

Reverence

A deep reverence for human life is worth more than a thousand executions for the prevention of murder; and is, in fact, the great security of human life. The law of capital punishment, whilst pretending to support this reverence, does in fact tend to destroy it.
JOHN BRIGHT

Lambs have the grace to kneel while nursing.
CHINESE PROVERB

The first mark of a Christian is a deep reverence for persons as destined for eternity with God.
MICHAEL RAMSEY

Reverence is the attitude which can be designated as the mother of all moral life, for in it man first takes a position toward the world which opens his spiritual eyes and enables him to grasp values.
DIETRICH VON HILDEBRAND

Revolution

(*See also* Reform and Reformation)

Every revolutionary ends by becoming either an oppressor or a heretic.
ALBERT CAMUS

The great revolution of the future will be nature's revolt against man.
HOLBROOK JACKSON

Those who make peaceful revolution impossible will make violent revolution inevitable.
JOHN F. KENNEDY

If omnipotent love did truly transform our hearts, the exterior work of reform would already be half done.
JACQUES MARITAIN

Revolutions are not made with rose-water.
ENGLISH PROVERB

Every revolution by force only puts more violent means of enslavement into the hands of the person in power.
COUNT LEO TOLSTOY

Every successful revolution puts on, in time, the robes of the tyrant it has deposed.
BARBARA TUCHMAN

Riches

(*See also* Materialism and Wealth)

I cannot call riches better than the baggage of virtue; for as the baggage is to an army, so is riches to virtue, it cannot be spared nor left behind, but it hindereth the march.
FRANCIS BACON

Theirs is an endless road, a hopeless maze, who seek for goods before they seek for God.
ST. BERNARD OF CLAIRVAUX

Riches are not forbidden, but the pride of them is.
ST. JOHN CHRYSOSTOM

Many speak the truth when they say that they despise riches, but they mean the riches possessed by other men.
CHARLES CALEB COLTON

The rich in this world cannot be made useful for the Lord, unless their riches have been cut out of them.
SHEPHERD OF HERMAS

The accumulation of vast wealth while so many are languishing in misery is a grave transgression of God's law, with the consequence that the greedy, avaricious man is never at ease in his mind: he is in fact a most unhappy creature.
POPE JOHN XXIII

Riches serve a wise man but command a fool.
ENGLISH PROVERB

Riches are like salt water, the more you drink the more you thirst.
ROMAN PROVERB

Right

One may go wrong in many different ways, but right only in one.
ARISTOTLE

Never claim as a right what you can ask as a favour.
JOHN CHURTON COLLINS

Let us have faith that right makes might, and in that faith let us to the end dare to do our duty as we understand it.
ABRAHAM LINCOLN

Right is right, even if everyone is against it; and wrong is wrong, even if everyone is for it.
WILLIAM PENN

Being in the right does not depend on having a loud voice.
CHINESE PROVERB

There is only one way of seeing things rightly, and that is seeing the whole of them.
JOHN RUSKIN

To be right with God has often meant to be in trouble with men.
A. W. TOZER

Always do right. This will gratify some people and astonish the rest.
MARK TWAIN

Righteousness

(*See also* Redemption and Salvation)

Christ came to reveal what righteousness really is, for nothing will do except righteousness, and no other conception of righteousness will do except Christ's conception of it – his method and secret.
MATTHEW ARNOLD

What is all righteousness that men devise?
What – but a sordid bargain for the skies?
WILLIAM COWPER

If there be ground for you to trust in your own righteousness, then all that Christ did to purchase salvation, and all that God did to prepare the way for it, is in vain.
JONATHAN EDWARDS

Righteousness is obedience to law, observance of duty, and fidelity to conscience.
J. P. HOPPS

The righteousness of Jesus is the righteousness of a Godward relationship of trust, dependence, receptivity.
MICHAEL RAMSEY

Sacraments

The symbolic actions of former and present times, which because of their pertaining to divine things are called sacraments.
ST. AUGUSTINE OF HIPPO

All the sacraments appear as vital acts of the Church in the process of its self-realisation as the primordial sacrament. In these acts the Church gives concrete form to its own essence, which is to be the eschatological, historical and social presence of God's self-communication to the world for the sake of individuals in the moments essential to their salvation.
KARL RAHNER

For mankind there are two unique sacraments which disclose the meaning and convey the experience of reality: they are the created universe and the person of Jesus Christ.
CHARLES E. RAVEN

The meaning of each sacrament is derived from two things: its reference to the paschal mystery and the particular situation of the individual or community upon whom the sacramental celebration focuses.
MARK SEARLE

Each sacrament is the personal saving act of the risen Christ himself, but realised in the visible form of an official act of the Church.
E. SCHILLEBEECKX

In the sacraments nature participates in the process of salvation. Bread and wine, water and light, and all the great elements of nature become the bearers of spiritual meaning and saving power. Natural and spiritual powers are united – reunited – in the sacrament.
PAUL TILLICH

Sacrifice

The sacrifice most acceptable to God is complete renunciation of the body and its passions. This is the only real piety.
ST. CLEMENT OF
ALEXANDRIA

Come, let us offer Christ the great, universal sacrifice of our love, and pour out before him our richest hymns and prayers. For he offered his cross to God as a sacrifice in order to make us all rich.
ST. EPHREM

Man's strongest instinct is to self-preservation; grace's highest call is to self-sacrifice.
PAUL FROST

Without sacrifice there is no resurrection. Nothing grows and blooms save by giving. All you try to save in yourself wastes and perishes.
ANDRÉ GIDE

Was anything real ever gained without sacrifice of some kind?
ARTHUR HELPS

I offer my life as a sacrifice for the successful outcome of the Ecumenical Council and for peace among men.
POPE JOHN XXIII

It is only through the mystery of self-sacrifice that a man may find himself anew.
CARL GUSTAV JUNG

The principle of sacrifice is that we choose to do or to suffer what apart from our love we should not choose to do or to suffer.
WILLIAM TEMPLE

Sadness

(*See also* Grief and Sorrow)

There is only one sadness, the sadness of not being a saint.
LEON BLOY

I have taken life on the sad side, and it has helped me to understand many, many failures, many utter ruins.
ABBÉ HUVELIN

I love everything in life, even to be sad.
ARTUR RUBINSTEIN

Saints

(*See also* Holiness and Perfection)

It is said that a saint is one who always chooses the better of the two courses open to him at every step.
ROBERT H. BENSON

A saint is never consciously a saint; a saint is consciously dependent on God.
OSWALD CHAMBERS

The great painter boasted that he mixed all his colours with brains, and the great saint may be said to mix all his thoughts with thanks.
G. K. CHESTERTON

And Satan trembles when he sees,
The weakest saint upon his knees.
WILLIAM COWPER

The saints are God's jewels, highly esteemed by and dear to him; they are a royal diadem in his hand.
MATTHEW HENRY

Many of the insights of the saint stem from his experience as a sinner.
ERIC HOFFER

A saint is one who makes goodness attractive.
LAURENCE HOUSEMAN

The way of the world is to praise dead saints and to persecute living ones.
NATHANIEL HOWE

What saint has ever won his crown without first contending for it?
ST. JEROME

God creates out of nothing. Wonderful, you say. Yes, to be sure, but He does what is still more wonderful: He makes saints out of sinners.
SØREN KIERKEGAARD

Nature requires the saint since he alone knows the miracle of transfiguration; growth and development, the very highest and most sustained incarnation, never weary him.
FRIEDRICH NIETZSCHE

Grace is indeed required to turn a man into a saint; and he who doubts this does not know what either a man or a saint is.
BLAISE PASCAL

The power of the soul for good is in proportion to the strength of its passions. Sanctity is not the negation of passion but its order. Hence great saints have often been great sinners.
COVENTRY PATMORE

The saint does everything that any other decent person does, only somewhat better and with a totally different motive.
COVENTRY PATMORE

A saint abroad and a devil at home.
ENGLISH PROVERB

Saint cannot, if God will not.
FRENCH PROVERB

It is easier to make a saint out of a libertine than out of a prig.
GEORGE SANTAYANA

Saints are persons who make it easier for others to believe in God.
NATHAN SÖDERBLOM

The saint is saint, not because he is 'good' but because he is transparent for something that is more than he himself is.
PAUL TILLICH

Salvation

(*See also* Redemption, Righteousness and Saviour)

Divine care supplies everybody with the means necessary for salvation, so long as he on his part does not put up obstacles.
ST. THOMAS AQUINAS

Salvation is seeing that the universe is good, and becoming a part of that goodness.
ARTHUR G. CLUTTON-BROCK

The knowledge of sin is the beginning of salvation.
EPICURUS

No man has the right to abandon the care of his salvation to another.
THOMAS JEFFERSON

The salvation of a single soul is more important than the production or preservation of all the epics and tragedies in the world.
C. S. LEWIS

The way to be saved is not to delay, but to come and take.
DWIGHT L. MOODY

Salvation is from God only.
LATIN PROVERB

God has shewn forth his saving righteousness in the sacrificial death of Christ, and the sole requirement of those who would avail themselves of this salvation is that they should believe and be baptised in the faith of Jesus Messiah.
ALAN RICHARDSON

The terms for 'salvation' in many languages are derived from roots like salvus, saos, whole, heil, which all designate health, the opposite of disintegration and disruption. Salvation is healing in the ultimate sense; it is final cosmic and individual healing.
PAUL TILLICH

Satan

(*See also* Devil)

Satan deals with confusion and lies. Put the truth in front of him and he is gone.
PAUL MATTOCK

Anyone who obeys Christ by making Christ's submission to God the basis of one's own life will be saved from bondage to Satan and from fear of death.
MARK SEARLE

Satan finds some mischief still
For idle hands to do.
ISAAC WATTS

Saviour

(*See also* Jesus Christ and Salvation)

While the Saviour does not reject the willing, He does not constrain the unwilling; while He does not deny Himself to those who seek Him, He does not strive with those who cast Him out.
ST. AMBROSE

To follow the Saviour is to participate in salvation; to follow the light is to perceive the light.
ST. IRENAEUS

The Saviour leaves his imprint on every single act of charity.
POPE JOHN PAUL II

If we really know Christ as our Saviour our hearts are broken and cannot be hard, and we cannot refuse forgiveness.
MARTYN LLOYD-JONES

To know Christ is not to speculate about the mode of his incarnation, but to know his saving benefits.
PHILIP MELANCHTON

Verbally in Scripture, visually in sacrament, Jesus Christ is set forth as the only Saviour of sinners.
JOHN R. W. STOTT

Scandal

(*See also* Gossip)

Scandal will rub out like dirt when it is dry.
THOMAS FULLER

Everything in turn, except scandal, whose turn is always.
ENGLISH PROVERB

Scandal is gossip made tedious by morality.
OSCAR WILDE

Science

We have too many men of science, too few men of God. We have grasped the mystery of the atom, and rejected the Sermon on the Mount. The world has achieved brilliance without wisdom, power without conscience.
OMAR BRADLEY

There is something in man which your science cannot satisfy.
THOMAS CARLYLE

Science without religion is lame, religion without science is blind.
ALBERT EINSTEIN

Science is not to be regarded merely as a store-house of facts to be used for material purposes, but as one of the great human endeavours to be ranked with arts and religion as the guide and expression of man's fearless quest for truth.
RICHARD GREGORY

In everything that relates to science, I am a whole encyclopaedia behind the rest of the world.
CHARLES LAMB

There is one thing even more vital to science than intelligent methods; and that is, the sincere desire to find out the truth, whatever it may be.
CHARLES SANDERS PEIRCE

Scripture

(*See also* Bible)

As in Paradise, God walks in the Holy Scriptures, seeking man.
ST. AMBROSE

Divine Scripture is the feast of wisdom, and the single books are the various dishes.
ST. AMBROSE

The whole series of the divine Scriptures is interpreted in a fourfold way. In all holy books one should ascertain what everlasting truths are therein intimated, what deeds are narrated, what future events are foretold, and what commands or counsels are there contained.
THE VENERABLE BEDE

It is a great thing, this reading of the Scriptures! For it is not possible ever to exhaust the mind of the Scriptures. It is a well that has no bottom.
ST. JOHN CHRYSOSTOM

Explain the Scriptures by the Scriptures.
ST. CLEMENT OF ALEXANDRIA

In the Scriptures be the fat pastures of the soul; therein is no venomous meat, no unwholesome thing; they be the very dainty and pure feeding. He that is ignorant, shall find there what he should learn.
THOMAS CRANMER

These writings bring back to you the living image of that most holy mind, the very Christ himself speaking, healing, dying, rising, in fact so entirely present, that you would see less of him if you beheld him with your eyes.
DESIDERIUS ERASMUS

Holy Scripture is a stream of running water, where alike the elephant may swim, and the lamb walk without losing its feet.
POPE ST. GREGORY I

There is only one real inevitability: It is necessary that the Scripture be fulfilled.
CARL F. HENRY

The book of books, the storehouse and magazine of life and comfort, the holy Scriptures.
GEORGE HERBERT

To be ignorant of the Scripture is not to know Christ.
ST. JEROME

Every Christian must refer 'always and everywhere' to the Scriptures for all his choices, becoming 'like a child' before it, seeking in it the most effective remedy against all his various weaknesses, and not daring to take a step without being illuminated by the divine rays of those words.
POPE JOHN PAUL II

The way to understand the Scriptures and all theology is to become holy. It is to be under the authority of the Spirit.
MARTYN LLOYD-JONES

God the Father is the giver of Holy Scripture; God the Son is the theme of Holy Scripture; and God the Spirit is the author, authenticator, and interpreter, of Holy Scripture.
J. I. PACKER

Scripture is full of Christ. From Genesis to Revelation everything breathes of Him, not every letter of every sentence, but the spirit of every chapter.
FREDERICK W. ROBERTSON

If we value the Scriptures very highly, this is not for themselves, but because they are the Father's testimony to Christ.
JOHN R. W. STOTT

The Scriptures of God, whether belonging to Christian or Jew, are much more ancient than any secular literature.
QUINTUS TERTULLIAN

Most people are bothered by those passages in Scripture which they cannot understand; but as for me, I always noticed that the passages in Scripture which trouble me most are those that I do understand.
MARK TWAIN

Second Coming

(*See also* Judgment)

There are three distinct comings of the Lord of which I know; His coming to men; His coming into men; and His coming against men.
ST. BERNARD OF CLAIRVAUX

We are not a post-war generation; but a pre-peace generation. Jesus is coming.
CORRIE TEN BOOM

Whatever resistance we see today offered by almost all the world to the progress of the truth, we must not doubt that our Lord will come at last to break through all the undertakings of men and make a passage for his word.
JOHN CALVIN

When Christ appears in the clouds he will simply be manifesting a metamorphosis that has been slowly accomplished under his influence in the heart of the mass of mankind.
P. TEILHARD DE CHARDIN

Christ designed that the day of his coming should be hid from us, that being in suspense, we might be as it were upon the watch.
MARTIN LUTHER

We are beginning to realise that the Parousia or Second Coming is not a once-and-for-all event in the historical future, whether near or remote, but part of a myth designed to clarify what it means − as well as what it will mean − to see all things 'new' in the Kingdom of God.
JOHN A. T. ROBINSON

Seeking God

(*See also* Knowledge of God)

It is in silence that God is known, and through mysteries that He declares Himself.
ROBERT H. BENSON

I hurry wherever I am beckoned, in search of what can bring men together in the name of the essential.
HELDER CAMARA

He is to be seen in the light of a cottage window as well as in the sun or the stars.
ARTHUR G. CLUTTON-BROCK

We must wait for God, long, meekly, in the wind and wet, in the thunder and lightining, in the cold and the dark. Wait, and he will come. He never comes to those who do not wait. He does not go their road. When he comes, go with him, but go slowly, fall a little behind; when he quickens his pace, be sure of it before you quicken yours. But when he slackens, slacken at once; and do not be slow only, but silent, very silent, for he is God.
FREDERICK W. FABER

Each conception of spiritual beauty is a glimpse of God.
MOSES MENDELSSOHN

Whosoever walks towards God one cubit, God runs towards him twain.
JEWISH PROVERB

Many millions search for God and find Him in their hearts.
SIKH PROVERB

To have found God is not an end in itself but a beginning.
FRANZ ROSENZWEIG

Self

(*See also* Selfishness and Self-Love)

We are all serving a life sentence in the dungeon of self.
CYRIL CONNOLLY

The true value of a human being is determined primarily by the measure and the sense in which he has attained liberation from the self.
ALBERT EINSTEIN

The living self has one purpose only: to come into its own fullness of being, as a tree comes into full blossom, or a bird into spring beauty, or a tiger into lustre.
D. H. LAWRENCE

A man needs self-acceptance or he can't live with himself; he needs self-criticism or others can't live with him.
JAMES A. PIKE

What other people think of me is becoming less and less important; what they think of Jesus because of me is critical.
CLIFF RICHARD

213

Nothing seems to me of the smallest value except what one gets out of oneself.
OSCAR WILDE

Self-Denial

(*See also* Unselfishness)

Inwardness, mildness, and self-renouncement do make for man's happiness.
MATTHEW ARNOLD

Self-admiration is the death of the soul. To admire ourselves as we are is to have no wish to change. And with those who don't want to change, the soul is dead.
WILLIAM BARCLAY

All great virtues bear the imprint of self-denial.
WILLIAM ELLERY CHANNING

The most satisfying thing in life is to have been able to give a large part of oneself to others.
P. TEILHARD DE CHARDIN

The true value of a human being is determined primarily by the measure and the sense in which he has attained liberation from the self.
ALBERT EINSTEIN

You give but little when you give of your possessions. It is when you give of yourself that you truly give.
KAHLIL GIBRAN

All along the Christian course, there must be set up altars to God on which you sacrifice yourself, or you will never advance a step.
ALEXANDER MACLAREN

They that deny themselves for Christ shall enjoy themselves in Christ.
JOHN MASON

One secret act of self-denial, one sacrifice of inclination to duty, is worth all the mere good thoughts, warm feelings, passionate prayers in which idle people indulge themselves.
JOHN HENRY NEWMAN

The cross that Jesus tells us to carry is the one that we willingly take up ourselves – the cross of self-denial in order that we might live for the glory of the Father.
COLIN URQUHART

Self-Discipline

(*See also* Self-Denial)

We must be anchored in self-discipline if we are to venture successfully in freedom.
HAROLD E. KOHN

There is endless room for rebellion against ourselves.
GEORGE MACDONALD

Self-discipline never means giving up anything, for giving up is a loss. Our Lord did not ask us to give up the things of earth, but to exchange them for better things.
FULTON J. SHEEN

He that commands others is not so much as free, if he doth not govern himself. The greatest performance in the life of man is the government of his spirit.
BENJAMIN WHICHCOTE

Selfishness

(*See also* Self and Self-Love)

Living in our selfishness means stopping at human limits and preventing our transformation into Divine Love.
CARLO CARRETTO

No indulgence of passion destroys the spiritual nature so much as respectable selfishness.
GEORGE MACDONALD

Nine-tenths of our unhappiness is selfishness, and is an insult cast in the face of God.
G. H. MORRISON

The man who lives by himself and for himself is apt to be corrupted by the company he keeps.
CHARLES H. PARKHURST

When a man is wrapped up in himself he makes a pretty small package.
JOHN RUSKIN

Selfishness is the only real atheism.
ISRAEL ZANGWILL

Self-Knowledge

What use do I put my soul to? It is a very serviceable question this, and should frequently be put.
MARCUS AURELIUS

He who knows himself best esteems himself least.
HENRY G. BOHN

Nothing is so easy as to deceive one's self.
DEMOSTHENES

A man has many skins in himself, covering the depths of his heart. Man knows so many things; he does not know himself. Why, thirty or forty skins or hides, just like an ox's or a bear's, so thick and hard, cover the soul. Go into your own ground and learn to know yourself there.
MEISTER ECKHART

A humble knowledge of yourself is a surer way to God than a deep search after learning.
THOMAS À KEMPIS

The highest and most profitable reading is the true knowledge and consideration of ourselves.
THOMAS À KEMPIS

Know yourself, and your neighbour will not mistake you.
SCOTTISH PROVERB

Other men's sins are before our eyes; our own are behind our backs.
SENECA

Most of us do not like to look inside ourselves for the same reason we don't like to open a letter that has bad news.
FULTON J. SHEEN

It is a great grace of God to practise self-examination; but too much is as bad as too little.
ST. TERESA OF AVILA

Self-Love

We would worry less about what others think of us if we realised how seldom they do.
ETHEL BARRETT

It is our self-importance, not our misery, that gets in His way.
DANIEL CONSIDINE

Self-love is cunning, it pushes and insinuates itself into everything, while making us believe it is not there at all.
ST. FRANCIS DE SALES

You have an ego – a consciousness of being an individual. But that doesn't mean that you are to worship yourself, to think constantly of yourself, and to live entirely for self.
BILLY GRAHAM

Your life is without a foundation, if in any matter, you choose on your own behalf.
DAG HAMMARSKJOLD

Self-love is a mote in every man's eye.
ENGLISH PROVERB

He who lives to benefit himself confers on the world a benefit when he dies.
QUINTUS TERTULLIAN

Self-centredness completely vitiates communication – with either God or man.
HUBERT VAN ZELLER

Self-Respect

(*See also* Pride)

Never esteem anything as of advantage to thee that shall make thee break thy word or lose thy self-respect.
MARCUS AURELIUS

First learn to love yourself, and then you can love me.
ST. BERNARD OF CLAIRVAUX

If you want to be respected by others the great thing is to respect yourself.
FEODOR DOSTOEVSKI

Self-respect and honour cannot be protected by others. They are for each individual himself or herself to guard.
MOHANDAS GANDHI

He who makes a beast of himself gets rid of the pain of being a man.
SAMUEL JOHNSON

No one can make you feel inferior without your consent.
ELEANOR ROOSEVELT

Self-respect is the noblest garment with which a man may clothe himself, the most elevating feeling with which the mind can be inspired.
SAMUEL SMILES

Take yourself as you are, and do not try to live by one part alone and starve the other.
JANET ERSKINE-STUART

Sentiment

(*See also* Emotion)

Sentiment is the main opponent of spirituality.
ART GLASSER

Trust not to thy feeling, for whatever it be now, it will quickly be changed into another thing.
THOMAS À KEMPIS

Seeing's believing but feeling is God's own truth.
IRISH PROVERB

Analysis, synthesis, reasoning, abstraction, and experience, wishing to take counsel together, begin by banishing sentiment, which carries away the light when it departs, and leaves them in darkness.
JOSEPH ROUX

Never trust a sentimentalist. They are all alike, pretenders to virtue, at heart selfish frauds and sensualists.
J. B. YEATS

Sermons

(*See also* Preaching)

Every man is a priest, even involuntarily; his conduct is an unspoken sermon, which is for ever preaching to others.
HENRI FRÉDÉRIC AMIEL

The sermons I like best are those that have more love for one's neighbour than indignation against him.
ST. FRANCIS DE SALES

It requires great listening as well as great preaching to make a great sermon.
JOHN ANDREW HOLMES

He that has but one word of God before him, and out of that word cannot make a sermon, can never be a preacher.
MARTIN LUTHER

The half-baked sermon causes spiritual indigestion.
AUSTIN O'MALLEY

A sermon is a proclamation of the generous love of God in Christ, or it is not a Christian sermon.
NORMAN PITTENGER

Some clergy prepare their sermons; others prepare themselves.
SAMUEL WILBERFORCE

Service

Ready service, according to our ability, even in very small things and even if rendered by women, is acceptable to God.
ST. BASIL

In Jesus the service of God and the service of the least of the brethren were one.
DIETRICH BONHOEFFER

No one gives himself freely and willingly to God's service unless, having tasted his Fatherly love, he is drawn to love and worship him in return.
JOHN CALVIN

If one were in a rapture like St. Paul, and there was a sick man needing help, I think it would be best to throw off the rapture and show love by service to the needy.
MEISTER ECKHART

The service we render for others is really the rent we pay for our room on this earth.
WILFRED GRENFELL

You have not done enough, you have never done enough, so long as it is still possible that you have something to contribute.
DAG HAMMARSKJOLD

Service is God's way of releasing the individual, whereas slavery is man's way of destroying him.
MICHAEL HARPER

The service that counts is the service that costs.
HOWARD HENDRICKS

He that serves God for money will serve the Devil for better wages.
ENGLISH PROVERB

He who serves is preserved.
LATIN PROVERB

There is no higher religion than human service. To work for the common good is the greatest creed.
ALBERT SCHWEITZER

If she (Martha) had been like the Magdalene, rapt in contemplation, there would have been no one to give to eat to this divine Guest.
ST. TERESA OF AVILA

Sex

About sex especially men are born unbalanced; we might almost say men are born mad. They scarcely reach sanity till they reach sanctity.
G. K. CHESTERTON

Whenever Christ was confronted by people in sexual disarray, he took good care to safeguard sexuality by reminding them that they had to avoid sin; that is to say to use their sexuality in a fully human way.
JACK DOMINIAN

Love may or may not include sexual attraction. It may express itself in sexual desire. But sexual desire is not love. Desire is quite compatible with personal hatred, or contempt, or indifference.
JOHN MACMURRAY

Sexuality throws no light upon love, but only through love can we learn to understand sexuality.
EUGEN ROSENSTOCK-HUESSY

Sex has become one of the most discussed subjects of modern times. The Victorians pretended it did not exist; the moderns pretend that nothing else exists.
FULTON J. SHEEN

A person who despises or undervalues or neglects the opposite sex will soon need humanising.
CHARLES SIMMONS

I lose my respect for the man who can make the mystery of sex the subject of a coarse jest, yet, when you speak earnestly and seriously on the subject, is silent.
HENRY DAVID THOREAU

Shame

It is a shame not to be shameless.
ST. AUGUSTINE OF HIPPO

He that has no shame has no conscience.
THOMAS FULLER

Where there is yet shame, there may in time be virtue.
SAMUEL JOHNSON

None but the shamefaced lose.
FRENCH PROVERB

I never wonder to see men wicked, but I often wonder to see them not ashamed.
JONATHAN SWIFT

I have known all evils; virtue can surmount them, but what generous heart can endure shame?
FRANÇOIS MARIE VOLTAIRE

Sickness

Before all things and above all things, care must be taken of the sick, so that they may be served in every deed as Christ himself . . . But let the sick on their part consider that they are being served for the honour of God, and not provoke their brethren who are serving them by their unreasonable demands. Yet they should be patiently borne with, because from such as these is gained a more abundant reward.
ST. BENEDICT

The best prayers have often more groans than words.
JOHN BUNYAN

Long illnesses are good schools of mercy for those who tend the sick, and of loving patience for those who suffer.
JEAN PIERRE CAMUS

Make sickness itself a prayer.
ST. FRANCIS DE SALES

The sick are to realise that they are sons of God by the very fact that the scourge of discipline chastises them. For unless it were his plan to give them an inheritance after their chastisements, he would not trouble to school them in afflictions.
POPE ST. GREGORY I

Jesus came to save persons, not just souls. He came to help the suffering in whatever way they were suffering. Sickness of the body was part of the kingdom of Satan he had come to destroy.
FRANCIS MACNUTT

Disease makes men more physical; it leaves them nothing but body.
THOMAS MANN

Sickness is every man's master.
DANISH PROVERB

Sickness shows us what we are.
LATIN PROVERB

I enjoy convalescence. It is the part that makes the illness worthwhile.
GEORGE BERNARD SHAW

Silence

(*See also* Quietness and Solitude)

To forbear replying to an unjust reproach, and overlook it with a generous or, if possible, with an entire neglect of it, is one of the most heroic acts of a great mind.
JOSEPH ADDISON

It is in silence that God is known, and through mysteries that He declares Himself.
ROBERT H. BENSON

Mere silence is not wisdom, for wisdom consists in knowing when and how to speak and when and where to keep silent.
JEAN PIERRE CAMUS

The very best and utmost of attainment in this life is to remain still and let God act and speak in thee.
MEISTER ECKHART

Christ is the still point of the turning world.
T. S. ELIOT

219

How can you expect God to speak in that gentle and inward voice which melts the soul, when you are making so much noise with your rapid reflections? Be silent, and God will speak again.
FRANÇOIS FENELON

The Father uttered one Word; that Word is his Son, and he utters him for ever in everlasting silence; and in silence the soul has to hear it.
ST. JOHN OF THE CROSS

Better to remain silent and be thought a fool than to speak and to remove all doubt.
ABRAHAM LINCOLN

'Rest in the Lord; wait patiently for Him.' In Hebrew, 'be silent to God and let Him mould thee.' Keep still, and He will mould thee to the right shape.
MARTIN LUTHER

With silence one irritates the Devil.
BULGARIAN PROVERB

Be silent about great things; let them grow inside you. Never discuss them: dicussion is so limiting and distracting. It makes things grow smaller. You think you swallow things when they ought to swallow you. Before all greatness, be silent – in art, in music, in religion: silence.
FRIEDRICH VON HUGEL

The greatest ideas, the most profound thoughts, and the most beautiful poetry are born from the womb of silence.
WILLIAM A. WARD

Simplicity

One can acquire 'simplicity', but 'simpleness' is innate. Education and culture may bring 'simplicity' – indeed, it ought to be one of their essential aims – but simpleness is a gift.
DIETRICH BONHOEFFER

All great things are simple, and many can be expressed in a single word: freedom; justice; honour; duty; mercy; hope.
SIR WINSTON CHURCHILL

Simple and sincere minds are never more than half mistaken.
JOSEPH JOUBERT

Blissful are the simple, for they shall have much peace.
THOMAS À KEMPIS

Sin

Everyone who commits sin is the slave of sin.
ST. AMBROSE

To sin is nothing else than not to render to God his due.
ST. ANSELM

Sin is not a monster to be mused on, but an impotence to be got rid of.
MATTHEW ARNOLD

The greatest fault is to be conscious of none.
THOMAS CARLYLE

To sin is human, but to persist in sin is devilish.
ST. CATHERINE OF SIENA

Keep yourself from opportunity and God will keep you from sins.
JACOB CATS

God loves us *in* our sin, and *through* our sin, and goes on loving us, looking for a response.
DONALD COGGAN

Sin is a power in our life: let us fairly understand that it can only be met by another power.
HENRY DRUMMOND

Can any sin be called light, since every sin involves some contempt of God.
EUCHERIUS

Sin is not hurtful because it is forbidden, but sin is forbidden because it is hurtful.
BENJAMIN FRANKLIN

Beware the pious fool, and the wise sinner.
IBN GABIROL

I see no fault that I might not have committed myself.
JOHANN WOLFGANG VON GOETHE

Let it be assured that to do no wrong is really superhuman, and belongs to God alone.
GREGORY OF NAZIANZEN

When thou attackest the roots of sin, fix thy thought more upon the God whom thou desirest than upon the sin which thou abhorrest.
WALTER HILTON

Sin is always a squandering of our humanity, a squandering of our most precious values.
POPE JOHN PAUL II

As long as we be meddling with any part of sin, we shall never see clearly the blissful countenance of our Lord.
JULIAN OF NORWICH

All the old primitive sins are not dead, but are crouching in the dark corners of our modern hearts.
CARL GUSTAV JUNG

Sin is essentially a departure from God.
MARTIN LUTHER

The ultimate proof of the sinner is that he does not know his own sin.
MARTIN LUTHER

The most serious sin is one of thought, the sin of pride.
POPE PAUL VI

Every sin brings its punishment with it.
ENGLISH PROVERB

Sin can be well guarded, but cannot be free from anxiety.
LATIN PROVERB

Almost all our faults are more pardonable than the methods we think up to hide them.
FRANÇOIS DE LA ROCHEFOUCAULD

The first step towards the soul's recovery is the knowledge of the sin committed.
SENECA

No sin is small. No grain of sand is small in the mechanism of a watch.
JEREMY TAYLOR

For the religious man to do wrong is to defy his King; for the Christian, it is to wound his Friend.
WILLIAM TEMPLE

Be ashamed of nothing but sin: not of fetching wood, or drawing water, if time permit; not of cleaning your own shoes or your neighbour's.
JOHN WESLEY

Sincerity

(*See also* Integrity)

Be what thou seemest! Live thy creed!
HORATIUS BONAR

Sincerity is never ludicrous; it is always respectable.
CHARLOTTE BRONTË

The sincere alone can recognise sincerity.
THOMAS CARLYLE

The Devil is sincere, but he is sincerely wrong.
BILLY GRAHAM

If you take heed what you are within, you shall not reckon what men say of you. Man looks on the visage and God on the heart. Man considers the deeds and God praises the thoughts.
THOMAS À KEMPIS

Be suspicious of your sincerity when you are the advocate of that upon which your livelihood depends.
JOHN LANCASTER SPALDING

Slander

Too often do we call the truths which offend us by the name of slander.
JEAN PIERRE CAMUS

Slander flings stones at itself.
THOMAS FULLER

Whispered insinuations are the rhetoric of the Devil.
JOHANN WOLFGANG VON GOETHE

If slander be a snake, it is a winged one – it flies as well as creeps.
DOUGLAS JERROLD

Slander is a shipwreck by a dry tempest.
ENGLISH PROVERB

What is slander: A verdict of 'guilty' pronounced in the absence of the accused, with closed doors, without defence or appeal, by an interested and prejudiced judge.
JOSEPH ROUX

The slanderous tongue kills three: the slandered, the slanderer, and him who listens to the slander.
THE TALMUD

Slavery

The peculiar characteristic of slavery is to be always in fear.
ST. AMBROSE

Whether slaves or freemen, we are all one in Christ, and have to serve alike in the army of the same Lord.
ST. BENEDICT

In Africa, as elsewhere, it was the practice of primitive tribes to war against one another and, when victorious, to massacre or enslave the conquered. From the latter process arose the practice of trading in and transporting slaves.
ARTHUR BRYANT

Excessive liberty leads both nations and individuals into excessive slavery.
MARCUS TULLIUS CICERO

Slavery still exists in some thirty countries and is likely to survive in many of them for a long time to come.
NOËL MOSTERT

But do you, who are slaves, be subject to your master, as to God's representative, in reverence and fear.
TEACHING OF THE TWELVE APOSTLES

Sleep

For what else is sleep but a daily death which does not completely remove man hence nor detain him too long? And what else is death, but a very long and very deep sleep from which God arouses man?
ST. AUGUSTINE OF HIPPO

Lying in bed would be an altogether perfect and supreme experience if only one had a coloured pencil long enough to draw on the ceiling.
G. K. CHESTERTON

Don't count sheep if you can't sleep. Talk to the shepherd.
PAUL FROST

Sleep is, in fine, so like death I dare not trust it without my prayers.
THOMAS FULLER

Sleep that knits up the ravell'd sleave of care.
WILLIAM SHAKESPEARE

The death of each day's life, sore Labour's bath,
Balm of hurt minds, great nature's second course,
Chief nourisher in life's feast.
WILLIAM SHAKESPEARE

Social Justice

Through love the supreme norm remains the will of God, who wants man's total well-being; what helps man, our neighbour or our neighbours, is right.
HANS KUNG

The aim and purpose of socialist doctrine is the promotion on earth of human equality and social justice. This – with different emphasis – is also part of the doctrine of Christianity.
JULIUS K. NYERERE

It is impossible to be just if one is not generous.
JOSEPH ROUX

Disbelief in Christianity is not so much to be dreaded as its acceptance with a complete denial of it in society and politics.
MARK RUTHERFORD

Society must be made to rest upon justice and love, without which it is but organised wrong.
JOHN LANCASTER SPALDING

If the Christian tries to spread the good news of salvation through Jesus Christ, he should also join in the fight against social injustice and political oppression.
JOHN R. W. STOTT

The preaching of the Gospel and its acceptance imply a social revolution whereby the hungry are fed and justice becomes the right of all.
LEON JOSEPH SUENENS

Society

What is not good for the hive is not good for the bees.
MARCUS AURELIUS

Human beings and human societies are not structures that are built or machines that are forged. They are plants that grow and must be tended as such.
SIR WINSTON CHURCHILL

To seek the society of others and to shun it are two blameworthy extremes in the devotion of those who live in the world.
ST. FRANCIS DE SALES

Civil society was renovated in every part by the teachings of Christianity. In the strength of that renewal the human race was lifted up to better things. Nay, it was brought back from death to life.
POPE LEO XIII

Society has always seemed to demand a little more from human beings than it will get in practice.
GEORGE ORWELL

The final decision as to what the future of a society shall be depends not on how near its organisation is to perfection, but on the degree of worthiness in its individual members.
ALBERT SCHWEITZER

There is no structural organisation of society which can bring about the coming of the Kingdom of God on earth, since all systems can be perverted by the selfishness of man.
WILLIAM TEMPLE

Solitude

(*See also* Quietness and Science)

Enter into the inner chamber of your mind. Shut out all things save God and whatever may aid you in seeking God; and having barred the door of your chamber, seek him.
ST. ANSELM OF CANTERBURY

This great misfortune – to be incapable of solitude.
JEAN DE LA BRUYÉRE

It is known to many that we need solitude to find ourselves. Perhaps it is not so well known that we need solitude to find our fellows. Even the Saviour is described as reaching mankind through the wilderness.
HAVELOCK ELLIS

It is easy in the world to live after the world's opinion; it is easy in solitude to live after your own; but the great man is he who in the midst of the crowd keeps with perfect sweetness the independence of solitude.
RALPH WALDO EMERSON

Solitude is a wonderful thing when one is at peace with oneself and when there is a definite task to be accomplished.
JOHANN WOLFGANG VON GOETHE

There is no true solitude except interior solitude.
THOMAS MERTON

He who does not enjoy solitude will not love freedom.
ARTHUR SCHOPENHAUER

A wise man is never less alone than when he is alone.
JONATHAN SWIFT

I never found the companion that was so companionable as solitude.
HENRY DAVID THOREAU

To go up alone into the mountain and come back as an ambassador to the world, has ever been the method of humanity's best friends.
EVELYN UNDERHILL

Practise the art of 'aloneness' and you will discover the treasure of tranquility. Develop the art of solitude and you will unearth the gift of serenity.
WILLIAM W. WARD

Sorrow

(*See also* Grief)

Sorrow is given us on purpose to cure us of sin.
ST. JOHN CHRYSOSTOM

Sorrow makes us all children again – destroys all differences of intellect. The wisest know nothing.
RALPH WALDO EMERSON

Nothing but sin should sadden us, and to this sorrow for sin it is necessary that holy joy should be attached.
ST. FRANCIS DE SALES

Sorrow is a fruit; God does not make it grow on limbs too weak to bear it.
VICTOR HUGO

Sorrow you can hold, however desolating, if nobody speaks to you. If they speak, you break down.
BEDE JARRETT

Sorrow, like rain, makes roses and mud.
AUSTIN O'MALLEY

Sorrow makes silence her best orator.
ENGLISH PROVERB

Where there is sorrow, there is holy ground.
OSCAR WILDE

Spiritual Life

Every advance in spiritual life has its corresponding dangers; every step that we rise nearer God increases the depths of the gulf into which we may fall.
ROBERT H. BENSON

He who believes himself to be far advanced in the spiritual life has not even made a good beginning.
JEAN PIERRE CAMUS

It is right that you should begin again every day. There is no better way to finish the spiritual life than to be ever beginning it over again, and never to think that you have done enough.
ST. FRANCIS DE SALES

Spiritual rose bushes are not like natural rose bushes; with these latter the thorns remain but the roses pass, with the former the thorns pass and the roses remain.
ST. FRANCIS DE SALES

Every man has two journeys to make through life. There is the outer journey, with its various incidents and the milestones . . . There is also an inner journey, a spiritual Odyssey, with a secret history of its own.
WILLIAM R. INGE

The more a man is united within himself, and interiorly simple, the more and higher things doth he understand without labour; because he receiveth the light of understanding from above.
THOMAS À KEMPIS

Spirituality really means 'Holy Spirit at work', a profound action of the Holy Spirit in his Church, renewing that Church from the inside.
LEON JOSEPH SUENENS

Interior growth is only possible when we commit ourselves with and to others.
JEAN VANIER

State

(*See also* Government)

What is a state but a multitude of men, brought together into some bond of agreement.
ST. AUGUSTINE OF HIPPO

A state is an association of families and their common affairs, governed by a supreme power and by reason.
JEAN BODIN

A state without the means of some change is without the means of its conservation.
EDMUND BURKE

The office of government is not to confer happiness but to give men opportunity to work out happiness for themselves.
WILLIAM ELLERY CHANNING

Stewardship

Stewardship is what a man does after he says, 'I believe'.
W. H. GREEVER

The two things which, of all others, most want to be under a strict rule, and which are the greatest blessings to ourselves and to others, when they are rightly used, are our time and our money.
WILLIAM LAW

Stewardship is the acceptance from God of personal responsibility for all of life and life's affairs.
ROSWELL C. LONG

Strength

When You are our strength, it is strength indeed, but when our strength is our own it is only weakness.
ST. AUGUSTINE OF HIPPO

It is a sign of strength, not of weakness, to admit that you don't know all the answers.
JOHN P. LOUGHRANE

When God wants to move a mountain, he does not take a bar of iron, but he takes a little worm. The fact is, we have too much strength. We are not weak enough. It is not our strength that we want. One drop of God's strength is worth more than all the world.
DWIGHT L. MOODY

When we feel us too bold, remember our own feebleness. When we feel us too faint, remember Christ's strength.
SIR THOMAS MORE

One has always strength enough to bear the misfortunes of one's friends.
ENGLISH PROVERB

Strenuousness is the open foe of attainment. The strength that wins is calm and has an exhaustless source in its passive depths.
RABINDRANATH TAGORE

Success

The figure of the Crucified invalidates all thought which takes success for its standard.
DIETRICH BONHOEFFER

Try not to become a man of success but rather try to become a man of value.
ALBERT EINSTEIN

The religious man is the only successful man.
FREDERICK W. FABER

Since modern man experiences himself both as the seller and as the commodity to be sold on the market, his self-esteem depends on conditions beyond his control. If he is 'successful', he is valuable; if he is not, he is worthless.
ERICH FROMM

Real success is not in having climbed the heights but in having maintained a foothold there.
PAUL FROST

Success consists of getting up just one more time than you fall.
OLIVER GOLDSMITH

Let us work as if success depended upon ourselves alone; but with heartfelt conviction that we are doing nothing and God everything.
ST. IGNATIUS LOYOLA

Success makes a fool seem wise.
ENGLISH PROVERB

Success, which is something so simple in the end, is made up of thousands of things, we never fully know what.
RAINER MARIA RILKE

Suffering

(*See also* Pain)

A Christian is someone who shares the sufferings of God in the world.
DIETRICH BONHOEFFER

One ounce of patient suffering is worth far more than a pound of action.
JEAN PIERRE CAMUS

When one is in very great pain and fear it is extremely difficult to pray coherently, and I could only raise my mind in anguish to God and ask for strength to hold on.
SHEILA CASSIDY

The strangest truth of the Gospel is that redemption comes through suffering.
MILO L. CHAPMAN

Jesus did not come to explain away suffering or remove it. He came to fill it with His Presence.
PAUL CLAUDEL

Take the cross he sends, as it is, and not as you imagine it to be.
CORNELIA CONNELLY

The only cure for suffering is to face it head on, grasp it round the neck, and use it.
MARY CRAIG

The hardest heart and grossest ignorance must disappear before the fire of suffering without anger and malice.
MOHANDAS GANDHI

The chief pang of most trials is not so much the actual suffering itself as our own spirit of resistance to it.
JEAN NICHOLAS GROU

The purest suffering hears and carries in its train the purest understanding.
ST. JOHN OF THE CROSS

He who knoweth how to suffer will enjoy much peace. Such a one is a conqueror of himself and lord of the world, a friend of Christ, and an heir of Heaven.
THOMAS À KEMPIS

Unearned suffering is redemptive.
MARTIN LUTHER KING, JR.

Know how sublime a thing it is to suffer and be strong.
HENRY WORDSWORTH LONGFELLOW

Our suffering is not worth the name of suffering. When I consider my crosses, tribulations, and temptations, I shame myself almost to death, thinking what are they in comparison of the sufferings of my blessed Saviour Christ Jesus.
MARTIN LUTHER

It is a glorious thing to be indifferent to suffering, but only to one's own suffering.
ROBERT LYND

The greatness of our God must be tested by the desire we have of suffering for his sake.
PHILIP NERI

We all suffer for each other, and gain by each other's suffering; for man never stands alone here, though he will stand by himself one day hereafter; but here he is a social being, and goes forward to his longed for home as one of a large company.
JOHN HENRY NEWMAN

He who suffers much will know much.
GREEK PROVERB

Torture us, rack us, condemn us, crush us; your cruelty only proves our innocence. That is why God suffers us to suffer all this.
QUINTUS TERTULLIAN

Suffering is the very best gift He has to give us. He gives it only to his chosen friends.
ST. THÉRÈSE OF LISIEUX

It is by those who have suffered that the world has been advanced.
COUNT LEO TOLSTOY

Suffering is the money with which one buys heaven.
THEOPHANE VÉNARD

Sunday

Sunday clears away the rust of the whole week.
JOSEPH ADDISON

God ended all the world's array,
And rested on the seventh day:
His holy voice proclaimed it blest,
And named it for the sabbath rest.
THE VENERABLE BEDE

There are many persons who look on Sunday as a sponge to wipe out the sins of the week.
HENRY WARD BEECHER

The Lord's Day is so called because, on that day, the joy of our Lord's resurrection is celebrated. This day the Jews did not observe, but it was declared by the Christians in honour of the Lord's resurrection, and the celebration began from that time.
ST. ISIDORE

Sunday, indeed, is the day on which we hold our common assembly because it is the first day on which God, transforming the darkness and matter, created the world; and our Saviour, Jesus Christ, arose from the dead on the same day. For they crucified Him on the day before, that of Saturn, and on the day after, Sunday, He appeared to His apostles and disciples, and taught them the things which we have passed on to you also for consideration.
ST. JUSTIN MARTYR

Everything has its weekday side and its Sunday side.
G. C. LICHTENBERG

The Sabbath is the golden clasp that binds together the volume of the week.
J. C. MACAULEY

Come day, go day, God send Sunday.
ENGLISH PROVERB

If you want to kill Christianity, you must abolish Sunday.
FRANÇOIS MARIE VOLTAIRE

Superstition

There is a superstition in avoiding superstition.
FRANCIS BACON

Superstition is a religion of feeble minds.
EDMUND BURKE

The Devil divides the world between atheism and superstition.
GEORGE HERBERT

Superstition is the cruellest thing in the world. Faith is to live in the sun. Superstition is to sit in darkness.
KATHERINE T. HINKSON

Sympathy

Next to love, sympathy is the dimmest passion of the human heart.
EDMUND BURKE

Harmony of aim, and identity of conclusion, is the secret of the sympathetic life.
RALPH WALDO EMERSON

Nothing is more salutary for those who are in affliction than to become consolers.
MAURICE HULST

Tact

Silence is not always tact, and it is tact that is golden – not silence.
SAMUEL BUTLER

Mention not a halter in the house of him that was hanged.
GEORGE HERBERT

Tact is the ability to describe others as they see themselves.
ABRAHAM LINCOLN

Talent

(*See also* Genius)

Doing easily what others find difficult is talent; doing what is impossible is genius.
HENRI FRÉDÉRIC AMIEL

Talents are distributed unevenly, it is true: to one ten, and to another five; but each has one pound, all alike.
ROBERT H. BENSON

If people knew how hard I have to work to gain my mastery, it would not seem wonderful at all.
MICHELANGELO
BUONARROTI

Iron rusts from disuse; stagnant water loses its purity, and in cold weather becomes frozen; even so does inaction sap the vigours of the mind.
LEONARDO DA VINCI

There is a great deal of unmapped country within us.
GEORGE ELIOT

No one respects a talent that is concealed.
DESIDERIUS ERASMUS

Talent is the capacity of doing anything that depends on application and industry; it is voluntary power, while genius is involuntary.
WILLIAM HAZLITT

Alas for those who never sing, but die with all their music in them.
OLIVER WENDELL HOLMES

Talent is God-given; be thankful. Conceit is self-given, be careful.
THOMAS LA MANCE

Nobody don't never get nothing for nothing nowhere, no time, no how.
AMERICAN PROVERB

Often the greatest talents lie unseen.
LATIN PROVERB

Nature has concealed at the bottom of our minds talents and abilities of which we are not aware.
FRANÇOIS DE LA
ROCHEFOUCAULD

No talent can survive the blight of neglect.
EDGAR A. WHITNEY

The real tragedy of life is not in being limited to one talent, but in the failure to use the one talent.
EDGAR W. WORK

Talk

(*See also* Communication, Conversation and Words)

Speaking without thinking is shooting without aiming.
WILLIAM G. BENHAM

Speak when you are angry and you will make the best speech you will ever regret.
AMBROSE BIERCE

I suspect that the real reason that an Englishman does not talk is that he cannot leave off talking. I suspect that my solitary countrymen, hiding in separate railway compartments, are not so much retiring as a race of Trappists escaping from a race of talkers.
G. K. CHESTERTON

If you don't say anything, you won't be called on to repeat it.
CALVIN COOLIDGE

Insinuations are the rhetoric of the Devil.
JOHANN WOLFGANG VON
GOETHE

The wise hand does not all that the foolish mouth speaks.
GEORGE HERBERT

Think twice before you speak and then say it to yourself.
ELBERT HUBBARD

Don't say all you'd like to say lest you hear something you wouldn't like to hear.
SEUMAS MACMANUS

A word rashly spoken cannot be brought back by a chariot and four horses.
CHINESE PROVERB

The greatest talkers are always the least doers.
ENGLISH PROVERB

Man is caught by his tongue, and an ox by his horns.
RUSSIAN PROVERB

He who talks much is sometimes right.
SPANISH PROVERB

Temperance

(*See also* Self-Denial)

Temperance is the moderating of one's desires in obedience to reason.
MARCUS TULLIUS CICERO

Temperance is to the body what religion is to the soul – the foundation of health, strength and peace.
TYRON EDWARDS

Temperance is the control of all the functions of our bodies. The man who refuses liquor, goes in for apple pie, and develops a paunch, is no ethical leader for me.
JOHN ERSKINE

If we give more to the flesh than we ought, we nourish our enemy; if we give not to her necessity what we ought, we destroy a citizen.
POPE ST. GREGORY I

Temperance is corporal piety; it is the preservation of divine order in the body.
THEODORE PARKER

To go beyond the bounds of moderation is to outrage humanity.
BLAISE PASCAL

Temperate temperance is best; intemperate temperance injures the cause of temperance.
MARK TWAIN

Temptation

He who with his whole heart draws near unto God must of necessity be proved by temptation and trial.
ST. ALBERT THE GREAT

The Devil tempts that he may ruin; God tempts that He may crown.
ST. AMBROSE

It is good to be without vices, but it is not good to be without temptations.
WALTER BAGEHOT

Temptations, when we first meet them, are as the lion that roared upon Samson; but if we overcome them, the next time we see them we shall find a nest of honey within them.
JOHN BUNYAN

No man is matriculated to the art of life till he has been well tempted.
GEORGE ELIOT

As the Sandwich-Islander believes that the strength and valour of the enemy he kills passes into himself, so we gain the strength of the temptations we resist.
RALPH WALDO EMERSON

Every moment of resistance to temptation is a victory.
FREDERICK W. FABER

To realise God's presence is the one sovereign remedy against temptation.
FRANÇOIS FENELON

If it takes temptation and sin to show God in his true colours and Satan in his, something has been saved from the wreck.
MICHAEL GREEN

No man is so perfect and holy as not to have sometimes temptations; and we cannot be wholly without them.
THOMAS À KEMPIS

There is no order so holy, nor place so retired, where there are not temptations and adversities.
THOMAS À KEMPIS

God chooses that men should be tried, but let a man beware of tempting his neighbour.
GEORGE MACDONALD

The heron's a saint when there are no fish in sight.
BENGALESE PROVERB

God promises a safe landing but not a calm passage.
BULGARIAN PROVERB

To pray against temptations, and yet to rush into occasions, is to thrust your fingers into the fire, and then pray they might not be burnt.
THOMAS SECKER

You are not tempted because you are evil; you are tempted because you are human.
FULTON J. SHEEN

Some temptations come to the industrious, but all temptations attack the idle.
CHARLES H. SPURGEON

The greatest of all evils is not to be tempted, because there are then grounds for believing that the Devil looks upon us as his property.
JOHN VIANNEY

Thanksgiving

(*See also* Gratitude)

No duty is more urgent than that of returning thanks.
ST. AMBROSE

Pride slays thanksgiving, but an humble mind is the soil out of which thanks naturally grows. A proud man is seldom a grateful man, for he never thinks he gets as much as he deserves.
HENRY WARD BEECHER

We should spend as much time in thanking God for His benefits as we do in asking Him for them.
ST. VINCENT DE PAUL

Awake with a winged heart, and give thanks for another day of loving!
KAHLIL GIBRAN

Joy untouched by thankfulness is always suspect.
THEODOR HAECKER

One act of thanksgiving when things go wrong with us is worth a thousand thanks when things are agreeable to our inclination.
JOHN OF AVILA

Give thanks frequently to God for all the benefits he has conferred on you, that you may be worthy to receive more.
ST. LOUIS IX

The thankful heart is the only door that opens to God.
JOE ORTON

Who does not thank for little will not thank for much.
ESTONIAN PROVERB

Three things for which thanks are due: an invitation, a gift and a warning.
WELSH PROVERB

Were there no God, we would be in this glorious world with grateful hearts: and no one to thank.
CHRISTINA ROSSETTI

Theology

Theology deserves to be called the highest wisdom, for everything is viewed in the light of the first cause.
ST. THOMAS AQUINAS

Theology is but our ideas of truth classified and arranged.
HENRY WARD BEECHER

Theology is only articulate religion.
G. K. CHESTERTON

The broad ethics of Jesus were quickly narrowed to village theologies.
RALPH WALDO EMERSON

Love is the abridgement of all theology.
ST. FRANCIS DE SALES

Your theology is what you are when the talking stops and the action starts.
COLIN MORRIS

The publican stood afar off and beat his breast and said, 'God be merciful to me, a sinner.' I tell you that man had the finest theology of any man in all England.
CHARLES H. SPURGEON

Theology, like gold, is where you find it.
BRUCE VAWTER

Thought

(*See also* Mind)

Thought is a kind of sight of the mind.
ST. AUGUSTINE OF HIPPO

When evil thoughts come into your heart, dash them at once on the rock of Christ.
ST. BENEDICT

Men have the power of thinking that they may avoid sin.
ST. JOHN CHRYSOSTOM

When the first spark of thought appeared on the earth, life found it had brought into the world a power capable of criticising it and judging it.
P. TEILHARD DE CHARDIN

There is no expedient to which a man will not go to avoid the real labour of thinking.
THOMAS EDISON

It isn't what people think that is important, but the reason they think what they think.
EUGENE IONESCO

Where all think alike, no one thinks very much.
WALTER LIPPMANN

Occupy your minds with good thoughts, or the enemy will fill them with bad ones: unoccupied they cannot be.
SIR THOMAS MORE

By space the universe embraces me and swallows me up like an atom, by thought I embrace the universe.
BLAISE PASCAL

Men fear thought as they fear nothing else on earth – more than ruin, more even than death.
BERTRAND RUSSELL

Time

It is the wisest who grieve most at loss of time.
DANTE ALIGHIERI

Time is a three-fold present: the present as we experience it, the past as a present memory, and the future as a present expectation.
ST. AUGUSTINE OF HIPPO

He who kills time commits suicide.
FREDERICK BECK

Time must always ultimately teach.
HILAIRE BELLOC

If a man has no time or only a short time for seeing people, you can be fairly sure that he is neither very important nor very busy.
JOHN S. CHURCHILL

The voice of Time cries to man, 'Advance'. Time is for his advancement and improvement, for his greater worth, his greater happiness, his better life.
CHARLES DICKENS

Time deals gently with those who take it gently.
ANATOLE FRANCE

Dost thou love Life? Then do not squander Time, for that's the stuff Life is made of.
BENJAMIN FRANKLIN

One always has time enough if one will apply it.
JOHANN WOLFGANG VON GOETHE

Time is a circus, always packing up and moving away.
BEN HECHT

Do not walk through time without leaving worthy evidence of your passage.
POPE JOHN XXIII

The great rule of moral conduct is, next to God, to respect time.
JOHANN K. LAVATER

Next to grace time is the most precious gift of God. Yet how much of both we waste. We say that time does many things. It teaches us many lessons, weans us from many follies, strengthens us in good resolves, and heals many wounds. And yet it does none of these things. Time does nothing. But time is the condition of all these things which God does in time. Time is full of eternity. As we use it so shall we be. Every day has its opportunities, every hour its offer of grace.
HENRY E. MANNING

Throughout the whole (New Testament) there runs the conviction that the time looked forward to by the prophets has in fact arrived in history with the advent of Jesus Christ . . . The time of Jesus is *kairos* − a time of opportunity. To embrace the opportunity means salvation; to neglect it, disaster. There is no third course.
JOHN MARSH

Time and tide wait for no man.
ENGLISH PROVERB

There is no mortar that time will not loose.
FRENCH PROVERB

The moment passed is no longer; the future may never be; the present is all of which man is the master.
JEAN JACQUES ROUSSEAU

He who neglects the present moment throws away all he has.
JOHANN C. F. VON SCHILLER

Come what, come may, time and the hour run through the roughest day.
WILLIAM SHAKESPEARE

Time is the deposit each one has in the bank of God and no one knows the balance.
RALPH W. SOCKMAN

Tolerance

I have seen gross intolerance shown in support of tolerance.
SAMUEL TAYLOR COLERIDGE

Tolerance is the posture and cordial effort to understand another's beliefs, practices, and habits without necessarily sharing or accepting them.
JOSHUA LIEBMAN

The modern theory that you should always treat the religious convictions of other people with profound respect finds no support in the Gospels. Mutual tolerance of religious views is the product not of faith, but of doubt.
ARNOLD LUNN

Torture

(*See also* Suffering)

To shelter or give medical aid to a man on the run, from a police force which will torture and perhaps kill him, is an act of Christian love demanded by Christ in the Gospel and is no more a political act than giving first aid and a cup of tea to a Member of Parliament who has a car smash outside your door.
SHEILA CASSIDY

Wild animals never kill for sport. Man is the only one to whom the torture and death of his fellow-creatures is amusing in itself.
JAMES A. FROUDE

Civilised mankind has of will ceased to torture, but in our process of being civilised we have won, I suspect, intensified capacity to suffer.
S. WEIR MITCHELL

Tradition

Scripture has been God's way of fixing tradition, and rendering it trustworthy at any distance of time.
HENRY ALFORD

Since it has been shown that the Church's traditions are subsequent to the Church, it follows that the Church does not derive its authority from the traditions but that the traditions derive their authority from the Church.
DANTE ALIGHIERI

There is a difference between apostolic tradition and ecclesiastical tradition, the former being the foundation of the latter. They cannot therefore be coordinated.
OSCAR CULLMANN

So that the river of tradition may come down to us we must continually dredge its bed.
HENRI DE LUBAC

Tradition is a guide and not a gaoler.
W. SOMERSET MAUGHAM

Tradition and conscience are the two wings given to the human soul to reach the truth.
GIUSEPPE MAZZINI

Tradition has its legitimate place and its true source. By tradition is meant, what has ever been held, as far as we know, though we do not know how it came to be held, and for that very reason think it true, because else it would not be held.
JOHN HENRY NEWMAN

Tradition is the living faith of the dead; traditionalism is the dead faith of the living.
JAROSLAV PELIKAN

Tradition will be our guide to the interpretation of the Bible through the appeal to the total life and experience of the Church from the ancient Fathers onwards.
MICHAEL RAMSEY

The Spirit who interprets the Scriptures is none other than the Risen Lord himself; the tradition of the Church is actually shaped and guided by the Spirit of the Risen Christ.
ALAN RICHARDSON

Ultimate authority is in Scripture, in God speaking through Scripture, for whereas tradition is oral, open and often self-contradictory, Scripture is written, fixed and always self-consistent.
JOHN R. W. STOTT

Trinity

(*See also* God)

The divine nature is really and entirely identical with each of the three persons, all of whom can therefore be called one: I and the Father are one.
ST. THOMAS AQUINAS

How can plurality consist with unity, or unity with plurality? To examine the fact closely is rashness, to believe it is piety, to know it is life, and life eternal.
ST. BERNARD OF CLAIRVAUX

The distinction of persons is true only for our knowledge of God, not for his inner Being, which we cannot know.
MILLAR BURROWS

The unity of Father, Son and Spirit is a unity of operation and revelation in which they are involved as three very diverse factors, to be described at best in analogical terms.
HANS KUNG

In God there can be no selfishness, because the three selves of God are three subsistent relations of selflessness, over-flowing and superabounding in joy in the perfection of their gift of their one life to one another.
THOMAS MERTON

Without belief in God's revelation the Trinity cannot be known at all; and even for believers it is incomprehensible in an exceptionally high degree, indeed, in the highest degree. There it is a mystery in the truest, highest, most beautiful sense of the word.
M. J. SCHEEBEN

God dwells in our heart by faith, and Christ by his Spirit, and the Holy Spirit by his purities; so that we are also cabinets of the mysterious Trinity; and what is this short of Heaven itself, but as infancy is short of manhood, and letters of words?
JEREMY TAYLOR

Trouble

He that seeks trouble never misses.
GEORGE HERBERT

If pleasures are greatest in anticipation, just remember that this is also true of trouble.
ELBERT HUBBARD

There is no man in the world without some trouble or affliction, though he be a king or a pope.
THOMAS À KEMPIS

Trouble will rain on those who are already wet.
SPANISH PROVERB

Trouble is a marvellous mortifier of pride and an effectual restrainer of self-will.
W. MORLEY PUNSHON

There were no troubles in my own life, except the troubles inseparable from being a spirit living in the flesh.
GEORGE SANTAYANA

Trust

(*See also* Confidence and Faith)

He who trusts in himself is lost. He who trusts in God can do all things.
ST. ALPHONSUS LIGUORI

The greatest trust between man and man is the trust of giving counsel.
FRANCIS BACON

Put your trust in God, but keep your powder dry.
OLIVER CROMWELL

Those who trust us educate us.
GEORGE ELIOT

What is more elevating and transport-ing, than the generosity of heart which risks everything on God's word?
JOHN HENRY NEWMAN

Trust in God, but mind your business.
RUSSIAN PROVERB

The more we depend on God the more dependable we find He is.
CLIFF RICHARD

God is faithful, and if we serve him faithfully, he will provide for our needs.
ST. RICHARD OF CHICHESTER

Consider seriously how quickly people change, and how little trust is to be had in them; and cleave fast unto God, Who changeth not.
ST. TERESA OF AVILA

God is full of compassion, and never fails those who are afflicted and despised, if they trust in him alone.
ST. TERESA OF AVILA

Trust is a treasured item and relationship. Once it is tarnished, it is hard to restore it to its original glow.
WILLIAM A. WARD

Truth

Truth is not only violated by falsehood; it may be equally outraged by silence.
HENRI FRÉDÉRIC AMIEL

Every truth without exception – and whoever may utter it – is from the Holy Ghost.
ST. THOMAS AQUINAS

If it is not right, do not do it; if it is not true, do not say it.
MARCUS AURELIUS

Truth which is merely told is quick to be forgotten; truth which is discovered lasts a lifetime.
WILLIAM BARCLAY

Truth exists, only falsehood has to be invented.
GEORGE BRAQUE

I thirst for truth, but shall not reach it till I reach the source.
ROBERT BROWNING

Truth is incontrovertible. Panic may resent it; ignorance may deride it; malice may distort it; but there it is.
SIR WINSTON CHURCHILL

The greatest friend of truth is Time, her greatest enemy is Prejudice, and her constant companion is Humility.
CHARLES CALEB COLTON

Truth is the foundation of all knowledge and the cement of all societies.
JOHN DRYDEN

If God were able to backslide from truth, I would fain cling to truth and let God go.
MEISTER ECKHART

If you tell the truth, you have infinite power supporting you; but if not, you have infinite power against you.
CHARLES GORDON

Truth does not allow us to despair of our opponents. The man of peace inspired by truth does not equate his opponent with the error into which he sees him fall.
POPE JOHN PAUL II

No truth can really exist external to Christianity.
JOHN HENRY NEWMAN

He who does not bellow the truth when he knows the truth makes himself the accomplice of liars and forgers.
CHARLES PÉGUY

Seven years of silent enquiry are needful for a man to learn the truth, but fourteen in order to learn how to make it known to his fellow men.
PLATO

The grave of one who dies for the truth is holy ground.
GERMAN PROVERB

Tell the truth and run.
YUGOSLAV PROVERB

Time discovers truth.
LATIN PROVERB

Truth is God's daughter.
SPANISH PROVERB

The truth is cruel, but it can be loved, and it makes free those who have loved it.
GEORGE SANTAYANA

Let us rejoice in the Truth, wherever we find its lamp burning.
ALBERT SCHWEITZER

No generation can claim to have plumbed to the depths the unfathomable riches of Christ. The Holy Spirit has promised to lead us step by step into the fullness of truth.
LEON JOSEPH SUENENS

Any human being can penetrate to the kingdom of truth, if only he longs for truth and perpetually concentrates all his attention upon its attainment.
SIMONE WEIL

Tyranny

Of all the tyrants that the world affords,
Our own affections are the fiercest lords.
WILLIAM ALEXANDER

Justice without force is powerless; force without justice is tyrannical.
BLAISE PASCAL

Men must be governed by God or they will be ruled by tyrants.
WILLIAM PENN

Nothing is more abhorrent to the tyrant than the service of Christ.
GIROLAMO SAVONAROLA

The tyrant is nothing but a slave turned inside out.
HERBERT SPENCER

Unbelief

(*See also* Atheism)

No man is an unbeliever, but because he will be so; and every man is not an unbeliever, because the grace of God conquers some, changes their wills, and binds them to Christ.
STEPHEN CHARNOCK

He who proselytises in the cause of unbelief is basically a man in need of belief.
ERIC HOFFER

Unbelief is blind.
JOHN MILTON

He who does not believe that God is above all is either a fool or has no experience of life.
CAECILIUS STATIUS

Understanding

Don't try to reach God with your understanding; that is impossible. Reach him in love; that is possible.
CARLO CARRETTO

Of course, understanding of our fellow beings is important. But this understanding becomes fruitful only when it is sustained by sympathetic feeling in joy and sorrow.
ALBERT EINSTEIN

Understanding a person does not mean condoning: it only means that one does not accuse him as if one were God or a judge placed above him.
ERICH FROMM

What we do not understand we do not possess.
JOHANN WOLFGANG VON GOETHE

What is most necessary for understanding divine things is prayer.
ORIGEN

Understanding is the wealth of wealth.
ARAB PROVERB

Universe

(*See also* Creation and World)

The more we learn about the wonders of our universe, the more clearly we are going to perceive the hand of God.
FRANK BORMANN

The universe is but one vast symbol of God.
THOMAS CARLYLE

The celestial order and beauty of the universe compel me to admit that there is some excellent and eternal Being, who deserves the respect and homage of men.
MARCUS TULLIUS CICERO

You will hardly find one among the profounder sort of scientific minds, without peculiar religious feelings of his own ... His religious feeling takes the form of rapturous amazement at the harmony of the natural law.
ALBERT EINSTEIN

I believe there is life on other planets with principalities and sovereignties, perhaps different from us, but all a part of God's universe.
BILLY GRAHAM

God showed me a little thing the size of a hazelnut in the palm of my hand, and it was as round as a ball. I thought, 'What may this be?' and was answered thus: 'It is the universe.'
JULIAN OF NORWICH

These are thy glorious works, Parent of good.
JOHN MILTON

The universe is a thought of God.
JOHANN C. F. VON SCHILLER

That the universe was formed by a fortuitous concourse of atoms, I will no more believe than that the accidental jumbling of the alphabet would fall into a most ingenious treatise of philosophy.
JONATHAN SWIFT

Unselfishness

(*See also* Generosity and Self-Denial)

The secret of being loved is in being lovely; and the secret of being lovely is in being unselfish.
JOSIAH HOLLAND

I find life an exciting business, and most exciting when it is lived for others.
HELEN KELLER

If people knew how much ill-feeling unselfishness occasions, it would not be so often recommended from the pulpit!
C. S. LEWIS

Neighbours praise unselfishness because they profit by it.
FRIEDRICH NIETZSCHE

Real unselfishness consists in sharing the interests of others.
GEORGE SANTAYANA

Vanity

(*See also* Pride)

Vanity is the pride of nature.
WILLIAM G. BENHAM

And the name of that town is Vanity; and at the town there is a fair kept, called Vanity Fair.
JOHN BUNYAN

At all times, but especially now, it is pertinent to say, 'Vanity of vanities, all is vanity.'
ST. JOHN CHRYSOSTOM

A vain man can never be utterly ruthless; he wants to win applause and therefore he accommodates himself to others.
JOHANN WOLFGANG VON GOETHE

The greatest magnifying glasses in the world are a man's own eyes when they look upon his own person.
ALEXANDER POPE

Vain-glory blossoms but never bears.
ENGLISH PROVERB

An ounce of vanity spoils a hundred weight of merit.
FRENCH PROVERB

Most of us would be far enough from vanity if we heard all the things that are said of us.
JOSEPH RICKABY

Provided a man is not mad, he can be cured of every folly but vanity.
JEAN JACQUES ROUSSEAU

Vice

We make a ladder of our vices, if we trample those same vices underfoot.
ST. AUGUSTINE OF HIPPO

This is the definition of vice: the wrong use, in violation of the Lord's command, of what has been given us by God for a good purpose.
ST. BASIL

In other living creatures the ignorance of themselves is nature, but in men it is vice.
AMICIUS M. S. BOETHIUS

Men wish to be saved from the mischiefs of their vices, but not from their vices.
RALPH WALDO EMERSON

There is a capacity of virtue in us, and there is a capacity of vice to make your blood creep.
RALPH WALDO EMERSON

If every year we rooted out one vice, we should soon become perfect.
THOMAS À KEMPIS

Vice is often clothed in virtue's habit.
ENGLISH PROVERB

Vices creep into our hearts under the name of virtues.
SENECA

Victory

If Christ is with us, who is against us? You can fight with confidence where you are sure of victory. With Christ and for Christ victory is certain.
ST. BERNARD OF CLAIRVAUX

The first step on the way to victory is to recognise the enemy.
CORRIE TEN BOOM

Unless the battle has preceded, there cannot be a victory . . . for the helmsman is recognised in the tempest; the soldier is proven in warfare.
ST. CYPRIAN

Even victors are by victory undone.
JOHN DRYDEN

The way to get the most out of a victory is to follow it up with another which makes it look small.
HENRY S. HASKINS

It is a great victory that comes without blood.
GEORGE HERBERT

He conquers twice who upon victory overcomes himself.
PUBLILIUS SYRUS

Violence

In some cases non-violence requires more militancy than violence.
CÉSAR CHAVEZ

Violence is always an offence, an insult to man, both to the one who perpetrates it and to the one who suffers it.
POPE JOHN PAUL II

It is well known that firearms go off by themselves if only enough of them are together.
CARL GUSTAV JUNG

Returning violence for violence multiplies violence, adding deeper darkness to a night already devoid of stars.
MARTIN LUTHER KING, JR.

The modern choice is between non-violence or non-existence.
MARTIN LUTHER KING, JR.

We are effectively destroying ourselves by violence masquerading as love.
R. D. LAING

Perseverance is more prevailing than violence.
PLUTARCH

A good portion of the evils that afflict mankind is due to the erroneous belief that life can be made secure by violence.
COUNT LEO TOLSTOY

Violent disorder once set in motion may spawn tyranny, not freedom.
CHARLES E. WYZANSKI

Virginity

(*See also* Chastity, Modesty and Purity)

Not because it is virginity is it held in honour, but because it is consecrated to God.
ST. AUGUSTINE OF HIPPO

Neither widowhood nor virginity has any place in Heaven but that which is assigned to them by humility.
ST. FRANCIS DE SALES

Virginity in the theological sense is basically an eschatological ideal which holds for all mankind equally, but not for all in the same way.
WALDEMAR MOLINSKI

Virgins are thorns that produce roses.
ARTHUR SCHOPENHAUER

Virginity is a life of angels, the enamel of the soul.
JEREMY TAYLOR

Virtue

Virtue is like a rich stone, best plain set.
FRANCIS BACON

Here and there people flee from public alteration into the sanctuary of private virtuousness. But anyone who does this must shut his mouth and his eyes to the injustice around him . . . What he leaves undone will rob him of his peace of mind.
DIETRICH BONHOEFFER

Love virtue rather than fear sin.
JEAN PIERRE CAMUS

Virtue is not the absence of vices or the avoidance of moral dangers; virtue is a vivid and separate thing, like pain or a particular smell.
G. K. CHESTERTON

So good a thing is virtue that even its enemies applaud and admire it.
ST. JOHN CHRYSOSTOM

Many wish not so much to be virtuous, as to seem to be.
MARCUS TULLIUS CICERO

Virtue and a trade are the best portion for children.
GEORGE HERBERT

Some of the most virtuous men in the world are also the bitterest and most unhappy, because they have unconsciously come to believe that all their happiness depends on their being more virtuous than other men.
THOMAS MERTON

Vocation

Do not despise your situation. In it you must act, suffer and conquer. From every point on earth, we are equally near to heaven and the infinite.
HENRI FRÉDÉRIC AMIEL

God chooses those who are pleasing to Him. He put a shepherd at the head of His people, and of the goat-herd, Amos, He made a prophet.
ST. BASIL

Our vocation is to live in the spirit – not to be more and more remarkable animals, but to be the sons and companions of God in eternity.
ANTHONY BLOOM

When I have learned to do the Father's will, I shall have fully realised my vocation on earth.
CARLO CARRETTO

It seems to me that it is the right thing for a director to discourage people who think they have a vocation. If it is real, it will vanquish all obstacles, and will stand out, not as a mere invitation, but as a categorical imperative.
JOHN CHAPMAN

A good vocation is simply a firm and constant will in which the called person has to serve God in the way and in the places to which Almighty God has called him.
ST. FRANCIS DE SALES

God has created me to do him some definite service; he has committed some work to me which he has not committed to another. I have my mission – I never may know it in this life, but I shall be told it in the next.
JOHN HENRY NEWMAN

Many are stubborn in pursuit of the path they have chosen, few in pursuit of the goal.
FRIEDRICH NIETZSCHE

The test of a vocation is the love of the drudgery it involves.
LOGAN PEARSALL SMITH

We must not forget that our vocation is so to practise virtue that men are won to it; it is possible to be morally upright repulsively.
WILLIAM TEMPLE

The vocation of every man and woman is to serve other people.
COUNT LEO TOLSTOY

War

(*See also* Peace and Violence)

An infalliable method of conciliating a tiger is to allow oneself to be devoured.
KONRAD ADENAUER

For a war to be just, three conditions are necessary – public authority, just cause, right motive.
ST. THOMAS AQUINAS

In peace the sons bury their fathers and in war the fathers bury their sons.
FRANCIS BACON

The Church knows nothing of the sacredness of war. The Church which prays the 'Our Father' asks God only for peace.
DIETRICH BONHOEFFER

There are many things worse than war. Slavery is worse than war. Dishonour is worse than war.
SIR WINSTON CHURCHILL

War can only be a desperate remedy in a desperate situation, used in order to spare humanity a still greater evil when all essentially reasonable and peaceful means have proved ineffective.
RENÉ COSTE

How vile and despicable war seems to me! I would rather be hacked to pieces than take part in such an abominable business.
ALBERT EINSTEIN

There is nothing that war has ever achieved we could not better achieve without it.
HAVELOCK ELLIS

We must have military power to keep madmen from taking over the world.
BILLY GRAHAM

Older men declare war. But it is youth that must fight and die. And it is youth who must inherit the tribulation, the sorrow, and the triumphs that are the aftermath of war.
HERBERT HOOVER

For a Christian who believes in Jesus and his Gospel, war is an inquity and a contradiction.
POPE JOHN XXIII

It is becoming humanly impossible to regard war, in this atomic age, as a suitable means of re-establishing justice when some right has been violated.
POPE JOHN XXIII

In modern warfare there are no victors; there are only survivors.
LYNDON B. JOHNSON

Henceforth the adequacy of any military establishment will be tested by its ability to preserve the peace.
HENRY KISSINGER

War is sweet to them that know it not.
ENGLISH PROVERB

A great war leaves the country with three armies – an army of cripples, an army of mourners, and an army of thieves.
GERMAN PROVERB

We (Christians in war) are called to the hardest of all tasks; to fight without hatred, to resist without bitterness, and in the end, if God grant it so, to triumph without vindictiveness.
WILLIAM TEMPLE

To be prepared for war is one of the most effectual means of preserving peace.
GEORGE WASHINGTON

Weakness

Weak things united become strong.
THOMAS FULLER

The acknowledgment of our weakness is the first step towards repairing our loss.
THOMAS À KEMPIS

There are two kinds of weakness, that which breaks and that which bends.
JAMES RUSSELL LOWELL

Men's weaknesses are often necessary to the purposes of life.
MAURICE MAETERLINCK

The weak go to the wall.
ENGLISH PROVERB

Weakness, not vice, is virtue's worst enemy.
FRANÇOIS DE LA ROCHEFOUCAULD

Wealth

(*See also* Materialism, Money and Riches)

Wealth is a good servant, a very bad mistress.
FRANCIS BACON

Surplus wealth is a sacred trust which its possessor is bound to administer in his lifetime for the good of the community.
ANDREW CARNEGIE

There is a time when a man distinguishes the idea of felicity from the idea of wealth; it is the beginning of wisdom.
RALPH WALDO EMERSON

Great wealth and content seldom live together.
THOMAS FULLER

Wealth is the relentless enemy of understanding
JOHN K. GALBRAITH

The greatest wealth is contentment with a little.
ENGLISH PROVERB

It is preoccupation with possession, more than anything else, that prevents men from living freely and nobly.
BERTRAND RUSSELL

If a rich man is proud of his wealth, he should not be praised until it is known how he employs it.
SOCRATES

Wholeness

(*See also* Body and Soul and Holiness)

If a man is not rising upwards to be an angel, depend on it, he is sinking downwards to be a devil. He cannot stop at the beast.
SAMUEL TAYLOR COLERIDGE

Seek not every quality in one individual.
CONFUCIUS

A weak person is injured by prosperity; a finer person by adversity, but the finest by neither.
PAUL FROST

God does not ask of a person anything that is false or beyond his power. Rather, God invites what is most human in every person to become aware of itself.
LOUIS M. SAVARY

Man must be lenient with his soul in her weaknesses and imperfections and suffer her failings as he suffers those of others, but he must not become idle, and must encourage himself to better things.
ST. SERAPHIM OF SAROV

It costs so much to be a full human being that there are very few who have the enlightenment or the courage to pay the price. One has to abandon altogether the search for security and reach out to the risk of living with both arms. One has to embrace the world like a lover. One has to accept pain as a condition of existence. One has to court doubt and darkness as the cost of knowing. One needs a will stubborn in conflict, but apt always to total acceptance of every consequence of living and dying.
MORRIS WEST

Wickedness

The belief in a supernatural source of evil is not necessary: men alone are quite capable of every wickedness.
JOSEPH CONRAD

No one ever became extremely wicked all at once.
DECIMUS JUVENAL

A wicked man is his own Hell.
ENGLISH PROVERB

Some wicked people would be less dangerous had they no redeeming qualities.
FRANÇOIS DE LA ROCHEFOUCAULD

None of us feels the true love of God till we realise how wicked we are. But you can't teach people that – they have to learn by experience.
DOROTHY L. SAYERS

Wife

(*See also* Marriage)

A good wife and health, are a man's best wealth.
HENRY G. BOHN

One shouldn't be too inquisitive in life Either about God's secrets or one's wife.
GEOFFREY CHAUCER

A wife is not to be chosen by the eye only. Choose a wife rather by your ear than your eye.
THOMAS FULLER

Who lets his wife go to every feast, and his horse drink at every water, shall have neither good wife nor good horse.
GEORGE HERBERT

The wife should be inferior to the husband; that is the only way to ensure equality between the two.
MARCUS MARTIAL

Let us teach our wives to remain in the faith taught them and in charity and purity to cherish their husbands in all truth, loving all others impartially in complete chastity, and to bring up their children in the fear of God.
ST. POLYCARP

The wife is the key of the house.
ENGLISH PROVERB

In buying horses and in taking a wife, shut your eyes tight and commend yourself to God.
TUSCAN PROVERB

A man too good for the world is no good for his wife.
YIDDISH PROVERB

Try praising your wife, even if it does frighten her at first.
WILLIAM ASHLEY SUNDAY

We always find it more acceptable to have God speaking to us directly rather than through our wives! But we may learn a great deal by listening to what He says to us through them.
PAUL TOURNIER

Will of God

In his will is our peace.
DANTE ALIGHIERI

The will of God is the measure of things.
ST. AMBROSE

All Heaven is waiting to help those who will discover the will of God and do it.
J. ROBERT ASHCROFT

Nothing, therefore, happens unless the Omnipotent wills it to happen: He either permits it to happen, or He brings it about Himself.
ST. AUGUSTINE OF HIPPO

No one may prefer his own will to the will of God, but in everything we must seek and do the will of God.
ST. BASIL

It needs a very pure intention, as well as great spiritual discernment, always to recognise the divine voice.
ROBERT H. BENSON

The centre of God's will is our only safety.
BETSIE TEN BOOM

If God sends us on stony paths, he provides strong shoes.
CORRIE TEN BOOM

Self-will should be so completely poured out of the vessel of the soul into the ocean of the will of God, that whatever God may will, that at once the soul should will; and that whatever God may allow, that the soul should at once willingly embrace, whether it may be in itself sweet or bitter.
LOUIS DE BLOIS

God's will is not an itinerary but an attitude.
ANDREW DHUSE

There are no disappointments to those whose wills are buried in the will of God.
FREDERICK W. FABER

Blessed are they who do not their own will on earth, for God will do it in heaven above.
ST. FRANCIS DE SALES

A possibility is a hint from God.
SØREN KIERKEGAARD

The hardness of God is kinder than the softness of men, and his compulsion is our liberation.
C. S. LEWIS

Let your will be one with His will, and be glad to be disposed of by Him. He will order all things for you. What can cross your will, when it is one with His will, on which all creation hangs, round which all things revolve?
HENRY E. MANNING

When we speak with God, our power of addressing Him, of holding communion with Him, and listening to His still small Voice, depends upon our will being one and the same with His.
FLORENCE NIGHTINGALE

Prayer is no other but the revelation of the will or mind of God.
JOHN SALTMARSH

Let each look to himself and see what God wants of him and attend to this, leaving all else alone.
HENRY SUSO

It is God's will that is the proper measure of reality; and that is expressed in Christ, who is his Will.
SIMON TUGWELL

The whole duty of man is summed up in obedience to God's will.
GEORGE WASHINGTON

Wisdom

The first key to wisdom is assiduous and frequent questioning. For by doubting we come in enquiry and by enquiry we arrive at truth.
PETER ABELARD

Wisdom is the foundation, and justice the work without which a foundation cannot stand.
ST. AMBROSE

Let your old age be childlike, and your childhood like old age; that is, so that neither may your wisdom be with pride, nor your humility without wisdom.
ST. AUGUSTINE OF HIPPO

A prudent question is one-half of wisdom.
FRANCIS BACON

Common sense, in an uncommon degree, is what the world calls wisdom.
SAMUEL TAYLOR COLERIDGE

There is this difference between happiness and wisdom: He that thinks himself the happiest man, really is so; but he that thinks himself the wisest is generally the greatest fool.
CHARLES CALEB COLTON

Fruitless is the wisdom of him who has no knowledge of himself.
DESIDERIUS ERASMUS

He is not wise to me who is wise in words only, but he who is wise in deeds.
POPE ST. GREGORY I

Wisdom is the ability to use knowledge so as to meet successfully the emergencies of life. Men may acquire knowledge, but wisdom is a gift direct from God.
BOB JONES

To have a low opinion of our own merits, and to think highly of others, is an evidence of wisdom. All men are frail, but thou shouldest reckon none as frail as thyself.
THOMAS À KEMPIS

Only a fool tests the depth of the water with both feet.
AFRICAN PROVERB

Wise men change their minds, fools never.
ENGLISH PROVERB

The great wisdom in man consists in knowing his follies.
FRENCH PROVERB

Wisdom comes by suffering.
GREEK PROVERB

There is often wisdom under a shabby cloak.
LATIN PROVERB

Nine-tenths of wisdom consist of being wise in time.
THEODORE ROOSEVELT

Never be ashamed to own you have been in the wrong, 'tis but saying you are wiser today than you were yesterday.
JONATHAN SWIFT

Wisdom is oftentimes nearer when we stoop than when we soar.
WILLIAM WORDSWORTH

Wit

(*See also* Humour)

Many get the name for being witty, only to lose the credit for being sensible.
GRACIAN

Wit is the salt of conversation, not the food.
WILLIAM HAZLITT

A person reveals his character by nothing so clearly as the joke he resents.
GEORGE G. LICHTENBERG

Wit is folly unless a wise man have the keeping of it.
ENGLISH PROVERB

Wit without learning is like a tree without fruit.
ENGLISH PROVERB

Witness

Witnessing is removing the various barriers of our self-love to allow Christ, living within us, to show himself to our neighbours.
PAUL FROST

The world is far more ready to receive the Gospel than Christians are to hand it out.
GEORGE W. PETERS

If Christ lives in us, controlling our personalities, we will leave glorious marks on the lives we touch. Not because of our lovely characters, but because of his.
EUGENIA PRICE

Our task as laymen is to live our personal communion with Christ with such intensity as to make it contagious.
PAUL TOURNIER

Woman

(*See also* Wife)

There is no limit to the power of a good woman.
ROBERT H. BENSON

A man's good work is affected by doing what he does; a woman's by being what she is.
G. K. CHESTERTON

Being a woman is a terribly difficult trade, since it consists principally of dealing with men.
JOSEPH CONRAD

The society of women is the foundation of good manners.
JOHANN WOLFGANG VON GOETHE

No one knows like a woman how to say things which are at once gentle and deep.
VICTOR HUGO

Women should remain at home, sit still, keep house, and bear and bring up children.
MARTIN LUTHER

Woman is the confusion of man.
ENGLISH PROVERB

Men shall always be what the women make them; if, therefore, you would have men great and virtuous, impress upon the minds of women what greatness and virtue are.
JEAN JACQUES ROUSSEAU

It was to a virgin woman that the birth of the Son of God was announced. It was to a fallen woman that his resurrection was announced.
FULTON J. SHEEN

Christianity brings liberation through the Gospel in faith and action. But the Christian Church has not been a sufficiently liberating institution for women, in the sense of not opening up to them the full range of possibilities.
PAULINE WEBB

Whatever women do, they must do twice as well as men to be thought half as good. Luckily, this is not difficult.
CHARLOTTE WHITTON

The history of women is the history of the worst form of tyranny the world has ever known. The tyranny of the weak over the strong. It is the only tyranny that lasts.
OSCAR WILDE

I think the great fault of the Catholic Church is that it has never really come to terms with women. What I object to, like a lot of other women in the Church, is being treated as Madonnas or Mary Magdalens, instead of being treated as people.
SHIRLEY WILLIAMS

Wonder

You will find something far greater in the woods than you will in books. Stones and trees will teach you what you can never learn from masters.
ST. BERNARD OF CLAIRVAUX

The man who cannot wonder is but a pair of spectacles behind which there is no eye.
THOMAS CARLYLE

Wonder is the basis of worship.
THOMAS CARLYLE

The world will never starve for want of wonders; but only for want of wonder.
G. K. CHESTERTON

Men love to wonder, and that is the seed of science.
RALPH WALDO EMERSON

To be surprised, to wonder, is to begin to understand.
JOSE ORTEGA Y GASSET

Wonder rather than doubt is the root of knowledge.
ABRAHAM JOSHUA HESCHEL

A wonder lasts but nine days.
ENGLISH PROVERB

God made us and we wonder at it.
SPANISH PROVERB

Wonder is especially proper to childhood, and it is the sense of wonder above all that keeps us young.
GERALD VANN

Words

(*See also* Communication, Conversation, Gossip and Talk)

Our words are a faithful index of the state of our souls.
ST. FRANCIS DE SALES

Words are nails for fixing ideas.
H. GIORNALE

The words of God which you receive by your ear, hold fast in your heart. For the word of God is the food of the soul.
POPE ST. GREGORY I

To the intelligent man a word is enough.
THOMAS À KEMPIS

Words are, of course, the most powerful drug used by mankind.
RUDYARD KIPLING

Cold words freeze people and hot words scorch them, and bitter words make them bitter, and wrathful words make them wrathful. Kind words also produce their image on men's souls; and a beautiful image it is. They smooth, and quiet, and comfort the hearer.
BLAISE PASCAL

The world pays itself with words; there is little plumbing of the depths of things.
BLAISE PASCAL

In love and divinity what is most worth saying cannot be said.
COVENTRY PATMORE

A man of words and not of deeds is like a garden full of weeds.
ENGLISH PROVERB

A word spoken is past recalling.
ENGLISH PROVERB

Better one word before than two after.
WELSH PROVERB

Little keys can open big locks. Simple words can express great thoughts.
WILLIAM A. WARD

Work

Nothing is really work unless you would rather be doing something else.
JAMES M. BARRIE

It appears, on close examination, that work is less boring than amusing oneself.
CHARLES BAUDELAIRE

He who labours as he prays lifts his heart to God with his hands.
ST. BERNARD OF CLAIRVAUX

Without work, all life goes rotten. But when work is soulless, life stifles and dies.
ALBERT CAMUS

The best worship, however, is stout working.
THOMAS CARLYLE

Hard work is a thrill and a joy when you are in the will of God.
ROBERT A. COOK

No one has a right to sit down and feel hopeless. There's too much work to do.
DOROTHY DAY

Work is love made visible.
KAHLIL GIBRAN

Happiness, I have discovered, is nearly always a rebound from hard work.
DAVID GRAYSON

Work is the greatest thing in the world, so we should always save some of it for tomorrow.
DON HEROLD

God gives every bird its food, but he does not throw it into the nest.
JOSIAH G. HOLLAND

I like work, it fascinates me. I can sit and look at it for hours.
JEROME K. JEROME

Work is not a curse, it is a blessing from God who calls man to rule the earth and transform it, so that the divine work of creation may continue with man's intelligence and effort.
POPE JOHN PAUL II

There is great fret and worry in always running after work; it is not good intellectually or spiritually.
ANNIE KEARY

A dairymaid can milk cows to the glory of God.
MARTIN LUTHER

It is our best work that he wants, not the dregs of our exhaustion. I think he must prefer quality to quantity.
GEORGE MACDONALD

It is a sublime mystery that Christ should begin to work before he began to teach; a humble workman before being the teacher of all nations.
POPE PIUS XII

Hats off to the past; coats off to the future.
AMERICAN PROVERB

A man grows most tired while standing still.
CHINESE PROVERB

Never was good work done without much trouble.
CHINESE PROVERB

Work is worship.
FRENCH PROVERB

Work is no disgrace: the disgrace is idleness.
GREEK PROVERB

Nothing is denied to well-directed labour; nothing is to be obtained without it.
SIR JOSHUA REYNOLDS

No amount of pay ever made a good soldier, a good teacher, a good artist, or a good workman.
JOHN RUSKIN

When love and skill work together, expect a masterpiece.
JOHN RUSKIN

Work is the natural exercise and function of man . . . Work is not primarily a thing one does to live, but the thing one lives to do. It is, or should be, the full expression of the worker's faculties, the thing in which he finds spiritual, mental and bodily satisfaction, and the medium in which he offers himself to God.
DOROTHY L. SAYERS

A man can do only what he can do. But if he does that each day he can sleep at night and do it again the next day.
ALBERT SCHWEITZER

Good for the body is the work of the body, and good for the soul is the work of the soul, and good for either is the work of the other.
HENRY DAVID THOREAU

No nation can prosper till it learns that there is as much dignity in tilling a field as in writing a poem.
BOOKER T. WASHINGTON

World

(*See also* Creation and Universe)

The very order, disposition, beauty, change, and motion of the world and of all visible things proclaim that it could only have been made by God, the ineffably and invisibly great and the ineffably and invisibly beautiful.
ST. AUGUSTINE OF HIPPO

My habitual feeling is that the world is so extremely odd, and everything in it so surprising. Why *should* there be green grass and liquid water, and *why* have I got hands and feet?
JOHN CHAPMAN

Man does not come to know the world by that which he extorts from it, but rather by that which he adds to it: himself.
PAUL CLAUDEL

This world and that to come are two enemies. We cannot therefore be friends to both; but we must resolve which we would forsake and which we would enjoy.
ST. CLEMENT OF ALEXANDRIA

The world is charged with the grandeur of God.
GERARD MANLEY HOPKINS

The world has become a global village.
MARSHALL MCLUHAN

The world is a sure teacher, but it requires a fat fee.
FINNISH PROVERB

You cannot please both God and the world at the same time. They are utterly opposed to each other in their thoughts, their desires, and their actions.
JOHN VIANNEY

Our very presence in the world gives a type of meaning to the world, but that meaning is the beginning and not the end of our lives.
A. A. VOGEL

I look upon the world as my parish.
JOHN WESLEY

We are citizens of the world; and the tragedy of our times is that we do not know this.
WOODROW WILSON

The world is too much with us; late and soon,
Getting and spending, we lay waste our powers:
Little we see in Nature that is ours.
WILLIAM WORDSWORTH

Worldliness

The unalterable law of 'the world' is that evil is fought with evil, and that the devil is driven out by Beelzebub. And so long as that remains unaltered, Christianity is not victorious.
THEODOR HAECKER

Whoever marries the spirit of this age will find himself a widower in the next.
WILLIAM RALPH INGE

More men live regardless of the great duties of piety through too great a concern for worldly goods than through direct injustice.
WILLIAM LAW

Be wisely worldly, be not worldly wise.
FRANCIS QUARLES

Worry

(*See also* Anxiety, Doubt and Trouble)

Worry does not empty tomorrow of its sorrow; it empties today of its strength.
CORRIE TEN BOOM

When I look back on all these worries I remember the story of the old man who said on his deathbed that he had had a lot of trouble in his life, most of which never happened.
SIR WINSTON CHURCHILL

There is nothing that wastes the body like worry, and one who has any faith in God should be ashamed to worry about anything whatsoever.
MOHANDAS GANDHI

Worry is interest paid on trouble before it falls due.
WILLIAM R. INGE

Worship

(*See also* Liturgy)

We are told to sing to the Lord a new song. A new man knows a new song. A song is a thing of joy and, if we think of it, a thing to love. So the man who has learned to love a new life has learned to sing a new song. For a new man, a new song and the New Testament all belong to the same kingdom.
ST. AUGUSTINE OF HIPPO

For the Christian who loves God, worship is the daily bread of patience.
HONORÉ DE BALZAC

It is only when men begin to worship that they begin to grow.
CALVIN COOLRIDGE

Glory to Christ. Come, let us offer him the great, universal sacrifice of our love, and pour out before him our richest hymns and prayers. For he offered his cross to God as a sacrifice in order to make us all rich.
ST. EPHREM

It is a man's duty to praise and bless God and pay him due thanks. Ought we not, as we dig and plough to sing, 'Great is God that He gave us these instruments wherewith we shall till the earth, great is God that He has given us hands to labour, and the power to draw our breath in sleep.' At every moment we ought to sing these praises, and, above all, the greatest and divinest praise, that God gave us the ability to understand His gifts and to use our human reason.
EPICTETUS

The glory of God is a living man; and the life of man consists in beholding God.
ST. IRENAEUS

A little lifting of the heart suffices; a little remembrance of God, one act of inward worship are prayers which, however short, are nevertheless acceptable to God.
BROTHER LAWRENCE

A man can no more diminish God's glory by refusing to worship Him than a lunatic can put out the sun by scribbling the word 'darkness' on the walls of his cell.
C. S. LEWIS

It cannot be that the instinct which has led to the creation of cathedrals, and of churches in every village, is wholly mistaken and misleading. There must be some great truth underlying the instinct for worship.
OLIVER LODGE

It is a law of man's nature, written into his very essence, and just as much a part of him as the desire to build houses and cultivate the land and marry and have children and read books and sing songs, that he should want to stand together with other men in order to acknowledge their common dependence on God, their Father and Creator.
THOMAS MERTON

Prayers travel faster when said in unison.
LATIN PROVERB

Do not forget that even as 'to work is to worship' so to be cheery is to worship also, and to be happy is the first step to being pious.
ROBERT LOUIS STEVENSON

Worship, then, is not a part of the Christian life; it is the Christian life.
GERALD VANN

Youth

(*See also* Children)

The principal trap which the Devil sets for young people is idleness. This is the fatal source of all evil.
JOHN BOSCO

Youth is not properly definable by age. It is a spirit of daring, creating, asserting life, and openly relating to the world.
MALCOLM BOYD

Young people will respond if the challenge is tough enough and hard enough. Youth wants a master and a controller. Young people were built for God, and without God as the centre of their lives they become frustrated and confused, desperately grasping for and searching for security.
BILLY GRAHAM

The young want to be challenged by something sacrificial. They are rejecting phoney values and standards. The only hope is to create a community that doesn't live by false values.
TREVOR HUDDLESTON

You yourself know how slippery is the path of youth – a path on which I myself have fallen, and which you are now traversing not without fear.
ST. JEROME

When we are out of sympathy with the young, then I think our work in this world is over.
GEORGE MACDONALD

The real lost souls don't wear their hair long and play guitars. They have crew cuts, trained minds, sign on for research in biological warfare, and don't give their parents a moment's worry.
J. B. PRIESTLEY

Who that in youth no virtue useth, in age all honour him refuseth.
ENGLISH PROVERB

Youth and age will never agree.
ENGLISH PROVERB

Praise youth and it will prosper.
IRISH PROVERB

I was born in the wrong generation. When I was a young man, no one had any respect for youth. Now I am an old man and no one has any respect for age.
BERTRAND RUSSELL

One other thing stirs me when I look back at my youthful days, the fact that so many people gave me something or were something to me without knowing it.
ALBERT SCHWEITZER

Don't laugh at youth for his affectations; he is only trying on one face after another to find his own.
LOGAN PEARSALL SMITH

Zeal

(*See also* Enthusiasm)

There are few catastrophes so great and irremediable as those that follow an excess of zeal.
ROBERT H. BENSON

Zeal without knowledge is always less useful and effective than regulated zeal, and very often it is highly dangerous.
ST. BERNARD OF CLAIRVAUX

Zeal without tolerance is fanaticism.
JOHN KELMAN

We are often moved with passion, and we think it to be zeal.
THOMAS À KEMPIS

Zeal dropped in charity is good; without it, good for nothing; for it devours all it comes near.
WILLIAM PENN

Misplaced zeal is zeal for God rather than zeal of God.
WILLIAM PETTINGILE

Zeal, when it is a virtue, is a dangerous one.
ENGLISH PROVERB

Zeal without knowledge is fire without light. Zeal without prudence is frenzy.
ENGLISH PROVERB

All true zeal for God is a zeal for love, mercy and goodness.
ROBERT E. THOMPSON

Nothing spoils human nature more than false zeal. The good nature of an heathen is more God-like than the furious zeal of a Christian.
BENJAMIN WHICHCOTE

Index to Quotations

Abelard, Peter (1079–1142) 126, 249
Abram, Morris (1879–1926) 98
Acton, Lord John (1834–1902) 21, 101
Adams, Arthur R. (b. 1861) 123
Adams, George M. (1878–1962) 73
Adams, Henry (1838–1918) 71, 82
Adams, James Truslow 167
Adams, John (1735–1826) 12, 33, 101
Adams, John Quincy (1767–1848) 130,
133
Addison, Joseph (1672–1719) 28, 50, 54,
56, 93, 109, 110, 136, 219, 228
Adenauer, Konrad (1876–1967) 56, 244
Adler, Alfred (1870–1937) 192
Aesop (c. 570, B.C.) 95
Ailred of Rievaulx, St. (1109–1166) 96
Ainsworth, P. 110
Albert the Great, St. (d. 1280) 47, 231
Alexander, William (1808–1884) 239
Alfieri, Vittorio (1749–1803) 56
Alford, Henry (1810–1871) 236
Alfred the Great, King (849–901) 88
Alfred, William 97
Alighieri, Dante (1265–1321) 17, 67, 104,
110, 111, 112, 145, 234, 236, 247
Allen, Woody (b. 1935) 67
Allport, Gordon W. (1897–1967) 190, 196
Alphonsus, Liguori, St. (1697–1787) 43,
135, 237
Ambrose, St. (340–397) 15, 21, 30, 43, 60,
64, 66, 73, 78, 84, 92, 94, 100, 101,
136, 143, 159, 169, 174, 195, 210, 211,
220, 222, 231, 232, 247, 249
Amerding, Howard (b. 1932) 7
Amiel, Henri Frédéric (1828–1881) 13,
24, 61, 76, 129, 143, 163, 166, 169,
174, 192, 217, 229, 238, 243
Andrew, Brother (b. 1928) 62
Andrewes, Lancelot (1555–1626) 96, 139
Angela, Merici, St. (1474–1540) 183
Anselm of Canterbury, St. (1033–1109)
20, 220, 224
Anthony of Padua, St. (1195–1231) 59,
186
Antonius, Marcus (83–30 B.C.) 130
Aquinas, St. Thomas (1225–1274) 15, 20,
23, 32, 34, 44, 54, 64, 77, 78, 101, 105,
114, 116, 126, 138, 139, 140, 149, 155,
169, 170, 177, 179, 182, 189, 191, 197,
203, 209, 233, 236, 238, 244
Arama, Isaac 21
Aristides, Marcianus (c. 450) 169
Aristotle (384–322 B.C.) 18, 76, 116, 140,
170, 182, 197, 206
Arnold, Matthew (1822–1888) 37, 58,
206, 214, 220
Arnold, Thomas (1795–1842) 202
Ashcroft, J. Robert 247
Ashmore, Harry 91
Asquith, Herbert Henry (1852–1928) 41,
60
Athanasius, of Alexandria, St. (295–373)
119, 155, 162
Athenagoras (c. 176) 115
Auden, Wystan Hugh (1907–1973) 182
Augsburger, David (b. 1938) 8, 106
Augsburger, M. S. 42
Augustine of Hippo, St. (354–430) 8, 12,
22, 23, 24, 25, 27, 28, 35, 36, 39, 42,
46, 48, 50, 54, 58, 61, 63, 66, 76, 77,
83, 90, 94, 96, 102, 106, 109, 112, 115,
119, 128, 132, 135, 136, 138, 143, 144,
155, 159, 161, 164, 165, 170, 174, 189,
192, 194, 198, 199, 207, 218, 223, 226,
233, 234, 241, 243, 248, 249, 254, 255
Aurelius, Marcus (121–180) 56, 152, 215,
216, 224, 238
Austin, Anne (b. 1921) 120
Austin, Henry (1613) 62, 179
Ayscough, John (1858–1928) 60, 85
Aznavour, Charles, pseud. for Varenagh
Aznavourian (b. 1924) 97

Babcock, Maltbie D. (1858–1901) 162
Bacon, Francis (1561–1626) 19, 24, 28,
60, 85, 86, 118, 123, 144, 163, 170,
171, 174, 176, 182, 194, 205, 229, 237,
243, 244, 246, 249
Bagehot, Walter (1826–1877) 184, 231
Baillie, John (1741–1806) 102
Balfour, Lord Arthur James (1848–1930)
199
Balguy, John (1686–1748) 50
Ballou, Hosea (1771–1852) 107

Balzac, Honoré de (1799–1850) 182, 185, 199, 255
Barat, Madeleine Sophie (1779–1865) 57
Barclay, Armiger 83
Barclay, William (1907–1978) 37, 38, 73, 183, 191, 214, 238
Baring, Maurice (1874–1945) 163
Barnardo, Dr. Thomas J. (1845–1908) 33
Baroka, Rabbi (1722–1801) 121
Barrett, Ethel 215
Barrett, William (b. 1900) 182
Barrie, James M. (1860–1937) 106, 134, 165, 252
Barrymore, Ethel (1879–1959) 120
Barth, Joseph 153
Barth, Karl (1886–1968) 62, 64, 83, 84
Barton, Bruce (b. 1886) 46
Baruch, Bernard Mannes (1870–1965) 129
Basil, St. (c. 330–379) 21, 29, 48, 79, 84, 100, 117, 128, 217, 241, 243, 248
Battista, O.A. 62
Baudelaire, Charles (1821–1867) 252
Baughen, Michael (b. 1930) 186
Baum, Vicki (1896–1960) 85, 133
Baxter, Richard (1615–1691) 139
Bayly, Joseph (1671–1720) 60
Beck, Frederick 234
Beckstrom, K. 130
Becque, Henry (1837–1899) 69, 76, 186
Bede, The Venerable (673–735) 84, 102, 112, 150, 177, 211, 228
Beecher, Henry Ward (1813–1887) 45, 46, 56, 59, 89, 90, 93, 109, 110, 115, 125, 174, 228, 232, 233
Bellarmine, Robert, St. (1542–1621) 34
Belloc, Hilaire (1870–1953) 9, 41, 48, 53, 85, 95, 127, 140, 191, 234
Benedict, St. (480–547) 46, 123, 168, 219, 222, 233
Ben-Gurion, David (1886–1973) 133
Benham, William Gurney (1859–1944) 112, 158, 230, 241
Bennett, Arnold (1867–1931) 8, 65, 122, 135, 159
Benson, Arthur C. (1862–1925) 74
Benson, Archbishop Edward (1829–1896) 116
Benson, Robert Hugh (1871–1914) 18, 21, 33, 39, 48, 52, 53, 57, 60, 62, 72, 73, 83, 86, 89, 93, 109, 120, 126, 130, 139, 150, 177, 179, 208, 213, 219, 225, 229, 248, 250, 257

Bentinck, Lord George (1802–1848) 76
Berdyaev, Nikolai (1874–1948) 19, 30, 55, 88, 152, 164
Berkeley, Bishop George (1685–1753) 116
Bernanos, Georges (1888–1948) 111, 134, 184
Bernard of Clairvaux, St. (1091–1153) 11, 49, 74, 84, 102, 104, 110, 117, 119, 120, 149, 155, 158, 174, 178, 181, 184, 195, 206, 216, 236, 242, 251, 252, 257
Bernardine of Siena, St. (1380–1444) 155
Bettelheim, Bruno (b. 1903) 45, 157
Bickmore, Lee (b. 1908) 151
Bierce, Ambrose (1842–1914) 123, 190, 230
Billings, Josh, pseud. for Henry Wheeler Shaw (1818–1885) 7, 14, 26, 75, 104, 106, 212
Binyon, Laurence (1869–1943) 13
Blackstone, William (1723–1780) 105
Blake, John (1788–1857) 16, 46
Blake, William (1757–1827) 90, 102, 155, 190, 193, 203
Blinco, Joseph D. 110, 189
Bloom, Archbishop Anthony (b. 1914) 8, 244
Blount, Sir Thomas Pope (1649–1697) 69
Bloy, Leon (1846–1917) 134, 180, 208
Blum, Leon (1872–1950) 91
Bodin, Jean (1530–1596) 226
Boehme, Jakob (1575–1624) 89, 134
Boethius, Amicius M. S. (c. 480–524) 98, 166, 241
Bohn, Henry George (1796–1884) 204, 215, 247
Boileau-Despreaux, Nicolas (1636–1711) 116
Bonaparte, Napoleon (1769–1821) 19, 66, 127, 200
Bonar, Andrew (1808–1889) 110
Bonar, Horatius (1808–1889) 222
Bonhoeffer, Dietrich (1906–1945) 35, 37, 39, 45, 47, 65, 66, 86, 102, 132, 135, 149, 217, 220, 227, 243, 244
Boom, Betsie Ten (1885–1944) 248
Boom, Corrie Ten (b. 1892) 212, 242, 248, 255
Boorstin, Daniel (b. 1914) 25
Booth, General William (1829–1912) 7
Boreham, F. W. 61
Bormann, Frank (b. 1928) 240
Bosco, St. John (1815–1888) 163, 256

Bossuet, Jacques Benigne (1627–1704) 23, 168

Bourdaloue, Louis (1632–1704) 57

Boyd, Malcolm (b. 1923) 256

Bradley, Francis H. (1846–1924) 35

Bradley, General Omar N. (b. 1893) 91, 211

Braque, Georges (1882–1963) 238

Braunstein, Richard (b. 1885) 14

Brenken, Gilbert 116

Brickner, Rabbi B. R. (1892–1958) 153

Bridges, Robert (1844–1930) 93

Bright, John (1811–1889) 205

Brodie, J. F. 55

Brontë, Charlotte (1816–1855) 222

Brooks, Phillips (1835–1893) 69, 81, 91, 102, 103, 186, 188

Broun, Heywood (1888–1939) 19

Browne, Sir Thomas (1605–1682) 9, 10, 158

Browning, Elizabeth Barrett (1806–1861) 86

Browning, Robert (1812–1889) 67, 110, 148, 238

Brunner, Emil (1889–1955) 116, 162, 203

Bryant, Sir Arthur (b. 1899) 222

Bryce, Viscount James (1838–1922) 177

Buber, Martin (1878–1965) 31, 63, 97, 143, 170

Buchan, John (1875–1940) 19

Buchman, Frank N. D. (1878–1961) 156, 177

Buck, Pearl (1892–1973) 68

Bulgakov, Sergius (1871–1944) 39, 44

Bunce, Oliver Bell 75

Bunyan, John (1628–1688) 14, 96, 127, 186, 196, 219, 231, 241

Buonarroti, Michelangelo (1475–1564) 7, 165, 230

Burke, Edmund (1728–1797) 14, 17, 25, 33, 34, 46, 79, 80, 89, 101, 104, 145, 171, 178, 226, 229

Burnett, A. Ian 38

Burrows, Millar (b. 1889) 237

Bushnell, Horace (1802–1876) 90

Butler, Nicholas Murray (1862–1947) 84

Butler, Samuel (1612–1680) 93, 113

Butler, Samuel, the Younger (1835–1902) 146, 229

Butterfield, Sir Herbert (b. 1900) 113, 172

Buttrick, George 147

Cadman, S. Parkes (1864–1936) 137

Cailliet, Émile 180

Calverton, V. F. 147

Calvin, John (1509–1564) 39, 170, 212, 217

Camara, Dom Helder (b. 1909) 32, 44, 114, 213

Campbell, Thomas (1733–1795) 203

Camus, Albert (1913–1960) 13, 31 82, 91, 94, 125, 140, 143, 183, 205, 252

Camus, Bishop Jean Pierre (1582–1652) 16, 34, 57, 63, 88, 92, 95, 131, 135, 181, 182, 219, 222, 225, 227, 243

Cantor, Eddie (b. 1892) 49

Carey-Elwes, C. 120

Carlyle, Thomas (1795–1881) 31, 52, 58, 77, 82, 88, 121, 143, 156, 179, 186, 201, 211, 220, 222, 240, 251, 252

Carmichael, Amy (1867–1951) 159

Carnegie, Andrew (1835–1909) 246

Carnegie, Dale 43, 93, 167

Carrel, Alexis (1873–1944) 79, 146, 167

Carretto, Carlo (b. 1910) 148, 185, 186, 215, 240, 244

Cary, Alice (1820–1871) 90, 149

Cary, Joyce (1898–1957) 67

Cassidy, Dr. Sheila (b. 1937) 227, 235

Castro, Jesus de 30

Catherine of Siena, St. (1347–1380) 16, 74, 110, 135, 149, 177, 220

Catherine II, Empress of Russia (the Great) (1729–1896) 90

Cats, Jacob 221

Cavell, Edith (1865–1915) 175

Cecil, Richard (1748–1810) 145, 188

Cerami, Charles A. 157

Cervantes, Miguel de (1547–1616) 77, 118, 122, 159, 193, 201

Chadwick, Samuel (1832–1917) 144

Chalmers, Thomas (1780–1847) 114

Chambers, Oswald 30, 131, 134, 208

Chamfort, Nicholas de (1741–1794) 124, 178

Chaneles, Sol 65

Channing, William Ellery (1780–1842) 82, 191, 214, 266

Chapman, Abbot John (1865–1933) 120, 186, 203, 244, 254

Chapman, John Jay (1862–1933) 113

Chapman, Milo L. 227

Chappell, Clovis G. 188

Charnock, Stephen (1628–1680) 239

Chaucer, Geoffrey (c. 1340–1400) 13, 159, 167, 181, 247
Chavez, César 242
Chazal, Malcolm de 16
Chekhov, Anton (1860–1904) 24, 36, 106, 135, 152
Chesterfield, Lord (1694–1773) 11
Chesterton, Gilbert K. (1874–1936) 9, 15, 18, 24, 26, 28, 37, 41, 42, 44, 50, 52, 53, 57, 62, 67, 71, 74, 80, 98, 103, 112, 117, 120, 121, 123, 132, 136, 140, 150, 152, 159, 163, 166, 180, 185, 200, 208, 218, 223, 230, 233, 243, 250, 251
Chrysostom, St. John (347–407) 12, 25, 27, 28, 48, 60, 61, 71, 79, 92, 104, 145, 159, 191, 206, 211, 225, 233, 241, 243
Churchill, John Spencer (1650–1722) 234
Churchill, Sir Winston S. (1874–1965) 14, 32, 46, 62, 64, 65, 76, 86, 90, 96, 97, 101, 103, 113, 141, 179, 220, 224, 238, 244, 255
Cicero, Marcus Tullius (106–43 B.C.) 53, 65, 102, 104, 130, 131, 169, 176, 188, 222, 231, 240, 243
Clarendon, Lord Edward (1609–1674) 81
Clark, Frank A. (1883–1956) 106
Clark, Glenn 186
Clark, Kenneth 58
Clarke, Arthur C. (b. 1917) 83
Claudel, Paul (1868–1955) 227, 254
Clement of Alexandria, St. (150–220) 19, 20, 106, 108, 112, 125, 126, 174, 186, 196, 202, 207, 211, 254
Clement I, Pope St. (c. 30–100) 29, 47
Clement II, Pope (d. 1047) 202
Climacus, St. John (570–649) 35, 195
Clutton-Brock, Arthur G. (b. 1906) 140, 209, 313
Coburn, John B. 193
Coggan, Archbishop Donald (b. 1909) 23, 33, 39, 137, 186, 188, 221
Coleridge, Samuel Taylor (1772–1834) 11, 37, 235, 246, 249
Collins, John Churton (1848–1908) 11, 75, 206
Colson, Charles (b. 1931) 52
Colton, Charles Caleb (1780–1832) 24, 93, 160, 206, 238, 249
Conant, James Bryant (1893–1978) 131
Confucius (c. 551–479 B.C.) 53, 110, 115, 163, 246
Conklin, Edwin (1863–1952) 54

Connelly, Mother Cornelia (1809–1879) 10, 227
Connolly, Cyril (1903–1974) 107, 213
Conrad, Joseph (1857–1924) 14, 56, 129, 247, 250
Considine, Daniel 216
Constable, John (1776–1837) 18
Conway, James 149
Cook, Robert A. (1646–1726) 252
Cook, Sidney 165
Cooley, Charles Horton (1864–1929) 48, 82
Coolidge, Calvin (1872–1933) 230, 255
Cooper, James Fenimore (1789–1851) 157
Copeland, William (1797–1868) 69
Corbishley, Thomas (1903–1976) 54
Corso, Gregory (b. 1930) 85
Coste, René 244
Coward, Noël (1899–1973) 56
Cowper, William (1731–1800) 45, 86, 87, 167, 194, 198, 206, 208
Cox, Coleman 179
Cox, Harvey (b. 1929) 61, 70
Craig, Archibald C. (b. 1888) 193
Craig, Mary (b. 1928) 227
Cranmer, Archbishop Thomas (1489–1556) 211
Crichton, Mgr. James D. 146, 197
Criswell, Marianne 105
Cromwell, Oliver (1599–1658) 114, 176, 237
Culbertson, William 186
Cullinan, Thomas (b. 1932) 162
Cullman, Oscar (1902–1972) 21, 236
Cummings, William T. 19
Curran, John Philpot (1750–1817) 143
Cuyler, Theodore 67
Cyprian, St. (c. 200–258) 14, 147, 191, 200, 242
Cyril of Jerusalem, St. (c. 315–386) 22, 173

Danielou, Jean (1905–1974) 132
D'Arcy, Martin C. (1888–1972) 180
Darwin, Charles (1809–1882) 14, 80
Davenant, Sir William (1606–1668) 14
Davies, J. G. (1565–1618) 78
Davies, Robertson (b. 1913) 75
Da Vinci, Leonardo (1425–1519) 18, 230
Davis, Charles (b. 1923) 112, 172
Dawson, Christopher (b. 1889) 200
Day, Dorothy (b. 1892) 252

de Beauvoir, Simone 169
de Blois, Louis 248
Debs, Eugene Victor (1855–1926) 41
de Caussade, Jean Pierre (1675–1751) 7, 10, 157, 170
de Chardin, P. Teilhard (1881–1955) 37, 80, 83, 137, 148, 202, 212, 214, 233
de Foucauld, Charles (1858–1916) 100
de Gaulle, Charles (1890–1970) 183
De Haan, Robert D. 132
Deiss, Lucien (b. 1921) 146
Deissmann, Adolf 100
de la Bruyère, Jean (1645–1696) 106, 163, 180, 224
Delacroix, Eugène (1798–1863) 18
de Lamartine, Alphonse 104
de la Salle, Jean Baptiste (1651–1719) 16, 35
de Lenelos, Ninon 89
de Lubac, Henri (b. 1896) 106, 236
Democritus of Abdera (c. 400 B.C.) 134
Demonax the Cynic (c. 150 A.D.) 140
de Montaigne, Michel (1533–1592) 167
Demosthenes (384–322 B.C.) 215
Denk, Hans 91
Dennis, Nigel (b. 1912) 53
de Paul, St. Vincent (1580–1660) 105, 109, 120, 141, 232
de Rosa, Peter (b. 1932) 172
Descartes, René (1596–1650) 190
de Tocqueville, Alexis (1805–1859) 40
de Vries, Peter 97
Dewey, John (1859–1952) 47, 48, 71, 131
Dhuse, Andrew 248
Dibble, Paul 185
Dickens, Charles (1812–1870) 28, 31, 34, 35, 38, 119, 125, 165, 199, 234
Didache (c. 2nd cent. A.D.) see Teaching of Twelve Apostles
Diderot, Denis (1713–1784) 16, 190
Dimnet, Ernest (b. 1869) 88
Disraeli, Benjamin (1804–1881) 9, 10, 37, 46, 56, 81, 104, 132, 136, 171
Dix, Gregory (1901–1952) 78
Dobson, James (b. 1936) 60
Dodd, Charles Harold (1884–1973) 137, 161, 202
Dominian, Doctor Jack (b. 1929) 29, 43, 154, 218
Donne, John (1572–1631) 22, 34, 119, 125, 200
Dostoevski, Feodor (1821–1881) 31, 111, 132, 216

Douglas, Frederick 118
Douglas, James (1837–1918) 169
Drummond, Henry (1851–1897) 136, 221
Dryden, John (1631–1701) 11, 14, 23, 49, 81, 106, 159, 175, 181, 238, 242
du Bose, Henry W. 137
Durant, (Will) William James (b. 1885) 32
Durrell, Gerald (b. 1925) 69
Dussault, Ed. 80
Dwight, Timothy (1752–1817) 25

Eastman, Max (1883–1969) 182
Eckhart, Meister (1260–1327) 97, 102, 128, 138, 143, 160, 171, 215, 217, 219, 238
Eddy, Mary Baker (1821–1910) 108
Edison, Thomas A. (1847–1931) 82, 234
Edwards, Jonathan (1703–1757) 96, 207
Edwards, Tyron (1809–1894) 41, 52, 60, 111, 231
Einstein, Albert (1879–1955) 55, 72, 94, 97, 133, 166, 200, 211, 213, 214, 227, 240, 245
Eixhter, Jean Paul 86
Elimelekh, Rabbi (1820–1892) 134
Eliot, George (1819–1880) 16, 36, 46, 62, 86, 98, 107, 129, 159, 168, 178, 192, 230, 231, 237
Eliot, Thomas Stearns (1888–1965) 15, 64, 172, 219
Elizabeth II, Queen (b. 1926) 175
Elliott, Elisabeth 148
Elliott, Walter 88, 162
Ellis, Henry Havelock (1859–1939) 70, 224, 245
Ellul, Jacques 161
Emerson, Ralph Waldo (1803–1882) 8 23, 24, 33, 41, 46, 56, 59, 65, 71, 75, 82, 86, 88, 93, 98, 105, 107, 113, 116, 125, 128, 153, 155, 166, 168, 192, 194, 224, 225, 229, 232, 233, 242, 246, 251
Emmons, Nathanael 168
Emrich, Richard S. 80
Ephrem of Syria, St. (c. 306–373) 207, 255
Epictetus (60–120) 8, 50, 255
Epicurus (342–270 B.C.) 157, 209
Erasmus, Desiderius (1469–1536) 11, 23, 37, 83, 107, 119, 155, 172, 211, 230, 249
Erskine, John (1509–1589) 51, 141, 202, 231

Erskine, Thomas (1750–1823) 171, 187
Esra, Abraham Ibn 107, 147
Estienne, Henri (1528–1598) 45
Ethelwold, Bishop of Winchester (908–984) 122
Eucherius (743) 221
Eudes, St. John (1601–1680) 132
Eusebius of Caesarea (264–349) 69, 133
Evely, Louis 97
Ezra, Moses Ibn 107

Faber, Frederick William (1814–1863) 9, 19, 51, 68, 72, 87, 88, 103, 110, 123, 125, 127, 136, 145, 174, 175, 213, 227, 232, 248
Farrell, Joseph 138
Farrer, Austin (1904–1968) 128
Faustus, Bishop of Riez, St. (c. 400–480) 47
Feltham, Owen (1602–1668) 193
Fenelon, Archbishop François (1651–1715) 53, 67, 137, 150, 178, 187, 194, 220, 232
Ferguson, John 39
Feuerbach, Ludwig (1804–1872) 45
Field, Henry Martyn 31
Fielding, Henry (1707–1754) 11, 42, 105, 163
Figgis, J. B. 176
Finney, Charles G. (1792–1875) 102
Fitzsimmons, Joseph 44
Flaubert, Gustave (1821–1880) 110
Fontaine, P. 154
Forbes, B. C. 35
Ford, Henry (1863–1947) 56, 142
Forsyth, Peter Taylor (1848–1921) 9, 25, 84, 126
Fosdick, Harry Emerson (1878–1969) 62, 83, 107
Foster, Richard (b. 1942) 50
Fox, George (1624–1691) 144, 160
France, Anatole (1844–1924) pseud. for Jacques A. Thirbault 90, 119, 125, 140, 234
Francis, Brendan 61, 122, 130, 147
Francis de Sales, St. (1567–1622) 2, 17, 31, 34, 48, 50, 51, 57, 70, 88, 92, 93, 95, 96, 99, 103, 109, 114, 120, 127, 131, 145, 150, 152, 154, 160, 168, 173, 175, 178, 179, 183, 188, 197, 201, 216, 217, 219, 224, 225, 233, 243, 244, 248, 252

Francis of Assisi, St. (1181–1226) 54, 60, 114, 153, 188
Frank, Waldo 72
Frankl, Viktor E. 81
Franklin, Benjamin (1706–1790) 12, 15, 16, 35, 60, 63, 74, 95, 97, 103, 123, 131, 136, 183, 201, 221, 234
Freud, Sigmund (1856–1939) 87
Fromm, Erich (b. 1900) 24, 71, 147, 165, 176, 180, 192, 227, 240
Frost, Evelyn 108, 109
Frost, Paul (b. 1938) 33, 72, 73, 87, 154, 207, 223, 227, 246, 250
Froude, James Anthony (1818–1894) 164, 235
Fry, Christopher (b. 1907) 76
Fuller, Andrew (1754–1815) 117
Fuller, David Otis 37
Fuller, Margaret Witter (b. 1871) 115, 138
Fuller, Thomas (1608–1661) 16, 19, 27, 29, 53, 74, 90, 103, 114, 150, 173, 176, 185, 187, 191, 196, 210, 218, 222, 223, 245, 246, 247
Furlong, Monica (b. 1930) 9
Fynn 147

Gabirol, Ibn, (c. 1022–1070) 221
Galbraith, John Kenneth (b. 1908) 44, 184, 246
Galileo, Galilei (1564–1642) 131
Gandhi, Mohandas K. (1869–1948) 32, 70, 74, 91, 97, 99, 118, 119, 120, 143, 150, 168, 176, 216, 227, 255
Gardner, John W. 59, 82, 142, 177
Garfield, James A. (1831–1881) 101
Garrick, David (1717–1779) 112
Garrigou-Lagrange O. P., Reginald (1877–1964) 10
Garrison, William Lloyd (1805–1879) 120
Gasset, Jose Ortega Y. 251
Gautier, Theophile (1811–1872) 148
Gayton, Edmund (1608–1666) 47
Geier, Woodrow A. 20
George, Henry (1839–1897) 33, 41
Gerould, Katherine Fullerton 63
Gibbon, Edward (1737–1794) 7, 113, 192
Gibbons, Cardinal James (1834–1921) 57, 124, 198
Gibran, Kahlil (1833–1931) 60, 67, 94, 142, 214, 232, 252
Gide, André (1869–1951) 18, 65, 74, 96, 107, 131, 208

Giles, Brother 23
Gill, Eric Rowton (1882–1940) 18, 62, 71, 103
Gillis, James M. 86, 121
Giornale, H. 252
Gissing, George (1857–1903) 192
Gladstone, William E. (1809–1898) 100
Glasgow, Arnold H. 122, 141
Glasser, Art 216
Goethe, Johann Wolfgang von (1749–1832) 12, 18, 48, 54, 55, 66, 67, 73, 75, 85, 89, 90, 92, 93, 97, 115, 118, 124, 127, 137, 142, 148, 154, 174, 221, 222, 224, 230, 234, 240, 241, 250
Goldsmith, Oliver (1730–1774) 81, 93, 227
Goldwyn, Samuel (1882–1974) 75
Goodier, Archbishop Alban (1869–1939) 51, 64, 75, 195
Gordon, General Charles George (1833–1885) 238
Gordon, Samuel 43, 79
Gore, Bishop Charles (1853–1932) 126, 145
Gorky, Maxim (1868–1936) 62
Gough, W. D. 176
Gracian, Baltasar (1601–1658) 250
Graham, Dom Aelred (b. 1907) 124, 146
Graham, Billy (b. 1918) 17, 21, 29, 37, 38, 48, 49, 73, 75, 79, 96, 100, 102, 111, 114, 132, 140, 163, 174, 189, 196, 216, 222, 240, 245, 256
Grant, Ulysses S. (1822–1885) 40
Gray, Thomas (1716–1771) 96
Grayson, David 51, 252
Greaves, J. P. 49
Green, Michael (b. 1930) 64, 232
Greene, Graham (b. 1904) 34, 83, 108, 129
Greever, W. H. 226
Gregory I, Pope St. (590–604) 9, 15, 20, 106, 158, 187, 211, 219, 231, 249, 252
Gregory of Nazianzen, St. (c. 330–390) 221
Gregory of Nyssa, St. (335–394) 178
Gregory, Richard (b. 1923) 211
Grenfell, Sir Wilfrid (1865–1940) 217
Greve, Fred 12
Grier, John P. 165
Griffiths, Dom Bede (b. 1906) 80
Grooms, Jordon 162
Grou, Jean Nicolas (1731–1803) 145, 227
Guardini, Romano (1885–1968) 37, 115
Guizat, François (1787–1874) 75

Haecker, Theodor 87, 94, 113, 121, 125, 128, 233, 254
Hague, William 127
Haig, Sir Douglas (1861–1928) 39
Hale, Edward Everett (1822–1909) 8
Halverson, Richard 132
Hamilton, James (1769–1829) 159
Hamilton, J. Wallace 48
Hammarskjold, Dag (1905–1961) 52, 64, 82, 97, 99, 114, 143, 202, 216, 217
Hammerstein, Oscar (1895–1960) 31
Hardie, James Keir (1856–1915) 197
Hardy, Thomas (1840–1928) 63, 110
Hare, Augustus W. (1792–1834) 36
Harper, Michael (b. 1931) 217
Harris, Sydney 90, 140, 165
Harrison, Paul W. 137
Hart, Elizabeth 190
Haskins, Henry S. 242
Hawthorne, Nathaniel (1804–1864) 118, 123, 125, 182
Haydn, Franz Joseph (1732–1809) 134
Hazlitt, William (1778–1830) 72, 103, 140, 143, 167, 171, 190, 230, 250
Hecht, Ben (1894–1964) 234
Hecker, Isaac T. (1819–1888) 55, 115, 178
Hegel, Georg Wilhelm F. (1770–1831) 92
Hello, Ernest 10
Helps, Sir Arthur (1813–1875) 137, 208
Hemans, Felicia (1793–1835) 12
Hembree, Charles R. 7
Hemingway, Ernest (1899–1961) 53
Hendricks, Howard 218
Henry, Carl F. (b. 1913) 23, 212
Henry, Matthew (1662–1714) 30, 103, 176, 208
Heraclitus (540–475 B.C.) 33, 190
Herbert, George (1593–1633) 35, 43, 50, 63, 88, 94, 103, 111, 113, 150, 181, 184, 185, 195, 196, 212, 229, 230, 237, 242, 243, 247
Hermas, Shepherd of (c. 155) 63, 64, 88, 129, 206
Herold, Don 253
Herrick, Robert 156
Hertz, Joseph H. (1872–1946) 45, 133
Hesburgh, Theodore M. 174
Heschel, Abraham Joshua (1907–1972) 138, 196, 251
Hession, Roy 89
Heywood, John (c. 1494–1578) 15, 28, 67, 75, 89, 122, 191

Hicks, Granville (b. 1901) 123
Hill, Rowland (1744–1833) 71, 187
Hilton, Walter (1340–1396) 34, 128, 167, 184, 200, 204, 221
Hinkson, Katherine (1861–1931) 229
Hippolytus, St. (c. 160–235) 47
Hobbes, Thomas (1588–1679) 113
Hodge, Charles (1797–1878) 164, 204
Hoecker, Theodor 63
Hoffer, Eric 92, 101, 118, 152, 208, 239
Holland, Josiah Gilbert (1819–1881) 29, 241, 253
Hollis, Christopher (1902–1977) 45
Holmes, John Andrew 54, 217
Holmes, Oliver Wendell (1809–1894) 7, 25, 26, 51, 95, 123, 130, 175, 230
Hooft, Dr. Visser't 71
Hooker, Herman 160
Hooker, Richard (1594–1662) 40
Hoover, Herbert (1874–1964) 36, 176, 245
Hope, Bob (b. 1903) 13
Hopkins, Gerard Manley (1844–1889) 73, 103, 254
Hopps, J. P. 207
Houghton, William H. (1736–1823) 25
Housman, Laurence (1865–1959) 208
Hovey, E. Paul 26
Howe, Edgar Watson (1854–1937) 100, 201
Howe, Nathaniel (1764–1837) 208
Hubbard, Elbert (1859–1915) 56, 74, 82, 100, 150, 157, 163, 201, 231, 237
Huddleston, Trevor (1913–1998) 197, 256
Hughes, Philip (1895–1967) 167
Hugo, Victor (1802–1885) 13, 26, 31, 53, 92, 107, 117, 187, 225, 250
Hui Hai 128
Hull, Clarence W. 69
Hulst, Maurice 229
Hume, Cardinal Basil (1923–1999) 186
Huskins, Henry S. 75
Huvelin, Abbé (1838–1910) 38, 64, 208
Huxley, Aldous (1894–1963) 24, 49, 82, 99, 176
Huxley, Sir Julian (1887–1975) 128
Huxley, Thomas Henry (1825–1895) 14, 25, 68, 92

Ibsen, Henrik (1828–1906) 92, 164
Ignatius of Antioch, St. (d. 110) 27, 35, 37, 71, 78, 79, 83, 154, 155, 179

Ignatius Loyola, St. (1491–1556) 66, 227
Inge, Dean William Ralph (1860–1954) 12, 16, 85, 94, 100, 121, 127, 225, 254, 255
Ingersoll, Robert G. (1833–1899) 36, 41, 120
Innocent I, Pope St. (d. 417) 47
Ionesco, Eugène (b. 1912) 234
Ireland, Archbishop John (1838–1918) 40
Irenaeus, St. (c. 125–202) 32, 126, 171, 210, 255
Irving, Washington (1783–1859) 38
Isidore of Seville, St. (c. 560–636) 27, 58, 69, 228

Jackson, Holbrook 90. 205
Jacobs, Margaret Moore 89
James, Eric 146
James, Fleming 194
James, Henry (1811–1882) 18
James, William (1842–1910) 17, 36, 43, 45, 47, 73, 153, 156, 171, 190
Jarrett, Bede 122, 166, 225
Jefferson, Thomas (1743–1826) 41, 101, 116, 124, 132, 145, 152, 165, 185, 192, 197, 209
Jeffrey, Edward (b. 1932) 42, 124
Jeffrey, Lord Francis (1773–1850) 201
Jennings, James (1854–1920) 26
Jeremias, Jeremias (1900–1979) 79
Jerome, St. (c. 340–420) 10, 27, 37, 42, 93, 110, 123, 183, 208, 212, 256
Jerome, Jerome K. (1859–1927) 253
Jerrold, Douglas W. (1803–1857) 122, 222
Jeschel, Abraham 80
Jewel, Bishop John (1522–1571) 27
Joachim of Flora (or Fiore) (c. 1130–1201) 19
John XXIII, Pope (1881–1963) 43, 58, 76, 77, 81, 87, 94, 149, 187, 197, 206, 208, 234, 245
John of Avila (1500–1569) 233
John of Damascus, St. (c. 675–749) 15, 189, 194, 204
John of Paris (1255–1306) 191
John of Ruysbroeck (1293–1381) 87
John of Salisbury (c. 1115–1180) 170, 182
John of the Cross, St. (1542–1591) 9, 47, 50, 70, 74, 99, 100, 118, 129, 148, 220, 228
John Paul I, Pope (1912–1978) 160, 187
John Paul II, Pope (b. 1920) 57, 71, 86,

134, 148, 153, 156, 157, 160, 176, 185, 192, 204, 210, 212, 221, 238, 242, 253
Johnson, Frank (b. 1922) 23
Johnson, Lyndon B. (1908–1973) 31, 183, 245
Johnson, Samuel (1709–1784) 29, 38, 42, 46, 72, 81, 117, 118, 131, 135, 138, 155, 164, 176, 179, 190, 216, 218
Jones, Bob 249
Jones, E. Stanley 200
Jones, Franklin P. 36
Jones, Rufus Matthew (1863–1948) 97
Joubert, Joseph (1754–1824) 13, 15, 36, 98, 125, 169, 220
Jowett, Benjamin (1817–1893) 67
Jowett, John Henry (1864–1923) 42, 133, 164
Julian of Norwich (1343–1443) 150, 179, 200, 221, 240
Jung, Carl Gustav (1875–1961) 52, 77, 129, 208, 221, 242
Justin Martyr, St. (c. 100–165) 136, 171, 180, 229
Juvenal, Decimus Junius (40–125) 56, 204, 247

Kant, Immanuel (1724–1804) 26, 92, 118, 164, 180
Keary, Annie 253
Keats, John (1795–1821) 23
Keble, John (1792–1866) 195
Keller, Helen (1880–1968) 17, 241
Kelman, John 40, 257
Kelsey, Morton T. 108, 158
Kemelman, Harry 58
Kempis, Thomas à (1379–1471) 10, 12, 24, 26, 42, 49, 57, 73, 77, 83, 96, 99, 102, 106, 121, 131, 134, 135, 138, 142, 165, 166, 167, 168, 171, 173, 174, 175, 176, 178, 184, 195, 215, 216, 220, 222, 226, 228, 232, 237, 242, 245, 249, 252, 257
Kennedy, Edward M. (b. 1932) 198
Kennedy, John F. (1917–1963) 31, 98, 176, 184, 205
Kettering, Charles F. (1876–1958) 83, 94
Khrushchev, Nikita S. (1894–1971) 44
Kierkegaard, Søren (1813–1855) 10, 11, 74, 90, 122, 170, 209, 248
Killey, Francis C. 53
King, Martin Luther Jr. (1929–1968) 85, 149, 150, 228, 242

Kingsley, Charles (1819–1875) 83, 92, 152, 172
Kipling, Elbert 7
Kipling, Rudyard (1865–1936) 100, 252
Kissinger, Henry A. (b. 1923) 245
Knowles, James S. (1784–1862) 47
Knox, Mgr. Ronald A. (1888–1957) 39, 51, 161, 183
Koenig, Franziskus 183
Koestler, Arthur (b. 1905) 43, 95
Koffler, Camilla 16
Kohn, Harold E. 214
Kordenat, Mildred E. 137
Korzybski, Alfred (1879–1950) 67
Kostka, St. Stanislaus (1550–1568) 59
Kraemer, Hendrik (1880–1965) 204
Kuebler-Ross, Elizabeth 12
Kulp, John C. (b. 1921) 65
Kung, Hans (b. 1928) 148, 198, 223, 237
Kuyper, Abraham (1837–1920) 130, 193

Lactantius, Lucius Caelius (c. 260–340) 163
Laighton, Albert (1829–1887) 130
Laing, R. D. 61, 242
la Mance, Thomas 230
Lamb, Charles (1775–1834) 157, 211
Lambert, D. W. 157
Langland, William (1330–1400) 9, 85
Laroe, William 40
Latimer, Bishop Hugh (1485–1555) 99, 179
Lavater, Johann Kasper (1741–1801) 9, 80, 234
Lavelle, Louis 60
Law, William (1686–1761) 43, 111, 123, 149, 181, 187, 191, 226, 255
Lawrence, Brother (Nicholas Herman) (1611–1691) 115, 145, 187, 255
Lawrence, David Herbert (1885–1930) 46, 55, 70, 73, 92, 146, 153, 164, 199, 213
Leary, Don 76
Lee, Vernon (1856–1935) 142
Lee, William Grant (1550–1610) 140
le Gallienne, Richard (1866–1947) 38
Leighton, Archbishop Robert (1611–1684) 10
Leo XIII, Pope (1878–1903) 41, 113, 180, 224
Lewis, Austin Alexander 9
Lewis, C. S. (1898–1963) 7, 11, 17, 24, 38, 52, 59, 72, 76, 91, 98, 107, 111, 118,

134, 147, 151, 161, 169, 172, 191, 209, 241, 248, 256
Lichtenberg, George C. (1742–1799) 28, 229, 250
Liebman, Joshua 235
Lincicome, F. 40
Lincoln, Abraham (1809–1865) 68, 81, 94, 119, 125, 143, 152, 165, 177, 206, 220, 229
Lincoln, John L. 65
Lindsell, Harold 103, 162, 176
Lippmann, Walter (1889–1974) 141, 234
Livingstone, David (1813–1873) 162
Livy, Titus Livins (59 B.C.–17 A.D.) 152
Lloyd-Jones, Jenkin 158
Lloyd-Jones, Martyn 23, 40, 71, 83, 87, 91, 100, 210, 212
Locke, Charles Edward 19
Locke, John (1632–1704) 34, 77, 141
Lodge, Sir Oliver (1851–1940) 256
Lonergan, Bernard J. T. (b. 1904) 16
Long, Roswell C. 226
Longfellow, Henry Wordsworth (1807–1882) 8, 11, 15, 18, 74, 228
Lortz, Joseph (b. 1887) 199
Loughrane, John P. 226
Louis IX of France, King St. (1226–1270) 233
Lowe, Arnold 78
Lowell, James Russell (1819–1891) 82, 120, 177, 245
Lubbock, Sir John (1803–1865) 135
Lucas, Edward Verrall (1868–1938) 58
Lucas, Samuel 48
Lumsden, Marshall 72
Lunn, Arnold (1888–1914) 52, 146, 160, 161, 235
Luther, Martin (1483–1546) 15, 22, 24, 26, 30, 43, 49, 65, 68, 76, 84, 100, 108, 111, 119, 124, 128, 133, 140, 148, 156, 166, 187, 189, 200, 201, 202, 213, 217, 220, 221, 228, 250, 253
Lynch, William F. 130
Lynd, Robert S. (1892–1970) 48, 54, 107, 228
Lyte, Henry Francis (1793–1847) 21, 98

Mabie, Hamilton 152
MacArthur, General Douglas (1880–1964) 177
Macauley, J. C. 103, 229

Macaulay, Baron Thomas B. (1800–1859) 26
McConnell, Francis J. (1871–1953) 63
McCraken, Robert 11
Macdonald, George (1824–1905) 12, 23, 59, 68, 111, 116, 145, 149, 151, 161, 177, 214, 215, 232, 253, 256
McKay, David O. (1873–1970) 38
Mackenzie, Compton (1883–1972) 152
McKeoun, Blanche 29
Mackintosh, Sir James (1765–1832) 51, 178
Maclaren, Alexander (1826–1910) 84, 157, 159, 214
Maclaren, Ian, pseud. for John Watson (1850–1907) 161
MacLeod, Lord George F. (b. 1895) 41, 71, 114, 128
McLuhan, Marshall (1911–1981) 254
MacManus, Seumas (b. 1869) 231
MacMurray, John 20, 73, 218
McNabb O. P., Vincent (1868–1943) 14, 19, 21, 23, 65, 101, 126, 133
McNamara, Robert (b. 1916) 17
MacNaughton, John 157
MacNutt, Francis 29, 108, 219
Macquarrie, John (b. 1919) 20
Maeterlinck, Maurice (1862–1949) 245
Main O.S.B., John (b. 1926) 158
Malraux, André (1901–1976) 141
Mann, Thomas 25, 219
Manning, Cardinal Henry E. (1808–1892) 57, 104, 124, 145, 168, 183, 192, 235, 248
Mansfield, Katherine (1888–1923) 83
Mao Tse-Tung (1893–1976) 44
Maritain, Jacques (1882–1973) 99, 180, 205
Markham, Edwin (1852–1940) 159
Marlowe, Christopher (1564–1593) 111
Marquis, Don (Donald Robert) (1878–1937) 70, 109, 131, 192
Marsh, John (1752–1828) 235
Marshall, Catherine (b. 1914) 8, 134, 168, 185, 187
Martial, Marcus Valerius (43–104) 85, 247
Martin, Hugh (1890–1964) 164
Martin, Paul 104
Martyn, Henry (1781–1812) 162
Marx, Groucho (b. 1895) 158
Marx, Karl (1818–1883) 184
Mason, John (1770–1829) 214

268

Mason, T.W. 137
Matthews, T. S. 43
Matthews, W. R. 77
Mattock, Paul 210
Maturin, Basil W. (1847–1915) 72, 129
Maugham, W. Somerset (1874–1965) 57, 205, 236
Mauriac, François (1885–1970) 57, 80, 121
Maurice, Frederick D. (1805–1872) 148, 200
Maurois, André (1885–1967) 154
Maximus the Confessor, St. (c. 580–662) 151
May, Rollo 94
Mazzarello, Mary (1837–1881) 34
Mazzini, Giuseppe (1805–1872) 171, 236
Mead, Margaret (1901–1978) 70, 86, 154
Melanchton, Philip (1497–1560) 210
Melville, Herman (1819–1891) 117, 135
Menander (342–291 B.C.) 80
Mencken, Henry Louis (1880–1956) 30, 60, 68, 76, 169
Mendelssohn Moses (1729–1786) 213
Menninger, Carl 149, 151
Mercier, Cardinal Désiré J. (1851–1926) 96, 138
Merton, Thomas (1915–1968) 14, 18, 38, 50, 57, 63, 68, 84, 107, 121, 149, 156, 160, 167, 189, 224, 237, 243, 256
Meyer, F. B. (1825–1898) 121
Middleton, Thomas (1570–1627) 60
Mill, John Stuart (1806–1873) 41, 58
Millar, J. F. 178
Miller, Henry (1891–1980) 64
Miller, Herbert 157
Miller, John (1923–1961) 103
Milligan, (Spike) T. A. (b. 1918) 143
Milton, John (1608–1674) 15, 99, 141, 171, 198, 239, 240
Mitchell, S. Weir (1829–1914) 236
Mizner, Wilson 72, 89, 90, 142
Moffat, Robert (1795–1883) 78
Molinski, Waldemar 243
Monaghan, George 95
Montaigne, Michel de (1533–1592) 47, 85, 131, 167, 190, 193, 199
Moody, Dwight L. (1837–1899) 20, 34, 81, 115, 149, 191, 209, 226
Moore, George (1853–1933) 197
Moore, Thomas (1779–1852) 108, 111
Moran, Gabriel (b. 1935) 79, 204

More, Sir Thomas, St. (1478–1535) 21, 28, 42, 85, 113, 226, 234
Morgan, G. Campbell 185
Morley, Christopher (1890–1957) 194
Morris, Colin (b. 1929) 233
Morris, Leon 185, 198
Morris, William (1834–1896) 23
Morrison, G. H. 215
Moseley, Rufus 57
Moss, C. B. 56, 204
Mostert, Noël 223
Mott, John R. (1865–1955) 106
Motyer, J. A. 22
Moule, Charles F. D. (b. 1908) 202
Muggeridge, Malcolm (b. 1903) 12, 41, 66, 158, 192
Müller, George 87
Mullins, Edgar Young (1860–1928) 126
Mumford, Lewis (b. 1895) 15
Munro, H. H. (Saki) (1870–1916) 199
Murdoch, Iris (b. 1919) 19
Murray, John C. (b. 1904) 32, 162
Myers, Cecil 154

Nash, Ogden (1902–1971) 193
Nathan, George Jean (1882–1958) 17
Necker, Madame (1739–1794) 110
Neill, Bishop Stephen (b. 1900) 143
Neri, St. Philip (1515–1595) 57, 228
Newman, Cardinal John Henry (1801–1890) 14, 18, 21, 24, 27, 28, 32, 33, 37, 49, 51, 55, 57, 61, 67, 68, 77, 84, 93, 95, 104, 105, 110, 111, 113, 118, 120, 124, 139, 141, 143, 155, 160, 161, 166, 172, 195, 197, 200, 204, 214, 228, 236, 237, 238, 244
Newquist, David 24
Newton, John (1725–1807) 52, 189
Newton, Joseph Fort (b. 1878) 84, 147, 158, 160
Nicholas, David 193
Nicholl, Donald (b. 1923) 114
Niebuhr, Reinhold (1892–1971) 63, 102
Nietzsche, Friedrich Wilhelm 30, 52, 56, 74, 128, 139, 209, 241, 244
Nightingale, Florence (1820–1910) 117, 144, 248
Nixon, Richard M. (b. 1913) 65
Nye, Harold 95
Nyerere, Julius K. (b. 1922) 223

O'Connell, Daniel (1775–1847) 183

Ogilvie, Lloyd John (b. 1938) 87
O'Malley, Austin 64, 107, 110, 136, 189, 196, 217, 225
Oman, John Wood (1860–1939) 198
Orchard, William Edwin (1877–1955) 40
Origen of Alexandria (185–254) 36, 66, 108, 126, 137, 240
Orione, Blessed Don (1872–1940) 194
Orton, Joe (John Kingsley) (1933–1967) 233
Orton, William A. 160
Orwell, George (Eric Blair) (1903–1950) 19, 44, 76, 224
Osborn, Alexander F. 55
Ovid (43 B.C.–17 A.D.) 142
Oxnam, G. Bromley 136

Packer, J. I. (b. 1926) 26, 182, 204, 212
Paine, Thomas (1737–1809) 34, 161
Pallotti, St. Vincent (1795–1850) 114
Palmer, Cecil 44
Panin, Count Nikita (1718–1783) 98
Parker, Theodore (1810–1860) 231
Parkhurst, Charles H. 196, 215
Pascal, Blaise (1623–1662) 15, 16, 24, 27, 30, 38, 52, 84, 96, 98, 101, 106, 107, 110, 114, 116, 121, 131, 136, 139, 145, 146, 150, 153, 161, 164, 167, 182, 195, 196, 209, 231, 234, 239, 252
Pasteur, Louis (1822–1895) 55
Patmore, Coventry (1823–1896) 47, 59, 209, 252
Paton, Alan (b. 1903) 70
Patrick, St. (c. 385–461) 187
Paul VI, Pope (1897–1978) 177, 198, 221
Peale, Norman Vincent 186
Péguy, Charles (1873–1914) 238
Peirce, Charles Sanders (1839–1914) 211
Pelikan, Jaroslav 236
Penington, I. 87
Penn, William (1644–1718) 37, 46, 51, 121, 164, 168, 175, 206, 239, 257
Pepplier, Agnes 122
Pepys, Samuel (1633–1703) 89
Perry, Bliss (1860–1954) 69
Peters, George W. 250
Pettingile, William 257
Petit-Senn, J. 89
Pfister, Oscar 119
Phelps, William Lyon (1865–1943) 95, 154

Phillips, Canon J. B. (1906–1982) 79, 115, 129, 198
Philo of Alexandria (b. 10 B.C.) 140
Pike, James A. 213
Pittenger, Norman (b. 1905) 189, 217
Pius X, Pope St. (1835–1914) 43
Pius XI, Pope (1857–1939) 32, 44, 72, 133
Pius XII, Pope (1876–1958) 35, 44, 141, 253
Pius, Raoul 59
Plato (427–347 B.C.) 137, 183, 239
Plautus, Fitus (254–184 B.C.) 86
Pliny the Elder (23–79) 115
Plomp, John 36
Plutarch (c. 66) 53, 242
Polycarp, St. (d. 167) 34, 137, 247
Pope, Alexander (1688–1744) 16, 21, 77, 90, 116, 117, 159, 167, 184, 190, 241
Porter, George 125, 132
Power, J. I. 55
Power, Richard (1630–1690) 130
Pratt, Ianthe (b. 1926) 146
Preston, Arthur 79
Price, Eugenia 250
Priestley, John B. (b. 1894) 257
Pringle-Pattison, A. S. 127
Prior, Matthew 193
Prochnow, Herbert V. 41, 61
Proust, Marcel (1871–1922) 55, 105
Proverbs:
African 91, 249
American 16, 70, 230, 253
Ancient 49
Arab 51, 95, 109, 136, 151, 171, 187, 240
Belgian 82
Bengalese 232
Bulgarian 107, 193, 220, 232
Chinese 7, 25, 34, 51, 59, 81, 86, 87, 88, 92, 93, 105, 115, 142, 175, 178, 179, 184, 205, 206, 231, 253
Croatian 194
Czech 89, 90, 106
Danish 12, 76, 82, 88, 95, 96, 112, 119, 123, 142, 151, 161, 187, 219
Dutch 111
English 9, 11, 13, 14, 16, 23, 25, 27, 28, 29, 30, 31, 34, 36, 40, 42, 47, 51, 52, 54, 57, 58, 59, 60, 61, 62, 63, 64, 65, 68, 69, 74, 75, 76, 77, 78, 80, 83, 85, 88, 91, 93, 95, 96, 97, 99, 104, 105, 109, 110, 116, 117, 122, 124, 129, 132, 136, 139, 140, 142, 153, 155, 167, 171,

172, 175, 177, 181, 182, 183, 186, 193, 195, 201, 205, 206, 209, 210, 216, 218, 221, 222, 225, 226, 227, 229, 231, 235, 241, 242, 245, 246, 247, 249, 250, 251, 252, 257
Estonian 233
Finnish 65, 254
French 14, 24, 28, 33, 40, 42, 49, 53, 62, 68, 74, 76, 81, 94, 95, 98, 103, 144, 154, 190, 195, 201, 209, 218, 235, 241, 249, 253
German 13, 15, 25, 63, 64, 76, 77, 80, 90, 96, 99, 101, 105, 107, 110, 111, 112, 116, 121, 123, 126, 163, 177, 187, 239, 245
Greek 13, 60, 68, 91, 104, 159, 168, 189, 228, 249, 253
Gypsy 87
Hebrew 15, 151, 184
Hindu 112
Hungarian 9
Irish 8, 82, 90, 147, 216, 257
Italian 31, 52, 53, 61, 105, 108, 109, 166, 184, 189
Japanese 68, 91, 137, 164, 186
Jewish 13, 27, 29, 46, 58, 86, 95, 97, 117, 121, 141, 151, 164, 165, 184, 190, 205, 213
Latin 47, 117, 168, 177, 184, 194, 209, 218, 219, 221, 230, 239, 249, 256
Malayan 137
Moroccan 86, 165
Nigerian 94
Oriental 134
Persian 96
Polish 16, 32, 68
Portuguese 112
Roman 206
Russian 27, 59, 61, 72, 88, 102, 107, 144, 152, 154, 156, 231, 237
Scottish 46, 47, 65, 215
Sikh 213
Spanish 55, 101, 111, 124, 129, 133, 140, 163, 192, 231, 237, 239, 251
Swiss 19, 151
Turkish 54, 88, 105, 194
Tuscan 247
Welsh 20, 65, 170, 233, 252
Yiddish 30, 49, 61, 74, 76, 133, 171, 187, 194, 247
Yugoslav 153, 239
Punshon, William Morley 237
Pusey, Edward B. (1800–1882) 145

Quarles, Francis (1592–1644) 255
Quillen, Robert (1887–1948) 154
Quintilian, Marcus Fabius (c. 35–95) 80
Quoist, Michel (b. 1921) 26, 122, 138, 164

Rabelais, Francis (1494–1553) 139
Rahner, Karl (b. 1904) 40, 92, 202, 207
Raine, A. 15
Raines, Richard C. 38
Ramakrishna, Sri. (1836–1886) 46
Ramsey, Archbishop Arthur Michael (b. 1904) 78, 124, 168, 169, 181, 205, 207, 236
Ramuz, Charles F. (1878–1947) 8
Raven, Charles E. 31, 207
Reding, Marcel 156
Rees, Jean 154
Rees, Paul S. 100
Renan, Joseph Ernest (1823–1892) 14, 133
Rest, Frederich 22
Reynolds, Sir Joshua (1723–1792) 253
Rice, John R. 39
Richard, Cliff (b. 1940) 22, 187, 213, 238
Richard of Chichester, St. (1198–1253) 238
Richards, Hubert J. (b. 1921) 130
Richardson, Alan (1905–1975) 10, 22, 27, 33, 79, 136, 156, 161, 203, 210, 236
Richter, Jean Paul (1763–1825) 34, 53, 91, 98
Rickaby, Joseph 180, 241
Rilke, Rainer Maria (1875–1926) 61, 105, 154, 199, 227
Riney, Earl 11
Roberts, Archbishop T.D. 114, 183
Robertson, Frederick W. (1816–1853) 212
Robinson, Don 104, 157
Robinson, Bishop John A. T. (b. 1919) 127, 139, 146, 172, 213
Robinson, N. H. G. 78
Rochefoucauld, François de la (1613–1680) 30, 51, 96, 117, 123, 132, 173, 201, 221, 230, 245, 247
Rogers, Will (1879–1935) 16, 76
Rolland, Romain (1866–1944) 166
Rolle, Richard (c. 1300–1349) 139
Romaine, William 103
Roosevelt, Eleanor (1884–1962) 216
Roosevelt, Franklin D. (1882–1945) 49, 89, 193

Roosevelt, Theodore (1858–1919) 7, 26, 123, 151, 152, 163, 185, 198, 249
Rosell, Merv. 20
Rosenstock-Huessy, Eugen (1888–1973) 20, 25, 218
Rosenzweig, Franz (1886–1929) 213
Rossello, Mary Joseph 59, 69
Rossetti, Christina (1830–1894) 168, 173, 233
Rossetti, Dante Gabriel (1828–1882) 20
Rousseau, Jean Jacques (1712–1778) 9, 29, 49, 61, 66, 100, 175, 193, 235, 241, 251
Roux, Joseph (d. 1794) 72, 95, 217, 222, 223
Rowland, Helen (1876–1945) 154
Royce, Josiah (1855–1916) 45
Rubinstein, Artur (b. 1886) 208
Ruffert, Ulrike 175
Runbeck, Margaret Lee 107
Ruskin, John (1819–1900) 19, 23, 25, 42, 46, 69, 72, 87, 98, 105, 138, 139, 191, 206, 215, 253
Russell, Bertrand A. W. (1872–1970) 53, 76, 196, 234, 246, 257
Russell, Lord William (1639–1683) 142
Rutherford, Mark, pseud. for W. H. White (1831–1913) 127, 204, 223
Rutherford, Samuel (1600–1661) 12, 102
Ruysbroeck, John of 87

Saadi (c. 1200) 137
Sahahib, Habib 94
Saint-Exupéry, Antoine de (1900–1944) 149, 202
Saltmarsh, John 248
Samuel, Viscount Herbert L. S. (1870–1963) 76
Samuel, Maurice 133
Sanford, Agnes 94, 108, 134
Santayana, George (1863–1952) 13, 65, 115, 175, 176, 181, 193, 209, 237, 239, 241
Sarnoff, David (1891–1971) 179
Savary, Louis M. (b. 1936) 246
Savas, E. S. 40
Savonarola, Girolamo (1452–1498) 239
Sayers, Dorothy L. (1893–1957) 56, 247, 253
Schechter, Solomon (1847–1915) 15
Scheeben, M. J. 237
Schillebeeckx, E. (b. 1914) 207
Schiller, Johann C. F. von (1759–1805) 159, 235, 240

Schlink, M. Basilea 97
Schnitzler, Arthur (1862–1931) 92, 155
Schaeffer, Francis A. 153, 196
Schopenhauer, Arthur (1788–1860) 19, 34, 46, 54, 81, 167, 191, 196, 203, 224, 243
Schreiner, Olive (1855–1920) 107
Schroeder, Johann H. (1642–1704) 99
Schuller, David 89
Schurz, Carl (1829–1906) 123
Schutz, Prior Roger (b. 1915) 50, 106, 146, 188
Schwab, Charles M. (1862–1939) 17, 32
Schweitzer, Albert (1875–1965) 20, 81, 85, 99, 104, 107, 111, 118, 131, 139, 144, 167, 189, 197, 202, 218, 224, 239, 253, 257
Scott, Sir Walter (1771–1832) 31, 52, 151
Scudder, Vida P. 10
Searle, Mark (b. 1938) 10, 207, 210
Secker, Thomas 16, 232
Selden, John (1584–1654) 54
Seneca (c. 5–65) 103, 129, 131, 151, 164, 168, 215, 221, 242
Sengai 118
Seraphim of Savoy, St. (1759–1833) 246
Seton, Elizabeth (1774–1821) 43
Sevareid, Eric 185
Shakespeare, William (1564–1616) 68, 80, 94, 104, 105, 123, 130, 194, 223, 235
Shaw, George Bernard (1856–1950) 28, 33, 36, 89, 99, 109, 113, 118, 119, 127, 134, 144, 176, 198, 219
Sheen, Archbishop Fulton J. 30, 34, 39, 41, 73, 89, 130, 150, 160, 166, 178, 214, 215, 218, 232, 251
Sheppard, Bishop David (b. 1929) 55, 162
Shoemaker, Samuel M. 118, 134
Silesius, Angelus, pseud for Johannes Scheffler (1624–1677) 92, 129, 156
Simmons, Charles 218
Simpson, A. B. 189
Singh, Sadhu Sundar 110
Smiles, Samuel (1812–1904) 216
Smith, Alexander (1830–1867) 39, 158
Smith, Hannah Whithall (1832–1911) 120
Smith, Harold J. 163
Smith, Logan Pearsall (1865–1946) 198, 244, 257
Smith, Roy L. 17, 39, 190
Smith, Sydney (1771–1845) 190
Smith, William Robertson (1846–1894) 26

Sockman, Ralph W. 150, 235
Socrates (469–399 B.C.) 124, 246
Söderblom, Nathan (1866–1931) 209
Sollitt, Kenneth 62
Solzhenitsyn, Alexander I. (b. 1918) 153
Soper, Lord Donald O. (1903–1998) 177
Sophocles (495–406 B.C.) 141
South, Prebendary Robert (1634–1716) 54
Spalding, John Lancaster 77, 82, 130, 184, 222, 223
Spencer, Herbert (1820–1903) 24, 120, 239
Spinoza, Benedict de (1632–1677) 42, 93, 177
Spurgeon, Charles Haddon (1834–1892) 11, 12, 17, 30, 57, 133, 179, 188, 191, 199, 232, 233
Stael Mme. Anne L. de (1766–1817) 61
Stalin, Joseph (1879–1953) 44
Stanislas I, King (1677–1766) 49
Stanton, Frank L. (1857–1927) 13
Statius, Caecilius (d. 168 B.C.) 239
Steele, Sir Richard (1672–1729) 174
Steere, Douglas 188
Steinbeck, John (1902–1963) 12, 156, 185
Stern, Gil 49
Sterne, Laurence (1713–1768) 54, 179, 194
Stevenson, Adlai (1835–1914) 124
Stevenson, Robert Louis (1850–1894) 7, 58, 89, 124, 152, 256
Stewart, James S. (1843–1913) 100
Stokowski, Leopold (1882–1977) 166
Stott, John R. W. (b. 1921) 29, 37, 43, 102, 199, 203, 210, 212, 223, 236
Strait, Neil C. 39, 87, 142, 196
Stuart, Janet Erskine 216
Studdert-Kennedy, G. A. 66, 203
Suarez, F. (1548–1617) 141
Suenens, Cardinal Leon Joseph (b. 1904) 38, 117, 153, 223, 226, 239
Sullivan, A. M. 78
Sunday, William Ashley (1863–1935) 247
Suso, Henry (1300–1366) 248
Sweeney, Paul 36
Swift, Jonathan (1667–1745) 13, 28, 218, 225, 240, 249
Swinburne, Charles A. (1837–1909) 29
Symeon the New Theologian, St. (c. 949–1022) 119
Syrus, Publilius (1st cent. B.C.) 60, 116, 157, 173, 242

Tabb, J. B. (1845–1909) 59
Tacitus, Caius Cornelius (55–117 A.D.) 85, 141
Tagore, Sir Rabindranath (1861–1941) 168, 182, 226
Talmud, The 46, 222
Tauler, Johnn (1300–1361) 63, 71
Tawney, Richard H. (1880–1962) 124
Taylor, A. E. (1782–1886) 59, 119
Taylor, James Bayard (1825–1878) 173
Taylor, Hudson (1832–1905) 98
Taylor, Jeremy (1613–1667) 7, 35, 64, 66, 150, 159, 221, 237, 243
Teaching of the Twelve Apostles (or Didache) (c. 2nd cent A.D.)14, 22, 108, 178, 194, 223
Tead, Ordway 72
Temple, Archbishop William (1881–1944) 20, 40, 43, 51, 55, 67, 72, 78, 91, 100, 138, 169, 173, 188, 194, 201, 203, 208, 221, 224, 244, 245
Templeton, Charles 123
Tennyson, Alfred, Lord (1809–1892) 25, 56, 68, 81, 174
Teresa, Mother (1910–1997) 188
Teresa of Avila, St. (1515–1582) 70, 82, 88, 117, 121, 151, 160, 188, 195, 197, 215, 218, 238
Tersteegen, Gerhard (1697–1769) 21, 196
Tertullian, Quintus (c. 150–230) 13, 22, 29, 35, 37, 40, 45, 56, 58, 61, 65, 67, 80, 154, 155, 163, 164, 173, 212, 216, 228
Thackeray, William Makepeace (1811–1863) 17, 165, 169
Thales (c. 624–546 B.C.) 117
Theophilus of Antioch (d.180) 109
Thérèse of Lisieux, St. (1873–1897) 165, 228
Thielecke, Helmut 151
Thieme, Dr. 199
Thom, James 81
Thompson, Francis (1859–1907) 20, 79, 150, 173
Thompson, Robert Ellis 257
Thoreau, Henry David (1817–1862) 13, 32, 68, 81, 121, 126, 136, 141, 142, 166, 190, 218, 225, 253
Tillich, Paul (1886–1965) 75, 147, 171, 180, 207, 209, 210
Tillotson, Archbishop John (1630–1694) 78

Tito, Marshal (1892–1980) 45
Tolstoy, Count Leo (1828–1910) 86, 98, 144, 185, 205, 228, 242, 244
Tournier, Paul 94, 135, 247, 250
Toynbee, Arnold (1889–1975) 41, 70, 75, 143, 149
Tozer, Aiden W. (1897–1963) 206
Trinité, Elizabeth de la 111
Trueblood, Elton 45, 80, 82
Tuchman, Barbara 205
Tugwell O.P., Simon (b. 1943) 8, 23, 248
Twain, Mark (1835–1910) 9, 10, 13, 31, 61, 78, 81, 116, 126, 144, 152, 153, 206, 212, 231

Ullathorne, Archbishop William B. (1806–1889) 17, 35, 50, 102, 124, 170, 184
Underhill, Evelyn (1875–1941) 38, 102, 135, 144, 155, 175, 225
Upham, T.C. 8
Urquhart, Colin (b. 1940) 8, 21, 66, 144, 193, 214

Van Dyke, Henry (1852–1933) 126
Van Gogh, Vincent (1853–1890) 139
Vanier, Jean (b. 1928) 45, 76, 105, 147, 150, 226
Vann O. P., Gerald (1906–1963) 48, 112, 200, 251, 256
Van Zeller, Hubert (b. 1905) 147, 177, 201, 216
Vauvenargues, Marquis de (1715–1747) 186
Vawter, Bruce (b. 1921) 233
Vénard, Theophane (1829–1861) 115, 228
Vianney, St. John (curé D'Ars) (1786–1859) 65, 115, 122, 149, 195, 232, 254
Virgil, Publius (70–19 B.C.) 36
Vogel, A. A. 254
Voltaire, François Marie (1694–1778) 27, 98, 106, 190, 218, 229
Von Balthasar, Hans Urs (b. 1905) 204
Von Hildebrand, Dietrich 205
Von Hugel, Friedrich (1852–1925) 44, 200, 220
Von Weizsacker, Carl F. (b. 1912) 29
Vos, Geerhardus 138

Wagner, Richard 93
Walcha, Helmut 166
Walesa, Lech (b. 1943) 142

Wallace, Lewis (1827–1905) 201
Wallis, Arthur (b. 1928) 31
Walton, Izaak (1593–1683) 28, 109
Walworth, Clarence 10
Wanamaker, John (1838–1922) 39
Warburton, William (1698–1779) 75, 172
Ward, Mary Augusta (1851–1920) 56
Ward, Ted 142
Ward, William A. (1812–1882) 8, 28, 83, 153, 169, 220, 225, 238, 252
Warner, Charles Dudley (1829–1900) 48
Washington, Booker T. (1859–1915) 202, 254
Washington, George (1732–1799) 49, 94, 116, 195, 199, 245, 248
Watson, David (b. 1933) 58, 66, 84
Watson, John (see Maclaren, Ian) (1850–1907) 137
Watts, Alan W. (1915–1973) 139
Watts, Isaac (1674–1748) 210
Weaver, H. G. 145
Webb, Pauline 251
Webster, Daniel (1782–1852) 40, 41, 101, 143, 202
Weil, Simone (1909–1943) 21, 63, 82, 119, 125, 129, 157, 195, 197, 239
Wellesley, Arthur (Duke of Wellington) (1769–1852) 148
Wells, Corrine V. 95
Wells, H. G. (1866–1946) 10, 20, 59, 98, 132, 197
Wesley, Charles (1707–1788) 63
Wesley, John (1703–1791) 79, 112, 164, 172, 178, 188, 189, 200, 222, 254
West, Jessamyn 91
West, Morris (b. 1916) 246
West, Dame Rebecca (b. 1892) 158
Whale, John S. 203
Wharton, Edith (1862–1937) 81
Whately, Richard (1787–1863) 58, 85, 116, 181
Whichcote, Benjamin (1609–1683) 214, 257
Whipple, Edwin Percy (1819–1886) 35
White, David 152
White, Gustav J. 11
White, William Allen (1748–1836) 143
Whitehead, Alfred North (1861–1947) 93, 125, 146, 172, 180
Whitmell, C. T. 59, 144
Whitney, Edgar A. 230
Whitton, Charlotte 251

Wiebe, Bernie 86
Wilberforce, Bishop Samuel (1805–1873) 38, 217
Wilde, Oscar (1856–1900) 31, 52, 58, 59, 107, 127, 144, 173, 210, 214, 225, 251
Wilkerson, David 174
Williams, H. A. (b. 1919) 203
Williams, Shirley (b. 1930) 251
Willis, Nathaniel Parker 103
Wilson, Bishop Thomas (1663–1755) 85, 88
Wilson, Woodrow (1856–1924) 9, 26, 32, 34, 120, 156, 195, 254
Wirt, Sherwood 79
Wolfe, Thomas (1900–1938) 147, 182
Woodhouse, Barbara 16
Wordsworth, William (1770–1850) 137, 156, 249, 254
Work, Edgar W. 230

Wren, Christopher (1632–1723) 18
Wright, Leonard (c. 1591) 54
Wright, Richardson 158
Wyon, Olive 130
Wyzanski, Charles E. (Jr.) 243

Xavier, St. Francis (1506–1552) 36
Xenophon (c. 430–355 B.C.) 178

Yasenak, Gene 199
Yeats, Jack B. (1871–1957) 146, 180, 217
Yeats, William B. (1865–1939) 53, 73, 130
Yoder, D. S. 106
Young, Edward (1683–1765) 192
Young, Leontine 36

Zangwill, Israel (1864–1926) 215
Zwingli, Ulrich (1484–1531) 47, 153, 181

Christian Lives

A

Abbot, Edwin *(1838–1926)*
Anglican schoolmaster and scholar who was headmaster of the City of London School for twenty-four years (1865–1889). He resigned to devote himself to theological study and writing aimed at the general public.

Abbot, Ezra *(1819–1884)*
United States Protestant biblical scholar who contributed widely to reviews and journals on New Testament textual criticism. His principal single production was *The Authorship of the Fourth Gospel* (1880), defending the Johannine authorship.

Abbot, George *(1562–1633)*
Archbishop of Canterbury. From an early date he supported the Puritan cause, which brought him into conflict with, among others, William Laud. In 1609 Abbot was made Bishop of Lichfield and Coventry, in 1611 Archbishop of Canterbury. In 1621 he accidently shot a gamekeeper; a commission met to consider if he was fit for the primacy. King James exercised his casting vote in his favour. Although Abbot crowned Charles I, he was continually in disagreement with the king and was suspended from his functions for a while in 1627.

Abelard, Peter *(1079–1142)*
Philosopher and theologian. Of Breton origins, Abelard showed early signs of a lively and independent mind. As a lecturer he stimulated and inspired large numbers of students, but his stubborn independence angered his elders. His career was cut short by the tragic consequences of his love affair with Héloise, daughter of Fulbert, a canon of Notre Dame. Abelard retired to the monastery of St Denis, and Héloise became a nun. His popular success as a theologian brought attacks from other theologians, particularly on his teaching about the Trinity. Later Abelard became abbot of St Gildas de Ruys in Brittany (1125–1132) but his reforming zeal offended the community. About 1140 St Bernard of Clairvaux denounced some of Abelard's teaching to the bishops of France; several selected passages were condemned at the Council of Sens. Abelard and St Bernard were eventually reconciled. Abelard was enthusiastically devoted to the search for the truth, but his considerable influence upon the shape of Western theology was more through his lectures than his writings.

Adam of Marsh *(d. c. 1258)*
An English Franciscan theologian, friend of Robert Grosseteste and Simon de Montfort; his influence was felt on the political and social life of the period,

and respect for his scholarship won him the title 'Doctor Illustris'.

Adam of St Victor *(d. between 1177–1192)*
Educated at Paris *c.* 1130, he entered the abbey of St Victor and is famous for writing a number of musical sequences used in the Roman liturgy.

Adam, Karl *(1876–1966)*
Catholic theologian who was ordained to the priesthood in 1900. After pastoral work he taught at the University of Munich, then at Strasbourg (1918) and finally at Tübingen. His writings, projecting a liberal and modern outlook to orthodox theology (the best-known example is *Das Wesen Des Katholizismus*, 1924) had a great influence, especially among the educated laity.

Adamson, Patrick *(1537–1592)*
Archbishop of St Andrews, Scotland, who was involved in a long controversy with the Presbyterian party in the Scottish Kirk. His writings and oratory caused much hostility and he was excommunicated by the Synod of Fife (1586). Having lost the favour of King James I he ended his days in poverty.

Adrian *(also Hadrian)* – There were six popes of this name, the most noteworthy being:

Adrian I *(d. 795)*
Pope from 772, who fought against the heresy of Adoptionism, and is remembered for his working relationship and rapport with Charlemagne. Their relationship symbolised the medieval ideal of State and Church working together in a united Christendom.

Adrian IV *(c. 1100–1159) (originally Nicholas Breakespear)*
The only Englishman to become pope, he originated from Abbot's Langley, Hertfordshire. Educated in France, he became an Augustinian monk and abbot in 1137, and while on a trip to Rome, retained in papal service, was elevated to cardinal *c.* 1150. As pope (1154) he crowned Frederick I (Barbarossa) and continued a stormy relationship with him; he is said to have granted the overlordship of Ireland to Henry II of England, but the document concerned, *Laudabiliter*, is now believed to be a forgery.

Aelfric *(c. 955–c. 1010)*
Abbot of the Benedictine community at Eynsham, Oxfordshire, and the greatest scholar of the English Benedictine revival, accorded the title 'the Grammarian'. His *Catholic Homilies*, sermons based on the Church Fathers, were cited by the sixteenth-century Reformers, especially in defence of their eucharistic teaching.

Aelred of Rievaulx, St *(c. 1110–1167) (also Ailred)*
Spiritual writer and outstanding Cistercian abbot. Brought up in the court of King David I of Scotland, he became a Cistercian monk at Rievaulx Abbey, Yorkshire, where later, in 1147, he became abbot. Adviser to both kings and bishops, he is best remembered for his influential spiritual writings, his most important being the *Speculum Caritates* ('Mirror of Love').

Affre, Denis-Auguste *(1793–1848)*
Archbishop of Paris, famous for his reforming spirit, who fearlessly opposed King Louis-Philippe (1843 ff) and welcomed the establishment of the Second Republic (1848). Grieved by the bloody insurrection of the Parisian workers, known as the June Days, he was accidently shot dead while trying to negotiate with them.

Agapetus – there were two popes of this name. The first, with the title 'saint', was pope from 535 to 536 and travelled to Constantinople where he deposed the Patriarch for his Monophysite beliefs.

Agatha, St – *See* Agnes, St

Agnes, St *(b. c. 304)*
As with St Agatha, also a virgin martyr, little reliable information is known of her life. Both were reputed to be beautiful Christian young women who refused to abandon their faith and were exposed and tormented in brothels (Agnes in Rome and Agatha in Palermo). Their sufferings ended in martyrdom.

Agricola, Johann *(c. 1494–1566) (original name: Schneider)*
Friend and follower of Martin Luther who studied theology under Luther at Wittenberg and introduced the Reformation to Frankfurt and Eisleben. He espoused Antinomianism, which brought him into conflict with Luther.

Aidan, St *(d. 651)*
Monk of Iona, missionary in Northumbria and the first Bishop of Lindisfarne. From his monastic centre at Lindisfarne Aidan evangelised northern England, founding churches and monasteries. He was renowned for his learning and charity.

Alain (or Alan) of Lille *(c. 1128–1203)*
Theologian, so celebrated in his day as to be called 'the Universal Doctor'. His work *The Art of the Catholic Faith* reveals the mystical slant of his theology. When he moved from teaching in Paris to Montpellier, he combated the Catharist heresy. In later life he joined the Cistercians at Citeaux.

Alban, St

The first British martyr. According to the Venerable Bede he was a pagan serving in the Roman army who, after conversion, sheltered a fugitive priest. Disguised in the priest's clothes, he was arrested and put to death in the priest's place. It is not clear whether this took place during the persecution of Septimius Severus (*c.* 209) or that of Diocletian (*c.* 305).

Albertus Magnus, St *(c. 1200–1280) (Albert the Great)*

Dominican philosopher, theologian and scientist. After studying in Italy and Germany, he was sent to Paris to lecture on the Bible and theology, one of his pupils being Thomas Aquinas, and there the newly translated works of Aristotle greatly influenced him. He was Bishop of Regensburg (1260–1261) and preached a crusade (1263–1264) on the order of Pope Urban IV, but he received the appellation 'Great' for his huge contribution to medieval learning. He was canonised and proclaimed a Doctor of the Church in 1931.

Alcock, John *(c. 1430–1500)*

Educated at Cambridge, where he later founded Jesus College; after ordination he rose rapidly in various posts to become successively Bishop of Rochester (1472), Worcester (1476) and Ely (1486); for a time he was also Chancellor of England. His most important work was *The Hill of Perfection* (1497).

Alcuin *(c. 732–804)*

Educator, poet, deacon and inspirer of the Carolingian Renaissance. Born and educated at York, where he became master of the cathedral school, in 781 he met Charlemagne and accepted his invitation to found an educational centre at Aachen. This centre suffused learning and culture throughout Europe, Alcuin being the foremost among many eminent scholars. His influential writings included history, poetry, educational manuals and theology (an attack upon the Adoptionist heresy), but lacked originality. He made important reforms in the liturgy and left more than three hundred Latin letters. Although he had a reputation for sanctity he was never proposed for canonisation.

Aldhelm, St *(c. 639–709)*

Abbot of Malmesbury (675), poet and first Bishop of Sherborne (705). While little is certain about the details of his life, he was highly regarded as the most learned teacher of his time and as a pioneer in Latin verse among the Saxons.

Alexander – Eight popes had this name, the most noteworthy being:

Alexander III *(1105–1181) (born Orlando Bandinelli)*
Canon Lawyer and lecturer at Bologna who rose rapidly to cardinal in the Church and then opposed the growing power of Frederick Barbarossa. As pope (1159) he was a vigorous defender of papal authority, opposing not only Barbarossa but also Henry II of England over the Thomas à Becket affair.

Alexander of Hales *(c. 1186–1245)*
Philosopher and theologian, accorded the title 'Doctor Irrefragabilis'. He originated from Halesowen, West Midlands, but studied and taught at Paris, where he lived most of his life. He joined the Franciscan Order (1236) and founded a Franciscan school of theology. He began a *Summa Theologica* which was completed by his followers.

Alexander, Michael Solomon *(1799–1845)*
First Anglican Bishop of Jerusalem. Born a strict orthodox German Jew; at twenty-one he came to England and was converted to Christianity. After ordination he worked for the conversion of Jews, first in Danzig (1827–1830) then in London (1830–1841) – he became the first Anglican Bishop of Jerusalem in 1841.

Alford, Henry *(1810–1871)*
Scholar of New Testament Greek and Dean of Canterbury who went from a Fellowship at Cambridge to pastoral posts. Remembered for his edition of the Greek New Testament (1849–1861) and several well-known hymns, including 'Come, ye thankful people, come'.

Alfred the Great *(849–899)*
Saxon king of Wessex (from 871) who saved England from conquest by the Danes and, himself an educated man, was successful in promoting a great revival of learning. He translated many Latin works, including spiritual classics, and founded several monasteries, although his monastic reforms did not receive support.

Allen, Richard *(1760–1831)*
First United States Negro bishop of the African Methodist Episcopal Church. Born of a slave family, he was converted to Methodism at seventeen and permitted to preach when twenty-two. After buying his freedom in 1786 he joined the Methodist Church in Philadelphia, but, unhappy with restrictions placed upon him, in 1787 he founded his own independent church for Negroes. He was officially ordained (1799) and after the foundation of the African Methodist Episcopal Church he was chosen as its first bishop in 1816.

Allen, William *(1532–1594)*
English cardinal and scholar who inspired the Roman Catholic Douai version of the Bible. A fellow of Oriel College, Oxford, he refused to acknowledge Elizabeth as head of the English Church and was ordained a priest on the Continent. He founded colleges for the training of priests to work on the English mission, at Douai (1568), Rome (1575–1578) and Valladolid (1589). He lost the support of many English Roman Catholics for his championing of the cause of Philip II of Spain and his Armada.

Aloysius Gonzaga, St *(1568–1591)*
Son of the Marquis of Castiglione, he was destined, after education as a page, for military service. Experiencing a vocation to the Religious life, after great family opposition and poor health, he joined the Jesuits (1585). With a reputation for personal austerity and care for the poor, he worked among the plague victims of Rome and died of the disease. He was canonised in 1726 and declared patron of Catholic Youth.

Alphege, St *(954–1012) (also known as Aelfheah or Elphege)*
Archbishop of Canterbury and martyr. Benedictine monk and anchorite who was chosen abbot of Bath then, in 984, Bishop of Winchester; in 1005 he became Archbishop of Canterbury. When the Danes sacked Canterbury they seized him for ransom but, because he would not permit his poor tenants to be taxed to raise the money, the Danes pelted him with ox bones and killed him. From earliest times he was venerated as a martyr.

Ambrose, St *(c. 339–397)*
Bishop of Milan, and biblical critic. Son of the Praetorian Prefect of Gaul, he was himself governor of Aemilia and Liguria and only a Christian catechumen when, by popular acclaim, he was chosen as Bishop of Milan. As a famous preacher and champion of orthodoxy he combated Arianism and paganism and stoutly upheld the independence of the Church from State interference. He is remembered for his vital part in the conversion and baptism of St Augustine, his literary works and his works of theology, particularly *De Sacramentis* and *De Officiis Ministrorum*.

Ambrose, Isaac *(1604–1664)*
A Lancashire Anglican priest, educated at Oxford, who became a Presbyterian (1641) and ministered in the Leeds area, but became caught up in the Civil War, twice being imprisoned by the Royalists. He published many religious titles, the most famous of which, *Looking unto Jesus* (1658), sprang from his own deep interior life.

Ames, William *(1576–1633)*

English Puritan moral theologian and controversialist who supported strict Calvinism in opposition to Arminianism. Compelled to leave England (1610) he settled in Holland and wrote and lectured in theology, particularly moral theology. Considered one of the greatest Calvinist theologians, his best-known work is *De Conscientia et ejus Jure vel Casibus* (1632).

Amsdorf, Nikolaus von *(1483–1565)*

German Protestant Reformer, theologian and friend of Martin Luther who sought to retain the purity of Luther's teaching in the face of liberalising elements.

Andrewes, Lancelot *(1555–1626)*

Anglican theologian, court preacher and Bishop of Winchester. An esteemed scholar, he served in several parishes from 1589 before becoming successively Bishop of Chichester (1605), Ely (1609) and Winchester (1619). He sought to defend and advance Anglican doctrine, criticising both Puritan and Roman Catholic teaching. In his time he was renowned for his preaching (some of his sermons were published as *Ninety-Six Sermons* in 1629), and his most famous book, *Preces Privatae* (1648), a collection of prayers, was still respected three hundred years later.

Angelico, Fra *(c. 1400–1455)*

Born Giovanni di Fiesole at Vicchio, Italy, between 1347 and 1400, it is unclear when he was first called 'Angelic', and whether it was for his saintliness or his skilled and graceful painting of angels. Giovanni trained as an artist before entering the Dominican Order (*c.* 1420) and his fame, as a Renaissance artist, rests upon his murals, particularly 'The Annunciation' and others, at the great Dominican Convent of San Marco, Florence.

Anselm, St *(c. 1033–1109)*

Archbishop of Canterbury and founder of Scholasticism. From Aosta, Italy, he became Benedictine monk at Bec, France, where (1063) he became prior and abbot in 1078, by which time he was renowned as a leader and original thinker; from which period dates his *Monologion* and *Proslogion*. Named Archbishop of Canterbury (1093) he became involved in the investiture controversy which led to exile from England (1103–1106). In his last two years he was engaged in a conflict with the See of York over primacy. The greatest of his many theological works, *Cur Deus Homo* ('Why Did God Become Man?'), is a classical presentation of the satisfaction theory of the atonement; he is also remembered as the originator of the ontological argument for God's existence. He was declared a Doctor of the Church in 1720.

Ansgar, St *(c. 801–865) (also Anskar)*
French Benedictine monk and outstanding missionary in northern Europe. He worked first in Denmark (826–829), then Sweden, being the first to introduce Christianity to the country (829–831). Recalled, he was appointed the first Bishop of Hamburg (832). He initiated missionary work to all the Scandinavian countries and was accorded the title 'Apostle of the North'. Despite the ravages of the Northmen, he combated the slave trade and converted Erik, King of Jutland (854). He was canonised shortly after his death and declared patron saint of Scandinavia.

Anthony of Kiev *(d. 1073) (also Anthony of Pechersky)*
The founder of monasticism in Russia. Introduced to the solitary life at a Greek Orthodox monastery on Mt Athos, he returned to Kiev and settled in a cave on Mt Berestov. This became a centre which grew into a community and there the 'Monastery of the Caves' was founded. This institution exerted a great influence upon the Russian Orthodox Church – for example, by the year 1250 fifty of its monks had become bishops.

Anthony of Padua, St *(1195–1231) (originally Ferdinand de Bulhoes)*
Born at Lisbon, he joined the Augustinian Canons (1210) transferring to the Franciscan Order (1221) in the hope of finding martyrdom as a missionary to the Moors. Illness forced him to return from Morocco and he was unexpectedly asked to preach at an ordination, revealing himself to be an eloquent preacher of great learning. He was sent to preach all over Italy with sensational success. After a number of teaching appointments he settled at Padua, where his fiery sermons denouncing corruption and wrongdoing resulted in a reformed city. He was particularly devoted to the care of the poor, and even in his own lifetime was credited with being a worker of miracles.

Antony of Egypt, St *(250–356)*
First Christian hermit and monk, founder of Christian monasticism. After distributing his family inheritance (269) he devoted himself to a solitary life of asceticism. About 285 he sought greater solitude on Mt Pispi, by the Nile. After twenty years he emerged to organise and write a Rule for the colony of ascetics that had developed around his retreat. He went twice to Alexandria, first in 311 to encourage the Christian community then suffering persecution and second (about 355) to support his friend Athanasius in his stand against Arianism.

Aphraates *(early fourth century) (also Afrahat)*
Earliest Syriac Christian writer. Knowledge of his life is limited, but it seems he was a monk who became a bishop, writing under the pseudonym of 'the Persian Sage'. Between 336 and 345 he composed twenty-three biblical

commentaries (inaccurately called 'Homilies') which are the earliest writings we have, casting invaluable light upon the simple presentation of Christian teaching at that time.

Aquaviva, Claudio *(1543–1615)*
Son of the Duke of Atri, he joined the Society of Jesus in 1567 and rose swiftly to become the Jesuits' youngest (and many have considered, the greatest) General of the Order. His remarkable leadership gifts were severely tested in a number of crises, and under him the Society more than doubled its numbers and widened its influence, particularly in missionary work.

Arminius, Jacobus *(1560–1609) (originally Jacob Harmensen)*
Celebrated theologian and minister of the Dutch Reformed Church who could not accept the strict Calvinist teaching on predestination and consequently developed a system of belief later named after him (Arminianism). He was educated at Leiden, where he later returned (1603) as professor of theology; later still he taught at Basel, then Geneva. The latter part of his life was dominated by controversy, particularly with the zealous Calvinist, Franciscus Gomarus.

Arnauld, Antoine *(1612–1694) (also Arnault)*
French philosopher and leading theologian of the Jansenist movement. Student of the Sorbonne, in law and theology, he was ordained a priest in 1641 and deeply associated himself with the Jansenist centre at the convent of Port-Royal. His book *De la fréquente communion* (1641) caused a storm and he was forced to withdraw from public life and the faculty of the Sorbonne. In his voluminous writing he defended Jansenism and attacked Calvinism. He finally settled in Brussels, where he died.

Arnauld, Jacqueline Marie Angélique *(1591–1661)*
Known as 'Mère Angélique', Abbess of Port-Royal convent. Sister of the above, she was committed to Religious Life at seven and took the veil in 1600, becoming abbess in 1602. After a conversion experience in 1608 she threw herself into the reform of her community and the new austere life attracted a big following. Directed by Francis of Sales for a time, later (1635) she turned to Jansenism and the convent of Port-Royal became an enthusiastic centre of the movement.

Arndt, Johann *(1555–1621)*
Lutheran theologian and mystical writer. Pastor of Badeborn (1583–1590) he was compelled to move on, first to Quedlinburg, then Brunswick, by the Calvinist hostility. Best remembered for his widely read and much appreciated *Four Books on True Christianity* (1606–1610), which was the inspiration of many Protestant and Catholic devotional works.

Arnold, Matthew *(1822–1888)*

Poet and literary critic whose criticism covered not only literature but also theology, history and science. Educated at Oxford (1841–1844) he spent the greater part of his working life as a government inspector of schools (1851–1883). Besides poetry, *e.g. Poems* (1853) and *New Poems* (1867), he published religious works, *e.g. St Paul and Protestantism* (1870) and *God and the Bible* (1875).

Arnold, Thomas *(1795–1842)*

Headmaster of Rugby School and father of the above. After studying at Oxford, where he proved to be a fine classical scholar, he was ordained and, in 1828, became headmaster of Rugby. He gradually raised the school to be a great public school much in demand. He developed a system of education firmly based upon a religious foundation; among other things he encouraged a prefect system which became the model of most English secondary schools. The Arnold tradition at Rugby had a wide and lasting effect upon English secondary education.

Asbury, Francis *(1745–1816)*

English Methodist lay preacher who volunteered for service in North America, where his unstinting efforts (he averaged five thousand miles a year on horseback), and leadership as the first United States consecrated bishop of the Methodist Episcopal Church, assured the continuance of the church in America.

Athanasius, St *(293–373)*

Theologian, Bishop of Alexandria and champion of orthodoxy. As secretary to Alexander, Bishop of Alexandria, he attended the Council of Nicaea (325), having written his famous treatise *De Incarnatione* some seven years earlier. He succeeded as bishop (328) and from Nicaea to the end of his life he was the champion of the Council's decrees and its struggle against Arianism. His Arian enemies forced him into exile (336), to flee to Rome (339), and caused the enmity of the emperor Constantius (356) and a second exile (365); but he never gave up the struggle and he brought about the final triumph of the Nicene party at the Council of Constantinople (381). Besides his important anti-Arian writings he also left letters and *The Life of St Antony.*

Athanasius, the Athonite, St *(c. 920–c. 1003)*

Originally named Abraham, he left urban monastic life in Constantinople and founded the first communal monastery on Mt Athos (961), which was already populated with scattered hermits. Despite fierce opposition he succeeded in his foundation, including the writing of a Rule, with the support of the emperors Nicephonus Phocas and John Tzimisces.

Athanasius I *(1230–1310)*

Monk and Patriarch of Constantinople who opposed the work for reunion between the Eastern and Western Churches of the Second Council of Lyons (1274). His own severe reforming measures for his clergy failed and brought about his resignation.

Athenagoras *(second century)*

Greek Christian philosopher and apologist. Believed to be a converted Platonist philosopher from Athens, he addressed his *Embassy for the Christians* (*c.* 177) to the Emperor Marcus Aurelius, answering current calumnies against the Christians, *viz.* atheism, cannibalism and incest. It is not certain that *On the Resurrection of the Dead*, although ascribed to him, is his work. An able apologist, he was the first to apply Neoplatonic concepts to interpret Christianity.

Augustine of Canterbury, St *(d. 604 or 605) (also called Austin)*

First Archbishop of Canterbury. While prior of St Andrew's Rome, he was dispatched with about forty monks, by the pope, St Gregory the Great, to evangelise the English (596). Although the group desired to turn back, Gregory encouraged them on and they landed in Kent in 597, being well received by King Ethelbert I of Kent. Within a few months the king and thousands of his subjects embraced Christianity and a centre was established at Canterbury. Augustine was consecrated archbishop and he sent for more missionaries. He was not so successful in building a relationship with the Celtic Church already existing in Wales and the North. By the time of his death a Benedictine monastery and a cathedral were founded at Canterbury and bishops had been consecrated for Rochester and London.

Augustine of Hippo, St *(354–430) (Latin name: Aurelius Augustinus)*

Bishop of Hippo and a Doctor of the Church. Born in North Africa of a pagan father and a devout Christian mother, Monica, he was educated as a Christian, but abandoned his faith and lived an immoral life, which he recounts in his *Confessions* (400). He taught rhetoric at Tagaste, Carthage, Rome (383) and Milan (384), where he fell under the influence of Ambrose, Bishop of Milan. He returned to the Christian faith at Easter 387. His mother, who had worked and prayed for his conversion, died (387) on the way back to North Africa; at Tagaste he founded a monastic community, but accepted priestly ordination (391) and eventually the See of Hippo in 396. His penetrating understanding of Christian doctrine, and brilliant exposition, was expressed in two hundred treatises, three hundred letters and nearly four hundred sermons, as valuable today as they have been throughout the centuries. He had embraced the Manichaean heresy in his youth, but as bishop he led the Church's fight against that heresy, Donatism and Pelagianism. After his *Confessions*, one of Christianity's great spiritual classics, his best-known work is the *City of God* (413–426), published in twenty-two books. He died while the Vandals were besieging Hippo.

B

Baader, Franz Xaver von *(1765–1841)*
Roman Catholic layman from Munich, influential theologian who contributed in 1815 to the Holy Alliance, a security pact between Russia, Austria and Prussia. He is now considered one of the founders of modern ecumenical activity.

Bach, Johann Sebastian *(1685–1750)*
German composer who, from 1723 until his death, was cantor at the Thomas School, Leipzig. It is to this period that his chief religious works belong. Originally written for and used by the German Lutheran Church, the music is now more usually performed outside divine worship.

Bacon, Roger *(c. 1214–c. 1292)*
A Franciscan philosopher who, with great energy, after studying in England (probably at Oxford) and at Paris, described futuristic mechanical inventions (flying machines, motorised ships *etc.*) and sought to reform the study of theology. A man of wide vision, Roger was commissioned by his friend, Pope Clement IV, to write an encyclopaedic work on the relationship of philosophy to theology, called *Maius Opus* (1267). He suffered imprisonment for his unconventional opinions after Clement's death.

Baillie, John *(1886–1960)*
Sometime professor of divinity at the University of Edinburgh and principal of New College; writer and author of the popular *A Diary of Private Prayer*.

Baillie, Robert *(1599–1662)*
Presbyterian minister and theological scholar; he led the Scottish movement to reject (1637) for Scotland the Church of England's Book of Common Prayer.

Baillie, Robert *(c. 1634–1684)*
Scottish Presbyterian executed for allegedly conspiring to assassinate King Charles II (the evidence was inconclusive). From 1676 Baillie had become associated with the struggle to free Scottish Presbyterianism from the control of the Anglican Church of England.

Baius, Michael *(1513–1589)*
Flemish theologian whose work on grace and justification, together with that of Jan Hessels, was censured by ecclesiastical authorities; his system of thought, Baianism, is often considered one of the foundations of Jansenism.

Baker, Augustine *(1575–1641)*
A convert to Roman Catholicism who became a Benedictine monk and an important writer on ascetical and mystical theology. Although his teaching was not new and was based upon his personal experience, it was vigorously attacked. Baker's spiritual writings were the fruit of his work as spiritual director to the English Benedictine nuns at Cambrai, France. After his death from the plague his better-known writings were collected and published in *Sancta Sophia* (1657) ('Holy Wisdom'). He also conducted important research into the history of the Benedictine Order in England.

Baldwin of Canterbury *(d. 1190)*
Cistercian monk who, although elected Archbishop of Canterbury, was constantly opposed by the monks of Christ Church, Canterbury. A scholar and writer who took part in one of the Crusades, it is said that he died of grief at the lack of discipline of the Christian armies.

Ball, John *(d. 1381)*
A priest, and one of the leaders of the Peasant Revolt in England; excommunicated for teaching Wycliffite doctrines on ownership and property. Ever popular with the people for his continual preaching on the equality of persons, he was executed as a traitor under King Richard II.

Barat, St Madeleine-Sophie *(1779–1865)*
Daughter of a French cooper, but well educated by her priest brother, Louis, Madeleine-Sophie desired to enter a Carmelite convent as a simple lay sister. Joseph Varin, Superior of the Sacred Heart Fathers encouraged her to lead a small community of women dedicated to the Christian education of girls. This led to the formation of the Society of the Sacred Heart, a congregation of Religious Sisters which, due to Mother Barat's efforts, became established in twelve countries, including the USA. She was elected Superior General for life, and the rules of the Society were adopted in 1815. She was beatified in 1908 and declared a saint of the Roman Catholic Church in 1925.

Barbara St
A virgin martyr who, in the third century, according to legend, was tortured and condemned to death by the authorities. On her refusal to abandon her Christian faith, her pagan father was ordered to kill her, which he did, but, according to the legend, he was afterwards immediately struck by lightning. There is no evidence to support this spurious legend of the seventh century.

Barberi, Dominic *(1792–1849)*

Of peasant origins, Dominic entered the Passionist Order as a lay brother, but in 1818 he was ordained a priest. He lectured and taught at several places in Italy, up to 1841, when a long-time desire to work as a missionary in England became a reality. He was given a house in Aston, Staffordshire, as a missionary base. In 1845 he received John Henry Newman into the Roman Catholic Church. Despite much abuse and opposition, Dominic persevered with his preaching and made many converts. By the time of his death, in 1849, he had established four Passionist houses in England. He was beatified by the Roman Catholic Church in 1963.

Barbon, Praise-God *(c. 1596–1680)*

Nicknamed 'Barebone' or 'Barebones', Barbon was a sectarian preacher from whom the Cromwellian 'Barebones' Parliament' derived its name.

Barclay, Robert *(1648–1690)*

Scottish Quaker writer and apologist. Robert was born at Gordonstoun, Morayshire, and at nineteen followed his father into the Society of Friends. In 1673 he published his *Catechism and Confession of Faith*, followed in 1675 by his principal work, his *Apology*. This early exposition of the Society's teaching defined Quakerism as a religion of the 'inner light'. He defended his teachings against Roman Catholic and Protestant attacks. Through his friendship with the Duke of York (later King James II) he was able to be of assistance to William Penn and the establishment of Quaker settlements in the New World.

Barclay, William *(1907–1978)*

Popular New Testament scholar and prolific writer of sixty religious books. Highly regarded as a spiritual guide and mentor to tens of thousands of Christians.

Barnes, Ernest William *(1874–1953)*

Anglican Bishop of Birmingham and leader of the Modernist movement in the Church of England; renowned as a pacifist during World War II. Bishop Barnes was very opposed to the Anglo-Catholic wing of the Church of England and he was vociferous in his attacks upon ritualistic practices. His scientific approach to Christianity brought him into conflict with his fellow bishops; his book *The Rise of Christianity* (1947) was condemned by the Archbishops of Canterbury and York.

Barnes, Robert *(c. 1495–1540)*

English Protestant martyr who helped to spread Lutheranism in England. Originally prior of the Austin Friars at Cambridge, due to the influence of Thomas Bilney he embraced the teachings of the Reformers and left England in 1528 for Germany, where he formed a lasting friendship with Martin Luther. Thereafter he travelled to and fro between England and Germany. A little more than a month after his protector, Thomas Cromwell, fell from favour, he was burnt as a heretic with two other Lutherans.

Barnett, Samuel Augustus *(1844–1913)*

Anglican priest and social reformer who, for twenty-one years as a parish priest, devoted himself to the cultural and religious improvement of the East End of London. From 1884 to 1896 Barnett was the first warden of Toynbee Hall. Through his pastoral concern, teaching and writing he worked for the reform of social conditions through the application of Christian principles. To foster the study of social problems Barnett House was founded at Oxford to his memory.

Baronius, Caesar *(1538–1607)*

Church historian and apologist for the Roman Catholic Church. He joined the Oratory of St Philip Neri and later succeeded him as superior. Hailed in Roman Catholic circles as the 'father of ecclesiastical history', his major massive work *Annales Ecclesiastici* is now recognised as biased, but acclaimed for its enormous accumulation of sources. He ended his life as a cardinal and the librarian of the Vatican.

Barrow, Henry *(c. 1550–1593)*

Congregationalist martyr and separatist. As a lawyer he had been converted from a dissolute life to the life of a strict Puritan. Friendship with John Greenwood, the separatist, led to the advocacy of separate and autonomous local churches. Greenwood and Barrow were imprisoned for their beliefs and later died together on the scaffold.

Barth, Karl *(1886–1968)*

One of the most influential Protestant theologians of modern times. Barth studied theology at Berne, Berlin, Tübingen and Marburg. His pastoral work began at Geneva (1909–1911) but it was while he was pastor at Safenwil for ten years that he wrote his sensational commentary *The Epistle to the Romans* (1918). Subsequently he held the chair of theology at Göttingen, Münster and Bonn. While at the latter Barth started work on his seminal four-volume work, *Die Kirchliche Dogmatik* ('Church Dogmatics'). His opposition to the rise of National Socialism and his work for and promotion of the anti-Nazi Confessing Church led to his suspension from his post at Bonn, when he refused the oath of allegiance to Hitler. As a Swiss subject he was able to accept the chair of theology at Basel, where he continued until his retirement in 1962.

Bartolomeo, Fra *(1472–1517) (also called Baccio della Porta)*
Florentine painter who was the most prominent exponent of the classical idealism of the High Renaissance style. An admirer of the Florentine Dominican reformer Savonarola, after Savonarola's death Bartolomeo joined the Dominican Order in 1500. He became a friend of Raphael and was also influenced by Bellini and Michelangelo. All his work was religious, from the early *Annunciation* (1497) to his gentle *Pietà* (1515).

Basil the Great, St *(c. 329–379)*
One of the great Fathers of the Church, brother of St Gregory of Nyssa and St Macrina. After the best possible education available at the time, Basil withdrew from the world to a hermit's life near Neo-Caesarea. He returned to public life at the call of his bishop, Eusebius of Caesarea, in Cappodocia, to join in the battle against Arianism. He was ordained priest to help Eusebius and in 370 succeeded him as bishop; this office he held until his death. In 371 he came into conflict with the emperor Valens, who divided Basil's province. Basil was renowned in his own lifetime for his learning, eloquence and personal sanctity. His exceptional organising ability left a lasting imprint upon the shape and form of Eastern monasticism and his charitable foundations to help the needy survived several hundred years. Not long after his death he was declared a saint and a little later a Doctor of the Church.

Baur, Ferdinand Christian *(1792–1860)*
German Protestant theologian and scholar who initiated the Protestant 'Tübingen School' of biblical criticism. Educated at Tübingen, Baur first taught at the seminary at Blaubeuren before becoming professor of theology at Tübingen, where he remained until his death. A disciple of F.D.E. Schleiermacher, he was also influenced by Hegel's conception of history. Baur applied Hegelian principles to the New Testament pastoral letters and the life and teaching of St Paul (his two-volume book, *Paul the Apostle of Jesus Christ*, 1873 and 1875). Later in life Baur concentrated upon Church history, taking ten years (1853–1863) to write his five-volume work *History of the Christian Church*. At first his pioneering work was rejected but later it was accepted as an important contribution to biblical scholarship.

Baxter, Richard *(1615–1691)*
Moderate Puritan minister who had a profound influence upon the Protestantism of seventeenth-century England. Largely self-educated, he was ordained into the Church of England in 1638, but two years later he rejected the current understanding of episcopacy in the Church of England and allied himself with the Puritan cause. From 1641 to 1660 he conducted a ministry at Kidderminster that was a model of pastoral care. His preaching drew large crowds and people travelled far to seek his spiritual counsel, yet throughout he suffered continual ill-health. He served briefly as a chaplain

to the Parliamentary forces during the Civil War but his moderation sought continual reconciliation; in 1660 Baxter helped in the restoration of the monarchy. His fight for moderate dissent in the Church of England and the refusal of a bishopric brought persecution for his views and imprisonment in 1685. Nearly two hundred writings were left, all reflecting his deep piety and moderation.

Baylon, St Paschal *(1540–1592)*
Spanish shepherd youth, self-taught, who after much persistence was admitted as a lay brother into the Franciscan Order. He served, for most of his life, as a porter at various Spanish friaries and won renown for his piety and care of the sick and needy. Baylon defended the Catholic teaching on the Eucharist in public debate and consequently after his canonisation by the Catholic Church in 1690 became patron of eucharistic confraternities and congresses.

Beaton, David *(1494–1546)*
Cardinal Archbishop of St Andrews, and papal legate in Scotland from 1544. Trusted counsellor of King James V, after whose death Beaton made a bid for the regency; although he failed in this he secured considerable influence over the regent, the Earl of Arran, and due to his efforts English attempts to subjugate Scotland failed. Beaton had a popular reformer, George Wishart, who was also politically involved, executed. In revenge a band of Protestant nobles assassinated him.

Beauduin, Lambert *(1873–1960)*
Belgian Benedictine liturgist and founder of Chevetogne; one of the original founders of the liturgical movement. In 1924, when Pope Pius XI encouraged the Benedictines to pray and work for Christian unity, Beauduin founded a monastery of Union; now at Chevetogne. His approach to the problems of unity did not win approval until the pontificate of John XXIII.

Becket, St Thomas *(c. 1118–1170)*
Educated in Paris, after three years as a city clerk Thomas was taken into the household of Archbishop Theobald of Canterbury. After ordination to deacon he was appointed Archdeacon of Canterbury in 1154; the following year Henry II chose him as his chancellor. Thomas enjoyed the close friendship of the king, sharing his interest in hunting and the pomp of royal occasions. He very reluctantly accepted the See of Canterbury in 1162, changing his lifestyle and becoming devout and austere. Thomas resigned the chancellorship and soon found himself in conflict with the king.

Thomas resisted Henry's attempts to take the trial of criminal clerks away from the church courts. As a result of a series of reprisals by the king, Thomas was summoned to trial, but fled the country and appealed to the pope. After the threat of an Interdict on England a reconciliation between king and archbishop was effected. Becket returned to his See and popular acclaim. A fresh disagreement brought hasty words from the king which sent four knights to Canterbury, and Thomas was murdered in his cathedral on 29 December 1170. Universal indignation swept Europe; miracles were recorded at Thomas' tomb and a cultus rapidly developed. In 1173 Pope Alexander III canonised him.

Bede the Venerable, St *(672/673–735)*
As an orphan at the age of seven, Bede was placed in the charge of the Benedictine monastery at Wearmouth, later transferred to Jarrow, under the care of St Benet (Benedict) Biscop. Apart from one visit to Lindisfarne and York, Bede spent the whole of his life at the Jarrow monastery. He devoted himself to the study of Scripture and teaching and writing. His early books appear to have been written for the pupils at the monastery school. His *De Temporibus* ('On Times') was for the clergy to help them calculate the date of Easter. In his own life, and through the middle ages, Bede was renowned for his Scripture commentaries. However, his fame in more recent centuries has rested upon his *Ecclesiastical History of the English People*. Of special interest is his method of dating events from the time of Christ's birth (AD); a method which became commonly accepted through the popularity of his writing. The title 'the Venerable' was bestowed within a hundred years of his death; Bede was formally canonised and declared a Doctor of the Church in 1899.

Beecher, Henry Ward *(1813–1887)*
American liberal Congregational minister who, through his social concern and oratorical skill, became one of the most influential Protestant preachers of his time. He vehemently opposed slavery and supported most liberal causes of the time – women's suffrage, evolution, scientific biblical criticism, *etc*. His later years were overshadowed by unproven charges of immoral affairs.

Bell, George Kennedy Allen *(1881–1958)*
Ordained in 1907 to the Anglican priesthood, a curacy followed at Leeds. After four years as a lecturer Bell became secretary to Archbishop Randall Davidson, later, in 1924, Dean of Canterbury and finally Bishop of Chichester in 1929. His great interest, dating from 1919, was the Ecumenical Movement. He supported the Confessing Church in Germany in its struggle against Hitler's regime. Through his German contacts he was instrumental in securing asylum in England for many Jews and non-Aryan Christians. During World War II he was outspoken in his condemnation of the saturation bombing by the Allies of German cities; he also opposed Britain's decision to make nuclear weapons. His European connections facilitated the first meeting of the World Council of Churches in 1948; he presided as chairman of its

central committee from 1948 to 1954 and as honorary president until his death in 1958.

Bellarmine, St Robert *(1542–1621)*
One of the most enlightened Jesuit theologians of the Counter-Reformation period and widely recognised as one of the most saintly. After entering the Society of Jesus in 1560, he was ordained in 1570. There followed twenty-nine years as a lecturer in theology during which he proved himself a vigorous and successful opponent of Protestant doctrine. Bellarmine was made a cardinal in 1599, but his great love of the poor prompted him to give away everything he owned and he died a pauper. He was canonised in 1930 and declared a Doctor of the Roman Catholic Church the following year.

Belloc, Hilaire *(1980–1953)*
French-born poet and Roman Catholic writer and essayist regarded as one of the most versatile of English writers of the early twentieth century. Educated at the Oratory School, Birmingham, and (after military service in the French army) at Balliol College, Oxford. In 1906 Belloc was elected as the Liberal MP for Salford; his individualism and liberalism cut short a political career, but he teamed up with G. K. Chesterton, who illustrated his satirical novels. He is best remembered for his light verse, but his interests and the breadth of his writing was wide, including humorous verse for children, history, biography, sailing and travel. The best example of the latter was his *Path to Rome* (1902), but his chief work was on a topic dear to him, *Europe and the Faith* (1912). His ardent profession of his faith shone through virtually everything he wrote.

Benedict – There were fifteen popes titled Benedict, from Benedict I (d. 579) to Benedict XV (d. 1992). Probably the most noteworthy were:

Benedict XII *(d. 1342) (original name: Jacaques Fournier)*
The third pope to reign at Avignon, from 1334 to 1342. Benedict devoted himself to the reform of the Church and its religious orders. A Cistercian monk, graduating in theology at Paris, he first served as an abbot, then bishop and cardinal in 1327. His ability as a theologian recommended him to his fellow cardinals, and as pope he immediately settled a theological dispute about the Beatific Vision (direct supernatural knowledge or vision of God) and set about a rigorous reform of the religious orders. This latter met fierce opposition and most of his reforming work was undone after his death.

Benedict XIV *(1675–1758) (original name: Prospero Lambertini)*
After a succession of appointments in Rome, Lambertini was chosen for the papacy; his intelligence and moderation won the admiration and respect not only of all Christians but also of the philosophers of the Enlightenment.

Benedict showed real interest in scientific learning and in the Papal States encouraged agricultural reform, free trade and reduced taxation. He was conciliatory in his relations with the secular powers and, as a scholar in his own right, wrote seminal books, the most important being on the canonisation of saints. Benedict also founded a number of academies in Rome and laid the groundwork for the present Vatican museum.

Benedict XV *(1854–1922) (original name: Giacomo Della Chiesa)*

After studying in Rome, Giacomo entered the papal diplomatic service. Pius X made him Archbishop of Bologna and, in 1914, a cardinal. Elected pope a month after the outbreak of World War I, he devoted himself to the relief of distress and the maintaining of a strict neutrality. Benedict worked hard to get both sides to state their aims, so these might be reconciled. Neither side co-operated, both accusing him of favouring the other side, and took no serious note of the peace plans Benedict proposed. (Had they done so several million lives would have been spared). The Italian Government, belligerent towards the Catholic Church, prevented the participation of the papacy at the Versailles peace conference. His last years were spent in readjusting the organisation of the Roman Catholic Church in the wake of the disastrous conflict, and in the promotion of missionary work.

Benedict (Benet) Biscop, St *(c. 628–689/690)*

Of noble birth, a thane of King Oswry of Northumbria, Biscop Baducing (his original name) came under the influence of St Wilfrid and, after two journeys to Rome, embraced the religious life in 666, taking the name Benedict. In 669 he was appointed abbot of the monastery of St Peter and St Paul, Canterbury (later St Augustine's), and, after a fourth journey to Rome, founded the Benedictine monastery of St Peter at Warmouth; in 682 a sister foundation was made at Jarrow, dedicated to St Paul. His repeated (five) journeys to Rome resulted in the introduction into England of glass windows, stone churches and many manuscripts and paintings. His most celebrated pupil was the Venerable Bede. Crippled about 686, he remained bedridden until his death. From his monastic foundations came a British tradition of learning and artistic achievement that was a strong influence throughout the north-west of Europe.

Benedict of Nursia, St *(c. 480–c. 547)*

Founder of the Benedictine monastic way of life (based upon his celebrated Rule); regarded as the father of Western monasticism and founder of the monastery at Monte Cassino. Benedict was born at Nursia and educated at Rome, where the permissiveness of the age prompted him to withdraw (*c.* 500) to a cave at Subiaco, about forty miles from Rome. After three years of solitude he became abbot of a local monastery, but his reforming zeal met with resistance and after an assassination attempt he returned to his cave.

Disciples flocked to him and with them he founded twelve monasteries composed of twelve monks at each, under Benedict's overall charge. As a result of the jealous intrigues of a local priest, Benedict left Subiaco with a small band of followers and settled on the summit of a steep hill at Cassino, half way between Rome and Naples. None of the dates of Benedict's life are certain, but he was buried at Monte Cassino in the same grave as his sister, St Scholastica, who had founded a convent nearby. As a tribute to the work of evangelisation and civilisation of the Benedictine Order through Europe in the Middle Ages, Pope Paul VI proclaimed Benedict the patron saint of Europe in 1964.

Bengel, Johann Albrecht *(1687–1752)*
German Lutheran biblical scholar. He worked on classical and patristic literature, but his chief work of importance was as the founder of Swabian Pietism and as a New Testament textual critic. His approach to New Testament exegesis is accepted as the beginning of modern scientific work in biblical studies.

Benson, Edward White *(1829–1896)*
Anglican priest, educator and, from 1883, Archbishop of Canterbury. He served first as an assistant master at Rugby School, Warwickshire, then in 1859 as headmaster of the New Wellington College, Berkshire. When the new diocese of Truro, Cornwall, was established Benson was consecrated as its first bishop. Enthroned as Archbishop of Canterbury in 1883, his period of office is memorable for the revival of the court of the Archbishop of Canterbury to pass judgment upon ritual charges brought against Edward King, the Bishop of Lincoln. Benson's interest in the study of St Cyprian contributed to a renewal in patristic scholarship and his influential *Cyprian* (1897) was published posthumously.

Benson, Richard Meux *(1824–1915)*
Anglican priest; vicar of Cowley. Inspired by John Keble he founded the Society of St John the Evangelist (the Cowley Fathers) in 1865. His sermons and writings reveal a deep spirituality.

Benson, Robert Hugh *(1871–1914)*
Son of E. W. Benson; ordained to the Anglican ministry, in 1894 he joined the Community of the Resurrection at Mirfield. In 1903 he was received into the Roman Catholic Church; the remainder of his life was devoted to preaching and writing. Benson is particularly remembered for his vivid religious novels, *e.g. By What Authority* (1904) and *Come Rack!, Come Rope!* (1912).

Beran, Josef *(1888–1969)*
Cardinal Archbishop of Prague, interned in 1949 by the communist regime in Czechoslovakia for refusing to allow his clergy to participate in political life. He was released and left Czechoslovakia in 1965.

Berengar of Tours *(c. 999–1088)*
After studying under the celebrated Fulbert at Chartres, Berengar returned to Tours, where he became head of the school there. His fame rests upon his very independent challenge to the current theological view of the Eucharist, particularly the theory of transubstantiation as handed down in the teaching of Paschasius Radbertus. His views were criticised and condemned by successive popes, and contemporary theologians vied with one another to argue against him. He ended his days in ascetic solitude. His teaching was clearly expressed in his *De Sacra Coena* and he forced the Church to re-examine its eucharistic teaching.

Berkeley, George *(1685–1753)*
Philosopher and Anglican bishop; educated at Trinity College, Dublin, and after travelling abroad and attempting to found a missionary college in America, appointed Bishop of Cloyne in 1734. As a philosopher he arrived at a radical theory of perception, and it is for his metaphysical doctrine that he is celebrated.

Bernadette of Lourdes, St *(1844–1879)*
Marie-Bernarde Soubirous (affectionately known by her family as 'Bernadette') was the eldest child of an impoverished miller and was always frail in health. Between 11 February and 18 July 1858, in a shallow cave on the bank of the river Gave, near Lourdes, she had a series of eighteen visions of a beautiful young woman. Her identity was revealed with the words, 'I am the Immaculate Conception.' The appearances of the Virgin Mary were accompanied by supernatural occurrences, some taking place in the presence of many witnesses. Bernadette suffered severely for some years from the suspicious disbelief of others, but steadfastly defended the genuineness of the visions. She eventually joined the Sisters of Notre Dame at Nevers where she lived a self-effacing life, loved for her kindliness and holiness, in spite of constant ill-health. She died in agony, cheerfully accepting her sufferings. She was declared a saint by the Roman Catholic Church in 1933, not for her part in the Lourdes apparitions but for the remarkable sanctity of her later life.

Bernanos, Georges *(1888–1948)*
French Roman Catholic novelist and writer, regarded as one of the most original and independent of his time. For Bernanos the supernatural world was very real and always close at hand. The constant theme of his many

novels was the struggle between the forces of good and evil for man's soul. This is perfectly exemplified in the most celebrated of his novels, *The Diary of a Country Priest* (1936).

Bernardino of Siena, St *(1380–1444)*

Of noble birth, at twenty-two Bernardino entered the Observants, a strict branch of the Franciscan Order. Deeply disturbed by the breakdown in morals and the lawlessness of the time, he set about the regeneration of the age with preaching tours, which resulted in the reform of many cities and a great reputation as an eloquent preacher. He sought to bring about moral reform through inculcating a deep personal love of Jesus Christ and he was an energetic promoter of devotion to the Holy Name of Jesus. He was canonised in 1450.

Bernard of Clairvaux, St *(1090–1153)*

Of noble parentage, when Bernard decided at twenty-two to become a Cistercian monk he took with him thirty young men, including brothers and uncles. His abbot at Citeaux sent him off after three years to found a new monastery at Clairvaux; this quickly became a centre of the Cistercian Order, famous throughout Europe. For ten years Bernard endured great hardships as he struggled to combine a mystical calling with service to others. The most active period of his life was from 1130 to 1145, when, due to his reputation for holiness, he was in constant demand, called to assist the pope of the time, preach the Second Crusade and serve on various civil and ecclesiastical councils. But Bernard always remained the ascetic Cistercian monk drawn to mysticism; his *De Diligendo Deo* was one of the most influential and outstanding books on mysticism to come from the Middle Ages. He was canonised in 1174 and declared a Doctor of the Church in 1830.

Bernard of Cluny *(c. 1140) (also known as Bernard of Moval or Morlaix)*

A monk of the Abbey of Cluny of whom little is known. Famous in his time as a preacher and writer, he is best remembered now for *De Contemptu Mundi* ('Condemning the World'), a poem of three thousand lines in which he attacks the monastic disorders of his age and stresses the transitory nature of life on earth. The poem is the source of many famous hymns, *e.g.* 'Jerusalem the Golden'.

Bernard of Montjoux, St *(d. c. 1081)*

As vicar general of the Aosta diocese in the Italian Alps, Bernard was concerned for travellers through two passes and established hospices to care for them. The dogs used by the hospices – and in time the passes themselves – were named after him.

Bersier, Eugène *(1831–1889)*
Writer and minister of a congregation of the Free Reformed Church in Paris, Eugène worked for Church unity and wrote on Church history and liturgy.

Bertold von Regensburg *(c. 1220–1272)*
Famous German Franciscan preacher who used his eloquence to insist that true repentance comes from the heart and all else are merely outward symbols.

Bérulle, Pierre de *(1575–1629)*
Cardinal, reformer and statesman who, as a prominent leader of the 'French School' of spiritual thought, played an essential role in reviving Catholicism in seventeenth-century France, principally by his teaching and by founding the Oratory (a congregation of priests without vows) which in turn founded seminaries and improved the standard of preaching.

Bessarion, John *(1403–1472) (originally Basil)*
Byzantine scholar and cardinal; a major contributor to the revival of Greek studies in the West; an ardent supporter of the reunion of the Eastern and Western churches.

Bessette, André *(1845–1937)*
Born near Montreal, Canada, at twenty-five André joined the Congregation of the Holy Cross and spent the next sixty-seven years in menial tasks. His heroic virtue and reputation for healing drew millions to Montreal to see him. His devotion to St Joseph occasioned the building of St Joseph's Oratory, Montreal, the most popular shrine in North America. He was honoured with the title 'Blessed' in 1982 by Pope John Paul II.

Beza, Theodore *(1519–1605)*
French Calvinist theologian; author and Bible translator. After studying law and publishing Latin verse, in 1548 Beza had a conversion experience and joined John Calvin at Geneva. On Calvin's death he succeeded him as leader of the Swiss Calvinists; he published a life of Calvin in 1564. Beza's Bible commentaries were widely read in his time and his Greek editions and Latin translations of the New Testament were basic sources for the later Geneva Bible and the Authorised version. In 1581 he donated the Codex Bezae (probably fifth century) to the University of Cambridge. Beza is considered Calvin's equal in the establishment of Calvinism in Europe.

Bilney, Thomas *(c. 1495–1531)*
Protestant martyr. At Cambridge he is believed to have converted Hugh Latimer to the doctrines of the Reformers. Arrested in 1527 for heresy, he recanted, but in 1531, for spreading ideas critical of the hierarchical structure of the Church and the cult of the saints, he was burnt at Norwich.

Binney, Thomas *(1798–1874)*
English Congregational minister who worked to obtain reunion with the Church of England. He introduced the chanting of psalms into Congregational worship as one step towards this. He wrote *Twenty-Four Reasons for Dissenting from the Church of England* (1848).

Birinus, St *(d. 649 or 650)*
Consecrated a bishop in Genoa, Birinus landed in Wessex and converted the local king. He was the first Bishop of Dorchester and is regarded as the apostle of the West Saxons.

Bishop, Edmund *(1846–1917)*
Lay liturgist and historian. His early working years were spent in government posts, but after his reception into the Roman Catholic Church in 1867, he sought admittance into the Benedictine Order. Poor health frustrated his desire and he devoted his life to studying and writing on liturgy, especially from a historical angle. His best-known work was *The Genius of the Roman Rite* (1899).

Blackburn, Gideon *(1772–1838)*
American Presbyterian clergyman and pioneer missionary to the Cherokee Indians. After preaching, teaching and introducing new agricultural methods to the Indians, failing health drove Blackburn to withdraw; taking up education, he founded a theological college that was subsequently named after him.

Blair, James *(1656–1743)*
Scottish Episcopalian minister who emigrated to America after being deprived of his Edinburgh parish for refusing the oath supporting the Roman Catholic Duke of York as heir to the throne. In Virginia he founded a college, which is now the second-oldest institution of higher education in the USA.

Blaise, St *(d.c. 316)*
Little is known of his life, but according to tradition Blaise was of noble birth, and Bishop of Sebastia. During the Emperor Licinius' persecution, the local governor of Armenia hunted down Blaise, who had become a hermit, and executed him. The blessing of throats associated with St Blaise arose from the miracle he is said to have worked in saving the life of a child choking to death on a fish bone.

Blake, William *(1757–1827)*
Apprenticed at fourteen to an engraver, Blake used his talent throughout his life in illustrating his own writings and poetry and that of others. His early

work also brought an appreciation of Gothic art, with which spirit he became imbued. In 1778 Blake became associated with the followers of the mystical sect of Swedenborg, but he was personally opposed to dogma and asceticism; his visionary genius developed a boundless sympathy with all living things. Blake's great allegorical poem *Jerusalem* took ten years to complete; his greatest work of art, the illustrations for the book of Job, was completed just a year or two before his death.

Blastares, Matthew *(fourteenth century)*
Greek Orthodox monk and theologian whose system of church and civil law influenced Slavic legal codes. Blastares is best known for his alphabetical handbook of Church law.

Blomfield, Charles James *(1786–1857)*
Anglican Bishop of London who worked for clerical reform and was a zealous church builder. He enjoyed a wide reputation as a classics scholar.

Blondel, Maurice *(1861–1949)*
Devout French Catholic philosopher whose *L'Action* (1893) gave birth to his 'philosophy of Action'; from which he developed a Christian philosophy of religion. Many later books amplified his original thought. For some years he was associated with the Modernist movement in the Roman Catholic Church.

Blosius, Franciscus Ludovicius *(1506–1566)*
Benedictine monastic reformer and spiritual writer. His concern for monastic renewal shone through his writings; his mystical writing was more popular, in his day, than *The Imitation of Christ*.

Bloy, Léon *(1846–1917)*
Fervent Roman Catholic French novelist who, principally through his writings, preached that spiritual renewal was to be attained through suffering and poverty. He made an impact upon many of his contemporaries, e.g. Maritain, Huysmans and Rouault.

Blumhardt, Johann *(1805–1880)*
Protestant evangelist whose preaching and ministry, attended by miraculous healing, drew large crowds to Möttlingen in Württemberg. The latter part of his life was spent at Bad Boll, near Göppingen, where an influential centre of missionary work developed.

Boehme (Böhme) Jacob *(1575–1624)*
Lutheran philosophical mystic who claimed that he was personally illuminated to write. His mystical experiences occurred while following the trade of shoemaker, but when published in 1612, in *Aurora*, the local Lutheran

pastor condemned the book. He was forbidden to write, but in 1619 he defied the ban, describing his mysticism in alchemical terms. His works included *The Way to Christ* (1622), *The Great Mystery* and *On the Election of Grace*.

Boethius, Anicius Manlius Severinus *(c. 480–c. 524) (St Severinus)*

Scholar, philosopher and statesman; consul under the emperor Theodoric the Ostrogoth. His most famous book, *De Consolatione Philosophiae* (written in prison), argues that the soul can attain to the vision of God through philosophy. This and other philosophical works had a profound influence in the Middle Ages, particularly upon Aristotelian studies. He also wrote a number of short theological treatises. Known also as St Severinus (canonised in 1883), his arrest and execution for treason by the Arian emperor brought him recognition as a martyr for the orthodox Christian faith.

Bolland, Jean *(1596–1665)*

Little is known of Bolland's life. A Jesuit ecclesiastical historian, he was chosen to continue the project of Rosweyde, whose idea was to compile the *Acta Sanctorum*, an exhaustive collection of the lives of the Christian saints using the best historical methods. Bolland (and those after him called Bollandists) travelled widely, combing through and examining all existing records. Work on the *Acta* has continued into the present time.

Bonar, Horatius *(1808–1889)*

Scottish Presbyterian minister whose poems, hymns and prayers were popular during the nineteenth century.

Bonaventure, St *(c. 1217–1274)*

Giovanni di Fidanza was an Italian by birth, but was educated in theology at Paris, where later he was head of the Franciscan School, having become a Franciscan in 1244. In 1257 he was elected Minister General of his Order, due to his personal holiness and his defence of the Order. Bonaventure wrote several spiritual books and an officially approved *Life of St Francis*. Created a cardinal in 1273, he was a leading figure at the Second Council of Lyons, and died before the end of it. Bonaventure made a real impact upon the theology of his day and his spiritual books had a long-lasting influence. Declared a saint in 1483, he was made a Doctor of the Church in 1589.

Bonhoeffer, Dietrich *(1906–1945)*

Lutheran theologian and pastor. Bonhoeffer received his theological education at Tübingen, Rome and Berlin, and subsequently lectured in theology at the Union Theological Seminary, New York, and at the University of Berlin. From the start Bonhoeffer was opposed to the Nazi movement and sided with the Confessing Church, for whom he headed a new seminary at

Finkenwalde. For his association with the resistance to Hitler and a link with the failed assassination attempt on the Führer, he was arrested in 1943 and hanged at Flossenbürg in 1945. In his theological thought, which matured while he was in prison, he sought to speak in a secular way to secular society about God; this comes across in *Letters and Papers From Prison* (1953). Bonhoeffer had an enduring interest in ecumenism and a link with the United Kingdom through his friendship with Bishop Bell of Chichester.

Boniface, St *(c. 675–754)*
Often known as 'the Apostle of Germany', Wynfrid or Wynfrith was born in Devon, England. From an early age he was in the care of the Benedictine Order, which he joined and in which he was ordained a priest. His first attempt in 716 to evangelise the Frisian Saxons met with no success, and he travelled to Rome where he was given papal authority; his second missionary journey, in 719, met with considerable success. He was recalled to Rome and consecrated a missionary bishop. From 725 to 735 he worked with success in Thuringia. After organising the Church in Bavaria, he was entrusted with a complete reform of the Frankish Church (740–747). Consecrated Archbishop of Mainz about 747, he was martyred by pagan Frisians on Pentecost Day 754.

Boniface – Nine popes bear this name; two, Boniface I and Boniface IV, were honoured with the additional title of 'Saint'.

Bonner, Edmund *(c. 1500–1569)*
An outstanding Oxford lawyer who from 1532 to 1543 served Henry VIII on various foreign missions, supporting the king in his antipapal measures. Bonner was made Bishop of London in 1540, but, during the reigns of Edward VI and Elizabeth I, would not impose Protestant doctrine and worship. As a result he was deprived of his See and imprisoned from 1549 to 1553). Under Mary Tudor he was restored to his bishopric but was rebuked by Mary's government for his reluctance to prosecute Protestants in London. He was deprived again of his See by Elizabeth I and spent the last ten years of his life in the London Marshalsea prison.

Booth family – The family associated with the foundation and development of the Salvation Army.

Booth, Catherine Mumford *(1829–1890)*
Wife of William Booth, but a famous preacher in her own right. The author of *Female Ministry*, she promoted the idea that the sacraments are unnecessary for salvation.

Booth, Evangeline Cory
Led and developed the Salvation Army in the United States.

Booth, William *(1829–1912)*
Apprenticed to a pawnbroker at the age of thirteen William became a
Methodist about the same time. In 1844 he had a conversion experience and
two years later became a revivalist preacher. In 1855 he married Catherine
Mumford. Leaving the Methodist Church, which was unhappy with his
style of evangelisation, he founded his own revivalist movement in the East
End of London, combining evangelism with social service; later, in 1878, this
was called the Salvation Army. As the movement spread General Booth
spent more and more time travelling and organising. In his book *In Darkest
England*, and in *The Way Out*, he outlined remedies for the social ills of his
time.

Booth, William Bramwell *(1856–1929)*
Succeeded his father as leader of the Salvation Army; he broadened out the
Army's Youth Service.

Borgia, St Francis *(1510–1572)*
The fourth Duke of Gandia, Borgia held various appointments in the court of
Charles V of Spain. After the death of his wife, Eleanor, in 1546, he entered
the Society of Jesus. He was a friend and adviser of St Ignatius Loyola and St
Teresa of Avila. Through his efforts and reputation for piety the Society of
Jesus spread through Europe. He was also responsible for the foundation of
many schools and colleges. He became the third General of the Order.

Borromeo, St Charles *(1538–1584)*
Created Cardinal Archbishop of Milan at the age of twenty-two, Charles
was concerned for the need of reform in the Roman Catholic Church and
took a prominent part in the reforming Council of Trent. At its close he
threw himself energetically into the implementation of its decrees. Considered
a model bishop, he regularly visited the thousand parishes in his diocese,
lived simply and won the admiration of all during the plague of 1576–1578
for the courageous care he gave his flock. His reforming zeal met with
opposition, and an assassination attempt was made on his life. He was
canonised by the Roman Catholic Church in 1610.

Bosco, St John *(1815–1888)*
Of peasant origins, after ordination John worked in a Turin suburb providing
for the needs of boys and young men. He opened workshops, schools, a
boarding house and, in 1859, founded the Society of St Francis of Sales
(Salesians) to care for the hundreds of youths that looked to him. The work
of the Salesians had spread to many countries by the time of his death.

Bossuet, Jacques-Benigne *(1627–1704)*
Ordained a priest in 1652, Bossuet has been accepted as one of the greatest preachers of all time. As Bishop of Meaux he taught the French Dauphin and became famous for his funeral orations, his fight against Jansenism and his clash with Fenelon over mysticism and Quietism. His later writings, *Meditation sur L'Évangile* and *Élevations sur les mystères*, rank as French spiritual classics.

Boulter, Hugh *(1672–1742)*
English Archbishop of Armagh, Ireland, and virtual ruler there representing the Protestant interest and ascendancy. He believed England's interests in Ireland were threatened by the large Roman Catholic majority, so he applied the penal laws with energy and Catholics were deprived of the vote. He was noted for his generosity to the poor.

Bourdaloue, Louis *(1632–1704)*
Famous French Jesuit preacher whose sermons on moral matters were a regular and beneficial part of the court of Louis XIV from 1670 onwards. He earned the title of 'king of preachers and preacher of kings'.

Bourgeois, Louis *(b. c. 1510–d. after 1561)*
Protestant Huguenot composer who wrote many melodic settings to the psalms, which appeared in the Genevan Psalter. He owed much to his close friendship with John Calvin.

Bourne, Francis *(1861–1935)*
Cardinal Archbishop of Westminster who proved a strong and resolute leader of English Catholics, and, during World War I, a patriotic Englishman.

Bousset, Wilhelm *(1865–1920)*
Biblical scholar and theologian; co-founder of the so-called 'History of Religions school'. In his principal work, *The Religion of the Jews in New Testament Times*, he investigated the relations between later Judaism and the early Christian Church.

Bradford, John *(c. 1510–1555)*
Protestant martyr. Bradford studied law first, then changed to theology. His strong preaching encouraged Nicholas Ridley, Bishop of London, to take him as secretary. Imprisoned under Mary Tudor, he was eventually burnt at Smithfield for his Protestant beliefs.

Bradwardine, Thomas *(1290–1349)*
Chaplain to King Edward III, theologian and mathematician; his principal work, *De Causa Dei contra Pelagium* (1344), won him the title 'the Profound

Doctor'; consecrated Archbishop of Canterbury while in Avignon, he died of the Black Death before being enthroned.

Brady, Nicholas *(1659–1726)*
Anglican priest and poet who graduated and first worked in Ireland but whose later life was spent in the pastoral ministry in England. Brady, with Nahum Tate, was author of a metrical version of the Psalms, licensed in 1696.

Brainerd, David *(1718–1747)*
Presbyterian missionary to the Seneca and Delaware Indians of New York and New Jersey. Famous for his diary, published post-humously, which aroused wide interest in missionary work to the American Indians.

Brant, Joseph *(1742–1807)*
Mohawk Indian chief, with the Indian name of Thayendanega, and fearless military ally of Britain in the War of Independence. Effective Christian missionary, he helped in the translation of the Book of Common Prayer and the Gospel of St Mark into Mohawk.

Bray, Thomas *(1656–1730)*
Anglican clergyman who founded the Society for Promoting Christian Knowledge (SPCK) in 1698, and in 1701 the separate Society for the Propagation of the Gospel (SPG). Selected by the Bishop of London to represent him in the colony of Maryland, Bray recruited missionaries and launched a free library scheme. By 1699 there were thirty, the SPCK being founded to support the libraries, which Bray also introduced into England. The latter part of his life was occupied in pastoral work as vicar of a London parish.

Brebeuf, St Jean de *(1593–1649)*
French Jesuit priest who dedicated his life to the conversion of the Huron Indians in Canada. Despite much opposition and danger he converted many thousands of Indians until he was captured by the Iroquois tribe and cruelly tortured to death. Known for his holiness and courage, Jean was canonised by the Roman Catholic Church in 1930.

Brendan, St *(c. 484–c. 577)*
Also known as Brendan the Voyager, or the Navigator. Little is known for certain of his life; he was reputedly born near Tralee, Country Kerry, became a monk and ordained a priest. He is credited with founding many monasteries in Ireland and Scotland. A noted traveller and voyager, he was immortalised in an Irish epic of the ninth century (*Navigatio Brendani*) which describes intrepid voyages of discovery in a leather craft.

Brenz, Johannes *(1499–1570)*
After studying theology at Heidelberg, Brenz was ordained priest in 1520, but by 1523 he had stopped celebrating mass and begun to support the work of the Reformers. In his book *Syngramma Suevicum* he expounded Luther's doctrine on the Real Presence in the Eucharist. He helped in the reconstitution of the University of Tübingen and was the author of two catechisms and several books.

Brewster, William *(1567–1644)*
At Scrooby, Nottinghamshire, where he had spent his early life, Brewster first became a Puritan leader. He migrated to Holland, where he printed Puritan books; he accompanied the Mayflower Pilgrims in 1620 and was the real religious leader, dominating the formation of doctrine and worship.

Bridget of Ireland, St *(d. c. 524) (also known as Bride or Brigit)*
Although she is one of the patron saints of Ireland, and ever popular there, little is known of Bridget's life, apart from legend and folklore. Born of a noble father and slave mother, she was later sold to a Druid, whom, tradition says, she converted. Restored to her father, a match was made for her with the King of Ulster. Her piety won her release and a grant of land at Kildare, where she is said to have founded the first convent in Ireland. She is also credited with founding other communities.

Bridget of Sweden, St *(c. 1303–1373)*
Patron saint of Sweden and founder of the Brigittine Order of Sisters; a mystic whose published revelations were influential in the Middle Ages.

Brooks, Phillips *(1835–1893)*
United States Episcopal clergyman who won an international reputation as a preacher. Pastor in Philadelphia and Boston (his ministry there lasted twenty-two years), in 1891 he was consecrated Bishop of Massachusetts. Widely known as the composer of the carol, 'O Little Town of Bethlehem'.

Brother Laurence – *See* Herman, Nicholas

Browne, Robert *(c. 1550–1633)*
Puritan separatist church leader, one of the original founders of the French Church movement among Nonconformist Christians. He led a separatist church at Norwich in 1580, and for this and similar activities he was imprisoned thirty-two times and exiled in 1582. He made submission to the Church of England in 1584 and accepted ordination for the Anglican Church. He finished his days in a pastoral role, but he exercised a great influence upon early Congregationalism.

Browne, Sir Thomas *(1605–1682)*
Physician and author who is best known for his book *Religio Medici* (1642), which describes his religious outlook and expressed a religious tolerance unknown at the time; the book was read throughout Europe.

Brunner (Heinrich) Emil *(1889–1966)*
Ordained in the Swiss Reformed Church, Brunner worked first as a pastor then, from 1924 to 1953, as professor of systematic and pastoral theology at the University of Zurich. He conducted many lecture tours in the USA, and his many books helped to shape the course of modern Protestant theology. He was one with Karl Barth in opposing theological liberalism but opposed him on the degree of knowledge of God attainable from creation.

Bruno of Cologne, St *(c. 1030–1101)*
Ordained at Cologne, he was made head of the cathedral school of Reims; among his pupils was the future Pope Urban II. Offered the See of Reims, he retired instead with six companions to Chartreuse, near Grenoble, where he founded the Carthusian Order (Trappists). In 1090 Pope Urban II summoned him to Rome as an adviser, but soon afterwards he retired to a desert in Calabria and founded another monastery, where he died.

Bruno of Querfurt, St *(c. 974–1009) (also known as Boniface)*
Missionary to the Prussians; a bishop martyred with eighteen companions in Poland after much success preaching to the Magyars.

Bruno the Great, St *(925–965)*
Youngest son of the Emperor Henry I, he became Archbishop of Cologne in 953 and, as such, exercised considerable influence over his brother, the Emperor Otto, in furthering peace and learning.

Bryennios, Philotheos *(1833–1914)*
Eastern Metropolitan, theologian and Church historian who in 1873, in Constantinople, discovered several early Christian documents, including *The Didache* and two epistles of St Clement of Rome.

Bucer, Martin *(1491–1551)*
As a Dominican monk Bucer became familiar with the teaching of Erasmus and Martin Luther. Released from his monastic vows in 1521, he preached Lutheranism, becoming leader of the Reformed Church in Switzerland on the death of Zwingli. Bucer moved to England in 1549 and was appointed Regius professor of divinity at Cambridge, advising Cranmer on the Anglican Ordinal of 1550.

Buchman, Frank *(1878–1961)*
A Lutheran minister, he worked in a parish in Philadelphia but resigned in disillusionment. Buchman took up evangelical work among students and travelled widely. The Group movement developed, and as its leader he travelled around the world and in 1938, in London, launched the Moral Rearmament movement.

Bugenhagen, Johannes *(1485–1558)*
A priest colleague of Martin Luther who organised the Lutheran Church in North Germany and Denmark; the *Brunswick Church Order* was mainly his work.

Bulgakov, Sergius *(1871–1944)*
Russian theologian and priest who started his adult life as a religious sceptic active in Marxism. Disillusioned, he gradually found his way back to the Church. Expelled from Russia, he became dean of the Orthodox Theological Academy at Paris from 1925. His involvement in the Ecumenical Movement and his theological writings ensured that he was well-known throughout Europe and America.

Bulgaris, Eugenius *(1716–1806)*
Greek Orthodox theologian and scholar of the liberal arts who spread knowledge of Western thought throughout the Eastern Orthodox world.

Bull, George *(1634–1710)*
Anglican bishop and High Church theologian who attacked Protestant theories of justification on the one hand, and *The Corruptions of the Church of Rome* (his celebrated book of 1705) on the other.

Bullinger, Heinrich *(1504–1575)*
Convert from Roman Catholicism to the teaching of Zwingli, on whose death in 1531 he succeeded as principal pastor of Zurich. He helped draft the First Helvetic Confession of 1536, and the Second Confession of 1566 was his own work. He corresponded with Henry VIII and Edward VI of England; Elizabeth I sought his support with her own settlement of Church affairs.

Bultmann, Rudolf *(1884–1976)*
New Testament scholar and theologian who studied at Tübingen, Marburg and Berlin; later he was appointed to teach at the Universities of Marburg, Breslau and Giessen, before, in 1921, his appointment as professor of New Testament studies at Marburg, where he stayed until 1951. Influenced by the German existentialist philosopher Martin Heidegger, Bultmann published many works, developing Form Criticism to reach his position on the demythologising of the New Testament message.

Bunsen, Christian Carol *(1791–1860)*
Liberal Prussian diplomat, scholar and theologian; while in office representing his country in England he was instrumental in the scheme for a joint Lutheran–Anglican Bishopric in Jerusalem. His writings were voluminous, the most important being *Signs of the Times* (1856), defending religious and personal freedom.

Bunting, Jabez *(1779–1858)*
Wesleyan Methodist minister who, as president of the first Wesleyan theological college, had the task of organising Methodism into a church, independent of the Church of England.

Bunyan, John *(1628–1688)*
Born of poor parents at Elstow, Bedfordshire, Bunyan fought for the Parliamentary side in the Civil War; about 1649 he married, and his gradual conversion dates from this time. Recognised as a preacher among the Independents of Bedford, most of the years 1660 to 1672 were spent in Bedford gaol, for holding unapproved services. There his writing began, which led to *The Pilgrim's Progress*, his autobiography *Grace Abounding*, and the allegory *The Holy War*. After release he worked among the Independents of Bedford.

Burgos, José *(1837–1872)*
Roman Catholic priest who spoke out against the oppressive power and privilege of Church and Spanish rule in the Philippines; he was arrested and executed. This 'martyrdom', as it was considered locally, initiated a movement which eventually achieved Burgos' desired reforms and the overthrow of Spanish domination.

Burrough, Edward *(1634–1663)*
Quaker preacher who defended Quaker doctrines against, among others, John Bunyan; arrested in 1662 for holding illegal meetings, he was committed to Newgate prison, where he died.

Bushnell, Horace *(1802–1876)*
American Congregationalist and controversial theologian, pioneer of liberal theology in New England. His seminal books, which examined and re-explained theological language and concepts, were bitterly attacked, but had a lasting impact.

Butler, Alban *(1710–1773)*
English Roman Catholic priest who returned to his seminary, the English College, Douai, France, as lecturer. After extensive research throughout the Continent he published (1756–1759) his classic *Lives of the Saints*. The four-

volume work with more than sixteen hundred hagiographies went through many editions and has never been out of print. (It was revised and updated in 1956.) Butler worked for a while as a mission priest in the English Midlands; from 1766 until his death he was president of the English College at Saint-Omer.

Butler, Christopher *(1902–1986)*
Benedictine abbot, theologian and writer. He was a brilliant student at St John's, Oxford, finishing with three Firsts – Mods., Greats and theology; he moved to Keble College as tutor and prepared for the Anglican ministry. In 1928 Butler became a Roman Catholic and joined the Benedictine Order; ordained in 1933 he became abbot of Downside in 1946. At the Second Vatican Council he made a creative contribution and was elected auxiliary Bishop of Westminster in 1966. Considered the foremost English Roman Catholic theologian of modern times, he made a substantial contribution to ecumenism, particularly on the Anglican-Roman Catholic International Commission (ARCIC) for fifteen years.

Butler, Joseph *(1692–1752)*
English bishop, moral philosopher and preacher in the royal court. As an author he was influential in defending revealed religion against the rationalists of his time.

Byrd, William *(1543–1623)*
Organist first at Lincoln Cathedral and then, from 1572, at the Chapel Royal, London, where he shared duties with his teacher, Thomas Tallis. Although a Catholic, this never prevented him composing and playing for the established Church. Considered the greatest English composer of the Shakespearean age, he wrote much secular as well as liturgical music.

C

Cabrini, St Frances Xavier *(1850–1917)*
The first American citizen to be canonised by the Roman Catholic Church (1946), Frances was born in Lombardy, Italy. At the direction of her local bishop she founded, in 1880, the Missionary Sisters of the Sacred Heart, who devoted themselves to the education of girls. Pope Leo XIII directed her attention to the USA, where she and her sisters worked among the needy Italian immigrants. Mother Cabrini, as she was known, became a naturalised citizen of the United States in 1909. Despite constant bad health and

innumerable obstacles she travelled widely in the United States and Europe, founding sixty-seven hospitals, schools, orphanages and convents.

Cabrol, Fernand *(1855–1937)*
Benedictine monk and abbot of St Michael's Abbey, Farnborough, Hants, who gained an international reputation as a liturgist and writer on the history of church worship.

Caedmon *(658–680)*
Little is known of his life except through the Venerable Bede, who tells how Caedmon, an illiterate herdsman at Whitby had a dream in which he was told to sing of 'the beginning of things'. By virtue of his hymn of creation, Caedmon has the distinction of being the first Old English Christian poet.

Caesarius of Arles, St *(c. 470–542)*
Monk and abbot who, in 503, became Archbishop of Arles and a leading prelate of the Gallican Church. Famed for his preaching, he energetically and decisively opposed Semi-Pelagianism.

Caird, Edward *(1835–1908)*
Scottish philosopher (chief representative of the New-Hegelian movement in British philosophy) and theologian. He wrote a critical review of Kant's philosophy and *The Evolution of Religion* (1893).

Caird, John *(1820–1898)*
Minister of the Church of Scotland, theologian and renowned preacher. Principal of Glasgow University, he followed, like his brother Edward, the New-Hegelian movement.

Cajetan, Thomas de Vio *(1469–1534)*
Entering the Dominican Order in 1484, Cajetan taught theology and philosophy at Padua, Pavia and Rome. As Master General of his Order (1508–1518) and cardinal he urged Church reform, particularly at the fifth Lateran Council (1512–1517). As papal legate in Germany, Cajetan met and reasoned with Martin Luther, and he opposed the divorce plans of Henry VIII of England. His profound commentary on Thomas Aquinas' *Summa Theologica* established his reputation as a scholar and founder of the revival of Thomism.

Calixtus *(also Calistus or Callistus)* – There were three popes with this name; the most significant was:

Calixtus I, St *(d. 222)*

Bishop of Rome from *c.* 217, he appears to have started life as a slave. Denounced as a Christian, he was sent to the Sardinian mines. After regaining his freedom he was elected pope. Attacked by a theologian, Hippolytus, he was accused of modalist doctrines. Calixtus, however, condemned Sabellius, the principal exponent of the modalist heresy.

Calixtus, George *(1586–1656)*

German Protestant theologian who persistently attempted, from 1613, to develop a theology which would reconcile Lutherans, Calvinists and Catholics. He expanded his system, given the name 'Syncretism', in many writings.

Calvin, John *(1509–1564)*

French theologian and one of the most important figures of the Protestant Reformation. After studying theology at Paris and law at Orleans, and the publication of his book *De Clementia*, Calvin had a religious experience in 1533 and broke with the Catholic Church. As a preacher and organiser he worked to found the Reformation at Geneva. Driven out of the city for three years, Calvin settled at Strasbourg, where he was pastor and lecturer. His master work, the *Institutes of the Christian Religion*, was published in 1536.

In 1541 he returned to Geneva and devoted the next fourteen years to the establishment of a theocratic regime on the Old Testament model. His opponents were tortured and executed. Calvin's Scripture commentaries date from this period as does his treatise on predestination. His mastery of the city by 1555 left Calvin free to devote more time to the spread of Reformed Protestantism in other countries. In 1559 the Academy of Geneva was founded to continue his teaching. Simple and austere in lifestyle, Calvin was a reticent man and little is known of his personal life. His wife died in 1549 and his only child died at birth in 1542. His great intellectual ability and charismatic leadership account for his enormous impact upon the course of Western Church history.

Camara, Helder *(1909–1999)*

Born at Fortaleza, north-east Brazil, Camara entered the theological seminary in his late teens, and was ordained in 1931. He immediately became committed to helping the poor of the local slums. Involved in education he became Secretary of State for Education in Ceara; in 1936 he became a member of the Supreme Council for Education. Consecrated bishop (1955), and then in 1964 Archbishop of Olinda and Recife, Camara was constantly working for the poor, living in the squalid shanty towns around Rio de Janeiro; he took these concerns to the Second Vatican Council (1963–1965) in Rome. The new (1964) dictatorship in Brazil closed down his education and land reform programmes; hundreds of his priests were tortured and he received many death threats. From the pulpit he courageously pursued his 'crusade for the poor' and denounced the brutality of the military dictators. Travelling in Europe and USA (1969 onwards) he addressed large rallies exposing the corrupt structures of injustice rampant throughout Latin America. In November 1975 he was awarded the World Humanity Award in London; he was nominated several times for the Nobel Peace Prize. He retired to live among the poor.

Camillus de Lellis, St *(1550–1614)*
Founder of the Ministers of the Sick. Camillus began life in Bucchianico, Italy, and served as a mercenary in the Venetian army against the Turks. A compulsive gambler, he lost all his money and became a labourer. After conversion in 1575 he worked, despite an incurable disease in his legs, as a nurse at St Giacomo's hospital in Rome. Under St Philip Neri's guidance he grew to great holiness and was ordained priest in 1584. Camillus was resolved to found an Order to be totally devoted to the care of the sick, with a fourth vow to care for all, especially those who were plague-stricken. His Order was revolutionary in its methods, for example, in providing the first medical corp for troops in battle; the separation of those with contagious diseases; well-aired wards, *etc.*; and above all for providing a caring which embraced the physical and spiritual needs of patients. Despite several painful illnesses Camillus continued caring for the sick until his death. He was canonised in 1746.

Campbell, Alexander *(1788–1866)*
Founder of the Disciples of Christ (Churches of Christ) or 'Campbellites'. Son of Thomas Campbell, a Presbyterian minister who emigrated to the United States, Alexander took the leadership of his father's reform movement, opposed both to speculative theology and emotional revivalism. He founded, in 1840, Bethany College and remained its president until his death. A prolific writer, he also founded and edited the *Christian Baptist*.

Campion, St Edmund *(1540–1581)*
Son of a London bookseller, Campion was teaching at Oxford University when he was ordained a deacon for the Anglican Church, in 1569. A crisis of conscience led him to be received into the Catholic Church. Travelling to Rome, he entered the Society of Jesus and was ordained in 1578. He joined the first Jesuit mission to England in 1580, preaching extensively, especially in the London area and Lancashire. The secret publication of his *Ten Reasons* (1581), defending the Catholic position, occasioned one of the most intensive manhunts in English history. He was betrayed at Lyford, near Oxford, and imprisoned in the Tower of London. When he would not renounce his Catholicism he was tortured, then hanged, drawn and quartered at Tyburn on 1 December 1581. In 1970 he was canonised as one of the forty English and Welsh martyrs.

Canisius, St Peter *(1521–1597)*
Educated at the University of Cologne, Peter became a Jesuit in 1543 and taught in various universities and founded colleges in six places. He lectured widely against Protestantism and composed several catechisms, the most famous of which was published in 1554 and ran through four hundred editions in 150 years. More than any other Catholic theologian, Canisius delayed the advance of Protestantism and advanced the Counter-Reformation in Southern Germany. In 1580 he settled in Fribourg and founded a Jesuit College, which became the University of Fribourg. He was canonised in 1925 and declared a Doctor of the Church.

Cantelupe, St Thomas de *(c. 1218–1282) (also known as Thomas of Hereford)*
English reforming Bishop of Hereford whose reforming spirit and ascetical life recommended him to King Edward I as confidential adviser. A dispute with John Peckham, Archbishop of Canterbury, sent Thomas to Rome to plead his cause, where he died.

Capgrave, John *(1393–1464)*
English historian and theologian who lectured at Oxford University; ordained priest, he later became a hermit of the Augustinian Order. He is credited with many theological works and is especially remembered for his *Life of St. Katharine.*

Carey, William *(1761–1834)*
Northamptonshire shoemaker, almost entirely self-taught, who left Anglicanism to become a Baptist in 1783; he became a preacher and pastor and moved to a ministry at Leicester. Three years later, in 1792, he published his famous *Enquiry* into the Christians' missionary obligation. This led to the formation of the English Baptist Missionary Society. In 1793 Carey left for Calcutta to fulfil a lifelong call. In five years he had translated the New Testament into Bengali and had visited two hundred villages. He moved to Serampore, which became his base. His prodigious work of translation continued and included the whole of the Bible in Bengali (1809) and parts of it in twenty-four other languages. His call to mission and his personal example touched the conscience of British Christians and inspired a renewed drive for mission.

Carlile, Wilson *(1847–1942)*
After a career in business, Carlile was accepted for ordination by the Anglican Church in 1880. In 1882 he founded the Church Army. He continued to help with its administration until his death.

Carpenter, William Boyd *(1841–1918)*
Anglican priest and prolific writer who established a reputation as a preacher, winning the admiration of Queen Victoria, who appointed him first Royal chaplain then Bishop of Ripon. He was responsible for the foundation of Ripon College, Oxford.

Carroll, John *(1735–1815)*
Born in Maryland, USA, but educated in Flanders, Carroll entered the Society of Jesus in 1753. He returned to Maryland in 1774 as a missionary, and ten years later became Superior of the Missions; subsequently he was the first Catholic bishop in America, consecrated in 1789 for the See of Baltimore.

Carstares, William *(1649–1715)*
Scottish Presbyterian theologian and statesman who was imprisoned for plotting to overthrow Charles II; later became William of Orange's chaplain and adviser. In 1703 he was made the principal of Edinburgh University and Moderator of the established Church of Scotland.

Cartwright, Peter *(1785–1872)*
Most famous of the nineteenth-century Methodist circuit riders in Kentucky, USA. He was an outspoken preacher, whose *Autobiography* (1856) gives an insight into the lives and travels of the itinerant preachers of the period.

Case, Shirley Jackson *(1872–1947)*
Canadian–United States theologian and educator. Dean of the University of Chicago Divinity School (1933–1938). His work on the interaction between Christianity and society provided principles for those engaged in the 'social gospel'.

Casel, Odo *(1886–1948)*
Benedictine monk and liturgist of international repute and influence. He studied and wrote widely on the theological aspects of liturgy. Casel was one of the forward-looking liturgists who prepared the way for the liturgical reforms of the Second Vatican Council.

Cassander, George *(1513–1566)*
Catholic theologian who sought, through his prolific writings, to draw Catholics and Protestants together. In 1564 the Emperor Ferdinand I called upon Cassander to assist in an official attempt at reconciliation, but his tireless efforts were not approved of by either side.

Cassian, John *(c. 360–435)*
Probably of Roman birth, Cassian became a monk and was trained by monks in Egypt; he was ordained deacon by John Chrysostom. Nothing is known of

the years 405–415, but immediately after that period he founded the Abbey of Saint-Victor at Marseilles. His writings, reflecting what he had learnt in Egypt, influenced all Western monasticism. He is honoured as a saint in the Eastern Church.

Caswall, Edward *(1814–1878)*
Anglican priest who converted to the Roman Catholic Church in 1847 and, after his wife's death in 1850, joined John Henry Newman's Oratory at Edgbaston. His fame rests upon his many popular hymns for Catholic usage and his successful translations of Latin hymns are still in popular use.

Catherine, Saint *(1522–1590)*
Baptised Alessandra dei Ricci, she entered the Dominican convent at Prato at thirteen and was prioress there for the last thirty years of her life. Famous for her stigmatisation, the ecstasy she was wrapt in for twenty-eight hours each week for several years, and her reputation for sanctity. Canonised by the Roman Catholic Church in 1746.

Catherine of Alexandria, St *(d. c. early fourth century)*
Her historicity is doubtful. Despite great devotion to her during the Middle Ages, and many popular legends, nowhere is Catherine mentioned before the ninth century. According to legend she was an exceptionally learned young girl of noble family who opposed the persecution of Christians by the Emperor Maxentius. She defeated eminent scholars sent to argue with her; arrested, she was tortured on a spiked wheel that broke (hence the Catherine wheel), and she was finally beheaded. The legend alleges that the body was taken by angels to Mt Sinai, where it was supposed to have been found in 800; there the great monastery of St Catherine still stands.

Catherine of Genoa, St *(1447–1510)*
Originally Caterina Fieschi, of a distinguished family, she was married at sixteen and led an unhappy life, until her conversion after a mystical experience in 1473. She gave herself to selfless care of the sick and her husband was subsequently converted. They agreed to live in continence, the husband joining the Third Order of St Francis. Catherine underwent a series of remarkable mystical experiences. Her spiritual teaching was contained in *Dialogo* and *Trattato del Purgatio*, published after her death.

Catherine of Siena, St *(1347–1380)*
Born Caterina Benincasa, from her earliest years she lived a devout and mortified life and began to have visions. At sixteen she joined the Third Order of St Dominic and gave herself to prayer and the service of the sick. Her evident holiness and mysticism won her many followers. When Florence was placed under an interdict by Pope Gregory XI, Catherine went to

Avignon to mediate and promote a crusade. With others she worked for the pope's return to Rome, and after the return she was invited to Rome as an adviser. She worked hard to have Urban VI accepted as the true claimant to the See of Rome. Catherine's spirituality and remarkable spiritual gifts continued to attract a large following. Her mystical experiences and teaching were recorded in her *Dialogo*, which, with over 350 letters and four treatises, is our chief source of her spirituality. Canonised in 1461, Catherine was declared a Doctor of the Church in 1970.

Caton, William *(1635–1665)*
Under the influence of George Fox, Caton became a Quaker and an itinerant preacher and missioner. He travelled through France and Holland where he was not always well treated. His *Journal* is still read in Quaker circles.

Caussade, Jean Pierre de *(1675–1751)*
Jesuit spiritual writer and preacher. His influence made mysticism once more acceptable after the Quietist period. His best-known work in the English language is *Abandonment to Divine Providence*, but there were also letters of spiritual direction and *An Instruction* on prayer.

Cecilia, St *(second and third century)*
Virgin martyr and patroness of music. Although one of the most famous of the Roman martyrs, her historicity is doubtful. According to a fifth-century legend she was of noble birth and married against her will to Valerian, a pagan, whom she converted together with his brother. They were martyred before Cecilia, who gave away all she had to the poor and then faced death by burning. When this failed she was beheaded. She is the patroness of church music.

Cedd, St *(d. 664)*
Brother of St Chad, and brought up with him at Lindisfarne under St Aidan. He worked among the people of Mercia and then of Essex and was consecrated bishop of the East Saxons in 654. He founded monasteries at West Tilbury, Bradwell-on-Sea and in Yorkshire at Lastingham, where he died of the plague.

Celestine – Five popes share this title; those of note were:

Celestine I, St *(d. 432)*
Pope from 422 to 432. He energetically fought against the heresy of Pelagianism, sending Germanus of Auxerre to Britain to deal with it; he wrote to Gaul against the Semi-Pelagianism of Cassian and condemned Nestorianism at a Roman synod in 430.

Celestine III *(c. 1106–98)*
Friend of Peter Abelard and Thomas à Becket, he was known for his moderation and patience. Elected pope at eighty-five years of age, he had continual difficulties with the German Emperor Henry VI, who oppressed the Church in Germany and, among other things, imprisoned King Richard the Lionheart.

Celestine V, St *(c. 1215–1296)*
Formerly a Benedictine monk he became a hermit with a wide reputation for austerity and sanctity, and founded the Celestines, a group of hermits. Elected pope when nearly eighty, in 1294, he abdicated after a few months when he realised his incapacity for the post. His successor, Boniface VII, had him imprisoned, where he died.

Chad, St *(d. 672)*
Brother of St Cedd and pupil of St Aidan of Lindisfarne. Succeeded Cedd as Abbot of Lastingham and was soon afterwards irregularly consecrated Bishop of the Northumbrians. When St Wilfred returned, Chad accepted the irregularity, stepped down and was sent instead as bishop to the Mercians, with his See at Lichfield. He founded monasteries at Lindsey and Barrow and is credited with the conversion of the kingdom of Mercia.

Challoner, Richard *(1691–1781)*
Born of Presbyterian parents, Challoner became a Roman Catholic before the age of fourteen, when he went to Douai, in Flanders, to train for the priesthood. He remained there after ordination, becoming vice-president. In 1730 he was sent to London to support the small, harassed Catholic community. He was consecrated Bishop (*in partibus*) of Debra and assistant to Dr Petre, the Vicar Apostolic whom he succeeded in 1758. He was the author of many books, including the ever-popular prayer book *The Garden of the Soul* (1740) and *Meditations for Every Day of the Year* (1753); both were frequently reprinted. He revised the Douai-Rheims version of the Bible and his historical works, including *Britannia Sancta* (1745), were well researched.

Chalmers, James *(1841–1901)*
Scottish Congregationalist member of the London Missionary Society; exploring the South-West Pacific, he was known as 'the Livingstone of New Guinea'. He tried to form an indigenous church but was killed by local tribesmen.

Chalmers, Thomas *(1780–1847)*
Presbyterian minister, theologian, social reformer and philanthropist. Famed as a preacher, on becoming minister at the largest and poorest Glasgow parish, St Johns, Chalmers concerned himself with the problems of the poor.

In 1823 he became professor of moral philosophy at St Andrews and, in 1828, professor of theology at Edinburgh. He was the acknowledged leader of the Evangelical party in the Church of Scotland, advocating the parishioners' right to choose their own minister. On 18 May 1843 the 'Disruption' occurred when 203 commissioners walked out of the General Assembly of the Church of Scotland. Chalmers became the first Moderator of the new Free Church of Scotland. He was subsequently chosen as principal of the New College at Edinburgh, for ministerial training.

Chanel, St Peter Mary *(1803–1841)*

French priest of humble origins who, after pastoral work, joined the Marist Order in 1831. In 1836 he was sent as a missionary to the New Hebrides in the Pacific and worked with success on the island of Futuna. He was murdered there by a chief when he discovered his son wanted to be baptised. He was canonised in 1954 as the first martyr of Oceania.

Channing, William Ellery *(1780–1842)*

Congregationalist minister who was a successful preacher and, from 1803, minister of the Federal St Church, Boston. He supported the liberal Congregationalist cause during the schism between conservative and liberal parties of that church. He preached against the doctrines of the Trinity and the atonement and was considered a Unitarian by 1820. While he disapproved of Unitarianism as a sect, this and the title 'apostle of Unitarianism' was forced upon him.

Chantal, St Jane Frances de *(1572–1641)*

Married in 1592 to the Baron de Chantal, who was killed in a hunting accident in 1601, and left a widow with four children, Jane Frances placed herself under the spiritual direction of St Francis of Sales in 1604. In 1610, with her family provided for, she founded, with St Francis, the Visitation Congregation of Sisters. Francis died in 1622 and her son was killed in battle in 1627. During the plague of 1628 she turned her convent into a hospital. At her death the Visitation Congregation had eighty-six houses. She was canonised in 1767.

Chapman, John *(1865–1933)*

Biblical and patristic scholar who converted from Anglicanism to the Roman Catholic Church in 1890. Two years later he joined the Benedictine Order. When the community on Caldey Island joined the Catholic Church in 1913, Chapman was sent as superior. He became Abbot of Downside Abbey in 1922. His works on Scripture were seminal, and his *Spiritual Letters* (1935) has proved to be a book of lasting value.

Charles I *(1600–1649)*
King of Great Britain and Ireland from 1625; Charles inherited from his father a firm belief in the divine right of kings. His authoritarian rule, at a time when aspirations for greater political and religious freedom were riding high, occasioned the Civil War. One result of the king's surrender in May 1646 was the disestablishment of the Church of England. His resolve not to surrender his principles led to his illegal execution, considered by many as a martyrdom. Churches have been dedicated to King Charles the Martyr and for nearly two hundred years the day of his death was honoured by the Church of England.

Charron, Pierre *(1541–1603)*
Famous French preacher, theologian and philosopher. His works *Les Trois Verites* (1593) and *De La Sagesse* (1601) made a major contribution to the new thought of the seventeenth century. Charron is noted for his sceptical tendency coupled with a traditional Catholicism.

Chemnitz, Martin *(1522–1586)*
Lutheran theologian who was one of the principal influences in consolidating and defending Luther's doctrines after his death, so much so that he was called 'the second Martin'. Refusing many important posts offered to him, Chemnitz spent most of his life in pastoral work and writing. Two of his principal works were the defence of Luther's teaching on the Real Presence in the Eucharist and an attack upon the decrees of the Council of Trent.

Cheney, Charles Edward *(1836–1916)*
Ordained a priest in the Protestant Episcopal Church of the USA, Cheney signed the 'Chicago Protest' against the 'unprotestantising' of the Church; and, after a conviction before an ecclesiastical court, helped to found the Reformed Episcopal Church, in which he served as a bishop.

Chesterton, Gilbert Keith *(1874–1936)*
Literary critic, poet, novelist and essayist. Chesterton was a master in the use of paradox, and used it to debunk Victorian pretensions. His voluminous works were enhanced by his interest in theology. Before turning from Anglicanism to Roman Catholicism in 1922, his *Heretics* (1905) and *Orthodoxy* (1908) appeared; after his conversion there was an edge to his controversial works, *The Catholic Church and Conversion* (1926), *The Everlasting Man* (1925), *etc*. His fiction is still well received, but his fame as a novelist rests principally upon his sleuth series, the Father Brown stories.

Cheverus, Jean-Louis Lefebvre de *(1768–1836)*
French priest who fled the French Revolution and on arrival in Boston, USA, served Indian missions, showing remarkable courage and charity during the

yellow fever epidemic of 1798. In 1808 Cheverus was consecrated the first Roman Catholic Bishop of Boston. He returned to France in 1823 and became Archbishop of Bordeaux; he was elevated to cardinal in the year of his death.

St Christopher *(c. third century)*
Although one of the most popular of saints, there is no certainty that he existed; for this reason he was dropped from the Roman Calendar in 1969. Tradition has it that he was martyred in Lycia under the Emperor Decius, about AD 250. There are many later legends about him, including the familiar story that represents Christopher as a giant who, after conversion, dedicated his life to transporting travellers across a river. One day a little child asked to be carried across, in mid-stream the burden became very heavy; the child was none other than the Christ-child and his care for the world (Christopher comes from the Greek, 'Christ-bearing').

Chrysostom, St John *(c. 347–407)*
As a hermit-monk, John lived the austere Pachomian Rule for eight years, which damaged his health. After his ordination in 386, his bishop instructed him to devote himself to preaching, which he did with such great talent for twelve years that he won the title 'Chrysostom' or 'golden-mouthed'. Against his wish, in 398 he was consecrated Patriarch of Constantinople, and his reforming zeal and plain-speaking pleased the common people and angered the wealthy. Powerful opponents had John convicted on false charges at the Synod of the Oak (403). Deposed from his See, Chrysostom was banished twice from Constantinople (403 and 404). His death was hastened in exile by an enforced march in severe weather conditions. While not an outstanding theologian, Chrysostom's fame rests upon his preaching (many scriptural homilies and sermons have survived) and his literal exegesis of the Bible, which was opposed to the allegorical sense popular at the time.

Church, Richard William *(1815–1890)*
Anglican priest, fellow of Oriel College and subsequently Rector of Whatley in Somerset, who worked to allay the outcry against his friends in the Tractarian Movement. Dean of St Paul's Cathedral from 1871, he wrote several biographies and his *Oxford Movement, Twelve Years 1833–1845* is regarded as the best record and judgment of the time.

Clare, St *(1194–1253)*
Influenced by St Francis of Assisi, Clare refused to marry as her parents wished and instead joined Francis. He placed her first in a Benedictine monastery then, when other women joined her, set up their own religious house, with Clare as abbess. So the Poor Clare Order began, and was soon housed at San Damiano, near Assisi, living in the 'privilege of perfect poverty'.

Many daughter houses sprang up throughout Europe in the thirteenth century. Famed for miracles during her life and after, Clare was canonised two years after her death.

Clarke, James Freeman *(1810–1888)*
Unitarian theologian and founder of the Church of the Disciples, Boston, USA. Close friend of many influential figures of his day; as a reformer opposing slavery Clarke supported the campaign of Grover Cleveland for the presidency. The editor of several journals and a prolific writer, it is said he had over a thousand articles and sermons published.

Clarke, Samuel *(1675–1729)*
Chaplain in turn to the Bishop of Norwich and, in 1706, Queen Anne, Clarke was not only a theologian but also a philosopher and exponent of the physics of his friend, Isaac Newton. In 1712 he caused a stir with his apparently Unitarian book, *Scripture Doctrine of the Trinity*. His condemnation was sought, but Clarke promised to write no more on the subject. His philosophical writings and correspondence brought him in touch with the philosophers Hume, Locke and Leibniz.

Claudel, Paul Louis Charles *(1868–1955)*
French poet, playwright and giant of French literature in the early twentieth century. His writing was achieved against the backcloth of an illustrious career in the French diplomatic service. Claudel served with distinction in the USA, the Far East and Central Europe; he was French ambassador in Tokyo (1921), Washington (1927) and Brussels (1933). His sudden conversion to the Roman Catholic faith gave a unique dimension to his writing, particularly his plays, which reveal a grand design in creation, a movement from man's lusts and appetites to a redemptive consecration of the world to Christ.

Clement – Fourteen popes shared this title, the most noteworthy being:

Clement I, St *(Clement of Rome) (pope from 88–97 or possibly 92–101)*
Probably the third Bishop of Rome after St Peter. It is feasible that he is the Clement referred to in Philippians 4:3. Certainly Irenaeus of Lyons speaks of him as a contemporary of the apostles. There is spurious Clementine literature, but the authorship of the *Letter to the Church at Corinth* (*c.* 96) is confidently ascribed to Clement. Many third and fourth-century Christians accepted it as part of Scripture.

Clement VII *(1478–1534)*
Born Guilio de Medici; despite being illegitimate, he became Archbishop of Florence and a cardinal in 1513, and pope ten years later. Of unreproachable

character, Clement was, however, personally weak and vacillating; he became caught up in the ambitious struggles of the emperor Charles V and Francis I of France. When Rome was sacked in 1527, Clement was imprisoned for seven months, during which Henry VIII of England asked for an annulment of his marriage to Catherine of Aragon. Clement vacillated, finally (in 1533) finding that Henry's marriage was valid. Henry's Act of Supremacy, declaring the kings of England to be head of the English Church, followed. Clement's indecisiveness allowed the Protestant movement to sweep Europe. To his contemporaries Clement appeared as a Renaissance prince concerned with the patronage of the arts.

Clement of Alexandria, St *(c. 150–c. 215)*
Of Greek origin, Clement became a pupil and convert of Pantaenus, who was leader of the catechetical school of Alexandria. While there Clement wrote his principal works, among them *An Exhortation* and *The Instructor*. He succeeded Pantaenus as head of the school in AD 190. During the persecution conducted by the Emperor Severus (201–202) Clement fled to Jerusalem and refuge with his friend Alexander, Bishop of Jerusalem.

Clifford, John *(1836–1923)*
Baptist minister and social reformer who started work at ten in a lace factory; after a conversion experience Clifford prepared for the Baptist ministry. His congregation at Paddington, London, became so large that a chapel at Westbourne Park was built and opened in 1877. In 1888 Clifford became president of the Baptist Union; theologically liberal, he defended the Union against Spurgeon's charges of heresy. Champion of the working classes, he came to national attention in 1902 with his passive resistance to Balfour's Education Act. Clifford served as president of the National Free Church Council (1898) and was the first president of the Baptist World Alliance.

Clitherow, St Margaret *(1556–1586)*
Wife of a butcher of York, Margaret was an Anglican who converted to Roman Catholicism in 1574. She was repeatedly fined and imprisoned for non-attendance at the Anglican church. Margaret allowed the Catholic Mass to be said secretly in her home and provided a hiding place for priests. During a sudden raid on 10 March 1586 she was seized and charged with the capital offence of harbouring priests. At her trial Margaret refused to plead to save her children being forced to witness against her. For this she was crushed slowly to death with an eight-hundred pound weight. Hence she won the title 'the martyr of York' and was canonised as one of the forty martyrs of England and Wales in 1970.

Cocceius, Johannes (or Koch) *(1603–1669)*
Biblical scholar and theologian of the Reformed Church who was a leading exponent of covenant theology. Prolific writer, his collected works were published as *Opera Omnia* in twelve volumes.

Coffin, Henry Sloane *(1877–1954)*
United States educator and Presbyterian minister who was known for his preaching, applying Christianity to social problems. Coffin also sought to raise the standard of theological education. Moderator of the General Assembly of the Presbyterian Church of USA (1943–1944).

Colenso, John *(1814–1883)*
Anglican clergyman and mathematics teacher at Harrow who in 1846 became vicar of Forncett St Mary, Norfolk. In 1853 he was appointed the first Bishop of Natal, where he was very pastorally involved with his Zulu congregation. In response to their needs he questioned the literal truth of the Pentateuch and followed an earlier critical book on Romans with work on the Pentateuch. His very liberal views led to his excommunication by the Archbishop of Cape Town. Colenso appealed to London and the Judicial Committee of the Privy Council, who decided in his favour. A schism followed, led, after his death, by his daughter, Harriette. Colenso always retained the affection of his people. The schism was finally ended in 1911.

Colet, John *(1466–1519)*
Dean of St Paul's who preached against the clerical abuses of his time and as one of the chief Tudor humanists promoted Renaissance culture in England. A friend of Erasmus and Thomas More, he never lost their support although he was several times suspected of heresy. From his father he inherited a fortune which he used, in part, to found St Paul's School.

Collier, Jeremy *(1650–1726)*
Anglican priest who wrote in support of King James II and was imprisoned on suspicion of treason. He became the bishop of the nonjurors (those clergy who refused the oath of allegiance to William and Mary in 1689) and wrote and preached against the current immorality of the stage.

Colman of Lindisfarne, St *(c. 605–676)*
Monk of Iona who succeeded St Finan as Bishop of Lindisfarne (661). In the clash between Celtic and Roman liturgical customs Colman supported the Celtic at the Synod of Whitby (664) while St Wilfred spoke for the Roman usage. The Synod decided in favour of the Roman and Colman resigned his See and retired to Iona. In Scotland he founded several churches and journeyed to Ireland, where he built monasteries at Innishboffin and Mayo.

Columba (Columcille) St *(c. 521–597)*
Of noble Irish family, ordained a priest (*c.* 551), Columba founded churches and monasteries in Ireland before building a monastery on Iona (*c.* 563) and setting out with twelve companions to convert Scotland, founding churches and monasteries in many places. As an abbot and missionary he has been credited with doing more than any other to convert Scotland to Christianity.

Contarini, Gasparo *(1483–1542)*
Theologian and humanist scholar who began life as a diplomat; as an advocate of reform and reconciliation he worked for an agreement with the Lutherans on justification. Although only a layman, he was elevated to cardinal and contributed to the preparatory work for the Council of Trent.

Conwell, Russell Herman *(1843–1925)*
Lawyer, publisher, educator and clergyman; Conwell was converted from atheism while recovering from a serious wound received during the American Civil War. He became a very successful Baptist minister in Philadelphia, where he founded the Temple University and three hospitals. He won world fame and great wealth through a lecture, 'Acres of Diamonds' (theme: opportunity lies in your own backyard), which he delivered approximately six thousand times. It was also published.

Cornelius à Lapide *(1567–1637)*
Flemish Jesuit and professor of biblical studies at Louvain and Rome. His celebrated series of biblical commentaries appeared gradually over a period of thirty years. These won acclaim and enduring popularity for their clarity and depth of scholarship.

Cosin, John *(1594–1672)*
While a chaplain at Durham Cathedral (1619) Cosin wrote, at the request of King Charles I, a daily prayer book, *Collection of Private Devotions*. Exiled during the Puritan Commonwealth Government, he was made Bishop of Durham at the Restoration. His literary works were controversial and as a liturgist he promoted a scholarly approach to worship which established him as one of the fathers of Anglo-Catholicism.

Cosmas & Damian, St *(trad. d. c. 303)*
Brothers who have been accepted since the fifth century as the patron saints of physicians. Little is known for certain of their lives or martyrdom. Tradition records that they were Christian physicians who would accept no money for their services. They were said to have been tortured and beheaded for their faith during the persecution of Diocletian.

Cottolengo, St Joseph *(1786–1842)*
Born near Turin, where he later worked as a pastoral priest, he was one day called to attend a poor dying woman, only to discover that there were no facilities for the poor. Joseph opened a small house ('Piccola Casa') which quickly expanded and expanded to cope with the need. His caring widened to include the aged, deaf, blind, crippled and insane. His 'Piccola Casa' grew into a great sprawling medical institution. To minister to the various patients and needs he founded fourteen different Religious Congregations of Religious sisters, brothers and priests. He was canonised in 1934.

Cotton, John *(1585–1652)*
Escaping the persecution of Nonconformists by the Church of England, Cotton became the New England Puritan leader. Within the First Church of Boston, from 1633–1652, Cotton was regarded as the spiritual leader and teacher.

Court, Antoine *(1695–1760)*
French minister of the Reformed Church and itinerant preacher who devoted his life, from the age of twenty-one, to the restoration of Protestantism in France.

Couturier, Paul Irénée *(1881–1953)*
French priest and educator who dedicated the latter part of his life to work for Christian unity. He popularised and extended the idea of an annual Week of Prayer for Christian Unity (18–25 January); from 1939 the Octave was observed as the Week of Universal Prayer. Through interdenominational conferences, vast correspondence and the writing of innumerable tracts, Couturier did more than any other Roman Catholic to further Christian unity over a period of twenty years.

Coverdale, Miles *(1488–1568)*
After ordination in 1514 Coverdale became an Augustinian friar; absorbing Lutheran opinions, he left the Order and preached against images and the mass. Forced to reside abroad, he produced the first complete English translation of the Bible. On his return to England he edited the Great Bible (1539). After Henry VIII's death he was made Bishop of Exeter in 1551. Exiled again under Queen Mary, on his return he assisted at the consecration of Matthew Parker as Archbishop of Canterbury, but felt unable to resume the See of Exeter. For the remainder of his life he was the leader of the Puritan movement.

Cox, Richard *(c. 1500–1581)*
Dean, first of Christ Church, Oxford, then of Westminster Abbey, he made important contributions to the Prayer Books of 1549 and 1552. A zealous

supporter of the Reform in England, he was imprisoned and then exiled during Queen Mary's reign. On his return he was briefly Bishop of Norwich, then of Ely.

Cranmer, Thomas *(1489–1556)*
Educated at Cambridge and ordained in 1523, he caught the attention of Henry VIII by his support for the king's royal divorce plans. He secretly married Margaret Osiander in 1532, while on a mission for Henry. In 1533 he was appointed Archbishop of Canterbury and the same year annulled Henry's marriage to Catherine of Aragon; in the following years he invalidated Henry's second, fourth and fifth marriages. In 1547, after Henry's death, Cranmer acted as counsellor to Edward VI and proceeded to Protestantise the Church of England and promote its union with the Reformed Churches of Europe. He promoted the publication of an English Bible and was largely responsible for the Prayer Books of 1549 and 1552. Tried for treason when Mary Tudor came to the throne, his life was spared by the queen. However, he was imprisoned and tried for heresy. After several recantations, which he later renounced, he died courageously at the stake on 21 March 1556.

Cromwell, Oliver *(1599–1658)*
Elected MP for Cambridge, Cromwell's religious fervour sustained him in his political struggles as a leader of the Puritan party. He viewed the Civil War as a religious struggle, his own role as God's instrument. Captain at the battle of Edgehill, he was second-in-command of the new Parliamentary Army at the battle of Marston Moor. Cromwell supported the Independents against the Presbyterians and worked for the execution of Charles I. He used his New Model Army to crush an Irish revolt and the Scots, and in 1653 he dismissed the Long Parliament. As Lord Protector of the Commonwealth he ruled from 1653 and attempted to instil 'true godliness' in England. On his death Cromwell was buried in Westminster Abbey but at the Restoration his body was disinterred and dishonoured.

Crowther, Samuel Adjai *(c. 1809–1891)*
Sold into slavery at twelve, but rescued by the British; Adjai's name was changed and he was educated at a mission school. The Church Missionary Society ordained him and sent him to his own Yoruba country (modern Nigeria). Crowther accompanied several expeditions in the Niger territory, for which he was consecrated as the first African bishop in 1864.

Cruden, Alexander *(1701–1770)*
Of Scottish Presbyterian upbringing, Cruden was famed for his eccentricities, bordering on insanity, and his *Concordance* of the Bible.

Cullen, Paul *(1803–1878)*
Ordained priest in Rome (1829), he stayed there as rector of the college, returning to Ireland as Archbishop of Armagh in 1850. He was appointed the first Irish cardinal in 1866 and played an important part in the First Vatican Council.

Cuthbert, St *(634–687)*
A monk of the monastery of Melrose from 651, Cuthbert became prior and, on Colman's resignation of the See of Lindisfarne, he and his abbot, Eata, took responsibility for Lindisfarne. They implemented the Roman liturgy as decreed by the Synod of Whitby. Cuthbert retired as a hermit in 676, but, nine years later, took Eata's place as Bishop of Lindisfarne. There followed two years of intense missionary activity. Due to Viking incursions Cuthbert's body was not given a permanent resting place until 999, in Durham Cathedral.

Cyprian, St *(c. 200–258)*
Thascius Caecilianus Cyprianus was converted from paganism about 246 and two years later was elected Bishop of Carthage. During the Decian persecution of 250 he hid and returned to Carthage in 251. He became involved in a dispute over re-baptism with Stephen, Bishop of Rome. A new persecution broke out under the Emperor Valerian. At first Cyprian was merely banished, but later, in 258, he was arrested and martyred at Carthage, becoming the first martyr-bishop of Africa. His theological writings were popular and of some lasting importance. His collected letters, some sixty-five of them, reveal Cyprian as an ideally pastoral bishop.

Cyril of Alexandria, St *(376–444)*
Born at Alexandria, nephew of the patriarch Theophilus, Cyril succeeded his uncle on his death in 412. He immediately waged war upon Novatianism and had the Jews expelled from the city. In 430 he became embroiled with Nestorius and worked for his condemnation, which occurred at the Synod of Rome in 430 under Pope Celestine. In 431 Cyril presided over the third General Council at Ephesus, which again condemned Nestorius. A brilliant theologian, Cyril wrote important treatises that clarified the Church's teaching on the Trinity and the incarnation. His writings have remained famous for their accurate thinking and precise exposition. He was declared a Doctor of the Church in 1882.

Cyril of Jerusalem, St *(c. 315–386)*
As Bishop of Jerusalem from 349, Cyril developed the idea of the Holy City as a centre of pilgrimage. By opposing Arianism Cyril was three times banished from his See. His work, the twenty-three *Catecheses* (*c.* 350), lectures for catechumens preparing for baptism, cast light on the method of preparation for baptism then customary.

Cyril, St *(826–869)* and Methodius, St *(c. 815–885)*

These brothers are always taken together; both were scholars and theologians in their own right, but together won the title 'the Apostles of the Slavs' for their joint missionary work among the Danubian Slavs. In their work they broke with custom and introduced a Slavonic liturgy and translated the Bible into Slavonic, having specially invented a Slavic alphabet. Conflict arose with the German bishops over the use of the vernacular for the liturgy. Cyril's death spared him the later harassment that Methodius experienced.

D

D'ailly, Pierre *(1350–1420)*

French theologian and bishop who was influenced by the teaching of William of Occam in his theology, which in turn influenced Luther and other Reformers. He worked for the healing of the Western Schism, seeking ways of reconciling the factions. His celebrated *Tractatus super Reformatione Ecclesiae* suggested reforms later adopted by the Council of Trent.

Damasus, St *(c. 304–384)*

Elected pope in 366, Damasus was energetic in suppressing various heresies. With the help of his secretary, St Jerome, he promulgated a canon of sacred Scripture and commissioned Jerome in 382 to revise the biblical text (known as the Vulgate).

Damien, St Peter *(1007–1072)*

Zealous reformer who first lived a hermit's life, then preached with great effect against contemporary abuses. Reluctantly made Bishop of Ostia and then cardinal (1057), he advised and served three successive popes, acting as their reconciling emissary. Damien's prolific writings denounced simony and promoted clerical celibacy. His life was an inspiring example of voluntary poverty.

Damien, Father *(1840–1889)*

Born Joseph de Veuster, of a Belgian family, he joined the Picpus Fathers in 1860 and requested to be sent to the Pacific Islands. After nine years of missionary work he asked to be allowed to devote himself to the lepers abandoned on the island of Molokai. In appalling conditions he administered to the needs of six hundred lepers, singlehanded, for ten years. He contracted leprosy in 1885 and for the last six years he was joined by a few priests and nuns. His body was taken back to Belgium in 1936 to an acclaim denied him in life.

Dante, Alighieri *(1265–1321)*
The greatest Italian poet, prose writer, moral philosopher and political thinker. His Christian epic *The Divine Comedy*, inspired by his love for Beatrice, is one of the landmarks in the literature of the world.

Darboy, Georges *(1813–1871)*
Archbishop of Paris and upholder of the Gallican tradition and episcopal independence, which brought him into conflict with Pope Pius IX. At the First Vatican Council he opposed the defining of papal infallibility, considering it inopportune. His concern for the destitute during the siege of Paris (1870–1871) was exemplary, but he was deliberately shot by the Communards, with four of his priests, on 24 May 1871.

D'Arcy, Martin Cyril *(1888–1976)*
Jesuit philosopher and theologian who was Master of Campion Hall, Oxford, from 1933 to 1945 and Provincial of the English Jesuits from 1945 to 1950. He was a prolific writer and exponent of Catholic philosophy and theology, his best-remembered works were *The Nature of Belief* (1931) and *The Mind and Heart of Love* (1945).

Davenport, Christopher *(1598–1680)*
Converted from Anglicanism to the Roman Catholic faith, he entered the Franciscan Order and became dedicated to trying to reconcile the Thirty-Nine Articles of Anglicanism with Roman Catholic theology. He served as chaplain to the queens of Charles I and Charles II.

David, St *(c. 520–c. 600)*
Patron saint of Wales of whose life no reliable account exists. Legend has it that he was of noble family and, after ordination to the priesthood, adopted a severe form of monastic life, eventually founding twelve monasteries. Chosen bishop, he transferred his See from Caerleon to Mynyw (now St Davids). The Synod of Victory is said to have been summoned by David, and this supposedly defeated the Pelagian heresy in Britain.

Davidson, Randall Thomas *(1848–1930)*
Educated at Harrow and Oxford, and ordained in 1875, he became chaplain to the Archbishop of Canterbury, A. C. Tait, and won the trust of Queen Victoria. Bishop of Rochester in 1891 and Winchester in 1895, he succeeded Frederick Temple as Archbishop of Canterbury in 1903. Respected as a moderate, Davidson steered the Church of England through a difficult period and his service to his church and nation was recognised on his retirement when he was made Baron Davidson of Lambeth.

Davies, Samuel *(1723–1761)*
American Presbyterian preacher who, in Virginia, helped lead the religious revival known as 'the Great Awakening'. The power of his preaching was experienced not only in the USA but also on a trip to Scotland and England. He is also remembered as the first American hymnwriter of note.

Day, Dorothy *(1897–1980)*
Social reformer from New York City, remembered for her work among the American poor, particularly in the cities, where she founded houses of hospitality. She originally trained as a nurse but then worked as a journalist and was the co-founder of the influential *Catholic Worker* newspaper (1930).

Dearmer, Percy *(1867–1936)*
Hymnologist and writer who popularised and adapted medieval church music for use in Anglican worship. As vicar of Hampstead he applied the ideals he set out in his *The Parson's Handbook* (1899). He wrote on a wide range of subjects and was also co-editor of various collections of hymns and religious music.

Delehaye, Hippolyte *(1859–1941)*
Belgian Jesuit priest who joined the Bollandists and spent his life studying and writing the lives of the saints. In 1912 he became President of the Bollandists; he wrote copiously and contributed regularly to the *Acta Sanctorum*.

De Lisle, Ambrose Lisle March Phillips *(1809–1878)*
Converted to Catholicism in 1824, he retained links with his Anglican past and, as a writer, worked for the reunion of Canterbury and Rome. His substantial gift of land, near Leicester, to the Cistercian Order made the foundation of Mount St Bernard Abbey possible (1835–1844).

Denck, Hans *(c. 1495–1527)*
German reformer who theologically opposed Lutheranism, becoming an Anabaptist; for his beliefs he was forced to wander Europe. His life and beliefs were markedly influenced by the mystic, Johann Tauler.

De Nobili, Robert *(1577–1656)*
Jesuit missionary to India who adopted the mode of life of the Brahmins in order to win converts. His methods were investigated, but he was permitted to continue and it is believed he made a hundred thousand converts. His gifts as a linguist are evident from his many religious and devotional works in Sanskrit, Tamil and Telugu.

Dibelius, Martin *(1883–1947)*
German New Testament scholar and one of the originators of form criticism; he was also an enthusiastic supporter of the Ecumenical Movement, being a leader of the Faith and Order Commission. His most influential publication was *From Tradition to Gospel* (Eng. trans. 1934).

Dibelius, Otto *(1880–1967)*
German Lutheran Bishop of Berlin (1945) who had been a supporter of the Confessing Church and an outspoken opponent of Nazism. Against atheistic Communism he presented the same opposition; in 1954 he became president of the World Council of Churches.

Dionysius, St *(c. 250) (also known as St Denis)*
Dionysius is the patron saint of France and, according to Gregory of Tours' (sixth century) history of France, he was the first Bishop of Paris and suffered martyrdom under the emperor Valerian.

Dionysius St *(d. 268)*
Little is known of the life of this pope, Bishop of Rome from 259; he had succeeded Sixtus II, who had been martyred. Caught up in the subordinationism controversy, there was also 'the affair of the two Dionysii', when he was in dispute with Dionysius, Bishop of Alexandria.

Dionysius, Exiguus *(c. 500–c. 560)*
Theologian and monastic expert on canon law and ecclesiastical chronology. In 525, at the request of Pope St John I, he worked out the Christian calendar still used today. Unfortunately he wrongly dated the year of Christ's birth. Also credited to him is a vast collection of church laws and council decrees.

Dionysius the Carthusian *(1402–1471) (Denys van Leaeuven or Denys Ryckel)*
Member of the Carthusian Order who wrote Old and New Testament biblical commentaries; these and his theological works were very popular in the fifteenth and sixteenth centuries. As a mystic he was one of the luminaries of the Rhenish school of spirituality and his *De Contemplatione* was considered a spiritual classic.

Dionysius the Great, St *(d. c. 264)*
Bishop of Alexandria and theologian who opposed Sabellianism and who suffered persecution under Valerian. Accused of Tritheism, he was in conflict with the pope of the same name; however, cleared of heresy, his teaching on the Trinity was later vindicated by the Church.

Dodd, Charles Harold *(1884–1973)*

Educated at Oxford and Berlin, Dodd was ordained in 1912 for the Congregational ministry. From 1915 he lectured successively in New Testament studies and divinity at Oxford, Manchester and Cambridge. His seminal works, *e.g. The Parables of the Kingdom* and *History of the Gospel*, put forward his 'realised eschatology' thesis. Dodd also defended the historical value of the Fourth Gospel and from 1950 was director of the *New English Bible* project.

Doddridge, Philip *(1702–1751)*

English Nonconformist minister in Leicestershire who is remembered for the large number of hymns he wrote, and for his scheme to distribute Bibles at home and abroad, which makes him one of the pioneers of Nonconformist missionary work.

Dollinger, Johann Joseph Ignaz von *(1799–1890)*

German Roman Catholic Church historian and theologian who, in his middle years, grew distrustful of the influence of the pope. He refused to accept the First Vatican Council (1871) decree on the infallibility of the pope and for the rest of his life supported the Old Catholic Church Movement in Germany.

Dominic, St *(1170–1221)*

Of Spanish birth, in 1199 he joined a community of canons in the diocese of Osma, leading an austere life of discipline; he was sent on a preaching tour among the Albigensian heretics and displayed great courage. In 1214 Dominic founded a new Order, the Order of Friars Preachers (Dominicans). He travelled widely, preaching and establishing the Order. Dominic led a simple austere life, his heroic sanctity leading to his canonisation in 1234.

Donne, John *(1572–1631)*

A chequered career in law, as a 'gentleman adventurer' on a military expedition, as a secretary to Sir Thomas Egerton, *etc.* preceded ordination to the Anglican ministry in 1615. In 1621 he was installed as Dean of St Paul's Cathedral, London, and became established as an eminent and popular preacher, a particular favourite at Court. As a leading poet of the seventeenth-century English 'Metaphysical school', Donne's secular poetry dates from his youth and his religious poetry from the troubled middle years.

Dositheus *(1641–1707)*

Theologian of the Greek Church, and important Church politician, who from 1669, as Patriarch of Jerusalem, stoutly supported Eastern Orthodoxy over the claims of Rome. To prevent Protestantism influencing the Greek Church he called the important Synod of Jerusalem in 1672. His extensive writings were to support his resistance to both Roman Catholic and Protestant influences upon the Orthodox Church.

Drexel, Katherine *(1858–1955)*
Daughter of a United States financier, she inherited a vast fortune on the death of her parents and she used it and dedicated her life to the welfare of American Indians and Negroes. In 1891 she founded the Congregation of Blessed Sacrament Sisters, who worked in the schools (sixty-three by the time of her death) that she built. In 1915 she founded the Xavier University in New Orleans for black girls.

Duff, Alexander *(1806–1878)*
Scottish Presbyterian missionary to India who, sent out as the first Church of Scotland missionary to Calcutta in 1830, joined the Free Church in 1843. His English school in Calcutta grew into a missionary college; when it was lost to him because of the Disruption of 1843, he started again. He was Moderator of the Free Church Assembly in 1851 and 1873.

Duns Scotus, John *(c. 1265–1308)*
Although he is regarded as the greatest medieval British philosopher and theologian, little is known of his life. He joined the Franciscan Order and studied at Oxford and Paris. Highly thought of as a scholar and lecturer, his teaching marks him out as the leader of the Franciscan school of thought. 'Scotist' philosophy was taught alongside the 'Thomist' school in European universities. His most important publication is his Commentary on the Sentences (*Sententiae*) of Peter Lombard.

Dunstan, St *(c. 909–988)*
Benedictine monk and abbot of Glastonbury, which he reformed and made famous for its learning. He served successive kings, eventually being elected Archbishop of Canterbury; with the king, Edgar, he carried through sweeping reforms in State and Church. He was also responsible for the restoration of monastic life in England.

Dupanloup, Felix *(1802–1878)*
French Catholic Bishop of Orleans, noted for his promotion and defence of education. A liberal in thought and an innovator in educational methods, he defended papal temporal sovereignty but led the small group of bishops at the First Vatican Council who considered the declaration of papal infallibility as inappropriate at that time. He later accepted the Council's decrees.

Duperron, Jacques Davy *(1556–1618)*
Converted from Calvinism to Roman Catholicism, Duperron brought about the conversion to the Roman Catholic Church of Henry IV of France in

1593. He was involved in conflict with the Huguenots and between the Gallicans and the Ultramontanists.

Duplessis-Mornay, Philippe *(1549–1623)*
French Statesman and leader of the Huguenots, he worked for the ideal of a united Protestant Church and toleration for the Huguenots; he was successful in bringing about the Edict of Nantes in 1598.

Durie, John *(1596–1680)*
Scottish Protestant minister who devoted himself to the union of the Lutheran and Calvinist Churches. In 1643 he was ordained priest in the Church of England, became a chaplain to the king and he espoused the royalist cause. Wavering in his allegiance eventually made him unacceptable to either party.

Du Toit, Jakob Daniel *(1877–1953)*
Afrikaans biblical scholar, pastor and poet, who compiled a famous Afrikaans Psalter and translated the Bible into Afrikaans. His Calvinism and patriotism are revealed in his many poetic works.

Duvergier de Hauranne, Jean *(1581–1643) (also known as Saint Cyran)*
One of the founders of the Jansenist movements, known for his remarkable erudition but hampered by an inability to communicate clearly. He sought to promote Augustinian thought in opposition to the prevailing scholasticism and proposed the reform of Catholicism through Augustinian principles. His friendship with C. Jansen, his connection with the community at Port-Royal, and his evident power, led to the opposition of Cardinal Richelieu and imprisonment for five years.

Dwight, Timothy *(1752–1817)*
One of the most influential intellectual leaders of the New American Republic. As an educator, minister and writer he helped to shape the educational pattern of New England. Many of his sermons were published and his ambitious poetic epic *The Conquest of Canaan*, in eleven volumes, was influential.

E

Eckhart, von Hochheim *(c. 1260–1327) (also known as Meister Eckhart)*
Dominican theologian, preacher and mystic. He rose to the position of
Provincial of his Order with the task of reforming the Bohemian religious
houses. In Germany, from 1313, Eckhart was acknowledged as the finest
preacher of his time and a mystic. His critics accused him of heresy and he
appeared before the Archbishop of Cologne in 1326. He appealed to the
pope and the next year recanted. After his death twenty-eight propositions
from his writings were condemned. Eckhart's mystical leanings and attempts
to express the inexpressible seem to have occasioned the condemnation, but
he succeeded in inspiring Tauler and Suso.

Edmund of Abingdon, St *(c. 1180–1240) (also known as Edmund Rich)*
He studied and later lectured at Oxford and Paris. Austere in lifestyle, he
accepted the post of treasurer of Salisbury Cathedral and in 1233 he was
elected Archbishop of Canterbury. A saintly and attractive man of lofty
ideals, he suffered, as archbishop, the opposition of the monks of Canterbury
and his own opposition to Henry III's policies led to a voluntary exile at
Pontigny in France.

Edmund the Martyr, St *(d. 869)*
King of the East Angles, in 865 his kingdom was invaded by the Danes, who
wanted Edmund to share his kingdom with their leader. He refused to
associate with a pagan and was used by the Danes for target practice. Almost
immediately he was honoured as a martyr. His body was moved in the tenth
century to Bury St Edmunds, which promptly became a place of pilgrimage.

Edward the Confessor, St *(1003–1066)*
Of Saxon birth, but brought up and educated in Normandy, Edward
succeeded his half-brother, Hardicanute, to the English throne in 1042. His
reign appeared peaceful but there were continual internal struggles between
the Saxons, led by the influential Earl Godwin, and Edward's Norman friends
and advisors. He showed more interest in religious matters than affairs of
state, acting more like a monk than a king. Edward was particularly concerned
with the building of the great abbey church of Westminster, where he was
buried. He was canonised in 1161.

Edwards, Jonathan *(1703–1758)*
Brought up in a Puritan atmosphere, Edwards showed great interest in
philosophy and science from an early age. His interest in stating Calvinism in
contemporary philosophical terms grew from 1727, after a conversion

experience. Ordained to the Congregational Church at Northampton, Massachusetts, he led the religious revival called 'the Great Awakening', but some excesses and his own extreme Calvinism led to his dismissal from Northampton. In missionary work at Stockbridge he worked among the Indians and wrote his most important works, *Freedom of the Will* and *Original Sin*. In 1757 Edwards accepted the presidency of Princeton College (later University) but died shortly afterwards. He is considered the greatest theologian of American Puritanism.

Egede, Hans *(1686–1758)*
Norwegian Lutheran minister and missionary who was the first to preach the gospel to the Eskimos of Greenland. In Copenhagen he founded a seminary (1736) to train missionaries for work in Greenland.

Elias of Cortona *(c. 1180–1235)*
One of St Francis of Assisi's earliest companions, mainly responsible for the building of the basilica at Assisi. Third General of the Franciscan Order, but deposed in 1239, and expelled from the Order. He established a monastery of his own at Cortona.

Eliot, John *(1604–1690)*
Born in Hertfordshire, England, and educated at Cambridge, Eliot emigrated to Boston in 1631, and from his Puritan church at Roxburg conducted a mission to the Indians, winning the title, 'apostle to the Indians'. He wrote a *Catechism* (1653) and a translation of the Bible for them.

Eliot, T. S. *(1888–1965)*
American-born British poet and critic, educated at Harvard, Paris and Oxford. Brought up a Unitarian, Eliot passed through an agnostic period, reflected in his early poetry. The poem which made him famous, *The Waste Land*, (1922) expressed his disenchantment with the post-war period and his own sense of emptiness. In 1927 Eliot became a British citizen and confirmed in the Church of England, in which he took an Anglo-Catholic position, which is reflected in his later verse, particularly *Ash Wednesday* (1930) and *Murder in the Cathedral* (1933). As a playwright he had little success, except for *The Cocktail Party* (1950), but he was highly regarded as a critic. His greatest poetry appeared in *Four Quartets* (1935–1942). Eliot won the Nobel Prize for Literature in 1948.

Elizabeth of France *(1764–1794) (also known as Madame Elizabeth)*
French princess, sister of King Louis XVI, who refused to escape and leave her brother and his wife, Marie Antoinette, at the French Revolution. She shared their imprisonment and death, and was notable for her courage and exemplary Christian virtue.

Elizabeth of Hungary (or of Thuringia), St *(1207–1231)*

Daughter of the king of Hungary, she was betrothed in infancy to Louis of Thuringia. Married at fourteen, there followed six happy years of marriage until Louis died on the way to the Sixth Crusade. Elizabeth had already shown great interest in an ascetic life and, driven from court, she settled at Marburg, where she built a hospice for the poor. She devoted the rest of her life to the care of the needy and was canonised in 1235.

Elizabeth of Russia, Grand Duchess *(1864–1918)*

Martyred in July 1918 by Bolshevik revolutionaries, Elizabeth was a famous beauty of her time. Partly brought up and educated in England, she later married the Grand Duke Sergei Alexandrovich, fifth son of the Tsar. After her husband's assassination in 1905, Elizabeth helped to found the Mary and Martha home in Moscow, to foster prayer and charity. She was one of the foundation's first Sisters of Love and Mercy. She was in the first group of sisters to be taken by the Bolshevik revolutionaries and thrown down a mineshaft. Elizabeth was recognised as a saint in 1992 by the Moscow Patriarchate. (Elizabeth is one of the ten modern martyrs honoured in sculpture with a place over the west door of Westminster Abbey, London.)

Embury, Philip *(1729–1775)*

Of Irish birth, Embury was converted by John Wesley and, after emigrating to American in 1760, became the first Methodist preacher in America and founder of the first Methodist chapel in New York.

Emerson, Ralph Waldo *(1803–1882)*

Prepared for the Unitarian ministry at Harvard College, Emerson ministered at Boston and established a reputation as a preacher. Although he continued to preach for a while, his extreme views occasioned his resignation from his pastorate. Settling at Concord, Massachusetts, Emerson developed his talents as a lecturer in literature and philosophy. His philosophy, a form of transcendentalism, and his freshness of style, won him wide popularity. All his works, mainly based upon his lectures, have an underlying moral-religious tone.

England, John *(1786–1842)*

Irish-born and educated, England was consecrated the first Roman Catholic bishop of the American diocese of Charleston (North Carolina, South Carolina and Georgia). He published a catechism and a missal for Americans and founded the first American Catholic newspaper. England began two schools, founded Religious Orders to care for the needy, and was the first Roman Catholic clergyman to address the United States Congress (1826).

Ephraem Syrus, St *(c. 306–373)*

Celebrated Syrian writer, biblical exegete and Doctor of the Church, he lived most of his life in his native Nisibis (Turkey), but moved to Edessa in 363, where most of his works were written. A prolific writer of biblical commentaries and homilies, he was more of a preacher than a theologian. His works are in verse and he composed over seventy hymns for the liturgy; while a popular writer with his contemporaries, his writings are difficult for modern readers.

Ephiphanius, St *(c. 315–403)*

Bishop of Constantia (Cyprus) from 367, he was dedicated to the spread of monasticism and the refuting of heresies. His major work, *Panarion*, gives an account of eighty heresies known to him and ends with a presentation of sound teaching.

Erasmus, Desiderius *(c. 1466–1536)*

Christened Herasmus, probably at Rotterdam, and educated in a humanist environment, he reluctantly entered the monastery at Steyn as an Augustinian canon. After he was ordained a priest, in 1492, he was allowed to leave his monastery as secretary to the Bishop of Cambrai. There began a quest for learning which took Erasmus all over Europe from Italy to England. In the latter he developed lasting friendships with scholars like John Colet, John Fisher and Thomas More; and he benefited from the patronage of William Warham, Archbishop of Canterbury. Released from his monastic vows in 1517, he continued to wander Europe, establishing himself as the great scholar and figure of the Northern Renaissance. He was very critical of the contemporary Church, and his satirical writing paved the way for the Reformation. When it broke, both sides appealed to him for support. He was first believed to be in support of Luther, but eventually wrote against him and withdrew to the stability of the traditional Church. However, after his death, his writings were forbidden by several of the popes. After his version of the Greek New Testament, his next important contribution was to make the works of the early Christian writers available and to promote patristic studies.

Erigena, John Scotus *(c. 810–877)*

Apart from his birth in Ireland and the patronage he secured of the West Frankish king, Charles the Bald, little is known of his life. Scotus was a deeply original philosopher, and a scholar of high repute, who took part in contemporary debates upon predestination and the Eucharist; he developed a theory of knowledge that was highly influential. His translation and commentaries of the works of the Pseudo-Dionysius were a great service to later scholars.

Erskine, John *(1509–1591)*
Educated at King's College, Aberdeen, Erskine, who was Lord of Dun, was a close friend of the reformers George Wishart and John Knox. He acted as an intermediary between Mary Queen of Scots and the reformers. Four times Erskine was elected Moderator of the General Assembly of the reformed Church of Scotland.

Ethelbert of Kent, St *(d. c. 616)*
King of Kent from *c.* 560, he is said to have extended his kingdom to south of the Humber. His marriage to the Frankish princess Bertha, who was a Christian, introduced Christianity into Anglo-Saxon England and Ethelbert was eventually converted. He welcomed St Augustine and his monks in 597 and gave his full support to Christianity, holding the distinction of being the first Christian king in England.

Etheldreda, St *(d. 679)*
Daughter of the Christian king of the East Angles who, although married twice, lived a life of consecrated virginity. Egfrid, her second husband, consented to her becoming a nun and she founded the double monastery (for men and women living separately in community) at Ely.

Eudes, St John *(1601–1680)*
Born in Normandy and educated at Caen by the Jesuits, John was ordained for the Roman Catholic priesthood in 1625. A gifted speaker, he devoted the next fifty years to parish preaching missions. In 1641 he established both a Congregation of Sisters (Order of Our Lady of Charity) to care for delinquent girls and women, and an association of priests (the Congregation of Jesus and Mary) to prepare candidates for the priesthood. One of his greatest achievements was to provide a theological foundation to the contemporary devotion to the Sacred Hearts of Jesus and Mary, which he had promoted.

Eusebius – There are seven famous Christians of the early centuries of Christianity with this title.

Eusebius, St *(fourth century)*
Pope and martyr who died in 309 (or 310) and was buried in the catacomb of Callixtus, Rome.

Eusebius of Caesaria *(c. 260–c. 340)*
Educated by the scholar and martyr, Pamphibus, about 314, he became Bishop of Caesarea. He was already an established scholar and writer when Arius propounded his views; Eusebius, always fearful of Sabellianism, tried to hold a middle course. Although suspected, he was exonerated of the charge of heresy. His Caesarean Creed, which he presented to the Council of

Nicaea, was not preferred to the Nicene Creed. Remembered as a Church historian – 'Father of Church History' – his voluminous works were mainly of an apologetical nature. His principal work (originally in seven volumes, but later extended to ten), was his *Ecclesiastical History*, which is our principal source for the history of the Eastern Church from apostolic times.

Eusebius of Dorylaeum *(fifth century)*
Bishop of Dorylaeum, he was ever the champion of orthodox teaching; even as a layman he was the first to publicly challenge the teaching of Nestorius. He suffered deposition by the 'Robber' Synod of Ephesus for challenging Monophysitism. The Council of Chalcedon reinstated him to his See.

Eusebius of Emesa *(d. c. 359)*
Bishop of Emesa, biblical exegete and scholar. Friend of the Emperor Constantius, he was suspected of Semi-Arian teaching and only fragments of his writings are extant.

Eusebius of Laodices *(c. 264–269)*
Eusebius risked his life to help Christian martyrs during the persecutions of Decius and Valerian; revered for his saintliness, he was persuaded to accept the See of Laodicea.

Eusebius of Nicomedia *(d. c. 342)*
Important Eastern bishop who was a proponent of the Arian heresy.

Eusebius of Samosata, St *(d. c. 379)*
Great opponent of Arianism, who, as Bishop of Samosata, was exiled for upholding orthodox beliefs.

Eutyches *(c. 378–454)*
Archimandrite at Constantinople whose fierce opposition to Nestorianism seems to have led him to be accused of the opposite heresy; his name has been given to the Eutychian heresy.

Evagrius Ponticus *(346–399)*
Ordained a deacon by St Gregory of Nazianus, he was first a gifted preacher then a monk living in the desert in Egypt. Highly regarded in his day as a spiritual guide and one of the first monks to write about spirituality, his writings were a formative influence on later spiritual writers.

Eymard, St Peter Julian *(1811–1868)*
French priest who, after some years of pastoral work, joined the Marist Order. His great devotion to the Blessed Sacrament resulted in the foundation of an Order of Priests and a separate Order of Nuns devoted to the perpetual

adoration of the Blessed Sacrament. St Peter also wrote several books on the Eucharist. He was canonised in 1962 by Pope John XXIII.

F

Faber, Frederick William *(1814–1863)*
Born at Calverley in Yorkshire, Faber was educated at Harrow and Balliol College, Oxford. Originally of Calvinist background, at Oxford he worked with J. H. Newman on the *Library of the Fathers* and in November 1845, a few weeks after Newman, he was received into the Roman Catholic Church. He founded a small community at Birmingham, but when Newman introduced the Oratory of St Philip Neri into England he joined that, becoming Superior of the London House in 1849. The author of popular spiritual books, *e.g. Growth in Holiness* (1854), he is best remembered for his popular hymns, *e.g.* 'Hark, Hark my soul', 'My God, how wonderful thou art', and others still in current use.

Fabiola, St *(d. 399)*
Of a wealthy Roman family, her divorce from a vicious first husband was disapproved of by her local Christian community and led her to a life of atonement. Under the direction of St Jerome, Fabiola gave away her wealth and dedicated herself to the care of the sick, founding the first public hospital in Europe.

Falconieri, St Juliana *(1270–1341)*
Of a Florentine family, she rejected her family's marriage plans and became instead a tertiary of the Servite Order at sixteen. After her mother's death, in 1304, she headed a group of women dedicated to prayer and charitable works and in time founded the Servite Order of nuns.

Faulhaber, Michael *(1869–1952)*
Born at Heidenfeld, Germany, ordained for the priesthood in 1892, he lectured in Old Testament studies at the universities of Wurzburg and Strasbourg. He became Archbishop of Munich in 1917 and cardinal in 1921. The Nazi movement was totally repugnant to him and he courageously opposed it every way he could. An attempt was made on his life in 1934 and his residence attacked in 1938.

Felix, St *(d. c. 647)*
Born and ordained in Burgundy, Honorius, Archbishop of Canterbury, consecrated him the first bishop of the East Angles. From his See at Dunwich, Suffolk, he spent seventeen years converting the heathen of East Anglia.

Felix of Valois, St *(1127–1212)*
A French hermit who in 1198 founded an Order of Monks, called the Trinitarians, to devote their lives to the redemption of Christian captives of the Saracens.

Fell, John *(1625–1686)*
Educated at Christ Church, Oxford, he supported the Royalist cause during the Civil War and, ordained in 1647, kept the Church of England services alive in Oxford during the Commonwealth. After the Restoration he became Bishop of Oxford, where he established the University Press and worked hard to restore the standards and traditions of the University.

Fénelon, Francois de Salignac de la Mothe *(1651–1715)*
Educated for the priesthood at St-Sulpice, he was ordained about 1675 and in 1678 was appointed Superior of the Nouvelles Catholiques (recent converts from Protestantism). Sent on missionary work among the Huguenots, he returned to tutor Louis XIV's grandson. In 1688 Fénelon met and began his support of Madame Guyon. He became implicated in the charges of Quietism made against her. Writing a defence of Christian mysticism, he became involved in a bitter controversy with Bossuet. As a result he was exiled from the French court in 1697 and thereafter worked humbly in his diocese of Cambrai. Highly respected for his writings on education, Fénelon was, above all, a master of the spiritual life and a mystical theologian and writer to whom history has not been kind.

Ferrar, Nicholas *(1592–1637)*
Educated at Cambridge, Ferrar studied abroad and in 1618 joined the council of the Virginia Company, but six years later entered Parliament. Leaving public life he was ordained a deacon in 1626 and set up a Christian community of about thirty persons at Little Gidding in Huntingdonshire, where he remained leader until his death. The community was visited three times by King Charles I but, along with most of Ferrar's writings, it was destroyed by the Puritans in 1646.

Ferrar, Robert *(d. 1555)*
Bishop of St Davids and a Protestant martyr who was condemned to death under Queen Mary for denying the Roman Catholic doctrine on the Eucharist.

Figgis, John Neville *(1866–1919)*
Anglican theologian and historian whose original thinking and writing on the relationship between Church and State sounded the alarm on the dangers to religion and human freedom from the all-competent modern state.

Fisher, Geoffrey Francis *(1887–1972)*
Anglican priest and educationalist who became Bishop of Chester (1932), London (1939), and finally Archbishop of Canterbury (1945). His abiding interest was the work for Christian unity, being Chairman of the World Council of Churches at its inauguration in 1948; he was the first Archbishop of Canterbury to visit the Vatican, where he met with Pope John XXIII.

Fisher, St John *(1469–1535)*
In 1504 Fisher became chancellor of the University of Cambridge, where he had been in turn a student and a lecturer. He made strenuous efforts to raise the standards at the university. Appointed Bishop of Rochester in 1504, he enjoyed a wide reputation as a scholar and a preacher and in both capacities worked to counter the Protestant influences spreading through England. As Catherine of Aragon's confessor he protested at Henry VIII's divorce plans; and for refusing the oath required by the Act of Succession he was arrested and imprisoned in the Tower of London. Tried and convicted, his elevation to the rank of cardinal by the pope did not save him from execution on 22 June 1535. He was acknowledged as a martyr by the Roman Catholic Church and canonised in 1935.

Fisk, Wilbur *(1792–1839)*
American Methodist clergyman and educator whose wide reputation raised the quality and standing of Methodism in New England.

Flaget, Benedict Joseph *(1763–1850)*
American Roman Catholic Sulpician priest who, after serving in education and as a missionary, was appointed the first bishop of the old north-west of the USA. His many educational foundations and the standards they maintained were legendary. He founded two Orders of Sisters to provide elementary education for girls.

Flemyng (Fleming), Richard *(d. 1431)*
Bishop of London (1420) who represented England at the Church Councils of Pavia and Siena and founded Lincoln College, Oxford.

Fletcher, John William *(1729–1785)*
An Anglican vicar who was an early supporter of the Methodist Movement and renowned for his sanctity and his devoted pastoral work.

Forbes, Alexander Penrose *(1817–1875)*
While studying at Oxford he came under the influence of the Tractarians. He was first a vicar in Leeds, Yorkshire, then Bishop of Brechin, where he worked to spread the Oxford Movement in Scotland.

Forbes, George Hay *(1821–1875)*
Brother of Alexander and also a High Churchman who proved to be, despite severe paralysis, a noted liturgist, patristic scholar and model priest of the Episcopalian Church of Scotland.

Forsyth, Peter Taylor *(1848–1921)*
Scottish Congregationalist theologian whose early liberal thinking developed to a position of great originality, and interpreted the faith of the Reformation in modern terms. He was also an experienced pastor, serving in five pastorates. His seminal works were many, the most famous being *The Person and Place of Jesus Christ* (1909).

Fosdick, Harry Emerson *(1878–1969)*
American Baptist minister and writer who for some years (1918–1925) served as a Presbyterian preacher. From 1926 to 1946 he was the Baptist minister at the Riverside Church, New York, His many books reflect a liberal-evangelical view of theology.

Foucauld, Charles Eugene de *(1858–1916)*
As a French calvary officer in Algeria, de Foucauld led a dissolute life, but on leaving the army undertook a dangerous expedition exploring Morocco. He was led back to the Catholic faith by the Abbé Huvelin and sought a life of austerity and solitude, first in the Trappist Order, then in the Holy Land and finally at the oasis of Tamanrasset in the Sahara. His life of prayer was augmented with work in the Tuareg language, compiling dictionaries, translations, *etc.* By the time of his assassination, despite much effort, he had failed to convert anyone. However, today, thousands of priests and Religious Brothers and Sisters (the 'Little Brothers' and 'Little Sisters') live by de Foucauld's rules of life, inspired by his writings and example.

Fox, George *(1624–1691)*
Born in Leicestershire, where his father was a weaver, at nineteen Fox left home and lived a wanderer's life for three years. In 1645, after long spiritual battles, he found the 'Inner Light' of the living Christ and experienced a lifelong call to bring people 'off' from false religion and the world. His preaching led to continual periods in prison, but his sincerity and enthusiasm attracted followers and in 1652 the Society of Friends (Quakers) was born. For the rest of his life Fox travelled widely, *e.g.* the West Indies, North America, Germany, Holland, appealing wherever

he went to 'that of God in every man'. His *Journal*, a survey of his life, which conveys his magnetic personality, was dictated in 1675 and published after his death.

Foxe, John *(1516–1587)*

At Oxford, as student and fellow, he promoted the Reformation in England but fled the country on Queen Mary's accession. Abroad he continued his history of persecutions and martyrdom which when published came to be known as *Foxe's Book of Martyrs*. This monumental work, extolling the heroism of the Protestant martyrs, went through several editions in his lifetime; it was marred as an objective historical work by the bitterness of the time and the uncritical use of some sources.

Francis of Assisi, St *(1181–1226)*

Born Giovanni Francesco Bernardine, son of a rich cloth merchant of Assisi, Francis was a normal high-spirited rich young man of his time. After a serious illnesss and a conversion experience he devoted himself to the service of the poor. His close identification with them led to rejection by his father, at which Francis turned to the service of lepers and the repair of the church of S. Damiano and then the church of the Portiuncula, near Assisi. Here he heard Matthew 10:7–19 as a personal call to follow literally Christ's way of renunciation. His preaching and example attracted followers, for whom he composed a rule of life. In 1212 he helped St Clare found a similar order for women. While on preaching tours to Spain, Eastern Europe and Egypt the Franciscan Order grew rapidly, was structured and then Francis left the leadership to others. While on Mt Alvernia, in 1224, he received the gift of the Stigmata, which he kept carefully hidden until his death. Francis' passionate love of God, his fellow man and nature have justly made him one of the most popular saints of modern times. His spirit is perfectly captured in his writings, for example in *The Canticle of the Sun*.

Francis of Paola, St *(1416–1507)*

A hermit whose early life was formed by contact with the Franciscans. About 1436, with companions, he founded the Order of the Hermits of St Francis of Assisi (later known as Ordo Minimorum or Minims). Renowned for his holiness, kings sought his spiritual guidance and many miracles were attributed to him. He was canonised in 1519.

Francis of Sales, St *(1567–1622)*

Bishop of Geneva and renowned spiritual counsellor and writer who refuted the error of his time that spiritual perfection was not possible for ordinary secular Christians. He was one of the leaders of the Counter-Reformation, converting the Chablais from Calvinism to Catholicism. In 1610, with Jane Frances de Chantal, he founded the Visitandine Sisters. His most famous spiritual books are *The Introduction to the Devout Life* and *Treatise on the Love of God*.

French, Thomas Valpry *(1825–1891)*
Anglican missionary sent by the Church Missionary Society to Agra, India. A good scholar and preacher, he was appointed the first Anglican Bishop of Lahore in 1877. Although saintly, he was not an able administrator and resigned his See in 1887. Always of uncertain health, he died as a result of a missionary enterprise of his own to Arabia.

Friedrich, Johannes *(1836–1917)*
German Church historian who opposed the definition of papal infallibility at the First Vatican Council; his refusal to acknowledge its decrees led to his excommunication. The Bavarian Government gave him protection and for a while he was one of the leaders of the Old Catholic Movement in Germany.

Froude, Richard Hurrell *(1803–1836)*
Educated at Eton and Oxford, where, as a tutor, he came under the influence of J. H. Newman. While health permitted, he worked with Newman and Keble in founding the Tractarian Movement. His posthumous writings, *Remains* (1838 and 1839), caused a sensation in the revelation of his own spiritual practices and his attack upon Reformed doctrines.

Fry, Elizabeth *(1780–1845)*
The daughter of a banker, Elizabeth was born of a Quaker family and in 1800 she married a strict Quaker. Eleven years later, while mother of a large family, she became a 'minister' of the Society of Friends. She devoted herself to the welfare of female prisoners at Newgate, but her prison work in earnest did not begin until 1817. The association she founded improved the lot of female prisoners in particular, and her energetic endeavours and travels bore fruit not only in Great Britain and Ireland, but throughout Europe.

Fuller, Andrew *(1754–1815)*
English Baptist theologian and minister who co-operated with John Ryland and John Sutcliff in assisting William Carey in the foundation and support of the Baptist Missionary Society, of which he was the first secretary.

Fuller, Thomas *(1608–1661)*
Anglican scholar, writer and preacher who held various pastoral appointments but is remembered for his historical accounts of the period, particularly *Worthies of Britain* and *Church History of Britain*, and his prolific, witty writing.

G

Gabriel, Severus *(1541–1616)*
Greek Orthodox metropolitan and one of the most learned Eastern theologians of the sixteenth and seventeenth centuries who disputed with Catholic and Protestant theologians.

Gairdner, William Henry *(1873–1928)*
Anglican missionary of the Church Missionary Society who went to Cairo in 1898 and studied Arabic and Islam. He reorganised the Arabic Anglican Church and pioneered Christian literature in Arabic.

Galen, Clemens August Graf von *(1878–1946)*
German Roman Catholic bishop and cardinal who offered the most effective resistance, among German Catholic bishops, to Nazism. From one of the oldest German noble families and conservative in outlook, Galen opposed the Nazis from the moment he became a bishop in 1933. He placed his life at risk by his open opposition in several major incidents, but survived to be made a cardinal a month before he died in 1946.

Gall, St *(c. 550–645)*
Irish missionary and companion of St Columbanus, who remained to convert Swabia (now Switzerland) when the latter travelled to Italy.

Gardiner, Stephen *(c. 1490–1555)*
Master of Trinity Hall, Cambridge, Gardiner was used by Henry VIII in the business of the annulment from Catherine of Aragon. In 1531 he became Bishop of Winchester and opposed the Reformation doctrines. Imprisoned under Edward VI, he was restored to his See and became Lord Chancellor under Mary Tudor.

Garnet, Henry *(1555–1606)*
English Jesuit and superior of the English Mission in 1587. He became implicated in the prior knowledge of the Gunpowder Plot, which he may have received through the confessional. Arrested some months after the plot, he was executed for not revealing his knowledge of it.

Gasquet, Francis Aidan *(1846–1929)*
Monk of the Benedictine Order, he became Prior of Downside in 1878, where he enlarged the priory and the school. He worked on Roman Commissions and was created cardinal in 1914. In 1919 he became Vatican

librarian; his seminal books on medieval monasticism were influential, particularly *Henry VIII and the Monasteries*.

Geiler von Kaisersberg, Johann *(1445–1510)*
An exceptionally forceful preacher who began his career as a scholar and lecturer at Freiburg University. Personally retiring and acknowledged as a mystic, he became known as the German Savanarola, for from his pulpit in Strasbourg Cathedral he denounced the evils of the day and won wide acclaim.

Gelasius – The name of two popes, the better known being:

St Gelasius I *(d. 496)*
He devoted most of his energies to combating the Acacian heresy and asserting the primacy of the Roman See over that of Constantinople. The *Gelasian Sacramentary* has been wrongly attributed to him.

Gentili, Luigi *(1801–1848)*
Abandoning Roman social life, Gentili joined Antonio Rosmini-Serbati and his new Institute of Charity (Rosminians). In 1835, in England, he helped organise a new Roman Catholic college at Prior Park, Bath; there followed years of fruitful missionary work, particularly among Irish immigrants in the new industrial cities. He died of cholera caught while preaching in a Dublin slum. He is credited with founding the Rosminian Order in England, and popularising devotions like the Stations of the Cross and the Forty Hours Devotion.

George, St
Patron saint of England who appears to have been an early martyr in the East, perhaps at Lydda, Palestine. Nothing for certain is known of his life, although his existence is generally accepted. Legends about him as a warrior saint became popular in about the sixth century, although the story of him rescuing a maiden from a dragon first appeared six centuries later. His popularity in England dates from the eighth century and returning crusaders popularised his cult.

Gerald, John *(1564–1637)*
English Jesuit missionary, trained in Rome, who from 1588 worked secretly in Norfolk, Suffolk and Essex. He was very successful, founding mass centres and making converts. In 1594 he was captured and imprisoned in the Tower of London for three years. In 1597 he escaped from the Tower (being the only prisoner in history to do so) and continued his missionary work. He returned to Europe and in 1607 wrote a vivid account of a life in hiding in Elizabethan England.

Gerhard, Johann *(1582–1637)*
German Lutheran theologian and highly regarded biblical and patristic scholar. Profoundly influenced in his early years by the Lutheran mystic Johann Arndt. His nine-volume *Loci theologici* (1610–1622) was the important and influential Lutheran work of theology of the era.

Germanus, St *(c. 378–448)*
Elected Bishop of Auxerre in 418, he visited Britain and fought Pelagianism; on a second visit he successfully led an army against the invading Picts and Saxons.

Germanus, St *(496–576)*
Patriarch of Constantinople. From the role of a human cleric at the great church of Santa Sophia, he rose to become the Patriarch. In this role he worked to refute monothelitism and became a key figure in the fight against iconoclasm. Only a few of his many writings survive, and in them he shows himself to be an ardent supporter of devotion to Mary, the mother of Jesus.

Gerson, Jean Le Charlier de *(1363–1429)*
French theologian, preacher and spiritual writer who had such a remarkable influence upon the Church of the fifteenth century that he was given the title 'Doctor Christianissimus'. Gerson's life was devoted to the reform of the Church from within; his biggest success was being personally responsible for the resolution of the Great Schism, when there were, at one time, three competing popes. He asserted the superiority of a General Council of the Church over an individual pope, and wrote of this in *De Unitate Ecclesiae* and *De Potestate Ecclesiae*. Gerson was influenced by nominalism in his theology, and his own mystical thought and writing, *e.g. The Mountain of Contemplation*, deeply influenced many later important spiritual writers.

Gertrude the Great, St *(1256–1302) (to be distinguished from the Belgian abbess (626–659) of the same name)*
Entrusted to the Benedictine convent of Helfta, Thuringia, at an early age, she remained there for the rest of her life; a conversion experience at twenty-five led her to a life of contemplation. Her book *Legatus Divinae Pietatis* was considered a spiritual classic. She is considered to be one of the first exponents of devotion to the Sacred Heart of Jesus, which she believed was revealed to her in the visions she experienced.

Ghéon, Henri *(1874–1944) (writing name of Henri Leon Vangeon)*
French Catholic playwright, biographer and writer whose modern, medieval-style, mystery plays portrayed the lives of the saints. His many biographies of modern saints, *e.g.* Curé D'Ars, reached an international readership.

Gilbert of Sempringham, St *(c. 1083–1189)*

Parish priest of Sempringham, Lincolnshire, who founded the only English medieval Religious Order of Sisters and Brothers. The Gilbertines lived by an Augustinian Rule and were distinctive in having double communities of men and women. At Gilbert's death there were nine of these communities in England.

Gillespie, George *(1613–1648)*

Leader of the Church of Scotland who negotiated with the Church of England for the freedom of his church to differ from the Anglican form of worship (1640). He drafted the church legislation sanctioning the Presbyterian form of worship (1645).

Gill, Eric *(1882–1940)*

English sculptor, engraver and essayist whose deep religious commitment, after his conversion to Roman Catholicism in 1913, was expressed through membership of the Third Order of St Dominic and his many works in lettering and stone – the most famous being the Stations of the Cross in Westminster Cathedral and the bas-reliefs of 'The Re-creation of Adam' in the Council Hall of the Palace of Nations at Geneva.

Gilpin, Bernard *(1517–1583)*

Gilpin was one of the most broad-minded upholders of the Elizabethan Church Settlement, refusing to espouse Calvinism outright or accept the decrees of the Council of Trent. He declined several posts of responsibility in favour of pastoral work, for which he was highly esteemed, and was often called 'the Apostle of the North' on account of his long missionary journeys in the North of England.

Gilson, Etienne *(1884–1978)*

French writer and lecturer in Thomist philosophy. His prolific writings on Scholastics and Scholasticism helped to introduce twentieth-century writers and thinkers to such medieval personages as St Bernard of Clairvaux, St Bonaventure, Duns Scotus, *etc.*

Gladstone, William Ewart *(1809–1898)*

One of the greatest Christian statesmen of the nineteenth century, four times Prime Minister of Great Britain (1868–1874; 1880–1885; 1886; 1892–1894). His evangelical upbringing was blended with the influence of the Oxford Movement and Gladstone first defended the establishment of the Church of England in *The State in its Relations with the Church* (1838) – a view he later reversed in *Chapter of Autobiography* – and its High Church doctrine in *Church Principles Considered in their Results* (1840). A strict moralist, Gladstone sought to apply his Christian principles to the conduct of domestic and foreign affairs.

Gomar, Francis *(1563–1641)*
Dutch Calvinist leader and professor of theology at Leyden, remembered for his rigid Calvinistic principles, which were evident in his bitter opposition to Arminius and all who followed him.

Goodrich, Thomas *(1480–1554)*
Bishop of Ely, biblical translator and supporter of Henry VIII's reforms of the English Church, assisting the king in his matrimonial problems. Goodrich later conformed to Roman Catholicism under Mary Stuart.

Gordon, Charles George *(1833–1885)*
British general who was hailed as a national hero for his exploits in China, and as a result earned the title 'Chinese Gordon'. He developed his own mystical brand of Christianity and after the fall of Khartoum, Sudan, where he was Governor and died at the hands of the rebels, the British public acclaimed him as a martyred warrior-saint.

Gore, Charles *(1853–1932)*
Anglican theologian, bishop and leader of the liberal school of thought in the Anglo-Catholic movement. Educated at Oxford he was the first principal of Pusey House, Oxford, and after the bishoprics of Worcester and Birmingham, he was translated, in 1911, to Oxford. Concerned with the foundation of the Community of the Resurrection, he served as its first superior (1892–1901). While he was widely known as a preacher and exegete, it was as a liberal theologian that he made his mark and his prolific works profoundly influenced the course of Anglican theology.

Goretti, Maria, St *(1890–1902)*
The twelve-year-old daughter of an Italian farmworker, she was stabbed to death by Alexander Serenelli, son of her father's partner, while resisting his attempts to seduce her. Held up as a model of modesty and purity, Pope Pius XII canonised her in 1950.

Gottschalk of Orbais *(c. 803–c. 869)*
Theologian, poet and monk of heterodox views who promoted an extreme form of predestination. Entered, by his parents, as a child into monastic life, he sought to leave in his twenties and the rest of his life was overshadowed by his failure to do so. His teachings were opposed by Rabanus Maurus and Hincmar and condemned by a succession of synods.

Grabmann, Martin *(1875–1949)*
German historian of medieval theology and philosophy; professor of Christian philosophy, first at Vienna (1913–1918) and subsequently at Munich. He was the first to show the development, extent and importance

of Scholasticism. His seminal writings stimulated later Thomist scholars like E. Gilson.

Grafton, Richard *(c. 1513–1573)*

London merchant who was an energetic supporter of the Reformation, but remembered as the printer of *Matthew's Bible* (1537) and the *Great Bible* (1539) also the first (1549) and second (1552) *Book of Common Prayer*. He suffered imprisonment and lost his title of 'King's Printer' under Queen Mary.

Gratian *(uncertain dates, d. before 1159)*

Little is known of his life. A Camaldolese monk, he lectured at Bologna and compiled what came to be known as *Decretum Gratiani*. This collection of nearly 3,800 texts touching all areas of Church discipline became the text book for the study of canon law for centuries. It became an important source for the Roman Catholic *Code of Canon Law* of 1917.

Gray, Robert *(1809–1872)*

First Bishop (1847) and Metropolitan Archbishop (1853) of Cape Town (South Africa). The Colenso affair, commencing in 1863, when he excommunicated the liberal Bishop John Colenso of Natal, brought him to the notice of the world. During his episcopacy he promoted the independence of the South African Church, adding five Sees.

Grebel, Konrad *(1498–1526)*

Principal founder of the Swiss Brethren, an Anabaptist movement which opposed the work of the Swiss Reformer Zwingli. The dispute centred upon adult baptism and in January 1525 Grebel performed the first adult baptism in modern history. This, and subsequent disobedience to civil authorities, produced harassment which pursued him to his death.

Gregory – There are sixteen popes of this name, those of interest being,

Gregory I, St *(c. 540–604)*

Often called 'Gregory the Great', he was one of the most influential of all the popes, receiving the title 'Doctor of the Church' in the eighth century. Of a Roman noble family, Gregory sold his vast property to help the poor and founded seven monasteries, becoming a monk in the Roman foundation. Later, while abbot, he passed, at the sight of British slaves in Rome, his much quoted remark: 'Non Angli, sed angeli.' As pope he centralised administration, reformed the Church and established its political independence in turbulent times. He sent St Augustine, with forty monks from his monastery, to convert England and began to call himself 'the Servant of the Servants of God', now a recognised papal title. His enthusiasm for the reform of the liturgy resulted in his name being given to church music, plainsong or Gregorian Chant. As an author his practical pastoral guide for bishops *Liber Regulae Pastoralis* (*c.* 591) became the manual for the medieval episcopate. His sermons and letters have proved of lasting importance and value.

Gregory VII, St *(c. 1020–1085) (known as Hildebrand)*

After a monastic education he was chosen by Pope Gregory VI as his chaplain; then followed nearly thirty years of service to successive popes, being elected himself by popular acclaim on 30 June 1073. Gregory worked energetically for the reform and moral revival of the Church. His desire to rid the Church of secular interference and manipulation led to the condemnation of lay investiture and a long drawn out battle with European princes, particularly the Emperor Henry IV, to enforce it.

Gregory of Nazianzus, St *(329–389)*

Son of the Bishop of Nazianzus (also Gregory), he studied at Athens with Basil (St) and afterwards adopted a monastic way of life. After two years he returned to Nazianzus to help his father, reluctantly accepting Orders and, in 372, consecration as bishop. He supported Basil's fight against Arianism and, after his death in 379, became leader of the orthodox party. His eloquent preaching at Constantinople restored the Nicene Faith. He took a prominent part in the Council of Constantinople which assured victory for orthodoxy. Intrigues forced him to resign the See of Constantinople and retire to Nazianzus. His most famous theological works are his *Five Theological Orations* and his *De Vita Sua*. He is known as one of the Cappadocian Fathers.

Gregory of Nyssa, St *(c. 330–395)*

Brother of St Basil, who influenced the direction of his life; Gregory was well grounded in philosophy but entered the monastic life. Gregory of Nazianzus enlisted his help in the fight against Arianism; he was ordained priest, then Bishop of Nyssa. A thinker of originality and a preacher of power and influence, he was a champion of orthodoxy and suffered considerable persecution for the Nicene cause. Gregory wrote numerous theological treatises, his greatest being his *Catechetical Discourse*, an exposition of the doctrines of the Trinity, incarnation and redemption, also the sacraments of baptism and the Eucharist. His reputation was such that the Sacred Council of Nicaea (680–681) hailed him as 'Father of the Fathers'.

Gregory of Thaumaturgus, St *(c. 213–270)*

A disciple of Origen, who converted him to Christianity. His name 'Thaumaturgus' ('Wonderworker') originates from the legends of the wonders which accompanied his preaching and pastoral work as Bishop of Neocaesarea. He guided his flock through the persecution of Decius and the invasion of the Goths (252–254). He wrote and preached against the heresies of Sabellianism and Tritheism. He is credited, by Gregory of Nyssa, with the first recorded vision of the Virgin Mary. He has always been honoured as a Father of the Church by the Greek Orthodox Church.

Grenfell, Sir Wilfred *(1865–1940)*
Medical missionary to Labrador who trained at the University of London and, influenced by Dwight L. Moody, initiated in 1892 a missionary service to the fishermen of Labrador. His autobiography *Forty Years for Labrador* (1932) tells of his dedicated desire to improve living conditions and the network of medical services he left on retirement.

Griesbach, Johann Jakob *(1745–1812)*
Rationalist Protestant theologian and New Testament scholar who was the first to make a systematic application of literary analysis to the Gospels. He originated the term 'Synoptic' to designate the first three Gospels and maintained that Mark was the latest of the three (the dependence theory). He also published a corrected Greek edition of the New Testament.

Grignion de Montfort, Louis Marie, St *(1673–1716)*
From early life he was dedicated to poverty and prayer and was ordained a priest in 1700. He founded two congregations of Religious, to care for the sick and to preach missions. His own missionary preaching, throughout Brittany, brought persecution from the Jansenists. His *True Devotion to the Blessed Virgin Mary* (later, from 1842, to have a devotional impact upon the Roman Catholic Church) and his popular preaching were tremendously successful, although critics charged him with emotionalism. He was canonised in 1947.

Groote, Geert de *(1340–1384) (also Gerardus Magnus)*
Brilliant and rich teacher who renounced his life of luxury in 1374 and, under the influence of the mystic Jan van Ruysboeck, became an outspoken missionary preaching against the laxity of the clergy. He drew around him followers who became the 'Brethren of the Common Life'. He was the father of 'Devotio Moderna' (the 'modern devotion'), which sought to root the spiritual life in daily life, favouring meditation rather than ritual. Groote's work contributed to the reform of the Church and had a long-lasting impact upon the direction of spirituality.

Grosseteste, Robert *(c. 1175–1253)*
Little is known of his early life; at Oxford he was the most influential teacher of his time and Chancellor of the University. After many clerical appointments he accepted the See of Lincoln (then the largest in England) in 1235 and proved a dynamic and demanding pastoral bishop. He fought against the practice of appointing clerics to sinecure pastoral posts for which they

exhibited no care. As a scholar he was the most famous Englishman of his time, excelling at mathematics, astronomy and science. He made available in Latin philosophical works of Greek and Arab origin. His writings included commentaries on several of the biblical books.

Grou, Jean Nicholas *(1731–1803)*
French Jesuit professor at the Jesuit College of La Flèche who fled to England at the French Revolution and settled at Lulworth, Dorset. 'Père Grou' wrote on Plato and the Jesuit Order but is best remembered for his acclaimed spiritual writings, *e.g. Meditations on the Love of God* and *Manual for Interior Souls*.

Grundtvig, Nikolai Fredrik Severin *(1783–1872)*
Danish preacher and poet, founder of a theological movement that revitalised the Danish church; he later accepted the title of 'Bishop'.

Guardini, Romano *(1885–1968)*
Italian-born German theologian of the Roman Catholic Church whose influential writings advocated a return to personal asceticism as the way to genuine human freedom.

Guéranger, Prosper-Louis-Pascal *(1805–1875)*
French Benedictine monk who re-established the Benedictine Order in France at the Abbey of Solesmes, which he made world-famous as the centre of a revival of interest in the Gregorian Chant and the pioneer centre of the modern liturgical movement. Voluminous writer, his works on the liturgy, *e.g. Institutions Liturgiques* and *L'Année Liturgique*, were seminal for all subsequent liturgical study.

Gunkel, Hermann *(1862–1932)*
German Protestant theologian and Old Testament scholar who was one of the first to develop the method of form criticism.

Guthrie, Thomas *(1803–1873)*
Scottish Presbyterian minister with remarkable pastoral gifts; he supported the Free Church at 'the Disruption' (1843) by raising considerable funds. After 1847 his energies were devoted to his famous 'Ragged Schools' for the poor.

Guyon, Madame (Jeanne-Marie de la Mothe) *(1648–1717)*
From a neurotic youth and an early unhappy marriage, she progressed, as a result of her mystical teaching (heavily influenced by the works of Molinos), to be the central figure in a seventeenth-century French religious controversy. Her Quietism (total passivity and indifference of the soul, even to eternal

salvation) was attacked by Bossuet and defended by Fénelon. Bossuet's charges of heresy were upheld by the Conference of Issy (1695) but this was not totally free of court/political intrigue. Madame Guyon's personal sincerity never seems to have been in doubt. Her chief mystical writings include *Moyen court et très facile de faire oraison* (1685) and *Le Cantique des Cantiques* (1688).

Gwyn, Richard St *(1537–1584)*
After studying at both Oxford and Cambridge, Richard opened a school at Overton, Flintshire. Married with six children, he became a Roman Catholic and in 1579 was arrested for this. He escaped, but after recapture and torture was hanged, drawn and quartered at Wrexham in 1584, becoming the first Welshman to die for the Catholic faith under Elizabeth I. He was canonised by his Church in 1970.

H

Halifax, Charles Lindley Wood *(1839–1934)*
Second Viscount Halifax, educated at Eton and Oxford, where he joined the High Church movement. He was associated with the foundation of the Cowley Fathers and, as president of the English Church Union, he was involved with the many and varied ecclesiastical controversies of his time. His lively interest in reunion between the Church of England and the Roman Catholic Church led to fruitless conversations at Rome (1894–1896) and the publication of his *Leo XIII and Anglican Orders* (1912). He arranged the Malines Conversations with Cardinal Mercier, but these ceased at Mercier's death; the documents relating to Malines he also published.

Hall, Joseph *(1574–1656)*
Bishop of Norwich, moral philosopher and English satirist of high repute who defended the episcopacy when it was attacked by Parliament, although he had been suspected by W. Laud of Puritan sympathies. Imprisoned in the Tower of London with the other bishops, on release he lived and died in poverty. A prolific writer, his *Heaven upon Earth* was reprinted by John Wesley.

Hall, Robert *(1764–1831)*
English Baptist preacher and social reformer who was famous for his commanding oratory and defence of workers' rights, particularly the Leicestershire lace workers.

Haller, Berchtold *(1492–1531)*
Swiss schoolmaster and canon of Berne Cathedral who, influenced by Zwingli, became the leader of the Reform Movement in Berne. He helped to develop a Protestant liturgy.

Hamilton, John *(1511–1571)*
Archbishop of St Andrew's who vehemently opposed the spread of Protestantism in Scotland. He led a number of reforming synods which gave rise to the *Archbishop Hamilton's Catechism* (1552). After imprisonment for saying Mass, he acted as adviser to Mary Queen of Scots, but, after her flight, he was hanged at Stirling.

Hamilton, Patrick *(c. 1504–1528)*
While only thirteen years of age he was made Abbot of Fern. Study in Paris introduced him to Luther's writings, whom he later met. In 1527 he returned to Scotland where he was formally charged with heresy and burnt at the stake.

Hannington, James *(1847–1885)*
First Anglican bishop of East Equatorial Africa (1884) where he was sent by the Church Missionary Society. While leading a perilous expedition the next year he was murdered by natives of Uganda.

Harnack, Adolf *(1851–1930)*
After his doctorate, Harnack lectured at several German universities – Leipzig, Giessen, Marburg and Berlin. Historian, theologian and the most outstanding scholar of his time on the early Church Fathers, he is more commonly remembered for his contributions to the study of the Synoptic problem and New Testament studies. He wrote copiously on all the scholarly areas that interested him.

Hastings, James *(1852–1922)*
Presbyterian theologian and editor of several religious dictionaries and an encyclopaedia. In 1889 he founded *The Expository Times*, of which he was editor until his death.

Havergal, Frances Ridley *(1836–1879)*
Daughter of William Havergal, composer of sacred music, and a popular Victorian hymnwriter, her 'Take my life, and let it be' being still popular.

Headlam, Arthur Cayley *(1862–1947)*
Bishop of Gloucester and biblical scholar who disliked ecclesiastical parties in the Church of England and attempted to mediate between them. One of the most influential bishops of his time, he collaborated on the important

International Critical Commentary on *Romans* and worked for Church unity, particularly with his book *The Doctrine of the Church and Christian Reunion* (1920).

Heber, Reginald *(1783–1826)*
Ordained an Anglican priest in 1807, his last years were dedicated to the spread of Christianity as Bishop of Calcutta; a hymnwriter of note, many of his hymns are still popular.

Hecker, Isaac Thomas *(1819–1888)*
Although of United States origin, he was ordained a Redemptionist priest in England (1849); he conducted missions with associates in America, where he later founded the Paulist Fathers, now a worldwide organisation, to work under local bishops. He also founded the Catholic Publications Society and two Catholic magazines.

Hegesippus *(d. c. 180)*
Jewish convert to Christianity who, after twenty years in Rome and visiting most of the important centres of Christianity, wrote the history of the first 150 years of the Church; hence considered the father of Church history.

Heiler, Friedrich *(1892–1967)*
German religious writer and scholar in the history of religion. Influenced by N. Söderblom, he converted from Catholicism to Protestantism, and later organised the German High Church movement and introduced an evangelical form of monasticism. His most important, long-lasting book was an analysis of prayer, *Das Gebet* (1918).

Helena, St (Helen) *(c. 248–c. 328)*
Wife of the emperor Constantius Chlorus; their son Constantine became emperor in 306, and due to his influence Helena became a Christian. In 326 she paid a visit to the Holy Land and founded basilicas on the Mount of Olives and at Bethlehem; according to a later tradition she at this time discovered the cross on which Christ had died.

Helwys, Thomas *(c. 1550–c. 1616)*
English Puritan leader who emigrated to Amsterdam and with J. Smith founded the first Baptist church there. Returning to London he founded the first General Baptist congregation in England. He was imprisoned for advocating religious tolerance.

Henderson, Alexander *(c. 1583–1646)*
Second only to John Knox as leader in the reformed Church of Scotland, he emerged from an Episcopalian background as a strong Presbyterian leader,

particularly over resistance to the Prayer Book of 1637. He clashed with Charles I and with his draft of the Solemn League and Covenant of 1643, which contributed to the king's defeat. He was the author of numerous tracts, one of the most famous being *The Bishops' Doom* (1638).

Henry VIII *(1491–1547)*
King of England from 1509, he showed an early interest in theology; in 1521 his opposition to the Reform Movement, with his *Assertio Septem Sacramentorum* won him, and his successors, the title 'Defender of the Faith' from Pope Leo X. In 1534, by the Act of Supremacy, Henry repudiated papal authority and assumed full authority over the Church in England. He showed tolerance to Protestantism for a brief period (1536–1539), evidently for political reasons, but reaffirmed Catholic doctrine in 1539 with the *Six Articles*. Persecution of Protestants continued spasmodically. His successive marriages marked the latter years of his reign.

Henry of Ghent *(c. 1217–1293)*
Scholastic philosopher and theologian, considered one of the most illustrious teachers of his time (accorded the title 'Doctor Solemnis'). He supported Augustianism against St Thomas Aquinas and, as a secular priest, fought against the privileges of the Mendicant Orders. His theological teaching is extensively represented in his *Quodlibeta* and his unfinished *Summa Theologica*.

Henson, Herbert Hensley *(1863–1947)*
Anglican theologian and Bishop of Durham who, through his many writings, tried to modernise Christian doctrine and proved to be a controversial figure. He was a strong establishment figure until Parliament rejected the Prayer Book revisions (1927–1928), when he became convinced that establishment was incompatible with the Church's freedom.

Herbert, George *(1593–1633)*
Devotional poet and Anglican priest whose early life, with its classical training, pointed towards a public life; however, he studied theology and was ordained in 1630 and devoted the last years of his life to the pastoral duties of a country vicar at Bemerton. His fame rests upon his exceptional poetic gifts, being one of the first and finest of the Church of England's devotional poets. His prose work *A Priest of the Temple*, presented the model of a pastoral priest; some of his poems are still in daily use as hymns.

Hermas *(second century)*
Author of *The Shepherd* (probably written 140–155), which was highly regarded by the Eastern Church for its early teaching on, among other things, the need for repentance. Little is known of the life of Hermas, although accorded the title of 'Apostolic Father'. He appears to have been

a freed slave-turned-merchant who repented of evil practices after a series of visions.

Herzog, Johann Jakob *(1805–1882)*
German Protestant theologian and Church historian, pupil of Schleiermacher and Neander, who was responsible for much original research and edited a twenty-two volume reference work; the English abridged version, *The New Schaff-Herzog Encyclopaedia of Religious Knowledge*, appeared 1951–1954.

Hesychius of Jerusalem *(d. c. 450)*
A Greek monk renowned in the Eastern Orthodox Church as a theologian, but particularly as a biblical commentator and preacher. Most of his writings, including a history of the Church, have been lost, but he is said to have commented on the whole Bible and was highly regarded by his contemporaries.

Hilary of Poitiers, St *(c. 315–367)*
A convert from Neoplatonism, he was elected Bishop of Poitiers and spent the rest of his life as a champion of orthodoxy against Arianism. Hilary was the most respected theologian of his time and was hailed as the 'Athanasius of the West'; he was declared a Doctor of the Church in 1851. Hilary's principal works were *De Trinitate* and *De Synodis*.

Hilda, St *(614–680)*
Of the Northumbrian noble lines, she was baptised by St Paulinus. After years as a noblewoman, at thirty-three she joined a convent and in 657 founded a double monastery for men and women at Whitby, becoming one of the foremost abbesses of Anglo-Saxon times. Her abbey was renowned as one of the great religious and cultural centres of England.

Hildegard *(1098–1179)*
German abbess and mystic who experienced visions from an early age; known as the 'Sybil of the Rhine' for her powers of prophecy; from her convent at Rupertsberg she exerted a wide influence, even upon the Emperor Barbarossa, kings and prelates. Her work *Scivas* (between 1141 and 1151) tells of twenty-six of her visions, but there were other theological and scientific writings. Long venerated as a saint, she was never formally declared such.

Hilton, Walter *(d. 1396)*
Devotional writer, of whose life little is known, who is considered one of the greatest English mystics of the fourteenth century. Hilton is thought to have studied at Cambridge and, after a period as a hermit, joined the Augustinian canons at Thurgarton Priory, Nottinghamshire. His spiritual writings exerted a great influence during the fifteenth century, and his most famous work, *The Scale of Perfection*, is still highly regarded.

Hincmar of Rheims *(c. 806–882)*
Archbishop, theologian and the most influential churchman of the Carolingian period. He defended the French Church's independence against papal claims and defended the orthodox view of divine predestination in a controversy with Gottschalk.

Hippolytus, St *(c. 170–236)*
A controversial Roman priest and theologian who allowed himself to be elected as an anti-pope for a time, but was later reconciled with the papacy. He suffered and died during the persecution of the Emperor Maximinus. His principal works were *A Refutation of All Heresies* and *The Apostolic Tradition.*

Hobart, John Henry *(1775–1830)*
American bishop of the Protestant Episcopal Church whose emphasis upon 'Evangelical Truth and Apostolic Order' during the post-Revolutionary period of American history helped Anglicanism to expand in the new nation. A famed preacher, to promote a proper view of the Church he wrote many manuals and founded the 'Protestant Episcopal Tract Society' in 1810, having founded what was to become the General Theological Seminary of New York in 1806.

Hodge, Charles *(1797–1878)*
Leading American Presbyterian theologian who spent most of his life lecturing in biblical studies at Princeton. Conservative in outlook, he resisted newer trends in his support of traditional Calvinism; his *Systematic Theology* was influential in this, and his New Testament commentaries stressed the verbal infallibility of the Bible.

Hofbauer, St Clement Mary *(1751–1820)*
Patron Saint of Vienna. Ordained a priest of the Redemptorist Congregation in 1785, he was authorised to establish Redemptorist houses throughout northern Europe. Centred for twenty years in Warsaw, he had considerable success. Driven from Warsaw by Napoleon, he settled in Vienna where he exerted a powerful pastoral influence. He was canonised in 1909.

Honorius – There were four popes of this name, of most interest is:

Honorius I *(d. 638)*
Modelling himself on Pope St Gregory the Great, Honorius gave great support to the Christianisation of the Anglo-Saxons, inducing the Celts to accept the Roman liturgy and date of Easter. The crux of his pontificate was his role in the Byzantine Church's controversy over Monophysitism; about 634, replying to a letter from Sergius, Patriarch of Constantinople, Honorius appears to give some support to the theory of 'one will' in Christ. He was

posthumously condemned for his reply, but modern scholars debate his real understanding of the matter.

Hontheim, Johann Nikolaus von *(1701–1790)*
Roman Catholic Auxiliary Bishop of Triers, West Germany, theologian and historian, who, concerned for Christian unity and the extent of papal power, wrote under the pseudonym of Justinus Febronius, proposing ideas which became known as Febronianism. His book *De Statu* and his theories were condemned by Rome in 1764; Hontheim later retracted in 1781.

Hooker, Richard *(1554–1600)*
Scholar and then Fellow of Corpus Christi College, Oxford, after ordination to the Anglican ministry he served as rector in several places, finally at Bishopsbourne, near Canterbury. A theologian and an apologist of note, he successfully developed and defended Anglican theology against both the Roman Catholics and the Puritans. His book *A Treatise on the Laws of Ecclesiastical Polity* presents his theological thought that the Church of England is a threefold cord consisting of Bible, Church and reason.

Hooker, Thomas *(1586–1647)*
Puritan minister who introduced innovations in his Chelmsford, Essex, church and fled to Holland to avoid investigation; thence he travelled to the American colonies and eventually settled in Connecticut as a founder of Hartford. Hooker's progressive political ideas led him to be called 'the father of American democracy'.

Hooper, John *(d. 1555)*
Educated at Oxford, an early interest in the continental Reformers led to exile in Zurich, where he developed a personal friendship with the Reformers. On his return (1549) to England he was chosen for the See of Gloucester, then of Worcester. Noted for his extreme Protestantism and his zealous pastoral care, when Mary came to the throne Hooper was tried for heresy (1553) and burnt at the stake. His books, particularly *A Godly Confession and Protestation of the Christian Faith*, influenced later Puritan teaching.

Hopkins, Gerard Manley *(1844–1889)*
Educated at Balliol College, Oxford. While there he became a Roman Catholic and in 1868 joined the Jesuits. He was professor of Greek at Dublin from 1884; unknown to his superiors, he had returned to writing poetry, the deep intensity of which revealed his priestly concern for others and a degree of personal mysticism. One of the most individual and influential of the Victorian poets, his work was unknown in his lifetime; it was published for the first time in 1918 by his friend R. Bridges.

Hopkins, Samuel *(1721–1803)*
American theologian and writer who, as minister of the Newport Congregationalist Church, was one of the first to fight slavery. His belief in the need for socal service is found in his major work *The System of Doctrines Contained in Divine Revelation* (1793).

Hort, Fenton J.A. *(1828–1892)*
Educated at Cambridge, where he later held various appointments, as a New Testament scholar he produced as a lifelong project, with Brooke Foss Westcott, one of the most important critical editions of the Greek New Testament.

Hoskyns, Sir Edwyn Clement *(1884–1937)*
Anglican biblical scholar and theologian who applied modern linguistic criticism to the New Testament. Hoskyns showed that the 'historical Jesus' of Liberal Protestant theory was unhistorical and the origins of Christianity were much more complex than supposed. His best-known work, *The Fourth Gospel*, was published posthumously.

Houghton, St John *(1487–1535)*
After serving for four years as a parish priest, he joined the Carthusian Order and was Prior of the London Charterhouse when Henry VIII ordered him to accept the Act of Supremacy. He was the first person tried for refusing the Act proclaiming the king as head of the English Church, so he was dragged through the streets of London, hanged, drawn and quartered at Tyburn. He was canonised in 1970 by Pope Paul VI.

Howard, St Philip *(1557–1595)*
Eldest son of the fourth Duke of Norfolk, he was baptised a Catholic but brought up a Protestant. A wastrel at Elizabeth I's court, after a conversion experience he returned to his neglected wife and his earlier Catholicism. Captured and imprisoned in the Tower of London, he was ordered to be executed but the sentence was never carried out and he died six years later in the Tower. He was canonised in 1970 by Pope Paul VI.

Howe, Julia Ward *(1819–1910)*
Famed for her 'Battle Hymn of the Republic', first published in 1862. She was a New York author and philanthropist who was especially concerned for equal educational and professional opportunities for women and for the welfare of Civil War widows.

Hubert, Walter *(d. 1205)*
As Bishop of Salisbury he accompanied Richard I on the Third Crusade and on his return raised the ransom when the king was imprisoned. Elected

Archbishop of Canterbury, he ruled England as justiciar for four years while Richard was away; in 1195 Pope Celestine III appointed him papal legate. King John chose him as his Chancellor in 1199. Hubert's position in the Church and State was unrivalled until Cardinal Wolsey in the sixteenth century.

Huddleston, Trevor *(1913–1998)*
The name 'Trevor Huddleston' is almost synonymous with the struggle against apartheid in South Africa; no one did more to highlight the evils of the apartheid system and alert worldwide opinion. He was born at Bedford; deciding to enter the Anglican priesthood, he was educated at Wells Theological College, Somerset; after ordination (1937) he served in a Swindon parish. In 1939 Huddleston joined the Anglican Community of the Resurrection at Mirfield and took his vows in 1941. The Community sent him to South Africa in 1943, to take charge of the missions at Sophiatown and Orlando, Johannesburg. With first-hand experience of apartheid, Huddleston confronted and denounced the authorities for their brutality. Expelled from South Africa (1956), he returned to England to preach, to write (*Naught for Your Comfort* was a disturbing bestseller) and to campaign against apartheid. He was one of the founders, and then president, of the Anti-Apartheid Movement. Appointed Bishop of Masasi, Tanzania (1960–1968) and then suffragan Bishop of Stepney, 1969, he maintained the pressure for change in South Africa. Honoured with a knighthood for his work by Queen Elizabeth II in January 1998, he died in April of that year.

Hughes, Hugh Price *(1847–1902)*
Welsh Methodist theologian and popular preacher who promoted liberal social reforms; founder of *The Methodist Times* (1885), in 1896 he became the first President of the National Council of the Evangelical Free Churches.

Hughes, John *(1797–1864)*
The first Roman Catholic Archbishop of New York, he was of Irish birth and served, after his ordination in America, in several Philadelphia parishes before becoming bishop, and then, in 1850, archbishop. He founded *The Catholic Herald*, fought for state support of parochial schools and helped end the Draft Riots in 1863. As President Abraham Lincoln's personal agent he visited Europe to counteract pro-Southern support during the Civil War. He founded what is now Fordham University and helped found the North American College in Rome.

Hughes, Thomas *(1822–1896)*
Famed for his book *Tom Brown's Schooldays* (which ran to fifty editions), he was also a jurist, called to the bar in 1848, and a social reformer. Influenced by F. D. Maurice he joined the Christian Socialists and was a founder-

member and later Principal (1872–1883) of the Working Men's College. His simple direct approach to Christianity is reflected in his tracts, *e.g. The Manliness of Christ* (1879).

Hugh of Cluny, St *(1024–1109)*
Abbot of the Benedictine Monastery of Cluny from the age of twenty-five until his death; as such, he was head of Cluny's extensive monastic network throughout Western Europe. Under Hugh, Cluny reached the highest point of its power and international influence in its long history. He wholeheartedly supported the Gregorian reforms within the Church and successive popes turned to him for advice and entrusted him with responsible missions. His integrity, generosity and saintliness influenced many contemporary international figures. Hugh supported the development of the Latin liturgy and championed orthodox doctrine at several Church Councils.

Hugh of Lincoln, St *(c. 1140–1200)*
When Henry II founded a Carthusian monastery at Witham, Somerset (1178), he asked for Hugh of Avalon, a French Carthusian already famed for sanctity, as the prior. In 1186 Hugh was appointed Bishop of Lincoln and set a shining example of pastoral care. He opposed the king, but retained his friendship, in defence of his people's rights and braved rioting mobs to defend the Jews of Lincoln. Internationally known for his courage, wisdom and justice, he was canonised twenty years after his death. Ruskin described him as 'the most beautiful sacerdotal figure known to me in history'.

Hugh of St Victor *(1096–1141)*
Of noble birth, he entered the Order of Augustinian Canons and about 1115 joined the Abbey of St Victor, Paris. There, from 1133, the school flourished under Hugh's guidance. An eminent scholastic theologian, his works cover a wide field, including geometry and Scripture commentaries, but for Hugh everything was subordinated to the life of contemplation and it was this mystical tradition which made St Victor famous in the twelfth century.

Hume, George Basil *(1923–1999)*
Son of Sir William Errington Hume and Marie Elizabeth (née Tisseyre), George Basil was born in Newcastle-upon-Tyne. After completing his secondary education at Ampleforth College, North Yorkshire, he entered the Benedictine monastic community of Ampleforth Abbey aged eighteen. From 1944 to 1947 he pursued his studies at Oxford, and than at Fribourg University, Switzerland, until 1951. Returning to Ampleforth College, Dom Basil was a senior master and housemaster. Abbot from 1963 to 1976, he was installed as the ninth Archbishop of Westminster on 25 March 1976. Pope Paul VI elevated him to the cardinalate on 24 May 1976. As leader of the Catholic Church in England and Wales he distinguished himself in many

responsible roles, including President of the Bishops' Conference of England and Wales, and President of the Council of European Bishops' conferences. As a cardinal, Basil Hume served on five different Roman congregations and councils. Sixteen British and American universities awarded him honorary degrees. He pastorally won a reputation for openness and prayerful moderation. 'Father Basil', as he liked to be called, was a familiar figure on British television and the author of several popular spiritual books. In the last few weeks of his terminal sickness, the outstanding contribution he had made to the life of British society was recognised personally by Queen Elizabeth II with the prestigous Order of Merit, presented in May 1999. He died on 17 June 1999.

Huntingdon, Selina Hastings, Countess of *(1707–1791)*
In 1793 she joined the new Methodist Society and on her husband's death devoted herself completely to spreading it among the upper classes. Her policy, as a peeress, of appointing numerous chaplains was disallowed by court and occasioned the founding of the body of Calvinistic Methodists known as 'The Countess of Huntingdon's Connexion'.

Huss, John *(c. 1372–1415)*
Educated at Prague University, where he later became rector, Huss was ordained and became a popular preacher and leader of the Czech National Reform Movement. Wycliffe's writings became an ever-increasing influence and he was excommunicated for upholding them. His chief work, *De Ecclesia* (1413), reflects his Wycliffite position. Huss appealed to a General Council at Constance but was tried for heresy and died at the stake.

I

Ignatius of Antioch, St *(c. 35–c. 107)*
Nothing certain is known of his life, except that he was Bishop of Antioch (according to Origen, the second bishop; according to Eusebius, the third) and was taken under guard to Rome for martyrdom. On the way he wrote seven important letters which had exceptional influence upon the early Church and are the source of early teaching upon the episcopacy. His letter to the church at Rome, to which he accords special respect, reveals a passionate devotion to Christ and a great desire to suffer martyrdom for him.

Ignatius of Loyola, St *(1491–1556)*
Born of a noble Spanish family, a leg wound sustained in battle (1521) enforced inactivity during which he read the Bible and experienced a conversion; he resolved to live an austere life and do penance for his sins. For a year, at Manresa, he lived such a life, had mystical experiences and began writing his *Spiritual Exercises*. He studied in Spain and at Paris for twelve years and while there gathered a group around him who became the first members of the Society of Jesus (The Jesuits). They took religious vows in 1534; several, with Ignatius, were ordained priest in 1537 and the Society was formally approved in 1540. Ignatius' paramount desire was to reform the Roman Catholic Church from within; the remainder of his life was devoted to this. He was canonised in 1622.

Inge, William Ralph *(1860–1954)*
Dean of St Paul's, London, and one of the best-known churchmen of his time. Educated at Eton and Cambridge, his fame derived principally from a long series of devotional and theological writings, including *Christian Mysticism* (1899) and *Faith and its Psychology* (1909).

Ireland, John *(1838–1918)*
First Roman Catholic Archbishop of St Paul, Minnesota; head of a liberal group of clergy who promoted the integration of immigrant parishes into the life of United States Church and society. He helped to found the Catholic University of America at Washington DC (1889) and St Paul's Seminary in 1894.

Irenaeus, St *(c. 130–c. 200)*
Little is known of his life; he was acquainted with Polycarp, became a missionary in Gaul and, after a persecution at Lugdunum (Lyons), was chosen as bishop and contended with the heresy of Marcion. Irenaeus is the first great theologian, his work *Adversus Haereses* (180) was directed against Gnostic errors and is a witness to the apostolic tradition.

Irving, Edward *(1792–1834)*
Church of Scotland minister whose teachings became the foundation of the Catholic Apostolic church or Irvingism. His later extreme eschatology lost him the impressive following he had enjoyed as a preacher in London.

Isaac the Great, St *(c. 345–439)*
After marriage and, as a widower, the life of an Orthodox monk, he was appointed 'Catholicos' (spiritual leader) of the Armenian Orthodox Church. He fostered Armenian ecclesiastical independence and culture, producing the first translation of the Bible in Armenian; he is also credited with many Armenian hymns.

Isidore of Kiev *(c. 1385–1463)*
Greek Orthodox Patriarch of Russia, theologian and humanist who worked for reunion between Greek and Latin Christendom, but the opposition of the Byzantine and Russian Orthodox Churches drove him into exile.

Isidore of Seville, St *(c. 560–636)*
Succeeding his brother, Leander, as Archbishop of Seville, Isidore put all his energy into spreading Catholicism in the face of Barbarism and Arianism; to this end his immense knowledge found expression in his *Etymologiae*, an encyclopaedia used for many centuries; his other influential theological writings contributed to his being known as a Doctor of the Church within twenty years of his death; he was canonised in 1598.

J

Jacopone da Todi *(c. 1230–1306)*
Baptised as Jacopo dei Benedetti, born at Todi, in Northern Italy, he was of noble family. On the sudden death of his wife (1268), he was converted from worldliness to a life of austerity, eventually becoming a Franciscan friar, advocating the most extreme poverty. A gifted poet, he was imprisoned and excommunicated for writing satirical verse against Pope Boniface VIII (1298), but freed by the next pope. He is remembered for more than a hundred mystical poems of great power and originality and for the hymn, the 'Stabat Mater', which was added to the Roman liturgy in the eighteenth century.

Jaegerstaetter, Franz *(1909–1943)*
Born, illegitimately, in the small village of St Radegund, Upper Austria, Franz became a member of the Jaegerstaetter family when his mother married a local farmer. From the age of fourteen he worked on the farm and disregarded religion until he married a devout Catholic in 1936. She changed Jaegerstaetter, who became involved in his parish and studied the Bible for himself. When Hitler took over Austria in 1938, Jaegerstaetter and his wife were deeply disturbed by the brutality and ideology of the Nazi regime. On 25 February 1943 he was ordered to report to the Nazi recruiting office, but Franz had no intention of doing military service. He knew his conscientious refusal meant death; he was beheaded in a Berlin prison six months later. Prison chaplains 'marvelled at his bravery and his simple, deep and genuine piety'.

Jansen, Cornelius Otto *(1585–1638)*

Roman Catholic Bishop of Ypres and founder of Jansenism. He studied at the University of Louvain, where he later became rector; his thorough study of the early Church Fathers, particularly St Augustine, led him to write *Augustinus* (1640) and lead a theological revival or reform movement, in opposition to the Roman Catholic Counter-Reformation theology and the Jesuits. His book and Jansenism were condemned after his death.

Jerome, St *(c. 347–420)*

His real name was Eusebius Hieronymus and he wrote under the name of Sophronius; educated at Rome, where he was baptised (366), he travelled widely. While living as a hermit in the Syrian desert for about four years, he learnt Hebrew; on his return to Rome, after ordination, he became secretary to Pope Damasus (382) but proved to be very outspoken. About 386 he settled in Palestine as leader of a new monastery at Bethlehem; the rest of his life was dedicated to study. One of the most learned of the early Church Fathers, his scholarship and writings, particularly his Latin translation of the Bible (the Vulgate), begun at the request of Pope Damasus, and his biblical commentaries profoundly influenced the Western Church.

Jewel, John *(1522–1571)*

Anglican Bishop of Salisbury who, influenced by Peter Martyr, became one of the intellectual leaders of the Reform movement in England. He opposed both the Roman Catholic and the Puritan positions and his masterly and celebrated *Apologia Ecclesiae Anglicanae* (1562) gave clarity and continuing strength to the Anglican position. Jewel proved to be a most caring and pastoral bishop and built the library at Salisbury.

Joachim of Fiore *(c. 1132–1202)*

Mystic, theologian and biblical commentator of whose life little is known, but whose influence was far-reaching. Called to the monastic life, he lived first as a Cistercian and then, in 1196, he formed his own local Religious Order. Of great personal sanctity, his writings on a trinitarian conception of history led to his optimistic hopes for the future and the spawning of revolutionary groups, like the Spiritual Franciscans.

Joan of Arc, St *(1412–1431)*

Second patron, and greatest heroine, of France. Joan was born of peasant family. A devout child, she first experienced visions at the age of 13; her voices revealed her mission to save France. Cleared by a panel of theologians, she convinced a doubting Dauphin and led the French army to victory at Orleans (1429) and the crowning of Charles VII at Rheims. Captured by the Burgundians in a later campaign, she was sold to the British; a politically motivated church court condemned her to the stake as a heretic. A later court, in 1456, found her innocent and she was canonised in 1920.

John – There are twenty-three popes with this name; the most famous is without doubt:

John XXIII *(1881–1963)*
One of the most popular and influential popes of all time. Angelo Giuseppe Roncalli originated from Bergamo, Northern Italy, of a poor farming family. After ordination (1904) and a period as bishop's secretary, he served in the First World War; afterwards he was called to Rome to serve in the Vatican Diplomatic Service. As Vicar Apostolic he served in Bulgaria (1925–1935), as Apostolic Delegate in Turkey (1935–1944) and as Papal Nuncio in Paris at the end of World War II. In 1953 he was created cardinal and Patriarch of Venice. Elected pope in 1958, he proposed three aims; to call a diocesan synod of Rome, an Ecumenical Church Council and a revision of Canon Law. The Second Vatican Council, which renewed the Roman Catholic Church, was his greatest achievement, but he also contributed much to the development of Church unity and wrote socially important encyclicals, especially *Pacem in Terris*. Although a diplomat, he was a pastor at heart and his simple, deep spirituality is reflected in his published diaries, *Journey of a Soul*.

John of Avila, St *(1500–1569)*
Known in Spain as 'the Apostle of Andalusia', he gave up a law career, sold his possessions and was ordained for missionary work (1525) in Mexico. However (1528), he was persuaded to preach throughout Andalusia and proved to be one of the greatest and most effective reforming preachers of his time. As author and spiritual director he influenced such people as Teresa of Avila, John of God and Francis Borgia. His writings, especially the spiritual classic *Audi Filia* (1530), reveal his own mystical experience and spirituality.

John Baptist de la Salle, St *(1651–1719)*
Born of a noble French family, he studied for the Roman Catholic priesthood (1678), but soon became involved in providing free schooling for the poor and the training of teachers. He distributed his fortune to the poor and gave himself completely to improving educational standards. He founded the Institute of the Brothers of the Christian Schools, a Religious Order of teachers, and established several teachers' colleges; his schools spread through Europe. Apart from his spiritual impact he was a significant pioneer in French education. He was canonised in 1900.

John Climacus, St *(c. 579–c. 649)*

A Byzantine hermit and later Abbot of St Catherine's on Mount Sinai, his name (John of the Ladder) derives from his book *The Ladder of Divine Ascent*, which, as a handbook on the ascetical and mystical life, has been regarded as a spiritual classic.

John of the Cross, St *(1542–1591)*

One of the greatest Christian mystics and reformers, Juan De Yepes Y Alvarez entered the Carmelite Order in 1563 and was ordained priest in 1567. He met Teresa of Avila, who persuaded him not to leave the Carmelites for the Carthusians but to work with her for the reform of the Carmelite Order. John set up a reformed Discalced Carmelite house (1568) and became spiritual director to Teresa's convent at Avila (1572). Violent dissent between the two forms of Carmelite life led to his imprisonment and great hardship (1576). He was finally banished to Andalusia, where he died. John's poetic sensitivity and Thomist theology, together with his deep mystical experience, produced Christianity's great spiritual classics *Dark Night of the Soul, Spiritual Canticle* and *The Living Flame of Love*.

John of Damascus, St *(c. 675–c. 749)*

Sometimes called 'John Damascene', he succeeded his father as 'Logothete' or representative of the Damascus Christians to the Muslim Caliph; soon after 730 he entered a monastery near Jerusalem. John played an important role in the eighth-century iconoclastic controversy, and the influence of his theological writings has reached through the Middle Ages to our own day; approximately 150 theological works, the most famous being *Fount of Wisdom* and *Sacra Parallela*, won him the title 'Doctor' of both the Greek and Latin Church.

John, Esther *(d. February 1960)*

Qamar Zia, Esther John's original name, was born (date uncertain) in India of a Muslim family, who moved to Pakistan after partition. She attended a Christian school and was a secret convert to Christianity. At the prospect of an arranged Muslim marriage she ran away from home and took the name 'Esther John'. Urged to return home and to accept the arranged marriage she went to the Punjab and worked in a mission hospital. Later she entered a Bible college in Gujranwala. In 1959 Esther John moved to Chichawatani to live and work with American Presbyterian missionaries. She was mysteriously found bludgeoned to death in her bed in February 1960. (Esther John is one of the ten modern martyrs honoured in sculpture with a place over the west door of Westminister Abbey, London.)

John of God, St *(1495–1550)*
Former shepherd and soldier converted to an ascetic way of life and great sanctity by John of Avila, he dedicated his life to the care of the poor and sick. He founded an Order of nursing brothers later known as the Hospitaller Order of St John of God; in modern times the Order has had the care of 225 hospitals worldwide.

John of Kronstadt *(1829–1909)*
Russian Orthodox theologian, known popularly as 'Father John', who as a priest-ascetic worked among the poor and promoted many pastoral and educational activities from his parish of St Andrew, Kronstadt. Of several spiritual writings the best known is *My Life in Christ*.

John of Odzun *(650–729)*
Learned theologian of the Armenian Church who, in 718, became the Catholicos (leader) of that church and encouraged orthodox Christology in the Eastern Church. His principal work, in defence of the human nature of Christ, was *Against the Fantastic*.

John Paul I, Pope *(1912–1978)*
Albino Luciani was the first pope to take a double name, to emphasise the ongoing renewal work of the two previous popes. After pastoral work and teaching he was chosen Patriarch of Venice, and cardinal (1973); while there his *Illustrissimi* was written. He died unexpectedly, five weeks after his election to the papacy, on 26 August 1978.

Jones, Rufus Matthew *(1863–1948)*
One of the most respected of American Quakers, professor of philosophy at Haverford College (1904–1934) he wrote over fifty books, many of them on Christian mysticism; he also founded the American Friends Service Committee, a worldwide charitable organisation.

Joseph of Volokolamsk, St *(1439–1515)*
Theologian and monk who has been accorded the title 'Father of medieval Russia'. His monastic reforms emphasised community life and inspired a spiritual renewal in the Russian Orthodox Church; he founded the celebrated monastery of Volokolamsk near Moscow.

Jowett, Benjamin *(1817–1893)*
Distinguished scholar with the reputation of being one of the finest teachers of his time. Educated at Balliol College, Oxford, where he was later Regius Professor of Greek (1855) and Master (1870). He was influenced by German philosophy and took a liberal stance in theology, this was reflected in *The Epistles of Paul* (1855) and his contribution to *Essays and Reviews* (1860).

Judson, Adoniram *(1788–1850)*
American Baptist missionary and linguist; one of the first missionaries to be sent abroad by the Nonconformist churches, he was ordained a Congregationalist minister but became a Baptist on arrival in India; in Rangoon (1813) he translated the Bible into Burmese and compiled a Burmese dictionary. His work in Burma was very successful, leading to a Christian community of about half a million.

Julian of Norwich *(c. 1342–after 1413)*
Celebrated English mystic of whom little is known (not even her real name), other than that she seems to have lived as an anchoress outside St Julian's Church, Norwich. According to her own account, she experienced in May 1373 a series of visions of the Passion of Christ and the Holy Trinity which, after years of meditation, she recounted in her influential *Revelations of Divine Love*, a book which is quite unparalleled in English religious literature.

Justin Martyr, St *(c. 100– c. 165)*
Philosopher-apologist of the early Church; he tried many pagan philosophies before embracing Christianity, and his writings, particularly the *Dialogue with Trypho the Jew* and two *Apologies*, represent the first encounter of Christian revelation with Greek philosophy and the first development of the idea of salvation history. Denounced as a Christian, he was scourged and beheaded.

Justus, St *(d. c. 637)*
Sent to England by Pope Gregory the Great to help Augustine, he was appointed by Augustine as the first Bishop of Rochester. He eventually succeeded as the third Archbishop of Canterbury (634) and dispatched St Paulinus to convert Northumberland.

K

Kagawa, Toyohiko *(1888–1960)*
Japanese social reformer and leader of labour and democratic movements that worked for the betterment of millions of Japanese. After conversion from Buddhism he studied modern social techniques at Princeton, USA, and on his return to Japan dedicated himself to the improvement of social conditions. He founded the first Labour Union (1921), the National Anti-War League (1928) and the Kingdom of God Movement in 1930. Toyohiko was imprisoned in 1921 and 1922 for his Labour activities and in 1940 as a pacifist. He wrote more than 150 books, several translated into English.

Keble, John *(1792–1866)*
Anglican priest, theologian and poet whose brilliant mind was evident in his educational success at Oxford, followed by a Fellowship at Oriel at the age of nineteen. From 1817 to 1823 he was a tutor at Oriel, but from then on embraced pastoral work, being vicar of Hursley, near Winchester, for the last thirty years of his life. As a poet he is remembered for *The Christian Year* and numerous hymn lyrics; as a theologian it was his sermon 'National Apostasy' (1833) that set the Oxford Movement, or Tractarians, in motion. He led and guided the Movement, with J. H. Newman and E. B. Pusey, writing nine of the *Tracts for the Times* and working on *A Library of the Fathers*. A brilliant scholar, but self-effacing, he was much sought after for his spiritual guidance.

Kempe, Margery *(c. 1373–c. 1440)*
Mother of fourteen children, from Lynn, Norfolk, who was a visionary and mystic, and whose autobiography is one of the earliest in English literature. In her dictated *Book of Margery Kempe* (she herself was illiterate) she describes her pilgrimages to Jerusalem, Rome and Germany and her mystical experiences.

Ken, Thomas *(1637–1711)*
Anglican Bishop of Bath and Wells, educationalist, hymnwriter and royal chaplain to King Charles II. He was one of the seven bishops who opposed James II's Declaration of Indulgence, but supported the king against William of Orange. This opposition led to his disposition from his See (1691) and he spent his last twenty years in ascetic retirement.

Kennicott, Benjamin *(1718–1783)*
English biblical scholar, educated at Oxford, whose fame rests upon his life-work of a critical study of the Hebrew text of the Old Testament. His research was published between 1776 and 1780 in two volumes.

Kentigern, St *(c. 518–603)*
Also known as Mungo ('dear one'), little is known for certain of his life. Brought up by St Serf, he lived at first as a hermit at Glasghu (Glasgow) and then worked as a missionary. Consecrated Bishop of Strathclyde (*c.* 540), he preached in Cumbria and Wales and eventually returned to work in the Glasgow area; he is reputedly buried in Glasgow Cathedral.

Khomyakov, Aleksey Stepanovich *(1804–1860)*
Russian Orthodox lay theologian, poet and founder of the nineteenth-century Slavophile Movement. He attacked Roman Catholic Scholasticism and German Idealism. His concept of the Church as 'Sobernost' ('togetherness' – symphony) was treated with suspicion during his life, but has been influential in twentieth-century theology.

Kierkegaard, Søren (Aabye) *(1813–1855)*
Danish religious philosopher and critic of rationalism who inspired the formation of existentialist philosophy. Originating from a wealthy but secluded background, Kierkegaard obtained a Master's degree in theology (1840) and from his book *Either/Or*, in 1843, there followed a succession of philosophical works of great originality and influence. His later writings attacked the established Church for its compromise, and his own ascetical life pointed to a sterner form of Christianity. His devotional works, *e.g. Christian Discourses* (1850), are less well known.

Kilham, Alexander *(1762–1798)*
English Methodist minister who, after John Wesley's death, became leader of the Methodist New Connexion, a radical wing that was expelled (1796) by the Methodist Conference.

King, Edward *(1829–1910)*
Theologian and Bishop of Lincoln with a reputation for pastoral care and great personal holiness. As a Tractarian, in 1888 he was involved in a famous prosecution over church rites; the court decided in his favour in 1890.

King, Martin Luther Jr *(1929–1968)*
Eloquent negro Baptist minister who championed the Civil Rights Movement in the USA from the mid-1950s. After theological training, including a PhD, he became a minister in Montgomery, Alabama (1954). He organised opposition to segregation on buses (1956), and in 1960 resigned his pastorate to devote himself completely to the Civil Rights Movement, advocating non-violent methods; this culminated in the massive march on Washington (1963), President Kennedy's sympathy and the Civil Rights Bill. In 1964 he was awarded the Nobel Peace Prize, but his leadership was challenged by more militant forces and he was assassinated in 1968.

Kingsley, Charles *(1819–1875)*
Anglican clergyman, teacher, social reformer and novelist whose novels influenced social developments in Britain. A graduate of Magdalene College, Cambridge, and ordained in 1842, he became vicar of Eversley, Hampshire (1844), where he spent most of his life. As a founder-member of the Christian Socialist Movement he was more interested in re-educating his own social class than changing political structures. He was one of the first churchmen to support Darwin's evolutionary theories. Disturbed by the Tractarian Movement, his novels, such as *Westward Ho!* (1855) and *Hereward the Wake* (1866), have an anti-Catholic slant.

Knox, John *(c. 1513–1572)*
Educated at Glasgow for the Roman Catholic priesthood, under the influence of George Wishart, he embraced the principles of the Reformation; by 1547 he was its acknowledged leader in Scotland. Chaplain to Edward VI, he fled to the Continent on Mary's accession, but on his return to Scotland assumed a leadership of enormous political and religious influence. His famous tract *The First Blast of the Trumpet against the Monstrous Regiment of Women* (1558), written in Geneva, earned him Elizabeth I's hostility. He worked on the *First Book of Discipline* and wrote a *Treatise on Predestination* (1560), but his principal work was the *History of the Reformation of Religion within the Realm of Scotland.*

Knox, Ronald Arbuthnott *(1888–1957)*
Theologian, author, preacher and translator of the Bible. Born into an Anglican family and educated at Eton and Oxford, he became a Roman Catholic in 1917. Ordained in 1919 to the priesthood, from 1926 to 1939 he acted as chaplain to the Oxford students. The author of several popular religious books, *e.g. The Creed in Slow Motion*, he is however best known for his translation of the Bible, commenced in 1939 and completed in 1949. This was followed by his New Testament commentaries (1953–1956). His own spiritual struggle appeared in his *Spiritual Aeneid* (1918).

Kolbe, St Maximilian Maria *(1894–1941)*
Polish Franciscan priest and founder of religious communities called Niepokalanow, in Poland, India and Japan. Arrested by the Gestapo in 1941, for aiding Jews, he was imprisoned in Auschwitz. He volunteered to take a married man's place in the death cell and was finally killed by an injection of carbolic acid. The man he saved, Gajowniczek, was present when Pope John Paul II declared him a saint in 1982.

Kuhlman, Kathryn *(1910–1976)*
Evangelist and charismatic faith healer. Of nominal Christian background, from Concordia, Missouri, she experienced a call from God at thirteen and began to preach at sixteen. Ordained by the Evangelical Church Alliance, she had a second religious experience in 1946, which set her upon a healing ministry. At her 'miracle services' thousands claimed to have been healed and she reached millions through her radio and TV programmes. Her best-known books are *I Believe in Miracles* (1962) and *God Can Do It Again* (1969).

Kuyper, Abraham *(1837–1900)*
Dutch theologian and statesman who was the leader of the Anti-Revolutionary Party. As a Dutch Reformed Church pastor he founded the Free University of Amsterdam (1880) for the training of Calvinist pastors. His

political party, in coalition, came to power in 1888 and he served as Prime Minister and Minister of the Interior (1901–1905).

L

Labouré, Catherine *(1806–1876)*
From a French farming family she joined the Sisters of Charity of St Vincent de Paul (1830) and immediately, at the Rue de Bac Convent, Paris, she experienced a series of visions of the Virgin Mary (declared authentic by an examining commission in 1836), who asked for a medal of the Immaculate Conception to be struck. World-famous as the Miraculous Medal, millions were reproduced. From 1831 until her death, Catherine worked at menial tasks in Hospice d'Enghien, but her evident sanctity led to her canonisation in 1947.

Labre, Benedict Joseph St *(1748–1783)*
Known as 'the beggar of Rome'; of a French family, he tried unsuccessfully to enter Religious Orders, all of whom declared him unfit for community life. Instead, alone, he set out to visit all the major shrines of Europe. From 1774 he was a well-known figure in Rome, living rough in the Colosseum and worshipping daily in the churches. He was declared a saint in 1883.

Lacordaire, Henri Dominique *(1802–1861)*
French theologian and preacher. As a young French lawyer influenced by Rousseau he lost his Christian faith, but in 1824, after conversion, he trained at St Sulpice for the priesthood. He worked for the separation of Church and State (1830) with F. de Lamennais, but broke off on Lamennais' excommunication. He won great fame as a Paris preacher, particularly for his Lenten Conferences, later published as *Conferences de Notre Dame de Paris* in four volumes (1844–1851). He sought the renewal of the French Church by re-establishing the Dominican Order, which he had joined in 1838.

Lactantius *(c. 240–c. 320)*
Sometimes called the 'Christian Cicero', he is one of the most reprinted of the Latin Church Fathers and an outstanding apologist whose *The Divine Precepts* (304–311) was the first systematic Latin account of the Christian attitude to life. Before his conversion he had worked for the Emperor Diocletian; later Constantine appointed him tutor to his son.

Lagrange, Marie Joseph *(1855–1938)*
Theologian and outstanding Roman Catholic biblical scholar. He became a member of the Dominican Order in 1879; he first taught before studying Oriental languages. His Order sent him, in 1890, to Jerusalem to found the famous 'École Pratique d'Études Bibliques' and (in 1892) the influential *Revue Biblique*. In 1902 he was appointed to the Roman Catholic Biblical Commission and in 1903 commenced his monumental Bible commentaries. He wrote several seminal books, including *Judaism before Jesus Christ* (1931).

Lake, Kirsopp *(1872–1946)*
Patristic and biblical scholar, educated at Lincoln College, Oxford. After ordination in the Anglican Church, and two curacies, he became professor of New Testament at Leyden (1904–1914) and later in the USA, at Harvard University. He challenged and provoked by his writings, *e.g. Historical Evidence for the Resurrection of Jesus Christ* (1907). His later work, in the five-volume *The Beginnings of Christianity: The Acts of the Apostles* and the series *Studies and Documents* (edited with his wife), has proved of lasting value.

Lamennais, Felicité Roland de *(1782–1854)*
French Roman Catholic priest and gifted philosophical and political writer who proved to be one of the greatest seminal influences on the social and political trends of the nineteenth and twentieth centuries. Converted from an early agnosticism he attempted to combine political liberalism with Roman Catholicism. His principal work, an *Essay on Indifference Towards Religion*, led to condemnation from Rome, excommunication and his eventual complete rejection of Christianity.

Lanfranc *(c. 1010–1089)*
Benedictine theologian from Northern Italy, Archbishop of Canterbury and trusted counsellor of William the Conqueror. Famed as a teacher and able administrator, in 1063 he became Abbot of St Stephen's, Caen; in 1070, as Archbishop of Canterbury, he conducted a successful reform and reorganisation of the English Church but supported William's policy of replacing English prelates by Normans.

Lang, William Cosmo Gordon *(1864–1945)*
Archbishop of Canterbury. Of Scottish Presbyterian background, after studying for the Bar he was ordained for the Anglican Church (1890). He worked as a curate in a Leeds parish then returned to Oxford as Dean of Divinity. From suffragan Bishop of Stepney (1901–1908) he went to York and twenty years later he was translated to Canterbury. He was involved in the abdication of Edward VIII and was a close friend and adviser to George VI. He retired as Baron Lang of Lambeth in 1942.

Langton, Stephen *(d. 1228)*
Considered one of the greatest of the medieval Archbishops of Canterbury, he was a renowned theologian for twenty-five years in Paris, before being chosen as a cardinal and Archbishop of Canterbury. He supported the barons in their struggle with King John, but later supported the regency against the barons. His voluminous writings included Bible commentaries and he was the first to divide the Bible into chapters and verses.

Latimer, Hugh *(1485–1555)*
English priest, educated at Cambridge, who from 1525 was gradually converted to Reformation principles. His vigorous preaching won him acclaim and preferment under Henry VIII, and it contributed to the spread of the Reformation in England. After opposing the Act of Six Articles (1539) he was forced to resign the See of Worcester, to which he had been elevated in 1535, and was confined in the Tower of London. Although at freedom during Edward's reign, he was committed to the Tower again (1553) on Mary's accession. Sent to Oxford to dispute with Catholic theologians, he was found guilty of heresy, and finally died courageously at the stake on 16 October 1555.

Laud, William *(1573–1645)*
Archbishop of Canterbury. Educated at Oxford and ordained in 1601, he opposed Calvinistic theology from the beginning and tried to restore, as bishop (first of Bath and Wells, then London), something of the pre-Reformation liturgy of the English Church. As religious adviser to Charles I his power increased, but he attracted the hostility of the Puritans and became increasingly unpopular. Attempting to impose Anglican liturgy on Presbyterian Scotland and, in 1640, a new set of canons, he was impeached before the Long Parliament, imprisoned, tried (1644–1645) and finally beheaded on Tower Hill, 10 June 1645.

Laval, Francois de Montmorency *(1623–1708)*
Born of one of France's most famous families, he was the first Roman Catholic bishop in Canada, and laid the foundation of his Church's organisation there. As Bishop of Quebec (1674) and member of the ruling council, he also had a powerful political influence. He founded the seminary at Quebec which later (1852) became Laval University.

Lavigerie, Charles *(1825–1892)*
French cardinal and Archbishop of Algiers and Carthage who worked for the conversion of Africa by founding the White Fathers (1868) and fought against slavery, forming several anti-slavery societies.

Law, William *(1686–1761)*
Author of works on mysticism and Christian ethics. Educated at Cambridge, he refused the Oath of Allegiance and became a non-juror; he was tutor to the Gibbon family from 1727 to 1737. From 1740 he lived in retirement, organising schools and almshouses, personally living a simple life of devotion and charity. He is best remembered for his *Treatise Upon Christian Perfection* (1726) and his spiritual classic. *A Serious Call to a Devout and Holy Life* (1728). His ethical works have seldom found acceptance among Christian moralists.

Lawrence (Laurence), St *(d. 258)*
One of the seven deacons of Rome serving Pope St Sixtus II, Lawrence suffered martyrdom a few days after his patron, during the persecution of Valerian. It is reported that his death by roasting on a gridiron was so heroically and patiently borne that mass conversions to Christianity took place in Rome.

Lawrence of Brindisi, St *(1559–1619)*
A member of the Capuchin Friars Minor, a gifted linguist and preacher who won the title of Doctor of the Church (1959) for his work in resisting the rise of German Protestantism. He was canonised by his Church in 1881.

Lawrence of Canterbury, St *(d. 619)*
One of the Benedictine monks who accompanied St Augustine to England (597) and succeeded him as Archbishop of Canterbury in 604.

Lawrence of the Resurrection, Brother *(c. 1605–1691) (originally named Nicholas Hermes)*
After serving as a soldier, and leading a hermit's life, he entered the Carmelite Order in Paris (1649), where he spent the rest of his life. In charge of the kitchen, amid the pots and pans, he developed a life of constant awareness of God's presence. His simple mystical writings, *Maximes Spirituelles* (1692) and *Moeurs et Entretiens du F. Lawrent* (1694), were edited by the Abbé de Beaufort and published after his death.

Leclerc, Jean *(1657–1736)*
Arminian theologian and the biblical scholar who championed freedom of thought and supported advanced theories of exegesis and theological method. He made a lasting contribution to biblical studies with three vast encyclopaedias.

Lee, Ann *(1736–1784) (also known as Mother Ann)*
The illiterate daughter of an English blacksmith from Manchester, she joined the radical Shaking Quakers. In 1774, with followers, she emigrated to

America and founded a settlement, near Albany, New York, from which the Shaker movement spread throughout New England.

Leo – Thirteen popes share this title, the most noteworthy being:

Leo I, St *(d. 461)*
Given the title 'Leo the Great', little is known of his life before becoming pope in 440 against the background of the disintegration of the Roman Empire. His papacy is noteworthy for the safeguarding of orthodox teaching and the advance of papal supremacy. In 449 his *Tome* was used to reject Eutychianism, an extreme form of the Monophysite heresy; his teaching was hailed as 'the voice of Peter' at the Council of Chalcedon (451). Leo's many letters and ninety-six sermons expound his teaching on papal primacy and reveal the liturgical practices of the time. Politically he negotiated with the invading barbaric tribes. He was declared a Doctor of the Church in 1754.

Leo XIII *(1810–1903)*
After a career in the Catholic Church's diplomatic service, he followed an authoritarian pope in 1878 and set out to pursue a more liberal programme. He brought the Kulturkampf in Germany to a finish and improved relations between the Vatican and Britain, Russia and Japan. His best-known contribution was his social teaching, enshrined in the letter *Rerum Novarum* (May 1891) and his encouragement to biblical study in *Providentissimus Deus* (November 1893). He did much to encourage ecumenism, although his letter *Apostolicae Curae* (1896) declared Anglican Orders invalid. Other letters encouraged the devotional and spiritual life of the Church.

Leslie, Charles *(1650–1722)*
Non-juring Anglican divine and writer who, as an ardent Jacobite, accompanied the Pretender to Rome after the 1715 rebellion. He wrote many highly regarded apologetical works against the deist philosophy, the Quakers and Roman Catholicism.

Lewis, C. S. *(1898–1963)*
Educated privately, he served in the British Army in the First World War; afterwards, in 1918, he proved to be an outstanding scholar at University College, Oxford. From 1925 to 1954 he was a tutor and Fellow of Magdalen College, Oxford; from 1954 to 1963 professor of medieval and Renaissance English at Cambridge. Lewis wrote nearly forty books, many of them on Christian apologetics, the most famous being *The Screwtape Letters* (1942) and his stories for children, the *Chronicles of Narnia* series. Also of note is his autobiographical *Surprised by Joy* (1955).

Liddon, Henry Parry *(1829–1890)*
Anglican priest and theologian who was ordained in 1852 and became vice-principal of the new seminary at Cuddesdon (1854) and vice-principal of St Edmund's Hall, Oxford, in 1859, where he was an energetic supporter of the Oxford Movement. As canon of St Paul's, London (1870), for the next twenty years his preaching attracted great crowds. Concerned for Church unity, he encouraged the growth of the Old Catholic Movement. A great admirer of E. B. Pusey, he commenced his biography in 1882, posthumously published in four volumes (1893–1897). The religious centre, Liddon House, London, was founded in his memory.

Lightfoot, Joseph Barber *(1828–1889)*
At Trinity College, Cambridge (1847), he was a pupil of B. F. Westcott and later lectured in theology and biblical studies; from 1875 he was Lady Margaret Professor of Divinity at Cambridge. He won international recognition for his work on the early Christian writers, his New Testament criticism and his famous commentaries. As Bishop of Durham (1878) he promoted ecclesiastical and social reforms.

Liguori, St Alphonsus *(1696–1787)*
A brilliant student, he received doctorates in civil and church law at the age of sixteen. He began a career as a lawyer, but turned to the Roman Catholic priesthood in 1726. Alphonsus helped a Sister Mary Celeste found a new order of nuns and himself founded (1732) the Redemptorist Congregation of Priests. Dissension tore at the new Order, but Alphonsus continued his work of preaching missions and devoted himself to writing. Although appointed bishop (1762), he resigned his See in 1775. Besides the Redemptorist Congregation he is best remembered for his extensive works of dogmatic and moral theology and his devotional writings. By the twentieth century these works had gone through eighteen thousand editions and been translated into sixty languages. Canonised by his Church in 1839, he was declared the patron of moralists and confessors in 1950.

Lingard, John *(1771–1851)*
English Roman Catholic priest and historian whose famous eight-volume work *The History of England* (1819) has proved of lasting value. He helped found Ushaw College, Durham, and reopened the English College in Rome (1817).

Livingstone, David *(1813–1873)*
Born at Blantyre, Scotland, he was basically self-educated and joined the London Missionary Society in 1838, first intending to go to China. Arriving in South Africa (1840), he worked with Moffatt (whose daughter he married) and from Kuruman conducted missionary/exploratory journeys. He became devoted to Africa, undertaking his first major expedition in 1853, which won

him international acclaim. He was the first white man to view the Victoria Falls (1855) and he sought the source of the Nile. More explorer than missionary, in his later travels he was sought and found exhausted in 1871 by Henry M. Stanley of the *New York Herald*. Loved by his African followers, after his death they carried his body to the coast, a journey of nine months, for eventual burial in Westminster Abbey.

Llull, Ramon (or Ramon Lull or Raymond Lully) *(c. 1235–1316)*
Lay missionary, mystic and poet. Educated as a knight, he acquired a knowledge of Islam from his upbringing on the island of Majorca. After a mystical experience he abandoned courtly life and devoted himself to the conversion of the Moors. He studied Arabic and Islamic culture to further his aim and succeeded in persuading State and Church to establish institutions for the study of Oriental languages. He is best remembered as a mystic, a forerunner of the great Spanish mystics.

Loisy, Alfred *(1857–1940)*
Biblical scholar, linguist and philosopher of religion. Ordained a priest, he devoted himself to modernising the teaching of the Roman Catholic Church and succeeded in founding Modernism, springing principally from his book *L'Évangile et L'Église*; this was condemned by Pope Pius X (1907). After the condemnation he parted with his Church, but continued to write prolifically.

Lossky, Vladimir *(1903–1958)*
Lay theologian, expelled from Russia in 1922. In the USA and Paris he expounded and spread knowledge of Orthodox teaching. He opposed the teachings of Bulgakov and studied and wrote upon Meister Eckhart.

Lovejoy, Elijah P. *(1802–1837)*
American lay preacher and editor, from St Louis, Missouri, of the Presbyterian newspaper the *St Louis Observer*. He wrote forthright editorials against the evils of slavery and died when his newspaper offices were burnt down by a mob.

Lowder, Charles Fuge *(1820–1880)*
Anglo-Catholic pastoral priest who served first in Pimlico, London, then as a missionary in the East End. He founded the church of St Peter, London Docks, and converted thousands of East Londoners.

Lucaris, Cyril *(1572–1638)*
Greek Orthodox theologian and Patriarch of Constantinople who sympathised with Calvinism and opposed Rome. He worked energetically for the reform of his own Church and he presented the Codex Alexandrinus to King Charles I (1628). He was put to death on a political charge by the Sultan Murad.

Lucius, three popes shared this name. The first (d. 254) was also honoured with the title of saint and he is the patron saint of Copenhagen, Denmark.

Ludlow, John Malcolm Forbes *(1821–1911)*
Educated in law and called to the Bar in 1843, he became a founder, with Maurice and Kingsley, of the Christian Social Movement. A member of the Church of England, he was largely responsible for the 1852 Industrial and Provident Societies Act and was co-founder of the Working Men's College.

Lunn, Sir Arnold *(1888–1974)*
World authority on skiing who invented the modern slalom race. Later in life he was converted to Roman Catholicism and became a vociferous apologist and writer. His own story was published as *Now I See*.

Luther, Martin *(1483–1546)*
Educated at the University of Erfurt; he joined the Augustinian Hermits in 1505, was ordained priest in 1507, and by 1515 he had become vicar of his Order. In 1508 he was lecturing at the new University of Wittenberg in theology and Scripture. Reacting fiercely against the preaching of Tetzel on indulgences, he posted his celebrated Ninety-Five Theses on various Church abuses (1517) and precipitated the Reformation movement. He refused to recant at the Diet of Worms (1521) and was placed under the ban of the Empire. He was rescued from physical harm by the Elector of Saxony, but returned to Wittenberg (1522) to restore order. Luther finally set aside his monastic habit in 1524 and married Catherine von Bora the following year. His many writings were mainly pamphlets and were principally to meet a particular need. His reply to Henry VIII's *Defence of the Seven Sacraments* lost him much support in England. From 1529, until his death, his disciples recorded the *Tischreden* which were table conversations with family and friends.

Luwum, Janani *(1922–1977)*
Janani Luwum was the Anglican Archbishop of Uganda, Rwanda, Burundi and Boga-Zaire, who dared to protest at the repeated brutal acts of Idi Amin, President of Uganda. He had been converted to Christianity as a young teacher and after studying for the ministry was ordained; he studied in England and won a reputation for creative leadership, energy and commitment. He was at first bishop of Northern Uganda (1969) and was elected archbishop in 1974. After bravely rebuking Idi Amin, Luwum disappeared and was murdered. His body was never found. (Janani Luwum is one of the ten modern martyrs honoured in sculpture with a place over the west door of Westminster Abbey, London.)

M

Macarius *(1482–1564)*
Metropolitan of Moscow, he began as a monk and became Archbishop of Novgorod in 1526. After his elevation to Metropolitan of Moscow and all Russia, he gave support to the autocratic monarchy to unite sacred and secular powers. He developed the idea of Moscow as the third 'Rome', replacing the first and Constantinople.

Macarius, St *(c. 300–c. 390) (also known as Macarius of Egypt and Macarius the Great; not to be confused with St Macarius of Alexandria, a fourth-century Egyptian hermit)*
Renowned for his sanctity, he founded a colony of monks which became one of the principal centres of Egyptian monasticism. He is regarded as one of the Desert Fathers and he had a considerable influence upon the development of the monastic life. The only authentic work to carry his name is *To the Friends of God*; later writings ascribed to him were influenced by his thought, but not written by him.

Macarius of Moscow *(1816–1862)*
Metropolitan of Moscow. Baptised Michael Bulgakov, he became a monk and, after lectureships and elevation to the See of Tambov (1857), and then to Kharkov and Vilna, he became Metropolitan in 1879. Considered one of the best Orthodox theologians of the nineteenth century, he wrote two influential theological works and a twelve-volume *History of the Russian Church*.

McAuley, Catherine Elizabeth *(1787–1841)*
Irish founder of the Congregation of the Sisters of Mercy, dedicated to education and social service. She opened the first 'House of Mercy' on 24 September 1827, took first vows in 1831, and henceforth the Sisters of Mercy spread rapidly, becoming one of the largest congregations of Religious Sisters in the world.

McDonald, George *(1824–1905)*
Scottish novelist, poet and writer of Christian allegories. He became a Congregationalist minister but, after 1853, devoted himself to writing. He is still remembered for his children's books, especially *At the Back of the North Wind* (1871) and *The Princess and the Goblin* (1872).

MacKay, Alexander Murdoch *(1849–1890)*

A Church Missionary Society missionary in Uganda, remembered for his engineering skills. He met with opposition and was expelled at a time of persecution. After expulsion from Uganda (1887) he translated the Bible into the Ugandan language.

Mackenzie, Charles Frederick *(1825–1862)*

Anglican priest and the first bishop of the British colony of Central Africa (1861). He was compelled to retire from missionary work due to ill health.

MacLeod, George *(1895–1991)*

In 1938 ten men set out from Glasgow, Scotland, to rebuild the ancient abbey on the historic island of Iona; their visionary leader was George MacLeod. The dynamic community there today is a living witness to their success. Born in 1895, of Scottish aristocratic background, MacLeod was educated at Winchester Public School, and the universities of Oxford and Edinburgh. Entering the Church of Scotland ministry, in the terrible Depression of the 1930s he worked in the industrial slum parish of Govan, Glasgow. His many projects for the unemployed and the young brought new hope for hundreds of people. The ruins on Iona seemed to beckon him and during and after restoration, from 1938 to 1967, he was the leader of the Community. He was Moderator of the Church of Scotland (1957–1958) and President of the International Fellowship of Reconciliation in 1963. Although he won the Military Cross for courage in the First World War, serving in the Argyll and Sutherland Highlanders, George became a dedicated Christian pacifist, campaigning strenuously in the 1970s for nuclear disarmament. Created a life peer – Lord MacLeod of Fuinary in Morven – from 1968 to 1971 he was Rector of Glasgow University. His many books include *Speaking the Truth in Love*.

McLeod, Norman *(1812–1872)*

Liberal minister of the Church of Scotland who worked to improve working-class conditions; the editor of the *Edinburgh Christian Magazine* (from 1849) and *Good Words* (from 1860). He was appointed chaplain to Queen Victoria (1857) and was elected Moderator of the General Assembly of the Church of Scotland in 1869.

McPherson, Aimée Semple *(1890–1944)*

Pentecostal evangelist of California and radio preacher who founded the International Church of the Foursquare Gospel. She won a large following, wealth and a certain notoriety; she died of an overdose of barbiturates.

Malachy, St *(1095–1148)*
Archbishop of Armagh who promoted reform in the Irish Church and is regarded as one of the most influential Irish churchmen of the Middle Ages. He introduced both the Roman liturgy into Ireland and, through his friendship with St Bernard of Clairvaux, the Cistercian Order. On a second journey to Rome to receive the pallium, he died at Clairvaux.

Manning, Henry Edward *(1808–1892)*
From an evangelical Protestant background, at Oxford he turned to the Tractarian Movement. Ordained for the Anglican ministry in 1833, he married the same year. Disturbed by the Gorham Judgment, he was received into the Roman Catholic Church in 1851. His wife having died, he was ordained to the Roman Catholic priesthood and founded the Oblates of St Charles. He rose rapidly in his Church, becoming the second Archbishop of Westminster, and later cardinal (1865). He was a staunch supporter of papal infallibility at the First Vatican Council and won national fame and respect for his successful mediation in the London Dock Strike of 1889.

Manning, James *(1738–1791)*
American Baptist minister who founded Brown University, first in Rhode Island, then at Providence, and served as its first president. He also helped to found the Warren Association of New England Baptists.

Mannix, Daniel *(1864–1963)*
Roman Catholic priest who studied and lectured at Maynooth College and rose to be college president. Appointed Archbishop of Melbourne in 1917, he was a forthright and controversial figure, *e.g.* demanding state support of church schools. After World War II he fought to prevent Communist infiltration of the Australian trade unions. An energetic supporter of Catholic Social Action, he founded over 180 schools and a hundred parishes.

Margaret Mary Alacoque, St *(1647–1690)*
French nun and visionary. Bedridden as a child with rheumatic fever, she later refused marriage and entered the Visitation convent at Paray-le-Monial in 1671. There, from December 1673, she received a series of visions of the Sacred Heart of Christ, in which she was told to promote devotion to the Sacred Heart of Jesus. Rebuffed for years, eventually her message was heeded and seventy-five years after her death the devotion was officially approved by the Roman Catholic Church. She was canonised in 1920.

Margaret of Scotland, St *(c. 1045–1093)*
Probably born in Hungary, she married Malcolm III of Scotland (1070). She instigated Church reform, inspired many with her own personal devotion and made many benefactions. She was canonised by Pope Innocent IV in 1250.

Margunios, Maximus *(d. 1602)*
Greek Orthodox bishop and scholar who was an exponent of Greek culture and the foremost Orthodox theologian of his age. His attempts to bring union between the East and West aroused his fellow churchmen to suspect his orthodoxy.

Marillac, St Louise de *(1591–1660)*
French co-founder of the Daughters of Charity of St Vincent de Paul. From her youth she wanted to be a Religious Sister, but was advised to marry (1613). Widowed in 1625, she met Vincent de Paul and devoted the rest of her life to assisting him in his charitable work. In 1633 Louise became the first superior of the new foundation and travelled all over France founding hospitals and orphanages. By modern times her congregation was the largest in the Roman Catholic Church.

Maritain, Jacques *(1882–1973)*
French Roman Catholic philosopher, respected worldwide for his interpretation of the thought of Thomas Aquinas, and the development of his own form of Thomism. A student of the Sorbonne, he held professorial chairs at the Institute Catholique Paris (1914–1933), the Institute of Medieval Studies, Toronto (1933–1945), and Princeton (1948–1952). His numerous books applied Thomism to all branches of philosophy and religious experience.

Marmion, Columba *(1858–1923)*
An Irishman who lived all his life in France. He entered the Benedictine House of Maredsous in 1886, where, from 1909, he was abbot. Famous as a spiritual director, he was also a gifted writer. His best-known book, *Christ the Life of the Soul* (1918), sold over a hundred thousand copies. He was declared 'Blessed' by Pope John Paul II in 2000.

Marshall, Stephen *(1594–1655)*
Popular Puritan leader and minister who helped to formulate the Presbyterian expression of faith (1643) and worked on the Shorter Westminster Catechism (1647). He was an influential preacher, but was always a popular leader rather than a seminal thinker.

Martensen, Hans Lassen *(1808–1884)*
Danish Protestant theologian who lived an academic life before becoming Bishop of Seeland (1854). He developed and interpreted the Lutheran system of doctrine and presented this in his best-known work, *Den Christelige Dogmatik* (1866).

Martin of Tours, St *(c. 316–397)*
The first great leader of Western monasticism and the patron saint of France. Of a pagan family, Martin was forced to serve in the Roman army from the age of fifteen. Five years later he had his famous vision of Christ, after sharing his cloak with a beggar. He accepted baptism and afterwards seems to have served as a medical officer in the army; after release in 358 he set up a religious community at Ligugé. Elected Bishop of Tours (371), he conducted church reforms and encouraged the spread of monastic communities throughout France. He died at Poitiers and his friend and biographer, Sulpicius Severus, tells how the men of Tours stole the body of their beloved bishop away, in the night, for burial at Tours.

Martyn, Henry *(1781–1812)*
Anglican missionary who, after ordination as a deacon (1803), became a chaplain of the East India Company at Calcutta. While involved in missionary work he translated the Book of Common Prayer and the New Testament into Hindustani (1807). His devotion to missionary work won him hero status at the time in Great Britain.

Masemola, Manche *(1912–1928)*
Manche Masemola was a member of the Pedi tribe, which lived in the barren reserved lands of the Transvaal, South Africa. Her family were animists, and very suspicious of Christians. The Anglican preacher, Father Augustine Moeka, made a great impression upon her and she accepted baptism at the age of sixteen. Persecuted by her family and beaten by her parents she resolutely held on to her faith. Finally, her parents took her to a remote place and beat her to death. (Manche Masemola is one of the ten modern martyrs honoured in sculpture with a place over the west door of Westminster Abbey, London.)

Massillon, Jean-Baptiste *(1663–1742)*
French Roman Catholic priest who, having joined the Oratory (1681), was ordained in 1691 and rose to become the most famous French preacher of his time, often preaching before Louis XIV. Elected Bishop of Clermont, he proved to be a model pastoral leader.

Mathews, Shailer *(1863–1941)*
American leader of the Social Gospel Movement. He taught at Colby College, Waterville, Maine, and the University of Chicago. His many books and hundreds of articles, *e.g. The Messianic Hope in the New Testament*, promoted the social dimension of salvation.

Matteo da Bascio *(c. 1495–1552)* *(or Matteo di Bassi)*
After entering the Observant Franciscans (1511), he was eager to return to
the early simplicity of St Francis of Assisi. He went bare-foot, grew a beard
and gathered a large following. His Order of Friars Minor Capuchin
(commonly called Capuchins) was approved by Rome in 1528. He acquired
a reputation as a powerful preacher.

Maurice, (John) Frederick Denison *(1805–1872)*
Anglican theologian, author and founder of the Christian Social Movement.
Originally of Unitarian background, he embraced the Anglican faith (1830)
and accepted ordination (1834). While chaplain of Guy's Hospital, London,
he wrote his *Kingdom of Christ* (1838), which established his reputation as a
theologian, but also aroused considerable suspicion. He joined with Kingsley
and Ludlow in founding the Christian Social Movement. His *Theological
Essays* (1853) caused his dismissal from his theological professorship at King's
College, London. Maurice founded and became the first principal of the
Working Men's College (1854). While lecturing in moral theology at
Cambridge (elected in 1866) he wrote his celebrated *Social Morality* (1869).

Mayhew, Jonathan *(1720–1766)*
Outspoken Boston, Massachusetts, preacher whose earlier fervour originated
from the Great Awakening, but who later distrusted religious emotionalism.
Ordained pastor of Boston's West Church in 1747 (where he served until his
death), he was famed for his preaching and his liberalism; his sermons were
published in New England and London.

Mayne, St Cuthbert *(1544–1577)*
The first of the English Roman Catholic priests trained in Europe to work
secretly in Elizabethan England to be executed, in Cornwall, for his pastoral
work. After arrest and a trial at Launceston he was executed there on 29 March
1577. He was declared a martyr of the Roman Catholic Church in 1970.

Mechtild of Magdeburg *(c. 1210–1285)*
German mystic who became a Beguine at Magdeburg and recorded the
visions she experienced there (1250–1269). She remained at Magdeburg for
forty years under the spiritual direction of the Dominican Friars. In old age
she retired to the convent at Helfta. (She is not to be confused with St
Mechtild of Helfta, who was a contemporary.) Her mystical experiences,
which had a powerful influence upon the course of German medieval
mysticism, are summarised in her book *The Flowing Light of Godhead*.

Melanchthon, Philip *(1497–1560)*
Educated at Heidelberg and Tübingen, he became the first professor of
Greek at the University of Wittenberg (1518) and developed a friendship

with Martin Luther. He helped to systematise Luther's teaching; his *Loci Communes* (1521) was the first ordered presentation of Reformation doctrine to appear. He founded many schools and reformed several universities, translated the Bible and wrote commentaries that were highly regarded. Melancthon was a leading figure at the Diet of Augsburg (1530) and is credited with writing the *Confession of Augsburg*. Although he helped to lead the reform movement after Luther's death, his standing was questioned by several controversies.

Melito of Sardis *(second century)*
Very little is known of his life, but, through his writings, he exerted a powerful influence upon the Church writers of the second and fourth centuries. Melito has been identified as an unmarried pastoral bishop of Sardis (Turkey). A prolific writer, he was virtually unknown until 1940; his masterly Easter treatise, *On the Pasch*, was discovered and first published in 1960.

Melville, Andrew *(1545–1622)*
Scottish scholar, educationalist and Presbyterian Reformer. After study in Scotland and France, in 1569 he studied in Geneva under the Reform leader, Theodore Beza. On his return to Scotland he reformed the educational system and helped Scottish universities to acquire an international reputation. He filled the vacuum caused by John Knox's death (1572) and gave the Reformed Church its Presbyterian character. His outspoken opposition to King James VI (James I of England) led to imprisonment and exile.

Mendes, Chico *(1944–1988)*
Francisco 'Chico' Alves Mendes was born in 1944 on the Cachoeira rubber estate, near Xapuri, north-west Brazil. The landowners forbade education to the rubber tappers; Mendes was at work by the age of nine. In 1962 a passing stranger taught him to read and introduced him to Christian teaching on social justice. Cattle ranchers were occupying the land and driving out the rubber tappers. He became dynamic in founding unions, encouraged by the Church. The unions developed a programme of nonviolent protests, called *empates*. Despite death threats, he led many peaceful protests at the massive illegal deforestation pursued by the landowners; who responded with violence. Mandes was shot dead by gunmen hired by the landowners. He left a wife and two young children.

Menno, Simons *(1496–1561)*
Roman Catholic priest who rejected his Church and became leader of the Dutch Anabaptists (1537). For twenty-five years, in constant danger as a heretic, he shepherded his communities, developing their teaching, which led to the formation of the Mennonite Church.

Mercier, Désiré-Joseph *(1851–1926)*
Belgian educator, philosopher and cardinal. As a leader of the nineteenth-century revival of Thomism and the first professor of Thomism at the University of Louvain, he applied its principles to modern philosophical and scientific thought. Created Archbishop of Malines in 1906 and cardinal the following year, he was an outspoken leader of Belgian resistance to the Germans during the First World War. Enthusiastic for Church unity, he was the Roman Catholic leader at the Malines Conversations (1921–1925).

Merry Del Val, Rafael *(1865–1930)*
Ordained to the Roman Catholic priesthood (1888), he was chosen by Pope Leo XIII for papal service; involved in momentous decisions, like the Schools Question in Canada (1890) and the question of Anglican Orders (1896), he became cardinal and the Vatican's Secretary of State (1903) and implemented the anti-Modernist policy of Pope Pius X. His influence was also powerfully felt within the Roman Catholic Church when he served as Secretary of the Holy Office.

Merton, Thomas *(1915–1968)*
United States journalist who, after a conversion, joined the Trappist Abbey of Gethsemane, Kentucky. He became the most influential proponent of traditional monasticism in modern times. His early autobiographical *The Seven Storey Mountain* gained him a wide readership and with his prolific writings he popularised Western spirituality. Before his sudden accidental death on 10 December 1968, he was exploring common ground with other forms of spirituality, notably in the Far East.

Methodius, St – *See* Cyril, St and Methodius, St

Meynell, Alice *(1847–1922)*
Poet and essayist. About 1872 she converted to Roman Catholicism, which was reflected in the many literary articles she wrote and religion formed an important part of her poetry. She married Wilfrid Meynell in 1877 and bore him eight children. Her poetry, which appeared in collections, from *Preludes* (1875) to the posthumous *Last Poems* (1923), was so popular that she was considered as a possible Poet Laureate.

Michael Cerularius *(d. 1058)*
Patriarch of Constantinople who was fiercely opposed to the Western Church and was so energetic in defence of the doctrinal, disciplinary and political independence of the Greek Church that the Eastern Schism became a permanent separation.

Michelangelo *(1475–1564)*

His full name was Michelangelo Di Lodovico Buonarroti Simoni. He was apprenticed to the painter Ghirlandaio (1488), from whom he learnt the basic skills which made him famous as one of the greatest artists of the Renaissance. His greatest sculptures include the *Pietà* (1499) in the Vatican, *David* (1504) at Florence, and *Moses* (1545), also in the Vatican. Pope Julius II commissioned him to paint the ceiling of the Sistine Chapel, on the themes of *Praeparatio Evangelica* (1508–1512) and the *Last Judgement* (1534–1541). At the time of his death he was the principal architect of St Peter's, Rome.

Middleton, Thomas Fanshawe *(1769–1822)*

Anglican missionary and first Bishop of Calcutta. He held various pastoral posts, and was widely recognised for his biblical scholarship, before his consecration in 1814 to the vast See of Calcutta, which at the time included responsibility for the whole of India and Australia!

Milton, John *(1608–1674)*

One of England's greatest poets. While at Cambridge (1625–1632), where he was highly regarded for his scholarship, he first wrote poetry in Latin, Italian and English. Disillusioned by the ways of the clergy, he gave up the idea of ordination and devoted himself to literature (1632–1638). Joining the Presbyterians in 1641, he attacked the clergy and defended the liberty of the Press in his *Areopagitica* (1642). Milton gave his support to Oliver Cromwell, became an Independent and defended the Government's action in executing Charles I. A prolific poet, his great epic *Paradise Lost* (1658–1665) and *Samson Agonistes* were written after he went totally blind in 1651. Milton's Christian beliefs, published posthumously in *De Doctrina Christiana*, were unconventional and individualistic.

Mindszenty, Josef *(1892–1975)* (*originally Josef Pehm*)

Hungarian Primate and Cardinal Archbishop of Esztergom (1945). From his ordination in 1915, he was for over fifty years an implacable enemy of fascism and Communism. He was imprisoned several times, twice in 1919, 1944 and 1948; the last was for refusing to permit the secularisation of Catholic schools by the Communists and led to a sentence of life imprisonment. Freed and hailed as a great patriot during the uprising of 1956, he took refuge in the United States Embassy in Budapest when the Communist government returned to power. The American president Richard Nixon persuaded him (1971) to leave Hungary for the Vatican. He died in Vienna, disappointed by the Vatican's policy of accommodation with Communism.

Moffatt, James *(1870–1944)*
Writer and biblical scholar. Ordained to the ministry of the Free Church of Scotland (1896), he taught at Oxford and Glasgow before becoming professor of Church history at Union Theological Seminary, New York (1927–1939). His translation of the New Testament appeared in 1913 and the Old Testament in 1924; he also edited a seventeen-volume *Commentary of the New Testament* (1928–1949).

Moffatt, Robert *(1795–1883)*
Missionary and Bible translator. A Scottish Congregationalist, he was sent to South Africa by the London Missionary Society in 1816. He eventually settled at Kuruman, where he developed, over forty-nine years, a major missionary centre and community. He travelled widely and translated the Bible, hymns and other literature into the native tongue. On a visit to England in 1839 he persuaded David Livingstone (later his son-in-law) to join him in Africa.

Mogila, Peter *(1596–1646)*
Russian Orthodox theologian and monk who became Metropolitan of Kiev (1632). His writings and leadership strengthened the Russian Church in its two-fronted controversy with Roman Catholicism and the Protestant Reformers. His most important work was *The Orthodox Confession of Faith* (1640), which brought order to Orthodox theology.

Möhler, Johann Adam *(1796–1838)*
Roman Catholic apologist, historian and theologian. He taught Church history at Tübingen (1826–1835) and Munich (1835–1838). He sympathised with Protestantism and worked untiringly for Church unity. His principal work, *Symbolik* (1832) (in English translation, *Unity in the Church*), prompted a theological revival in the Church.

Molina, Luis de *(1535–1600)*
Spanish Jesuit theologian who taught at Coimbra (1563–1567) and Evora (1568–1583) and in 1588 published his work *The Union of Free Will and Divine Grace*, in which he tried to clarify the relationship between God's foreknowledge and man's free will. The book gave rise to a theological system called 'Molinism' and over three hundred years of fierce theological debate between the Jesuits and Dominicans.

Molinos, Miguel de *(1628–1696)*
After ordination in Spain (1652) and obtaining his doctorate in theology, he was sent to Rome (1663) as a spiritual director. There he became a celebrated confessor and gained great fame after the publication of his *Spiritual Guide* (1675). He advocated a perpetual union with God and taught that perfection

was to be obtained by the total abandonment of the will. His extreme Quietism led to his arrest (1685), the examination of twenty thousand letters and a trial for heresy and immorality. He recanted the heresy but was imprisoned for life for the immorality.

Monica, St *(c. 332–387)*
Mother of St Augustine of Hippo and responsible for his conversion by her prayers and example. Widowed when forty, Monica followed Augustine to Rome (383) and on to Milan, where she was greatly influenced by St Ambrose and where Augustine was baptised. She became a popular saint in the Middle Ages, being regarded as the patron of mothers.

Monod, Adolphe-Theodore *(1802–1856)*
Reformed theologian of Swiss origin who was considered the foremost preacher of his time in France. He held pastorates at the Reformed Church, Naples (1826), the Free Evangelical Church. Lyons (1833), and the Church of the Oratoire, Paris (1847).

Montalembert, Charles *(1810–1870)*
French politician and Roman Catholic Church historian (born in London) who helped to lead the struggle to free the Church from state control in France. He joined Lamennais and Lacordaire in the publication of *L'Avenir*, the opposition of the Gallican Church faction led to the closing of the newspaper and the condemnation of liberalism by Pope Gregory XVI (1832). Montalembert submitted, but continued in Catholic journalism and politics, where he championed Catholic principles.

Montecorvino, Giovanni da *(1247–1328)*
Franciscan missionary, from Italy, who worked in Armenia and Persia (*c.* 1280), then in the Madras region of India and there wrote the earliest Western account of the area. In 1294 he entered Peking, founding the first Christian mission in China. He opened several mission stations and was consecrated the first Roman Catholic Archbishop of Peking in 1307. His missionary work was destroyed in the fourteenth century with the fall of the Mongol Empire.

Moody, Dwight Lyman *(1837–1899)*
American evangelist who began as a successful shoe salesman in Chicago; after conversion from Unitarianism to Congregationalism (1856) he worked with the YMCA, becoming President of the Chicago YMCA. The Moody Church was founded, and he conducted mission work in the slums. After meeting Ira D. Sankey they launched upon successful evangelistic tours. Moody made a first visit to Great Britain in 1867 and returned with Sankey for an extended term in 1873–1875, and again in 1881–1884. It was during

the first of these tours that the *Sankey and Moody Hymn Book* (1873) appeared. He preached 'the old-fashioned gospel' message with literal interpretation of the Bible. At Northfield, Massachusetts, he conducted annual Bible conferences, founded a seminary for young women (1879) and one for young men (1881), and also founded what is now the Moody Bible Institute (1889).

Moore, George Foot *(1851–1931)*
American Presbyterian pastor and theologian who established a reputation as an Old Testament scholar with a remarkable knowledge of rabbinical source literature. He held academic posts at Andover Theological Seminary (1883–1902) and at Harvard. His most influential work was probably *Judaism in the First Century of the Christian Era*.

More, Hannah *(1745–1833)*
Popular religious writer and philanthropist. A blue-stocking as a young woman, after the death of her friend David Garrick (1779) she turned to religion. Guided by William Wilberforce, she established schools in the West of England, worked to relieve poverty and wrote the *Cheap Repository Tracts* to educate and encourage the working classes.

More, Henry *(1614–1687)*
English philosopher of religion and poet. Educated at Cambridge and elected a Fellow in 1639, he spent the whole of his life there. He was concerned to counter the secular philosophy of his day, corresponding with Descartes (published in 1659 as *The Immortality of the Soule*).

More, Sir Thomas *(1478–1535)*
Educated first in the classics, then in the law, he became a barrister in 1501. Attracted to the religious life at Charterhouse, he decided against celibacy and married in 1505, having entered parliament the year before. Highly regarded as a scholar, his home at Chelsea became a centre for men of learning; More gave particular support to his friend Erasmus. He rose speedily after Henry VIII's accession, becoming a Privy Councillor in 1518, a knight in 1521 and eventually Lord Chancellor in 1529. His best-known work, *Utopia*, appeared in 1516. When Henry's intentions were clear, More resigned his post in 1532 and refused the oath on the Act of Succession eighteen months later. He was imprisoned in the Tower of London, where he wrote *Dialogue of Comfort against Tribulation*. On 6 July 1535 he was beheaded on Tower Hill, having been found guilty of treason for opposing the Act of Supremacy. In 1935 the Roman Catholic Church canonised him as a martyr.

Morison, James *(1816–1893)*
Theologian and founder of the Evangelical Union. He trained for the ministry of the United Seccession Church, but his preaching at Kilmarnock (1840)

caused him to be accused of teaching against the Westminster Confession and he founded his own church. This later (1897) united with the Scottish Congregationalists to form the Congregational Union of Scotland.

Mornay, Philippe de *(1549–1623)*
French Protestant diplomat and writer. He wrote many political tracts in support of the Huguenots, for whom he also fought. A counsellor of Henry of Navarre, he won a reputation of being the most outspoken publicist of the Protestant cause.

Morone, Giovanni *(1509–1580)*
Italian Bishop of Moderna who served in the papal diplomatic service and, sympathetic to the Reformers' grievances, worked for a General Council to bring peace. Appointed cardinal in 1542, his reforming zeal led to suspicion and charges of heresy and, in 1557, imprisonment. The next pope, Pius IV, cleared him and Morone presided over the final session of the Council of Trent (1562), his diplomatic skill saving it from disaster. In his last years, as Cardinal Protector of England, he helped to administer the English College in Rome.

Morrison, Robert *(1782–1834)*
Presbyterian minister and first Protestant missionary to China. After ordination in 1807, the London Missionary Society sent him to Canton. With a colleague, William Milne, he translated the New Testament into Chinese (1813) and published a Chinese Grammar (1815). The whole Bible appeared in 1823. An Anglo-Chinese College was founded and was moved to Hong Kong in 1843. Morrison ended his days in China.

Morse, St Henry *(1595–1645)*
After studying at Cambridge and for the law he became a Roman Catholic in France in 1614. On a private visit to England he was imprisoned for four years for being a Catholic; he returned to France, where he was ordained a priest in 1623. Sent to England, he was almost immediately arrested and spent three years in a York gaol. Although exiled, he returned in 1633 and worked among the plague victims in London (1636–1637). Again arrested and exiled, he returned once more in 1643. Eventually captured and convicted at the Old Bailey of being a Roman Catholic priest, he was hanged, drawn and quartered at Tyburn on 1 February 1645. In 1970 he was declared a martyr by the Roman Catholic Church.

Mott, John Rayleigh *(1865–1955)*
American Methodist layman. He was student secretary of the International Committee of the YMCA (1888–1915) and assistant general-secretary of the YMCA in 1901. Mott was one of the organisers of the World Missionary

Conference which met at Edinburgh in 1910, from which dates his involvement in the Ecumenical Movement. He played an important part in the foundation of the World Council of Churches and was elected honorary president (1948). He served on the international scene in various posts of responsibility, and was awarded the 1946 Nobel Peace Prize (shared with Emily Greene Bech) for his work in international Church and missionary movements. His many writings included *The Future Leadership of the Church* (1909) and *The Larger Evangelism* (1944).

Mott, Lucretia *(1793–1880)*
Quaker and pioneer reformer who founded the Women's Rights Movement in the USA. She married a fellow Quaker teacher and became a Quaker minister in 1821. The couple were actively involved in the anti-slavery campaign. With Elizabeth Stanton, in 1848 she held a convention at Seneca Falls, New York, on women's rights and devoted the rest of her life to writing and lecturing for the cause.

Moule, Handley Carr Glyn *(1841–1920)*
A brilliant scholar at Cambridge, where he was elected Fellow in 1865 and Master of Marlborough College (1865–1867). In 1881 he became the first principal of the new evangelical theological college, Ridley Hall, Cambridge, and thereafter a leading light in English evangelicalism. He became Bishop of Durham in 1901. He wrote many books, including *Veni Creator* (1890) and *Christus Consolator* (1915).

Mowinckel, Sigmund *(1884–1965)*
Norwegian biblical scholar who spent his whole teaching career at the University of Oslo (1917–1954). He made important contributions to Old Testament studies, but particularly to the study of the book of Psalms. His *The Psalms in Israel's Worship* (1962) is regarded as one of the major twentieth-century commentaries.

Müller, George *(1805–1898)*
Of German origin, most of his life was spent in England. Converted to Christianity at twenty, he joined the Plymouth Brethren and became a preacher. From 1832 he dedicated himself to caring for orphans on a large scale. The last seventeen years of his life were devoted to a world preaching tour.

N

Nayler, James *(c. 1618–1660)*
Converted by George Fox to the Quaker teaching of the inner light (1651), he became Fox's deputy, preaching widely in Northern England and leading the Society in London (1655). About that time, due to the influence of the Ranters, he was separated from Fox, imprisoned for blasphemy and only reconciled with Fox and the Society of Friends in 1660.

Neale, John Mason *(1818–1866)*
Anglican priest, author and hymnwriter. While at Cambridge he became a High Churchman, founded the Cambridge Camden Society with B. Webb (1839) and was ordained in 1842. Ill-health bedevilled his pastoral work, but he founded the Sisterhood of St Margaret, (1885) a Religious Community to care for the education of girls and tend the sick. He is best known for his hymns, many of which are still in popular use.

Neander, Joachim *(1650–1680)*
German pastor and hymnwriter. Converted to Christianity in 1670, he was attracted by the Pietist Movement and this and his love of nature shine through his many hymns. The popular 'Praise to the Lord, the Almighty' is just one which found its way into English translation.

Neri, St Philip *(1515–1595)*
Of Florentine origins, he went to Rome about 1533, where he tutored, studied and lived privately an austere life. Concerned for the care of the poor, convalescents and pilgrims, he founded a society to assist them (1548). Ordained in 1551, he joined a community of priests at the Church of San Girolamo, where later (1564–1575) he was the rector. So many boys and men came to his conferences that a special large room was built, called the Oratory, from which developed the Institute of the Oratory. (The Institute also encouraged music, hence 'oratorio'.) The Congregation of the Oratory for Priests was approved in 1575 and Philip became the most sought-after figure in Rome, known for his gentleness and gaiety. He had numerous ecstatic experiences and was regarded as a saint long before being officially declared such in 1622.

Neumann, St John Nepomucene *(1811–1860)*
Roman Catholic Bishop of Philadelphia and the first American male to be canonised by the Roman Catholic Church, by Pope Paul VI in 1977. After study in Prague and ordination in New York in 1836, he joined the Redemptorist Congregation of Priests and rose to become their United States

Superior. Devoted to education, he was a leader of the parochial school system in the USA. Appointed Bishop of Philadelphia in 1852, he built many schools, churches and asylums in his diocese and, at the time of his death, was renowned for his holiness, charity and pastoral care.

Neumann, Therese *(1898–1962)*
A German stigmatic of Konnersreuth, Bavaria, on whose body appeared, from 1926, the marks resembling those on Christ's hands, feet and side. She also claimed to have visions of the Passion and the wounds were observed to bleed on most Fridays and during Lent. Examinations by the church authorities were inconclusive but, despite the local Roman Catholic bishop's caution, thousands flocked to visit her every year until her death.

Newman, John Henry *(1801–1890)*
Leader of the Tractarian Movement and later cardinal. Educated at Trinity College, Oxford, after ordination he became vicar at St Mary's, Oxford. A leading figure in the Oxford Movement from its beginning (1833), his sermons at St Mary's (published as *Parochial and Plain Sermons*) had a powerful influence upon its spread. He wrote twenty-four of the *Tracts for the Times* (1833–1841), the most famous and controversial being no. 90. His doubts about the Anglican Church grew, and retiring from public life to a community he had founded at Littlemore (1842), he was finally received into the Roman Catholic Church in 1845. His *Essay on the Development of Christian Doctrine* followed. Newman established the Oratory (see 'Neri, Philip') at Birmingham (1849); while serving as rector to the Catholic University, Dublin (1854–58), his *Idea of a University* was published. He was restored to national prominence with his *Apologia pro Vita Sua* (1864), which plotted his spiritual journey; but it was *A Grammar of Assent* (1870) which presented his mature thought. Newman was made a cardinal in 1879 by Pope Leo XIII.

Nicephorus, St *(c. 758–829)*
Greek Orthodox historian, theologian and Patriarch of Constantinople who wrote and struggled in the cause of the Byzantine iconoclastic (veneration of images) controversy. Following in his father's footsteps, he supported the use of images in his *Apologeticus Minor* and *Apologeticus Major* (1817). His works of history were highly regarded.

Nicholas, St *(d. c. 350)*
One of the most popular saints honoured in both the Eastern and Western Churches; however, outside of tradition, nothing is known for certain of his life, except that he was probably Bishop of Myra (fourth century), in modern Turkey. According to tradition he suffered during the Diocletian persecution

and, as bishop, attended the Council of Nicaea. There was a shrine to him at Myra in the sixth century and Italian merchants seem to have removed the body to Bari in 1087. Other colourful traditions of his coming to the rescue of children *etc.* were added later. Nicholas is the patron saint of several countries, including Russia and Greece, and of sailors and children. His modern popularity centres on his transformation, via the Dutch Protestant settlers in New Amsterdam (New York), into 'Sinter Claes', hence Santa Claus.

Nicholas – Five popes chose this name, the most noteworthy being:

Nicholas I, the Great, St *(d. 867)*
After years in papal service, he was elected pope in 858 and proved one of the most forceful of the early medieval popes. He was justly famed for his courage and firmness in dealing with emperors and kings. His support for the illegally deposed Ignatius, Patriarch of Constantinople, led eventually to the Photian Schism; he upheld the dignity of marriage against King Lothiar of Lorraine and King Charles the Bold of Burgundy. He sent missionaries to Scandinavia and Bulgaria. Nicholas was held in high regard for his personal integrity, care of the poor and pursuit of reform among the clergy.

Nicholas of Cusa *(1401–1464)*
Cardinal, scholar, mathematician, experimental scientist and influential philosopher. As a leading churchman he worked for reconciliation, *e.g.* of the Hussites with the Church, and for reform; his *On Catholic Concordance* (1433) was a complete programme for reform. He began as a supporter of the supremacy of a General Council, but in time reversed his opinion in favour of the supremacy of the papacy over the Council. In his greatest work *On Learned Ignorance* (1440) he used mathematical principles to propound his philosophy. In breadth of learning and intellectual interests he was a forerunner of the Renaissance.

Nicholas of Flue, St *(1417–1487)*
Affectionately recalled in Swiss history as 'Bruder Klaus', after serving with distinction as a soldier (1439), cantonal councillor and judge, he consistently refused the post of Governor. Happily married with ten children, at the age of fifty, with the approval of his family, he became a hermit at Ranft. He was famed for his holiness and wise counsel, which he used to avert a civil war between the Swiss cantons in 1481. He was canonised in 1947.

Nicole, Pierre *(1625–1695)*
Theologian and author whose controversial writings were, in the main, in support of Jansenism, a seventeenth-century movement within the Roman Catholic Church. He taught at Port-Royal and co-operated with A.

Arnauld. He opposed Calvinistic teaching and wrote against Molinos and Quietism. Among his many works, the most famous is the *Essays on Morality* (1671).

Niebuhr, Reinhold *(1892–1971)*
American theologian and writer. Ordained in 1915, he served at the Bethel Evangelical Church, Detroit, until 1928, when he accepted the post of professor of applied Christianity at Union Theological Seminary, New York City, where he remained until retirement. First-hand experience of labour problems led him to advocate socialism, but he broke with the party in the 1930s. Theologically opposed to the liberalism of the 1920s, he was influenced by Barth and Brunner, but his own theology expounded 'a vital prophetic Christianity'. Niebuhr's best-known work was *The Nature and Destiny of Man* (1941–1943).

Niemöller, Martin *(1892–1984)*
The son of a pastor, he served Germany as a submarine commander in the First World War and after ordination (1931) pastored the Lutheran Church in Dahlem, Berlin. He protested against Nazi interference in church affairs and founded the Pastors Emergency League, which developed into the Confessing Church. Arrested by the Gestapo, March 1938, he was imprisoned, eventually, in Dachau Concentration Camp. After the war he helped to rebuild the Evangelical Church and served as head of its Foreign Relations Department (1945–1956). In 1961 Niemöller was elected as one of the presidents of the World Council of Churches.

Nightingale, Florence *(1820–1910)*
Born at Florence, Italy, after which she was named, she was educated largely by her father. From an early age she felt called by God to nursing; she studied, among other things, the approach of the Sisters of Charity of St Vincent de Paul and in 1851 undertook training with the Protestant deaconesses at Kaiserwerth, Germany. She offered to go to the Crimean War in 1854 and coped with conditions appalling in every way. Her devotion and expertise revolutionised nursing standards and became legendary. On her return to England (1856), the Nightingale School and Home for Nurses was founded (1860) in recognition of her services at St Thomas's Hospital, London.

Nilus of Ancyra, St *(d. c. 430)* (*also called Nilus the Ascetic*)
Greek Byzantine abbot and author of ascetical literature. A disciple and supporter of St John Chrysostom, he became a monk and eventually abbot of a monastery near Ancyra. He wrote many tracts on moral and monastic subjects; he refuted Arianism and wrote about a thousand letters of spiritual direction. His writings show him to be a master of Christian spirituality, and

his influence on the direction of Eastern and Western monasticism was considerable.

Norbert, St *(c. 1080–1134)*
Archbishop of Magdeburg and the founder of the Premonstratensians (also called White Canons or Norbertines). Ordained as a subdeacon, he led a worldly life until a sudden conversion led him to accept ordination to the priesthood (1115). He became dedicated to preaching reform of life; renowned for his eloquence, he travelled throughout Europe. In 1119 Pope Calixtus II asked him to found a Religious Congregation at Premontre, France, to be dedicated to preaching. Chosen as Archbishop of Magdeburg (1126), he exerted great influence in church affairs for the rest of his life. He was declared a saint in 1582.

Nouwen, Henri J. M. *(1932–1996)*
One of the most prolific and popular spiritual writers of the late twentieth century, Henri Nouwen saw writing as his primary vocation in life. He was a Dutch Roman Catholic priest who left academic life, as a professor at Harvard Divinity School, to commit himself to practical Christianity, living and working among people with developmental disabilities at L'Arche Daybreak Community, Toronto, Canada. His many bestselling books include *The Inner Voice of Love*, *Bread for the Journey* and *The Return of the Prodigal*. He died, in his native Holland, of a heart attack in September 1996, while on a sabbatical year from the L'Arche Community.

Nowell, Alexander *(c. 1507–1602)*
Anglican priest, scholar and dean of St Paul's Cathedral, London, where his preaching often offended Elizabeth I. He wrote three Catechisms (1520) the *Large*, the *Middle* and the *Small*; the last, in substance, appears in the Book of Common Prayer and is still the official Catechism of the Church of England.

Oberlin, Johann *(1740–1826)*
A former teacher, he became a Lutheran pastor at Walderbach in the Vosges and dedicated his life to raising the living standards of all the people of the five isolated villages, regardless of their religion. He won an international reputation for his advanced thinking in social and educational methods. He transformed the area with schools, adult education, improved farming techniques, *etc.* His name was given to Oberlin House at Potsdam and to Oberlin College, Oberlin, Ohio, USA.

O'Bryan, William *(1778–1868)*

A Methodist minister who founded, in Devon, England, the Bible Christian Church (1815), which split away from Methodism. It spread to the USA (1846) via Canada. O'Bryan left and took up an itinerant preaching career in 1831. The Bible Christians joined the United Methodist Church in 1907.

Ochino, Bernadino *(1487–1564)*

After an illustrious background in the Franciscan Order, *e.g.* twice Vicar-General of the Capuchins and sought after as an eloquent preacher, he became a Lutheran and accepted a pastorate at Augsburg. Invited to England by Cranmer, he enjoyed a clerical appointment at Canterbury. Renowned for his violent anti-Roman views, he wrote *The Usurped Primacy of the Bishop of Rome* (1549). He went to Zurich on Queen Mary's accession, but due to his unsound teaching in *Thirty Dialogues* (1563) he was expelled; he was also driven from Poland when he tried to settle there. He died of the plague while travelling in Moravia.

Oecolampadius, John *(1482–1531)* (*German name: Johannes Huszgen*)

Lecturer, linguist, preacher and humanist. As a Roman Catholic he worked with Erasmus. His admiration of Martin Luther prompted him to join the Reform Movement in 1522. At Basle he established a reputation as a lecturer and preacher and developed a friendship with Zwingli, whose teaching on the Eucharist he defended.

Ogilvie, John *(c. 1579–1615)*

A Scottish Calvinist, son of the Baron of Drum-na-Keith, while studying abroad he became a Roman Catholic (1596). He joined the Jesuits and was ordained at Paris in 1610. Using the disguise of a horse trader he worked secretly among the persecuted Catholics of Edinburgh and Glasgow (1613–1615). Betrayed, he was imprisoned and tortured for several months. Refusing to acknowledge the spiritual supremacy of the king, he was condemned to death and hanged at Glasgow.

Oldham, Joseph Houldsworth *(1874–1969)*

Born in India, educated in Scotland and at Oxford, he was secretary of the YMCA in Lahore (1897–1901). While working for the Student Christian Movement, he was appointed organising secretary of the Edinburgh World Missionary Conference (1910). His dedication to Africa, and his assistance to missions and missionaries as the colonial powers withdrew, is generally considered his greatest achievement. He helped prepare for the launch of the World Council of Churches and held the post of secretary to the Council on the Christian Life (1939–1942) and the Christian Frontier Council (1942–1945).

Olier, Jean-Jacques *(1608–1657)*
Ordained a Roman Catholic priest (1633), he became a popular preacher conducting parish missions (1634–1639). He founded a seminary at Vangirard which transferred to Saint Sulpice, Paris. A community of secular priests he founded there, called the Sulpicians, specialised in the training of priests. St Sulpice became the model for other seminaries through Europe and further afield, *e.g.* Montreal, in 1657.

Oman, John Wood *(1860–1939)*
Presbyterian theologian, lecturer and principal of Westminster College, Cambridge (1907–1925). His teaching on the uniqueness and independence of the religious consciousness was expressed in his book *The Natural and the Supernatural* (1931).

Orchard, William Edwin *(1877–1955)*
Presbyterian minister who attracted large congregations to King's Weigh House Congregational Church, London. He became nationally known for his efforts to draw Protestants and Roman Catholics together. He led prolonged ecumenical negotiations with the Church of England which collapsed. Orchard became a Roman Catholic in 1932 and was ordained a priest in 1935. His many writings included the popular *The Temple* (1913).

Origen *(c. 185–c. 254) (Latin name: Origenes Adamantius)*
On the martyrdom of his father, Leonidas, at Alexandria (202) Origen was appointed head of the catechetical school there. He led an austere, ascetic life, travelled and studied pagan philosophy. From *c.* 218 to 230 he devoted himself to writing. On a visit (230) to Palestine he was ordained priest, but his own Alexandrian bishop declared it irregular and Origen settled at Caesarea (231), where he established a famous school. In the persecution of Decius (250) he was severely tortured, from which he never really recovered. Many of Origen's writings are lost. He was principally a biblical scholar, his *Hexapla* being a synopsis of several versions of the Old Testament. His greatest theological work was *On First Principles* (before 231), which reveals why he is regarded as one of the most influential theologians and biblical scholars of the early Church.

Osmund St *(d. 1099)*
Bishop of Salisbury (the old Sarum) and Chancellor of England who followed William I to England. He helped compile the Doomsday Book and is credited with the introduction of the Sarum Rite.

Oswald St *(c. 605–642)*
King of Northumbria who appealed to Iona for monks to establish Christianity; St Aidan responded and received Oswald's support. He was killed in

battle with King Penda of Mercia and ever afterwards was honoured as a martyr.

Oswald, St *(d. 992)*
Archbishop of York who established many monastic houses, particularly at Ramsey in Cambridgeshire. Also famed for his energetic reform of abuses and the education of the clergy.

Overbeck, Johann Friedrick *(1789–1869)*
German Romantic painter and leader of the Lucas Brotherhood, or the Nazarenes, who were devoted to depicting, in precise outlines and clear bright colours, Christian religious subjects, his major work being the 'Rose Miracle of St Francis' (1829) at Assisi.

Owen, John *(1616–1683)*
Puritan minister, writer and preacher. Originally a Calvinist, he became an independent, holding pastoral posts at Fordham and Coggeshall, Essex; his outstanding preaching before Parliament led to his appointment as Dean (1651) and vice-chancellor of Christ Church, Oxford. After the Restoration he devoted himself to preaching and voluminous controversialist writing.

Ozanam, Antoine Frédéric *(1813–1853)*
Brilliant French scholar in law and literature; in his Catholicism he was influenced by Montalembert, Lacordaire and other liberal thinkers. His concern for social conditions led to the foundation of the Society of St Vincent de Paul (SVP), an association of lay people devoted to the service of the poor, and *Ère Nouvelle*, the journal of the French Catholic Social Movement.

P

Pachomius, St *(c. 290–346)*
Of Egyptian origins, after serving in the Emperor Constantine's North African army he became a Christian (*c.* 314) and embraced a hermit's life. About 320 he founded the first communal settlement, with a Rule of Life, for monks. His Rule, the first of its kind, influenced later more famous Rules, *e.g.* that of St Benedict. He was so popular an abbot that at his death there were eleven monasteries (nine male and two female) with a total of seven thousand monks.

Palestrina, Giovanni Pierbuigi da *(c. 1525–1594)*
Originating from Palestrina (Italy), he moved to Rome as a boy and lived and worked there, filling a variety of musical appointments, rising eventually to Composer of the Papal Chapel (1570) and choirmaster of St Peter's Basilica (1571). His motets and masses filled a vacuum in church music and he was influenced by and wrote music for St Philip Neri and his Oratory. Palestrina's deeply religious polyphony, welcomed by the Roman Catholic Church, was enormously influential in the subsequent development of church music.

Paley, William *(1743–1805)*
Anglican priest, theologian and writer, educated at Christ's College, Cambridge, where he became a Fellow in 1766. His most famous work, *View of Evidences of Christianity* (1794), became required reading for entrance to Cambridge, and his *Natural Theology* (1802) developed his theology of the teleological argument for the existence of God.

Palladius *(c. 365–425)*
After a period with monks in Egypt, under the direction of Evagerius Ponticus, he became Bishop of Helenopolis and suffered exile for his faith. He is remembered for his famous Lausiac History, entitled *Friends of God* (c. 419), being the first history of early monasticism.

Papias *(c. 60–130)*
Bishop of Hierapolis of whom nothing is known beyond the remarks of Irenaeus, the second-century Bishop of Lyons, that Papias was a disciple of the apostle John and a companion of St Polycarp. His work *Expositions of the Oracles of the Lord*, which now exists only in quotations in other writings, authenticates and casts light upon the Gospels of Matthew and Mark.

Parker, Matthew *(1504–1575)*
Archbishop of Canterbury, of scholarly inclination, chosen (1559) by Queen Elizabeth I from relative obscurity. A moderate reformer, he strove to maintain the settlement of 1559, guiding the Church of England to a distinct identity apart from Roman Catholicism and Protestantism. Involved in the formulation of the Thirty-Nine Articles and the *Bishops' Bible*, he also wrote several scholarly works in English Church history.

Parsons (or Persons) Robert *(1546–1610)*
After resigning a Fellowship at Balliol College, Oxford (1568–1574), he became a Jesuit priest in Rome and returned secretly (1580) to minister to English Catholics. Forced to return to the Continent he directed the Jesuit Mission to England and established seminaries for English priests in Spain, at Valladolid and Madrid. He helped with the running of the English College, Rome (1597–1610), where he died.

Pascal, Blaise *(1623–1662)*
French mathematician, inventor, religious philosopher and theologian. Mathematically gifted as a child, Pascal was later responsible for the invention of the barometer and the first digital calculator (1644), the syringe and the hydraulic press (1647–1654). He experienced what he called a 'first conversion' when he 'discovered' the Jansenist teaching at Port-Royal (1646), and underwent his 'definitive' conversion in 1654, which led to regular visits to the Port-Royal Community, his famous *Les Provinciales* (1654) in defence of Jansenism and his posthumously published *Pensées*.

Paschasius Radbertus, St *(c. 790–865)*
French Benedictine abbot of Corbie, near Amiens, who is best known for his work *De Corpore et Sanguine Christi* (831), which became the dominant interpretation of the doctrine of the Eucharist for hundreds of years. He was also the author of commentaries on the book of Lamentations and Matthew's Gospel.

Patmore, Coventry (Kersey Dighton) *(1823–1896)*
Roman Catholic poet and essayist who began writing poetry at an early age and was employed at the British Museum. His best-remembered poetry, containing a mystical view of divine love and married love, is in *The Unknown Eros and Other Odes* (1877). He translated *St Bernard on the Love of God* and wrote a long novel in five parts, *The Angel in the House* (1854–1863).

Paton, John Gibson *(1824–1907)*
Presbyterian missionary to the New Hebrides who, after ten missionary years in Glasgow, Scotland, lived an austere and dangerous life on the island of Tanna. There his wife and child died. From 1866 to 1881 he was centred on Aniwa before moving to Melbourne.

Paton, William *(1886–1943)*
Presbyterian minister and writer. In 1911 he became secretary to the Student Christian Movement; from 1922 to 1927 he was general secretary of the National Christian Council of India, Burma and Ceylon. The author of several works on mission, he also edited the *International Review of Missions*.

Patrick, St *(c. 389–c. 461)*
The life of the apostle and patron saint of Ireland is shrouded in myth and legend. He is known from two short works, his *Confessio* and *Epistola*. Apparently, at sixteen he was captured from Roman Britain by Irish pirates and spent six years as a shepherd in Ireland. After escaping back to Britain he studied for the priesthood (some say in Gaul), probably being ordained *c.* 417. He returned to Ireland as a bishop *c.* 432 and spent the rest of his life travelling the length and breadth of the country, meeting a fierce

opposition, but successfully converting the Irish. He probably set up his episcopal See at Armagh. Later traditions added embellishments of uncertain authenticity.

Patrick, Simon *(1625–1707)*
Originally a Presbyterian minister, he was ordained for the Anglican ministry in 1654, and after a succession of pastoral posts became a bishop, first of Chichester, then of Ely. A sincere Latitudinarian, he helped to found the Society for Promoting Christian Knowledge and the Society for the Propagation of the Gospel. He wrote many treatises and the notable *The Parable of the Pilgrim* (1664).

Patteson, John Coleridge *(1827–1871)*
Missionary Bishop of Melanesia. Educated at Eton and Balliol College, Oxford, in 1855 he set out to work in the South Seas, where he was very successful, also founding a college for boys on Norfolk Island. Consecrated bishop in 1861, his murder by the natives of Nukapu caused great interest and concern in Great Britain.

Paul – Six popes chose this name, the most noteworthy being:

Paul VI *(1897–1978)*
Baptised Giovanni Battista Montini and ordained in 1920, he entered the Vatican diplomatic service and, over a period of thirty years, rose through various posts of responsibility. He was appointed Archbishop of Milan in 1954 and cardinal by Pope John XXIII four years later. He succeeded John XXIII in 1963, guided the Second Vatican Council through its remaining sessions and then the task of carrying out its reforming decisions. His encyclicals appeared conservative, especially *Humanae Vitae* (1968), on birth control, and *Matrimonia Mixta* (1970), on mixed marriages. He was the first pope to travel abroad; for example he met Athenagoras, the Greek Patriarch, on a pilgrimage to the Holy Land (1964) and travelled to the United States (1965) to plead for peace in an address to the United Nations General Assembly.

Paul of the Cross, St *(1694–1775)*
Originally Paolo Francesco Danei, he led an austere life of prayer and, in 1720, he began to have visions which inspired him to found a Religious Order, or Congregation, devoted to the suffering of Christ on the cross, known as the Passionists. Faced with great difficulties, he worked as a missionary and was famed as a preacher and spiritual director. At his death he had founded twelve monasteries in Italy, but the Passionist Order soon spread around the world. He was canonised in 1867.

Paulinus – There are four saints with the name Paulinus; that of most interest to English readers is:

Paulinus, St *(c. 584–644)*
Missionary of Northumbria. Sent to England in 601 to support and help the missionary work of St Augustine of Canterbury, he accompanied Ethelburga of Kent to York when she married Edwin of Northumbria in 625. A cathedral was begun at York and his missionary work was successful, but on the defeat of Edwin by Cadwallon he returned to Kent and occupied the See of Rochester.

Peake, Arthur Samuel *(1865–1929)*
Methodist lay biblical scholar, first to hold the Rylands Chair of Biblical Criticism and Exegesis at Manchester University (1904). He was the author of several biblical works, including *The Bible, Its Origin, Its Significance and Its Abiding Worth* (1913), but is best remembered for his editorship of the *Commentary* (1919) that bears his name.

Peckham, John *(c. 1225–1292)*
Theologian, poet and Archbishop of Canterbury. He joined the Franciscan Order at Oxford (*c.* 1250), where he studied and later taught. From 1269 to 1271 he occupied the Franciscan chair of theology at Paris. After a period in Rome he was elected to Canterbury and immediately promoted Church reform. Theologically he supported the Franciscan tradition, especially against the Dominicans; his works include Bible commentaries and his poetic work, *Philomena*.

Péguy, Charles *(1873–1914)*
French poet, philosopher and patriot. He gave up the study of philosophy to manage a bookshop in Paris which became an intellectual centre supporting Christian Socialism: this was promoted by his journal *Cahiers de la Quinzaine*. An ardent Roman Catholic and a socialist, his works, including two on Joan of Arc (1897 and 1910), express this. His last massive poetic work, *Eve* (1913), reflects meditatively on the human condition. While serving in the French army, he died at the Battle of Marne, 1914.

Pennington (or Penington), Isaac *(1616–1679)*
Originally a Puritan, educated at Cambridge, he heard George Fox speak and joined the Society of Friends (1657). For his Quaker beliefs he was imprisoned and lost his property. He wrote many books which, with his example, promoted the growth of the Society.

Penn, William *(1644–1718)*
Son of Admiral Sir William Penn, he was educated at Oxford, where he refused to conform to Anglicanism. In 1665 he joined the Society of Friends; for writing *The Sandy Foundation Shaken* (1668) he was imprisoned in the Tower of London, where he wrote the classic *No Cross, No Crown* (1669). Acquitted in a famous court case, he obtained authorisation (1682), founded the 'Free Society of Traders of Pennsylvania' and sailed for America, where the American Commonwealth of Pennsylvania was founded. The rest of his life was dedicated to developing this colony and defending Quaker principles and practices. Further works included *The Fruits of Solitude* (1692) and *Primitive Christianity* (1696).

Perkins, William *(1558–1602)*
English Puritan theologian, Fellow of Christ's College, Cambridge (1584–1594), famed for his powerful anti-Romanist preaching and systematic exposition of Puritan theology. His works, highly regarded in the seventeenth century, included his *Reformed Catholike* (1597).

Peter Chrysologus, St *(c. 400–c. 450)*
Archbishop of Ravenna, Italy, who, supported by the Empress Galla Placida, put through a vast building programme. A champion of orthodoxy, which earned him the title of 'Doctor of the Church' in 1729, he was renowned for his preaching (hence the Greek name 'Chrysologus', 'Golden-worded').

Peter Claver, St *(1581–1654)*
A Jesuit missionary to South America, he called himself 'the slave of the negroes', dedicating thirty-eight years of his life to the total service of the slaves shipped from West Africa to Cartagena, South America's principal slave market. Despite fierce official opposition, Peter visited, defended, nursed and taught the negro slaves. It is estimated that he instructed and baptised over three hundred thousand of them. He was declared a saint in 1888.

Peter Lombard *(c. 1100–1160)*
Theologian and Bishop of Paris whose fame rests chiefly upon the authorship of *Sententiarum libri quatuor* (the *Sentences*, in four volumes), which is a clear systematic presentation of theology, especially on the sacraments. It became the standard theological textbook for hundreds of years and won him the title 'Master of the Sentences'.

Peter the Hermit *(1050–1115)* (*also Peter the Little*)
Influential preacher and monastic founder, who, after Pope Urban II called for a crusade to liberate the Holy Places (1095), toured Europe preaching the crusade. Eventually he entered Jerusalem with a victorious army and later

returned to Europe (1100) as prior of the monastery at Neumroutier, which he had founded.

Peter of Verona, St *(1205–1252)* (*also known as Peter Martyr*)
Son of parents who were members of the Cathari sect, he studied at Bologna and joined the Dominican Order. He gained a great reputation as a preacher, founded several religious centres to combat heresy and was appointed Inquisitor for Northern Italy by Pope Gregory IX (1251). He successfully preached among the Cathari, although some were forced into exile. Returning to Milan from a preaching tour, he was killed, with a companion, by two Cathari assassins.

Peter Martyr *(1500–1562)* (*also Pietro Martire Vermigli*)
Named after Peter of Verona, he was born in Florence and joined the Augustinian Order. A Bible scholar, he was much in sympathy with the Reformers and fled to Zurich, Basel and Strasbourg, where he was appointed professor of theology. Invited to England, he was made Regius professor of theology at Oxford (1548) and was involved in the Book of Common Prayer of 1552. After a short imprisonment under Queen Mary he was allowed to return to his former post at Strasbourg (1554). He later removed to Zurich because of his views on the Eucharist.

Peter Nolasco, St *(c. 1189–1258)*
The precise details of his life are uncertain. Of a French family, at fifteen his father died and he used his inherited fortune to ransom Christian prisoners from the Moors. Between 1218 and 1234 he founded the Order of Our Lady of Ransom (the Mercedarians), with St Raymond of Penafort, to ransom Christians from the Saracens. (The Order was later dedicated to hospital work.)

Peter of Alcantara, St *(1499–1562)* (*original name: Pedro Garavito*)
Ordained for the Order of Observantist Franciscans (1524), he emphasised the penitential aspects of St Francis of Assisi's teaching and became superior of several houses and Provincial in Spain. His ideals of austerity were popular and *c.* 1557 he founded his own Order, the Alcantarines, or Barefooted Friars Minor. Admired by St Teresa of Avila, who he helped in her reform work, he was much in demand as a spiritual director. His friars spread to Italy, Germany and France.

Petrarch, Francesco *(1304–1374)*
Italian humanist and poet of international standing. His most famous poetry, which influenced all subsequent European Romantic poetry and is collected in the *Canzoniere*, was addressed to an idealised beloved, Laura. He travelled widely, copying classical manuscripts, but he also spent long periods in solitude. His religious poetry meditates upon the transitory nature of life.

Petri, Laurentius *(1499–1573)*
Swedish churchman and the first Protestant Archbishop of Uppsala. He was responsible for the Swedish Bible of 1541. His *Kyrkoordning* ('Church Order') of thirty years later defined the church–state relations which led to the independence of the Swedish Church.

Petri, Olaus *(1493–1552)*
Swedish churchman, and brother of the above, who played an important role in the reformation of the Swedish Church. He rose to prominence in 1531, as chancellor to the king, but fell from favour by his later opposition. His preaching and his literature, including a Swedish New Testament, the Swedish liturgy, a hymnbook, *etc*, made him the leading exponent of reform in Sweden.

Philaret, Drozdov *(1782–1867)*
Russian Orthodox monk, theologian and Metropolitan of Moscow. Well known for his scholarship and his preaching, he was a skilled administrator and was considered an exemplary bishop. His best-known work, the *Christian Catechism of the Orthodox Catholic Eastern Greco–Russian Church* (1823), exerted a great influence upon nineteenth-century Russian theology.

Phillpotts, Henry *(1778–1869)*
Anglican Bishop of Exeter and a conservative high churchman who supported the Oxford Movement, he had a special interest in the liturgy and the monastic life. His refusal to institute George C. Gorham to the living of Bampford Speke gave rise to one of the most famous law-suits of the nineteenth century.

Photius *(c. 820–891)*
Elected Patriarch of Constantinople while still a layman and professor of philosophy (858), he defended his Church against the papacy. He is remembered for objecting to the insertion of the *Filioque* clause in the creed and for the schism which grew out of the break with Rome.

Pilkington, James *(c. 1520–1576)*
The first Protestant occupant of the See of Durham (1560) and a prominent leader of the Protestant party in the Church of England. He contributed to the revision of the Book of Common Prayer and, as Regius professor of divinity at Cambridge, promoted Protestant theology in and through the University.

Pire, Dominique *(1910–1969)*
Belgian Dominican priest and educator who won the Nobel Peace Prize (1958) for his energetic aid to displaced persons in Europe after World War II. In 1949 he founded the 'Aide aux Personnes Déplacée' and (1950–1954)

four 'homes of welcome' in Belgium, as well as seven European 'villages' to help refugees. Later he worked for peace with the University of Peace, Huy, and his 'Islands of Peace' project in India.

Pius – There were twelve popes of this name. Noteworthy are:

Pius II *(1405–1464)*
Areneas Sylvius Piccolomini was elected pope in 1458, having established a reputation as a humanist, scholar, poet and astute politican. After the fall of Constantinople in 1453 he worked for a Crusade against the Turks' threat to Europe; however he failed to unite the European princes.

Pius V, St *(1504–1572)*
An Italian Dominican, Antonio Ghislieri was an ascetic reformer who, from the post of Inquisitor (1551) and Grand Inquisitor seven years later, then Bishop of Nepi and Sutri (1556), rose to cardinal (1557). Elected pope in 1566, he inaugurated one of the most austere periods in the Roman Catholic Church, eliminating Protestantism from Italy and putting the decrees of the Council of Trent into effect.

Pius IX *(1792–1878)*
Originally Giovanni Maria Mastai-Ferretti, he served as Bishop of Spoleto (1827) and Bishop of Imola (1832) before being chosen pope in 1846. His was the longest pontificate in history and marked a transition from liberalism to conservatism. His pontificate began with liberal reforms in the Papal States, but when these were lost in 1870, Pio Nono remained a virtual prisoner in the Vatican and became more conservative. He restored the Catholic hierarchy to England and Wales (1850), defined the dogma of the Immaculate Conception (1854) and issued the *Syllabus of Errors* (1864) and *Quanta Cura* (1864), which reaffirmed traditional Catholic beliefs. He summoned the First Vatican Council (1869–1870) that defined papal infallibility. He strengthened the spiritual authority of the papacy as its temporary power disappeared.

Pius X, St *(1835–1914)*
Born Giuseppe Melchiorre Sarto, of a poor Italian family, he rose through pastoral posts to Cardinal Patriarch of Venice (1893). Elected pope in 1903, he set his heart upon a spiritually orientated pontificate, but was compelled to issue two encyclicals against the French Government over its confiscation of church property. Viewing Modernism as an insidious new heresy, he issued the decree *Lamentabili* (1907) and the encyclical *Pascendi Gregis* (1907). He is best remembered for his pastoral concern, personal sanctity and as 'the Pope of frequent Communion', which he promoted and encouraged. Venerated as a saint in his own lifetime, he was canonised in 1954.

Pius XI *(1857–1939)*
Originally Ambrogio Damiano Archille Ratti, of scholarly background and interests, he taught, becoming the Prefect of the Vatican Library in 1912. Nuncio to Poland (1919), he became a cardinal and Archbishop of Milan (1921) and was elected to the papacy in 1922. He concluded the Lateran Treaty with Mussolini and issued several influential encyclicals, *viz. Divini Illius Magistri* (1929), on education, *Casti Connubii* (1930), on the dignity of marriage, and *Quadragesimo Anno* (1931), on social justice. He encouraged the Apostolate of the Laity through the Catholic Action Movement. While he encouraged missionary work he did not encourage the Ecumenical Movement.

Pius XII *(1876–1958)*
After ordination (1899) Eugenio Pacelli entered the Vatican Secretariat of State, and after serving in Bavaria (1917) and Berlin (1925) he was created a cardinal and Secretary of State to the Vatican (1929). Elected pope ten years later, he tried to prevent the Second World War with his *Five Peace Points*, but, having failed, he worked in neutrality for refugees and prisoners. A prolific writer, some encyclicals were very influential, *e.g. Mystici Corporis Christi* (1943), on the Church as the Mystical Body of Christ, *Divino Affante Spiritu* (1943), an encouragement and guide to the study of Scripture and *Mediator Dei* (1947), which encouraged reform of the liturgy. He reformed several liturgical practices, especially Holy Week. With the decree *Munificentissimus Deus* (1950) he defined the teaching on the Assumption of the Virgin Mary. In the aftermath of the war he guided his Church through reconstruction.

Plunket, St Oliver *(1629–1681)*
Of a noble Irish family, he was educated and ordained in Rome, where he later lectured in theology. Appointed Roman Catholic Archbishop of Armagh and primate of all Ireland (1668), he returned to a disorganised and dispirited Irish Church. In the face of constant hardship he raised the standards of order, education and discipline. In 1673, under renewed persecution, he continued his pastoral work in secrecy. Betrayed (1679), there followed imprisonment, protracted farcical legal proceedings and his execution for treason at Tyburn, London. He was canonised as a martyr in 1975.

Pole, Reginald *(1500–1558)*
English cardinal and Archbishop of Canterbury who was of royal descent through both parents, in recognition of which Henry VIII paid for his education at Oxford and Padua. He, however, broke with Henry over his anti-papal policies (his two brothers and mother, Margaret, were subsequently executed by Henry for treason without evidence). Trained in humanism, he was the leader of those Catholic clerics who sought reform and reconciliation

with Protestantism. A powerful figure in Mary Tudor's Government, he pursued a reforming policy in the Church, but Pope Julius II cancelled his Legatine authority and accused him of unsound doctrine. He died, demoralised, twelve hours after Queen Mary.

Polycarp, St *(probably c. 69–c. 155)*
Greek bishop of Smyrna (modern Turkey) and a leading Christian figure in second-century Roman Asia. His importance lies in his intermediary position between the times of the apostles (St Irenaeus says he knew St John) and the great Christian writers of the end of the second century, as well as for his energetic defence of orthodoxy against the Marcian heresy, the Valentians and the Gnostics. His important *Letter to the Philippians* is a testimony to the New Testament texts from which he quotes. After a visit to Rome at the age of eighty-six, he was arrested and, refusing to sacrifice to the gods, was burnt to death.

Porres, St Martin de *(1579–1639)*
Dominican lay brother of Lima, Peru, who served in his monastic community as barber, infirmarian, *etc*, and who became famous throughout the city for his kindness, particularly his care of the sick and African slaves. He founded an orphanage and a foundling hospital. Canonised in 1962, he is the Peruvian national patron of social justice.

Prokopovich, Feofan *(1681–1736)*
Orthodox theologian and Archbishop of Novgorod. After an Orthodox education he became a Roman Catholic and studied in Rome. Returning to Kiev (1701), he reverted to his Orthodox faith, becoming a monk and later an abbot. In 1716 he became an adviser to the Tsar and was eventually responsible for the legislative reform of the Russian Church. As a theologian he is considered the father of Russian systematic theology, and his principal work is an exposition of the entire corpus of doctrinal theology.

Prosper of Aquitaine, St *(c. 390–c. 463)*
Monk and theologian of Marseilles, known for his defence of orthodoxy against the Semi-Pelagian heresy and for his friendship and support of Augustine of Hippo. After Augustine's death (430) he went to Rome and won support for Augustine's teaching on grace and predestination; he also wrote in his defence, particularly *The Book of the Sentences of St Augustine*. Towards the end of his life he was secretary to Pope Leo the Great.

Proud, Joseph *(1745–1826)*
Baptist churchman and exponent of Swedenborgian religious principles and co-founder of the New Jerusalem Church, centred upon Manchester and Lancashire. He wrote many hymns for use in the new church.

Provoost, Samuel *(1742–1815)*
The Anglican rector of Trinity Church, New York, who won the title 'patriot rector' for his loyalty to the American Revolution and overcame American diffidence towards the Anglican episcopacy. A chaplain to Congress (1785) and the United States Senate (1789), he was elected the first Episcopal Bishop of New York in 1786.

Prynne, William *(1600–1669)*
An English lawyer and member of Parliament of unbending Puritan beliefs whose denunciation of the theatre (interpreted as an attack upon both Charles I and his theatrically inclined wife) and of Archbishop Laud led to persecution by the Government, imprisonment and disfigurement. A prolific writer and controversialist, he wrote against the Independents, the papists and the Quakers.

Pseudo-Dionysius the Areopagite *(c. 500)*
Historical research has failed to reveal the identity of this writer who assumed the pseudonym of one of Paul's converts (Acts 17:34). He was probably a Syrian monk who wrote a series of treatises and letters for the purpose of uniting Neoplatonic philosophy with Christian theology and mystical experience. His influence has pervaded almost all theological thought from the Venerable Bede to the sixteenth-century Spanish mystics.

Pugin, Augustus Welby Northmore *(1812–1852)*
An architect and author who was the principal leader and inspirer of the English Roman Catholic Gothic revival. He was responsible for many new churches, including St Chad's Cathedral, Birmingham, and St George's Cathedral, Southwark. He also wrote extensively on church architecture, including *Contrasts* (1836) and *An Apology for the Revival of Christian Architecture in England* (1843).

Purcell, Henry *(1659–1695)*
English composer and organist at Westminster Abbey (from 1679) and the Chapel Royal (1682). Regarded as the most important English composer of his time he is famous for both vocal and instrumental music. Besides secular music, he wrote many anthems for worship, his most famous sacred music being settings for the *Benedicite, Magnificat* and *Nunc Dimittis* and for his *Te Deum* and *Jubilate in D* (1694).

Pusey, Edward Bouverie *(1800–1882)*
Anglican theologian and leader of the Oxford Movement. Fellow of Oriel College, Oxford (1823), he studied in Germany and in 1828 was appointed Regius professor of Hebrew at Oxford. Associated with the Tractarian Movement from 1833, he wrote important Tracts on baptism and the

Eucharist; he assumed leadership of the movement when Newman withdrew. A fine preacher, he was suspended for two years as a result of his teaching on the Real Presence. In 1845 he helped to found in London the first Anglican Sisterhood. Known for his sincerity and humility, he built St Saviour's Church, Leeds, at his own expense and cared for the sick in the cholera epidemic of 1866. His sermons were as influential as his many writings, which included *The Doctrine of the Real Presence* (1855) and *Daniel, the Prophet* (1864).

Q

Quarles, Francis *(1592–1644)*
Anglican religious poet who is famous for his popular books *Emblemes* (1635) and *Hieroglyphikes* (1638). (Emblem books were popular devotional aids, highly regarded in seventeenth-century England.) Earlier he had produced many biblical paraphrases, such as *Job Militant* (1624).

Quesnel, Pasquier *(1634–1719)*
French theologian and writer who led the Jansenists and was the centre of continuing controversy in seventeenth-century France. His greatest work, *Nouveau Testament en francais avec des reflexions morales* (1692), was condemned by Pope Clement XI's bull *Unigenitus* (1708) and Quesnel spent the last years of his life defending his teaching.

R

Rabanus Maurus *(c. 780–856)*
Benedictine abbot of Fulda and Archbishop of Mainz, recognised as one of the most influential churchmen and theologians of his age. He was accorded the title of 'Teacher of Germany' for his development of German language and literature. Elected abbot of Fulda (822), he developed the monastery into a renowned centre of learning and culture and a base for extensive missionary work throughout Germany. As Archbishop of Mainz he convened synods to refute doctrinal error. His many works include several commentaries on books of the Bible and a vast twenty-two volume encyclopaedia of knowledge entitled *On the Nature of Things*, also known as *On the Universe* (842–847).

Rabaut, Paul *(1718–1794)*
Protestant minister of the French Reformed Church who assumed leadership of the Huguenots on the death of Antoine Court. His patient restraint helped to achieve the Edict of Toleration of 1787.

Rad, Gerhard von *(1901–1971)*
German Old Testament scholar, educated at Tübingen University, who later lectured at Jena, Göttingen and, from 1949 to 1966, at Heidelberg. He specialised in the study of Old Testament theology and of the first six books of the Bible, applying to them the principles of literary analysis and form criticism.

Raikes, Robert *(1736–1811)*
English journalist, philanthropist and founder of Sunday schools. From a concern for prison reform, Raikes turned his attention to the unsupervised children on a Sunday of his native Gloucester, and in 1780 he opened a Sunday school for them. In spite of opposition he persevered and reported success in 1783 in his paper, the *Gloucester Journal*. There followed the Sunday School Society in 1785.

Rancé, Armand-Jean le Bouthillier de *(1626–1700)*
Abbot of La Trappe, France, whose early life as a priest was very worldly; after a sudden conversion, in 1657, he entered the Cistercian noviate at Perseigne and became regular abbot of La Trappe (which he had held as a benefice); he then devoted himself to the reform of the Cistercian Order. His book *Treatise on the Holiness and Duties of the Monastic Life* (1683), in which he forbade study for monks, led to controversy with other Religious Orders.

Raphael *(1483–1520)*
Painter and architect, one of the great masters of the Italian High Renaissance style. After an apprenticeship and collaboration with Perugino in Perugia (*c.* 1495–1504) he painted the *Crucifixion* (1502) and *Espousals of the Virgin* (1504). Moving to Siena and Florence he was influenced by Leonardo da Vinci and Michelangelo; there followed the first of his famed series of Madonnas. Pope Julius II summoned him to Rome, where he executed many biblical scenes, including *St Peter Released from Prison* and the celebrated *Sistine Madonna* (*c.* 1512). In 1514 he was appointed principal architect in the reconstruction of St Peter's Basilica.

Rapp, George *(1757–1847)*
German Lutheran lay preacher who emigrated to the USA in 1803 and, with about six hundred disciples, founded communities, in particular Harmony, Pennsylvania. Known as Rappites (or Harmonists), they founded Economy, Pennsylvania, in 1825; however, torn apart by internal disputes, the colony did not survive long after Rapp's death.

Rauschenbusch, Walter *(1861–1918)*
Minister, theologian and leader of the United States Social Gospel movement. Ordained (1886) for the Second German Baptist Church, New York, he became acutely aware of social problems and formed, with Williams and Schmidt, the Brotherhood of the Kingdom and launched the periodical, *For the Right*. As professor of Church history at Rochester Theological Seminary he published *Christianity and the Social Crisis* (1907); his other writings include *Christianizing the Social Order* (1912) and *A Theology for the Social Gospel* (1917).

Raymond of Penafort, St *(c. 1185–1275)*
Spanish Dominican friar and canon lawyer who studied and taught Church law at Barcelona. He joined the Dominican Order in 1222 and about that time wrote his celebrated *Summa de casibus poenitentiae*. Pope Gregory IX commissioned him to codify the papal statutes; the resulting *Decretals*, published in 1234, remained operative for nearly seven hundred years. Appointed General of the Dominican Order, he revised the constitutions. After resigning his post he devoted his time to promoting missionary work among Jews and Moors.

Reinkens, Josef Hubert *(1821–1896)*
German historical scholar and bishop. At the First Vatican Council (1869–1870) he opposed the definition of papal infallibility and, following his excommunication, was elected first bishop of the Old Catholic Church (1873). The rest of his life was dedicated to defending and promoting the Old Catholic cause.

Renan, Joseph Ernest *(1823–1892)*
French historian, philosopher and theologian. After a crisis of faith he left the seminary of Saint Sulpice and the Roman Catholic Church (1845). He wrote on the history of religious origins and after a visit to the Holy Land he wrote his famous *Vie de Jesus* (1863) which caused a sensation throughout Europe.

Revels, Hiram *(1822–1901)*
American minister of the African Methodist Episcopal Church who worked among Negroes of the Midwest, Kentucky and Tennessee. In the post-Civil War period he became the first black member of the United States Senate (1870–1871).

Ricci, Matteo *(1552–1610)*
Italian Jesuit missionary to China. After an early education in classics and law he joined the Society of Jesus (1571) and showed a special interest in the sciences. Sent first to Goa (1578) and then to Macao (1582), he succeeded in

gaining entrance to the interior of China, normally closed to outsiders, because he adopted the Chinese language and culture. His knowledge of the sciences won him entrance to the imperial city and he stayed in Peking, making many converts until his death. His skilful adaptation of Christianity to the Chinese way of life led to protracted controversy and final disapproval in 1704 and 1715.

Richard of Chichester, St *(c. 1197–1253) (also known as Richard of Wych)*
After study at Oxford he became chancellor there (*c.* 1235) and then chancellor to his friend Edmund of Abingdon, at Canterbury. When Edmund died, Richard was ordained priest and elected Bishop of Chichester (1244). After initial opposition from King Henry III he took possession of his See, proved to be a model bishop and won renown for his sanctity of life. He was canonised in 1262.

Richard of St Victor *(d. 1173)*
Theologian of Scottish origins who went to study at the Abbey of St Victor, Paris, and stayed to become eventually the prior (1162). Although he wrote the important treatise *De Trinitate* in six volumes, as well as many books of scriptural exegesis, he is best remembered for his influential works on Christian mysticism.

Richelieu, Armand Jean du Plessis *(1585–1642)*
French cardinal and politician, he is the prime example of the use of power for ecclesiastical and secular ends. Consecrated Bishop of Lucan, he became adviser to Maria de Medici, the mother of Louis XIII, and Secretary of State in 1616. Exiled for a while, he wrote his famous catechism, *Instruction du Chrétien* (1619). Restored to power, he became cardinal (1622), president of the Council of Ministers and actual ruler of France (1624). His major goals were the establishment of royal absolutism in France and the destruction of Hapsburg–Spanish power in Europe. He fought the Protestant Huguenots to achieve the first and co-operated with the Protestant German princes to achieve the latter.

Ridley, Nicholas *(c. 1503–1555)*
Educated at Cambridge, the Sorbonne and Louvain, he was ordained a priest about 1524 and ten years later showed sympathies with Protestant teachings. Appointed chaplain to Cranmer, Archbishop of Canterbury, he rose rapidly in the Church until he was appointed Bishop of Rochester (1547), then of London (1550). He helped with the compilation of the Book of Common Prayer (1549) and the establishment of Protestantism at Cambridge University. He supported the claim of the Protestant Lady Jane Grey to the throne and was arrested upon the accession of Mary Tudor. He was excommunicated and burnt at the stake at Oxford on 16 October 1555.

Ripalda, Juan Martinez de *(1594–1648)*

One of the most famous theologians of his time, a Spanish Jesuit, he lectured in theology at Salamanca and in moral theology at Madrid. His most important works were *De Ente Supernaturali* (1634–1648) and *Brevis Expositio Magistri Sententiarum* (1635).

Ritschl, Albrecht *(1822–1889)*

Lutheran theologian who lectured at the University of Bonn (1846–1864) and at Göttingen (1864–1889). His influential work *Die Christliche Lehre von der Rechtfertigung* (1870–1874), which presents most of his thinking, resulted in the 'Ritschlian School' of theologians, which stressed the role of 'community' in New Testament theology and ethics.

Robinson, Henry Wheeler *(1872–1945)*

Baptist Old Testament scholar and theologian. Principal of Regent's Park College (1920–1942), Speaker's Lecturer at Oxford and President of the Baptist Historical Society, his interest in Old Testament theology was reflected in many books, including *The Religious Ideas of the Old Testament* (1913) and *Inspiration and Revelation in the Old Testament* (1946).

Robinson, Edward *(1794–1863)*

American Bible scholar. After study in German universities he returned to the United States in 1830. Professor of biblical literature at Union Theological Seminary, New York, from 1837, he became renowned for his geographical study trips to the Holy Land. The publication of his researches, *e.g. Biblical Researches in Palestine* (1841), led to his being considered the father of biblical geography.

Robinson, John Arthur Thomas *(1919–1983)*

Anglican Bishop of Woolwich, theologian and New Testament scholar. He was educated at Cambridge, where he later lectured in theology (1953–1959 and again 1969–1983). He was a prolific writer, from his first success *In the End, God . . .* (1950) to his posthumously published *The Priority of John* (1985). While serving as Bishop of Woolwich (1959–1969) he wrote his sensational *Honest to God* (1963), which stimulated a long-lasting debate; he also supported what was called 'the South Bank Theology', with which he was closely associated. His other works included *The Human Face of God* (1973) and *Wrestling with Romans* (1979).

Robinson, John *(c. 1575–1625)*

Puritan minister who was originally ordained for the Anglican ministry, but joined the Separatist congregation at Scrooby, Nottinghamshire. The community was forced to move to Holland (1608), settling at Leiden, where Robinson built up and encouraged the members. He prepared them for their journey to America on the *Mayflower* (1620). Called 'the pastor of the Pilgrim Fathers', he was an able controversialist and his writings, such as *A Justification of Separation from the Church of England*, were influential and supportive to the Pilgrim Fathers.

Rogers, John *(c. 1500–1555)*

Educated at Cambridge, while serving as a chaplain to English merchants at Antwerp Rogers met William Tyndale, whose influence drew him to Protestantism. After Tyndale's execution (1536) he edited the Bible translation published in 1537 as 'Matthew's Bible'. On his return to England (1548) he was given pastoral work in London and appointed divinity lecturer at St Paul's Cathedral. On Queen Mary's accession he was imprisoned for preaching Protestant doctrine and, after a year in Newgate Prison, in February 1555 he died, the first British Protestant martyr at Smithfield.

Rogers, Mary Joseph *(1882–1955)*

American founder of the Maryknoll Sisters of St Dominic (popularly known as Maryknoll Sisters). Her interest in foreign missions developed through working on *Field Afar*, the Catholic Foreign Mission Society of America's magazine. With companions she started a lay group called Teresians (1912), which evolved into the Foreign Mission Sisters of St Dominic. Mother Rogers founded the Motherhouse at Maryknoll, New York, and at her death there were over eleven hundred Maryknoll Sisters who had served in all parts of Asia.

Rogers, William *(1819–1896)*

Anglican priest and educational reformer, known as 'Hang-Theology Rogers' because in his large network of schools in his London slum parish, he proposed that doctrinal training be left to parents and clergy. He tackled the problems of middle-class schools while rector of St Botolph's Bishopsgate, London.

Rolle, Richard *(c. 1300–1349)*

English mystic, hermit and author of tracts on Christian mysticism. A Yorkshireman, he studied at Oxford, but broke off his studies at the age of eighteen to become a hermit, first on the estate of John Dalton of Pickering (North Yorkshire), but later in various places. His last years were spent near a convent at Hampole, where he acted as spiritual adviser to the nuns. He was highly regarded up to the Reformation for his sanctity and his many spiritual writings, which make reference to his own mystical experiences.

Romero, Oscar *(1917–1980)*

From a family of seven, Oscar Romero was born in El Salvador, and after training for the priesthood in Rome was ordained there in 1942. An academic by inclination, Romero worked as secretary to the diocese of San Miguel and built a reputation as a preacher and broadcaster. After his consecration as archbishop of San Salvador (1977), he was shocked into action for human rights at the murder of his friend, Rutilio Grande, at Aguilares. Romero espoused the poor and the persecuted, confronted those in power and preached a gospel of social justice. A succession of his priests were murdered and he received countless death threats. In 1979 Romero presented seven dossiers of atrocities to the Pope. On 24 March 1980 he was shot dead while celebrating Mass in a hospital chapel at San Salvador. His people immediately hailed their 'monseñor' as a martyr and a saint. (Oscar Romero is one of the ten modern martyrs honoured in sculpture with a place over the west door of Westminster Abbey, London.)

Rose of Lima, St (1586–1617)
Patron saint of South America and the Philippines, she lived her whole life in Lima, Peru. Noted for her beauty, she resisted all efforts to make her marry, having dedicated herself to virginity and an austere spiritual life, taking St Catherine of Siena as her model. Living the life of a recluse in a garden shed, she suffered great opposition, but her sanctity attracted many to her for spiritual help. At twenty she joined the Third Order of St Dominic. Her short life ended after a long illness. She was canonised in 1671.

Rosmini-Serbati, Antonio (1797–1855)
Italian priest, philosopher, theologian and founder of the Institute of Charity or Rosminians. Ordained a priest in 1821, with the support of successive popes he dedicated himself to reconciling Catholicism with modern political and scientific thought. He also attempted to influence the nineteenth-century Italian nationalist movement. His Institute of Charity grew out of his dissatisfaction with the spiritual and educational state of the Church. His philosophical works, contained in *The Origin of Ideas* (1830) and *Maxims of Christian Perfection* (1849), were examined and declared free of censure in 1854.

Rossetti, Christina Georgina (1830–1894)
Poetess and member of the famous Anglo-Italian family of letters, she was associated with the Pre-Raphaelite Brotherhood. A devoted Anglican, her poetry expresses her strong Christian faith. She is best remembered for *Goblin Market* (1862), *Princes' Progress and Other Poems* (1866) and the carol 'In the Bleak Mid-Winter'.

Rossetti, Dante Gabriel (1828–1882)
Elder son of the Rossetti family, and named after the Italian poet who influenced the family so markedly, he was both a poet and a painter. His poetic works include *The Blessed Damozel* (1850) and *The House of Life* (1881).

He founded the Pre-Raphaelite Brotherhood (1848), which was devoted to a 'truth to nature' policy.

Rowntree, Joseph *(1836–1925)*
Quaker, philanthropist and social reformer. The head of the great cocoa business which had been founded by his father, he pioneered better working conditions, higher wages and provision for old age. He founded the model village of New Earswick, promoted adult education and fought intemperance.

Rublev (also Rublyov) Andrei *(c. 1360–c. 1430)*
Honoured by the Russian Orthodox Church as St Andrew, Rublev is best remembered for his famous icon, 'The Hospitality of Abraham' (also known as 'The Old Testament Trinity'). One of the greatest icon painters of the Russian Church, he became a monk and learnt iconography from the famous artist, Theophanes the Greek.

Rufinus, Tyrannius *(c. 345–410)*
Priest, writer and translator. A friend of St Jerome, he studied Origen and became suspected of Origenism; although an original writer, he is best remembered for his translations from the Greek.

Ruskin, John *(1819–1900)*
Writer, art critic and social reformer who championed the Gothic revival, supported in *The Seven Lamps of Architecture* (1849). By his writings, *e.g. Unto This Last* (1862), and the foundation of the Guild of St George (1871) he promoted the dignity and moral destiny of men.

Ruysbroeck, Jan van *(1293–1381)*
Flemish mystic, originating from Ruysbroeck, near Brussels, he was ordained (*c.* 1317) and held the chaplaincy of St Gudule, Brussels (1317–1343). He retired to a hermitage in 1343, with several others, and founded a Community of Canons Regular at Groenendaal. His influential writings spread rapidly and anticipated the fifteenth-century Devotio Moderna. His masterpiece *The Spiritual Espousals* (1350) is a guide for the soul in search of God.

S

Sabatier, Auguste *(1839–1901)*
French educator and Protestant theologian who helped to revolutionise the interpretation of the Bible by applying the principles of historical criticism and by promoting the development of liberal theology, which influenced not only French Protestantism but also prepared the way for the Modernist movement in the Roman Catholic Church.

Sabatier, Paul *(1858–1928)*
Calvinist pastor, holding from 1885 to 1889, a pastorate in Strasbourg. An interest in St Francis of Assisi grew and he became an internationally acknowledged specialist, giving great impetus to Franciscan studies, especially by his *Vie de St François* (1893). He founded the 'Societa Internazionale di Studi Francescani' at Assisi (1902) and the 'British Society of Franciscan Studies' in London (1908).

Sabatier, Pierre *(1682–1742)*
Benedictine Bible scholar who, trained in historical methods, compiled, over many years, the exhaustive collection of pre-Vulgate Latin texts of the Bible. This was published posthumously in three volumes as *Bibliorum Sacrorum Latinae Versiones Antiquae*.

Salmon, George *(1819–1904)*
Theologian, writer and mathematician who, educated at Trinity College, Dublin, remained there to become Fellow (1841), Regius professor of divinity (1866) and Provost (1888). Strongly Protestant, he wrote *Cautions for the Times* and his *Introduction to the New Testament* (1885) was also popular.

Sancroft, William *(1617–1693)*
For refusing to take an oath of allegiance to the Government of the Commonwealth he was dismissed as Fellow of Cambridge. Rising swiftly through church appointments, he helped in the revision of the Book of Common Prayer (1662) and the rebuilding of St Paul's Cathedral, becoming Archbishop of Canterbury in 1677. As leader of seven bishops who opposed James II's Declaration of Indulgence (1688) he was imprisoned in the Tower of London. After his acquittal, and the king's flight, he refused to recognise William of Orange and was deprived of his See (1690).

Sanday, William *(1843–1920)*
English New Testament scholar who, through his numerous books, was a pioneer in introducing to English students and the Anglican world the continental research in biblical criticism. His principal writings were the *International Critical Commentary* (with A. C. Headlam), *Romans* (1895) and *Outlines of the Life of Christ* (1905).

Sankey, Ira David *(1840–1908)*
The colleague of the American evangelist Dwight L. Moody, Sankey was the musician and accompanist on Moody's preaching tours. Together they produced the *Sankey and Moody Hymn Book* (1873).

Sarapion, St (also Serapion) *(d. after 360)*
Egyptian monk, theologian and Bishop of Thmius, on the Nile Delta. A key figure in early monasticism, with his friend Athanasius he championed orthodox teaching against the Arians and wrote his celebrated treatise *Against the Manichees*. His other work of note is the *Euchologion*, which contains important collected prayers and liturgical texts.

Savile, Henry *(1549–1622)*
English mathematician and scholar who helped in the preparation of the Authorised Version of the Bible; he collected and published the works of St John Chrysostom and founded two Savilian professorships in astronomy and mathematics at Oxford University (1619).

Savio, St Dominic *(1842–1857)*
A student of John Bosco at Turin, while only a young boy he formed the Company of the Immaculate Conception to assist Bosco. Though young he had spiritual gifts beyond his years and reputedly received visions. He was canonised in 1954 and declared patron of choirboys.

Savonarola, Girolamo *(1452–1498)*
Florentine Dominican friar, preacher and reformer. At the Priory of San Marco, Florence (from 1482), he attracted great attention by his prophetic and reforming sermons. He boldly preached against the ruling Medici and, after their downfall in 1494, became leader of a democratic republic. After refusing to obey several papal summonses and preaching against the papal court, he was excommunicated in 1497. Savonarola ignored the excommunication and continued preaching; he lost popular support, was imprisoned, tried and hanged.

Sayers, Dorothy L. *(1893–1957)*
English scholar and writer whose fame rests mainly upon her stories of mystery and detection. One of the first women graduates of Oxford University

(1915), her first major work, *Whose Body?*, appeared in 1923. Later in life she turned her attention to theological writing, *e.g. Creed or Chaos?* (1947) and her much-admired, if a little controversial, series of plays for the BBC, *The Man Born to be King* (1941–1942).

Schaff, Philip *(1819–1893)*
American Church historian, theologian and ecumenist who originated from Switzerland, was educated at Tübingen, Halle and Berlin. His works, especially *Creeds of Christendom* (1877) and his *History of the Christian Church*, in twelve volumes (1883–1893), set standards in the USA for scholarship in Church history.

Scheeben, Matthias Joseph *(1835–1888)*
German Roman Catholic theologian, professor of dogmatic theology at a Cologne seminary, whose speculative work and erudite books, especially *Mysterien des Christenthums* (1865), were widely translated and admired.

Scheffler, Johannes *(1624–1677)*
Better known under his pen name Angelus Silesius. Of Polish Lutheran background, he became a Roman Catholic (1653) and ordained priest (1661); afterwards he devoted his time to writing. Although he wrote many controversial tracts he is best known for his mystical poetry and songs, which celebrate, in vivid imagery, the soul's union with God. These were published under the titles *Heilige Seelenlust* (1657) and *Der Cherubinisch Wandersmann* (1675).

Schleiermacher, Friedrich Daniel *(1768–1834)*
German Protestant theologian who is considered the founder of modern Protestant theology. Of Moravian background, his education began in a Moravian seminary but he moved to Halle University in 1787. After ordination (1794) he became pastor at the Charité Hospital, Berlin. His famous *Religion. Speeches to its Cultured Despisers* (1799) and his developing belief that religion is based on intuition and feeling, independent of dogma, led to the professorship of theology at Halle (1804). Moving to Berlin, he became pastor of Trinity Church and professor of theology at the new University of Berlin (1810). In his time widely regarded as a preacher, his theological thought appears fully in his *Der Christliche Glaube*. Schleiermacher's emphasis upon feeling was a reaction to contemporary rationalism and immensely influenced subsequent Protestant theology.

Schürer, Emil *(1844–1910)*
German New Testament scholar who held the biblical studies chair at Göttingen and is famous for his monumental five-volume work, *A History of the Jewish People in the Time of Jesus Christ* (1890–1891).

Schweitzer, Albert *(1875–1965)*
German theologian, philosopher, mission doctor and organist. Educated at Strasbourg University, he was a pastor in Strasbourg and a lecturer at the university following the publication of his *The Mystery of the Kingdom of God* in 1901. His influential work *The Quest of the Historical Jesus* (1906) established him as a world figure in theological studies. In 1905 he announced his plan to prepare for missionary work, and after qualifying as a doctor (1913) left with his wife for Lambárené in French Equatorial Africa. There he founded a hospital, re-sited in 1924, to which a leper colony was added. Renowned as an organist and acclaimed for his interpretations of Johann Sebastian Bach, he never abandoned his musical or scholarly interests, writing up to his death. He was awarded the Nobel Peace Prize in 1953.

Schwenckfeld, Kasper *(1489–1561)*
Silesian Reformation theologian, writer and preacher who led the Reform Movement in Silesia. Initially impressed by Martin Luther, he later parted company with some Protestant teachings, founding the movement called 'Reformation by the Middle Way'. He established societies which still survive in the United States as the Schwenckfelder Church.

Scott, George Gilbert *(1811–1878)*
The most prominent church architect of the Victorian period, being the most successful exponent of the Gothic Revival style. In 1838 he designed his first church, St Giles, Camberwell, London; but his reputation was established after he was selected to work on the Martyrs' Memorial at Oxford (1841). His travels abroad widened his knowledge, which he applied to restoration work at Ely, Hereford, Salisbury and Gloucester cathedrals. In 1849 he was appointed architect to Westminster Abbey. His work of restoration was not without criticism and some controversy.

Scrivener, Frederick Henry Ambrose *(1813–1891)*
New Testament textual scholar, and headmaster of Falmouth School (1846–1856), who is remembered for his comprehensive study of New Testament manuscripts, published as *Plain Introduction to the Criticism of the New Testament* (1861), a reference book which went through many editions.

Seabury, Samuel *(1729–1796)*
After studying theology in America and medicine in Scotland, he was ordained for the Episcopal Church of America in 1753, serving first as a missionary in New Brunswick. Loyal to the British Government during the War of Independence, he was consecrated the first bishop of the Protestant Episcopal Church of America by Scottish bishops, thus causing problems of a separate Episcopal line in the USA until 1789.

Sebastian, St *(d. c. 288)*
Little is known for certain of his life, although it is believed he was martyred during the persecution of the Emperor Diocletian. According to legend, graphically portrayed by Renaissance painters, he was a Christian officer in Diocletian's army, condemned to be shot by archers for converting other soldiers.

Sellon, Priscilla Lydia *(c. 1821–1876)*
Founder of the first post-Reformation Religious Community in the Church of England. With E. B. Pusey's assistance, her charity work among the destitute grew into the 'Devonport Sisters of Mercy'. Schools and orphanages were founded and the Sisters heroically nursed the sick in the cholera epidemic of 1848.

Selwyn, George Augustus *(1809–1878)*
Educated at Eton and St John's College, Cambridge, and consecrated the first missionary Bishop of New Zealand in 1841. His heroic and inventive methods won him wide respect and he had a marked influence upon the subsequent development of the New Zealand Church. On his return to England (1867) he was appointed to the See of Lichfield.

Seraphim of Sarow, St *(1759–1833)*
Originally Prokhor Moshnin, he took the name Seraphim on entering the Monastery of Sarow in 1777. After fifteen years in community, he withdrew to a hermit's life. After a further twenty-five years he returned to pastoral care, devoting the remainder of his life to spiritual direction. He was accorded the title 'Starets' (spiritual teacher) and acknowledged as one of the greatest spiritual counsellors in Russian Orthodox history. His Church declared him a saint in 1913.

Sergius *(1867–1944)* *(originally Ivan Nikolayevich Stragorodsky)*
Theologian and Patriarch of Moscow under whose leadership the Russian Orthodox Church rallied against Hitler's armies (1941) in a united effort with the Soviets. He thus obtained Soviet acknowledgement of the role and position of the Orthodox Church in Russia.

Sergius – There were four popes of this name, the most noteworthy being:

Sergius I, St *(d. c. 701)*
Considered one of the most important seventh-century popes, he resisted moves to make Constantinople an equal See to that of Rome. He showed an interest in English affairs, baptising Caedwalla, king of Wessex (689); he also consecrated Willibrord Bishop of the Frisians and ordered St Wilfred to be restored to his See of York (c. 700). He is further credited with introducing the *Agnus Dei* ('Lamb of God') into the Mass.

Sergius of Radonezh, St *(1314–1392)*
Originally Bartholomew Kirillovich, he took the name Sergius when he became a monk (1337). He founded the famous Monastery of the Trinity, which re-established the monastic life after the ravages of the Mongol invasions; it became the inspiration of seventy-five other monasteries and a centre and symbol of religious renewal. Sergius was famed for his ascetical life, his compassion for the needy and the help he gave in developing better methods of agriculture. He is credited with stopping four civil wars. Honoured as the greatest of Russian saints, he was canonised at some time before 1449.

Serra, Junipero *(1713–1784)*
The apostle of California, Serra was a Franciscan missionary priest whose work in North America won him acclaim. From missionary work among the Indians of Mexico he moved up into California (1769) and founded eight mission centres, including San Francisco in 1776. He was an energetic supporter of the rights of the native Indians.

Seton, St Elizabeth Ann *(1774–1821)*
Born in New York City, educated by her father, she was involved early in life in social work, helping to found the Society for the Relief of Poor Widows with Small Children (1797). Herself widowed with five children in 1803, she converted from Anglicanism to Roman Catholicism in 1805, resulting in her ostracism by family and friends. Opening a school with companions, a Religious Community developed which was approved as the Sisters of Charity (the first American religious society) in 1812. Known as 'Mother Seton', she is credited with being the founder of the Catholic Parochial School System of the USA. At her death Mother Seton's Order had branched into twenty communities. She was the first American-born saint to be canonised, in 1975.

Shaftesbury, Anthony Ashley Cooper, Seventh Earl of *(1801–1885)*
Educated at Harrow and Christ Church College, Oxford, he entered Parliament in 1826 and proved to be one of the most effective social and industrial reformers in nineteenth-century England. He was largely responsible for the Ten Hours Bill (1847), which limited the working day in textile mills, the Mines Act (1842) and the Factory Act of 1874. President of the Ragged Schools Union for thirty-nine years, he also served as President of the British and Foreign Bible Society. He was the acknowledged leader of the evangelical movement within the Church of England; although opposed to ritualism, he supported, however, Catholic emancipation.

Sharp, James *(1613–1679)*
Church of Scotland minister who worked secretly for the Restoration and for the reintroduction of the episcopacy in Scotland. He was subsequently

rewarded with the See of St Andrew's in 1661; however he was murdered by a party of Presbyterians, whose church he was working to suppress.

Sheed, Francis Joseph *(1896–1981)*

Roman Catholic lay theologian, apologist and writer. Born and educated in Sydney, Australia, on arrival in England he worked full time for the Catholic Evidence Guild and remained one of the best-known apologists for fifty years. With his wife Maisie Ward he founded the well-known Catholic publishing house Sheed and Ward. His many writings include *A Map of Life* (1933), *Communism and Man* (1938) and *Theology and Sanity* (1947). He is best remembered for opening up the specialist world of theology to lay people.

Sheen, Fulton J. *(1895–1979)*

United States Roman Catholic archbishop, preacher, writer and celebrated media personality. Ordained in 1919, his talents as a communicator took him to radio and TV work, including *The Catholic Hour* for NBC and the hosting of *Life is Worth Living* (1951–1957). The recipient of many awards for media work, he was also the national director of the Society for Propagation of the Faith (1950–1966) and Archbishop of Newport from 1969. His many books include *Walk with God* (1965) and *That Tremendous Love* (1967).

Sheldon, Charles Munroe *(1857–1946)*

American Congregational preacher, founder of the Central Congregational Church, Topeka, Kansas, and inspirational writer. He is famous for his best-selling novel *In His Steps* (1897), which was the largest-selling book, apart from the Bible, in the United States for sixty years.

Sheldon, Gilbert *(1598–1677)*

Archbishop of Canterbury who was an active supporter of William Laud's reforms, particularly at his old college, Trinity, Oxford. The Bishop of London in 1660, he was chosen Archbishop of Canterbury in 1663.

Sheppard, Hugh Richard Lowrie *(1880–1937)*

Immensely popular (as 'Dick Sheppard') vicar of St Martin-in-the-Fields, London, who made his parish church the most lively and well-known in the British Empire. An enthusiast for Church reform, the use of broadcasting by the Church and, in his retirement, the cause of Christian pacifism. His best-known book was *The Impatience of a Parson* (1927).

Shorthouse, Joseph Henry *(1834–1903)*

Anglican man of business whose fame rests upon his novel *John Inglesant* (1881), which revived interest in the seventeenth-century community at

437

Little Gidding. The book was widely admired by a wide cross-section of nineteenth-century Christians.

Simeon, Charles *(1759–1836)*
Vicar of Holy Trinity Church, Cambridge, and leader of the Evangelical Revival. He established the Simeon Trust to further this cause and helped to found the Church Missionary Society (1797), also assisting the newly founded British and Foreign Bible Society (1804). Renowned as a preacher, he also proved to be an able biblical commentator with his seventeen-volume *Horae Homileticae*, which annotated the entire Bible for sermon material.

Simeon Stylites, St *(c. 390–459)*
The first known pillar hermit, or stylite. (He is not to be confused with a later, sixth-century stylite of the same name.) At first a monk, he was expelled from the community because of his excessive austerities and became a hermit. To avoid the attention of pilgrims he mounted first a low pillar then one of about fifty feet. He remained there until death but exerted an extraordinary influence upon the world of his time through those who flocked for counsel, those who imitated him and through his correspondence.

Simeon the New Theologian *(949–1022)* (*also Symeon*)
Byzantine monk, mystic and spiritual writer. Called 'New Theologian' to distinguish him from the fourth-century theologian and spiritual writer 'Gregory the Theologian' (in the West, St Gregory Nazianzen). Simeon became a monk at Studius and priest (980) and Abbot of the Monastery of St Manas, near Constantinople. He was compelled to resign in 1009 because of his austere monastic policy. Considered the greatest of Byzantine spiritual writers, with deep mystical experience, his works include sermons, 'catecheses' and the *Hymns of the Divine Loves*, which describes his spiritual experiences.

Simon Stock, St *(c. 1165–1265)*
Born at Aylesford, Kent, he became a hermit ('Stock' may have originated from a legend that as a young hermit he lived in a tree trunk) and on a pilgrimage to Jerusalem joined the Carmelite Order. He brought the Order to England, promoted its expansion and became Superior General of the Order in 1247.

Simon, Richard *(1638–1712)*
Roman Catholic biblical scholar, regarded as the founder of Old Testament criticism. His *Histoire Critique du Vieux Testament*, denying Moses as the author of the Pentateuch, resulted in his expulsion from his Order, the French Oratory.

Slessor, Mary *(1848–1915)*
United Presbyterian missionary on the Calabar coast of West Africa. From work in an Aberdeen factory she went to a role of great influence in Africa. 'Ma Slessor' successfully brought tribal abuses, including human sacrifice and the murder of twins, to an end.

Smet, Pierre Jean de *(1801–1873)*
Courageous American Jesuit missionary and friend of the Indian tribes west of the Mississippi River. His pioneering efforts, involving journeys totalling some 180,000 miles in primitive conditions, to Christianise and act as mediator, won him the title 'Black Robe' from his beloved Indians. Towards the end of his life he was disillusioned by the exploitation of the Indians and continual violation of treaties by the Government and their agents.

Smith, Bernard *(1630–1708)*
Familiarly known as 'Father Smith', he originated from Germany but established a reputation as a master organ-builder in Restoration England. Appointed king's organ-maker (1681), he thereafter built many important instruments, for example for St Paul's Cathederal, London.

Smith, Sir George Adam *(1856–1942)*
Scottish biblical scholar and preacher who helped to establish the acceptability of the higher criticism of the Old Testament. His many books include *The Early Poetry of Israel* (1916) and *Jeremiah* (1923). He was knighted in 1916.

Smith, Sydney *(1771–1845)*
Ordained to the Anglican ministry, he proved to be one of the foremost preachers of his time. Renowned for his wit and powers of persuasion, he supported parliamentary reform and Catholic emancipation.

Smith, William Robertson *(1846–1894)*
Scottish Semitic scholar and theologian whose writings, especially in the *Encyclopaedia Britannica* on the higher criticism of the Old Testament, caused him to lose his Free Church appointments. Moving to Cambridge, he was elected Fellow of Christ's College (1885) and continued to exert great influence through his books, particularly *The Old Testament in the Jewish Church* (1881) and *The Prophets of Israel* (1882).

Smyth, (Smith) John *(1554–1612)*
Se-Baptist and founder of the General Baptists. Ordained for the Church of England ministry, he became a Puritan preacher, then a Separatist pastor, which led to exile in Amsterdam. Baptising himself (*c.* 1609), hence 'Se-Baptist', he set up the first modern Baptist church. In the year of his death a

group of his followers travelled to England to establish the first Baptist church in Britain.

Söderblom, Nathan *(1866–1931)*

Ordained a Lutheran minister in 1893, he served first as a chaplain to the Swedish Legation in Paris, then he became professor of theology at his old University of Uppsala (1901), later (1912–1914) at Leipzig. Appointed Archbishop of Uppsala (1914), he travelled widely, developing his interests in comparative religion and ecumenism. Due to his efforts, the first Life and Work Conference met at Stockholm in 1925; he was awarded the Nobel Peace Prize in 1930 for his work for peace through Church unity.

Soper, Donald *(1903–1998)*

Renowned as a public speaker, popular evangelist and pacifist, Donald Soper attracted thousands to his Sunday evening services at the Methodist West London Mission where he was superintendent from 1936 to 1978. He was already a dedicated socialist influenced by the conditions of industrial life that he had witnessed in Derby at the age of twenty-one. He made broadcasting history when he gave the first ever evening epilogue on BBC television in 1947; but the BBC banned him during the Second World War because of his firmly held pacifist views. For many years he was President of the Fellowship of Reconciliation. Soper was a familiar weekly speaker, first at Tower Hill (starting in 1927) and then at Speakers' Corner, Hyde Park, London (from 1942). He was one of the founders of the Christian Socialist Movement, and its first chairperson from 1960 to 1975. In 1965 his social work, through the West London Mission, was recognised when he became Baron Soper of Kingsway; in the House of Lords he was a very active Labour peer. He insisted on continuing to work after his wife, Marie, died in 1994 and in spite of many physical disabilities.

Southcott, Joanna *(1750–1814)*

A domestic servant who became a religious fanatic with a following of some forty thousand devotees; these were attracted by her allegedly inspired divine messages. She joined the Methodist Society in 1791 and wrote and sealed 'prophecies'. After her death, from brain disease, a box of these was left; finally opened in 1927, it contained nothing of value or interest.

Southwell, St Robert *(1561–1595)*

Poet and Roman Catholic martyr, remembered not only for his saintly life but also for his religious poetry, which anticipated George Herbert and later poets. Ordained a Jesuit priest in 1585 in Rome, he returned to England as a missionary and became chaplain to the Howard family. He worked secretly until his betrayal in 1592; he was arrested while saying mass, severely tortured, and brought to trial three years later. Much of his poetry was written while in the Tower of London. He was hanged, drawn and quartered; soon afterwards collections of his religious poetry became widely available, appreciated by Protestants and Catholics alike. He was canonised in 1970.

Southworth, St John *(1592–1654)*
Ordained a secular priest at Douai (1618) to work secretly as a Roman Catholic missionary in England, Southworth was arrested and condemned to death in 1627. He was released three years later, but was back in prison again in 1632. While there, he worked among the prison inmates who had the plague (1635–1636). Released again, he worked secretly until 1654, when, arrested on suspicion, he proclaimed he was a Catholic priest and was executed at Tyburn on 28 June. His body now rests in Westminster Cathedral, London; he was canonised in 1970.

Spener, Philipp Jakob *(1635–1705)*
Theologian, author and founder of Pietism. Answering a call to revivify the Lutheran Church, he introduced his devotional gatherings ('collegia pietatis') and by preaching and correspondence encouraged personal spiritual growth. By the time of his death Pietism was well established in Germany, and its influence spread via England to the British colonies in America.

Spurgeon, Charles Haddon *(1834–1892)*
English Baptist minister of strong Calvinist and fundamentalist views who was extremely successful as a preacher, his sermons being translated into many languages and filling over fifty volumes. He preached first at the age of sixteen (1850) and two years later had his own church at Waterbeach in Cambridgeshire; he moved to New Park Street Chapel, Southwark, London, where the crowds attending were so large that the Metropolitan Tabernacle at Newington Causeway, for six thousand, had to be built. Spurgeon edited a monthly magazine and founded a college for ministers (1856) and an orphanage (1867). Some of his extreme views led to a break with the Baptist Union in 1887. He wrote several books, including *Commenting and Commentaries* (1876) and *John Ploughman's Talk* (1869).

Stainer, Sir John *(1840–1901)*
Church organist and composer, he began his musical career as a choirboy at St Paul's Cathedral, London (1849), and at sixteen was organist at St Michael's College, Tenbury. Eventually he became organist at St Paul's Cathedral (1872), where he made important reforms in church music. Stainer founded the Musical Association (1874), was Principal of the National Training School for Music (1880) and was knighted in 1888. His many compositions included oratorios, cantatas (his best known, *The Crucifixion* (1887), being widely performed), anthems and hymns, many of which are still in regular use.

Stanislaus, St *(1030–1079)*
Bishop of Cracow (1072) who reproved the Polish king, Boleslav II, for his scandalous life. Murdered by the king, according to tradition, he was hailed as a saintly martyr by the people. Canonised in 1253, he has been patron of Poland since then. However, historians are uncertain about the true facts of his death, some suggesting that Stanislaus was executed for treason.

Stanley, Henry Morton *(1841–1904)*
Explorer and journalist who, on behalf of the *New York Herald*, made the famous discovery of Dr Livingstone in Central Africa in 1871. He afterwards picked up Livingstone's work as an explorer, charting over two million square miles of the African interior; and, as a missionary, corresponded with the CMS, an activity which led to the beginning of missionary work in the Uganda area.

Staupitz, Johann von *(1468–1524)*
Vicar-General of the Augustinian Order at the time of Martin Luther's revolt. As Luther's superior he counselled, advised and supported him until the Reformer broke with Rome. Staupitz then withdrew his support, joined the Benedictine Order and became Abbot of St Peter's Abbey, Salzburg.

Stein, Edith *(1891–1942)*
Born of a rich orthodox Jewish family, she renounced her faith for atheism, studied phenomenology under Edmund Husserl and, impressed by the mystic St Teresa of Avila, converted to Roman Catholicism in 1922. She joined the Carmelite Order in 1934 and took the name Sister Teresa Benedicta of the Cross. She continued writing, translating and lecturing on the application of phenomenology to Thomism. Moved suddenly from Cologne to Holland, to save her from Nazi persecution, she was eventually arrested in 1942 and died in the gas chambers of Auschwitz with her sister Rosa. Widely regarded as a modern saint and martyr, her philosophical writings are still published and studied.

Stephen – There were ten popes of this name, the most memorable being:

Stephen I, St *(d. 257)*
A Roman, and pope from 254, details of his life are known only through the correspondence which arose from his dispute with Bishop St Cyprian of Carthage over baptism. He upheld the teaching authority of the Bishop of Rome against Cyprian and three African Councils; he died during the Emperor Valerian's persecution of Christians, before the matter could be resolved.

Stephen Harding, St *(d. 1134)*
An Englishman from Dorset who, after travelling widely, embraced the religious life at Molesme, France; he moved to Citeaux with companions and became abbot in 1109. The community was faced with extinction when unexpectedly (1112) Bernard of Clairvaux arrived with thirty companions; following this Citeaux became the centre of a large network of Cistercian monasteries.

Stern, Henry Aaron *(1820–1885)*
Anglican missionary of German–Jewish origins who dedicated himself, after his own baptism in 1840, to the mission to the Jews. He travelled widely and after ordination worked principally in Abyssinia among the Falasha Jews, the last years of his life being fruitfully spent in London. His writings include *Dawn of Light in the East* (1854).

Stone, Barton Warren *(1772–1844)*
American Presbyterian minister who was dedicated to seeking Christian unity; he founded the *Christian Messenger* to promote this and was one of the principal founders of the Disciples of Christ denomination (1832).

Stowe, Harriet Beecher *(1811–1896)*
Daughter of a well-known Congregationalist minister and married to a clergyman, she is remembered principally as the author of *Uncle Tom's Cabin*, which promoted popular feeling against slavery. She followed her success with many other novels, studies and religious poems.

Stratford, John *(d. 1348)*
Archbishop of Canterbury, and a native of Stratford-upon-Avon, of which town he was a benefactor. He was Chancellor of England and counsellor of the young Edward III. He admired St Thomas à Becket and imitated him in standing up to the king over a peer's right to be judged by his equals in Parliament.

Strauss, David Friedrich *(1808–1874)*
German controversial Protestant philosopher, theologian and biographer who used dialectical philosophy in biblical interpretation. He is famous for his *Leben Jesu* (1835–1836), in which he denied the historical value of the Gospels and applied his myth theory to the life of Christ. Although he lost his own faith, his work heavily influenced liberal schools of biblical study and the search for the 'historical Jesus'.

Street, George Edmund *(1824–1881)*
Architect noted for his many English churches in the Gothic Revival style. His extensive travels through Europe influenced his commissions; he was

diocesan architect to York, Winchester, Oxford and Ripon, and was also professor of architecture at the Royal Academy.

Streeter, Burnett Hillman *(1874–1937)*
Anglican priest, theologian and biblical scholar, remembered for the results of his study of the Synoptic problem. His most important work was *The Four Gospels* (1924). In a series of publications he dealt with many different modern problems from a Christian viewpoint.

Strossmayer, Joseph Georg *(1815–1905)*
Patriot and Roman Catholic bishop who led the Croatian national party in Yugoslavia. At the First Vatican Council he was a leading and vocal opponent of the move to define the infallibility of the pope.

Studd, Charles Thomas *(1862–1931)*
Protestant missionary of the China Inland Mission (popularly known as C.T.) who worked in China (1885–1894), India (1900) and Central Africa (1910). He inspired the foundation of the Student Volunteer Movement and thought up the idea of a 'World Evangelisation Crusade', which spread to many countries.

Studdert-Kennedy, Geoffrey Anketell *(1883–1929)*
Anglican priest, remembered as the best-known military padre of the First World War and known affectionately by the soldiers as 'Woodbine Willie'. Rector of St Edmund, King and Martyr, Lombard Street, London, from 1922, he continued his preaching and published several popular books, including *The Hardest Part* (1918) and *The Wicket Gate* (1923).

Stumpf, Johannes *(1500–1578)*
One of the most important figures of the Swiss Reform Movement, also remembered as a chronicler. A friend of Zwingli, he dedicated his life, after years as prior of the Knights of St John, to the work of building up the Reformation in Switzerland.

Suarez, Francisco De *(1548–1617)*
Spanish theologian and philosopher, the most important of the Jesuit Order and one of the most prominent of scholastic philosophers. His *Defensio Fidei Catholicae* (1613), which opposed the divine right of kings, was burnt in England upon the steps of St Paul's Cathedral. He wrote other apologetical works and *De Legibus* (1612), on political theory. Credited with being the founder of international law, he was so highly regarded by successive popes that he was accorded the title 'Doctor Eximius'.

Suenans, Leon Joseph *(1904–1996)*
Born (1904) of a poor Belgian family, living in Brussels, Leon Suenans rose to be one of the most influential churchman of the 1970s and 1980s. Convinced of a vocation to the priesthood from an early age, he studied in Rome; he became committed to work in education, lecturing as Professor of Philosophy at Malines Seminary. During the Second World War he was vice-rector of the Catholic University of Louvain. From 1945 to 1961 Suenans was auxiliary bishop to the Cardinal Archbishop of Malines-Brussels, who he succeeded in 1962. A close friend of Pope John XXIII, he was a key figure at the Second Vatican Council, being one of the four chairmen of the Council sessions. He led the Catholic Movement for Renewal in the post-Council years; his book *A New Pentecost?* was most influential. Totally dedicated to ecumenism, he shared pulpits, in Anglican and nonconformist churches in Britain and throughout Europe. Highly regarded by all denominations he was awarded the Templeton Prize for Progress in Religion in 1976. Cardinal Suenans retired in 1979; his last major book was *The Testimony of a Life* (1995) – a biography of his friend, King Baudouin of the Belgians, who he admired.

Sulpicius Severus *(c. 363–c. 420)*
Early Christian historian, ascetic and hagiographer, principal authority on Christian life in contemporary Gaul. A friend of Paulinus, Bishop of Nola, and Martin of Tours, his life of the latter, *Vita S. Martini*, was highly influential on later hagiography and his literary masterpiece *Dialogue* (404) reveals his interest in the development of monasticism.

Sunday, Billy *(1863–1935)* *(full name: William Ashley Sunday)*
American revivalist preacher and evangelist. Prior to ordination as a Presbyterian minister, in 1903, he had been a professional baseball player and YMCA worker. He led more than three hundred revivals and claimed one million converts to Christ.

Surin, Jean Joseph *(1600–1665)*
French Jesuit spiritual writer and mystic whose influential book *Catéchisme Spirituel* (1659) was suspected, for a while, of Quietism. His many other works reveal his deep spirituality, especially his belief in the need for purification and self-abnegation.

Suso, Henry *(c. 1295–1366)*
German Dominican and one of the principal German mystics; he studied under Eckhart (1322–1325), for whom he retained a great admiration. Suso's spirituality shines through his *Little Book of Truth* (1327) and his masterpiece *Little Book of Eternal Wisdom* (1328). For defending Eckhart he lost his professorship but continued as a successful preacher and spiritual director.

He died at Ulm after much persecution and slander. One of the most attractive and easiest to understand of the Rhineland mystics, his works were highly influential through the fourteenth and fifteenth centuries and admired by writers like Thomas à Kempis.

Suzuki, Bunji *(1885–1946)*
Japanese Christian who was active in issues of social justice and founded the Japanese Federation of Labour (1919). He helped to organise the new Social Democratic party and served several times in the Diet.

Swedenborg, Emmanuel *(1688–1772)*
Swedish scientist, philosopher and mystic. Educated at the University of Uppsala, he at first travelled in Europe, developing his interest in science. Appointed to the Swedish Board of Mines (1716), he demonstrated extraordinary scientific ability, inventiveness and mental agility. In his philosophical writings he sought to demonstrate that the universe had essentially a spiritual structure. After 1743 Swedenborg had continual mystical, visionary experiences which radically changed his life. Convinced that he was to form the 'New Church' to make his teaching known, he left his position in 1747 and dedicated himself to study and the defence of his philosophy. After his death, Swedenborg Societies appeared which developed into the Church of the New Jerusalem (1897). His works are extensive and include the eight-volume *Arcana Coelestia*.

Swithun, (or Swithin) St *(d. 862)*
Priest of Wessex who, from chaplain and counsellor to King Egbert of the West Saxons, went to Winchester as bishop in 852. He built several churches and was renowned for both his humility and his concern for the needy. The long-established superstition in England, associated with forty days of rain from his feast day, 15 July, is of unknown origin.

Sylvester – Three popes bore this name, the best known being:

Sylvester I, St *(d. 335)*
Pope at a crucial period of Church history. Although little is known of his life, according to legend he converted and baptised the Emperor Constantine. He allegedly received the 'Donation of Constantine' and during his reign he was represented at the Council of Nicaea, which condemned Arianism.

T

Tait, Archibald Campbell *(1811–1882)*
Archbishop of Canterbury who, as Bishop of London and later (1868) as archbishop, opposed the spread of the Oxford Movement. While a Fellow of Balliol College, Oxford (1834–1842), he had protested at Tract 90, but as bishop he worked for reconciliation between the evangelical and High Church wings.

Tallis, Thomas *(c. 1510–1585)*
Little is known of his early life, although he was apparently organist at Waltham Abbey at some time before 1540. His unprinted compositions of vocal works for worship were circulating when he was appointed gentleman of the Chapel Royal. He is considered the most important English composer of sacred music before Byrd, with whom he had a monopoly of printed music for over twenty years. His first printed works appeared in 1560, but *Cantiones Sacrae* (1575) was the first publication, shared with Byrd, containing sixteen motets by Tallis. His *Responses*, made popular in the nineteenth century, are his best-remembered compositions.

Tapiedi, Lucian *(1921–1942)*
Born in Papua New Guinea, Tapiedi was the son of a sorcerer. His mother converted to Christianity after his father's death. After training to be a teacher Tapiedi, who was a talented organist, joined the staff of the Sangara mission school; he also worked energetically as an evangelist. With the missionaries, Tapiedi struggled to evade capture when the Japanese invaded Papua New Guinea, and fled to a village of the Orokaiva people. There he was hacked to death. A shrine marks the spot where he died. (Lucian Tapiedi is one of the ten modern martyrs honoured in sculpture with a place over the west door of Westminister Abbey, London.)

Tauler, Johann *(c. 1300–1361)*
German Dominican mystic, influenced by Meister Eckhart and Heinrich Suso, who was immensely popular and exerted a great influence upon the Gottesfreunde (devout Rhinelanders of like mind) by his preaching and example. His mystical teaching, which impressed Martin Luther and is found in his sermons, is solidly based upon the teaching of St Thomas Aquinas.

Tausen, Hans *(1494–1561)*
Roman Catholic monk and language scholar who converted to Lutheranism and, for his work in establishing the Reformation in Denmark, became known as the 'Danish Luther'. After the final triumph of the Reformation in Denmark (1536) Tausen accepted the Lutheran Bishopric of Ribe.

Taylor, James Hudson *(1832–1905)*
Medical missionary who founded the China Inland Mission. In spite of ill-health, he travelled extensively and courageously faced many problems in inland China. His books include *China: Its Spiritual Needs and Claims* (1865) and *Union and Communion* (1894).

Taylor, Jeremy *(1613–1667)*
Anglican bishop and spiritual writer. Ordained in 1633 after an education at Cambridge, he attracted the patronage of Archbishop Laud, then of the king himself; Charles I made him a doctor of divinity by royal decree. After serving as chaplain to the Royalist army, and a period of imprisonment, he retired to Wales, where much of his writing took place. Made Bishop of Down and Connor, after the Restoration (1660) he helped to reconstitute the University of Dublin. He is remembered today for his devotional books, particularly the classics, *The Rule and Exercises of Holy Living* (1650) and *The Rule and Exercises of Holy Dying* (1651).

Teilhard de Chardin, Pierre *(1881–1955)*
French Jesuit philosopher, theologian and palaeontologist. From an early age he showed in interest in geology, which continued through his preparation for ordination as a Jesuit priest (1911). Serving as a stretcher bearer in the First World War, he was decorated for bravery. He established a notable reputation for his palaeontological work in China, being involved in the discovery of Peking Man. Theological mediation upon evolution resulted in the manuscript *The Phenomenon of Man* (1956; English translation 1965), in which he presents a theology of evolution, with the theory that man is presently evolving toward a final spiritual unity. His devotional work *Le Milieu Divin* also reflects his philosophical theology. Both he and his writings were unknown outside scientific circles until after his death.

Temple, Frederick *(1821–1902)*
Archbishop of Canterbury and educational reformer. Ordained priest (1847) after teaching and serving as Inspector of Schools, he became headmaster of Rugby (1857–1869) and prominent in the education movement. Appointed Bishop of Exeter (1869–1885), he did much for church schools and at London (1885–1897) came into conflict with the High Church wing. He was appointed Archbishop of Canterbury in 1897.

Temple, William *(1881–1944)*
Archbishop of Canterbury and a leader of the Ecumenical Movement and labour and educational reforms. The second son of the above, he progressed from lecturer at Queen's College, Oxford (1904–1910), headmaster of Repton (1910–1914), Rector of St James', Piccadilly, London (1914–1917), and Archbishop of York (1929–1942) to being Archbishop of Canterbury (1942–

1944). Prominent in national life, he gave enthusiastic support to the Faith and Order Movement, and influenced the formation of both the British Council of Churches and the World Council of Churches. An independent thinker and philosopher, his many works include *Mens Creatrix* (1917), *Nature, Man and God* (1934) and *Christianity and Social Order* (1942).

Teresa, Mother *(1910–1997)*
Agnes Gonxha Bojaxhiu was born in Skopje, Yugoslavia, of a devout Albanian Catholic family. Desiring to be a missionary in India she joined the Sisters of Our Lady of Loreto (1928), and trained at the Loreto Abbey in Dublin, Ireland, taking the name 'Teresa'. After her arrival in India (1929), she trained as a geography teacher and by 1937 was principal of St Mary's High School for girls in Calcutta. After receiving what Teresa called 'her second call', to serve the poorest of the poor, she obtained permission (August 1948) to leave the convent and live among the poor of Calcutta. Her total dedication to the sick and the dying attracted hundreds of young women to join her and she founded her own congregation, the Society of the Missionaries of Charity (approved in 1963). This spread first throughout India and then worldwide. Mother Teresa travelled the world stimulating and supporting the work of her sisters and others caring for the poor. Her work came to the attention of the general public and she was awarded the Nobel Peace Prize in 1979. She died on 5 September 1997 loved and admired by millions of people of all faiths around the world.

Teresa of Avila, St *(1515–1582) (her Religious name: Teresa of Jesus)*
Spanish mystic, spiritual writer and founder of the Discalced Carmelites. She entered the Carmelite Convent, Avila, at the age of twenty but suffered bad health. Within the convent she lived a lax life until she experienced a religious awakening in 1555. Her mystical experiences began soon afterwards, and in 1558 she resolved to reform the Carmelite way of life. This was achieved, in the face of fierce opposition, with official approval, at the Convent of St Joseph, Avila, in 1562. From this period dates her *Life* and *The Way of Perfection*; both are outstanding spiritual classics, along with the later *The Interior Castle* (1588). From 1567, with the help of John of the Cross, who reformed the male Carmelites, Teresa, in spite of great difficulties, founded sixteen more convents. Her ascetic teaching has been regarded as the classical exposition of the contemplative life.

Tersteergen, Gerhard *(1667–1769)*
German Protestant spiritual writer and director. After a conversion experience (1687) he retired to a solitary life. After 1727, when he had founded his Pilgrim's Hut at Otterbeck, near Mulheim, he spent his life as a spiritual director and translator of devotional works. He is best remembered now for his hymns, some of which have been translated into English.

Tertullian, Quintus Septimus Florens *(c. 160–c. 225)*
Early Christian theologian and writer. Converted to Christianity *c.* 196, he emerged as a leader of the African Church. Always a teacher, he developed as an apologist for Christianity and his many writings include apologetical and theological works. About 210, disturbed at the laxity in Christian life, he joined the Montanist sect; this too proved to be lacking in rigour, so he founded his own sect, which lasted until the fifth century in Africa.

Tetzel, Johann *(c. 1465–1519)*
German Dominican friar whose preaching and selling of indulgences reflected the Church abuses of the period, caused great scandal throughout Germany and was the occasion of Martin Luther's Ninety-Five Theses in 1517. Tetzel replied, but soon after retired to Leipzig Priory, where he died.

Theobald *(c. 1090–1161)*
Benedictine monk and Abbot of Bec, France, who became Archbishop of Canterbury in 1138. He proved to be an exceptional administrator, strengthning the position of the Church in England. He introduced the study of Roman law and, as an educator, he trained other leading churchmen for high office.

Theodore, St *(c. 602–690)*
A Greek from Tarsus, he was appointed by Pope Vitalian as Archbishop of Canterbury. Arriving at Canterbury in 669, he established a school there and set about reorganising dioceses and reforming Church government. His greatest achievement was to create a centralised Church in England according to the Roman model. He also called the first synod of the whole English Church (673).

Theodore of Mopsuestia *(c. 350–428)*
Controversial theologian and biblical exegete. Influenced by St John Chrysostom, he entered a monastery near Antioch, where he spent ten years. He became Bishop of Mopsuestia (392) and started writing about 402. He wrote commentaries and theological works which had a big impact upon the Eastern Church of the time.

Theodore Studites, St *(759–826)* *(also known as Theodore of Studius)*
Abbot of the Monastery of Studius, he was a leading opponent of iconoclasm. He fought for Church independence from imperial power, which caused him to be exiled twice. Working to reform monastic life, his monastery became a famous centre; his published works include homilies and nearly six hundred letters.

Theodoret *(c. 393–466)*
Controversial theologian and Bishop of Cyrrhus. From a monastic background, as a bishop he was energetic in fighting heresy, writing several treatises

of apologetics, the most famous being *Therapeutike*. He tried to shed more light on the Christological discussions of the time with his *On the Incarnation* (431) and *Eranistes* (446). This led to a famous conflict with Cyril of Alexandria and an eventual condemnation of some of Theodoret's teaching at the Council of Constantinople in 553.

Thérèse of Lisieux, St *(1873–1897)* *(original name: Marie Francoise Thérèse Martin)*
Carmelite nun. From a very pious home, at the age of fifteen, after much opposition, she entered the convent at Lisieux, where two of her own sisters were already nuns. Professed in 1890, she longed to go to the foreign missions, but ill-health made it impossible. Neurotic as a child, in the convent she never exhibited anything but an unselfish pleasant manner. Her struggle to achieve this and her 'little way' to sanctity are recorded in her autobiography *Histoire d'une âme*, written in obedience. It was the huge popular success of this book, recording her courageous coping with the affliction of tuberculosis, that attracted a tremendous following. She was canonised in 1925 and named a patron of Roman Catholic Foreign Missions and co-patron of France (1947).

Thierry of Chartres *(c. 1100–1151)*
Theologian, medieval philosopher and eminent teacher. He taught at Chartres (1121) and then at Paris (1124), John of Salisbury being one of his pupils; he was one of the first to introduce Arabian knowledge of science into the West. His unpublished *Heptateuchon* (book in seven volumes) and his commentary on Genesis reveal him as an exponent of the application of Platonist philosophy to the mysteries of the Christian faith.

Tholuck, Friedrich August Gottreu *(1799–1877)*
German Protestant theologian who lectured at Berlin (1820–1826) and Halle University. He exerted great influence upon his students through pastoral care and in his works he reveals his Pietistic leanings, doing much to check the spread of rationalism in Germany.

Thomas à Kempis *(1379/80–1471)* *(originally Thomas Hemerken)*
Probable author of *The Imitation of Christ*, the devotional book which has been considered the most influential Christian work (excepting the Bible). He studied at the religious centre, Deventer, Netherlands, founded by the Brethren of the Common Life. In 1399 he joined the Augustinian Canons Regular Community at Agnietenberg, where he spent the rest of his life, directing novices, writing, preaching and giving spiritual direction. His writings, of different kinds, are all permeated with the same devotional spirit of *Imitatio Christi*, which is the best representation of the 'Devotio Moderna', a religious movement founded by Gerhard Groote.

Thomas Aquinas, St *(c. 1225–1274)*
Foremost philosopher and theologian of the Roman Catholic Church. Educated by (and destined by his family for membership of) the Benedictine Abbey at Monte Cassino, he chose, in the face of fierce opposition, to join the newly founded Dominican Order. Furthering his education at the University of Paris, he was a pupil of the renowned Albertus Magnus, who introduced him to the thought of Aristotle. He taught at Paris and was appointed theological adviser to the Papal Curia (1259–1265). In 1272 he returned to Italy to found a Dominican House of Studies at the University of Naples. He defended the application of Aristotelian principles to theology against the Franciscan scholar Bonaventure. At Naples he worked hard to produce his celebrated *Summa Theologica*, the classical systematisation of Latin theology. He died on his way to the Second Council of Lyons. Thomas's many theological and philosophical works, and biblical commentaries, reached a culmination in his two 'Summae', the first being *Summa contra Gentiles*, the other being the *Summa Theologica*. His spiritual poetry lives on in several eucharistic hymns still used in the Church's liturgy.

Thompson, Francis *(1859–1907)*
English Roman Catholic poet best remembered for his famous poem *The Hound of Heaven*. He left his training for the priesthood at Ushaw, for medicine; this too proved unsuccessful, and he lived in destitution in London for three years before he and his poetry were discovered by Wilfrid Meynell.

Thurneysen, Eduard *(1888–1974)*
Protestant theologian from Switzerland who successively held pastoral posts at Zurich, Bruggen (near St Gall) *etc.* He associated with Karl Barth in developing dialectical theology, himself supplying the pastoral dimension. His own works included *Das Wort Gottes und die Kirche* (1927).

Tikhon *(1866–1925)* *(originally Vasily Ivanovich Belavin)*
Patriarch of the Russian Orthodox Church after the Revolution of 1917. He became a monk (1891) and rose swiftly in the Church, serving as bishop for the Orthodox community, for two years, in New York (1905–1907). Returning to Russia, he was elected to the restored Patriarchate of Moscow. Harassed by the Soviet Government, he none the less wielded considerable moral authority.

Tillich, Paul *(1886–1965)*
Protestant theologian, educated at Tübingen and Halle (1904–1912). Ordained for the Lutheran ministry, he served as a chaplain in the First World War, after which he joined the Religious Socialists. While lecturing in theology and philosophy successively at Marburg (1924), Dresden (1925) and Frankfurt (1929), he developed his theology through many publications, including his major three-volume work *Systematic Theology* (1951–1963) and

Kirche und Kultur (1924). Criticism of the Nazi movement led to his leaving Germany and settling in the United States, taking teaching posts at the Union Theological Seminary (1933–1955), Harvard (1955–1962) and the University of Chicago (1962–1965). A prolific writer, some of his books reached a large public audience, *e.g. The Courage to Be* (1952).

Tillotson, John *(1630–1694)*
Archbishop of Canterbury who reluctantly accepted the See (1691) and whose archiepiscopate was marked by his fierce opposition to Roman Catholics, Puritans and atheists. A famous preacher, many later preachers modelled themselves upon him.

Tischendorf, Constantin *(1815–1874)*
German biblical critic. Starting as a student at Leipzig University, and continuing as Professor of Theology, he devoted himself to the New Testament text, publishing eight editions of the Greek text (1841–1869). His invaluable contributions to biblical textual criticism included the search for manuscripts. His most famous find was of the *Codex Sinaiticus* at the Monastery of St Catherine in the Sinai Peninsula.

Toplady, Augustus Montague *(1740–1778)*
Author, hymnwriter and vicar of Broad Hembury, Devonshire, Toplady is remembered particularly for 'Rock of Ages', which first appeared in print in 1775. His most important prose work was *The Historic Proof of the Doctrinal Calvinism of the Church of England* (1774), which reflected his turning from support for John Wesley to extreme Calvinism.

Traherne, Thomas *(1637–1674)*
Ordained for the Anglican ministry (1660), he lived a pastoral life as rector and chaplain, having only one book published in his lifetime, the controversial *Roman Forgeries* (1673). His *Poetical Works* was discovered and published in 1903 and he was acknowledged as a religious poet of great originality of thought and depth of feeling. In 1908 his *Centuries of Meditations*, a collection of reflections on ethics and religion, was published.

Tremellius, John Immanuel *(1510–1580)*
Of Jewish origins, he was converted to Christianity (1540) and in 1541 became a Protestant. On leaving Italy, as a Hebrew scholar, he taught successively at Strasbourg, Cambridge, Heidelberg and Sedan. His greatest achievement was his translation of the Bible into Latin; this was the standard Protestant Latin translation for a long period.

Trench, Richard Chenevix *(1807–1886)*
Archbishop of Dublin and biblical scholar. As a writer he stimulated popular interest in New Testament studies with his *Notes on the Parables of our Lord* (1841) and *Notes on the Miracles of our Lord* (1846); he also wrote religious poetry. As archbishop he opposed the disestablishment of the Irish Church.

Trimmer, Sarah *(1741–1810)* *(née Kirby)*
English authoress and mother of twelve children, she promoted the Sunday school movement with writing and the production of religious text books for charity schools. A woman of great piety and charity, she is best remembered for her children's book *The History of the Robins* (1786).

Truth, Sojourner *(c. 1797–1883)* *(legal name: Isabella Van Wagener)*
American black evangelist. Born and reared as a slave, she was set free by Isaac Van Wagener, whose name she took. Deeply religious from childhood, she had visions and believed herself called by God. From 1843 she adopted the name 'Sojourner Truth', and her personal magnetism made her a famous itinerant preacher. She energetically supported the abolition of slavery and the Women's Rights Movement.

Tubman, Harriet *(1821–1913)*
Harriet Tubman was born a slave in Maryland, in the American South. After escaping in 1849, she spent much of her life helping other runaway slaves to evade capture and find their way to the freer North. She helped to set up and run the 'Underground Railway', a series of safe barns and cellars where slaves could hide and receive money and clothing. When slavery was abolished she devoted the rest of her life to providing education for the children of former slaves.

Tunstall, Cuthbert *(1474–1559)*
Bishop of Durham (1530–1552 and 1553–1559) who reluctantly implemented the Reformation in England, demonstrating his conservatism in his treatise *De Veritate Corporis et Sanguinis Domini Nostri Jesu Christi in Eucharistia* (1554). He had proved valuable to Henry VIII in overseas diplomatic missions. Imprisoned under Edward VI, reinstated by Mary, he was once again deprived of his See and imprisoned under Elizabeth I.

Tyndale, William *(c. 1494–1536)*
English Reformer, biblical translator and Protestant martyr. A student of Oxford and Cambridge, he was refused permission to publish an English version of the Bible, so he began the work in Cologne (1525) and completed it at Worms. His translation later became the basis of the Authorised Version. His other works include *Parable of the Wicked Mammon* (1528) and *Obedience of a Christian Man*. Arrested in 1535, and condemned for heresy, he was burnt at the stake.

Tyrrell, George *(1861–1909)*
English Roman Catholic theologian who advocated Modernism. Of evangelical origins, he converted to Roman Catholicism (1879) and joined the Society of Jesus (Jesuits) in 1880. He served at Stonyhurst College, Lancashire, and Farm Street, the principal Jesuit Church in London. His friendship with Friedrich von Hugel and the influence of A. Loisy led to his Modernist publications; some of the many works were published under pseudonyms. He was expelled from the Jesuit Order in 1906 and excommunicated by the Roman Catholic Church. Pope Pius X condemned Modernism in his encyclical letter *Pascendi Gregis* (1907).

U

Ullathorne, William Bernard *(1806–1889)*
Benedictine missionary to Australia and the first Roman Catholic Bishop of Birmingham. After years as a cabin boy, he entered the Benedictine Order in 1824 and volunteered to work in the convict penal colonies of Australia and Norfolk Island (1832–1842). His *Horrors of Transportation Briefly Unfolded* (1836) helped to bring the abolition of the transportation system. On his return to England he became Vicar Apostolic of the Western District of England (1846) and Bishop of Birmingham in 1850. His most popular work, his autobiography *From Cabin Boy to Archbishop* (1856), was often reprinted.

Underhill, Evelyn *(1875–1941)*
Anglican mystical poet and exponent of mysticism. Educated at King's College, London, after a conversion experience (1907) she studied the mystics and her books *Mysticism* (1911), *The Mystic Way* (1913), *The Essentials of Mysticism* (1920) and others, helped to establish mystical theology as a reputable discipline for contemporary study. From 1924 she was much sought after as a spiritual counsellor, retreat giver and lecturer.

Ursula, St *(fourth century)*
According to pious legend she was the leader of eleven, or possibly eleven thousand, virgins reputedly martyred at Cologne by fourth-century Huns (nomadic invaders from South-East Europe). The story is based upon an inscription found at Cologne; a later form of the legend suggests Ursula was a British princess killed on her way to Rome. The patron of many educational establishments, she is known today through the Ursulines, a congregation of Religious Sisters dedicated to education.

Ussher, James *(1581–1656)*
Archbishop of Armagh and a highly regarded scholar of his day. Memorable for his work on patristic texts, especially upon the writings of Ignatius of Antioch, and upon the chronology of the Old Testament. After the Civil War he worked for reconciliation between churchmen and dissenters.

V

Vadianus, Joachim *(1484–1551)*
Swiss poet and humanist who rose to be Mayor of St Gallen (1526), where he also practised medicine and was a popular preacher. He was influential in establishing the Reformation in Switzerland.

Valdés, Juan de *(c. 1490–1541)*
Spanish humanist and religious writer who developed religious ideas similar to Erasmus; publication of these as *Dialogue on Christian Doctrine* (1529) caused him to flee to Italy from the Spanish Inquisition (1531). Although formally remaining a member of the Roman Catholic Church, his ideas paved the way for the Reformation.

Valentine, St *(third century)*
The name of two legendary martyrs: a Roman priest who died during the persecution of the Emperor Claudius (c. 269), and a Bishop of Terni, Italy, martyred probably in Rome. It is possible that the legendary accounts have some basis in historical fact and may derive from one original person. The association of St Valentine's Day with a lovers' festival derives probably from the pagan Roman fertility festival of Lupercalia.

Valignano, Alessandro *(1539–1606)*
Italian Jesuit missionary who helped to introduce Christianity to the Far East. He trained missionaries, including Matteo Ricci, in Portuguese India (from 1574) and went personally to Japan, where he successfully converted several Japanese feudal lords. There he was highly esteemed, establishing a centre for the education of native priests; at his death there were over 115 Jesuits in Japan and an estimated three hundred thousand Christians.

Van Espen, Zeger Bernhard *(1646–1728)*
Belgian canon lawyer and supporter of Gallican theories who is remembered for his learned *Jus Ecclesiasticum Universum* (1700) and his judgment, in 1723, in the 'Chapter of Utrecht' case, in which he supported Jansenism, which led to his suspension and condemnation.

Van Eyck, Hubert *(1366–1426)* and Jan *(1390–1441)*
Flemish painters. Jan was probably pupil to his elder brother and settled at Bruges. Hubert started the famous *Adoration of the Lamb* altar piece for the Cathedral of St Bavon, which was finished by his brother in 1432. This remarkable work is considered one of the masterpieces of Christian art.

Vane, Sir Henry *(1613–1662)*
English Puritan, usually called 'the Younger', to distinguish him from his statesman father. He travelled widely in Europe, then went to New England (1635), where he served as Governor of Massachusetts for a year. Returning to England and entering politics, he worked against the episcopacy and was chief negotiator in arranging the Solemn League and Covenant with Scotland (1643). He opposed Cromwell's dictatorial methods, retired from politics and wrote several religious books, including the obscure *Retired Man's Meditations* (1655). At the Restoration he was imprisoned and executed for his parliamentary activities.

Vaughan, Henry *(1622–1695)*
Welsh poet, doctor and mystic. He practised medicine at Brecon and Newton-by-Usk and about 1650, after a spiritual experience, he produced religious poetry of great depth. His *Silex Scintillans* (1650) shows the influence of George Herbert. *The Mount of Olives* followed in 1652. Largely disregarded in his own day, his poetry had a great influence upon William Wordsworth.

Vaughan, Herbert *(1832–1903)*
Archbishop of Westminster and cardinal. Vice-President of St Edmund's Seminary, Ware, and founder of St Joseph's Missionary College, Mill Hill (1866). He championed the Ultramontanist cause prior to the First Vatican Council through his editorship of *The Tablet*. Appointed first to the See of Salford (1872), he was elevated to Westminster (1892) and made cardinal in 1893. As archbishop he commenced the building of Westminster Cathedral and was involved in the Education Bill of 1902.

Venantius Fortunatus *(c. 530–c. 610)*
Poet and Bishop of Poitiers. As the result of a pilgrimage to the shrine of St Martin of Tours from Treviso, near Venice, he settled at Poitiers, France. He was impressed by the holiness of Radegunda, formerly a queen, who had founded a monastery there. He served the community as steward, then as chaplain, and finally became Bishop of Poitiers. Although author of several lives of saints, he is remembered for his poetry which combines the style of the classical Latin poets with the mystical spirit of Christianity. His genius is best seen in the hymns still in use, the *Pange Lingua* and *Vexilla Regis*.

Venn, Henry *(1725–1797)*
One of the leading evangelical divines of his time and one of the first to have a parish, that of Huddersfield, where he had a reputation for piety and zeal. Author of the popular book *The Complete Duty of Man* (1736), he was also one of the founders of the Clapham Group.

Vermigli, Pietro Martire – *See* Peter Martyr

Veronica, St
Renowned woman of Jerusalem, who, according to legend, wiped the face of Christ as he carried his cross to Calvary. Although this incident is one of the Stations of the Cross, it has no foundation in Scripture. The origin of the legend may spring from a misapplication of a story in Eusebius of Caesarea's *Historia Ecclesiastica*; it seems to be of French origin.

Vianney, St Jean-Baptiste *(1786–1859) (also known as the Curé d'Ars)*
Attracted early to the priesthood, he had severe difficulties with study; drafted into Napoleon's army, he deserted and after an amnesty (1810) he returned to the seminary. Eventually ordained (1815), he was first a curate at Ecully; he was appointed curé of Ars (1818), from where his fame as a model parish priest and saintly confessor with supernatural powers spread throughout Europe. By 1827 the remote village of Ars was a pilgrimage centre and from 1845 approximately twenty thousand visitors a year sought spiritual direction and confession from the curé. He was canonised in 1925 and declared patron saint of parish priests in 1929.

Victor – There were three popes of this name, the most significant being:

Victor I, St *(d. 199)*
Pope from 189 and believed to be an African by birth. He is memorable for imposing on the Eastern patriarchs the Roman date for Easter, strongly asserting papal authority. He also replaced Latin for Greek as the official language of the Roman Church.

Victor III *(1027–1087)*
Benedictine monk (known as Desiderius) of the monastery of Monte Cassino who, as abbot (1058), promoted the abbey as a centre of learning and culture and radically rebuilt it. Chosen pope against his will, he was driven out of Rome by the emperor and became embroiled in problems with an anti-pope. He condemned lay investiture by the emperor and died at Monte Cassino, where he had taken refuge.

Vieira, Antonio *(1608–1697)*
Portuguese Jesuit theologian, missionary and master of classical Portuguese prose. Continually drawn to missionary work, his outstanding preaching drew him, however, to royal attention and several diplomatic missions. His befriending of converted Jews and Amazon Indians gained him enemies and his theology attracted the attention of the Spanish Inquisition. He played a positive role in both Brazilian and Portuguese history.

Vigilius *(d. 555)*
Pope from 537 to 555, and remembered for his part in the Three Chapters Controversy, a complex theological dispute which arose over the struggle with Monophysitism in the Eastern and Western Churches. Vigilius succeeded Pope Silverius, who was forcibly removed by the civil authorities for his support of the Council of Chalcedon, which had condemned Monophysitism. Great imperial pressure was put upon Vigilius, whose *Constitution*, an attempt to resolve the problem, only resulted in a number of bishops deserting him, a schism which lasted 150 years.

Vilmar, August Friedrich Christian *(1800–1860)*
Lutheran theologian who rigorously opposed rationalism with his 'theology of facts', defending the retention of the early Christian creeds. He compiled a hymn book and wrote many theological works, the most widely known being *Geschichte der Deutschen Nationalliteratur*.

Vincent de Paul, St *(c. 1580–1660)*
Of a French peasant family, he was ordained a Roman Catholic priest in 1600 but was captured by pirates (1605) and enslaved in Algeria for two years. Chaplain to Queen Margaret of Valois in Paris, his preaching and work among the city's poor attracted much attention. Tutor to the household of Count de Gondi, general of the galleys (1613–1625), he ministered to the galley slaves. In 1625 he founded the Congregation of the Mission (known as Vincentians or Lazarists), devoted to mission work among French peasants. Influenced by Francis de Sales, he founded, with Louise de Marillac, the famous Sisters of Charity and established hospitals, orphanages and seminaries to train priests for the missions. His whole life was devoted to the alleviation of human suffering. He was canonised in 1737.

Vincent Ferrer, St *(c. 1350–1419)*
Spanish Dominican friar and famous preacher. Professor of theology at Valencia, he became confessor to the anti-pope Benedict XIII (1394), but after five years he devoted his life to preaching missions to huge crowds, with great effect, throughout Southern Europe. He tried to persuade Benedict XIII to abandon his claims and worked successfully to end the schism.

Vincent of Lérino, St *(d. c. 450)*
Theologian and monk of the Mediterranean island of Lérino, near Cannes, at that time a monastic centre of education and culture. Little is known of his life beyond his reputation for scriptural knowledge and theology, and for his work *Commonitoria* (*c.* 435), a reply to current heresies.

Vinet, Alexandre Rudolf *(1797–1847)*
French–Swiss Reformed theologian, moralist and literary critic who was influential in establishing the Reformation in Switzerland. An energetic defender of freedom of worship and the separation of Church and state, he believed that conscience, not dogma, is man's basis for religion; these views found expression in his works, particularly *Memoire Sur Les Libertés des Cultes* (1826).

Vitoria, Francisco de *(c. 1485–1546)*
Dominican priest and one of the greatest of Spanish theologians. He lectured in theology at the Universities of Paris, Valladolid and Salamanca, where he inaugurated a new school of theology. He is often regarded as 'Father of International Law' for his teaching on the conditions for a just war and his spirited defence of the rights of the Indians of the New World. His moral teaching was presented in his *Reflections*, based upon lectures given between 1527 and 1540.

Vladimir, St *(956–1015)*
First Christian ruler in Russia, considered 'Apostle of the Russians'. Steeped in paganism, he embraced Christianity to further his military conquests and ambitions but became an ardent promoter of his new faith, erecting many churches, promoting education and aiding the poor; however, his methods of spreading Christianity were sometimes heavy-handed.

Voetius, Gisbertus *(1589–1676)*
Dutch Reformed theologian of strong uncompromising convictions who stoutly defended the Calvinistic doctrine of predestination and condemned the rationalistic thought of the seventeenth-century French philosopher Descartes. He would allow no concessions to Roman Catholic thought, as his *Diatribe de Theologia* (1668) reveals.

Von Hügel, Baron Friedrich *(1852–1925)*
Roman Catholic philosopher, theologian and spiritual counsellor. A naturalised British citizen, after a cosmopolitan education he lived most of his life at Hampstead (1876–1903) and Kensington, London (1903–1925). A conversion experience (1870) brought him to a deeper faith and with a keen interest in science, biblical criticism and philosophy he sympathised with the Modernist movement. He founded the London Society

for the Study of Religion (1905) and wrote many works of lasting value, including *Eternal Life* (1912) and the posthumous *The Reality of God* (1931).

Voss, Gerhard Jan *(1577–1649)*
Dutch Protestant theologian and humanist who was suspected of Remonstrant teaching and involved in the disputes arising. He was invited to England and, refusing a post at Cambridge, accepted one offered by Archbishop Laud at Canterbury. All his works made a solid contribution to learning.

W

Wach, Joachim *(1898–1955)*
One of the foremost German Protestant theologians, he specialised in the modern science of religion. He lectured at Leipzig (1929–1935) and Chicago (1945–1955); in his works, which include *Sociology of Religion* (1944), he explored religious experience as well as the sociology of religion.

Wake, William *(1657–1737)*
Archbishop of Canterbury who engaged (1717–1720) in negotiations for reunion with the French Roman Catholic Church, represented by the Gallian theologian, Dupin; the project ended with Dupin's death. He sympathised with the Nonconformists and advocated changes to accommodate them. His *Principles of the Christian Religion* (1700) proved very popular.

Waldenström, Paul Peter *(1838–1917)*
Swedish Free Churchman and theologian who was active in the revivalist movement, editing *Pietisten*. He proposed theories contrary to traditional Lutheran theology; hence he founded a large sectarian movement in Sweden and took over direction of the Swedish Mission Society (1905).

Walther, Carl Ferdinand Wilhelm *(1811–1887)*
Conservative Lutheran theologian, of German origin, who settled in Missouri and worked to unite the various Lutheran groupings in the USA, becoming President of the Missouri Synod of American Lutheranism (1847).

Walton, Brian *(1600–1661)*
Bishop of Chester, remembered for his six-volume *Biblia Sacra Polyglotta*, or *London Polygot Bible*, which was begun in 1653 and never superseded. Walton lost his living and was imprisoned for supporting Laud, but the Restoration brought him recognition and the See of Chester.

Warburton, William *(1698–1779)*
Anglican Bishop of Gloucester and controversialist. After ordination (1727) he held various livings before accepting the See of Gloucester. His works included many of literary criticism, and *The Alliance between Church and State* (1736) and his famous *The Divine Legation of Moses* (1737–1741). He attacked the new Methodist movement in *The Doctrine of Grace* (1762) and was an early, outspoken opponent of slavery.

Ward, Mary *(1585–1645)*
A Yorkshirewoman, she entered the Poor Clares Religious Order (1606) but left to found her own more active Religious Congregation in 1609. After opening houses in Liege, Cologne and Vienna, her request for papal approval (1629) was refused and the Congregation was suppressed. Later approval was given by Urban VIII and the houses reopened. The most famous in Britain is the Bar Convent at York, originally founded in 1642.

Ward, Wilfrid *(1856–1916)*
Son of W. G. Ward, he gave up training for the Roman Catholic priesthood in favour of literary work. Biographer of his father, Cardinal Wiseman and Cardinal Newman, he also edited the *Dublin Review* and raised it to a high standard.

Ward, William George *(1812–1882)*
Anglican theologian, philosopher, Fellow of Balliol College, Oxford, and keen supporter of the Oxford Movement. His book *The Ideal of a Christian Church* (1844) praised the Roman Catholic Church, which he joined in 1845. Constantly engaged in controversial writing, he lectured at St Edmund's College, Ware, and supported the Ultramontanist party in the English Roman Catholic Church.

Warham, William *(c. 1450–1532)*
Archbishop of Canterbury. Educated in civil law he rose rapidly, becoming Master of the Rolls (1494) and, after ordination (1493), Bishop of London (1502), Lord Chancellor and Archbishop in 1504. A quiet intellectual, he had to continually give way to Cardinal Wolsey in ecclesiastical policy. Although he supported Henry VIII's divorce petition (1530) he was not in sympathy with the Protestant movement and resolutely opposed the king's anticlerical policies towards the end of his life.

Waterland, Daniel *(1683–1740)*
Anglican theologian and writer. Educated at Magdalene College, Cambridge, of which he became Fellow (1704) and Master (1713), he rose through other ecclesiastical preferments, but he is remembered as a learned theologian and author of several influential books, including *Eight Sermons in Defence of the Divinity of Our Lord Jesus Christ* (1720).

Watson, David *(1933–1984)*
Anglican priest, preacher and author. Educated at Cambridge, he was ordained (1959) and served as a curate at St Mark's, Gillingham, Kent. After moving to York (1965) he dedicated himself to student work and led over sixty university missions. From 1974 David led many festivals worldwide, using a team of singers, dancers and musicians (from 1976) in corporate acts of worship. He wrote thirteen books, including his auto-biography *You are my God* and his last, *Fear No Evil*, which describes his struggle with cancer.

Watts, Isaac *(1674–1748)*
Nonconformist pastor and writer, also considered the father of English hymnody. While assistant (1699) and later full pastor at Mark Lane Congregational Chapel, London, he wrote his famous hymns, *e.g.* 'When I survey the Wondrous Cross' and 'O God, our help in ages past', which were published in *Horae Lyricae* (1706) and *Hymns and Spiritual Songs* (1707). He did much to establish hymn singing, previously suspect, as an essential part of Nonconformist worship. Ill-health forced his resignation from pastoral work in 1712 and he lived the rest of his life at Abney Park, Stoke Newington. He wrote many books, including text books, but little, beyond his hymns, is remembered.

Weiss, Bernhard *(1827–1918)*
German New Testament scholar and theologian. Professor of New Testament exegesis at Kiel (1863–1877) and Berlin (1877–1908), his two important works are *Biblical Theology of the New Testament* (1868) and *The Life of Christ* (1882).

Weiss, Johannes *(1863–1914)*
Son of the above and a New Testament scholar of originality who laid the foundations for the development of form criticism. Professor at Marburg (1895) and Heidelberg (1908), his *Die Predigt Jesu vom Reiche Gottes* (1892) explored the eschatalogical dimension of the gospel and his many other works were equally influential.

Welch, Adam Cleghorn *(1864–1943)*
Scottish biblical scholar who was a pastoral minister and preacher, and became professor of Hebrew and Old Testament exegesis in New College, Edinburgh (1913–1934). A critic of Wellhausen, he is remembered particularly for his development of an alternative theory, published in five books, concluding with *The Work of the Chronicler* in 1939.

Wellhausen, Julius *(1844–1918)*

German biblical scholar and critic. After several posts he became professor in Semitics at Marburg (1885–1892) and Göttingen (1892–1913). His work of higher criticism, particularly upon the structure of the book of Genesis, transformed Old Testament studies. His principal works were *Die Geschichte Israels* (1883) and *Das Evangelium Marci* (1903). His New Testament theories were not so readily accepted.

Wenceslas, St *(c. 903–929) (also known by his Czech name Vaclav)*

Prince-duke of Bohemia, martyr and patron saint of the Czechs. Raised and educated as a Christian by his grandmother, St Ludmila, after the death of his father and the violent anti-Christian regency of his mother Wenceslas became ruler. He promoted Christianity, encouraged missionary work and enjoyed a reputation for piety. His political friendship with Germany and his religion provoked his murder on his way to Mass. Immediately there were stories of miracles and he was venerated as a martyr. His virtues are still extolled in the famous Christmas carol.

Wesley, Charles *(1707–1788)*

Anglican priest (1735), evangelist, and hymnwriter. Educated at Westminster School and Christ Church, Oxford, while at the latter he joined his brother John's study group, nicknamed 'Methodists' because of their methodical approach. He went to Georgia, North America, with John and founded Methodist Societies there; on his return to England, and after a conversion experience, he began an itinerant preaching ministry. He established himself as the greatest of English hymnwriters, writing over 5,500, the first collection being published as *Hymns and Sacred Poems* (1739).

Wesley, John *(1703–1791)*

Anglican priest (1728), evangelist and founder of Methodism. Educated at Charterhouse and Christ Church, Oxford: while there he gathered around him a study group of serious Christians, nicknamed 'Methodists'. After an unsuccessful missionary trip to Georgia, North America, he became influenced by Moravian teaching, experienced a conversion and devoted the rest of his life to preaching. Churches were closed to him, so he preached in the open, travelling an average of eight thousand miles a year on horseback. Although he wanted the Movement to remain within the Church of England, by 1784 the Methodists had removed themselves from it. John Wesley's journeys took him to Scotland and Ireland and at his death there were over seventy-one thousand members in Great Britain and over forty-three thousand in America.

Westcott, Brooke Foss *(1825–1901)*

Anglican Bishop of Durham, best remembered for his theological works and his celebrated edition of the Greek New Testament, prepared with F. J. A.

Hort (1881). Regius professor of divinity at Cambridge, he founded the Cambridge Clergy Training School (which became 'Westcott House'). As bishop he was concerned with social issues, mediating in the Coal Strike of 1892. In the same year his substantial theological work *The Gospel of Life* was published.

Weston, Frank *(1871–1924)*
Anglican Bishop of Zanzibar (1908) who developed great empathy with his African people. Involved in the Kikuyu Dispute (1913) he, however, worked for and inspired the drive for Christian unity at the Lambeth Conference of 1920.

Whately, Richard *(1787–1863)*
Anglican Archbishop of Dublin, educator, logician and social reformer. Educated at Oriel College, Oxford, while there he wrote his satirical *Historic Doubts Relative to Napoleon Bonaparte* (1819). As Archbishop of Dublin, in co-operation with the Roman Catholic authorities, he devised a nonsectarian programme of religious education which was later abandoned.

Wheelock, Eleazar *(1711–1779)*
American Congregational minister, educator and founder of Dartmouth College, established in New Hampshire at the new town of Hanover, which he helped to settle. A popular preacher, he played an important part in the Great Awakening.

White, William *(1748–1836)*
First bishop of the United States Episcopal Church. Ordained an Anglican priest in England (1772) he returned to Philadelphia where he became rector of Christ Church. He led the foundation of the Protestant Episcopal Church, independent of the Church of England, with its own bishops; he was himself the first presiding bishop of that Church.

Whitefield, George *(1714–1770)*
Anglican priest and evangelist whose popular and powerful preaching supported the foundation of the Methodist movement and stimulated other dissident Churches. His *Journal* began publication in 1739 and he prompted the foundation of nearly fifty colleges and universities in the USA.

Whitgift, John *(c. 1530–1604)*
Archbishop of Canterbury. Prominent at Cambridge, where he was educated, as Fellow, Master of Trinity College and professor of divinity, he was first Bishop of Worcester (1577–1583) before going to Canterbury. He sought to strengthen and unify the Church of England, opposing both papal and Puritan influences. He founded almshouses and a school at Croydon, where he is buried.

Whitman, Marcus *(1802–1847)*
American Congregational missionary and physician who ministered to the Cayuse Indians of Waiilatpu, near Walla Walla. As a pioneer he helped to open up the Pacific North West; his valiant efforts failed and he and his family, with others, died in a massacre by the Indians in 1847.

Whittier, John Greenleaf *(1807–1892)*
American Quaker author, abolitionist and poet. At first just a journalist and poet, after 1832 he became a fervent anti-slavery advocate, using his poetry to good effect. His writing developed during the period 1843–1865, his Quaker poetry coming to the fore from 1866 to his death. His best-known poem, *Snow Bound* (1866), was followed by others, including *The Pennsylvania Pilgrim* (1872). Some of his poems, e.g. 'Dear Lord and Father of Mankind', became famous hymns.

Wilberforce, Robert Isaac *(1802–1857)*
Theologian of the Oxford Movement, second son of W. Wilberforce; his writings include *The Doctrine of the Incarnation* (1848). Close friend of Froude and Newman, he joined the Roman Catholic Church in 1854.

Wilberforce, Samuel *(1805–1873)*
Anglican bishop, first of Oxford then of Winchester, and third son of William Wilberforce. He was considered a model bishop for his pastoral reforms and innovations, founding new churches, establishing religious communities and the first Anglican theological college at Cuddesdon (1854). He opposed Liberalism and attacked Darwinism, having a famous debate with Thomas Huxley (1860) on the issue. In 1870 he initiated the revision of the Authorised Version of the Bible.

Wilberforce, William *(1759–1833)*
Politician, philanthropist and promoter of the abolition of the slave trade. He entered Parliament (1780) with his lifelong friend William Pitt the Younger, and his parliamentary work was guided, after 1785, by his strict evangelicalism. He gained a reputation for radicalism, supporting the Roman Catholic political emancipation, and devoting much energy to bringing the slave trade, and then slavery, in British territories to an end. He was one of the founders of the Clapham Sect, and helped to establish the Church Missionary Society (1798) and the Bible Society (1803). His *Practical View of the Prevailing Religious System of Professed Christians* (1797) was widely popular and demonstrated his reputation as a leading evangelical.

Wilfrid, St *(634–709)*
Monk and Bishop of York. He started his monastic life at the Celtic Lindisfarne (648) but later moved to Canterbury and studied the Roman

form. Ever after he promoted Roman usage and papal authority, especially evident at the Synod of Whitby (664) and in the establishment of the Benedictine Rule at the Hexham monastery. A great builder at Hexham, Ripon and York, he improved the liturgy and, showing a lively missionary zeal, promoted the idea of Anglo-Saxons working as missionaries among the Germanic peoples. He is commonly considered to be one of the greatest English saints.

Wilkes, Paget *(1871–1934)*
Protestant missionary in Japan, where he travelled in 1897 under the auspices of the Church Missionary Society to work with B. F. Buxton. He founded the Japanese Evangelistic Band and dedicated his whole life to his missionary work.

Wilkins, John *(1614–1672)*
Anglican Bishop of Chester, author and scientist who helped to found the Royal Society; as bishop he advocated tolerance for dissenters and wrote, among many works, *The Discovery of a World in the Moon* (1638).

William de la Mare *(d. 1290)*
English Franciscan theologian and philosopher who criticised the Aristotelian thought of Thomas Aquinas, against whom he wrote his *Correctorium Fratris Thomas*; this was approved for the whole Franciscan Order in 1282.

William of Auvergne *(1180–1249)* (*also known as William of Paris*)
French scholastic theologian and philosopher who lectured in divinity at the University of Paris (1223) and was author of the monumental *Magisterium Divinale* (1223–1240).

William of Ockham *(c. 1285–1349)*
Originating from Ockham, Surrey, he trained in logic at Oxford and later lectured there. His radicalism eventually caused his philosophy to be examined but, although censured by papal authority, it was never condemned. He was embroiled in the dispute between the Franciscan Order and the papacy, and his resultant excommunication caused him to attack the supremacy of papal power. A vigorous and independent thinker, Ockham was the most influential of fourteenth-century scholastic philosophers and the founder of Nominalism.

William of Saint-Thierry *(c. 1085–1148)*
Monk, theologian and mystical writer. After entering the Benedictine monastery in Reims (1113), he became a specialist in Scripture and patristic writings; he devoted much of his life to synthesising the theology of East and West with these. Elected abbot of Saint-Thierry, near Reims, his friend St

Bernard of Clairvaux encouraged his copious theological writing. To this period belong *On the Nature and Dignity of Love* and *On the Contemplation of God*. He retired to the Cistercian monastery of Signy, from where his more developed mystical writing comes, for example, *The Mirror of Faith* (1140) and the celebrated *Golden Letter* (1144).

Williams, Isaac *(1802–1865)*
Oxford-educated Anglican priest, poet and theologian, member of the Tractarian Movement, who contributed to *Lyra Apostolica* (1836) and the famous Tract 80, *Reserve in Communicating Religious Knowledge*. Losing the chair of poetry at Oxford (1842), he retired to concentrate upon his own poetry.

Williams, John *(1796–1839)*
Missionary sent out by the London Missionary Society to the Pacific (1817). He laboured among the islands, translating parts of the Bible into a local language until one day, landing at Dillon's Bay, Erromanga (1839), he was killed by cannibals. News of his death inspired much enthusiasm and support for missionary work in England.

Williams, Roger *(1603–1683)*
Pioneer and champion of religious toleration; founder of the colony of Rhode Island. After an Anglican ordination he sailed to North America (1630) in search of religious liberty. After many civil and religious disagreements he bought land from the Indians, later known as Rhode Island, which became a haven for Nonconformists and dissenters. He himself adhered to a Calvinist theology.

Williams, William *(1717–1791)*
Anglican minister who, by his preaching and poetry, did much to spread Methodism in Wales. He wrote more than eight hundred hymns and has been hailed as the first Welsh Romantic poet. His best-known hymn is 'Guide Me, O Thou Great Jehovah'.

Willibrord, St *(c. 658–739)*
Benedictine monk, archbishop and missionary. He was educated by the Benedictine monks of Ripon, Yorkshire, under the direction of St Wilfrid. Called to Ireland, he was ordained there. In 690, with companions, he was sent to evangelise West Frisia and he was consecrated archbishop of the Frisians in 695. Willibrord founded the monastery of Echternach and the success of his missionary work won him the title of 'Apostle of Friesland'. He is also patron saint of Holland.

Wilson, Gordon *(1927–1998)*
A shocking act of terrorism at Enniskillen, Northern Ireland, in November 1987, threw the humble Gordon Wilson into the public eye. He and his 20-

year-old daughter Marie were buried under rubble; Marie died but, broken-hearted, Gordon survived. He amazed the world, through a BBC report initially, by his forgiveness of the bombers. Born of a devout Methodist family – his father was a draper and his mother a nurse – Gordon Wilson entered the family business, marrying Joan in 1955. Their deeply Christian home was always open to all, Protestants and Catholics. Over the ten years following the terrorist bombing he was regularly on TV and radio, gently but firmly promoting the Christian message of forgiveness and peace. His book *Marie – A Story from Enniskillen* was a bestseller.

Winchelsey, Robert *(c. 1245–1313)* *(also known as Robert of Winchelsea)*
Theologian and Archbishop of Canterbury who championed ecclesiastical rights and found himself in constant opposition to both Edward I and Edward II.

Windthorst, Ludwig *(1812–1891)*
German Roman Catholic political leader of the Centre Party, which he founded to unify German Catholics and which struggled successfully against Bismarck's 'Kulturkampf'. Twice minister of Justice (1851–1853 and 1862–1865) he had the 'May' Laws directed against the Catholic Church gradually repealed (1888–1890); he is considered one of the greatest of German parliamentary leaders.

Winifred, St *(d. c. 650)* *(also known as Gwenfrewi)*
According to legend she was the beautiful daughter of a wealthy family living in North Wales. She refused the advances of Prince Caradog of Hawarden. Beheaded (or wounded) by him, she was healed by her uncle, St Beuno, and thereafter dedicated her life to God, becoming a nun and later abbess. A spring known as Holywell or St Winifred's Well marked the spot of her restoration (cure) to life, and this has been a great pilgrimage centre over the centuries. Patron saint of North Wales.

Winslow, Edward *(1595–1655)*
One of the *Mayflower* pilgrims who emigrated to New England; he was delegated to build relations with the local Indians, forming a friendship with Massasoit, their chief. He rose to become governor of the colony (1644–1645). What remains of his writings are of great interest, particularly the *Glorious Progress of the Gospel Amongst the Indians in New England* (1649).

Wipo *(d. c. 1050)*
Little is known of this priest and chaplain to the emperors Conrad II and Henry III who wrote poetry (most of which is lost); he is best recalled for his Easter hymn *Victimae Paschali Laudes*.

Wiseman, Nicholas Patrick Stephen *(1802–1865)*
First Cardinal Archbishop of Westminster. Of an Anglo-Irish family, he was educated in Rome and became rector of the English College there (1828–1840), also holding a position at the Vatican library. Appointed Vicar Apostolic, first of the Midland District then (1847–1850) of the London District, he was chosen as the first Archbishop of Westminster and cardinal when the Catholic Hierarchy was re-established in 1850. An Ultramontanist, he faced opposition from the long-established English Roman Catholics, but won respect by his tact and constructive achievements; his writings include the widely read historical novel *Fabiola* (1854).

Wishart, George *(c. 1513–1546)*
Scottish Reformer. At Cambridge, where he had fled from a heresy charge, he met Hugh Latimer; further charges caused him to flee to the Continent. On his return to his native Scotland he preached Reformation doctrine, strongly influencing John Knox; arrested by the Earl of Bothwell, he was tried for heresy and burned at the stake at St Andrews.

Wolsey, Thomas *(c. 1474–1530)*
Cardinal and statesman. Son of a Suffolk butcher, and educated at Oxford, after ordination (1498) he rose swiftly through ecclesiastical benefices to be Bishop of Lincoln (1514) and later the same year Archbishop of York; he was made a cardinal in 1515. Henry VIII chose him as Chancellor of England and Wolsey proceeded to amass a vast personal fortune, showing himself to be an able diplomat but worldly, greedy and unchaste as a cleric. His unpopularity contributed to his downfall, the occasion of which was his failure to secure an annulment from Pope Clement VII of Henry's marriage to Catherine of Aragon. Pleading guilty to a Praemunire charge, he was stripped of all his offices, except the See of York; he died before he could answer a charge of treason.

Woodard, Nathaniel *(1811–1891)*
Anglican priest and founder of the 'Woodard Schools', which provided a middle-class public school education in an Anglican ambience. His ideas were outlined in the controversial *Plea for the Middle Classes* (1845) and furthered by the Society of St Nicolas, which he founded.

Woolman, John *(1720–1772)*
American Quaker preacher and campaigner against slavery. From 1743 he made long, arduous preaching journeys on foot, and in great simplicity, rallying Quaker communities against slavery. His *Journal* (1744) is recognised as a spiritual classic.

Wordsworth, Christopher *(1807–1885)*
Educator and Bishop of Lincoln. Fellow of Trinity College, Cambridge, he was headmaster of Harrow (1836–1844), then held various appointments before accepting the See of Lincoln (1869). A conservative High Churchman, he compiled a Bible commentary, was respected for his writings on the early Church Fathers, and wrote many hymns, some of which are still in use.

Wordsworth, John *(1843–1911)*
Bishop of Salisbury. Son of Christopher Wordsworth, he was a specialist in Latin and worked on a critical edition of the Vulgate New Testament (1911); he was appointed the first Oriel professor of the interpretation of Scripture in 1883. As bishop he worked for the reunion of the Church of England with the Swedish and Old Catholic Churches; he also wrote in defence of Anglican Orders.

Wordsworth, William *(1770–1850)*
Greatest poet of the English Romantic movement. Educated at St John's College, Cambridge, in his early twenties he rejected religious belief and espoused revolutionary ideals. A creative friendship with Samuel Taylor Coleridge produced the *Lyrical Ballads* (1798). He returned, with his sister Dorothy, to the Lake District (1799), where he lived the rest of his life. His autobiographical poem *The Prelude* (1805) was not published until after his death. Nature was his greatest inspiration, which brought him near to pantheism; but his devotion to the Church of England was deep and sincere.

Wulfstan, St *(c. 1008–1095)* *(also known as Wulstan)*
Bishop of Worcester and the last English bishop after the Norman Conquest. A Benedictine monk, he reluctantly accepted the office, but in his humility, austerity of life and able administration he proved to be a model bishop. He helped to suppress the slave trade between England and Ireland, assisted in compiling the Domesday Book and rebuilt Worcester Cathedral.

Wulfstan *(d. 1023)*
Monk and author of many sermons, treatises and codes of law; Bishop of London (996–1002), Archbishop of York (1002–1023) and Bishop of Worcester (1002–1016). Little is known of his life prior to becoming bishop; his greatest achievement was his copious and influential writing. His most famous work is a call to reform, *Sermo Lupi ad Anglos* (he sometimes used the pen name 'Lupus'); as adviser to the kings Aethelred and Canute, he drafted their codes of law.

Wycliffe, John *(c. 1330–1384)*
Philosopher, theologian and reformer. Wycliffe was educated at Oxford, where he became Master of Balliol (1360–1361). At the time Edward III

appointed him rector of Lutterworth (1374) he came into the political service of the Black Prince and John of Gaunt; it was their families who appear to have shielded him from later ecclesiastical censure. As a philosopher he reacted against the current scepticism, and as a theologian he looked to the Bible and the Fathers of the Church; this was clear in his *De Ecclesia, De Veritate, Sacrae Scripturae* and *De Potestate Papae* (1377–1378). It was, however, his teaching on the Eucharist which brought condemnation of heresy down upon him. An energetic preacher, he inspired many followers who continued his teaching (taking popular expression in the Lollards) and his project of a Bible translation was seen through by his disciples.

Wyszynski, Stefan *(1901–1981)*
Archbishop of Warsaw and Primate of Poland who was imprisoned (1953–1956) by the Communist authorities for protesting at the false accusations directed at the Polish hierarchy.

X

Xavier, St Francis *(1506–1552)*
Of Spanish origin, he was one of the original founder-members of the Society of Jesus (Jesuits), having met Ignatius of Loyola at the University of Paris (1525). Ordained a priest in 1537, he left for the missions three years later. He spent these highly successful years (1542–1545) in Goa, then travelled to the Malay Archipelago, and eventually travelled on to Japan, where he founded a Christian community. In 1552 he returned to Goa, then set out for China, but died before arriving. He is generally considered the greatest Roman Catholic missionary of modern times, credited with over seven hundred thousand conversions; hence he is often called the 'Apostle of the Indies' and 'of Japan'. He was canonised in 1622 and declared 'Patron of Foreign Missions'.

Ximenez de Cisneros, Francisco *(1436–1517)*
Cardinal Archbishop of Toledo. A Spanish secular priest who became an austere Franciscan and, through the office of chaplain to Queen Isabella (1492), became first a reformer of his Religious Order and then, reluctantly, Archbishop of Toledo and Chancellor of Castile with heavy political responsibilities and involvements. He was a zealous patron of education, founding the university of Alcala and re-establishing the Mozarabic Rite in the Spanish Church.

Y

Yonge, Charlotte Mary *(1823–1901)*

English novelist who dedicated her life and talents to the service of the church. For seventy-one years she taught Sunday school in her village of Otterbourne and from 1851 edited *The Monthly Packet*, an uplifting magazine for girls. She is best remembered for her support for the Oxford Movement, especially through her novels, including *The Heir of Redclyffe* (1853), her first, *Heartsease* (1854), *The Young Step-mother* (1861) and many others.

Z

Zaccaria, St Antonio Maria *(1502–1539)*

Italian physician who became a priest and founded the Congregation of Clerks Regular of St Paul (also known as Barnabites) to revive spirituality in the Church (1530). He dedicated the remainder of his life to reform and missionary work in Vicenza, Italy. He was canonised in 1897.

Zahn, Theodor *(1838–1933)*

German New Testament and patristic scholar who successively held professorships at five different German universities and whose work was notable for its erudition and thoroughness. He did pioneer work on the New Testament canon, edited a commentary on the New Testament and contributed many valuable books on the study of the Fathers of the Church.

Zhiming, Wang *(1903–1973)*

Educated in Christian mission schools, Wang Zhiming became a Christian and in 1951 he was ordained a pastor. He showed loyalty to the Chinese state but refused to take part in 'denunciation' meetings. In December 1973, at a rally of more than 10,000 Chinese Christians who had been forced to attend in an attempt to frighten them into submission, Wang Zhiming was publically executed. His whole family, who had been arrested with him in 1969, survived the imprisonment. Wang Zhiming is one of the ten modern martyrs honoured in sculpture with a place over the west door of Westminster Abbey, London.

Zinzendorf, Nikolaus Ludwig, Graf von *(1700–1760)*

After studying law at Wittenberg University he entered politics, but left in 1727 as his religious interests, particularly the Herrnhut community on one of his estates, grew. Ordained a Lutheran pastor (1734) and a bishop of the

Moravian Episcopal Church ('Unitas Fratrum') in 1737, he travelled widely, establishing Moravian communities in the Netherlands, the Baltic States, England, the West Indies and North America. He sought to create an ecumenical Protestant movement. He was equally opposed to rationalism and rigid Protestantism, proclaiming a 'religion of the heart'. His emphasis upon the role of the emotions found lasting expression in the later Protestant theology of Schleiermacher.

Zwingli, Ulrich *(1484–1531)*
Leader of the Protestant Reformation in Switzerland. Educated at the Universities of Vienna (1498) and Basel (1502), he was ordained priest in 1506 and became pastor at Glarus (1506–1516), then at Einsiedeln. In 1518 he accepted the post of People's Preacher at the Great Minister in Zurich. Well read in humanism and the early Christian writers, with a knowledge of New Testament Greek, his preaching began to reflect the new Reformation teaching. He published and defended his sixty-seven theses in 1523, receiving much local support. He opposed the Anabaptists and disagreed with Luther on the theology of the Eucharist. His movement spread to some other cantons, but violent conflict developed (1531) between these and cantons that remained Catholic. Zwingli, acting as chaplain with a force from Zurich, was killed in battle.

Zygomalas, Theodore *(1544–1581)*
Greek Orthodox theologian and author. The Orthodox Patriarch, Jeremias II, engaged Zygomalas to respond to the Confession of Augsburg, the Lutheran statement of belief. In so doing, and through the subsequent correspondence with the Lutherans, he highlighted the areas of disagreement and wrote an invaluable presentation of Orthodox theology.